W9-CGY-899

·Cultural Anthropology·

Second Edition

David Hicks
Margaret A. Gwynne

State University of New York at Stony Brook

HarperCollinsCollegePublishers

Chapter opener art: The four figures used in the corners of the first pages of each chapter are "generalized monumental figures representing the various races" from the *Detroit Industry* murals by Diego Rivera in the Detroit Institute of Arts. The frescoes, done in 1932 and 1933, are considered the finest example of Mexican muralist work in the United States and a highlight of Rivera's career. The images appear by kind permission of the Institute.

Acquisitions Editor: Alan McClare
Developmental Editor: Michael Kimball
Project Editor: Shuli Traub
Cover Designers: John D. Sparks/Amy Trombat
Text Designer: John D. Sparks
Cover Photographs: Top left, Bob and Ira Spring; top right, Gerard Fritz, 704/333-5330; bottom left, image provided by © 1994 PhotoDisc, Inc.; bottom right, Ron Chapple/FPG International Corp.
Art Studio: John D. Sparks/Burmar Technical Corp.
Photo Researcher: Julie Tesser
Electronic Production Manager: Alexandra Odulak
Manufacturing Manager: Hilda Koparanian
Electronic Page Makeup: Interactive Composition Corp.
Printer and Binder: R. R. Donnelley & Sons Company
Cover Printer: New England Book Components

For permission to use copyrighted material, grateful acknowledgment is made to the copyright holders on p. 443, which is hereby made part of this copyright page.

Cultural Anthropology, Second Edition

Copyright © 1996 by HarperCollins College Publishers

HarperCollins© and ♛° are registered trademarks of HarperCollins Publishers, Inc.

All rights reserved. Printed in the United States of America. No part of this book may be used or reproduced in any manner whatsoever without written permission, except in the case of brief quotations embodied in critical articles and reviews. For information address HarperCollins College Publishers, 10 East 53rd Street, New York, NY 10022. *For information about any HarperCollins title, product, or resource, please visit our World Wide Web site at **http://www.harpercollins.com/college**.*

Library of Congress Cataloging-in-Publication Data

Hicks, David, 1939–
    Cultural anthropology / David Hicks, Margaret A. Gwynne—2nd ed.
       p. cm.
    Includes bibliographical references and index.
    ISBN 0-673-99875-4
    1. Ethnology.   I. Gwynne, Margaret Anderson.   II. Title.
    GN316.H52   1995
    306—dc20   95–21274
                                    CIP

95 96 97 98 9 8 7 6 5 4 3 2 1

To
Emma and Paul
and
to the memory of
Margaret Spencer Wood Anderson

Brief Contents

Detailed Contents

Preface

Before we embarked on the preparation of *Cultural Anthropology,* neither of us had ever found a textbook entirely suitable for our first-year anthropology students. Our colleagues sometimes mentioned the same problem. Some available textbooks seemed unnecessarily pedantic; others dwelt on material that was obviously remote from students' interests; still others seemed to us to be too abstract. We were looking for something that was clearly and engagingly written; that was as comprehensive as any single textbook could reasonably be, covering the basic subjects to which instructors would wish to expose their introductory students; that would introduce certain new materials commonly shortchanged in currently available textbooks (such as women and culture, the human body as a vehicle for cultural expression, and sexuality from a cross-cultural point of view); and that would genuinely interest and even excite its undergraduate readers.

We wrote *Cultural Anthropology* to address these needs. We were, and are, guided by two related and equally fundamental premises: that American college students are interested in their own cultural experience, and that the comparative study of their own culture with others will result in a deeper appreciation of all cultures. In *Cultural Anthropology* we deliberately focus on familiar aspects of Western culture that find parallels in other cultures, since we believe this will foster readers' awareness of, and tolerance for, the ethnic diversity that constitutes an ever-increasing element in the lives of American students.

Themes

Cultural Anthropology is designed around four distinctive themes we regard as fundamental to the education of anthropology students in the last decade of the twentieth century.

1. **Cultural relativism**. Most introductory cultural anthropology texts promote the notion that some invisible dividing line separates Westerners from non-Westerners. In *Cultural Anthropology* we reject what we consider the improper distinction between "us" and "them," and following from this general stance, consistently advocate what we take to be the most important lesson cultural anthropology has contributed to human understanding: cultural relativism, the willingness to evaluate a culture in terms of its own values rather than those of another culture. Throughout the book, we contrast this ideal with its opposite, ethnocentrism.

2. **Holism.** Despite its traditional fragmentation into four subfields customarily treated in separate courses, anthropology remains a holistic discipline, and "American anthropologists . . . credit the quality of their insights, research and teaching in one field to past and present influences of the remaining three. Trained in one subdiscipline, they still are affected by other parts of the whole. The persistent power of holism continues today as American anthropology's essential and coveted reality" (Givens and Skomal 1992:1).

   The same concept is also used by anthropologists to convey the idea that the various aspects of any culture are closely interrelated, even as the different but interconnected parts of a car's engine work together to keep the car running smoothly. Anthropologists study cultures holistically because the synchronic interconnections among the different aspects of a culture help to impart meaning to that culture. We continue this tradition here.

3. **Women and anthropology.** A major theme of *Cultural Anthropology* is that ways of living, the beliefs that encapsulate them, and the institutions by which they are brought into action belong not to one gender but to both. Until recently, even though much anthropological fieldwork was carried out by women, most published work in anthropology was dominated by the presumption that culture was male culture and society was male society. This unrealistic

and outmoded stance is currently in the process of being replaced by one that emphasizes the complementary influences of males and females in fashioning the communal worlds in which they live. While not wholly uncritical of contemporary feminist research, we draw on it frequently in our attempt to fashion a coherent, balanced account of the contributions women make to the cultures they have helped create.

4. **The value of applied anthropology.** In the first half of the 1990s, the proportion of anthropology graduates who applied their training outside of academia increased to such an extent that these anthropologists now outnumber their academic colleagues. However, the importance of applied anthropology continues to be underestimated in comparison with academic anthropology in the majority of textbooks. In contrast, *Cultural Anthropology* emphasizes this newly recognized and growing subdiscipline in the form of "Anthropologist at Work" boxes, which appear in most chapters. Each of these focuses on a practicing anthropologist and her or his work, or else suggests a way students might apply an undergraduate education in anthropology to a specific career path.

Theoretical Approach

Cultural Anthropology has no theoretical axe to grind; we treat the most influential perspectives and approaches in cultural anthropology with an even hand. Still, as teachers of anthropology we have found that we can best express our holistic view of culture through two approaches, the structural-functionalist and the cultural-materialist. Since holism is a lesson we regard as fundamental to understanding cultures, and therefore an essential one for our readers to grasp, we emphasize these two approaches rather more than, say, the psychological or structuralist approaches. This is perhaps especially true for Chapters 6 and 7, which provide cultural-materialist treatments of subsistence strategies and economics, and Chapters 10 and 13, which provide structural-functionalist interpretations of marriage and religion.

Special Features

Unique Coverage

While generally following the now-standard format and list of topics found in other major introductory anthropology textbooks, *Cultural Anthropology* offers additional materials not available in any introductory text with which we are familiar.

- *Unique chapters on sexuality and the human body.* We devote an entire chapter (Chapter 8) to a cross-cultural look at social constructions of sex, gender, and sexuality, and another (Chapter 15) to consideration of how people in different cultures reconstruct the human body to reflect their own cultural images.

- *"Ask Yourself" boxes.* We believe a good textbook should provide intellectual challenge, actively encouraging its readers to think for themselves. To promote independent thinking, we have placed inserts, titled "Ask Yourself," throughout each chapter. These boxes ask readers to formulate their own personal answers to questions—many of them of an ethical nature—related to the text. We hope they will also stimulate discussion in class.

- *"Anthropology and the Environment" boxes.* This second edition includes a new series of boxes, titled "Anthropology and the Environment," reflecting the contemporary concerns of anthropologists and nonanthropologists alike about the natural environment. These boxes appear in most chapters to draw links between major chapter topics and environmental matters.

- *"The Anthropologist at Work" boxes.* As we mentioned above, these highlight the relevance of studying anthropology for a wide range of interesting and challenging careers.

- *Locator maps.* New maps, found in each chapter, locate regions and peoples at the points in the text where we first mention them. These are intended to help readers quickly and easily place the groups and places mentioned in their appropriate geographical contexts.

Student Accessibility

Unfamiliar material, especially when combined with technical jargon, can intimidate newcomers to anthropology. We have taken pains to ensure that our special features and style of writing will make this book accessible to undergraduate students.

- *Chapter-opening vignettes.* Each chapter of *Cultural Anthropology* opens with a brief vignette, selected from Western culture, calculated to evoke immediate interest and recognition in student readers. Many of these vignettes are drawn from the popular press. The chapter on marriage, for instance, begins with a back-page news story about a brother-sister marriage in Massachusetts, and discusses this episode in the context of familiar Western marriage customs before going on to consider the different forms of marriage encountered cross-culturally.

- *Student-oriented writing.* We have taken to heart our students' preferences for brevity, informality, and even humor. Each chapter is short enough to be read comfortably at a single sitting; our writing style is nonpedantic; and here and there, we hope, the material will bring a smile to our readers' faces.

Cultural Anthropology is the product of our combined teaching experience of over forty years. Our hope is that students who read it will become well-informed about the contemporary world and the place of a wide range of cultures, theirs and others, within "the world system."

Accompanying Supplements

- We have written our own Instructor's Manual and Test Bank to aid instructors in the classroom use of *Cultural Anthropology*. Each chapter of this manual includes suggested additional lecture topics with substantial discussion, a suggested class activity, recommended reference materials, essay-type exam questions, and a test bank of multiple-choice questions.

- To assist students in their review and comprehension of the text material, a Student Study Guide has been developed by Diane Barbolla at San Diego Mesa College. Each chapter of the study guide contains a chapter outline, chapter learning objectives, key points for review, identification exercises, a practice test of multiple-choice questions (including an answer key), and three practice essay questions that require the student to synthesize the chapter material.

- For this edition we have prepared an accompanying reader consisting of sixteen texts, each corresponding to one of the book's sixteen chapters. Some of these texts were written by well-known anthropologists; others are drawn from popular literature. Each is prefaced by a short introduction. The readings are intended to supplement the text by providing further information and helping to develop our discussions of topics introduced in the book.

Note to Specialists

Cultural anthropology poses special challenges to scholars seeking to synthesize its theories, hypotheses, and philosophical approaches. On the one hand, we see our discipline as holistic. On the other, we acknowledge that its elements may not only be disparate but controversial or even contradictory as well.

One problem is definitions. Anthropologists are notorious for disagreeing, and nowhere is this more obvious than in their attempts to define terms such as "marriage" or "religion." The more general a definition, the more specific instances it can accommodate; the more precise the definition, the fewer. Broad or narrow: which to choose?

Another problem is empirical generalizations. Anthropologists have been conditioned by experience to avoid these, yet in interpreting features of social life we find it impractical to do so. Topical and geographic specializations are essential, but paradoxically they must be transcended if our discipline is to progress, for without cross-cultural generalization, cultural anthropology would have no academic justification. So we generalize, but our generalizations almost invariably result in some distortion.

We ask colleagues who may be concerned—and rightly so—about the distortions that our particular definitions or generalizations may have introduced into *Cultural Anthropology* to help us find our way through the semantic or conceptual minefields we have no doubt wandered into by interpreting our material for their students in their own ways.

Acknowledgments

We owe a great debt of thanks to the following colleagues, friends, and family members, whose generous support and in many instances painstaking labor have helped us immeasurably.

For editorial help, we thank our developmental editor, Michael Kimball of HarperCollins, and especially our acquisitions editor, Alan McClare, also of HarperCollins, whose continuing encouragement and support has sustained us through years of work. HarperCollins project editor Shuli Traub capably steered us through the final stages of manuscript preparation.

For thoughtful criticism of the manuscript we are grateful for the help of Diane E. Barbolla, San Diego Mesa College; Richard Bordner, Chaminade University of Honolulu; William Coleman, University of North Carolina–Greensboro; Kim M. King, Hiram College; Victoria Lockwood, Southern Methodist University; Barbara Mueller, Caspar College; Martin Ottenheimer, Kansas State University; Evan C. Ragsdale, Yavapai College; Michael R. Rhum, Northern Illinois University; Jill B. Smith, University of South Dakota; Jeffrey P. Williams, Cleveland State University; and Dorothy D. Wills, California State Polytechnic–Pomona.

More often than not, we incorporated the suggestions of these reviewers, whose opinions and criticisms we valued highly, into the final version of *Cultural Anthropology*. Lack of space and our inability to reconcile the diversity of reviewers' opinions made it impossible to include every suggested change or addition, but this does not at all lessen our appreciation of each reviewer's efforts.

For specialist advice, we are grateful to our colleagues Najwa Adra, W. Arens, Michael Clatts, Shirley Fiske, Nancie Gonzalez, Roger McConochie, Lorna McDougall, Maria Messina, Dolores Newton, Loretta Orion, Paul B. Roscoe, Edwin S. Segal, John Shea, Elizabeth Stone, Dan Varisco, Zhusheng Wang, and Patricia Wright.

For photographic help, we appreciate the assistance of Julie Tesser and our talented spouses.

For constant and stimulating feedback, we affectionately salute our undergraduate students at SUNY/Stony Brook since 1968.

For personal support, we acknowedge, with love and gratitude, our spouses and children: Maxine, Tom, Cathy, Ellen, Emma, Meg, Nik, Paul, and Thad.

David Hicks
Margaret A. Gwynne

About the Authors

David Hicks studied anthropology at the University of Oxford, where he earned his Ph.D. after carrying out nineteen months of field research on the island of Timor, in eastern Indonesia. He has taught at the State University of New York at Stony Brook since 1968, and has returned to Indonesia for further research on several occasions. He has received research awards from the National Science Foundation, the Wenner-Gren Foundation for Anthropological Research, and the American Philosophical Foundation. He has also served as a consultant for the World Bank. He is the author of four previous books.

Margaret A. Gwynne received her Ph.D. in anthropology from the State University of New York at Stony Brook. She has taught anthropology at SUNY/Stony Brook and Dowling College, and as a specialist in international health and development, has worked as a consultant, mainly in Eastern Caribbean countries, on projects sponsored by the World Health Organization, the United States Agency for International Development, private foundations, and consulting firms. She is the recipient of two teaching awards from SUNY/Stony Brook and of research grants from SUNY/Stony Brook and The Pew Charitable Trusts.

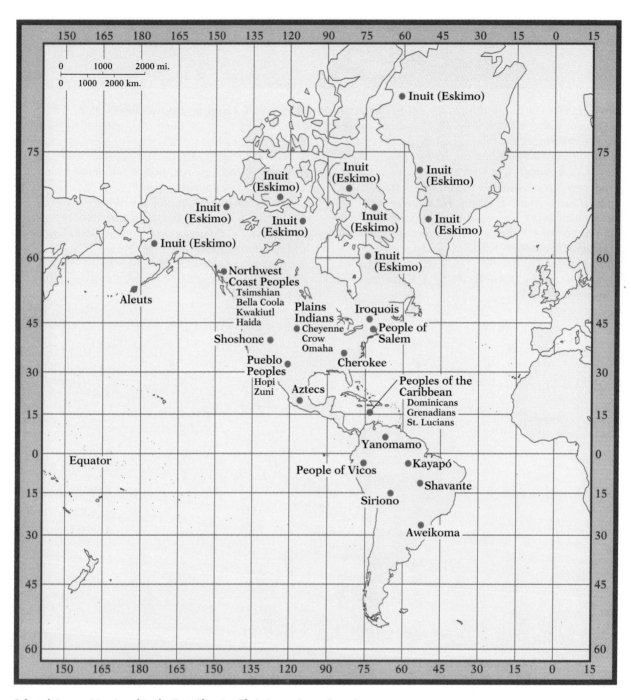

Selected Groups Mentioned in the Text, Showing Their Approximate Locations.

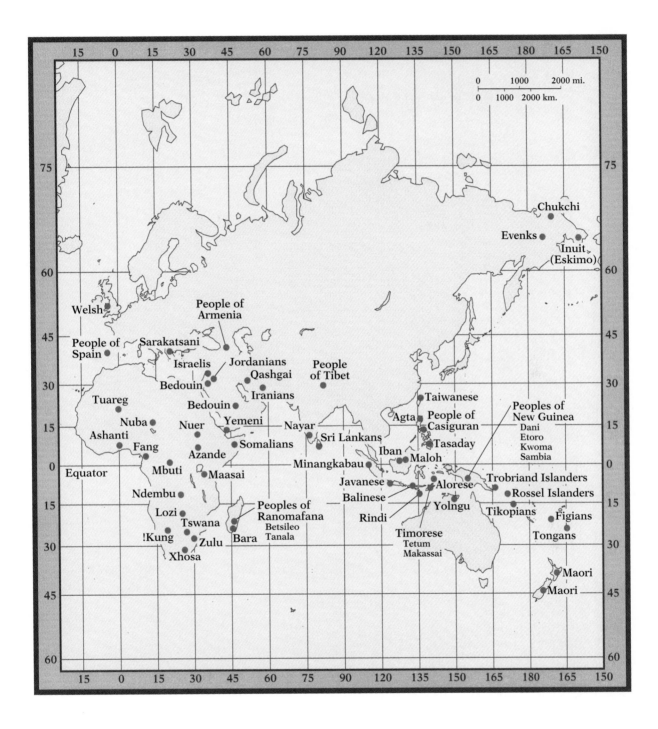

Cultural Anthropology

Second Edition

David Hicks
State University of New York
at Stony Brook

Margaret A. Gwynne
State University of New York
at Stony Brook

ISBN 0-673-99875-4

While writing *Cultural Anthropology*, authors Hicks and Gwynne were guided by two related and equally fundamental premises: that American college students are interested in their own cultural experience, and that the comparative study of their own culture with others will result in a deeper appreciation of all cultures. Hence, the authors' focus of familiar aspects of Western culture that find parallels in other cultures fosters readers' awareness of, and tolerance for, ethnic diversity. *Cultural Anthropology* is designed around four distinct themes: cultural relativism, holism, women and anthropology, and applied anthropology. While treating the most influential perspectives in cultural anthropology with an even hand, the authors use the structural-functionalist and cultural materialist approaches to express their holistic view of anthropology.

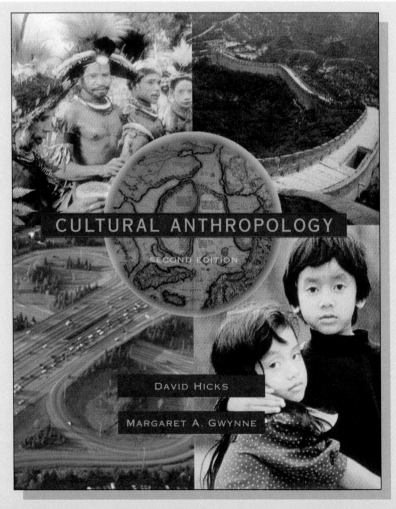

EMPHASIS ON CULTURAL RELATIVISM

The authors reject the improper distinction between "us" and "them," and consistently promote one of cultural anthropology's most important lessons: cultural relativism, the ability to evaluate a culture in terms of its own values rather than those of another culture. The result is a refreshing and distinguished treatment of the discipline of cultural anthropology.

Cultural Relativism

A fourth concept central to modern cultural anthropology, and one of the most important in this book, is **cultural relativism.** This is the idea that a culture must be evaluated in terms of its own values, not according to the values of another culture. For example, the marriage of one man to two women at the same time, unacceptable in Western culture, is entirely acceptable in certain other cultures. Who is to say that the Western custom of limiting individuals to only one spouse at a time is superior?

The concept of cultural relativism has an opposite, **ethnocentrism,** the idea that one's own ethnic group, society, or culture is superior to others. This notion is inconsistent with the findings of cultural anthropology, which have repeatedly shown that—in the absence of any universal yardstick against which cultures can be measured and compared—no ethnic group, society, or culture can be said to be superior to any other.

Sometimes the concept of cultural relativism has been interpreted narrowly, as implying that anthropologists must suspend their cultural values when studying the cultures of others. But this is tantamount to saying that people have the right to engage in any practice, however reprehensible, simply because it is "part of their culture" (Maybury-Lewis 1988:378). In the wider sense, cultural relativism means that an anthropologist should refrain from making value judgments about other peoples' beliefs and practices until she has understood these beliefs in their own cultural terms (Maybury-Lewis 1988:378–379). Under this definition, the Holocaust could never be justified on the grounds that it was part of Nazi culture, nor the racism practiced in South Africa on the grounds that it was a part of South African culture.

Cultural relativism a central idea in modern cultural anthropology—that a culture must be evaluated in terms of its own values, not according to the values of another culture

Ethnocentrism the belief that one's own society or culture is superior to all others

Nonliterate lacking a tradition of reading and writing

Illiterate lacking the ability to read and write while living in a literate society

• Specialties in Cultural Anthropology •

In the past, cultural anthropologists almost exclusively studied societies that were small-scale and **nonliterate**—lacking a tradition of reading and writing. (The term *nonliterate* distinguishes such people from **illiterate** people, who do not read or write either, but who live in societies in which others do). Nonliterate societies used to be called *primitive* societies, but because Westerners are inclined to equate that word with inferiority, most anthropologists today prefer using either *nonliterate* or *small-scale* when referring to such societies. They do not consider nonliterate societies to be inferior to literate societies, nor do they equate them with prehistoric societies (as scholars of the Victorian

Small-scale, nonliterate societies are characterized by simple technologies. On the island of Flores in Eastern Indonesia, a Manggarai man, wearing a hat made from half a coconut shell, sets a rat trap.

Although males as well as females are matrigroup members, the core of a matrigroup consists of women of different generations bound together by consanguineal ties. Above, three generations of matrilineal Navajo women.

grew older, did a husband acquire some standing in his wife's household.

In economic matters, a Zuni husband was a contributing member of his wife's household, but for religious purposes he remained a member of his sister's. He grew corn for his wife's household, not for his sister's, but returned to the latter's house to officiate at rituals. A man's allegiance as brother carried more weight than his allegiance as husband because of his importance in his sister's home as the performer of her household's rituals. This conflict of loyalties brought about frequent divorces. An ex-husband would return to his sister's house, leaving his children (who, of course, belonged to his wife's matrigroup, not his) with his ex-wife. A Zuni woman had no similar conflict of interest. The only family to which she owed allegiance was her own household, which was one of many that made up her matrigroup.

Matrilocal residence does not accompany matriliny in all matrisystems. In some matrilineal societies, a male resides with his mother's brother, a custom known as **avunculocal residence.** This is a more efficient way than matrilocal residence of keeping matrilineal property under the control of the men who have a stake in it. If widely practiced in a society, avunculocal residence also tends to keep brothers together after they have married because, unlike matrilocal residence, wives must come to live with their husbands, not vice versa. Among the matrilineal Tsimshian, neighbors of the Kwakiutl, children of both sexes spend their early years living with their parents. A daughter remains with her parents until she marries, when she goes to live with her husband. A son, however, usually leaves his father's household sometime between the ages of 8 and 14 to live with his mother's brother. One result of avunculocal residence is that a core of males, related matrilineally, is established as a local group. Since it is these males who control their matrilineage's property, their common residence makes it easier for them to protect it than if they lived dispersed in matrilocal fashion like Zuni husbands (Vaughan 1984:60–61).

avunculocal residence the residence pattern by which male ego resides with his mother's brother

FOCUS ON WOMEN AND ANTHROPOLOGY

This new edition features strong coverage of women's roles and gender issues. Coverage features the contributions of female anthropologists, as well as a wide range of anthropological research on women. While not wholly uncritical of contemporary feminist research, the authors draw upon it frequently in their attempt to fashion a coherent, balanced account of the contributions of women to the cultures they have helped create.

UNIQUE FULL-CHAPTER TREATMENTS ON "SEX, GENDER, AND SEXUALITY" AND "CULTURE AND THE HUMAN BODY"

These two unique chapters provide insightful examinations of cross-cultural constructions of sex, gender, and sexuality and the cultural implications of the human body. From premarital sex, postmarital sex, and extramarital sex to body adornment, body alteration, and body language, the authors also explore how a broad range of cultures reconstruct the human body to reflect their own cultural image.

Premarital, Extramarital, and Postmarital Sex

Some societies forbid premarital sex entirely, but many more either permit or encourage it. In fact, the idea that young people should not have sex before marriage is quite unusual, cross-culturally. Western society is one of only a few in which premarital sexual activity short of intercourse is common among the unmarried as a way of preserving virginity and/or avoiding pregnancy (Masters, Johnson, and Kolodny 1985:627).

The Maasai of East Africa provide an example of a society in which premarital sex is encouraged. After rituals marking the end of boyhood, young Maasai males leave the villages where they were born and go to live in remote camps called *kraals*. For the next 10 or 15 years, which a young man spends as a warrior, the kraal is his home. Here, older warriors teach him how to fight and to raid other tribes' herds of cattle. The warriors cannot marry, but they are permitted to have sex with young women who live with them in the kraal. Such liaisons are not expected to lead to marriage. A girl who gets pregnant returns to her village, where she marries. She is not stigmatized for having had premarital sex nor for having become pregnant, because the Maasai welcome children—and anyway, at one time or another the majority of Maasai females have sexual relations with the warriors in the kraal. When his period as a warrior comes to an end, a man returns to his village, marries, and assumes the rights and duties of a husband and father (Saibull 1981; Saitoti 1988).

In contrast, there are various societies around the Mediterranean where girls must remain virgins until they marry or else suffer public shame and greatly reduced chances of marriage. Since marriage is the "overriding criterion for a fulfilling life" for females in this region (Brandes 1985:113), parents vigorously protect the chastity of their unmarried daughters. In the town of Monteros, Spain, for instance, the "main prerequisite to marriage for women . . . is virginity" (118). Since potential husbands believe that premarital sex for females (but not for males) is somehow defiling, an unmarried woman's chances of marrying are much reduced if she loses her virginity, but a virtuous daughter can readily find a husband. Parents in Monteros tell their daughters "Good linen, preserved in a trunk,

In Kenya, unmarried Masai men live in remote cattle camps called kraals. Here they have sexual relationships, not expected to lead to marriage, with young Masai women. Above, Masai youths and their girlfriends clasp hands.

called the **double standard,** is the notion that the rules governing sexual behavior should be different for males and females living in the same society. Of a sample of 61 societies compared by Frayser (1985:203), 18 percent sanctioned premarital sexual activity for males but not for females. In contrast, not a single society permitted females to engage in premarital sex while forbidding the same behavior to males. Cross-culturally, then, the double standard is strongly biased in favor of male premarital sex. Frayser adds, however, that in 82 percent of the societies she sampled, no double standard exists. In these societies, members of both sexes must either avoid premarital sex, or else both males and females are allowed to indulge themselves.

The second idea, often found where premarital sex is permitted, is that the females involved must not become pregnant (Frayser 1985:204). Premarital sex is permissible for enjoyment but not for reproduction. Sexual relationships are, in other words, classified as physical rather than social. One might assume that this restriction would characterize modern societies with access to reliable birth control methods, but it applies in nonindustrial societies as well. Typically, if a girl becomes pregnant the pregnancy must be terminated through abortion or the child must be killed. Alternatively, by marrying its father the girl may be permitted to transform a physical relationship between two indi-

... tal sex are encountered ... universally. The first,

Double standard the notion that within a single society the rules governing sexual behavior should be different for males and females

Cosmetics

Another way in which people adorn their bodies is by temporarily decorating their skin with **cosmetics,** the general term for preparations designed to improve the appearance of the body, or part of it, by directly but temporarily applying them to the skin. In Western society, cosmetics take the form of various mass-produced, petroleum-based, colored creams, oils, or powders. These are usually applied to the face, and are much more frequently used by females than by males. In other societies, the term *cosmetics* may refer to body as well as face paints, usually made by combining animal or vegetable oils with colored powders made from naturally occurring minerals.

The extent to which cosmetics are used in human societies, from the remote jungles of South America to the high-fashion capitals of western Europe, suggests that the notion of adorning or enhancing the surface of the body, like the idea of covering it with clothing, comes close to being a human universal. There are differences of placement, emphasis, and extent among various traditions of cosmetic use, but the reasons for wearing cosmetics are similar.

In every society with a cosmetic tradition, including Western society, one reason bodies are decorated is to enhance them—to make them appear more perfectly in accord with society's ideals of beauty (although, as we shall see at the end of this chapter, what is considered attractive varies widely from society to society). But in some societies, the use of cosmetics quite consciously provides other benefits as well. Cosmetics may protect people from harm, express their social status, or identify them as members of particular classes or families. Benefits of this kind are probably part of the reason behind Western cosmetic use also, although Western cosmetics users may not be aware of it.

If Westerners differ little from members of other societies in their primary motivations for applying cosmetics, they do differ from some in the relatively modest extent to which they decorate themselves. Cosmetic use in some societies is so extensive it

would make the heavy-handed application of cosmetics to a female American screen star by a Hollywood makeup artist seem moderate.

A well-turned-out Nuba male from Kordofan Province in the Sudan of northern Africa is literally painted from head to foot. Among the Nuba, body painting begins in infancy, when a baby's scalp is decorated with either red or yellow paint, depending on its family membership (Faris 1972:30). Thereafter, body painting is used to suggest one's social and physical status as well as to beautify, and it becomes more and more complex with advancing age. A young Nuba boy, for example, wears simple, inconspicuous, red and greyish white decorations on his scalp, gradually earning the right to use increasingly elaborate, colorful, and extensive designs as he matures (38). Each change of age and status means a new kind of decoration for the boy, as with advancing years he earns the right to use more products in a wider range of colors and designs. (Westerners, too, sometimes use cosmetics as an age marker, as when an American girl is forbidden by her parents to wear lipstick until she has reached a certain age.)

Cosmetics are universally used to beautify people, protect them from harm, express their social status, or identify them as members of particular groups. In Liberia, a Bassa girl being initiated into the Sande, an all-female secret society, is elaborately decorated with a chalky white clay.

Cosmetics preparations designed to improve the appearance of the body, or part of it, by directly but temporarily applying them to the skin

For cultural anthropologists, much of what motivates the desire to follow up on earlier work is the pace of change in today's world. Technologically complex cultures are affecting technologically simpler ones at an ever-increasing rate, and the thrust of ethnographic research has shifted in response. Many cultural anthropologists today are interested in studying the process of change at "their" research sites. At the end of this chapter we discuss the work of Napoleon Chagnon, who in the course of his anthropological career revisited his original fieldwork site in the Amazon jungle some twenty times.

•Ask Yourself•

What changes have taken place in the community into which you were born, in the time that has passed since then? What factors best account for these changes?

▶ Applied Fieldwork

Fieldwork is sometimes undertaken not to test hypotheses but to achieve some practical end. This work, as noted in Chapter 1, is called *applied research*, and it is quite different from theoretical research. In the last decade or two, applied anthropology has grown dramatically in both scope and popularity. Today virtually every field and subfield of anthropology incorporates applied as well as theoretical research.

Cultural anthropology, because of its origins in the collection of data on foreign cultures for commercial or political reasons, has always included an applied component of sorts. However, the reasons for undertaking applied work have changed significantly in recent years, along with the proportion of cultural anthropologists engaged in such work. No longer a tool used for global political advantage, applied cultural anthropology today may have either commercial or social objectives. In many instances it serves the practical and humanitarian needs of governments, other public institutions, or private agencies such as charitable organizations or relief agencies.

A project undertaken by English anthropologist Emma Crewe, who worked for a nonprofit British [organization] . . . g in helping people in the . . . world to develop clean, . . . riate technologies, pro- . . . 95). Crewe did applied

fieldwork in Sri Lanka to help find a solution to a long-standing health problem: indoor air pollution caused by the wood- and dung-burning clay cook-stoves traditionally used in Sri Lankan households (Crewe 1995). When wood or dung are burned in a traditional Sri Lankan stove, the resulting smoke contributes to a variety of serious ailments, including cancer and acute respiratory infection (ARI). A woman using such a stove in an unventilated room is exposed to the equivalent of more than a hundred cigarettes a day, and ARI is the single biggest killer of children in the developing world, annually taking the lives of 4 to 5 million children under age 5. Living in a Sri Lankan village, Crewe observed how the clay stoves were made, bought, used, and cleaned, as well as the social and economic contexts in which they were used. Later she helped introduce a safer, cleaner-burning stove. Inexpensive and locally made, it gives off less smoke, retains heat better, uses fuel more efficiently, and reduces cooking time. Today the new stoves are helping to improve local people's health, conserve their resources, and protect their environment.

• Field Methods •

In this section, we describe and explain the array of methods and tools used by ethnographers to collect data. These methods and tools differ depending on whether the fieldwork is theoretical or applied, and also on the theoretical perspective and cognitive or topical specialty of the anthropologist. At the end of the chapter, we will describe how two modern ethnographers collected data in the field and coped with the unexpected difficulties that often arise during fieldwork.

Participant Observation

As remarked in Chapter 1, participant observation is the most important strategy used by cultural anthropologists to collect data in the field. Rather than reading about or briefly visiting the people they are interested in studying, ethnographers—like Emma Crewe, whose work in Sri Lanka we mentioned a moment ago—live among the members of a community under study, usually for many months or even years at a time, participating in the people's lives, speaking their language, and observing their behavior and customs.

In addition to participant observation, ethnographers also use other research methods and tools, some in conjunction with participant observation

---

APPLIED ANTHROPOLOGY

Hicks and Gwynne emphasize this growing subdiscipline and give it special attention in four different chapters,"Anthropology and Anthropologists," "Field-work" (another unique chapter), "Economics," and "Culture Change and Anthropology's Response," as well as in "The Anthropologist at Work" boxes throughout the text.

The Anthropologist at Work

Patricia Wright

In Madagascar, a huge island lying off the southeast coast of Africa, lies Ranomafana National Park, one of the richest yet at the same time most endangered natural areas in the world. The park is so extensive and remote that parts of it have yet to be explored. At one time, Ranomafana was home to a thriving population of lemurs, rare primates that exist only in Madagascar. By 1985, however, environmentally destructive practices such as hunting by local people, slash-and-burn agriculture, and cattle herding in the forest, as well as deforestation resulting from fuelwood collection and industrial logging, had seriously depleted Ranomafana's lemur population. If the lemurs and their habitat were to be protected, these practices would have to be halted.

An international conference was convened to help the Malagasy government decide how both the rainforest and its rare denizens could best be protected. Participants realized they needed to formulate policies that would simultaneously preserve the land and its animal and plant species, and also address the economic needs of the local people, the Tanala and Betsileo, who depended on the rainforest for their livelihood. A project to achive these goals was established.

Anthropologist and primatologist Patricia Wright was appointed director of the new Ranomafana National Park Project. Wright quickly realized that any plan of

action that failed to combine conservation with development, or to win the cooperation of the Tanala and Betsileo people in maintaining the park, would be doomed to failure. To learn what the villagers' needs would be if the use of their traditional lands were denied to them, she led a survey team on foot over rugged hillsides to Tanala and Betsileo villages. In each village, the team first met with the elders, then called a general meeting of village members at which their need for schools, health clinics, women's cooperatives, and agricultural assistance could be discussed. As the team listened, the scope of the project increased (Wright 1992:28).

Madagascar

Ranomafana National Park

"THE ANTHROPOLOGIST AT WORK" BOXES

These boxes highlight the contributions of anthropologists and the ways in which their real-world applications relate to the discussion of the material at hand. Each of them focuses on a practicing anthropologist and his or her work, or suggests a way that students might apply an undergraduate education in anthropology toward a specific career path. Highlights include the works of Roger McConochie, Elizabeth Briody, Applied Medical Anthropology, Fieldwork Coordination, and many others.

---

owned three ranches, several cars, and an airplane with his likeness painted on the fuselage. Two years later he died of hypertension, his doctor placing some of the blame on the chief's fondness for "white man's food"—chocolate and sugar.

In some Pacific island nations, the customary diet is changing from one based on high-fiber, low-fat

foods like root crops, fresh fish, green leaves, and coconuts to one based on white flour or rice, canned meat and fish, and large quantities of sugar and salt. In Fiji, the proportion of total energy deriving from less nutritious imported foods has steadily increased: high enough at 43 percent in 1977, it had risen to 63 percent by 1981 (Hull 1991:25).

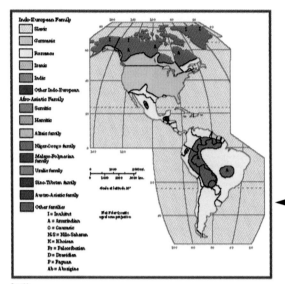

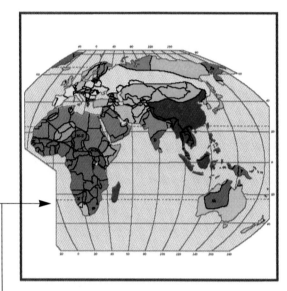

Figure 5.2
The distribution of the major language families in the world. (Source: From Jordan et al. 1994.)

If this is said in a way that the speaker's voice falls on the second *he*, the utterance is probably intended as a flat statement, with which the speaker expects the listener to agree. However, if the words are spoken so the second *he* is uttered with a rising tone, the meaning changes. In this case, the speaker is in doubt about the validity of the statement, and is making a request for information (Crystal 1975:165–166).

One important focus of contemporary paralinguists is the ways in which paralanguage affects communications between the sexes, a subject discussed later in this chapter (see Gender and Language, below). Another is the overlap between paralanguage and body language—the nonverbal ways human beings convey ideas, feelings, and intentions through bodily movements and facial expressions,

unconscious or conscious (see Chapter 15). Paralanguage manifests itself differently depending on who is speaking, what language is being used, and the context of the conversation, but it is a feature of all spoken languages.

Historical Linguistics
Historical linguistics approaches the study of language diachronically, rather than synchronically as

descriptive linguistics does. Historical linguists are interested in the histories of the world's living, or currently used, languages (see Figure 5.2) and in the decipherment of dead, or obsolete, languages.

historical linguistics the branch of linguistics that studies the histories of languages, both living and dead, and the relationships between languages and dialects

---

MAPS EMPLOYED THROUGHOUT THE TEXT

The pedagogical program incorporates maps to cross-reference and shed further light on the material covered within each chapter. These maps illustrate a wide range of key topics, including the distribution of major language families and the distribution of the world's major religions.

Allocate Goods and Services
In many societies, including Western society, marriage may involve the transfer of goods and services among affines, either at the time of marriage or later (Goody and Tambiah 1973). The terms *bridewealth, bride-service,* and *dowry* are used to

not come to *your* aid when you and your clan were attacked.

Affinal alliances require regulations that spell out how suitable marriages can be brought about. The rule of exogamy, of course, requires descent group members to choose spouses from groups other than their own, thus bringing two groups into alliance. But in many cases a society will not want its members to choose spouses from groups so distant or so alien that useful affinal alliances cannot be formed. So, in addition to rules of exogamy, many societies have rules of **endogamy:** spouses must be chosen from *within* a certain group. Usually the endogamous group within which one is encouraged to find one's spouse is relatively large, such as a religious or ethnic group. Indeed, one reason for endogamy is to preserve a religious or ethnic tradition. Many people living in Jordan, for instance, identify themselves as Palestinian rather than Jordanian, and are encouraged to choose spouses from within the Palestinian

endogamy the custom in which one's spouse must be chosen from within one's own group

---

LOCATOR MAPS FOR GEOGRAPHICAL REFERENCE

Found throughout the text, these helpful guides supplement extended discussions of indigenous peoples and ethnographic material while enabling students to easily locate the cultures discussed within their appropriate geographical contexts.

"ANTHROPOLOGY AND THE ENVIRONMENT" BOXES

Each isolating a particular environmental issue, these sections illustrate how different cultures view and interact with the environment, as well as how the condition of the environment affects them socially, economically, and in other ways.

Anthropology and the Environment

Women and Water in Kenya

Water covers nearly three-quarters of the earth's surface, but only 3 percent of it is fresh, and most of that amount is frozen in the polar ice caps, buried underground, or otherwise inaccessible for human use. Thus fresh, clean water accounts for less than 1 percent of the total water on earth (Miller 1994:336), and the supply is constantly decreasing due to pollution by human beings. Today over one-fifth of the world's population—1.2 billion people, most of them in developing countries—do not have adequate access to the clean water they need for drinking, bathing, cooking, laundering, disposing of wastes, or irrigating crops. Yet adequate amounts of clean water are essential for human life.

Especially in developing countries, women are primarily responsible for obtaining the fresh water their families need. Many do not have running water at home, so they must walk to a well, stand in line for a turn at the hand pump, draw water to the surface, and carry it home in heavy jars or cans. At home, women are the managers of the water they have procured, since they are the family members who are usually responsible for cooking, dishwashing, and laundry. When supplies of fresh water are scarce or located at great distances from homes, it is women who pay the greatest price, and when new wells are dug that bring clean water closer to their homes, they are the primary beneficiaries.

Kwale, a poor, rural district on the coast of Kenya, East Africa, with a rapidly growing population, lies in an area of seasonal droughts. By the mid-1970s, the wells in Kwale no longer provided sufficient quantities of clean water reliably all year round (Mwangola 1995). To supply her family with fresh water, a village woman, carrying heavy water containers, would have to walk two or more miles to a slippery-sided, dangerous well—even further, when local wells dried up (Mwangola 1995). Depending on family size, some women had to make this round trip as many as eight times a day. When water was available, it was often tainted, causing a wide variety of illnesses; 80 percent of all illnesses in developing countries can be attributed to unsafe water and poor sanitation (WASH 1992:2). There was an urgent need for new, reliable sources of clean water.

In 1975, Kenya's National Council for Women, made up of some 40 small women's groups, took on the challenging task of increasing rural Kenyan

---

that each male has a limited quantity of "life force," some of which he loses each time he has sex with a woman. Beliefs of this kind encourage the segregation of males from females, and New Guinea is famous for its men's associations.

Other men's groups exist for different reasons. **Military associations,** common to many traditional and modern societies, are groups of males who have fought or may fight together. In some societies, military associations are combined with age grades. Among the Shavante, for instance, the role of warrior belongs to the mature men's age grade. In other societies, military associations exist without age grades, although in any society men who go to war together are likely to be members of the same generation.

Military associations formed an important part of the culture of the Native Americans of the Great

military association a group of males who have fought or may fight together

---

• The Concept of Culture •

What Is Culture?

The concept of culture is fundamental to anthropology, yet it is so complex a notion that anthropologists have never agreed on a single (much less a simple) definition of the term. We provided one definition in Chapter 1, briefly introducing culture as all the things people collectively think, do, say and make—in other words, their shared ideas, behaviors, languages, and artifacts. These include institutions (such as marriage), political ideas (such as democracy), religious beliefs (such as witchcraft), customs (like fireworks on the Fourth of July), rituals (like saluting the flag), objects, stories, art styles, games, and much more. But culture cannot adequately be defined in terms of its outward manifestations alone; we must also take account of its other properties.[1]

Ask Yourself

What does the term *culture* mean to you? As popularly used, the word is often defined in terms of certain activities, such as going to the opera or reading poetry. What is the relationship between that definition and the one we are proposing?

Culture Is Unique to Human Beings. Cultural anthropologists sometimes define culture as that which distinguishes human beings from all other forms of life. This definition has not gone unchallenged; some scholars, most of them in disciplines other than cultural anthropology, feel it is either insufficient or incorrect. Among them are some primate ethologists, students of the behavior of nonhuman primates (human beings' closest biological relatives), who argue that the nonhuman "higher primates" (all the monkeys and apes, and especially chimpanzees and gorillas ("great apes,") possess culture of an elementary kind. We will take this subject up again in a moment (see the section entitled "Animal Symbols," below). For now, suffice it to say that as cultural anthropologists we do not consider the behavior of any nonhuman creatures

[1] We need to distinguish between culture as we defined it in Chapter 1, and the coulture of a particular society, which is all the cultural things that characterize that particular society.

Because they are deprived of culture, children who grow up in isolation behave differently from other human beings. Kamala, found living alone in the jungle in India, may have been deprived of culture since babyhood. She moved about on all fours and ate from her caretaker's hand.

to be cultural. At the same time, however, we recognize that the concept of culture is only incompletely understood in terms of the distinction between human beings and other creatures.

Culture Is Patterned. The ideas, behaviors, languages, and artifacts that constitute the outward manifestations of any culture are elements of patterns that are widely recognized and repeated within that culture, both in the present (synchronically) and down through the generations (diachronically). Therefore, nothing that is unique to one individual can be considered an element of that individual's culture. Someone native to the United States might create a flag with alternating purple and green stripes and a pink field of stars in one corner. This unique object would not be considered art of American culture, although a similar flag with alternating red and white stripes and a blue field of stars in one corner would be. As we pointed out in Chapter 1, however, caution is in order: just because an idea, behavior, word, or artifact cannot be considered an

---

THOUGHT-PROVOKING "ASK YOURSELF" SECTIONS

Sprinkled throughout each chapter, these brief, open-ended questions encourage students to formulate their own personal opinions while answering questions—many of which are ethical in nature—as they relate to the text.

also true. A culture cannot be understood without an understanding of its economic system.

Summary

- Economic anthropology is the study of how societies allocate their resources (means) to achieve their wants and needs (ends).

- The concepts underlying the formal academic discipline of economics are based on Western economic behaviors, so economic theory cannot fully explain economic behavior in non-Western societies.

- For both economists and economic anthropologists, economic behavior consists of production, distribution, and consumption. Together, these add up to a society's economic system. Beyond this, however, economic anthropology rests on a cross-cultural, rather than a Western, view of economic behavior.

- Production, the transformation of resources into things people can use, is affected by what resources the environment provides, the technology available, the organization of the producers' labor, and their cultural values.

- Distribution—allocating products to those who need or want them—can involve moneyless giving and receiving (reciprocity—generalized, balanced, or negative); the pooling and disbursal of commodities, also moneyless (redistribution); or a market system, in which transactions are impersonal and negotiated with money.

- Consumption refers to all the ways in which the goods, services, and nonmaterial things produced within a society are used, for purposes including the satisfaction of basic wants and needs, symbolizing social prestige, or establishing political clout.

- The term *economic development* refers to a variety of strategies designed to increase the capacities of national economic systems to improve human welfare.

- Although some economic development projects have successfully improved people's lives, others have not, and anthropologists continue to [...] r they should be involved in [...] nscientific endeavors.

- Anthropologists are increasingly using their expertise to help businesses improve their efficiency, a form of applied anthropology called *business anthropology.*

- Business anthropologists analyze the internal operations of companies, sometimes carrying out cultural audits; survey the market potential for products; and advise companies that conduct business abroad how they might interact more smoothly with customers and workers of different cultures.

Key Terms

balanced reciprocity
barter
business anthropology
capital
capitalist mode of production
consumption
cultural audit
dependency ratio
destructive potlatch
distribution
economic development
economic system
economy
ends
generalized reciprocity
general-purpose money
kin-oriented mode of production
leveling mechanism
market exchange
means

Suggested Readings

Leach, Jerry W., and Edmund Leach. 1983. *The Kula: New Perspectives on Massim Exchange.* Cambridge: Cambridge University Press. A thought-provoking collection of articles, remarkable for its comprehensive treatment of the kula. Provides new insights into the ideas and behavior associated with the kula as practiced by societies other than the Trobrianders.

Plattner, Stuart. (ed.). 1989. *Economic Anthropology.* Stanford: Stanford University Press. Twelve scholars discuss a wide range of economic topics in the context of gatherer-and-hunter, horticultural, peasant, and urban societies. An essay on the roles women play in economic institutions is particularly interesting.

STUDENT-FRIENDLY PEDAGOGY

Supplementing the authors' extremely accessible presentation are chapter-opening introductory vignettes, a general outline of the material to be covered in each chapter, running glossaries, chapter-ending conclusions, summaries, key terms, and annotated suggested readings.

Introduction

On the streets of the South Bronx in New York City, they were known as the Bombers. Depending on your point of view, they were either juvenile delinquents who

Introduction

Ollege student, standing in doorway of anthropology professor's office: "I found this really weird-looking rock on the beach, and I was wondering if you could identify it for me."

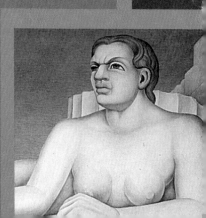

Medical technician, making small talk while taking patient's pulse: "I see on your personal history form that you're an anthropologist. Doesn't that have something to do with old bones?"

Small nephew, climbing into grown-up aunt's lap: "Mom told me you're an anth-ro-pol-o-gist, so I wanna show you my model dinosaurs."

Dubious parent to college student: "You want to major in *what?* Are you sure it's something that will help you find a job?"

Misconceptions about anthropology abound. The confusion stems from the fact that there are several different kinds of anthropologists, who study many different things. Some are interested in rocks and bones (although not dinosaurs), but only insofar as these can reveal something about human beings. The word *human* is the key to understanding what anthropology is about: it is the study of human beings and their ancestors, from before the emergence of the human species on this earth up to the present day, and of anything and everything that helps explain human beings' existence and behavior.

Almost every anthropologist is a specialist in some particular aspect of the study of human beings, whether it be their ancestry, physical development, history, or present behavior. On any given day, somewhere around the world, some anthropologist may be asking

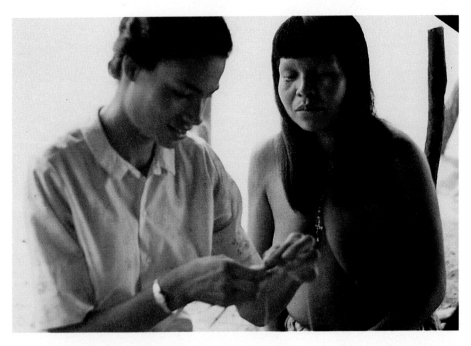

While all anthropologists study people, each anthropologist has his or her own specific interests. In Amazonian Brazil, an Apinaye woman demonstrates a traditional knitting technique, unique to the New World, to anthropologist Dolores Newton.

residents of the Amazon jungle how they determine the boundaries of their banana gardens, while another anthropologist may be sitting in a university laboratory peering through a microscope at a sample of human blood, and a third may be interviewing the patrons of a run-down urban bar. Yet another may be admiring an ancient stone arrowhead just dug out of the ground, while still another may be sitting cross-legged in a tent, entering into a portable computer the different terms by which the inhabitants of a Pacific island refer to their various cousins. A sixth anthropologist may be delivering a lecture to American college students on the evolutionary ideas of Charles Darwin, while a seventh, binoculars and notebook in hand, may be silently stalking a small group of wild chimpanzees through the forests of Zaire.

Different jobs, but all anthropologists. What do they have in common? **Each of them—in his or her own way—is engaged, directly or indirectly, in the study of some aspect of human life.**

• The Four-Field Discipline • of Anthropology

An academic discipline as broadly defined as "the study of human beings and whatever helps explain their existence and behavior" is, of course, an extraordinarily far-ranging and comprehensive one. No single individual can be an expert in every aspect of such a broad discipline. Thus, since its nineteenth-century origins as an academic discipline, anthropology has embraced a number of distinct fields or subdisciplines, each devoted to the analysis of a different aspect of human existence and behavior. Traditionally, there are four of these fields: **biological (or physical) anthropology, cultural anthropology, archaeology, and anthropological linguistics** (Figure 1.1).

Each takes a different view of humanity and is usually taught separately from the others. But the four subdisciplines share a major philosophical perspective: all four are both comparative (rather than dedicated to the study of any one group of people) and comprehensive (in that they include all of humankind). Occasionally the four subdisciplines overlap, but most anthropologists specialize in only one.

Three of the four fields of anthropology—cultural anthropology, archaeology, and anthropological linguistics—share a common theme: they are primarily concerned with **culture.** Defined in the broadest and simplest terms, culture is everything that human beings collectively do, think, make, and say, anywhere in space or time, including their customs, ideas, the physical objects they create, and the ways in which they communicate and interact with one another. Of the four fields of anthropology, only biological anthropology—the study of the biological aspects of what it means to be human—is not primarily about culture. For the other three fields, the concept of culture is fundamental. Cultural anthropology is concerned with the culture of contemporary people, archaeology with the culture of people who lived in the past, and anthropological linguistics with the links between communication and culture.[1]

---

biological (physical) anthropology the field of anthropology that focuses on the biological aspects of being human

cultural anthropology the study of culture

archaeology the field of anthropology that focuses on the material remains of people of the past

anthropological linguistics (linguistic anthropology) the field of anthropology that focuses on languages

culture everything that people collectively do, think, make, and say

---

[1] Despite these three subdisciplines' common concern with culture, the term *cultural anthropology* usually refers only to the study of the culture of contemporary people, and this is the way in which the term is used in this book.

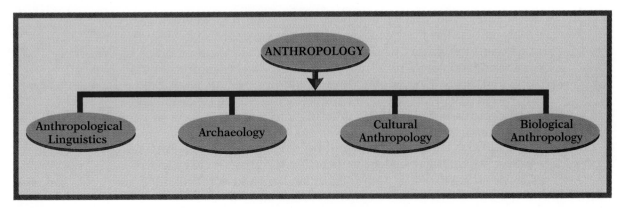

Figure 1.1

Fields and Subfields of Anthropology. We usually divide anthropology into four major fields, each of which focuses on a different subject. This book is about cultural anthropology, a field that embraces a number of subfields, such as urban anthropology, feminist anthropology, and applied cultural anthropology.

Below, before describing in detail what cultural anthropology is about, we briefly introduce each of the four subdisciplines, in order to convey a sense of how cultural anthropology relates to and complements biological anthropology, archaeology, and anthropological linguistics to add up to a broad, comprehensive discipline whose area of interest is everything human.

Biological Anthropology

Biological anthropology, unlike the other three subdisciplines, emphasizes the biological, or physical, rather than the cultural aspects of being human. Major specialties within the subdiscipline include the origins and physical evolution of human beings; the study of the physical makeup and behavior of human beings' closest animal relatives, the nonhuman primates (such as apes and monkeys); and physical variation among contemporary human populations. While these subjects have an important bearing on the study of human beings, our frame of reference in this book is culture, not biology.

Cultural Anthropology

Cultural anthropology (sometimes called **ethnology**) is the study of the culture of contemporary people. The word *contemporary* in this instance covers both people who are living today and those who lived in the relatively recent past, about whom written or oral information exists.

Cultural anthropologists study, describe, and try to explain and understand the behavior of contemporary people: their customs, beliefs, values, and social interactions; the physical products of their minds and hands; and the ways in which they communicate with one another. Sometimes cultural anthropology focuses on the members of one group—how they get the basic things they need for survival; how they interact with one another; how they clothe themselves, express their creative impulses, impose order on their lives, organize themselves into families and other groups, regulate their sexuality, worship their deities. But cultural anthropology also takes a broader view, comparing cultures with one another in order to address wider questions of human existence—why cultures are so different from one another; why some people favor political equality while others prevent it; why some worship many gods, others only one; why some discourage premarital sex while others encourage it; whether there is any behavior that occurs in only one human group and no others; whether any kind of human behavior occurs so commonly around the world as to be considered "average" or "normal." In the range of questions it addresses, cultural anthropology is the broadest of the four fields of anthropology.

ethnology an alternative term for cultural anthropology

Archaeology

The primary focus of **archaeology** is the material remains of human beings who lived in the past.[2] These remains take two forms: **artifacts**—human-made objects such as tools, pottery, garbage, and even huge walled cities—and **ecofacts**—natural objects once used or altered by human beings, such as grains of pollen or pieces of charcoal from ancient hearths. Since artifacts and ecofacts are apt to be buried under layers of soil by the passage of time and the action of wind and water, the primary research method of archaeologists is excavation, augmented by a variety of scientific tests, conducted in laboratories, to determine the composition, age, and function of excavated artifacts and ecofacts.

Archaeology includes two major subfields, prehistoric and historic. The cultures of prehistoric people, those who left no written records, can be studied only through excavation and laboratory analysis, so were it not for archaeology we would know nothing about such people. In the case of historic people, those who left written records that have survived to the present day, excavation and laboratory analysis supplement the written record, which is often incomplete because people tend not to write down information that is well known to members of their community.

Archaeologists are anthropologists who study the material things left by people of the past. In Iraq, archaeologist Elizabeth Stone excavates the site of Mashkan-Shapir, an ancient city that had been forgotten for nearly four thousand years.

• Ask Yourself •

Have you ever taken the time to record in a diary a description of your home, the names and ages and occupations of your relatives, the foods you eat, the kinds of transportation you use, or other ordinary details of your life?

Anthropological Linguistics

Anthropological linguistics (sometimes called **linguistic anthropology**) is the anthropological study of languages, ancient and modern, written and unwritten. Among the many interests of anthropological linguists are the origins of human communication, clues to which may be found by studying how apes, our closest nonhuman relatives, communicate with one another; how the parts of the brain and body used in speaking developed in modern human beings; how ancient languages, handed down to us either in the form of written texts or as words incorporated into other languages, developed and changed through time; how children learn to speak; how certain sounds and tones of voice combine to make up a spoken language; and how language and culture mutually affect one another. This last topic is especially important to cultural anthropologists because it is culture, of which language is an essential constituent, that distinguishes human beings from all other living creatures.

"Language," as defined by anthropological linguists, is more than just spoken words; it includes any kind of patterned communication between people, such as sign language, body language, and even electronic communication. Since the ways in which people communicate constitute an integral constituent of culture, the subject of this book, we devote a chapter (Chapter 5) to this topic.

---

[2] Some anthropologists define archaeology as the study of the material remains of all people, past or present.

artifact any material thing created by people

ecofact a natural object used or modified by human hands

• Fundamental Concepts in • Cultural Anthropology

Culture

Difficult to define in few words, culture is nevertheless the most important and most frequently mentioned concept in this book, because it embodies what it means to be human. Earlier we defined culture as everything that human beings collectively do, think, make, and say, anywhere in space or time—in other words, their collective behavior, ideas, artifacts, and forms of communication. The word *collective* is fundamental here: cultural anthropologists are interested in the behavior of human beings in groups, for culture is a group phenomenon, shared among group members and passed along by older members to younger ones.

One reason why culture is difficult to define precisely is that what constitutes a component of the culture of one group may not be cultural in the context of another. For example, if a young woman, reared in the context of Western culture, were to cut her chest with a knife and then rub ashes into the wounds to ensure visible scarring, this would be considered aberrant behavior; the woman would be thought of as mentally ill, and perhaps referred to a psychiatrist. However, in the context of some non-Western cultures, such as that of the Korongo people of the Sudan in Africa, this behavior on the part of young women is both normal and appropriate. Thus any attempt to explain what culture consists of must take into account the context in which a particular custom, idea, object, or mode of communication occurs.

---

society a group of people whose members live in the same place and whose lives and livelihoods are interdependent

social anthropology especially in England, the brand of anthropology focusing on societies rather than on culture

social structure the web of relationships binding members of a society

sociocultural anthropology a term for cultural anthropology that emphasizes society

ethnicity the identification of individuals with particular ethnic groups

ethnic group a group whose members share basic cultural traditions and values and a common language, and who identify themselves (and are identified by others) as distinct from other such groups

Society

A second major topic of interest to cultural anthropologists is **society,** a term that has been defined in so many ways that even anthropologists are not in agreement on its meaning. For our purposes, a simple definition will do: a society is a group of people whose members live in the same place and whose lives and livelihoods are interdependent. A society's members do not have to be alike. They may come from the same or different traditions, their skin color may be the same or different, and they may speak the same or different languages. Thus we may refer to "North American society," which incorporates many different traditions, shades of pigmentation, and languages, just as we speak of "Trobriand society," referring to people who live on several tiny islands in the Pacific and share a single tradition, skin color, and language.

In England, where anthropologists have emphasized societies and the relationships among people within them rather than culture, the term **social anthropology** is often used. It was given prominence by A. R. Radcliffe-Brown (1881–1955), who advocated the study of **social structure,** the web of relationships that bind members of a society. Since social anthropology (with its emphasis on society) and cultural anthropology (with its emphasis on culture) overlap, one sometimes encounters the term **sociocultural anthropology.** In this book we avoid this cumbersome term; our use of *cultural anthropology* is sufficiently flexible to include the British concept of society.

• Ask Yourself •

As a member of a particular society, what makes you similar to other members of your society? Do you see yourself as different in some ways from other members? Is it possible for a person to be a member of more than one society at the same time?

Ethnicity

Another major concept in cultural anthropology is **ethnicity,** one's identification with a particular **ethnic group.** An ethnic group is a community of people whose members share basic cultural traditions and values and in most cases a common language, and who identify themselves (and are identi-

A society's members live in the same place and interact with one another, but they may or may not be similar in other ways. North American society incorporates people from many different cultural backgrounds. Chinese society is much more uniform.

fied by others) as distinct from other groups. All of us belong to at least one and sometimes to several such groups; a single society may contain many.

• Ask Yourself •

Do you identify yourself as a member of a particular ethnic group? Have you ever questioned older relatives about your common ethnicity? If so, whose ethnic identity is stronger, yours or your older relatives'?

The reason ethnicity is of so much interest to cultural anthropologists is that it has a profound effect on people's beliefs, values, and behavior, and can thus help to explain cultural differences. For example, in the United States, a multiethnic society, members of different ethnic groups often use language, wear clothes, and affect hairstyles that symbolize their affiliation with one ethnic group and at the same time set them apart from the members of other ethnic groups.

Cultural Relativism

A fourth concept central to modern cultural anthropology, and one of the most important in this book, is **cultural relativism.** This is the idea that a culture must be evaluated in terms of its own values, not according to the values of another culture. For example, the marriage of one man to two women at the same time, unacceptable in Western culture, is entirely acceptable in certain other cultures. Who is to say that the Western custom of limiting individuals to only one spouse at a time is superior?

---

cultural relativism a central idea in modern cultural anthropology—that a culture must be evaluated in terms of its own values, not according to the values of another culture

The concept of cultural relativism has an opposite, **ethnocentrism,** the idea that one's own ethnic group, society, or culture is superior to others. This notion is inconsistent with the findings of cultural anthropology, which have repeatedly shown that—in the absence of any universal yardstick against which cultures can be measured and compared—no ethnic group, society, or culture can be said to be superior to any other.

Sometimes the concept of cultural relativism has been interpreted narrowly, as implying that anthropologists must suspend their cultural values when studying the cultures of others. But this is tantamount to saying that people have the right to engage in any practice, however reprehensible, simply because it is "part of their culture" (Maybury-Lewis 1988:378). In the wider sense, cultural relativism means that an anthropologist should refrain from making value judgments about other peoples' beliefs and practices until she has understood these beliefs in their own cultural terms (Maybury-Lewis 1988:378–379). Under this definition, the Holocaust could never be justified on the grounds that it was part of Nazi culture, nor the racism practiced in South Africa on the grounds that it was a part of South African culture.

• Specialties in Cultural • Anthropology

In the past, cultural anthropologists almost exclusively studied societies that were small-scale and **nonliterate**—lacking a tradition of reading and writing. (The term *nonliterate* distinguishes such people from **illiterate** people, who do not read or write either, but who live in societies in which others do). Nonliterate societies used to be called *primitive* societies, but because Westerners are inclined to equate that word with inferiority, most anthropologists today prefer using either *nonliterate* or *small-scale* when referring to such societies. They do not consider nonliterate societies to be

inferior to literate societies, nor do they equate them with prehistoric societies (as scholars of the Victorian period did). Some aspects of life in nonliterate societies, such as technology, are simpler than their equivalents in literate societies, but other aspects, such as kinship systems or oral traditions, may be more sophisticated.

Also of long-standing interest in cultural anthropology, perhaps because the number of small-scale, nonliterate societies has diminished steadily since anthropology became an academic discipline, are the cultures and societies of **peasants.** These are people who are typically found within the geographical and cultural boundaries occupied by larger and more technologically complex societies, whose traditions they share. In most cases, peasants are agricultural people whose lives and work revolve around their households and farms, and whose subsistence technologies are simpler than those used in industrialized societies. Despite the rapid pace of

Small-scale, nonliterate societies are characterized by simple technologies. On the island of Flores in Eastern Indonesia, a Manggarai man, wearing a hat made from half a coconut shell, sets a rat trap.

---

ethnocentrism the belief that one's own society or culture is superior to all others

nonliterate lacking a tradition of reading and writing

illiterate lacking the ability to read and write while living in a literate society

peasants typically agricultural people who share the same general cultural tradition as members of the larger and more technologically complex societies in which they live

change in the twentieth century, there are millions of people, in India, China, Latin America, and elsewhere, who live this way of life. Once largely illiterate, peasants today are increasingly likely to have some formal education.

Today, cultural anthropologists' interest in nonliterate people and peasants continues, but people who live in contemporary large-scale societies, both non-Western and Western, have also become a major focus of study. Large-scale societies are so culturally diverse that cultural anthropologists who specialize in them usually concentrate on smaller subgroups within them—for example, the members of a particular ethnic group, occupational group, or social class.

Cultural anthropologists often specialize in specific topics, viewed cross-culturally, rather than in particular cultures (although every cultural anthropologist has expertise in at least one culture, and sometimes several). Some cultural anthropologists, for instance, are interested in how people in large-scale societies adapt to city life; their specialty is called urban anthropology. Others focus on the place of women in society (feminist anthropology); medical beliefs and practices, particularly those of people in non-Western societies (medical anthropology); or the ways in which people of different cultures adapt to their natural and cultural environments (cultural ecology).

These specialties are described in more detail in Chapter 3. In addition, because the focus of cultural ecology is now widely understood as crucial not only to our understanding of culture but also to our understanding of how human life may be sustained on this planet, there are boxes entitled "Anthropology and the Environment" throughout

Anthropology and the Environment

What Is "The Environment"?

The word *environment,* as it is commonly used, refers to our natural surroundings: the planet Earth and the soil, rock, air, water, plants, and animals that compose it. Our concern in this book, however, is not with the physical environment by itself, but rather with the complex and interactive relationships between human beings and these natural phenomena. Wherever they live, people and their environment are inextricably linked; we cannot hope to understand the relationships between them if we conceive of nature as separate from human behavior (Bradford and Gwynne 1995:1).

We are by no means the first to recognize that what human beings do (or do not do) helps to create what is called the environment. The term is seldom equated with, or limited to, the "green" environmental agenda of natural resource management and biodiversity conservation. Today *environment* is widely understood

also to include the humanly caused "brown" environmental problems so troublesome in most of the world, such as air and water pollution, soil erosion and degradation, and the misuse of energy resources.

In this book, however, the term is used in an even broader sense. *Environment* refers not only to our physical, natural surroundings, and the concerns of the green agenda, not only to human beings' pollution and degradation of natural resources and "brown" environmental concerns, but also to the environment we human beings have created, the cultural climate in which we live, whether it be clean or polluted, affluent or impoverished, safe or dangerous. After all, cultural phenomena, such as poverty, violence, and racism, negatively affect our environment even as deforestation, industrial pollution, and nuclear waste do. Viewing the environment in such expansive terms helps us understand not only what environmental problems human beings face, but also what we can do about them.

The Anthropologist at Work

Roger McConochie

A twin-engine passenger jet taxis to the end of the runway, turns and brakes. The control tower operator clears the plane for takeoff, and the captain advises his flight crew to take their seats. The engines rev to full power and the jet begins to roll. Suddenly, as the plane lifts into the air, the voice of a flight attendant crackles over the intercom. "Captain, the right engine is on fire!" Quickly the captain shuts down the right engine . . . and the plane drops from the sky. Later, in reconstructing the accident, investigators discover that at the time of the crash the flight attendant was properly strapped into her jumpseat at the front of the passenger compartment—facing the rear of the aircraft. Thus her "right" was the captain's "left." The captain shut down the one good engine.

Preventing such miscommunication through the design of training programs in aviation safety is one of the many assignments handled by Chicago-based corporate anthropologist Roger McConochie, presi-

dent of Corporate Research International and a specialist in how people communicate with one another in the workplace. Other assignments include formulating programs to develop global management teams for international corporations.

McConochie followed a circuitous route to his present position. After college, he spent four years in the army, in Europe and Vietnam. Having learned to speak German, he qualified for a fellowship for graduate study in anthropology, including three years of predoctoral fieldwork among German-speaking peasants in the Italian Alps. "I felt that I had found my niche in life and that I was on the fast track to becoming an Alpine peasant specialist," he says. "With the clear certainty of youth, I knew that I would be teaching Anthro 101 and spending summers in the Alps for the rest of my life" (McConochie 1994).

After graduate school, however, McConochie learned that academic jobs were scarce. A casual conversation on campus led to a temporary

---

this book that describe interactions between culture and environment.[3]

• Applied Anthropology: A • Fifth Field?

In the past, most people with advanced degrees in anthropology either became university or college professors, or did not make direct professional use of their anthropological training. Over the last several decades, however, a different kind of anthropology has gained prominence, less theo-

retical than the academic anthropology that has been practiced since the nineteenth century and more oriented to practical ends. This is **applied anthropology,** in which anthropological ideas and methods are used to address problems and achieve specific goals in areas such as business, government, or social services. Some anthropologists consider applied anthropology to be so distinct from the four other fields of anthropology as to constitute a fifth field, although it is more commonly viewed as cross-cutting the other four; there are applied physical anthropologists,

---

[3] Cultural ecology has become more publicly prominent since the United Nations sponsored the World Conference on Environment and Development (the "Earth Summit"), which focused much-needed media attention on global environmental problems. The conference was held in Rio de Janeiro, Brazil, in 1992.

applied anthropology the use of anthropological ideas and methods to achieve practical ends outside the academic community

assignment with a local business firm. "When they paid me with a check that read 'Roger McConochie, Consultant,' I realized that a door had opened for me, and within a week I had set up my own consulting firm as a business anthropologist. Later I learned that a dozen of my colleagues in anthropology had been through parallel experiences, each of us coming independently to the discovery that anthropology had direct applications in the world of business."

For students who have decided to major in anthropology and who are perhaps considering careers as corporate anthropologists, McConochie advises: "Consider all your options. While anthropology has essential lessons for business, want-ads specifying 'corporate anthropologist' are few. As your primary specialty, consider earning a degree in science, engineering, law, or business. Then, to that, add your interest and expertise in anthropological matters. The combination will give you a unique skill-set. And remember—the best jobs will go to those who never stop learning, whether in formal programs or in self-directed study."

Even though advertised jobs in applied anthropology are few, McConochie thinks that opportunities in this field are "uncountable," limited only by the ability of anthropologists to apply their

insights to products, processes, and services with direct and immediate effect on people's lives. Students who thrive on challenge, novelty, and unpredictability—qualities that are increasingly required of us all—may be able to follow in the footsteps of this internationally recognized pioneer by carving out their own niches as corporate anthropologists.

In carving out his career as a corporate anthropologist, Roger McConochie combined anthropology with his other interests, among them aviation. Today, as a specialist in cross-cultural communication, one of his areas of expertise is aviation safety.

applied cultural anthropologists, applied archaeologists, and applied anthropological linguists.

Applied anthropology is growing rapidly. In 1972, an estimated 2 percent of anthropologists with doctoral degrees worked outside academia; the remainder were teachers (Dunkel 1992:10). Today, nearly a third of all graduates holding Ph.D. degrees in anthropology and even more of those holding M.A. degrees work outside of academics, and the range of jobs from which they can choose—in health care, law, business, environmental conservation, journalism, and many other fields—continues to grow. Some work full time as employees of businesses, governmental agencies, or nonprofit groups. Some serve as independent consultants to such organizations. Some have established their own consulting firms. Some work for the media. Some work internationally, in areas

such as health care, education, or agriculture. The potential list of nonacademic anthropological occupations would seem to be limited only by anthropologists' imaginations.

Undergraduate anthropology majors rarely find applied anthropology jobs waiting for them after graduation; usually one must have an advanced degree to find a job as an applied anthropologist. Yet for anthropology majors willing to go on for further study, we see many opportunities to apply anthropological expertise professionally outside of academics, a fact that might help to relieve the doubtful parent upon whom we eavesdropped at the beginning of this chapter. To illustrate how studying cultural anthropology can prepare people for jobs outside academia, this book includes a number of boxes titled "The Anthropologist at Work." Each illustrates one way in which the academic study of cultural anthropology can be translated into a job in some area of applied cultural anthropology. Some "Anthropologist at Work" boxes contain short profiles of applied anthropologists, their academic backgrounds, and the work in which they are currently engaged; others describe ways in which the study of anthropology might provide the qualifications needed to begin a particular career.

• Pioneers •

The Beginnings of Cultural Anthropology

Anthropology as a formal academic discipline is only a little over a hundred years old, but from the beginning of recorded history (and probably before that as well) people have been observing and obtaining information about other people. Much of this information was collected to serve the ends of conquest, trade, or missionary work, but some of it—more and more as time went on—was gathered simply to further people's understanding of others.

As far as we can tell from ancient records, the first person to travel to foreign places to collect information on the cultures of their inhabitants was the Greek historian Herodotus (ca. 485–425 B.C.), who in the fifth century B.C. explored the lands bordering the Mediterranean Sea. His work had a practical purpose: he traveled mainly to provide his own government with information to guide its interaction with foreign countries. We might thus view him not only as the first cultural anthropologist, but also as the founder of applied anthropology.

After Herodotus, but still before the time of Christ, Romans traveled to Gaul (now France); later, seventh-century Arabians journeyed northeast to Persia and northwest to France; eleventh-century Norsemen traveled west to America; and Genghis Khan and Marco Polo traveled west and east, respectively, in the twelfth and thirteenth centuries. In the fifteenth and sixteenth centuries, an "Age of Exploration" began, as western Europeans fanned out around the globe, coming into contact with cultures that until then had not existed for Westerners, even in their imaginations. By the eighteenth and early nineteenth centuries, numerous systematic attempts had been made to explain the origins and organization of human societies, the wide variety of people's customs, and how societies changed.

Although most of these attempts were undertaken in conjunction with Western efforts to gain economic or political advantages or spread Christianity among non-Christians, some had more scholarly purposes.

The nineteenth century witnessed cultural anthropology's rapid growth. As the colonial empires of Great Britain, France, the Netherlands, and Germany expanded all over Africa, the East Indies, South America, and Asia, so did the data collected on the cultures of these lands. Information was gathered by administrators, merchants, missionaries, and soldiers, who greatly expanded the West's knowledge of non-Western people.

One reason for this surge of interest in the customs of other people was that such information had increasing practical application. Western European governments needed the information collected by missionaries and explorers to assist them in administering the people whose lands they had conquered. Similarly, the U.S. government established the Bureau of American Ethnology (BAE) in 1872 to study Native Americans,[4] partly to gather scientific information about their cultures but also to be better positioned to control them. One famous study carried out with the support of the BAE was James Mooney's 1895 investigation of the Ghost Dance ritual of the Plains Indians. The government suspected that this religious ritual, still being practiced by the Native Americans five years after the infamous massacre at Wounded Knee effectively ended their resistance, might bring about another uprising. Mooney's mission was to suggest to the United States Department of War how to respond to the Ghost Dance and ultimately to predict and control the Native Americans' behavior. We cannot escape the fact that some of anthropology's roots lie in Western efforts to exploit, contain, or control other societies.

By the late nineteenth and early twentieth centuries, anthropology had become a distinct academic discipline, and departments of anthropology

---

[4] Some people object to the term *native* because they feel it implies being non-Western or inferior. We use the term to refer to people who are members of a given local culture by both birth and tradition. Native Americans have different opinions on the issue of what they should call themselves; some prefer *Native Americans,* some prefer *American Indians,* and some prefer to use the ancient terms by which their ancestors referred to themselves.

*In the late nineteenth century, U.S. government anthropologists studied Native Americans so the
government could "protect" and control them. James Mooney studied the Ghost Dance
performed by Native Americans of the Great Plains, who believed this ritual would end their
intense suffering at the hands of white people.*

were being formed, most of them in England and the United States. While economic and political interests continued to motivate some Westerners who visited foreign lands, the quest to understand what it means to be human had by now become a formal, scholarly pursuit. Among the greatest contributors to the development of the new academic discipline were Frank Hamilton Cushing, Franz Boas, and Bronislaw Malinowski.[5]

Frank Hamilton Cushing (1857–1900)

The late nineteenth-century American cultural anthropologist Frank Hamilton Cushing was untrained in anthropology, which was not yet being taught in the United States as a formal discipline. Yet by going to live among a group of people he was studying and by participating in their everyday lives, he became a pioneer in the discipline.

In 1875, still in his teens, Cushing was appointed to a U.S. government post in the Bureau of

American Ethnology, and settled down to what he probably thought would be a desk job. But four years later, in 1879, the Smithsonian Institution underwrote an expedition to the lands of the Pueblo Indians in the Southwest, to collect American Indian artifacts. In November of that year, Cushing joined the expedition as its official anthropologist. His instructions were generous: he could choose for himself where to collect his anthropological data, and could use his own methods. All he had to do was 'get the information,' which could probably be done, said his boss, in three months (Cushing 1990:3). Cushing stayed for four and a half years, from September 1879 to April 1884.

Arriving in western New Mexico, the Smithsonian expedition made camp near a Pueblo village called Zuni, home to a community of Native American people of the same name. The 22-year-old Cushing, without benefit of formal training in data collection, began his work by observing, sketching, and mapping the pueblo, and starting to learn the Zuni language. At first, the Zuni treated their uninvited guest with aloofness. When he asked for permission to sketch scenes of ceremonial activities, he received a curt refusal. Later he

---

[5] Most anthropologists at this time were men.

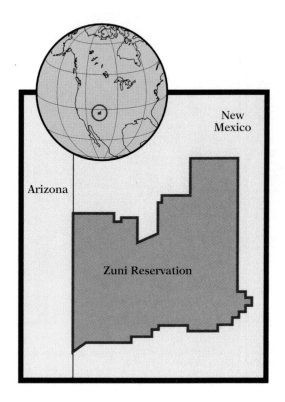

Arizona

New
Mexico

Zuni Reservation

wrote that the Zunis' suspicion of him resulted from the fact that his expedition had unwittingly set up camp on the property of the local missionary, whom the Zuni disliked. Naturally, they associated Cushing with the missionary, whose nickname was *Dust-eye*.

Cushing realized that to win the confidence of the Zuni he must not only observe them, but also participate in their lives. So he abandoned his expedition tent-mates and hung his hammock in the house of the Zuni governor, the man who held the highest political office in the village. The Smithsonian authorities had advised Cushing to learn all he could about the ways of the Pueblo people by concentrating his attention on one community, rather than by traveling throughout Native American lands. This was an unusual approach for the time; previously what little anthropological research had been done consisted of collecting artifacts and information from as many communities as possible in as short a time as possible. When his Smithsonian colleagues left for other parts of the Southwest, Cushing had not yet learned all he could about the Zuni, so he chose to remain behind in the governor's house.

Trouble soon arose. Although the expedition had left supplies for Cushing with "Dust-eye," the missionary now informed him that everything left behind now belonged to him as compensation for the use of his land as a campsite. Cushing would not get any of it. Left to fend for himself, he had little choice but to throw himself on the generosity of the Zuni.

Over the months, as Cushing settled into the community and improved his facility in the Zuni language, the Zuni seem to have developed some fondness for their anthropologist. Perhaps his run-in with the missionary made him more popular than he would otherwise have been. Whatever the reason, within two years the community had accepted Cushing to such an extent that the governor, with whom he was still living, adopted him into his family and gave him a Zuni name, *Medicine Flower*. From then on, Cushing ate Zuni food and wore Zuni clothing. He received instruction in every aspect of the local culture, much as though he were a child. A measure of his integration into the community was his initiation into a religious and fraternal men's club called the Priesthood of the Bow, membership in which ensured his welcome at meetings of all such Zuni clubs. He even played an important part in local government as an advisor to the Zuni nation. All this seems not only to have delighted Cushing but also to have given him the impression that he had become a person of authority in Zuni society.

According to Zuni marriage practices, a bachelor who accepted a gift of cornmeal from an unmarried girl was officially betrothed to her. On two separate occasions, Zuni girls offered Cushing presents of cornmeal, but by the time of the first such marriage proposal he had already learned enough about local customs to insist on paying for the offering, and so avoided marital entanglement.

On one occasion, Cushing's confidence in his own importance in Zuni society caused him to abandon his customary cultural relativism temporarily, bringing about a situation that could have compromised his fieldwork. A man the Zuni believed to be a magician was brought to trial for casting evil spells. Cushing considered the crime absurd, probably because, like most Americans of European descent, he did he not believe in magic. During the trial, he intervened, even engaging in a scuffle with some of the accusers, but failed to prevent the accused from

In the late nineteenth century, pioneering American ethnologist Frank Cushing studied the pueblo-dwelling Zuni people of the American Southwest. Cushing lived with a Zuni family and adopted Zuni dress.

being found guilty and executed. Whether anthropologists should try to impose their own ethical values when doing fieldwork remains a matter for discussion in the discipline.

By the spring of 1881, the Smithsonian wanted Cushing back in Washington, and he reluctantly complied. On April 26, he boarded a train at Albuquerque for his return. Subsequently, he engaged in other anthropological projects, including an archaeological dig in Florida, but never returned to New Mexico for further fieldwork among the Zuni.

Cushing's most important contribution to anthropology was his invention of the fieldwork technique called **participant observation**—sharing in the lives of the people being studied as well as observing their behavior. In this regard he was 35 years ahead of the anthropologist who is usually credited with having devised this technique, Bronislaw Malinowski (see below). Cushing also published insights into Zuni culture that no outsider had previously been able to obtain. He discovered, for example, the significance to the Zuni of the number 7, which pervaded their culture. Conceptually the Zuni divided the universe into seven sectors, a structure that found expression in Zuni myth, ritual, the architecture of Zuni houses, and even agricultural techniques.

Cushing's record of scholarly activity was far less impressive than his achievement as a fieldworker, and insignificant when compared with the life's work of many other anthropologists. He wrote few papers, never published a scholarly book, and, since he never held an academic job, passed no scholarly legacy along to students. Today, publishing research data so that other cultural anthropologists can compare them with their data from other societies is considered a basic requirement for good anthropology, since only in this way can anthropologists add in some substantial way to what is known about society and culture. It has been said that Cushing felt himself one of the Zuni to such a degree that he could not publish data on customs he knew his hosts wished kept secret. The truth may be less romantic: he may have thought there was plenty of time to organize, write about, and publish the countless facts he had collected. But he miscalculated. In April 1900, at the age of 43, Cushing choked to death on a fish bone. He is remembered mainly for his major contribution to anthropological research methods, an achievement all the more remarkable for its early date.

---

participant observation ethnology's major research tool, involving sharing in people's lives as well as observing them

At the turn of the century, anthropologist Franz Boas assembled a huge collection of artifacts while studying the Native Americans of British Columbia, Canada. Now housed at the American Museum of Natural History in New York, the collection includes household utensils, hats, boxes, ceremonial blankets, totem poles, and even a war canoe.

Franz Boas (1858–1941)

Visitors to the American Museum of Natural History in New York are sometimes awed by the huge collection of objects made around the turn of the century by the Native Americans of British Columbia on the Pacific coast of Canada. Dominated by towering totem poles carved with animal faces, the collection also includes kitchen utensils, boxes, hats, decorated ceremonial blankets, and even an enormous, high-prowed war canoe bearing the model figures of more than a dozen men in traditional costumes. This impressive collection is only one of the legacies left to anthropology by the foremost American anthropologist of his time, Franz Boas.

Boas was born in Germany, where in 1881 he obtained his doctorate in geography. Two years later this interest prompted him to join a geograph-

ical expedition to eastern Canada, where he encountered a group of Native Americans, the Central Eskimo or Inuit,[6] whose adaptation to a hostile environment he found interesting. Boas became so intrigued by the Inuit way of life that he turned to anthropology, eventually becoming a specialist in the cultures of the nonliterate people of the northwest coast of North America.

To prepare himself for anthropological research, Boas read the works of nineteenth-century scholars who purported to explain the astonishing variety of human behavior, and found many of their ideas unsatisfying. How could sweeping statements about humanity be made on the basis of so few

---

[6] Although *Eskimo* is by far the more familiar term, in some regions these people prefer to call themselves *Inuit*. The word *Eskimo* means "eater of raw meat."

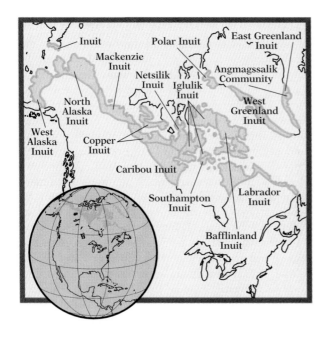

which all cultures must eventually pass, and that similar environments, similar economic systems, and similar population sizes would produce similar cultural results. Boas disagreed, and eventually formulated a different idea about what was responsible for the many different kinds of human cultures. Each culture is unique, Boas argued, for each is the individual product of unique historical circumstances. This approach came to be known in anthropology as **historical particularism.**

Boas also developed a new and important anthropological research method. While living among the Kwakiutl, he realized that by himself he would be unable to absorb the enormous amount of data these people could provide. He needed help. In 1893, he turned to George Hunt, a local man whose father was of European descent and whose mother belonged to the neighboring Tlingit ethnic group. Boas trained Hunt to collect myths, legends, poems, and descriptions of the lives and customs of the Kwakiutl in their own language, which—since he had been raised in the Kwakiutl town of Fort Rupert—Hunt spoke fluently. It was the first time an indigenous person had been recruited by an anthropologist as a research assistant. Today, although the use of local research assistants by anthropologists is by no means universal, this practice is recognized as one way of overcoming the barriers between the collector of anthropological information and the individuals who are providing it (Goldman 1980:335).

Adding Hunt's material to the results of his own inquiries, Boas was able to provide detailed information, often in the actual words of Kwakiutl people, on many different topics, including hunting, fishing, local myths, food gathering, recipes, the life cycles of men and women, marriage, songs, prayers, death, sweat baths, the status of women, art, curses, names, the significance of dog hair, spirits, tributes to chiefs, blood revenge, wars, family quarrels, village organization, kinship, chieftain-

anthropological data? It was clear to Boas that, before anthropologists could hope to understand human behavior, an enormous amount of detailed information about individual cultures was needed. In an effort to contribute detailed data on one culture and society to this effort, Boas traveled in 1886 to the west coast of Canada to begin an intensive study of one of the native populations of British Columbia, the Kwakiutl.[7] For years afterward, Boas collected information about Kwakiutl culture, eventually amassing an enormous amount of data.

Boas's reputation as a major contributor to the anthropology of British Columbia won him eminence, but this was by no means his only accomplishment in the discipline. He also made a significant contribution to anthropological thought. In the late nineteenth century, the idea of **cultural evolution** had many followers. This is the notion that in human culture, as in biology, change—usually slow, steady, and in the direction of greater efficiency and complexity—tends to occur. Many cultural evolutionists believed that this process of change involved a set series of stages through

---

cultural evolution the notion that cultures evolve, usually gradually, steadily, and in the direction of greater efficiency and complexity

historical particularism the idea that every culture, because it is the product of specific historical circumstances, is unique

---

[7] Strictly speaking, the term *Kwakiutl* refers only to the people of Fort Rupert, British Columbia. The generic term for this Native American group is *Kwakwaka'wakw peoples.*

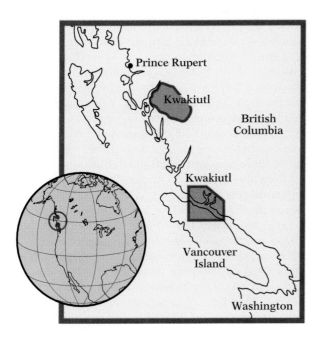

Bronislaw Malinowski (1884–1942)

Like Boas, Bronislaw Malinowski came into anthropology almost by accident. He began his career by studying natural science in his native Poland, but his interests ranged well beyond that field. One day he picked up a copy of Sir James George Frazer's *The Golden Bough* (1890), a book describing the religious beliefs, magical practices, and myths of hundreds of cultures, past and present. Enchanted by what he read, Malinowski decided to study anthropology. In 1908, having earned a Doctor of Philosophy degree from the University of Cracow, he left for England to study anthropology at the University of London.

A few years later, in 1914, Malinowski joined an expedition to the Western Pacific. Arriving on the island of Boyowa off the east coast of New Guinea (one of several islands that form the Trobriand islands group), he pitched his tent in a tiny village called Omarakana. He did not speak the local language, so quickly found himself an interpreter, but after six months or so felt sufficiently confident in the native language to discard this help, and thereafter carried out his inquiries in the Trobriand tongue.

In 1914, field methods in cultural anthropology were still not sufficiently well established for Malinowski to have learned how to conduct research in a nonliterate community, but it seemed that there was more than one way to accomplish this goal. He rejected the idea of remaining apart from the daily lives of the Trobrianders as he collected his data, choosing instead, like Cushing, the participant observation method. In addition to asking anthropological questions of the islanders, he took part, also like Cushing and to a much greater extent than Boas, in community events. He closely observed the activities going on about him and listened carefully to anecdotes and local gossip, so that he could provide much fuller accounts of Trobriand customs than would have been possible had he relied only on formal questioning.

Living among the Trobrianders throughout the year instead of just a few months at a time, Malinowski was impressed with the fact that the customs, ideas, artifacts, and language of the islanders all served their needs (for food, shelter, companionship, and so on) very well. At first, some Trobriand customs, such as elaborate and time-consuming religious rituals to accompany boat-building and seafaring, seemed quite useless or ran-

ship, and social status. Boas's ultimate goal was to document every aspect of Kwakiutl culture. Long before he was finished, he had amassed so much information that it seemed to him that, if similar amounts of data were available for other societies, no unified explanation of human behavior could ever emerge. His idea that every culture must be the unique product of its own particular circumstances was thus reinforced by his detailed research.

Unlike Cushing, Boas published many of his findings in a huge number of books and papers (e.g., Boas 1897, 1911, 1948)—a total, by one estimate, of over 5000 printed pages (Goldman 1980:335). He never abandoned the historical particularist approach, and argued all his life that anthropologists should avoid grand theorizing and focus on assembling as comprehensive a collection of data as possible on as many individual cultures as possible. For over four decades, he taught this Boasian approach to students such as Alfred Kroeber, Ruth Benedict, and Robert Lowie, who were later to become some of the most eminent scholars in the discipline. The influence of "the father of American anthropology" has waned over the years as other ideas about culture have arisen, but in his time no one had a greater influence on American cultural anthropology than Franz Boas.

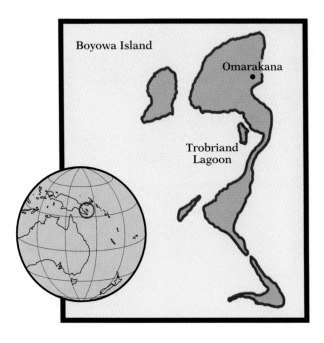

given the credit. Nor did Malinowskian functionalism ever win widespread acceptance in anthropological circles. But the huge amount of data Malinowski collected and published established participant observation as the principal fieldwork technique for serious anthropological research, and set the standard followed by subsequent anthropologists. Moreover, after his stay among the Trobrianders, Malinowski became an academic luminary, spending most of his life at the University of London, England, where he attracted a following of students such as E. E. Evans-Pritchard and Raymond Firth, who in their turn were to become the leading British anthropologists of their generation. Thus it is as an empirical collector of data and as a teacher, rather than as a theorist, that history most remembers him. In 1939, Malinowski accepted a position as a visiting professor at Yale University, where he died three years later.

Conclusion

Cultural anthropology is about human beings—ourselves as well as others—and the different cultures we have created. The reason for studying human beings and their cultures goes well beyond the desire for academic knowledge. Over 60 years ago, Bronislaw Malinowski (1984:517–518) eloquently summed up both the need for anthropological work and its desired result. Exploring the almost infinite variety of human experiences is important, Malinowski wrote, yet

> There is . . . one point of view deeper and [even] more important. . . , and that is the desire to turn such knowledge into wisdom. . . . [O]ur [ultimate] goal is to enrich and deepen our own world's vision, to understand our own nature and to make it finer, intellectually and artistically. In grasping the essential outlook of others, with . . . reverence and real understanding . . . we cannot help widening our own. We cannot possibly reach the final Socratic wisdom of knowing ourselves if we never

dom, but Malinowski eventually saw even these as fitting into the scheme of things in biological or psychological ways. His idea that aspects of culture are functional in that they fulfill the biological, psychological, or other needs of human beings is known as Malinowskian **functionalism.**[8]

Malinowski worked among the Trobrianders for 26 months between 1914 and 1918. The many books and papers resulting from his research were enormously successful, in part because he placed himself squarely in the center of local life and described exactly what he saw. The effect, on paper, is not one of abstract analysis removed from daily life, but "a picture of the living reality of Trobriand society" (Evans-Pritchard 1951:94). The titles Malinowski chose for his books, such as *Crime and Custom in Savage Society* (1978, originally published in 1926) and *The Sexual Life of Savages in Northwestern Melanesia* (1962, originally published in 1929), did nothing to discourage either scholarly or popular interest.

As we saw earlier, Malinowski was not the inventor of participant observation, though he is often

---

[8] Since Malinowski's day, the term *functionalism* has been applied to other, very different ideas, proposed by other anthropologists. We distinguish between two different kinds of functionalism in Chapter 3.

functionalism the idea that aspects of culture function to fulfill the biological, psychological, or other needs of individuals

Early twentieth-century cultural anthropologist Bronislaw Malinowski, one of the first to practice participant observation, spent over two years with the Trobriand Islanders of the South Pacific. Rather than studying the Trobrianders from a distance, Malinowski lived among them and learned to speak their language.

leave the narrow confinement of the customs, beliefs, and prejudices into which every man is born. Nothing can teach us a better lesson ... than the habit of mind which allows us to treat the beliefs and values of another man from his point of view. [Anthropology] should lead us to such knowledge, and to tolerance and generosity, based on the understanding of other men's point of view.

Summary

- Anthropology is the study of people.

- Anthropology is divided into four major subdisciplines: biological anthropology (the study of

the biological aspects of being human), cultural anthropology (the study of the culture of contemporary people), archaeology (the study of people of the past through their material remains), and anthropological linguistics (the study of languages from an anthropological point of view).

- Archaeology, cultural anthropology, and anthropological linguistics are all concerned with culture, which we define as all the things people collectively do, think, make, and say.

- This book introduces the subdiscipline of cultural anthropology.

- Like the other subdisciplines of anthropology, cultural anthropology is comparative in that it seeks to compare the similarities and contrast the differences among human societies and cultures, and comprehensive in that no group of people is excluded.

- Central to cultural anthropology are the opposing concepts of ethnocentrism—the erroneous belief that one's own ethnic group, society, or culture is superior to others—and cultural relativism—the idea that a culture must be evaluated in terms of its own values, rather than according to the values of another culture.

- Cultural anthropology as an academic discipline originated during the late nineteenth century. Its development is illustrated through the lives and work of the early anthropologists Frank Hamilton Cushing, Franz Boas, and Bronislaw Malinowski.

- These portraits introduce an important anthropological research method, participant observation, and three different theoretical perspectives: cultural evolution, historical particularism, and Malinowskian functionalism.

Key Terms

anthropological linguistics (linguistic anthropology)
applied anthropology
archaeology
artifact
biological (physical) anthropology
cultural anthropology
cultural evolution
cultural relativism
culture
ecofact
ethnic group
ethnicity
ethnocentrism
ethnology
functionalism
historical particularism
illiterate
nonliterate
participant observation
peasants
social anthropology
social structure
society
sociocultural anthropology

Suggested Readings

Birdsell, Joseph. 1987. Some Reflections on Fifty Years in Biological Anthropology. *Annual Reviews of Anthropology* 16:1–12. This is a personal view by an eminent scientist of some key developments in the field of physical anthropology.

Diamond, Stanley. (ed.). 1980. *Anthropology: Ancestors and Heirs.* The Hague: Mouton. Twenty essays presenting topics, personalities, and interests from most of the countries where anthropology is an academic subject. The collection gives an excellent idea of the different anthropological traditions worldwide.

Fagan, Brian M. 1994. *In the Beginning: An Introduction to Archaeology* (8th ed.). New York: HarperCollins. A basic text in the field of archaeology, offering a comprehensive overview of the subject incuding methods of field research and numerous examples of the reconstruction of cultures of the past.

Greenberg, Joseph H. 1986. On Being a Linguistic Anthropologist. *Annual Reviews of Anthropology* 15:1–24. A leading linguistic anthropologist describes how he became a practitioner of this field of anthropology, and in doing so provides especially useful insights into the study of languages in their cultural context.

Kaplan, Abraham. 1984. Philosophy of Science in Anthropology. *Annual Reviews of Anthropology* 13:25–39. Kaplan provides a brief overview of issues involved in the question of whether or not anthropology should be considered a science.

Silverman, Sydel. (ed.). 1981. *Totems and Teachers: Perspectives on the History of Anthropology.* New York: Columbia University Press. Describes the contributions of eight major figures in anthropology, with an emphasis on American anthropologists.

Weatherford, Jack. 1991. *Native Roots: How the Indians Enriched America.* New York: Crown. This readable book describes the impact of Native American cultures on mainstream life in the United States. Among the topics discussed are the history of European–Native American relations, how the Native American fur trade influenced the American economy, and the trade in Native American slaves.

Introduction

In 1799, a strange, filthy, nearly naked boy was found wandering in the wooded countryside near the village of Aveyron, France. He appeared to be 11 or 12 years

old, and had apparently been living alone in the woods for many years. Brought to Paris, this "dirty, scared, inarticulate creature who trotted and grunted like the beasts" became an object of great curiosity (Itard 1962:vi). He could neither speak nor behave like a normal person, and was assumed by Parisians to be an incurable idiot. But a young French doctor, Jean-Marc-Gaspard Itard, doubted that the child, dubbed the "Wild Boy of Aveyron," was simply mentally deficient. Itard thought that if the child had grown up in isolation from other human beings, deprived not only of French culture but also of any culture, this might explain his odd behavior. Itard made up his mind to try to "cure" the "idiot."

Itard attempted to introduce the Wild Boy to French culture by giving him language lessons, dressing him like a typical French boy, and trying to persuade him to imitate the behavior of others, whether at the dinner table, in the classroom, or on the dance floor. Sadly, however, the doctor's treatment was not a great success. Despite five years of effort, Itard was unable to teach the Wild Boy to behave like a normal human being. For one thing, the boy may indeed have had less than normal intelligence, although various observers disagreed on this point. But the main reason why Itard was unable to transform the Wild Boy into a typical nineteenth-century Parisian was because of the boy's apparently total lack of exposure to anything cultural during his impressionable early years, a time when "the ordinary child is learning to be a human being" (Itard 1962:xi). It seems that human beings must absorb the details of some specific culture—it does not matter which one—early in life, or we will not absorb any. For the Wild Boy, the opportunity came too late.

• The Concept of Culture •

What Is Culture?

The concept of culture is fundamental to anthropology, yet it is so complex a notion that anthropologists have never agreed on a single (much less a simple) definition of the term. We provided one definition in Chapter 1, briefly introducing culture as all the things people collectively think, do, say and make—in other words, their shared ideas, behaviors, languages, and artifacts. These include institutions (such as marriage), political ideas (such as democracy), religious beliefs (such as witchcraft), customs (like fireworks on the Fourth of July), rituals (like saluting the flag), objects, stories, art styles, games, and much more. But culture cannot adequately be defined in terms of its outward manifestations alone; we must also take account of its other properties.[1]

---

[1] We need to distinguish between culture as we defined it in Chapter 1, and "the culture" of a particular society, which is all the cultural things that characterize that particular society.

• Ask Yourself •

What does the term *culture* mean to you? As popularly used, the word is often defined in terms of certain activities, such as going to the opera or reading poetry. What is the relationship between that definition and the one we are proposing?

Culture Is Unique to Human Beings.   Cultural anthropologists sometimes define culture as that which distinguishes human beings from all other forms of life. This definition has not gone unchallenged; some scholars, most of them in disciplines other than cultural anthropology, feel it is either insufficient or incorrect. Among them are some primate ethologists, students of the behavior of nonhuman primates (human beings' closest biological relatives), who argue that the nonhuman "higher primates" (all the monkeys and apes), and especially chimpanzees and gorillas ("great apes"), possess culture of an elementary kind. We will take this

Because they are deprived of culture, children who grow up in isolation behave differently from other human beings. Kamala, found living alone in the jungle in India, may have been deprived of culture since babyhood. She moved about on all fours and ate from her caretaker's hand.

because an idea, behavior, word, or artifact cannot be considered an aspect of one culture does not mean it could not be part of another.

Culture Is Compulsory. Individuals who wish to get along successfully have no option but to take their society's culture into account in their dealings with others. Even people who do not accept one or more aspects of their culture usually behave the way most others behave, because the penalty for not doing so can be severe. One might not believe personally in representative government, an important element of mainstream American culture, but to barge into the United States Senate and insist on representing oneself would probably result in a jail term. Some cultures permit more individual variation than others (a classic treatise on this subject is Lee 1959); contemporary U.S. culture, for example, accords women more freedom in matters of dress and behavior than Iranian culture. Still, all cultures demand some degree of conformity from their members, and penalize nonconformists.

• Ask Yourself •

Are there aspects of Western culture that you don't like or with which you disagree? Do you behave as if you accept these cultural features? What would the penalty be if you publicly rejected them?

subject up again in a moment (see the section titled "Animal Symbols?" below). For now, suffice it to say that as cultural anthropologists we do not consider the behavior of any nonhuman creatures to be cultural. At the same time, however, we recognize that the concept of culture is only incompletely understood in terms of the distinction between human beings and other creatures.

Culture Is Patterned. The ideas, behaviors, languages, and artifacts that constitute the outward manifestations of any culture are elements of patterns that are widely recognized and repeated within that culture, both in the present (synchronically) and down through the generations (diachronically). Therefore, nothing that is unique to one individual can be considered an element of that individual's culture. Someone native to the United States might create a flag with alternating purple and green stripes and a pink field of stars in one corner. This unique object would not be considered part of American culture, although a similar flag with alternating red and white stripes and a blue field of stars in one corner would be. As we pointed out in Chapter 1, however, caution is in order: just

Culture Is Adaptive. Culture enables people to form families and communities, to communicate with each other, to work cooperatively to make a living, to maintain order in their lives, to give meaning to life by believing in something, to express themselves creatively, and to raise new generations of people who can continue to live and work together. Thus we can view a given culture as a complex set of problem-solving strategies for satisfying people's needs within a particular social and natural environment. How do people in Trobriand society (see map on page 19) get the protein they need? They fish. How do people in North American society achieve the same goal? They purchase what they need in a supermarket or restaurant. These examples illustrate the fact that while cultures incorporate different mechanisms for solving the problems of human existence, each is adaptive given its own circumstances.

In the 1994 movie Nell, *actress Jodie Foster portrays a 30-year-old woman, deprived of culture, who had up to that time lived virtually alone in the Smoky Mountains of North Carolina. The movie chronicles Nell's introduction to "civilization."*

Culture Is Holistic.   The various aspects of any culture are interrelated, something like the parts of a car's engine that, when functioning both individually and together, keep the whole car running smoothly. The English scholar Sir Edward Burnett Tylor acknowledged this well over a hundred years ago when he defined culture as "that complex whole which includes knowledge, belief, art, morals, law, custom, and any other capabilities and habits acquired by man as a member of society" (1873:1). In his use of the word *whole*, Tylor recog-

nized the connectedness of the different aspects of any culture. Cultures differ in the extent to which they form coherent wholes, but the idea that a culture is an integrated system, termed *holism*, is basic to the concept of culture. Yet it is an idea that is sometimes difficult for North Americans to understand, because North American culture, large-scale and varied, is in general less integrated than many others. North Americans tend to compartmentalize aspects of their culture, such as politics and religion. This is uncharacteristic of many societies; in the Middle East, for example, politics and religion are intimately connected, and one cannot fully understand one without also studying the other.

Culture Is Dynamic.   Both cultures and car engines are dynamic, meaning constantly changing rather than remaining static. This is not to say that aspects of culture change at uniform rates; in Western culture, the economy changes much more rapidly, and with more immediate cultural impact, than religion. Still, even a small change to one of the parts of an engine—a little wear and tear, for instance—can cause the whole engine to operate differently. Likewise, a change in one aspect of culture may produce much broader cultural changes. The causes of culture change are so important to cultural anthropology that Chapter 16 of this book is devoted to them. They include changes in response to direct contact with or indirect influence from another culture, exerted through trade, war, population movements, missionary activity, or—today—global communications systems; collectively, the process of change resulting from such causes is called **acculturation.** Culture change can also result from internal or environmental factors. The mosaic of cultures existing in the world today reflects both different environments and the past and present spread of customs and beliefs among the world's people—some beneficial, others destructive.

Cultures differ from one another, but the six defining characteristics listed above are universal. The institution of marriage, practiced in all cultures but according to different rules, illustrates this point. Marriage is, first of all, unique to human beings; other animals, even monogamous ones, do not marry. Marriage is patterned in that in any culture it is universally recognized, constantly repeated, and governed by rules passed down through the generations. Marriage is compulsory in that people who wish to function successfully in their society have no choice but to recognize its existence and importance.

---

acculturation the process by which important changes take place within a culture as the result of contact with another culture

The causes of culture change include contact with or indirect influence of another culture. Here, in an example of acculturation, an Irish family enjoys a meal of potatoes, a vegetable native to the New World.

If a Westerner ignored his society's marriage customs and asked a married woman for a date, she and her husband might both be offended. Marriage is adaptive in that it helps people to satisfy a number of requirements: among others, it creates efficient economic units called households, provides a nurturing environment for child rearing, and regulates sexual access. (Imagine the problems that would occur in a society in which there were no rules about who could have sex with whom.) Marriage is intimately related to other aspects of culture, such as residential arrangements and child-rearing practices, and is thus integrated holistically with other elements of culture. Finally, marriage is dynamic, changing in response to other cultural changes. A comparison of American rates of marriage and divorce now with those of the 1950s illustrates this for North America.

Culture Versus Nature

Besides examining the properties of culture, a second way to understand this concept is to compare culture with its opposite, nature. Culture is something human beings have created; *nature* (as the term is applied to the human species) is all the things human beings inherit biologically and cannot modify. One's eye color is natural; one's haircut is cultural. The shape, size, and state of health of one's body is a combination of natural and cultural influences, among them genetic inheritance, diet, and exercise.

Although human beings are creatures of both nature and culture, people in some societies distinguish strongly between the two, deemphasizing the natural aspects of what makes them human and instead emphasizing the cultural. Invariably, culture is viewed as superior to nature. Sometimes this culture/nature opposition is formlated as a confrontation; Westerners, for example, speak of "conquering" nature. As long ago as 2000 B.C., the ancient Babylonians incorporated the culture/nature opposition into the earliest story to have come down to us in written form, the *Epic of Gilgamesh,* a sprawling

The institution of marriage is part of the culture of every society, although the details of what marriage entails differ from society to society. In North America (but not everywhere), marriage is a legal and social union between one man and one woman.

tale consisting of 72 poems written over the course of a thousand years. On its surface, the epic recounts the strange adventures of Gilgamesh, a great king who ruled the city of Uruk (Warka in Iraq today). Symbolically, however, as the hero Gilgamesh, the epitome of culture, confronts Enkidu, who was raised among animals in the wild, the epic chronicles the separation of what is human or cultural from what is natural (Gardner and Maier 1985:15).

• The Transmission • of Culture

Culture, as the story of the Wild Boy of Aveyron illustrates, is not inherent in human beings; it has to be learned. We call the process by which an individual absorbs the details of his or her particular culture, starting from the moment of birth,

---

enculturation the process by which an individual absorbs the details of his or her particular culture, starting from birth

symbol something that stands for something else

enculturation. There are three main, and somewhat overlapping, ways in which the process of enculturation takes place: through symbols, through imitation, and through experience.

Symbols

> The flag of the United States of America . . . should be displayed on all days when the weather permits. . . . No disrespect should be shown to the flag; [it] should not be dipped to any person or thing. . . . The flag should never be carried flat or horizontally, but always aloft and free, [and] when the flag is passing . . . , all persons present should face the flag, stand at attention, and salute.
>
> *Public Law 623 of the 77th Congress of the United States of America*

A **symbol,** to use the simplest definition of the term, is something that human beings use to stand for something else (Needham 1979:7). A rectangular piece of cloth imprinted with a design consisting of a conventional arrangement of stars and stripes in specific colors symbolizes the United States of America, and for U.S. citizens displaying this object, reciting the Pledge of Allegiance to it, or saluting it symbolizes their loyalty to their country and their agreement with the ideals on which the U.S. government is based.

This everyday example suggests four important properties of symbols. First, a symbol can be an object (such as a flag), a series of words (such as a pledge), or an action (such as a salute). Second, to use a symbol is to communicate something—an attitude, a feeling, or an abstract idea (such as freedom or democracy). Third, symbols are arbitrary; there is no intuitively obvious connection between a piece of printed cloth and the concept of democracy. And fourth, the meaning of a symbol is not necessarily immediate; it may convey meaning back into the past or forward into the future.

In every society, symbols are the most important vehicles by which culture is transmitted. Whether in the form of language, actions, or objects, people constantly employ symbols in doing, thinking, saying, and making things. Moreover, the symbols used by members of a society often coalesce into integrated symbolic systems. A language, for instance, is made up of many sounds, many gestures, and many tones of voice, every one of which not only has meaning in its own right but also takes on added meaning when employed in conjunction with all the others.

The Anthropologist at Work

Daniel Varisco

Some anthropologists combine their interests in both culture and nature by focusing on the relationship between people and the natural environments in which they live (a specialty, as we mentioned in Chapter 1, called *cultural ecology*). Applied anthropologist Daniel Varisco, who worked for the World Wildlife Fund in the small country of Yemen on the Arabian peninsula (see map on page 357), is one of them. In Yemen, virtually all adult men wear daggers at their waists. Many of these daggers have handles carved from rhinocerous horn, the traditional material (Varisco 1989:215). Rhinos are not native to Yemen, so horn for dagger handles is imported from East Africa. But the rhino is a gravely endangered species. Unless the killing of rhinos for their horns ceases, these creatures will soon become extinct. In 1982, in response to this problem, the Yemeni government banned the import of rhino horn, but some Yemenis value it so highly that international smuggling of rhino horns continues.

In 1987, Varisco went to Yemen to study the cultural significance of the Yemeni dagger, assess local awareness of the plight of the rhino, develop a strategy to reduce the demand for rhino horn, and thus help promote conservation of these endangered animals. He found that wearing a dagger symbolizes a Yemeni man's honor and ability to defend himself, and serves as a "potent symbol of Yemeni identity" (Varisco 1989:217). While there seems to be no intrinsic reason why a dagger's handle should be made of rhino horn, this material is valued because it becomes translucent with age, eventually resembling highly prized amber. Thus, daggers with rhino horn handles, expensive (at around $1500) to begin with, increase in value with age. So even though younger Yemeni males are not as interested in daggers as their fathers were, most fathers still want to purchase rhino-horn daggers for their sons because of their increasing value in a part of the world where there are relatively few safe investments. Varisco predicts that rhino horn will be in great demand in Yemen for some time to come.

He also predicts it will be impossible to stop the trade in rhino horn until alternative materials acceptable to the local people are promoted. Warning that there are no easy, short-term solutions to the problem, he has proposed a multistep plan to help save the rhino. The steps include developing a synthetic alternative to rhino horn and promoting efforts to conserve Yemen's own wildlife species, an initiative that would raise awareness of the value of conservation and might eventually create a climate more favorable for reducing the demand for rhino horn. But perhaps the most important step is education. Most Yemenis do not even know the rhino is in danger of extinction.

Animal Symbols?   Animals often use sounds, colors, scents, and bodily movements to indicate their physical or psychological status. With a flash of colorful plumage, for example, a male bird of paradise sends a message about its maleness, a dog purposefully urinates to mark the edges of its turf, a horse whinnies with alarm at the approach of a dangerous snake. These behaviors may, as Needham says, "stand for something else," but they are not symbolic in the human sense, for they lack both the arbitrary quality and the nonimmediacy of human symbols. To distinguish the kinds of representative behaviors of which animals are capable from human symbol making, anthropologists use the word *signs* (or sometimes *signals*) for the nonhuman behaviors.

A symbol is something that stands for something else. A flag bearing a particular arrangement of stars and stripes symbolizes the United States of America, and saluting this flag symbolizes loyalty to the nation.

Just as they have sometimes suggested that higher primates possess culture of a rudimentary kind, some animal ethnologists have argued that apes occasionally use symbols, or at least have the capacity to do so. Researchers studying these animals' ability to acquire language have taught captive chimpanzees and gorillas to communicate with human beings, and even occasionally with one another, by using some symbolic system, such as sign language (the language of the deaf), colored plastic shapes, or computer keys. Some apes have been taught to recognize and use hundreds of such symbols.

symbolic anthropology the anthropological study of symbols

However, this kind of symbolizing in the primate-studies laboratory is a product of human culture. Apes do not communicate with each other by these methods in the wild. They do occasionally seem to employ objects to represent concepts: an angry chimpanzee, for instance, may snatch up a stick and wave it over his head in a threatening gesture. But the stick, as well as the threatening posture and movements, are signs, not symbols. Their message is immediate, and they are hardly arbitrary.

Other important differences exist between animals' use of signs and human beings' use of symbols. We use symbols much more frequently, in a far wider range of situations, and to convey a much broader range of ideas than animals use signs. Furthermore, rather than repeating the same symbols over and over again, as animals do with signs, we constantly vary and elaborate on our symbols, frequently inventing new ones. Finally, like other aspects of culture, the symbols used by humans are conventional: widely understood and shared among members of the same group. So distinctive is our symbolic behavior that we might define *Homo sapiens sapiens* as the only species of animal capable of complex, infinitely varied, constantly elaborated, and widely understood symbolic behavior.

Languages, human beings' most frequently employed and therefore most important symbolic systems, illustrate the complexity, variety, conventionality, and unlimited potential for elaboration that characterize symbols. A language, whether in the form of speech, writing, or gestures, consists of a complex set of symbols in which every syllable, word, gesture, punctuation mark, inflection, or pause stands for something else—some object, action, idea, or combination of these. Every one of the world's thousands of languages is a symbolic system so variable that it can express any concept of which the human mind can conceive, so flexible that meaningful groupings of words or gestures never before combined are continually and easily created, and so conventionalized that even new combinations of words or gestures can be readily understood.

Symbolic Anthropology. Symbols play such an important part in culture and its transmission that a subfield of cultural anthropology, **symbolic anthropology,** is devoted to the study of symbols, both within cultures and cross-culturally. Symbolic anthropologists have repeatedly shown that analyzing the symbols used by members of a soci-

Our closest nonhuman relatives, the apes, occasionally employ symbols to convey ideas. Using sign language taught him during a study of primates' ability to use language, a chimpanzee tells his trainer that he's thirsty.

ety can help uncover hidden patterns of meaning within their culture and decipher the significance of their behavior. Language, art, games, rituals, colors, and stories are all subjects for symbolic analysis, which is now considered a major approach to understanding culture.

While some symbols are unique to the cultures that employ them, others are found in several or many different cultures. The human eye, for example, has profound symbolic meaning around the Mediterranean, southward into Africa, eastward into South Asia, northward into Europe, and westward into parts of Latin America. Throughout this vast area, the eye symbolizes much the same thing: evil or the potential for evil. People in the cultures of the region believe that individuals can cause illness or misfortune to befall others merely by *looking* at them or their property (Dundes 1981).

To ward off the evil eye, people in these areas of the world wear or display charms, such as chili peppers, snakeskins, or horns, which are believed to distract the evil eye or to absorb the evil directed toward a particular person or object. A typically Middle Eastern way of diverting the evil eye is to wear or display a blue bead, with or without an eye painted on it. This is often the first gift a baby receives, and it is pinned to the inside of the cradle. Blue beads are also used to protect animals and property; they decorate the radiator grilles of cars, trucks, and buses, or dangle from the harnesses of donkeys.

Since the evil that is transmitted by the evil eye is often the common human feeling of envy, anything excessively good or beautiful and thus enviable, like a pretty child or a ewe that is a particularly good milk producer, is an appropriate target for the evil eye. To ensure oneself against becoming its victim, and to avoid "casting the evil eye" oneself, one neither accepts nor gives compliments, and avoids displaying perfection or good fortune. It is considered poor form, for example, to tell a mother what a beautiful baby she has. For her part, the mother may protect her child from the consequences of the evil eye by smudging its forehead with dirt so that it is less than perfect.

Why should the eye have become a symbol for evil in so much of the world? Anthropologist Joe Delmonaco (1986) believes the evil eye symbolically embodies some of the problems inherent in human communication and social interaction. In many societies, he has found, the evil eye is associated with a fear of the violation of privacy, and conse-

The belief that people can cause harm to other people or their property with an evil glance is widespread, and various symbols are used to ward off this "evil eye." In India, vehicles are protected from the evil eye with old shoes or, as in this case, pictures of shoes.

quently with the loss of the self-control and security that privacy creates in social life.[2] Delmonaco argues that the evil eye is an "exposing" eye. Frequently it is the overly curious person—the so-called busybody—who is suspected of causing misfortune by casting the evil eye. This individual can be someone familiar, such as the neighborhood gossip, but the individuals most strongly suspected of casting the evil eye are outsiders who exhibit excessive curiosity—such as anthropological fieldworkers!

Another way in which symbolic anthropologists uncover the hidden meanings of symbols is to analyze them as parts of systems of communication within cultures. For example, cultural anthropologist Victor Turner (1967:48–55) has shown how the Ndembu of Zambia combine symbols of at least three different kinds—objects, actions, and institutions—to express a complex value system.

To the Ndembu, a local tree called the *milk tree* is as important a symbol as "Old Glory" is to people born and raised in the United States. When the thin bark of the milk tree is scratched, a milky white sap oozes out. For the Ndembu, this sap is the tree's most important physical property, on which is

based an ever-widening series of symbols that ultimately entails six different referents. The white sap (actually beads of latex) symbolizes (a) human milk, which symbolizes (b) the female breast from which human milk flows. The breast in turn symbolizes (c) the suckling of infants, which symbolizes (d) the mother–child bond. This important tie symbolizes (e) the family, a social group crucial to Ndembu society, and the family, finally, symbolizes (f) Ndembu society in its entirety.

The Ndembu have thus incorporated into their culture an orderly progression of symbols in which each object, action, or institution serves as a symbol for another (see Figure 2.1). The chain starts with tangible symbols—beads of latex, milk, the female breast—and progresses to abstract ones—first an action (breastfeeding), then social institutions (the mother–child relationship, the family, Ndembu society as a whole). No single referent conveys the full symbolic meaning of the milk tree to the Ndembu; its meaning lies in the combination of all six referents, any one of which can be fully understood only within the holistic context provided by all the referents.

Some symbols are so widely used cross-culturally that they seem to be virtually universal. For example, in all cultures about which we have the relevant information, the right hand or right side is consid-

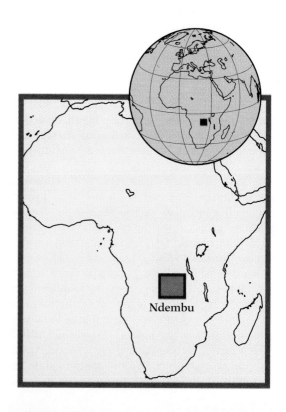

Ndembu

---

[2] According to animal ethologists, staring is a basic threat mechanism among the higher primates.

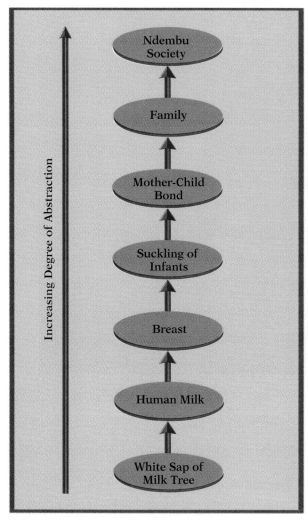

Figure 2.1

In the Ndembu series of symbols, each object, action, or institution can serve as a symbol for another.

ered superior to the left. Further, "right" usually symbolizes goodness and strength, whereas "left" is associated with evil and weakness. This symbolism may date back to our Palaeolithic ancestors. In a cave in Kenya, Stone Age skeletons were discovered with the males lying on their right sides, the females on their left sides, suggesting that females may have been considered the inferior sex in this society (Turner 1967:78).

These universal left/inferior and right/superior associations may result from the fact that about 90 percent of human beings are either exclusively or predominantly right-handed. Whatever their origin, however, these associations often create disadvan-

tages for left-handed people. In Western culture, for instance, writing goes from left to right, which is more difficult for left-handed persons. Ordinary scissors and baseball gloves fit the hands of right-handed, but not left-handed, individuals, for whom special scissors and baseball gloves must be made. Other cultures have different ways of accommodating the approximately 10 percent of people who are left-handed or ambidextrous. For the Nuer of the Sudan (see map on page 217), the right hand symbolizes what is strong, virile, and vital, while the left hand symbolizes evil (Evans-Pritchard 1956:233–235). Nevertheless, left-handed Nuer are not discriminated against, nor considered inherently evil. The Nuer simply say of a left-handed person that his left hand is his right!

The meaning of many symbols varies widely cross-culturally. Colors, for example, have different symbolic meanings the world over. White, black, and red are those used the most frequently, but the three colors may have different meanings in different parts of the world (Turner 1967:72–77). In Western cultures, brides traditionally wear white, and black is associated with death. But in India and many other Asian countries, white symbolizes death, and brides dress in red. The same three colors seem to have had symbolic importance in the past. Archaeologists have discovered evidence of the apparently symbolic use of these colors in a prehistoric South African Stone Age burial site, which contained half an ostrich eggshell, coated internally with a black substance and externally with red, lying beneath the arms of a skeleton (Turner 1967:78–79). Unfortunately, archaeologists have no means of establishing the significance of the colors.

Imitation

While symbols (including words) are the most important means by which culture is transmitted, human beings also transmit culture by wordless, nonsymbolic, imitative behavior. This is also an important way in which nonhuman primates learn. A chimpanzee, after watching another strip a twig of its leaves and insert it into a termite nest in order to fish out a meal, will often attempt to do the same thing.

Among human beings, imitation is an important way in which children are enculturated, because it does not depend on language. When a rural woman on a small Caribbean island washes clothes in a stream, her small daughter, squatting beside her, gravely imitates every motion. The mother is communicating an aspect of her culture

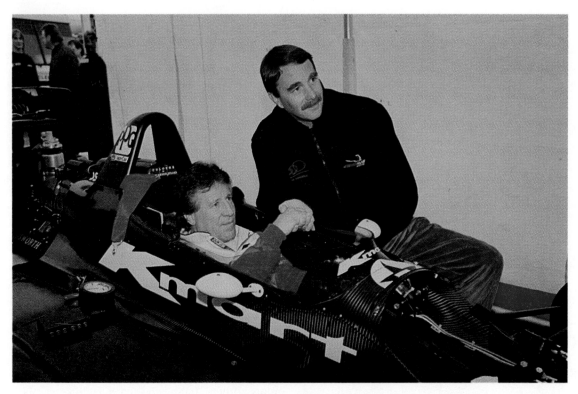

All over the world, "right" symbolizes goodness and strength while "left" represents the opposite. Thus, in cultures in which greetings take the form of handshakes, the right hand is used, never the left. Champion drivers Mario Andretti and Nigel Mansell greet each other prior to the Indianopolis 500 race in January 1993.

to her daughter, and the daughter is learning it, even though neither is using symbols. Imitation seems especially important in the acquisition of early motor skills in children. While children in all cultures begin to walk, on average, at between 13 and 15 months, a child who does not have the opportunity to observe others walking may not learn to do so. The Indian feral child Kamala, whose picture appeared earlier in this chapter, is an example. Apparently reared among animals, Kamala learned to move about not by walking but by imitating, as well as a human being can, animals' quadripedal form of locomotion.

Learning by imitation is not confined to children. For many young adults with new driver's licenses, learning to drive was not primarily the result of listening to a driving instructor, watching a safety video, or studying a driver's manual; instead, successfully passing the road test was the result of many years of watching others (especially their parents) drive, and then imitating that behavior.

Experience

A third way culture is transmitted is by experience, negative and positive, gained through trial and error. Learning through experience, like learning by imitation, is a mechanism human beings share with other animals. Early in this century, American behavioral psychologist John B. Watson, influenced by the well-known salivating dog experiments of Russian physiologist Ivan Pavlov, studied both human beings and animals, and discovered how strongly positive and negative stimuli affected their learning. In Watson's view, even complex human behavior could be seen as a product of experience. Later, Watson's intellectual successor, B. F. Skinner, trained (or "conditioned") laboratory rats, confined in so-called Skinner boxes, to feed themselves by using a system of rewards (such as food pellets) and punishments (mild electric shocks). Today the growing popularity of behavior modification—a method of encouraging or (more usually) discouraging certain

Because it does not depend on language, imitation is a particularly important way of enculturating the young. In Zaire, Africa, an Efe child learns to prepare leaves for thatch by imitating her mother.

culture. Negative experience would soon teach them to avoid this behavior, while imitation would teach them to smile and shake hands instead.

Positive experience also promotes enculturation, which is why rewarding children's appropriate behavior is such an effective teaching method. But experiential enculturation, like imitation, is not limited to children. A first-time visitor to a Middle Eastern bazaar turns away in disappointment when a merchant quotes an excessive price for a silver bracelet. "Wait!" the merchant calls after her, and lowers the price. She has just learned that in this particular culture, prices are negotiable. Next time she needs to buy something, she will be ready to haggle over its cost.

All societies have institutionalized ways of transmitting cultural rules to their members through positive and negative experience. By sanctioning some behaviors and disapproving of others, either formally (that is, under the tenets of the society's legal system) or informally (for example, by rejection or ridicule), societies encourage their members to adhere to certain standards and abide by certain rules. Conventionalized, societywide responses to approved or disapproved behavior, called sanctions, are discussed in more detail in Chapter 12.

Enculturation may rely on a combination of modes of cultural transmission. Instruction (including formal education), for example, enculturates through a combination of symbols (such as the instructor's words), imitation (such as the students' replication of the instructor's behavior, as in a language class or science lab), and experience (such as trial and error during test taking).

• Translating Cultures •

The most important, and perhaps the most difficult, task cultural anthropologists face is interpreting the data on a given culture in such a way as to make them intelligible to members of their own culture. This attempt at cross-cultural explanation is sometimes called the *translation* of culture, since the anthropologist seeks to translate the ideas, values, symbols, and institutions of one culture for members of another. Translating a culture is not simply a matter of presenting the observable facts. When a culture is being analyzed, meaning and interpretation are at least as important as facts—perhaps more so. The significance of interpretation was stressed as early as 1950 by the English anthropologist Edward Evans-Pritchard (1902–1974), who

behaviors, such as smoking, by using a system of rewards and punishments—is one legacy of the work of Pavlov, Watson, and Skinner.

Enculturation by negative experience is in a sense the reverse of enculturation by imitation, in that instead of learning by doing what others are doing, one learns by avoiding doing what others do not do. In Tibet (see map on page 255), it is considered appropriate for a person to stick his tongue out at another as a greeting and a sign of respect; in America, the same behavior would engender a negative or even hostile reaction. Tibetan visitors to America might be expected to realize quickly that sticking the tongue out has a meaning other than a polite greeting in American

considered anthropology to be more akin to the humanities than to the sciences.

> [Cultural anthropology] is a kind of . . . philosophy or art, [which] implies that it . . . is interested in design rather than in process, and that it therefore seeks patterns and not scientific laws, and interprets rather than explains. (Evans-Pritchard 1962:26)

It was not until the 1970s, twenty-some years after Evans-Pritchard argued for interpretation over explanation in anthropology, that Clifford Geertz (1973) popularized this view. He used the term **interpretive anthropology** to convey the idea that a cultural anthropologist's job is not merely to describe cultures but also to interpret them—to discover what the members of a culture under study find meaningful, and why. A culture may be regarded, said Geertz, as a sort of text that its members constantly "read" and which its anthropologist must interpret.

In seeking to make sense of what the people in a society under study are doing and what their behavior means, a cultural anthropologist must distinguish among four perspectives. The first is the set of rules that defines ideal behavior in that culture. Such guidelines, which may be related to people's religion or philosophy of life, are understood by all members of the society: accepted as right and proper by most, and adhered to by many. These guidelines ensure that the behavior of most members of the society will be predictable.

Individuals are not cultural robots; they have their own personalities, desires, and goals. Thus, even though they may accept their culture's ideals and rules as behavioral standards, they do not necessarily always obey them. Consider the difference between the ideal and the actual in the case of marriage. Ideally, in Western society, a man and a woman fall in love, get married, set up a household, sometimes have children, and spend their lives together. In reality, a large proportion of all marriages in Western countries today—in the United States, roughly half—end in divorce. The second perspective on culture, often quite different from the cultural ideal, is what the members of a society actually do.

Cultural anthropologists, like the members of the cultures they study, are individuals, with certain kinds of personalities, certain preconceptions, certain desires and goals. Inevitably, as they strive to understand and interpret cultures, they are influenced by subjective, personal factors. No matter how objective they try to be, the results of their fieldwork will, in the end, always reflect their individuality; two fieldworkers investigating the same culture at the same time would view the culture somewhat differently. The third perspective, then, is the cultural anthropologist's conception of what is actually happening in a culture. This personal slant is sometimes referred to as the **etic perspective** (see Headland et al. 1990).

Finally, individuals in any society will have their own ideas of what is happening around them. Usually well aware of cultural ideals, they may feel that deviations from them are justified at times, or they may not even realize that rules are being breached. The fourth perspective from which to

Individuals do not always follow their society's rules. At a cricket match in England, a nude "streaker," breaching cultural rules regarding proper dress, is apprehended by the police.

---

interpretive anthropology the idea that an ethnographer's job is to describe and interpret what members of the culture being studied find meaningful

etic perspective the anthropological use of the concepts meaningful to the anthropologist to understand a culture

understand a culture is what the people themselves think is actually happening. The first and fourth perspectives are sometimes classified together as the **emic perspective,** and contrasted with the etic.[3]

Each of the four perspectives—the ideal (what the people say should happen), the real (what is "objectively" happening), the ethnographer's view (what the ethnographer thinks is happening), and the people's view (what the people themselves think is happening)—is important to anthropologists as they struggle to find meaning in other cultures. Taking each perspective into account is necessary for the full "translation of culture" in all its shades of meaning.

• **The Politics of Culture** •

Race and Culture

To biologists, a **race** is a subpopulation within a single species of plant or animal, which is distinguished from other subpopulations in the same species on any basis. When applied to human beings, the term is generally used to distinguish groups of people from one another on the basis of physical attributes such as skin color, hair texture, and facial features. Beginning with the Age of Exploration, and especially in the Victorian era, some scholars (including some anthropologists) argued that in human beings, causal links exist between "race" and cultural attributes such as academic achievement, religious beliefs, or economic development.

Anthropologists continued to use the term *race* until the 1960s, in the belief that it was useful to classify human beings, like plants and animals, into discrete categories based on physical attributes (see, e.g., Coon 1962). This attempt at scientific rigor was complicated, however, by a history of conscious and unconscious cultural and political associations between specific "races" and specific cultures, lifestyles, or worldviews. The term fell into general disfavor among anthropologists, but continued to be used by scholars in other disciplines as well as by ideologues with political agendas detrimental to one or another "race."

The argument that "race" can be correlated with factors usually thought to be at least in part culturally derived (such as artistic achievement or economic status), or with factors whose origin has not yet been determined (such as intelligence quotient, or IQ), has never subsided entirely. In the United

States in 1994, it gained renewed media attention with the publication of a book by two biological determinists, Richard Herrnstein and Charles Murray (Herrnstein and Murray 1994). Having documented small differences in average IQ between members of different "races" in the United States, Herrnstein and Murray attempted to determine whether IQ or another variable, socioeconomic status, could be associated more strongly with social problems such as crime, unemployment, and single parenthood. Their answer was that in the United States these problems are more closely associated with IQ than with socioeconomic status.

Since Herrnstein and Murray believe IQ, in turn, to be associated with "race," the implications of their book are both far-reaching and controversial. For example, if it were true that, on the average, the members of some "races" were immutably limited intellectually, this would have profound implications for the educational system. But critics were quick to find flaws in Herrnstein and Murray's analysis. Some pointed out that IQ tests are culturally biased; others doubted that human intelligence can be rendered as a single number in any case; still others put forth other explanations for IQ differences, such as environmental factors. Herrnstein and Murray themselves point out that there is very little average genetic difference between members of different "races," and that when it comes to achievement, individuals are strongly influenced by culture.

The term "race" has also been used to distinguish groups of people based mainly on cultural differences rather than physical attributes (see, e.g., Sowell 1994). A recent American court case illustrates the point (Pohorecky 1992). The case involved an accusation of racial discrimination by whites against darker-skinned Pakistanis. Lawyers defending the whites called on scientific experts who testified that Pakistanis are classified as members of the Caucasian or "white" race, raising an interesting legal question: how can something termed *racial discrimination* have occurred

---

emic perspective the anthropological use of the concepts meaningful to the members of a society to understand their culture

race a term commonly used to identify groups of people supposedly sharing certain specific physical attributes, or, alternatively, physical plus cultural similarities. The word is not useful for distinguishing either biological or cultural categories of people

---

[3] The two terms were first used in anthropology by Marvin Harris, who adapted them from a distinction originally used by the linguist Kenneth Pike.

between members of the same race? Lawyers representing the Pakistanis then called their own expert witness, a cultural anthropologist, who argued that the court should rely not on the supposed biological classification of Pakistanis as "white," but on the common usage of the term *white*, since it was the *cultural* interpretation of "race" that was relevant in this context. The anthropologist's view prevailed, and the court found that racial discrimination had indeed occurred.

Today, the political connotations of the term "race" aside, many biologists and anthropologists believe that human "races," as discrete biological categories, do not exist (Shanklin 1994). Indeed, they argue that the long-term evolution of distinct human races would have been impossible. With two parents, four grandparents, eight great-grandparents, and so on, each of us has, in theory, billions of ancestors. Yet the population of the world did not reach even one billion until the eighteenth century (G. Moffett 1994:7). Thus the human species, over the long term, is highly inbred. Over shorter periods of time, the geographical isolation of some human groups from others, combined with the influence of particular environmental circumstances, did result in the development and intensification, in many populations, of the physical characteristics later used as defining characteristics of "races." But even this manifestation of genetic pooling is now a thing of the past, as physical characteristics are continually being combined and recombined in the human species. Human physical characteristics today do not converge to define clear-cut races, if they ever did in the past.

In any case, since the meaning of "race" can change to suit the context in which it is used, it is clear that the term is of limited utility, whether used to designate a biological *or* a cultural category.

Cultural Pluralism

When people with different biological characteristics or cultural traditions form a single society, the result is termed **cultural pluralism.** This is most characteristic of large-scale, modern societies, since they

are most apt to incorporate many different **subcultures:** small groups, always found within larger ones, whose members distinguish themselves (or are distinguished by others) as different from other such groups on any cultural basis.

Subcultures should not be confused with ethnic groups, discussed in Chapter 1. *Subculture* is the broader term. The members of a subculture may be distinguished from the members of other groups on any basis, including biological similarities, cultural traditions, current lifestyles, or even common interests. In contrast, the members of an ethnic group share specific attributes, such as cultural traditions, values, and language. In addition, subcultures are always found within the context of larger groups; ethnic groups are not. Thus, prisoners might be considered members of a subculture, but Trobriand Islanders are members of an ethnic group.

• Ask Yourself •

Many of the world's cities are plagued by violence perpetrated by gangs, which often distinguish themselves on ethnic grounds (Public Health Reports 1991). From Los Angeles to New York to London to Capetown, there are Asian gangs, Latino gangs, Irish gangs, and so on. In a debate, could you assume a "politically correct" stance and defend the behavior of members of an ethnic gang? How would you go about doing so?

How do societies handle problems inevitably deriving from cultural pluralism? In some, such as South Africa before the end of apartheid, political or religious regulations exist to control the behavior of people of different ethnic groups, religions, sexual orientations, or classes. In modern democracies, democratic ideals tend to limit the number of such regulations. Yet the ethnic, religious, sexist, and other biases that characterize modern democracies show that these societies have not yet come to grips with their cultural pluralism so as to protect the members of all subcultures from discrimination. Some nations, including the United States, have antidiscrimination laws, but in no culturally pluralistic society have these been completely successful.

One response to cultural pluralism, and a recent subject of debate on North American college cam-

---

cultural pluralism the meeting of many cultural traditions within a society, particularly a large-scale, modern society

subculture a small group within a larger one, whose members distinguish themselves (or who are distinguished by others) as different from others on any cultural basis

"Political correctness" demands that we avoid saying or doing anything to demean people of any gender, sexual orientation, physical status, or subculture. Fans of the Atlanta Braves baseball team feel they are honoring their team's mascot, the Native American warrior, with a gesture called the tomahawk chop, but critics view the gesture as demeaning to Native Americans who, they assert, should never have been chosen as a mascot for a baseball team in the first place.

puses, is called *political correctness* (see Berman 1992). The idea behind political correctness is that everyone should avoid saying or doing anything to demean or degrade the members of any subculture, whether based on ethnicity, gender, age, religion, physical status, or any other characteristic. But this ambition, worthy at first glance, raises a troubling question. Should we give equal treatment (assuming that we can agree on what constitutes this) to members of every subculture, or would such extreme cultural sensitivity lead to the nondiscriminatory affirmation of any person, behavior, or view (even, of course, the reprehensible), and the neglect of cultural and historical realities?

Those favoring political correctness argue that demeaning the members of any subculture is inconsistent with the American ideal of equality. Those who question its value point out that special treatment for certain groups, such as individualized college curricula for minority students, is in itself demeaning, and that political correctness, with its implicit guidelines about what one may and may not say, restricts free speech. The continuing debate

• Ask Yourself •

Do you see yourself as a member of a specific subculture? If so, do you feel that nonmembers should be compelled to avoid giving you offense on the basis of your membership? Would you favor a law making it illegal to behave disrespectfully to members of your subculture?

may have an important impact on how North Americans view subcultures within their culturally pluralistic society.

Culture and Personality

The nineteenth-century founder of psychoanalysis, Sigmund Freud, claimed that childhood occurrences, even those we do not remember, strongly influence our adult personalities. Freud's ideas exerted considerable influence on some early twentieth-century cultural anthropologists, to whom it seemed plausible that a link could be found between culture and individuals' psychological makeup. They supposed that not only could one's cultural surroundings influence one's personality, but also that the personalities of individuals could also help to shape a culture.

The idea gained followers in the first few decades of this century, and by the 1930s members of the **culture and personality** school of anthropology were testing their ideas in the field. One of them was Cora DuBois (1903–1991), who hypothesized that the way adults treated young children in a given society—how long they are breast-fed, how they are toilet trained, and so on—affected the personalities of those children when they became adults, thus providing a basic "personality structure" for the society (Kardiner 1945). In 1937, DuBois traveled to the island of Alor in eastern Indonesia, where she spent nearly a year and a half studying Alorese personality (DuBois 1961). In addition to gathering what had by this time become the customary types of ethnographic data, DuBois also administered psychological tests to her Alorese hosts, collected children's drawings, and recorded dreams.

DuBois's data showed that Alorese mothers customarily resumed their full-time gardening work

culture and personality an area of special interest within anthropology, whose adherents see a significant link between culture and human psychology

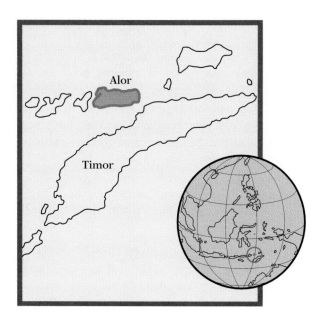

When you were a child, how did your mother and father punish you? How did they show affection? Do you think these aspects of your childhood helped to make you the person you are today? With your own children, will you handle these matters the way your parents did, or differently?

and ignores others. Is money important to members of the culture or not? How are adolescents treated? Is warfare encouraged, tolerated, or completely avoided (Benedict 1934:35)? A society's cultural choices give it a distinct flavor. Benedict claimed that the Zuni of New Mexico (see map on page 14), for example, were a sober, moderate, formal, somewhat puritanical, nonviolent, and restrained people, who placed the good of society above that of the individual. The Kwakiutl of Vancouver Island (see map on page 18), on the other hand, seemed to Benedict to be almost the direct opposite.

These characterizations of cultures on the basis of typical or average personality types led to studies of what was called *national character*. A number of such studies were undertaken in the United States

shortly after childbirth, leaving their infants in the care of others, such as grandmothers or aunts (1961:34). If they could, these caretakers sometimes breast-fed their charges in the mother's absence. Otherwise they fed the babies soft or liquid foods more or less conscientiously, but from an etic perspective DuBois felt this feeding was "neither very effective nor satisfactory" (1961:35). As the children grew up, it seemed to her, as an American, that they were given little consistent direction or love. Aggressive teasing was common, and punishments were often harsh (1961:61).

DuBois found Alorese adults to be hostile, suspicious, jealous, and given to temper tantrums. Married couples seemed to share little warmth. People took great delight in teasing one another, but otherwise seemed apathetic. These traits, DuBois concluded, resulted from the local child-rearing practices. She went on to suggest that certain features of any society, such as widespread mutual hostility and suspicion, could be explained with reference to the **modal personality**—the statistically most common personality type—of that society (DuBois 1961:xix).

Among the most influential members of the culture and personality school were Ruth Benedict and her student Margaret Mead. Benedict argued that from among limitless possibilities every society selects the cultural attributes that characterize it

On the island of Alor, anthropologist Cora DuBois noted that parents seemed to give their children little love, a tendency she associated with the hostile personalities of Alorese adults. Frightened by the photographer, an Alorese child clings to its mother, whose response seems to lack warmth.

modal personality in any culture, the personality type that is statistically the most common

Anthropology and the Environment

Native Americans, Human Rights, and the Environment

Of the 5000 or so indigenous cultures in the world today, some 700 are found in North America (Butler and LaDuke 1995:113). For at least ten thousand years (some archaeologists say thirty thousand), these Native American cultures enjoyed a sustainable relationship with their natural environment, on which they depended for all their subsistence necessities. In recent times, however, unplanned economic development has increasingly abridged the right of Native Americans to pursue their traditional way of life in healthy, productive natural surroundings. Today, a disproportionate number of environmentally harmful activities, from logging to fuel processing to nuclear waste disposal, are sited on or near Native American lands, polluting the air, water, and soil; depriving Native Americans of their traditional livelihoods; and posing a variety of environmental health risks.

To combat environmental degradation, Native Americans are becoming increasingly involved in the "environmental justice movement," begun by participants in the First National People of Color Environmental Leadership Summit, held in Washington, D.C., in October 1991. Advocates of environmental justice view human societies and the natural environment as inextricably linked; the health of one depends on the health of the other, and social exploitation is viewed as inseparable from the exploitation of the natural world (Bullard 1993:57).

The premise has led to the creation of a number of new, community-based, indigenous environmental protection organizations. For example, a recent battle against the placement of a toxic waste incinerator on Navajo lands in the Southwest led to the formation of Deneh Care, a Native American grassroots organization devoted to restoring the reservation to environmental health.* Over the last four years Deneh Care has grown rapidly, and now addresses issues ranging from forestry management to asbestos regulation to alternative energy planning. Other Native American environmental protection organizations, mostly in the Midwest, West, and Northwest, are doing likewise. Without funding or paid staff, these organizations are nevertheless having a notable impact on local environmental problems.

Native Americans once constituted 100 percent of the population of the Americas and controlled 100 percent of American lands. Today they represent approximately 1 percent of the population and control less than 4 percent of the land (Butler and LaDuke 1995:113), much of which is no longer productive. In recognition of similar problems worldwide, the United Nations in December 1994 launched the Decade of Indigenous People (1994 to 2004). Its goals include heightening public awareness of worldwide threats to the right of members of indigenous subcultures to live and work in healthy local environments.

* Deneh is the indigenous term for the Navajo Nation.

around the time of World War II, in the hope of gaining insights into the thinking of the Japanese and the Germans. In 1939, a group that included Margaret Mead worked with the Committee for National Morale "to consider ways in which the sciences of anthropology and psychology . . . could be applied to the problems of morale building in wartime" (Bock 1988:80). Later, other American anthropologists, among them Ruth Benedict, moved to Washington, where they took part in national character studies. After the war ended, research was extended to include the Russians. However, national character studies bore few results that scholars found reliable.

In the 1940s, 1950s, and 1960s, the culture and personality school branched out to include studies of the differences between normal and abnormal personality and the relationship between culture and mental illness. Today, although the idea that psychology can help us to understand culture continues to interest anthropologists (Paul 1989), most cultural anthropologists believe that, in addition to psychological explanations, there are additional, or different, explanations for cultural differences. The result has been that by no means all of today's anthropologists accept the validity of this perspective. Nevertheless, thanks to the pioneering field-work of Benedict, Mead, DuBois, and their many colleagues and successors, the connection between culture and personality remains an area of contemporary anthropological interest.

Conclusion

Animals do not need culture to survive. They adjust to their natural environments, over the long term, by evolving physical traits (such as a covering of hair to keep them warm in cold climates, a specialized set of teeth for chewing certain raw foods, large eyes that permit them to see in mimimal light) and behavioral traits (like hibernation or predator alarm calls) that favor their survival. Human beings, too, adapt physically through time; more important, however, we adapt culturally, employing cultural means—such as fire for warmth, cooking to soften raw foods, and electric lights for night vision—to achieve not merely our long-term survival as a species but also our short-term comfort, safety, health, and well-being as individuals.

So flexible is culture that—unlike other species, most of which inhabit particular environmental niches—human beings have been able to adapt to life in Arctic regions, deserts, tropical rainforests, and temperate zones, as well as places where temperature, rainfall, and climate vary widely from season to season. Human beings have not simply found a special niche and managed to hold their own in the world of nature: they have expanded into almost every environmental niche, and exploited the world of nature to their own advantage.

Human beings are unique. Originally purely natural creatures like all other living things, we are now the only species on the planet that depends for its existence on something other than nature, something we ourselves invented: culture. So dependent have we become on our own invention that we could not, as a species, survive without it.

Summary

- A central concern of cultural anthropology is the concept of culture: the customs, ideas, artifacts, and languages that human beings in groups share with and learn from one another.

- Culture is unique to human beings; not even our closest animal relatives, the great apes, can be considered to have cultures.

- Culture is patterned, in that the ideas, behaviors, languages, and artifacts of which it is constituted are familiar to all and continually repeated, both in the present and down through the generations.

- Culture is compulsory, in that individuals who wish to get along successfully have no option but to take their society's culture into account in their dealings with others.

- Culture is adaptive, consisting of a complex set of problem-solving strategies for satisfying people's needs within a particular social and natural environment.

- Culture is holistic in that the various elements of any culture are interrelated.

- Culture is dynamic because it is constantly changing.

- Culture, a creation of human beings, is often compared with and viewed as superior to nature, everything human beings did not create and cannot modify.

- The primary means of transmission of culture, both among people who are contemporaries and from one generation to the next, is through symbols: things that stand for something else. Words may be human beings' most important symbols.

- Symbolic anthropology, a subfield of cultural anthropology, is devoted to the study of symbols, both within cultures and cross-culturally, in order to help uncover hidden patterns of meaning within cultures.

- Imitation and experience also transmit culture and contribute to enculturation, the process by which individuals learn to become functioning members of specific cultures.

- Cultural anthropology's task is to "translate" the ideas, values, symbols, and institutions of cultures so that they can be understood by members of other cultures. In order to find meaning, this translation entails interpretation as well as the reporting of facts.

- To describe what members of a culture find meaningful, the anthropologist distinguishes among four perspectives: the ideal rules by which the members of a society say they should lead their collective lives, the real behavior of the society's members, the reality that the ethnographer perceives, and the reality that the people themselves perceive.

- The utility of the term *race* is limited either as a biological or a cultural category, since its definition varies according to context.

- Cultural pluralism results from the interaction of people of different subcultures within the same large-scale society. "Political correctness" is one recently devised way of dealing with the problem.

- According to the culture and personality school of anthropology, cultures can be characterized in terms of isolable cultural attributes and typical personality types. Members of this school examined the effects of childhood experiences on adult personality, attempted to identify the most common personality type (modal personality) for particular cultures, and studied national character. Today, the approach has lost much of its conviction.

- Culture is the human mechanism for coping with the demands of survival, enabling human beings to form families and communities, communicate, make a living, maintain order, find meaning in existence, express aesthetic values, and perpetuate their species.

- So dependent is *Homo sapiens sapiens* on culture, its own creation, that the species could not survive without it.

Key Terms

acculturation
cultural pluralism
culture and personality
emic perspective
enculturation
etic perspective
interpretive anthropology
modal personality
race
subculture
symbol
symbolic anthropology

Suggested Readings

Barnouw, Victor. 1985 (orig. 1963). *Culture and Personality* (4th ed.). Belmont, CA: Wadsworth. An introduction to this topic, covering all the basic information.

MacLaury, Robert E. 1992. From Brightness to Hue: An Explanatory Model of Color-Category Evolution. *Current Anthropology* 33(4):137–186. The most recent contribution to the controversy about whether the meanings of certain colors vary cross-culturally or are similar for all cultures. The author adopts an in-between position.

Sebeok, Thomas A., and Jean Umiker-Sebeok. (eds.). 1980. *Speaking of Apes: A Critical Anthology of Two-way Communications with Man.* New York: Plenum Press. A collection of articles that includes contributions by all the major researchers of language behavior in apes up to 1980.

Sowell, Thomas. 1994. *Race and Culture: A World View.* New York: Basic Books. A neoconservative thinker argues for the primacy of culture over biology, postulating that differences between groups once thought of as separate "races" can best be explained in terms of the different skills and values characterizing such groups.

Turner, Victor. 1967. *The Forest of Symbols: Aspects of Ndembu Ritual.* Ithaca, NY: Cornell University Press. Ten essays dealing with the use of symbols in ritual in a central African society, by one of the most eminent contributors to symbolic anthropology.

White, Leslie A. (ed.), with **Beth Dillingham.** 1973. *The Concept of Culture.* Minneapolis: Burgess. An overview of the culture concept, by one of its most famous interpreters.

Introduction

Once upon a time, so the old story goes, there was a city in which all the inhabitants were blind. One day an elephant was brought into town, and word

spread rapidly among the sightless residents. Eventually, three of the most curious—none of whom had any idea how an elephant looked—approached the beast and began to grope about, gathering information by touching various parts of its body. Soon each blind man was convinced that he knew just what an elephant was. The one who had chanced to seize an ear exclaimed, "It's obvious to me that an elephant is a large, rough thing, flat and wide. It's very much like a rug." Another, who had handled the trunk, disagreed. "Not at all," he protested. "An elephant is like a big, flexible pipe." A third, who had grasped one of the legs, announced as confidently as his fellows, "You're both wrong. An elephant is upright, sturdy and straight, like a pillar!"

"The Blind Men and the Elephant" is only a children's fable, but it illustrates an important point: if we wish to understand a subject as fully as possible, we must examine it from as many angles as we can. No single point of view is likely to give us a comprehensive interpretation. This is as true of culture as it is of elephants. In this chapter, we look at several basic theoretical perspectives and a number of specialty areas—some conceptual orientations, some specific topics—in cultural anthropology. Each has something significant to contribute to our understanding of culture.

• Synchronic Versus • Diachronic Approaches

One way to learn about an elephant would be to examine its ears, trunk, and legs, attempting to find out how they work together to keep the whole animal functioning. We call this approach **synchronic** (Figure 3.1), meaning "at one point in time," because it seeks to understand how the various parts of the elephant fit together at a particular moment in time, rather than looking at how the animal developed through time. To try to understand and interpret a culture using this approach, a cultural anthropologist collects data on the different institutions, ideas, and customs of the culture, and attempts to fit them together into a general, comprehensive picture of the culture at one moment in time.[1] This is an especially useful way of

organizing, summarizing, and understanding data on cultures that lack written or other records of the past.

A very different approach to the study of culture, the **diachronic** approach, takes a dynamic, historical point of view. The term *diachronic* means "through time." The diachronic approach is based on the assumption that to understand the elephant fully, one must not only examine its ears, trunk and legs, but also study how the animal was conceived, was born, and grew. Followers of this approach believe that we cannot understand cultures unless we know something of their origins and how they developed through time.

Both approaches, the synchronic and the diachronic, are valid for studying culture, and the choice of which to use depends on the circumstances. Using both is preferable to using only one, and most contemporary cultural anthropologists would make use of both if they could. But for some contemporary cultures, no archaeological data exist, and for some nonliterate ones there are no historical documents to help the anthropologist understand change and development through time. Cultural anthropologists attempting to understand such cultures today are therefore usually limited to the synchronic approach. Throughout this book, we will make a strong case for examining cultures using both approaches, whenever possible.

---

[1] This point in time may be contemporary with the anthropologist or not. The French scholar Emmanuel LeRoy Ladurie (1979) wrote a book about life in a village in southern France in the early 1300s, and the fact that the community he studied existed seven hundred years ago made his study no less synchronic.

synchronic approach the study of how aspects of societies and cultures fit together at any given point in time

diachronic approach the study of societies and cultures as they develop through time

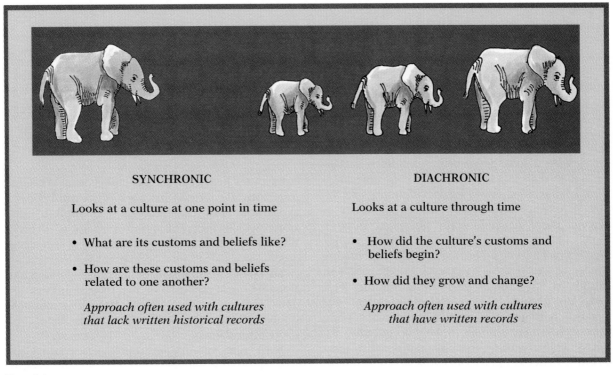

SYNCHRONIC

Looks at a culture at one point in time

- What are its customs and beliefs like?

- How are these customs and beliefs related to one another?

Approach often used with cultures that lack written historical records

DIACHRONIC

Looks at a culture through time

- How did the culture's customs and beliefs begin?

- How did they grow and change?

Approach often used with cultures that have written records

Figure 3.1

Synchronic and Diachronic Approaches to Studying a Culture. Two approaches to studying a culture are the synchronic, in which the culture is viewed at a single point in time, and the diachronic, in which the culture is viewed as it developed through time.

• Theoretical Perspectives •

In cultural anthropology there are several fundamental, different, but not mutually exclusive ways of looking at and interpreting data. We call these different intellectual orientations *theoretical perspectives*. Three of the most basic to cultural anthropology are cultural evolution, functionalism, and cultural materialism.

Cultural Evolution

In Chapter 1, we introduced the theory of cultural evolution, the idea that cultures tend to evolve or change, usually slowly, steadily, and in the direction of greater complexity and efficiency. Although predating the nineteenth-century work of Charles Darwin on biological evolution, cultural evolution received a boost from his ideas. When the cultural evolutionists—foremost among whom were the British anthropologist Edward Tylor and the American lawyer/anthropologist Lewis Henry

Morgan—compared the many cultures about which they had read, they thought, ethnocentrically, that some cultures seemed exceedingly "primitive," others somewhat more advanced, and still others (especially their own) quite civilized. They concluded that cultures must progress through stages, from "savagery" to "barbarism" and finally to "civilization."[2]

• Ask Yourself •

In your view, are there any societies in existence today that you would consider "primitive"? What are the features that make them primitive? Can you think of anything primitive about your own society?

---

[2] The historical particularism of Franz Boas, described in Chapter 1, was in part a reaction to cultural evolution, with its generalizations about human progress. Boas saw every culture as unique, rather than passing through the same predictable stages. We have not included a discussion of historical particularism in this chapter because this perspective has few contemporary proponents.

The initially rather rigid nineteenth-century concept of cultural evolution has been greatly modified in the twentieth century to produce several new ideas, collectively called **neoevolution.** Thus cultural evolution still has many followers in anthropology.

One important contribution of the neoevolutionists was a refinement of the concept of culture change. To neoevolutionists, the term *change*, when applied to a culture, does not necessarily imply progress or betterment; whether a culture is "better" today than it was in the past is a value judgment best avoided. Indeed, neoevolutionists recognize that cultures do not inevitably get better or become more technologically advanced through time, but may remain stable for long periods, or even become less capable of adaptation to changing circumstances. This is as true of North American culture as any other. The twentieth-century tendency to degrade the natural environment, for instance, hardly seems adaptive in the long run. So the neoevolutionists prefer to avoid using terms like *change* and *progress*. Instead, they use the term **cultural process** to describe what happens to cultures through time, whether this is change or stability, greater complexity or greater simplicity.

A second contribution of the neoevolutionists was to modify the nineteenth-century idea of **unilineal evolution,** the notion that all cultures follow the same trajectory, from savagery to barbarism to civilization. There did seem to be some empirical support for unilineal evolution: ancient cultures between which there had apparently been no contact and which thrived at different times (such as the cultures of long-ago Egypt and Mexico) nevertheless shared some similar cultural characteristics, such as the building of pyramids. To explain this, Julian Steward (1955) proposed that the environment in which a given society exists

---

neoevolution any of several twentieth-century variations on cultural evolution

cultural process what happens to cultures through time, whether change or stability, increasing or decreasing complexity

unilineal evolution the notion that all cultures follow the same trajectory, from "savagery" to "civilization"

multilineal evolution the notion that different cultures evolve along multiple, if similar, lines, depending on their natural and cultural environments

---

• Ask Yourself •

Native American cultures today are characterized not only by increasing involvement in mainstream American culture but also by disproportionately high rates of poverty and alcoholism. Do you think these cultures are "better" now than they were before Western European contact?

---

contributes heavily to its particular developmental trajectory. He termed his perspective **multilineal evolution,** after the multiple, but similar, lines along which different cultures seem to evolve. While societies in similar settings may evolve along parallel tracks, Steward added, any society, at any given point in time, will be at a particular point along its track, a point at which its cultural institutions are appropriate to its particular circumstances. Steward called these points "levels of sociocultural integration."

Most contemporary anthropologists would probably agree that, although exceptions occur, ever more complex and adaptive cultural characteristics tend to evolve in most societies over the long term.[3] Does this notion help us to understand a given society? A familiar phenomenon of contemporary American culture provides an example. Since the 1970s, an increasing number of long-distance truckers have been using Citizens Band (CB) radios. A modern cultural evolutionist might declare that this phenomenon can best be explained as an adaptive response to certain environmental changes, both general (such as the country's increasing population size and the development of a national system of linked superhighways) and specific (such as the 1973 fuel crisis and the 55-mile-an-hour speed limit). This view is evolutionary in that a more complex, more adaptive, more efficient cultural characteristic—instant communication among truckers through CB radios—is understood to have developed out of a less adaptive, less efficient one (headlight blinking, horn honking, and hand waving). In Steward's terms, CB radio is a particularly efficient and effective method of communication among

---

[3] We must stress that we are speaking in general terms. A culture does not have to be complex (by modern, Western standards) to be adaptive; the culture of prehistoric gathering and hunting people—simple by modern, Western standards—was nevertheless highly adaptive.

Multilineal evolution may explain why ancient cultures that arose and fell at different times shared similar cultural characteristics. Pyramids built at different times and in different places by Aztecs (left) and Egyptians (right) show striking similarities.

long-distance truckers, given American society's level of sociocultural integration.

Functionalism

Another viewpoint from which cultural anthropologists seek to understand their data is **functionalism**. As anthropologists use this term, it has several applications, two of which are associated with Bronislaw Malinowski (Firth 1960). The first is the idea that cultures can be viewed as systems, made up of individual elements that work (or function) both individually and together. A fundamental premise of this kind of functionalism is that if one element in a system is altered, this will have an effect on the others, and indeed on the performance of the whole system. Applied to cultures, this viewpoint suggests that if one aspect of a culture changes, this will eventually cause culturewide changes. If, for example, a culture is beset by a new and deadly disease, this change to the physical health of some of its members will have a cascading effect, eventually changing other aspects of the culture such as the health-related behavior of its members, its system of health care delivery, and perhaps even the way the members of the society think about illness.

The influence of this version of functionalism was considerable, as the important work of Malinowski's followers demonstrates. His student Raymond Firth (1901–) begins his *We, the Tikopia* (1963), a classic in cultural anthropology, with a description of family life among the Tikopians, technologically simple agriculturalists living on a South Pacific island. Firth presented the Tikopian family

Cultures tend to become more complex and adaptive through time. From a cultural-evolutionary point of view, long-distance truckers' increasing use of CB radios is an adaptive response to environmental changes such as the development of a national superhighway system and the 55-mile-an-hour speed limit.

functionalism any of several approaches to the study of culture and society that emphasizes the functional interactions of aspects of culture or of individuals in terms of its primary "functions," reproduction and enculturation. Later, the study branched out to other Tikopian institutions with links to the family, and from these institutions to still others. *We, the Tikopia* has been criticized for relying too much on mere description and not enough on abstract analysis, which would have given the book a greater sense of coherence. Firth simply described one aspect of culture before moving on to describe another, examining each as it interacted with the others, with little indication of what he believed was basic to understanding the culture and what was of only marginal significance. Lacking a sense of proportion, Firth appeared to attempt to describe every aspect of Tikopian life, so much so that one critic wondered why, in a book that runs to hundreds of pages, he stopped at the particular point he did (Kuper 1985:73).

The second variety of functionalism is quite different. This is the idea that aspects of a culture function to fulfill the biological and psychological needs of individuals. For instance, one of the most interesting aspects of Trobriand culture (see map on page 19) to Malinowski was the Trobrianders' constant interisland trading, which involved—in addition to boat-building and long, dangerous

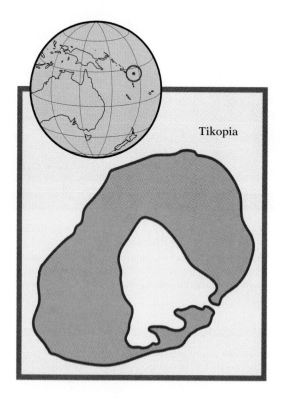

Tikopia

sea voyages—many seemingly useless activities, such as elaborate magical rituals, which on the surface lacked any obvious, tangible result. (The Trobrianders, of course, were not alone in undertaking apparently useless activities. In our own culture, to cite only one example, people sometimes expend much money and effort on restoring antique cars not intended for transportation, a seemingly nonfunctional endeavor.) How might one explain the Trobriand islanders' magic rituals? From the second Malinowskian functionalist perspective, these complex rites and spells can be understood as serving a psychological function: reassurance. Magic helped to relieve the islanders' anxiety about traveling over dangerous seas in canoes, in the face of uncertain weather conditions and without navigational aids (Malinowski 1954:90).

The third variety of functionalism is similar to the first, the main difference being that it is rather more abstract in its application since it is concerned with social structure. It focuses on the social relationships between individuals in a group, and the way in which these relationships function to maintain the social structure (see Chapter 1) of the group. Hence this third variety of functionalism is labeled **structural-functionalism,** an anthropological perspective in which aspects of culture are viewed in terms of the part they play in maintaining the social structure. The origins of functionalism in this sense lay with a French sociologist, Emile Durkheim (1858–1916), but the viewpoint was greatly popularized by the British anthropologist A. R. Radcliffe-Brown. It dominated British social anthropology and in the United States had strong support at the University of Chicago during the 1940s and 1950s.

Radcliffe-Brown explained his version of functionalism in the following way:

> When I pick up a particular sea shell on the beach, I recognize it as having a particular structure. I may find other shells of the same species which have a similar structure, so that I can say there is a form of structure characteristic of the species. . . . I examine a local group of Australian aborigines and find an arrangement of persons

---

structural-functionalism an anthropological perspective in which aspects of culture are viewed in terms of the part they play in maintaining the social structure

Apparently nonfunctional activities occur in all cultures. In North America, for example, some people spend a great deal of money and effort on restoring antique cars not intended for transportation.

in a certain number of families. This, I call the social structure of that particular group at that moment of time. Another local group has a structure that is in important ways similar to that of the first. . . . By examining a number of different species [of shells], I may be able to recognize a certain general structural form. . . . By examining a representative sample of local groups in one region, I can describe a certain form of structure. (quoted in Kuper 1985:53–54)

As it turned out, finding cultural groups that were "representative" of a "certain form of structure" proved virtually impossible: too many cultural phenomena were peculiar only to one society. Nevertheless, other anthropologists took up the structural-functionalist perspective. The best known was Edward Evans-Pritchard, who produced a classic structural-functionalist study of a nonliterate group of people in the Sudan and Zaire, Africa, called the Azande. The Azande believe that some people are witches. When a Zande person dies, witchcraft is frequently thought to be the cause, and the dead person's relatives are entitled to avenge the death by using "vengeance magic." But before they

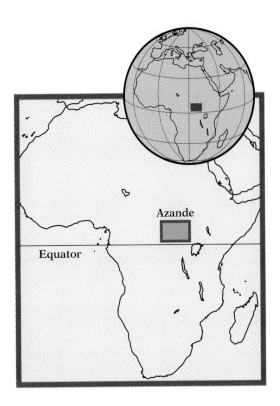

The Azande of Africa believe that death may be caused by witchcraft. A victim's relatives may use magic to avenge the death, but they must first get permission from their village headman. From a structural-functionalist point of view, the need to seek permission functions as a reinforcement of a headman's authority. Above, a Zande village headman.

The structural-functionalist perspective has been criticized for two reasons. First, its synchronic emphasis makes culture change (a constant feature of human life) impossible to understand clearly. And second, it did not fufill the claim made for it by Radcliffe-Brown: that it would eventually enable us to discover laws governing human social behavior. Despite these limitations, however, functionalism in general remains a major theoretical orientation in cultural anthropology. In numerous field studies, its adherents have revealed a great deal about individual societies—how they function and what makes them unique. All three types of functionalist perspective, Malinowski's two versions and structural-functionalism, continue to contribute to our understanding of society.

Cultural Materialism

Some anthropologists think it is concrete, observable factors that most strongly influence people's institutions and beliefs. These factors include the natural environment, a society's level of technological development, its population size and distribution, and the specific ways its people get food and shelter. Like cultural evolution and unlike functionalism, this way of looking at cultural phenomena, called **cultural materialism,** is often diachronic rather than synchronic, because the aspects of culture on which it most relies for interpretation—environment, technology, demographic change—are all dynamic rather than static. The assumptions underlying this point of view are found in the ideas of the nineteenth-century German political philosopher Karl Marx, who sought explanations for social customs in one of the most concrete, observable aspects of any culture: the ways in which the culture produces the goods it needs. Today its best known anthropological advocate is Marvin Harris (1980).

To illustrate how the cultural materialist perspective can help interpret a culture, we return once again to the Trobriand Islands, the site of the interisland trading voyages and associated rituals that so interested their first Western investigator, the early functionalist Bronislaw Malinowski. One aspect of Trobriand trading that Malinowski found

can do so, they must first seek their local village headman's permission (Evans-Pritchard 1985:6–7). Every time such a request is made, the headman's authority is reinforced. If villagers ceased to believe in magic, perhaps as the result of acculturation, the headman's authority would be weakened, because villagers would no longer have to ask for permission to avenge deaths. From a structural-functionalist point of view, one function of Zande witchcraft and magic is that they help maintain the political authority of the village head, and thus the village's political organization.

cultural materialism the idea that concrete, measurable things, such as the natural environment or technology, are more responsible for specific aspects of culture than other factors

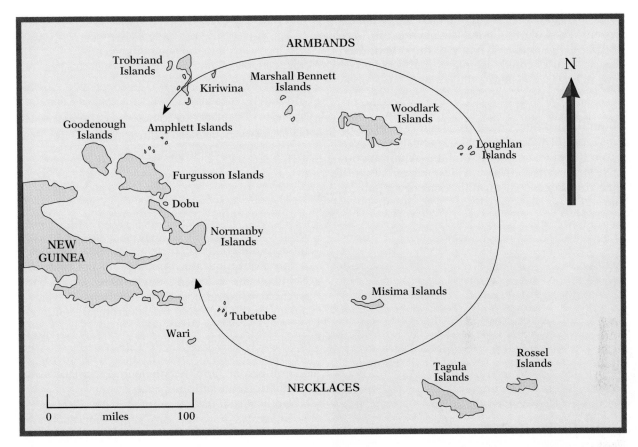

Figure 3.2

The Kula Ring. In the kula ring, residents of different islands in the western Pacific give one another the same gifts—shell necklaces and armbands—over and over again. Necklaces always pass from hand to hand in one direction, armbands in the other. Giving or receiving these items wins prestige for both givers and receivers.

particularly intriguing but seemingly nonfunctional if judged only on its outward appearance was called the kula ring (see Figure 3.2), a ritual exchange of certain gifts between people living on different islands of the Trobriand Islands chain. As part of this reciprocal trading arrangement, the islanders made dangerous canoe trips across the open seas between islands, in order to exhange the same gifts—always shell necklaces and armbands—over and over again. These objects circulated endlessly among island traders, sometimes eventually winding up in the same hands that had given them away years ago. Even though the recipient of a kula gift was only its temporary owner, the transfer of a particularly desirable shell necklace or armband from one person to another won both donor and recipient great prestige.

For Malinowski, the explanation for the kula trade lay not in anything directly observable but rather in something that was neither concrete nor obvious: the islanders' social and psychological needs, such as their craving for prestige. But a later cultural anthropologist who worked in the region, R. F. Fortune (1989:206–210), took a less functionalist, more cultural materialist view. Fortune pointed out that, in addition to their ceremonial component, the kula ring voyages also had an economic purpose: food, tools, and other necessities were distributed among the islanders along with ritual objects. This practical exchange was important because nature had distributed the necessities of life unevenly throughout the Trobriand Islands. Some islands produced yams, others stone for ax heads, and still others pottery, all of which needed to be distributed through some sort of exchange system. The kula ring provided a context in which the purely economic exchange of important, everyday necessities could take place in a friendly fashion, among islanders who did not have equal access to everything they needed.

The kula ring example illustrates how a single cultural phenomenon can be usefully approached from more than one philosophical viewpoint. From the more subjective Malinowskian functionalist perspective, the activities surrounding the kula ring can be explained in terms of the satisfaction of the islanders' social and psychological

• Ask Yourself •

Cross-culturally, the idea that certain objects are desirable not simply because of their monetary worth, but for other reasons as well, is a common one. Can you find similarities—or differences—between kula ring objects and American football players' Super Bowl rings or Olympic champions' medals?

needs; from the more objective cultural materialist perspective, they can be seen as a matter of economic production and distribution. The two views of this institution are different, but not mutually exclusive: the kula ring might have served both psychological and economic functions. Similarly, looking at the kula ring from a cultural evolutionary point of view (if one had the relevant data about the past) would not be incompatible with the cultural materialist view, in that both focus on environmental and technological variables as explanations for cultural process.

Another example of cultural materialist analysis illustrates how the diachronic approach can serve the cultural materialist perspective. Like the twentieth-century Azande, the late seventeenth-century residents of Salem, Massachusetts, believed in witchcraft, accusing over 100 villagers of this crime and executing 20. Unlike the Azande, however, the villagers of Salem were literate and kept records of various kinds, so recorded changes that took place in Salem during the time of the witchcraft accusations and trials were available for later analysis. Thus, while Evans-Pritchard was limited to a synchronic interpretation of Zande witchcraft, cultural materialists Paul Boyer and Stephen Nissenbaum (1974) were able to bring a diachronic perspective to understanding what caused the frenzy of witchhunting in Salem in the late 1680s and early 1690s.

Boyer and Nissenbaum's research showed that, at the time of the Salem witchcraft accusations and trials, the land owned by one of Salem's families, the Porters, lay nearer to the growing commercial prosperity spreading out from the town of Boston than the holdings of other families. Other documents showed that the economic strength and prestige of the Porters was on the rise. At the same time, the economic situation of a more established fam-

The idea that certain objects are desirable for reasons other than their monetary value is common cross-culturally. To U.S. speed skater Bonnie Blair, the medal she won at the 1994 Winter Olympics at Lillehammer, Norway, is worth much more than its weight in gold.

ily, the Putnams, was deteriorating, in part because the location of their land denied them ready access to commerce. When Boyer and Nissenbaum tried to make sense of the witchcraft furor by determining who were the accusers and who the accused, they realized that those who brought the accusations were related to or allied with the economically deteriorating Putnam family, while the accused were allied with the economically successful Porters. Boyer and Nissenbaum concluded that the Putnams, in the face of their declining power and influence in the village, were striking out against members of a family benefiting from the economic changes taking place.

A synchronic, structural-functionalist approach, such as Evans-Pritchard's study of Zande witchcraft, is appropriate when no records of the past exist. In the case of the Salem study, however, a cultural materialist stance, in which material factors such as the siting of farmlands and economic realities were viewed as explanatory factors, was combined with the diachronic perspective that the existence of historical documents permitted, thus yielding a fuller understanding of the culture.

In seventeenth-century Salem, Massachusetts, over 100 villagers were accused of witchcraft, and 20 were executed. Historical records describing changing economic relationships among the villagers permit an analysis of the Salem witchcraft accusations that is at once synchronic, diachronic, and cultural materialist.

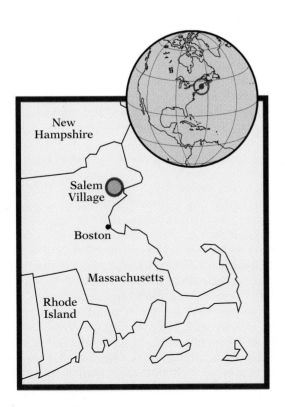

• Specialties •

We pointed out in Chapter 1 that cultural anthropology is an extraordinarily broad discipline; it covers all contemporary human cultures and includes many ways of interpreting data and hundreds of specialized topics. Most cultural anthropologists organize their professional careers around the study of one or several societies or cultures, and also one or several topics, usually viewed from a single broad philosophical perspective. A cultural anthropologist might, for example, specialize in the study of symbols (a topic we discussed in Chapter 2) among the Ndembu of Africa (a society mentioned in Chapter 2; see map on page 32) from the functionalist perspective (a perspective described above). In addition to broad theoretical perspectives, narrower topical specialties, and individual societies, some cultural anthropologists also specialize in particular interpretive stances—ways of looking at data and interpreting findings. There are many more topics and interpretive stances in cultural anthropology than we can discuss here, so below we discuss those we think are most important. Each is a focus of interest for a group of like-minded anthropologists who have organized their research around it.

We begin with four interpretive stances. Because cultural anthropologists study living human beings, it is possible for them not only to observe and participate in their subjects' outward behavior and customs, but also to ask their subjects about their inward thoughts and feelings. Moreover, cultural anthropologists, no matter how objective they try to be, have thoughts and feelings of their own, which cannot help but affect their interpretation of cultures. As a result, several specialties concerned with the study of thoughts and emotions have emerged. Among them are cognitive anthropology, structural anthropology, psychological anthropology, and postmodernism.

Cognitive Anthropology

Cognitive anthropology is the attempt to explain cultures by examining the different categories by which human beings organize their thinking. Since these categories order and classify thoughts, they affect the way in which individuals organize their experience of the world. Cognitive anthropologists consider their speciality to be essential for an understanding of culture.

The roots of cognitive anthropology go back to the seventeenth century, when the human mind became a topic of great interest to scholars. Most (e.g., Locke 1979 [1690]) believed that people were born with minds that were like empty cabinets, devoid of content, and that they filled these empty cabinets with information throughout their lives. Almost two hundred years later, the German Adolf Bastian (1826–1905) disagreed, arguing in support of what he called the *psychic unity* of all humankind (Needham 1970:lxxii). According to Bastian, fixed patterns of thought, which he called **mental univer-**

sals, are common to human beings all over the world. The details of these universal patterns, which produce human beings' ideas and institutions, differ from society to society because of differences in the natural environments and the stages of cultural evolution that various cultures have reached.

There is some validity in this notion, which has been recently modified to reflect biological notions of universal cognitive structure. Cultures that are widely separated, in time or geographically, do often contain striking similarities, an observation that has suggested to some scholars that human behavior is indeed influenced by mental universals (see D. Brown 1991). Similarities among myths from around the world lend some support for this possibility. The biblical story of Noah and the flood, familiar to most Westerners, is an example: other cultures also have stories describing great floods caused by divine actions. Typically, the deluge causes the subsequent extinction of most of humanity; the few people who are saved eventually repopulate the earth.

One such tale was told by the ancient Greeks. In it, the god Prometheus foresees that Zeus, the mightiest of all gods, plans to flood the earth. Prometheus warns his son Deucalion of the coming deluge, instructing him to build an ark in which to save his life and that of his wife, Pyrrha. Just as the vessel is completed, torrential rains begin, which flood the earth and drown all life except for the occupants of the ark. When the rain stops, Deucalion and Pyrrha emerge into an empty world. They thank Zeus for their lives, and are instructed by him to throw their "mothers' bones," the rocks of Mother Earth, over their shoulders. As they do so, human beings spring up where the stones land, and repopulate the earth.

Cognitive anthropologists stress the fact that human beings require order in their lives to survive. We must distinguish things that are edible from things that are not, things that are safe from things that are dangerous, and so on (Gombrich 1979a; see also Gombrich 1979b). The order we perceive in the natural world, such as the procession of the seasons and the regularity of the sunrise and sunset, may serve as a model for the cultural patterning we noted in Chapter 2. For example, the Zunis' perceptions of their natural world were reflected in their social order (Cushing 1896). The Zuni (see map on page 14) viewed most natural phenomena as divided into sevenths of some larger whole. The physical world, they believed, contained seven spatial regions

---

cognitive anthropology a specialty whose practitioners attempt to explain cultures by examining the different categories people create in order to organize their universe

mental universals fixed patterns of thought common to human beings all over the world

All cultures have some system of order, and in many of these systems, numbers play an important part. In cultures in which the predominant religion is Christianity, things are often organized into threes. Above, sixteenth-century Flemish painter Joos van Cleve's three-part Crucifixion with Donors.

or sectors—north, south, east, west, the zenith (or heavens), the nadir (or depths), and the center—and everything in the world belonged in one or another of these regions. Zuni social organization, with seven subtribes, reflected this principle. In the past, the subtribes had occupied seven towns, but by the time of Cushing's fieldwork they had congregated into a single village organized into seven sectors, each corresponding to one of the seven divisions of space (Cushing 1896:367). This "mythic division of the world," as Cushing called it (1896:369), was so comprehensive and integrated that "not only the ceremonial life of the people, but all their governmental arrangements as well" were thoroughly systematized according to the same pattern (1896:372).

The problem of how young children develop their capacity to classify and therefore to think was of central concern to a Swiss psychologist, Jean Piaget (1896–1980), who (although not an anthropologist) contributed much to cognitive anthropology. Beginning in the 1920s, Piaget examined children's concepts of time, space, numbers, and logic to discover whether their intellectual development occurred in fixed stages. In the first or "sensorimotor" stage, children between

birth and the age of 2 gain motor control and skills (turning over, sitting up, reaching and grasping, crawling, walking, running), and learn about reality by observing the physical objects, people, and actions around them. Next, in the "preoperational" stage (between the ages of 2 and 7), they learn to speak, a crucial developmental step that forms the mental underpinnings for their later ability to reason. In the third or "concrete-operational" stage, from 7 to 12, children gain the ability to understand abstract concepts. A 9-year-old, for

• Ask Yourself •

It has been said that the number three has assumed a special importance in American culture (Dundes 1968). One example is the Holy Trinity—the Father, Son, and Holy Spirit—of Christianity, American culture's predominant religion. Can you think of other examples of important groupings of three in American society? Is there another number that seems to you to be more culturally important?

Swiss psychologist Jean Piaget contributed to cognitive anthropology with studies of how young children develop their capacity to classify and therefore to think. No matter what their culture, children go through the same stages of cognitive development.

example, fully understands that when her mother leaves the house for work in the morning she does not disappear but continues to exist in another place; a 3-year-old may not understand this. Finally, in the "formal-operational" stage between the ages of 12 and 15, children refine their ability to reason logically and consistently.

Since cognitive anthropologists are interested in discovering what is inherent in the process of human intellectual development and what is the product of culture, Piaget's ideas have been of great interest to them. Piaget insisted that his findings on cognition in Swiss children could not legitimately be extended to children of other cultures, but his research nevertheless suggested to some cognitive anthropologists that all children, no matter what their culture, go through the same stages of cognitive development. Whether and to what extent Piaget's stages of learning can be modified by culture, however, is still a matter of research and debate (Bock 1988:176–177).

Structural Anthropology

Closely related to cognitive anthropology is a specialty called **structural anthropology,** pioneered by French anthropologist Claude Lévi-Strauss. Lévi-Strauss analyzed cultural phenomena such as languages, myths, and kinship systems to discover what ordered patterns, or structures, they seemed to display. These, he suggested, could reveal the structure of the human mind.

Lévi-Strauss was struck by the contrast between the extraordinary variety of beliefs and customs throughout the world and the fact that the human brains that created this great variety are essentially the same everywhere. How could brains that are structured in the same way create different cultures? He reasoned that beneath the surface of individual cultures there must exist natural properties (universals) common to all.[4] In the belief that universals underlying human culture are to be found at this deeper level, rather than at the more superficial level of individual cultural differences, Lévi-Strauss focused his attention not on the customs and beliefs of specific cultures, but on the patterns or structures existing beneath the customs and beliefs of all cultures.

One such pattern is called **opposition.** The ancient Greek philosopher Heraclitus noted many opposites in the natural and social worlds: good is opposed to bad, life to death, right to left, male to female, and so on. He suggested that the entire world could be conceptualized in this dualistic way,

---

structural anthropology a specialty within cultural anthropology whose followers attempt to discover orderly patterns common to languages, myths, kinship systems, and other aspects of culture

opposition thinking in terms of opposing categories

[4] This notion is quite similar to Bastian's concept of mental universals, but Lévi-Strauss lays greater emphasis on the way in which universals are ordered. In particular, he stresses the importance of thinking in terms of opposition.

and others have agreed. The reason people of all cultures tend to think in terms of opposites is that to think, we must classify, which means we must be able to distinguish between things. Thinking of two things as opposites is the simplest way to do this. Thus much of Chinese philosophy is based on the idea of two opposing life forces: yin (the passive, female principle or force) and yang (the active, masculine principle or force). More recently, the German philosopher Georg Hegel (1770–1831) proposed that every idea implied its opposite and that by uniting an idea and its opposite (a process termed *synthesis*), the two of them would create a single new idea, which in turn would give birth to its opposite, and so on. This idea was later employed by the influential German political philosopher Karl Marx, one of the authors of communism, who interpreted human history as a continuous struggle between two opposite classes, the rulers and the ruled.

So important is opposition in human thinking that it would seem a basic component of human thought. A familiar example might help to illustrate this. In the industrialized world, the red light of a traffic signal means "stop"; green means "go." To Lévi-Strauss, this is a mere external of culture, devoid of any deeper significance. Much more meaningful is how these facts convey information to drivers and pedestrians: through the contrast or opposition between red and green, and the switching from one color to another. Red has a meaning (stop) only in relation to green (go). It is the structure or pattern of opposites that provides the messages, not the specific colors considered independently of each other. This dual structure constitutes the meaning of "stop/go." Both structure and meaning, therefore, are present only under the surface of this particular custom.[5]

Lévi-Strauss's (1983) inspiration for his structural anthropology were the models formulated by linguists, among whom an early figure was Ferdinand de Saussure. In 1916, de Saussure (1983) made a distinction that was to become very important in structural anthropology—that between *language* and *speech*. A spoken communication system, de Saussure noted, consists of a set of sounds, the rules (grammar) governing their organization, and a limitless number of meaningful utterances. These sounds and rules we call *language*, and the utterances, *speech*. Lévi-Strauss likened people's language to the "rules" that govern society, in that the governed are largely unconscious of what they know. He likened speech—the use of the sounds and rules, mainly in the form of sentences—to the ideas and behaviors that result from the application of largely unconscious social rules. Members of a society are much more likely to be conscious of their actual ideas and behaviors than they are of the deeply structured rules that make these ideas and behaviors possible, but the ideas and behaviors of a given group of people can be understood if the unconscious structures in their minds can be discovered.

Psychological Anthropology

Anthropologists who believe that culture can best be accounted for by intangibles such as feelings, dreams, and artistic impulses have developed **psychological anthropology,** an important specialty in contemporary anthropology (see Schwartz et al. 1992). Like cognitive anthropology, psychological anthropology focuses on thought processes, and indeed the two orientations overlap, but psychological anthropology stresses feelings and experiences, whereas cognitive anthropology stresses the different categories people create to organize their universe and, therefore, how they think and learn. By focusing on topics such as the interrelationship of personality and culture (see Chapter 2), how concepts of mental illness vary cross-culturally, or the interpretation of dreams in different cultures (see below), psychological anthropology examines the relationship between culture and the psychological makeup of individuals and groups.

Some recent cross-cultural studies undertaken by psychological anthropologists have focused on the analysis of dreams, and how their content may be influenced by the culture of the dreamer. The brains of human beings in all cultures are equally active during sleep. However, the content of dreams varies. In some cultures, solutions to personal problems are expected to come during sleep, and often

---

[5] For an example of how cognitive and structural anthropologists use the concept of opposition in their attempts to understand societies, see our description of how the Fang people of West Africa view their world, found on pages 359–360.

psychological anthropology an anthropological specialty focusing on the relationship between culture and the psychological makeup of individuals and groups

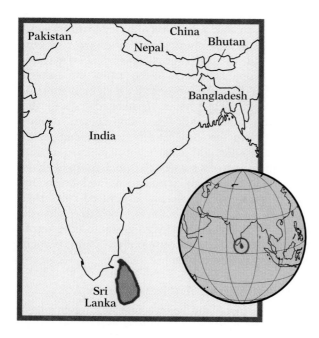

ble hidden meaning behind the long locks of matted hair worn by Sri Lankan priestesses of a Hindu-Buddhist cult. When Obeyesekere first saw a priestess of this cult, her hair reminded him of snakes, and he was seized with anxiety. Immediately he thought of a paper by Freud in which the snake-covered head of the mythical figure Medusa was linked to the terror of castration. Was it this association that caused Obeyesekere's anxiety? Did Sri Lankan people have similar feelings when they saw the matted locks of hair worn by priestesses? Could

do. In other cultures, the dreamer's hidden enemies are revealed. In still others, people wake with ideas for songs, poems, or visual images they later fulfill in artistic creations.

In Chapter 2, in our discussion of symbols as transmitters of culture, we introduced symbolic anthropology, a topical area of cultural anthropology devoted to the cross-cultural analysis of symbols. Psychological anthropologists are also interested in symbols, but in a broader context: they concern themselves with all processes and products of thought insofar as they relate to culture. An example is the relationship between the psychology of the individual and symbolic meanings shared widely within his or her culture. While working in Sri Lanka, an island off the south coast of India, psychological anthropologist Gananath Obeyesekere (1981:6–7) brought two interesting ideas together: Freud's concept of the unconscious as a motivating factor in individuals' behavior, and the anthropological notion that culture imposes meaning on every aspect of human existence. Obeyesekere was able to show how certain cultural symbols can become "personalized" by individuals, who interpret them in their own distinctive ways. When cultural symbols take on highly individualized meanings, these meanings are typically marked by intense emotion. This aspect of the individual in culture had been rarely discussed by previous cultural anthropologists.

Obeyesekere's first analytical focus was the possi-

Psychological anthropologists are interested in the relationship between the psychology of individuals and the symbolic meanings shared by individuals of the same culture. One ethnographer felt anxious when he first saw the long, matted hair of a Sri Lankan priestess. On learning that Sri Lankans have similar feelings, he concluded that his own reactions could help him learn something about Sri Lankan culture.

Obeyesekere utilize his own feelings and reactions to learn something broader about Sri Lankans—or about human psychology in general?

Obeyesekere (1981:9) soon learned that Sri Lankans "are indeed often anxious when they see the matted hair" of their religious practitioners. From this experience, he realized that his own reactions were useful for understanding "what goes on in the minds of others," since he reacted in the same way others did. He went on to analyze symbols that operated at both the personal and the cultural levels in Sri Lankan society. Such symbols, because they have meaning at both levels, help to integrate culture and the individuals who share it.

Postmodernism

The written works about individual cultures produced by cultural anthropologists are called **ethnographies,** and cultural anthropologists in the process of collecting data on contemporary people are called **ethnographers.** A traditional ethnography claims to create a realistic picture of a culture, often a holistic one. It suggests that the different aspects of the culture can be organized in a systematic, understandable way, and that the ethnographer's representations of his or her findings is a more or less objective analysis of the culture.

But some ethnographers are critical of traditional ethnographies, claiming that the cultural "realities" they portray are more subjective than they are made out to be. Aware of the subjective nature of cultural anthropology and how the relationship between the anthropologist and the people being studied can influence the data collection process, these ethnographers believe that ethnographies should include—in addition to cultural "facts"—the feelings that researchers experience in the field, their personal relationships with the people they meet and interview, and any other subjective observations that might help readers to understand the culture under study. This kind of ethnographic writing is termed *reflexive ethnography,* because the ethnographer is aware that his or her personality and experiences reflect a personal interpretation of what is going on, and because feelings and reactions to the experience of fieldwork are reflected in written descriptions of the culture.

Reflexivity is closely tied to a wider development in cultural anthropology called **postmodernism,** which emerged during the 1980s. The postmodernist movement's leaders—James Clifford, George E. Marcus, and Stephen Tyler—distinguish more clearly

than do most of their predecessors between doing field research and writing up the data collected in the form of books or articles. They argue that a more accurate description of a culture would be possible if anthropologists adopted more self-conscious attitudes about their own methods, assumptions, and ideas. Instead of regarding anthropological reports based on field research as accurate reflections of a culture, postmodernists view ethnographies as the unique products of particular researchers, local people, and field methods (Marcus and Cushman 1982; Clifford and Marcus 1986). Thus postmodernists focus on ethnography itself as their central object of study, not the cultures ethnographers portray. For example, they analyze the style in which an ethnography is written and determine whether individuals in the society under study have been allowed to voice their own thoughts and feelings—or whether the ethnographer has either chosen not to mention individuals at all or edited what they said, thus only *appearing* to give them their own voice.

A number of postmodernists have experimented with the process of creating ethnographies. Some, for instance, have written portraits of fictitious members of a culture under study, or included descriptions of fictitious incidents, in the belief that these efforts will provide a clearer sense of reality than the mere presentation of data. Fictionalization must be clearly labeled as such, of course; otherwise, a reader will be confused, unable to discern what is factual from what is invented.

As with most advocates of any theoretical position, postmodernists tend to oversell the novelty of what they claim to have discovered, and some anthropologists are put off by the jargon that confuses much of what the postmodernists are attempting to say (Sangren 1992). But by emphasizing that the analysis of how ethnographies are written is as valid a type of research as the more traditional analyses of the cultures these ethnographies claim to describe, postmodernists have again

---

ethnography a written work about a particular culture; also, the collection of data on contemporary people

ethnographer a cultural anthropologist in the process of collecting data on contemporary people

postmodernism an anthropological specialty, developed in the 1980s, that encourages anthropology to focus on the analysis of ethnographies, examining how they are written from a reflexive point of view

raised the problem of whether a culture can be represented objectively.

Cognitive anthropology, structural anthropology, psychological anthropology, and postmodernism do not exhaust the list of approaches to understanding how human beings think and feel, but they are among the most important anthropological specialties. In addition to these specialized "slants" on data interpretation, most cultural anthropologists also specialize in one or more topics, often studied cross-culturally.

Urban Anthropology

Since the late nineteenth century, when cultural anthropology started to become an academic discipline, the number of small-scale, nonliterate societies around the world has decreased rapidly, and peasant societies have become increasingly large and Westernized. At the same time, cultural anthropologists discovered that their theories and research methods were as useful for studying human behavior in literate, urban societies as in nonliterate and peasant societies (see Gmelch and Zenner 1980). Thus a topical specialty in cultural anthropology was born—**urban anthropology,** or the anthropological study of urban dwellers. Today its practitioners, some of whom have joined together in the Society for Urban Anthropology within the American Anthropological Association (AAA), study life in the cities of the world, addressing topics such as urban planning and policy, social networks among city dwellers, and the adaptation of urban ethnic minorities. Numerous examples throughout this book involve urban anthropology.

Feminist Anthropology

By the 1970s, it was becoming increasingly clear that cultural anthropology had not previously taken sufficient account of the contributions women make to culture. Part of the reason for this was that most early cultural anthropologists were men, due mainly to a general lack of equal educational opportunities for women. Thus much anthropological research had a male bias. To rectify it, cultural anthropologists since the 1970s, an increasing number of them women, have focused their research on the roles of women. Today **feminist anthropology** is a major area of research for both female and male anthropologists (Mukhopadhyay and Higgins 1988) who "seek to understand and dismantle gender hierarchies in their intellectual as well as personal worlds" (Wolf 1992:1). Some are members of the Association for Feminist Anthropology within the AAA. The last few years have seen intriguing new studies—just to mention a few examples—on cultural attitudes toward Indian women in Hindu society (Mitter 1991), women's roles in the household and the workplace in the eastern Caribbean (Senior 1991), and the relationships between women and men on Vanatinai, a remote island in the western Pacific (Lepowsky 1993).

In addition to the emphasis they place on the roles of women in different societies, feminist anthropologists also stress the importance of women in anthropology. Their concern is thus both scholarly (females as objects of anthropological research) and political (females as anthropological researchers) (di Leonardo 1991). Throughout this book, there are numerous references to the work of feminist anthropologists.

Medical Anthropology

Some ethnologists specialize in understanding the attitudes, beliefs, and practices surrounding physical or mental illness and healing in different cultures, a topical specialty called **medical anthropology.** Like practitioners in other specialty areas, these cultural anthropologists are represented by a unit within the AAA—in this case, the Society for Medical Anthropology. Illness and health may be treated largely as biological concerns in our own culture, but (even in our own culture) they are rich in social interaction, folklore, symbolism, and ritual, making them appropriate for cultural analysis. What—in any given culture—is believed to cause disease? What attitudes exist toward illness and health? How does a person who is ill behave? What does the healing process involve? How do **biomedicine** (the Western system of medical belief and practice) and **ethnomedicine** (non-Western

---

urban anthropology a topic within ethnology that focuses on the adaptations of urban dwellers

feminist anthropology a topic within cultural anthropology that focuses on women

medical anthropology a topic within cultural anthropology that focuses on the attitudes, beliefs, and practices surrounding illness and healing in different cultures

biomedicine the Western system of medical belief and practice

ethnomedicine non-Western systems of medical belief and practice

Since the 1970s, the attention of cultural anthropologists, many of them female, has focused increasingly on women. On the island of St. Lucia in the West Indies, female farmers gather in town on market day to sell their produce.

systems of medical belief and practice) differ? In addressing such questions, medical anthropologists constantly draw attention to the close connections between health and other aspects of culture.

Cultural Ecology

As we noted earlier in this chapter when discussing cultural materialism, some cultural anthropologists emphasize the contribution of material things to the formation of cultures. A cultural materialist perspective can take several forms, depending on what aspect of the material world is emphasized. When the emphasis is on the environment, this field of interest, as we mentioned in Chapter 1, is called **cultural ecology** (see, e.g., Vayda and McCay 1975; Ellen 1982).[6] Not all cultural materialists are cultural ecologists—some cultural materialists emphasize that material factors other than the environment,

such as technology, influence culture—but cultural ecology is, by definition, a materialist stance.

Introduced into American anthropology by Julian Steward in 1955, this perspective won many followers in the environmentally conscious 1960s. It continues to engage many cultural anthropologists today, because it provides a useful framework within which to examine otherwise puzzling human behaviors. From the cultural-ecological point of view, a human group and its environment are viewed as part of an integrated system (in this regard, cultural ecology has much in common with functionalism). Why, for example, did some migratory Inuit (Eskimo) groups abandon elderly and infirm members, allowing them to die alone in the

---

[6] The term *ecological anthropology* is synonymous with "cultural ecology."

cultural ecology a cultural materialist perspective emphasizing the natural environment as a factor influencing culture

The Anthropologist at Work

Applied Medical Anthropology

The Hmong people are an ethnic group native to southeast Asia. Many Hmong, particularly in Laos, were displaced by the Vietnam War, and some eventually resettled in the United States as refugees (Donnelly 1994). Now at home in the United States, most have become Christians and have given up those traditional Hmong medical beliefs and practices that were incompatible with Christianity. They have retained other aspects of their traditional medical system, however. Thus, when they fall ill, Hmong people in the United States sometimes seek Western medical care, but in many instances prefer traditional Hmong care, which includes magic and herbalism. The Hmong view these alternative ways of healing not only as superior to Western biomedicine, but also as a way of "enhancing their sense of membership in a distinct ethnic group" (Capps 1994:163).

Recently a Hmong woman living in the United States developed chest pains, which a Western physician diagnosed as symptoms of indigestion and depression. His prescribed treatment was antacid and antidepressant medicines (Capps 1994:172). The patient then went to a Hmong herbalist, whose diagnosis was quite different: the woman's symptoms signified that her ancestors were hungry. This time the treatment prescribed consisted of massage and prayer. The patient recovered.

Medical anthropologists' knowledge of differences in beliefs and attitudes surrounding illness and curing from a cross-cultural point of view presents opportunities for them to help people in different societies to understand the cultural construction of illness in themselves and others, and to cope with the healing process. Some applied medical anthropologists, for instance, serve the ill as cultural translators. Dealing with illness is difficult enough within the context of one's own belief system, but more and more frequently, as traditional cultures become increasingly Westernized, people in these cultures must cope not only with their own system of medical beliefs and practices, but the Western one as well. For undergraduates thinking of careers in medicine, psychiatry, nursing, or public health, the examples of applied medical anthropology in this book may suggest ways in which studying cultural anthropology can contribute a new, cross-cultural dimension to their plans.

---

frigid Arctic? From the cultural-ecological perspective, such abandonment is seen as a product of an especially harsh environment, in which feeding and transporting an elderly family member would lessen the survival chances of the rest of the group.

Combining Specialties

Urban, feminist, and medical anthropology, as well as cultural ecology, are examples of topical specialties. There are many others. Some, such as Marxist anthropology, educational anthropology, and legal anthropology, are not included here for reasons of space; others, such as development anthropology and advocacy anthropology, are discussed later.

Cognitive, structural, psychological, and postmodernist anthropology, in contrast, are specialized ways of interpreting findings, and they cross-cut these topics. The work of many cultural anthropologists involves both expertise in a particular topic and the interpretation of that topic from a particular frame of reference.

An example is Margery Wolf, who combined her topical specialty, feminist anthropology, with postmodernism. Wolf (1992) carried out fieldwork on Taiwan, an island off the coast of mainland China. In addition to doing traditional realistic ethnographic work, she wove her fieldwork data into a long, fictionalized account of a Taiwanese woman

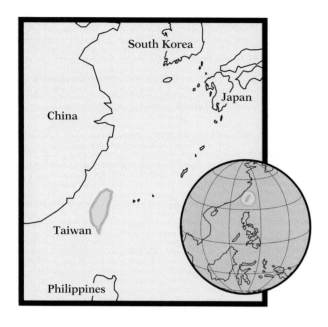

within many different, overlapping contexts. What is the historical or evolutionary context in which a particular custom or artifact occurs? What are the material correlates of the setting in which it is found? What is its functional meaning: how does it connect with other aspects of culture? And what meanings do the data collected about the people, artifact, or custom have for the people themselves, and for the cultural anthropologists who study them?

One reason such an eclectic approach is useful is that it does not depend on the assumption that grand theories to explain all human behavior exist and will one day be discovered. The long anthropological search for theories of human behavior has not proven particularly successful, partly because human behavior is so varied. As soon as a cultural anthropologist comes up with what appears to be a custom that can be found in human societies everywhere, another points to a society in which this generalization about people does not hold true.

Looking at cultures through a number of different lenses gives cultural anthropologists the option of using any perspective that involves the quest for orderly patterns (recall Gombrich on the importance of order in human existence) and encourages them to look for different ways in which facts and ideas can be understood. It does not limit them to particular assumptions or preconceptions. After examining an idea or institution from as many angles as possible, a cultural anthropologist might well decide that one perspective reveals most of its properties. Naturally, he or she will stress that perspective as a general interpretive framework. But no matter what aspect of culture is under consideration, it will reveal at least some of its meaning from other angles, and these need to be taken into account. The cultural elephant is a many-sided creature.

she calls *Mrs. Tan*. The result yields compelling insights into what it is like to be a female Taiwanese villager. As the author of a piece of fiction, Wolf was free to invent her own "truth," and was thus able to give us straightforward explanations of how and why Mrs. Tan behaved as she did in the context of her Taiwanese culture. A **realistic ethnography** rather than a work of fiction would have obliged her to be faithful to a complex set of facts, and would have compelled her to explore all the other—some contradictory—pressures that cause Taiwanese women to act as they do. By creating an account that, while fictional, could well be true, this anthropologist gave us a clear-cut view of a Taiwanese woman's social world unobscured by the contradictions of ethnographic reality.

Conclusion

"The Blind Men and the Elephant" makes the important point that no single perspective is sufficient when one's goal is a thorough understanding of some many-sided whole. The most productive approach to the study of culture, past and present, is to consider all potentially useful ways of understanding this complex subject, and to use one or another approach as the particular conditions of a study suggest. Often a certain aspect of culture will yield secrets when looked at multidimensionally, for every idea, institution, mode of behavior, or artifact occurs

Summary

- Attempting to understand what it means to be human requires examining culture from as many different angles as possible.

- Three different (if partially overlapping) theoretical perspectives used in cultural anthropology

realistic ethnography an ethnography that claims to represent a "real" portrait of a culture or society

are cultural evolution, functionalism, and cultural materialism.

- Cultural evolution—the idea that cultures change, usually in a gradual, continuous, and adaptive way—takes several different forms: neoevolution, unilineal evolution, and multilineal evolution.

- Functionalism is the idea that cultures can be viewed as systems, made from individual parts that function both individually and together. A fundamental premise of functionalism is that changing one part of a system will have an effect on the functioning of the whole culture.

- Functionalism takes three forms, the first two associated with Malinowski. In the first, cultures are viewed as systems made up of individual elements that function both individually and together. In the second, aspects of culture are viewed as functioning to satisfy biological or psychological needs. The third, called structural-functionalism, focuses on the social relationships between individuals in a group and the way in which they contribute to maintaining the social structure.

- Cultural materialism is the idea that concrete, observable, measurable things, such as the natural environment or technology, are more responsible for specific aspects of culture than other factors.

- Cultural evolution, functionalism, and cultural materialism are complementary rather than mutually exclusive viewpoints.

- Cultural anthropologists, because their research (in contrast to that of archaeologists) involves the living, can study what and how people think. This field therefore incorporates several specialties that facilitate the analysis of human thought: cognitive anthropology, structural anthropology, psychological anthropology, and postmodernism.

- Cognitive anthropologists examine the different categories people create to organize their universe.

- Structural anthropologists search for structures common to languages, myths, kinship systems, and other aspects of culture.

- Psychological anthropologists focus on the relationship between culture and the psychological makeup of individuals and groups.

- Postmodernism encourages anthropologists to focus on the analysis of ethnographies and to be reflexive in their ethnographic work.

- Cultural anthropologists also focus on specific topics, such as urban anthropology, feminist anthropology, medical anthropology, and cultural ecology.

- The most useful approach to the study of culture is to consider all potential ways of understanding it and to use one or another approach as the particular conditions of a study require.

Key Terms

biomedicine
cognitive anthropology
cultural ecology
cultural materialism
cultural process
diachronic approach
ethnographer
ethnography
ethnomedicine
feminist anthropology
functionalism
medical anthropology
mental universals
multilineal evolution
neoevolution
opposition
postmodernism
psychological anthropology
realistic ethnography
structural anthropology
structural-functionalism
synchronic approach
unilineal evolution
urban anthropology

Suggested Readings

Harris, Marvin. 1977. *Cannibals and Kings: The Origins of Cultures.* New York: Random House. The well-known cultural materialist discusses how human behavior can be explained using the cultural ecological approach.

Kuper, Adam. 1980. Great Britain: Functionalism at Home, a Question of Theory. In *Anthropology: Ancestors and Heirs,* Stanley Diamond (ed.), pp. 293–315. The Hague: Mouton. An excellent summary statement of functionalism.

Roland, Alan. 1988. *In Search of Self in India and Japan: Toward a Cross-Cultural Psychology.* Princeton: Princeton University Press. In this series of case studies, an American psychoanalyst explores the notion of self among Japanese and Indians, and concludes that there are fundamental differences between their "selfhoods" and those of Westerners.

Sahlins, Marshall D., and Elman R. Service. (eds.). 1960. *Evolution and Culture.* Ann Arbor: University of Michigan Press. Neoevolutionists distinguish specific from general evolution.

Introduction

Late on a summer afternoon, a professorial-looking middle-aged man carrying a battered leather briefcase dropped in at a small cafe somewhere in

the American Southwest. Seating himself at the counter, he began to spread around him numerous looseleaf notebook pages and index cards. Next he drew from his briefcase a portable tape recorder, to which he listened intently as he sipped his coffee and added to his already voluminous notes. The curious proprietor, never at a loss for words, asked the man whether he might be an agent for the Internal Revenue Service or perhaps even the FBI, but the man shook his head with a smile. "No," he replied, "I'm an anthropologist, and I'm interested in studying changing speech patterns among Navaho youths. This town is the place I've chosen for my fieldwork."

The next day it rained. The cafe was disappointingly empty until lunchtime, when a damp threesome of local women, whom the proprietor recognized as members of the local church's morning sewing group, entered in the company of an unfamiliar younger woman. Curious about the stranger, the proprietor kept his ears open as he served the women dessert. "All of you have been enormously helpful," the young woman was saying to the others. "But my search for data on the changing roles of rural women is getting more complicated that I'd expected. I'm beginning to think I should extend my fieldwork by a couple of months." Now the cafe owner was truly confused. In *his* day, *fieldwork* meant getting out of bed early, grabbing a hoe, and spending a hot morning weeding the corn. He wished he understood what was going on.

In Chapter 1, we pointed out that anthropology is not limited in time or space; the anthropologist is interested in *people,* no matter where, when, or how they live or lived. In anthropology, the process of collecting original information about people, ancient or modern, is called **fieldwork,** a general term for several data-collecting strategies that differ according to what kind of information is being collected. Fieldwork in cultural anthropology—the process of collecting original information from living people—is termed *ethnographic fieldwork.*

• **Why Do Fieldwork?** •

While early fieldworkers such as Cushing, Boas, and Malinowski (see Chapter 1) were strongly motivated by a desire to collect information about populations unknown to the outside world, cultural anthropologists today usually go into the field for more specific reasons. Three common ones are (1) to test new anthropological hypotheses, (2) to check up on previously tested hypotheses that may have been insufficiently examined or may no longer be valid because of change, and (3) to apply anthropological principles and methods to achieve specific, practical ends. A fieldwork expedition may combine all these aims; testing new ideas, checking up on old ones, and achieving practical goals are not at all incompatible. No matter what the reason, fieldwork represents the primary way in which cultural anthropologists get data, which they use to add to our knowledge of cultures all over the world.

Hypothesis Testing

A major goal of modern anthropological fieldwork is to provide new insights into human behavior. Many fieldwork projects are undertaken to do just

---

• Ask Yourself •

Can you see yourself doing ethnographic fieldwork? If so, where would you like to do your fieldwork, and why?

---

fieldwork the process of collecting original information about people, ancient or modern

During fieldwork, anthropologists collect the data they need to test specific hypotheses.
Later they analyze these data to see whether or not the hypotheses hold true.
Anthropologist Loretta Orion uses a computer to analyze the data she collected during
fieldwork in North America.

this, by testing anthropological hypotheses and, ultimately, contributing to the formulation of anthropological theories. This kind of research is called *theoretical,* or *basic, research.*

The accumulated knowledge of any science is contained in its body of hypotheses and theories. Given that human behavior is almost infinitely variable, there is an ongoing debate about whether any legitimate anthropological theories actually exist. Most anthropologists use the term in a somewhat generous sense: an anthropological theory is a statement about some observable, testable, human phenomenon that has been examined repeatedly and is widely accepted as true. Thus, cultural evolution is widely referred to as an anthropological theory. An anthropological hypothesis, in contrast, is an educated guess about what people will do, and why. Here is a possible hypothesis based on the theory of cultural evolution: "The introduction of a daily National Weather Service radio broadcast into a village of rural Iranian peasant farmers will result

in the abandonment of traditional but less accurate methods of weather prediction and a new reliance on the radio, since more accurate weather information is highly adaptive for such farmers." An anthropological hypothesis, when tested, has the potential to help explain something about some aspect of human behavior.

Much anthropological research centers on the testing or retesting of specific hypotheses among particular groups of people. Using the methods described below, fieldworkers collect the data they need to test their hypotheses and then analyze these data to see whether the hypotheses hold true. In the case of the hypothesis about peasant farmers, will the anthropologist's expectation—that the radio broadcast will quickly replace former methods of weather prediction—be upheld? If so, this would justify our increased confidence in the capacity of cultural evolutionary theory to predict and explain human behavior (Agar 1980:64). Or will the hypothesis be shown to be false? This would suggest that the theory requires rethinking, or else that the hypothesis testing was not carried out properly.

Confirming the validity of previously tested hypotheses, one's own or another researcher's, also takes anthropologists into the field. Most fieldworkers wish to return, sooner or later, to the places where they carried out earlier work. Sometimes they are unsure of some of the information they collected and want to confirm details. Sometimes there are data they missed the first time around. Or in the process of working with their own or others' fieldwork data and comparing them with data from other cultures, they may think of ways to rework their original hypotheses. They may even develop entirely new ones.

An example of hypothesis testing and retesting is provided by nineteenth-century cultural anthropologist Edward Burnett Tylor (1832–1917) and his twentieth-century successor E. E. Evans-Pritchard (1985:203). In his book *Primitive Culture* (1873:133–136), Tylor raised an interesting question: why do many people around the world believe in magic, while others (including Tylor himself) are skeptical? Based on the theory that people all over the world, literate or nonliterate, think in much the same logical manner, Tylor proposed several hypotheses. One was that in societies with strong beliefs in magic, "magical" rituals are performed at the same time as other, more mundane activities, and it is these other activities that really make the wished-for "magical" results occur. For example, magicians might help their predictions of life or death come true with medicines that cure or kill.

Tylor was an **armchair anthropologist,** meaning that instead of carrying out fieldwork, he collected his data secondhand from books, articles, and letters written by others. His hypothesis that magicians combine their "magic" with other actions that have more predictable results waited 50 years to be tested in the field. In 1926, Evans-Pritchard went to live among the Azande of central Africa (see page 52), with the testing of this hypothesis as one of his several goals. Evans-Pritchard learned that Zande leaders use "magic" to attract

followers—but that they hand out free food at the same time (1985:203). These findings supported Tylor's hypothesis.

For cultural anthropologists, much of what motivates the desire to follow up on earlier work is the pace of change in today's world. Technologically complex cultures are affecting technologically simpler ones at an ever-increasing rate, and the thrust of ethnographic research has shifted in response. Many cultural anthropologists today are interested in studying the process of change at "their" research sites. At the end of this chapter we discuss the work of Napoleon Chagnon, who in the course of his anthropological career revisited his original fieldwork site in the Amazon jungle some twenty times.

• Ask Yourself •

What changes have taken place in the community into which you were born, in the time that has passed since then? What factors best account for these changes?

Applied Fieldwork

Fieldwork is sometimes undertaken not to test hypotheses but to achieve some practical end. This work, as noted in Chapter 1, is called *applied research,* and it is quite different from theoretical research. In the last decade or two, applied anthropology has grown dramatically in both scope and popularity. Today virtually every field and subfield of anthropology incorporates applied as well as theoretical research.

Cultural anthropology, because of its origins in the collection of data on foreign cultures for commercial or political reasons, has always included an applied component of sorts. However, the reasons for undertaking applied work have changed significantly in recent years, along with the proportion of cultural anthropologists engaged in such work. No longer a tool used for global political advantage, applied cultural anthropology today may have either commercial or social objectives. In many instances it serves the practical and humanitarian needs of governments, other public institutions, or private agencies such as charitable organizations or relief agencies.

---

armchair anthropologist an anthropologist who collects data from documents written by others rather than carrying out fieldwork

A project undertaken by English anthropologist Emma Crewe, who worked for a nonprofit British organization specializing in helping people in the poorer countries of the world to develop clean, inexpensive, locally appropriate technologies, provides an example (Crewe 1995). Crewe did applied fieldwork in Sri Lanka (see map on page 60) to help find a solution to a long-standing health problem: indoor air pollution caused by the wood- and dung-burning clay cookstoves traditionally used in Sri Lankan households (Crewe 1995:95 ff.). When wood or dung is burned in a traditional Sri Lankan stove, the resulting smoke contributes to a variety of serious ailments, including cancer and acute respiratory infection (ARI). A woman using such a stove in an unventilated room is exposed to the equivalent of more than a hundred cigarettes a day, and ARI is the single biggest killer of children in the developing world, annually taking the lives of 4 to 5 million children under age 5. Living in a Sri Lankan village, Crewe observed how the clay stoves were made, bought, used, and cleaned, as well as the social and economic contexts in which they were used. Later she helped introduce a safer, cleaner-burning stove. Inexpensive and locally made, it gives off less smoke, retains heat better, uses fuel more efficiently, and reduces cooking time. Today the new stoves are helping to improve local people's health, conserve their resources, and protect their environment.

• Field Methods •

In this section, we describe and explain the array of methods and tools used by ethnographers to collect data. These methods and tools differ depending on whether the fieldwork is theoretical or applied, and also on the theoretical perspective and cognitive or topical specialty of the anthropologist. At the end of the chapter, we will describe how two modern ethnographers collected data in the field and coped with the unexpected difficulties that often arise during fieldwork.

interview a conversation between an ethnographer and one or more informants

informant an individual who provides an ethnographic researcher with information

Participant Observation

As remarked in Chapter 1, participant observation is the most important strategy used by cultural anthropologists to collect data in the field. Rather than reading about or briefly visiting the people they are interested in studying, ethnographers—like Emma Crewe, whose work in Sri Lanka we mentioned a moment ago—live among the members of a community under study, usually for many months or even years at at time, participating in the people's lives, speaking their language, and observing their behavior and customs.

In addition to participant observation, ethnographers also use other research methods and tools, some in conjunction with participant observation and some not. Participant observation is an effective way to undertake a holistic study of a culture, but sometimes, rather than providing a broad-brushed picture of a society, an ethnographer may want to focus on a narrower issue: why a rural community has a high rate of emigration to urban areas, for example, or why people in a particular society reject modern birth control methods. These are legitimate topics for ethnographic research, but do not necessarily require total immersion in the life of a community. They may be researched by studying documents, collecting information and opinions from one or two knowledgeable individuals rather than many community members, or distributing questionnaires (Clammer 1984:63–85).

Among the most useful research tools and procedures ethnographers have at their disposal, whether used in conjunction with participant observation or not, are interviews, surveys, sampling, genealogical research, life histories, case studies, filmed and taped records, network analysis, and team research.

Interviews

Probably the most common technique for gathering ethnographic data, an **interview** is a conversation between an ethnographer and one or more **informants:** individuals who provide the researcher with information.[1] Almost any member of a community under study is a potential informant, and the type and quantity of information each can offer

---

[1] Some anthropologists, concerned that the term *informant* may carry negative connotations, prefer to call these local people *assistants*.

One commonly used ethnographic field method is the interview, a conversation between an ethnographer and one or more informants. In Botswana, Africa, anthropologist Richard Lee interviews informants living a gathering-and-hunting way of life in the Kalahari desert.

vary (Cohen 1984:224–225). Most people are **casual informants,** from whom an ethnographer obtains general or specialized information from time to time. Certain individuals, however, will be **key informants,** on whom the ethnographer relies more heavily. They may be "key" because they have specialized knowledge, or just because they know more than others. Or, while not especially knowledgeable themselves, they may be politically powerful, and thus able to help the ethnographer obtain information from those who might otherwise be reluctant to share it. Or they may be popular characters, at the center of social activities or networks of gossip, and

hence in constant touch with others. Most ethnographers try to assemble a mix of informants, both casual and key.

The ethnographer may ask an informant a series of prearranged questions on preselected topics, or engage the informant in a free-ranging, open-ended interview. Usually the ethnographer records the informant's answers in writing (often with the help of a portable computer) or on tape. The length, content, and scope of interviews vary greatly, depending on the number of questions asked, the degree of predetermination in the questions, the broadness of the questions, the type of interview (individual or group), the interviewer's personal style, and the informant's willingness to cooperate with the interviewer.

In general, the more informal and casual the interviewer's style, the more "negotiable" the interview, since "the informants can criticize a question, correct it, point out that it is sensitive, or answer in

---

casual informant an informant from whom an ethnographer obtains information from time to time

key informant an informant on whom, because of specialized knowledge or influence, an ethnographer relies heavily

any way they want to" (Agar 1980:90)—including turning the interview around and questioning the ethnographer (Clammer 1984:231–232). An informant's willingness to cooperate is affected not only by the interviewer's demeanor, but also by the informant's natural degree of reticence or forthrightness, the setting (e.g., is the interview private or might others overhear?), the topic (are the questions politically or socially sensitive?), and the informant's sense of coercion (did the informant volunteer to be interviewed, or feel somehow pressured into it?).

For reasons ranging from a need to keep certain information private to a wish to have a little fun at a visitor's expense, informants sometimes deliberately mislead ethnographers. Our account of the fieldwork of Napoleon Chagnon, later in this chapter, contains an example of such deception.

Focus Groups

If a group of informants is involved, it may be a small gathering called a **focus group,** consisting of no more than about six or eight people brought together for a couple of hours to help explain a particular topic of interest (Krueger 1988; Stewart and Shamdasani 1990). The ethnographer leads the discussion, focusing it tightly on the subject of the research. Focus groups may be used to identify issues of potential importance, get an overview of a topic that the ethnographer will later explore more intensively, provide an explanation for some puzzling aspect of culture, or confirm ethnographic findings. Focus groups are popular with applied ethnographers, often to collect data for social marketing or planning purposes. For example, if the Ministry of Health in a small country is planning to launch an AIDS information campaign, it may, in preparation for the campaign, call upon an ethnographer to conduct focus group sessions to determine what the local people already know, believe, and do with regard to AIDS.

Surveys

Cultural anthropology shares several basic research methods with other disciplines, among them surveying. In any discipline, a **survey** is a broad overview of a particular subject. Surveys are especially useful tools for ethnographers, since much ethnographic fieldwork includes collecting statistical information on events or opinions. There are a variety of methods that can be used. One is the **personal survey** in which a researcher personally counts items or

events—for example by standing at the entrance to a village market and counting the number of people of a certain ethnic group who enter. Afterwards the researcher analyzes the results.

In a **respondent survey,** a prearranged series of questions, either spoken or written in questionnaire form, is asked of informants called **respondents,** and the results are tallied (Mitchell 1984). For example, a cultural anthropologist might visit all of the heads of households in a community to collect information about household composition or the educational status of family members.

In conducting a respondent survey, the wording of questions is crucial. They must be precise enough to leave little room for individual interpretation (by the interviewer or the respondent) and neutral enough to avoid tilting respondents toward positive or negative answers (Wallman and Dhooge 1984:261–262). The degree of openness of the questions is also important. There is a big difference between the open-ended question "What are your religious beliefs?" and the much more restricted question "Do you believe in God?" which can be answered only with "yes," "no," or "don't know."

Sampling

A fieldworker undertaking our hypothetical research project among Iranian peasants would be challenged by several methodological questions. Should the population studied consist of all of the farmers in a village or only some of them? Should only wheat farmers be studied, or should people with small kitchen gardens also be included? Should another group of farmers, similar in size and composition, be chosen, perhaps from a second village, as a **control group,** in order to provide

---

focus group a small group of informants brought together to shed light on a particular topic

survey the counting and classifying of items, events, or opinions

personal survey a survey undertaken personally by a researcher

respondent survey a survey consisting of a prearranged series of questions, in questionnaire form, asked of respondents

respondent a person who provides information for a survey

control group a group similar in size and composition to a study group, used for purposes of comparison or as a cross-check on the data provided by the study group

comparative data or to cross-check data provided by the farmers? Fieldworkers in anthropology, like practitioners in other disciplines, must decide whether to base their research on an entire population or to "sample" it. The decision depends on the scope of the research and the size of the population. The technique of **sampling**—in which only a small part of something, representative of a larger whole, is investigated—is used more and more frequently as anthropologists become increasingly computer-literate, since computers are well suited to assessing the statistical validity of sample results.

Genealogies

Genealogies are essential to the study of descent (Chapter 9) and marriage (Chapter 10). Genealogical research involves tracing the genealogical links between individuals to discover who is related to whom and in what way. When written records are not available, genealogical data are limited by what present-day members of a community can remember.

Life Histories

A **life history** is the personal story of an informant's life and the cultural and economic influences on it (Clammer 1984:75). Life histories can provide personal, vivid pictures of a culture from within, through the eyes of its own members. One of the most interesting, the story of an African woman named Nisa who lived a gathering-and-hunting way

---

sampling using a small part of something to represent a larger whole

genealogy a record of a person's relationships by blood or marriage

life history an informant's story of his or her life and the influences on it

case study a detailed ethnographic study focusing on a single individual or episode

network analysis gathering and organizing data by focusing on individuals or small groups and their interrelationships, in order to establish patterns of association and assess their effects

set-centered network a network based on groups of individuals linked to one another

ego-centered network a network centering on a particular individual and including all the links between this person and others in his or her community

---

of life, is listed in the Suggested Readings at the end of this chapter.

Case Studies

An ethnographic **case study** focuses on a single individual or episode, rather than on the wider actions of whole families or communities of people. A detailed narrative about how a conflict between two people was resolved in the context of a given culture would be an example. By analyzing several individual case studies from the same society on the same topic, we can learn much about the society—in this case, its rules for conflict resolution.

Filmed and Taped Records

Photographs and videos are excellent ways to record ethnographic information. Photos capture details of daily life, such as styles of dress or housing, and record the memberships of extended families, clubs, or teams. Videos accurately preserve public or private performances, such as religious rituals, for later study and analysis. Showing group photographs to informants is one way of identifying individuals and tracing genealogies. A tape recorder is also essential if a fieldworker wants to record precise information from informants in certain contexts, such as story-telling sessions or meetings. Some ethnographers use tape recorders to take their own notes. Finally, the camera-toting anthropologist is often asked to take portraits. A Polaroid photo is a fine way to repay informants for the help they have provided.

Network Analysis

This is a way of gathering and organizing information about communities by focusing on individuals or small groups and their relationships with others. The goal of **network analysis** is to establish patterns of association among people and assess the effects of such patterns (Mitchell 1984:267–272).

Networks may be of two kinds, set-centered and ego-centered. **Set-centered networks** assume the existence of groups, or sets, of individuals with contacts or links with one another. Participant observation is the best way to get information on set-centered networks. Details for later network analysis are selected only after the broader ethnographic data have been collected (Mitchell 1984:270). **Ego-centered networks** focus on a particular individual (called *ego*), and include all the links between this person and other individuals

Cameras of various kinds are useful pieces of equipment for fieldworkers. In central China, villagers look at a Polaroid photo of themselves.

in the community under investigation. Data are typically provided in interviews with ego.

An example of network analysis is the work of cultural anthropologist Elizabeth Bott. Prior to the work of Bott and her fellow researcher, J. H. Robb, there had been few anthropological studies of Western families inside their homes. In a pioneering study using network analysis (Bott 1971:17–22), Bott and Robb studied families in London to formulate hypotheses about how family members interact with people outside their homes and what effect these relationships have on family life. The researchers visited 20 families an average of 13 times each, exploring the relationship between wife and husband and the radiating networks of relatives and nonrelatives in which the spouses were involved. Bott and Robb found that each wife had her network of social ties outside the family, and each husband had his. These extrafamilial ties both strengthened and weakened families. They strength-

ened them in that wives and husbands tended to deal with the outside world as a couple. At the same time, they weakened families in that both wives and husbands were sometimes more interested in and involved with members of their own networks than with their spouses. Several interesting hypotheses emerged from these observations. One was that the denser the network of ties, the weaker the bond between wife and husband, and vice versa.

Team Research

In the past, cultural anthropologists usually went into the field alone, sometimes hiring local people to help in their work. (By "alone," we mean unaccompanied by other professionals. It is not uncommon for an anthropologist to take a husband, wife, or other companion—even children—into the field, since fieldwork generally lasts for months or even years.) Today, an ethnographer may be part of a team that includes either fellow

The Anthropologist at Work

Fieldwork Coordination

Large, multidisciplinary field teams require close coordination, both among the researchers in the field and between the fieldwork site and home office. For this reason they usually include a field coordinator, whose job it is to take care of the fieldworkers' basic needs, manage their schedules, provide secretarial and other services, administer funds, and maintain contact with the project's directors and sponsors.

A multidisciplinary field team recently spent three months in an African nation, helping its government analyze and control the ever-increasing costs of its public hospital system. The team consisted of a political economist, a doctor, a hospital cost accountant, an anthropologist, and a field coordinator: a young woman just out of college. Her job included renting hotel rooms and offices for the team members; hiring a car and driver; arranging appointments with hospital administrators, medical personnel, and government officials; recording the team's daily meetings; transcribing field notes; and reminding team members to take their malaria pills. She also coped with various unexpected emergencies, even managing to find someone to repair an American-made portable computer. An anthropology major and a minor in a foreign language, plus business skills and perhaps travel experience, are excellent qualifications for this kind of job.

cultural anthropologists or experts in other disciplines. Ethnographers may accompany specialists in medicine, agriculture, or economics into the field. Multidisciplinary field teams are increasingly common, especially on large-scale projects.

Complementing the fieldwork activities described above is a growing list of specialized field techniques, some of them highly sophisticated technologically and borrowed from other disciplines. Depending on the project, inkblot or other psychological tests may be administered, census data studied, or blood analyzed. In addition, most fieldworkers search their field sites for documents such as maps, censuses, government reports, or local histories. Data derived from these sources can provide field research with some historical depth.

• Doing Fieldwork •

Getting There

To do fieldwork in most foreign countries, an ethnographer must have not only the government's consent but also, because of the length of time usually spent in the field, a special residence visa. Sometimes both the approval and the visa are easily and swiftly obtained, but delays of up to a year are not unheard of, and occasionally one cannot obtain permission at all.

Why would it be difficult for a cultural anthropologist to get permission to do fieldwork? Patriotic, ethical, and other considerations affect whether a country will grant a foreigner a residence visa for fieldwork. With educational levels generally rising all over the world, the leaders of some countries feel that local scholars are best suited to undertaking anthropological studies in their own countries. Governments may also be concerned about outsiders' interfering in their constituents' lives, or about the health and safety of fieldworkers (Hicks 1984:192–197).

Culture Shock

Upon entering a new and unfamiliar setting, the cultural anthropologist is immediately faced with strange faces, sights, sounds and smells, a language she or he cannot understand, a different climate, and people acting in ways that may seem very peculiar.

The English cultural anthropologist Rodney Needham (1975:vii–ix) compared the feelings of an ethnographer newly arrived in the field to those of a person who has been blind since birth, but who has just regained the gift of sight. Such a person does not see the world as it exists for someone who has never been blind. Instead, he or she is overwhelmed by a chaos of forms, movements, and colors—as Needham puts it, a "gaudy confusion of sensual impressions," none of which seems related to the others.

We call this unpleasant sense of confusion and disorientation upon entering the field **culture shock** It may be heightened by feelings of loneliness, homesickness, anxiety, and even depression, suspicion, or anger. Occasionally, these feelings are so intense that a fieldworker cannot handle them, and chooses to return to a more familiar setting. Usually, however, he or she manages to remain in the field, and discovers that culture shock is only temporary. Gradually and with great effort, the fieldworker begins to feel more comfortable, to discern order amidst disorder, to classify things and ideas along the lines of the host society.

Special Problems

Stages of Fieldwork. Each ethnographic field-work experience is unique, yet many ethnographers find that, broadly speaking, their field research might be thought of as dividing into fairly distinct stages. With the warning that we risk oversimplifying what is really always more complicated in reality, we outline three stages: adjustment, involvement, and achievement. Again we ask you to imagine that you are an ethnographer just entering the field.

Stage 1: Adjustment. During the first few months of your project, you use much of your energy simply adjusting to your new environment and overcoming culture shock. Your inquiries are cautious, since (unless this is an applied project) you are an uninvited stranger. Even with prior study, you are unlikely to know the local language well enough to enter into detailed discussions about anything; people treat you as hopelessly stupid, and indeed you feel as if you are. In any case you take pains to avoid topics that might offend, embarrass, or arouse hostility in your informants. Personal contacts are few; you rely mainly on your eyes for information. You learn to find your way around, map the area, take photographs—activities

Not all anthropologists study exotic, foreign people and their cultures; some pursue their fieldwork close to home. Fieldworker Jack Haas studied the lives of construction workers, like these Chicago steelworkers, whose specialty is building skyscrapers.

that do not require the assistance of local people or involve more conversation than you are capable of. You spend a lot of time writing letters home and eagerly awaiting return mail.

You also learn to schedule your activities. Since ethnographers usually go into the field not only with definite goals in mind, but also with a limited amount of time in which to achieve them, most construct rough timetables. Few fieldwork plans are more certain to be changed than those contained in such timetables, so they have to be flexible enough to allow for unforseen events. But they are absolutely necessary. The "let's see, what should I do today" attitude is no substitute for a systematic plan of inquiry.

culture shock the sense of confusion and disorientation fieldworkers may experience upon entering the field

In an unfamiliar setting, it may be easier for a visitor to establish initial rapport with children than with other adults. On Woodlark Island in the Trobriand Islands chain, a Westerner makes friends with children dressed for a dance.

Just how long this period of adjustment, contact making, language learning, and preliminary data gathering lasts depends on local circumstances and your particular talents and personality. Some fortunate fieldworkers are "adopted" into a local host family during this first stage, which helps immeasurably in establishing rapport, friendships, and a group of informants on whom to call for help.

Stage 2: Involvement. Most likely, after a few months you will have entered a second stage of fieldwork. Increasingly involved in and dependent on your informants' daily round of activities, you alter your own schedule to fit theirs. By now you know the most favorable times of the day to approach informants. At work they will not usually wish to talk, so during the day you visit old people at home or youngsters not yet old enough for school—if there is one. A convenient time to engage

the workers of a community in conversation is after the evening meal, so the evening loneliness you experienced at the beginning of your fieldwork is lessened, but you still feel estranged.

Your Stage 2 questions, focusing directly on your research hypothesis, are organized around specific themes—local death rituals, perhaps, or the rules of land ownership, or some other topic relevant to your hypothesis. By gearing your conversations with informants directly to the anthropological problems you have come all this way to address, your time in the field, always too brief, is allocated economically.

Although you have by now weathered culture shock, some continuing strain is inevitable. You feel you are always on stage, your schedule of meals and rest is different from what you are used to, you feel dependent on people's willingness to cooperate, and you worry that your work is not coming along fast enough or that the data you are getting are not of sufficient interest or depth. A break from the tension is usually called for after several months of Stage 2. If your budget does not permit returning home, you retreat for some well-earned rest to a city or town where things are more comfortable and less stressful than at your field site. Your short vacation comes as a welcome alternative to both the strains and the boredom that accompany ethnographic research.

Upon returning to the field, you may well find you are now welcomed as a friend rather than merely tolerated as a stranger, and that your informants are pleased to strengthen ties established earlier.

Stage 3: Achievement. With your more confident command of the language, your greater familiarity with your informants, and your ever-deepening roots in the community, you now feel fully capable of achieving your fieldwork goals. You discover that the quantity and quality of the data you are acquiring is far greater than seemed possible when you were stumbling along in Stages 1 or 2. Now, although you must still exercise caution, topics once too sensitive to introduce with strangers can be put—gently—to carefully chosen members of the community.

By now you will have come to appreciate the personal nature of ethnographic research. You will have had an emotional and intellectual impact on the people around you; they, in turn, will have had

an impact on you. Fieldwork, you realize, is not just about collecting facts waiting out there for you to write down in your notebooks. Your informants are your companions, associates, teachers, and friends. How is the character of your human relationships, you wonder, being reflected in the kind of questions you are now asking? How is your involvement in the lives of people around you affecting the way you perceive the customs and beliefs you are trying to understand? Does the very fact of being asked questions that may never have been asked before change, in however modest a way, your informants' own thinking about their culture? Reflections such as these are likely to influence your research. Far from seeming a straightforward job of collecting data, ethnographic fieldwork emerges as an extremely human kind of activity.

Ethnographic fieldwork is thus a dialogue between the ethnographer and local people that affects everyone concerned. This feedback process, which was mentioned in Chapter 3 in our discussion of postmodernism, is known as *reflexivity*. You may think about this process again later, when you sit down to analyze and write up your field notes and realize how subjective your account is. Today, as we saw in the work of Margery Wolf (Chapter 3), some ethnographers are experimenting with ways to represent more accurately what it means to live in the cultures they attempt to describe. In addition to "facts," the ethnographer may describe his or her

Table 4.1
Three Stages of Fieldwork

Stages	Sample Activities
Stage 1: Adjustment	Coping with culture shock, beginning to learn the local language, establishing contacts, learning to schedule activities, making maps, taking photographs
Stage 2: Involvement	Continuing with language acquisition, collecting data relevant to research hypothesis, strengthening friendships
	A SHORT BREAK FROM THE FIELD
Stage 3: Achievement	Strengthening ties with community, widening range of topics, reflecting on the reflexive nature of your fieldwork

inner thoughts, feelings, or emotional reactions to local people's words or actions, thus hoping to give readers a better feel for the culture being portrayed.

The Problem of Gender. The sex of a cultural anthropologist can make a difference in the collection of ethnographic data. People in some cultures—perhaps most notably Muslim cultures—will not permit easy relationships between female ethnographers and male informants, and vice versa. But sometimes being female is an advantage. A woman can enter women's public bathhouses or other traditionally female settings that are strictly prohibited to men, while at the same time being at least tolerated in sports arenas or other traditionally male spheres. A man, while able to move freely within the world of men, is much more apt to be completely excluded from the world of women (Ardener 1984:124). Describing how gender influenced her fieldwork in Greece, one cultural anthropologist wrote:

> Often . . . I could not be involved in specified "male" activities or areas [like] coffee shops [or] football matches, [but] the limitations were not nearly as severe as they might seem. . . . I had the great advantage of free access to homes. Here it was possible to get to know *all* members of the family, male and female. In this respect, a single woman field worker has a distinct advantage over the male counterpart. (R. Hirschon in Ardener 1984:124)

Later in this chapter, we will describe the fieldwork experience of Nancie Gonzalez and how being female affected her work in the Dominican Republic.

The Ethics of Fieldwork. Not long ago, a female ethnographer, interested in feminist issues and funded by a generous grant from a private educational foundation, went to live and work for a year in a rural West African society in order to study gender differences in this setting. One way in which females reinforced their self-identity and their worth in this society was by being initiated into adulthood, a process all girls of 11 or 12 seemed eager to undergo. In different stages of the long initiation ritual, girls symbolically "died," were removed for a time from other members of the society, were then "reborn" and given new names, and finally were accepted back into their community as marriageable adult women. The ceremonies accompanying the initial phases of this series of highly

Female anthropologists can sometimes gain access to fieldwork settings where males would be unwelcome. In Morocco, parties at which a bride's hands are decorated with an orange-red dye called henna, prior to marriage, are women's affairs.

symbolic activities were fascinating, and the anthropologist happily observed, interviewed, scribbled notes, and took photographs for a future comparative study.

Then a dilemma arose. In the next stage of the proceedings, the ethnographer learned, the young initiates were to undergo a surgical procedure, without anaesthesia, to alter the outward appearance of the genitalia. The ethnographer was surprised that such procedures were still practiced in her fieldwork area.[2] What, if anything, should she do? Could

---

[2] Female genital mutilation was officially condemned by the World Health Organization in 1979, but continues to be practiced, although its incidence is apparently declining. For more information, see Lightfoot-Klein 1989.

she possibly stand by and observe this event silently? Should she intervene, and if so, how? Should she try to impose her personal feminist values on the people who had permitted her to share their lives? Did her responsibilities to her grant-making organization, or to anthropology, outweigh her responsibilities to the initiates, or vice versa?

• Ask Yourself •

What would you do if faced with the fieldwork dilemma described above? Would you decide what to do yourself, or consult someone else for advice? If you learned that the surgery would not actually happen, but the initiates would not know this ahead of time, how would this change your response?

Cultural anthropology, to a far greater extent than most other sciences, involves intimate contact between researchers and those who are the focus of anthropological inquiry. Thus, also to a far greater extent than most other sciences, the behavior of the researcher as a human being counts. No matter how objective the researcher tries to be, there is always the possibility that any of the many relationships that can exist between individuals— secrecy or openness, affection or dislike, trust or mistrust—may develop, and may color the research. And the data collected, if made known to outsiders, may have the potential to embarrass or perhaps even to harm the members of a society under study.

Those who practice cultural anthropology know that there is far more to research than collecting and publishing as much accurate information about people as possible. They realize only too well that they must try to balance their responsibilities to the people they are studying, to their sponsors, to the governments of countries that permit them to undertake research, to the profession of anthropology, and to their own consciences. Most ethnographers would probably agree that, in the balance,

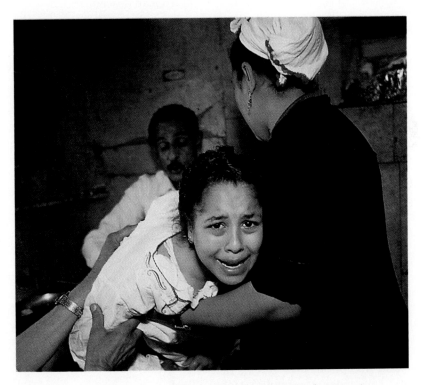

Fieldworkers may face situations that challenge their objectivity by presenting difficult ethical dilemmas. In Egypt, a young girl undergoes a traditional but dangerous procedure known as female circumcision.

their responsibility to the people they study should come first. But this is easier said than done: deciding how best to protect the interests and welfare of a society under study may not be at all simple.

The first public statement on ethics as an anthropological concern was contained in a letter written in 1919 by Franz Boas to *The Nation* (Weaver 1973:51–52). Boas claimed that several North American anthropologists, hired as U.S. government agents and using anthropology as a cloak, were spying against other governments. Boas was outraged. Anyone who "prostituted science" in this way, he declared, forfeited the right to be considered a scientist. The American Anthropological Association did not agree. Stating that Boas's scathing letter was "unjustified," the AAA censured him and stripped him of his membership in its governing council.

Nearly half a century later, in 1965, a research project devised by the United States Department of Defense reopened the Pandora's box of controversy over the ethics of social scientific research (Horowitz 1967). Beginning in Latin America, "Project Camelot" was to call on social scientists to investigate the conditions under which social unrest arose in foreign countries, and collect information on how to prevent uprisings against pro-American leaders. Such gross interference in the internal politics of other countries angered many anthropologists, who were among the most vocal opponents of the project. Project Camelot was cancelled, and partly in response to the controversy, the American Anthropological Association (AAA) commissioned an inquiry into the relationships between sponsors and anthropologists, created a Committee on Research Problems and Ethics, and passed a Statement on Problems of Anthropological Research (Ackroyd 1984:135). In 1971, it finally established an official code of ethics (American Anthropological Association 1971).

Even the AAA code of ethics has not made anthropologists' ethical choices easy. As J. Barnes (1981:2, 22–23) puts it, "Ethical and intellectual compromise is an intrinsic characteristic of social research." Compromises must be made between commitment to the people one is studying and impartiality; between openness and secrecy; between honesty and deception; and among the pursuit of scientific knowledge, the public's right to know, and the individual's right to privacy and protection.

• Contemporary Fieldworkers •

In Chapter 1, we discussed the work of three pioneering cultural anthropologists: Frank Cushing, Franz Boas, and Bronislaw Malinowski. Each undertook anthropological fieldwork many decades ago and contributed significantly to the subject. Two contemporary ethnographers, Napoleon Chagnon and Nancie Gonzalez, show how fieldwork is carried out today.

Napoleon Chagnon (1938–)

Napoleon Chagnon is well known for his fieldwork among the Yanomamo Indians, who live in the Amazon jungle of South America. For his first visit to the Yanomamo in the mid-1960s, Chagnon was part of a multidisciplinary team assembled by a university Department of Human Genetics to do medical research. At that time, the Yanomamo had had little contact with other cultures. They lived in small villages scattered widely throughout the remote tropical forest, and spoke only their own language. Many had never seen anyone of European descent.

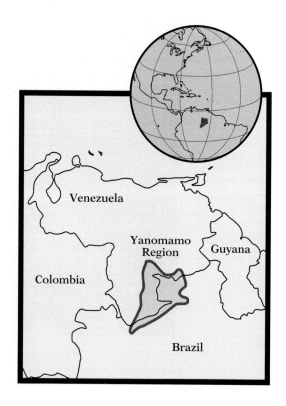

In the 1960s, the world know little about the Yanomamo, yet given the pace at which small-scale societies were becoming swallowed up by larger ones, it was inevitable that the Yanomamo way of life would eventually change—indeed, it was already changing. Thus Chagnon's most compelling goal as the anthropologist on his team was to preserve ethnographic data about this threatened culture. More specifically, his research hypothesis addressed the question of Yanomamo settlement patterns. Why were all those Yanomamo villages scattered throughout the jungle, how had this pattern come into being, and how long was it likely to last?

As a related goal, Chagnon also wanted to collect data on genealogical ties, which would help him to understand whether family relationships provided the basis of Yanomamo village composition. This proved difficult, since the Yanomamo observed a strict taboo against mentioning the names of individuals, living or dead, out loud. Chagnon nevertheless set to work with energy and determination, and after five months "smugly thought I had cracked the system" (1992:20) of Yanomamo family organization. He enthusiastically constructed several elaborate family trees. Soon, however, his "anthropological bubble burst" when he discovered that the names he had been so carefully writing down in his notebooks were inventions. Not only were the names entirely fictional, many were Yanomamo insults! Chagnon describes the reactions, from "stunned silence" to "uncontrollable laughter," that afflicted one group of villagers when he "named" the wife of a community headman (1992:21). He had to begin again. Having originally collected names during public interviews, he now began conducting private sessions, thereby reducing his informants' clowning (1992:21).

As his command of the Yanomamo language improved and the people grew more comfortable with his "pesky" questions, Chagnon's body of data increased, until at last he was able to begin to explain his initial research problem. He discovered that many currently occupied Yanomamo villages were recent colonies, splintered off from larger villages. A fascinating pattern began to emerge. There appeared to be cause-and-effect connections between the size of villages, their genealogical compositions, the age and sex distributions of their members, and marriage alliances between families. Warfare emerged as a factor controlling the size and distribution of villages. Chagnon realized

he must visit many villages to document the genealogical aspects of Yanomamo society, make detailed censuses, and map the locations of existing villages and others that had been abandoned. He adjusted his research strategy and began visiting village after village, collecting oral histories about Yanomamo wars, village breakups, and migrations (1992:31–32).

Following Cushing's and Malinowski's leads, Chagnon committed himself to full participant observation. On one occasion, he was working on genealogical notes in his hut when two of his Yanomamo friends appeared at the door. The local Christian missionary, they reported, had been telling the villagers that unless they stopped their traditional custom of chanting to the *hekura* (spirits), God would destroy them. Chagnon, whose attitude toward the missionary appears to have resembled that of the Zuni toward "Dust-eye" (Chapter 1), was angry. To show the missionary how he felt, he said to his friends, "Let's *all* go chant to the hekura!" (1983:207).

Preparations for the chant began. The Yanomamo decorated Chagnon with feathers and painted his face and chest so he would look his best for the spirits. Then, just like a Yanomamo, he permitted his companions to puff a hallucinogenic powder into his nostrils through a long wooden tube. It was painful. Coughing and retching, he rubbed the back of his head to reduce the pain. More powder, more retching—but the pain diminished. The Yanomamo, too, were taking the drug, but bit by bit Chagnon lost interest in them. His knees grew rubbery and his peripheral vision faded (1983:208). Soon he began to feel as if he were filled with a strange power. Yanomamo songs began to whirr though his brain, and "almost involuntarily" he began to sing. Blips of light flashed before his eyes. He began to dance in the manner of Yanomamo men, calling to the spirits, inviting them to come into his chest and dwell within him. Feeling great confidence, he sang ever louder, and danced with ever more complex steps. Taking up a friend's arrows, he struck magical blows, searching the horizon for spirits, sensing "intimately why [some Yanomamo] went daily through the pain of taking their drugs, for the experience was exhilarating and stimulating" (1983:208–209). As his "high" reached ecstatic proportions, he broke the arrows over his head and pranced wildly with the splinters clutched tightly in his fists (1983:209–210). Later he reported that what thrilled him the most about this episode was "the freedom to give complete reign to the imagination . . . to shed my cultural shackles and fetters, to cease being a North American animal up to a point and be Yanomamo" (1983:209). Participant observation cannot go much further.

Not only was Chagnon interested in studying Yanomamo culture synchronically; its diachronic aspects also concerned him. After collecting base-line ethnographic data during 15 months of field-work between 1964 and 1966, he went back to visit these people many more times during a long-term research project that by 1983 added up to a total of 42 months in the field. Between 1964 and 1983, as more and more missionaries, settlers, and miners ventured into Yanomamo territory (an area rich in gold, diamonds, and zinc), the Yanomamos' origi-nal way of life began to fade very rapidly. Chagnon took a filmmaker on subsequent visits, and helped shoot over 80,000 feet of ethnographic film. By 1983 he had completed some 20 documentaries on the Yanomamo. Together with numerous articles and several highly regarded books, Chagnon's films have transformed one of the least known of nonlit-erate peoples into one of the best known.

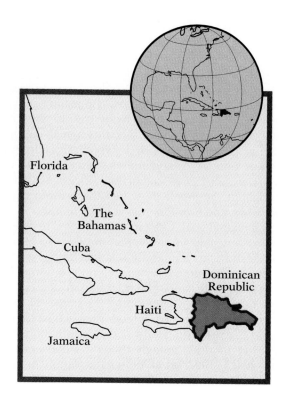

Nancie L. Gonzalez (1929–)

In the mid-1960s, few anthropological field studies had yet dealt with migration from rural to urban settings and the cultural changes that result in both areas. Nancie Gonzalez decided to study these top-ics, choosing the Dominican Republic, which shares the large Caribbean island of Hispaniola with Haiti, as her field site. Combining features of Latin American and Caribbean urbanization, previ-ously studied only in Puerto Rico, the country's political and social atmosphere seemed well suited to anthropological work (Gonzalez 1974:21).

Gonzalez began her 14 months of fieldwork in July 1967, in the city of Santiago de los Caballeros, at that time home to some 85,000 people. Far from being the typical lone ethnographer, she was accompanied by her two sons, 7 and 9, as well as a pair of married graduate students who were collect-ing data for their Ph.D. theses.

Gonzalez found a humble place to live on the out-skirts of the city, but this soon proved to be a mis-take. Although surrounded by immigrant neighbors, she soon realized that to incorporate herself into the life of the city as a whole it was essential to live in

the center of town, for only there could she be around when things happened. So Gonzalez and her sons moved into a once-fashionable but now deteri-orating neighborhood only a block off the main plaza. Wealthier informants remembered the area's former prestige and even the splendor of the man-sion she rented, while poorer ones did not feel uncomfortable visiting. Moreover, her new house had a telephone, indispensable for urban research.

Taking her sons with her into the field had its advantages, too. Gonzalez enrolled them in school, where they were quickly accepted into a local group of neighborhood children (Gonzalez 1974:24). From this "insider" position they were able to enlighten their mother on aspects of life in Santiago she could never have learned about alone. As infor-mal field assistants, the boys provided their mother with data on children's games, problems, and atti-tudes toward adults. For example, Gonzalez knew that members of the city's middle and upper classes celebrated Christmas with Christmas trees, Santa Claus, and gifts. But until her youngest son told her, she did not know that poor children had to wait until the 6th of January ("King's Day") to receive

In the Dominican Republic, fieldworker Nancie Gonzalez's young sons acted as their mother's informal assistants. Gonzalez's two sons were indistinguishable from their Dominican playmates.

their presents, since, they said, their working mothers did not get paid until January 1st.

Since she was also interested in the effects of immigration into Santiago on the rural communities the immigrants had left, Gonzalez had to pick a second suitable research site, a rural village. Her two graduate students moved into this community, beginning their field research with a census of the local population (Gonzalez 1974:25). In this way they were able to learn the names and addresses of local people who had immigrated to Santiago, so Gonzalez could look them up and collect information about family and marital patterns, household economics, and reasons for migration (Gonzalez 1974:26).

As her fieldwork progressed, Gonzalez realized that Santiago's elites controlled the social and economic opportunities available to the immigrants. Thus she could not restrict her inquiries to informants of lower status; studying the elites would be just as important. But this presented problems. Her previous experience as a participant observer had been in rural areas, and she was unprepared to

work among urban elites. Her fieldwork wardrobe, for example, consisted mainly of jeans and casual shirts, but silk dresses would have been more appropriate for dealing with upper-class people. Having learned to dress in a particular style, speak in a certain way, and use one kind of table manners, she was now obliged to "acquire different patterns in order to establish rapport with another group in the population" (1974:27–28).

Gender, too, affected her social status. The elites of heavily Catholic Santiago, among whom divorce was almost nonexistent, were not used to the idea of a single female as the head of a household (Gonzalez 1984:104). Upper-class women in particular, perhaps viewing Gonzalez as a competitor for the attentions of the local males of their class, were reluctant to accept a young, attractive, unattached American woman. Her relationships with middle-class women were somewhat closer, but only among lower-class women could she truly relax.

Working with the elites of Santiago also raised an interesting ethical problem. Gonzalez's upper-class informants were both relatively few in number and prominent in city life. Moreover, on occasion they shared information with her that she felt was politically sensitive. If she were not careful with her research data, the anonymity of her informants might be compromised, much to their embarrassment. So concerned was Gonzalez to protect her informants that she decided not to publish the book she later wrote about her Santiago research. In an article resulting from her fieldwork, she carefully disguised her informants' identities (Gonzalez 1972).

Nancie Gonzalez was confronted with other problems as well. For example, Santiago's residents stayed up late, and the activities Gonzalez wanted to study would often last far into the night. Other problems were due to the "extreme pressures" of her particular circumstances. Trying to fulfill many different and even contradictory roles—reseacher, mother, teacher, friend—and having to shift quickly and frequently from one form of behavior to another were emotionally exhausting. To add to these problems, Gonzalez's intended study of immigrants' interactions with their home communities proved impossible. (This is not a rare experience for fieldworkers; many a research hypothesis has had to be adjusted in the field, or even abandoned for a new one.) The final results of her fieldwork bore little resemblance to the research design she had initially planned (Gonzalez 1974:34).

Despite these difficulties, Gonzalez's fieldwork produced findings of considerable importance to urban anthropology. She was able to demonstrate that to understand how cities work, ethnographers need to pay more attention to the roles of upper- and middle-class inhabitants (Gonzalez 1974:19). More specifically, she demonstrated that rural-urban differences in the Dominican Republic were far less marked than social scientists had generally assumed. And she showed that in the ranking system of this particular urban center, differences in life-styles and the associated values and expectations of immigrants and longtime city dwellers were the result not so much of the contrast between rural and urban origins as between the "haves" and the "have-nots," regardless of where they came from (Gonzalez 1974:38).

Nancie Gonzalez's experience offers a good lesson in urban fieldwork methods. Like all cultural anthropologists, urban anthropologists rely heavily on participant observation, but they also make use of other research techniques sometimes denied to ethnographers of isolated, nonliterate peoples. First, urban anthropologists have access to written documents—which in some cases go back as much as six thousand years, to the time when urban centers first appeared. Second, because urban communities are large, geographically concentrated, and usually literate, the field technique of using surveys and questionnaires is particularly helpful. And third, because of its great quantity and comparability, information collected in surveys and from documents and questionnaires lends itself especially well to statistical analysis.

Conclusion

As the work of Napoleon Chagnon and Nancie Gonzalez shows, the techniques by which cultural anthropologists obtain information about cultures have improved since the time of Cushing, Boas, and Malinowski. But if jet travel, computers, and sophisticated new data-gathering techniques have made the job of fieldwork easier, the impetus behind fieldwork and the kinds of information cultural anthropologists seek in the field remain much the same. The discipline is still concerned with finding, describing, and explaining human behavior, past and present.

Summary

- Fieldwork in cultural anthropology may be undertaken to test new hypotheses, to retest old ones, or to address practical problems.

- The major strategy of cultural anthropologists is participant observation. Techniques that accompany (or sometimes substitute for) this strategy include interviewing, collecting genealogies, surveys, sampling, life histories, case studies, filming and taping, network analysis, and team research.

- Doing fieldwork involves difficulties that may include obtaining permission to do research, culture shock, and difficult gender relations in the field.

- A particularly awkward problem facing ethnographers is that ethnographic data, if not handled appropriately, may embarrass or even harm people.

- Successful fieldworkers typically experience three stages of fieldwork: adjustment, involvement, and achievement.

- The chapter ends with a description of the ways in which two modern fieldworkers, Napoleon Chagnon and Nancie Gonzalez, obtained their research findings.

Key Terms

armchair anthropologist
case study
casual informant
control group
culture shock
ego-centered network
fieldwork
focus group
genealogy
informant
interview
key informant
life history
network analysis
personal survey
respondent
respondent survey
sampling
set-centered network
survey

Suggested Readings

Agar, Michael H. 1980. *The Professional Stranger: An Informal Introduction to Ethnography.* New York: Academic Press. An account of how research in anthropology is carried out. The author brings his own experiences into his suggestions to the reader. We have relied heavily on this book in the present chapter.

Bernard, H. Russell. 1994. *Research Methods in Anthropology: Qualitative and Quantitative Approaches* (2nd ed.). Thousand Oaks, CA: Sage. An excellent manual on anthropological research, focusing on preparing for field research, collecting data, and analyzing qualitative and quantitative data.

Ellen, Roy. (ed.). 1984. *Ethnographic Research: A Guide to General Conduct. ASA Research Methods in Social Anthropology 1.* London: Academic Press. A comprehensive guide to carrying out ethnographic research, with contributions from experts in various specialties. As with Agar's book, we have made extensive use of this book in the present chapter.

Mead, Margaret. 1972. *Blackberry Winter.* New York: Simon & Schuster. An autobiography describing the early fieldwork of one of the world's most famous anthropologists.

Parkin, Frank. 1986. *Krippendorf's Tribe.* New York: Dell. A comic novel about an anthropologist whose fieldwork documents the bizarre customs of a particularly savage group: members of his own family.

Rabinow, Paul. 1977. *Reflections on Fieldwork in Morocco.* Berkeley: University of California Press. This short but perceptive book argues cogently that the fieldwork setting and the individuals the fieldworker encounters strongly affect the fieldworker, the material collected, and its interpretation.

Sanjek, Roger. (ed.). 1990. *Fieldnotes: The Makings of Anthropology.* Ithaca, NY: Cornell University Press. A well-balanced collection of articles illustrating the fieldwork not only of traditional but also of feminist and postmodernist anthropologists.

Shostak, Marjorie. 1983. *Nisa: The Life and Words of a !Kung Woman.* New York: Vintage Books. An evocative portrayal of a woman's life among African gatherers and hunters.

Whitehead, Tony L., and **Mary Ellen Conaway.** (eds.). 1986. *Self, Sex and Gender in Cross-Cultural Fieldwork.* Urbana: University of Illinois Press. Sixteen case studies dealing with the reciprocal impact of fieldworkers' personalities and behavior and those of people under study. A special focus is how the gender of the ethnographer affects this interaction.

Introduction

In February 1964, with the temperature hovering around 35° F below zero, a missionary from Illinois and his pregnant wife arrived in the Northwest Territories of

Canada. During the next 14 months, Herb and Judy Zimmerman and their baby lived in an isolated encampment of tents and tiny huts in which all of the other occupants were Native Americans called Dogribs. From the moment of their arrival, the Zimmermans worked at learning the Dogrib language, because, as members of the Evangelical Free Church of America, they considered it their divine mission to translate the Bible into Dogrib. Since this language had never been written down nor its grammatical rules ever defined, the missionaries were faced with a real linguistic challenge.

"Translating the Bible into another tongue is a difficult assignment," wrote a newspaper reporter who covered the missionaries' story, since the Zimmermans "must also translate the Bible into another culture" (Malcolm 1981:14). Isolated in the frigid Canadian wilderness, the Dogribs had of course never heard of many of the biblical objects and concepts familiar to Western-educated people. So the "Three Wise Men" had to be translated into Dogrib words meaning the "three chiefs," and these chiefs were given horses to ride instead of camels. For people who had no farm animals and whose survival depended in part on killing any mountain sheep they came across, the metaphor of the good shepherd—one who cares spiritually for a flock of dependents—meant nothing to the Dogribs, so instead of "shepherd" the Zimmermans had to settle for the Dogrib word *gikedi*, which meant "communal baby sitter"!

To make the Bible meaningful to the 2500 Dogrib-speakers, the Zimmermans needed a thorough understanding of Dogrib culture, aspects of which were reflected in their language. Unlike North Americans, for example, the villagers placed great emphasis on the communal ownership of property, at the same time devaluing individual property ownership. The dominance of community over individual rights was reflected in the Dogribs' use of possessive pronouns (mine, yours, his, hers, ours, theirs). These could be used only for parts of a person's own body and for relatives. Instead of saying, for instance, "my sled," as English-speakers would, Dogrib speakers' looser sense of ownership was expressed through the use of prepositional phrases such as "this sled is to me."

Fortunately for the Zimmermans, the Dogribs were very friendly—so friendly that they considered it rude for newcomers to their community to wait for a formal invitation before visiting their neighbors. In their view, visitors should immediately make a "walk-around" to every village home, beginning with that of the chief, to pay their respects. So it wasn't long before the Zimmermans found themselves socializing, and at the same time learning Dogrib customs and manners. They quickly discovered that participation in Dogrib daily life made learning the language easier, so—like ethnographers using the participant observation field method (Chapter 4)—they immersed themselves in community activities, and their project was under way.

Since many aspects of culture are reflected in language, understanding a culture involves understanding its language as well. Herb and Judy Zimmerman of Yellowknife, Northwest Territories, had to immerse themselves in Dogrib culture before they could accurately translate the Bible into the previously unwritten Dogrib language.

In every society there are close links between culture and language; indeed, language is the major means by which culture is transmitted. Thus, anyone who wishes to understand a culture must understand the language spoken by its members. Only by learning the Dogrib language could the Zimmermans properly understand the way these people thought, why they behaved as they did, and how they viewed their world.

This chapter is about language, the major medium of human interaction (Collinge 1990:xv). Human beings also convey meaning through other means, such as symbols or gestures. The semaphore system, in which signal flags rather than words constitute the medium of communication, is an example. But language is the most complex kind of human communication and—in the view of many anthropologists—the feature that most sharply distinguishes human beings from other living creatures. (For a consideration of other kinds of human communication, see Chapter 2, which treats nonlinguistic symbols, and Chapter 15, which discusses communication through bodily gestures.)

We begin this chapter by exploring the origins and development of two main expressions of language, speech, and writing. Next, we discuss the varied work of anthropological linguists. Some of them seek to understand contemporary languages, written or unwritten, by studying the sounds and sound combinations making up a language and the ways in which these can be arranged to convey meaning. Others focus on the world's ancient languages. Some of these are represented by written texts, while others exist only in the form of a few words that managed to survive and were included in other languages. Finally, we examine the nature of the links among language, thought, and culture. Each of these topics is essential for understanding language, but the last one, termed *sociolinguistics*, is of the most compelling interest to the cultural anthropologist

Language is the principal but not the only medium of human interaction; symbols and gestures are others. The semaphore system, which employs signal flags rather than words, is a nonlinguistic means of human communication.

because of the importance of language in transmitting culture, from generation to generation within a society and also from one society to another.

• The Origins Of Human • Communication

To help understand the origins of language and other forms of human communication, we can draw on evidence from several fields. Primatology, the study of the nonhuman higher primates, has taught us something about how the great apes (gorillas, chimpanzees, and orangutans) communicate (see Animal Symbols, Chapter 2, page 29). Ape communication is relevant to our understanding of human communication since apes are biologically our closest relatives among the world's animal species. Comparative

anatomy has revealed significant anatomical differences between human beings and these close relatives. Questions of intelligence or innate ability aside, the size and structure of the larynx and oral cavity of nonhuman primates does not permit humanlike speech in these creatures. Biological anthropology has traced the physical evolution of modern human beings from early **hominids** (our prehuman ancestors), showing how the physical apparatus of language developed in human beings through the millennia. Archaeology has documented some of the ways in which members of past human societies communicated symbolically. Finally, elementary education has contributed to our knowledge of how children learn to speak.

Hominid Communication

Our earliest hominid ancestors appear to have had much in common with contemporary great apes. Physically these ancestors had many apelike characteristics (such as short stature, small braincases,

hominids contemporary human beings' prehuman ancestors

and large jaws) and their remains, recovered in Africa by biological anthropologists and archaeologists, suggest that their lifestyle was in many ways similar to that of contemporary great apes in the wild. For example, they appear to have lived in small, migratory foraging groups, even as modern-day chimpanzees do. Because of these similarities, the behavior of apes in the wild provides us with a model around which to construct hypotheses of early hominid behavior.

Some anthropologists argue that early hominid communication was primarily vocal, resembling the hoots and grunts of the "call system" used by modern-day apes in the wild. Apes are able to vocalize information not only about their physical and emotional states (such as pain or anger) but also about the world around them (such as impending danger). Other researchers think early hominid communication was in large part gestural, a notion supported by recent studies of the capacity of higher primates for symbolic behavior (see Animal Symbols, Chapter 2, page 29). One hypothesis for the development of hominid communicative ability—whether vocal, gestural, or a combination of the two—is that it arose as an adaptation to a food-getting strategy based on group foraging (Parker and Gibson 1979). Successfully obtaining food in this way would have required planning and teamwork, which in turn would have required some reliable way of communicating what kinds of food were located where.

Origins of Speech

How Did Speech Evolve? It is reasonable to suppose that speech was a gradual outgrowth of the system of communication used by our prehuman ancestors—calls, gestures, or a combination of the two.

Apes' calls are mutually exclusive; they cannot convey two ideas at the same time. For example, there may be one vocalization that means "food," and another that means "danger." If a chimp notices a ripe banana nearby, but at the same time spots a leopard waiting to pounce, it can send only one of these messages to its fellows, because a call system lacks a way of combining the messages "food" and "danger." Speech, on the other hand, permits such combinations. Even new statements, never uttered before, can be understood. Some researchers think that prehuman creatures learned, over a long period of time, to combine two calls to

produce a new one. Suppose one of our ancestors found herself simultaneously confronting food and danger, both important to her and her companions. Perhaps she uttered a unique cry incorporating the elements of both the food and danger calls, and the members of her troop successfully reached the food and avoided the danger. The association between the cry and successful food getting and danger avoidance had been made. Over time, she or other prehumans might have recognized this cry as meaning "food-*and*-danger." This scenario may suggest how speech evolved (see Landsberg 1988).

An ape-sized brain is inadequate for this kind of communication, but beginning about 2.5 million years ago, the brain size of early hominids grew relatively rapidly. Archaeologists have shown that hominids were making stone tools at about the same time. Biological anthropologists believe that toolmaking and language involve some of the same mental processes, such as step-by-step planning and foresight. They hypothesize that brain enlargement, increased tool-making skills, and increased ability to communicate may all have stimulated each other simultaneously, even though the vocal apparatus of hominids could not have produced speech as we know it (Lieberman 1984). Whether or not this is true, it does seem likely that by the time anatomically modern human beings emerged some 35,000 years ago, they could speak.

Communication through gestures has also been suggested as an avenue to speech. Gordon W. Hewes (1973) sees the basis of spoken language in hand and arm gestures. He suggests that apes' ability to use signs (Chapter 2) shows that prehumans could have developed a simple **sign language.** This evidence from primate behavior, plus archaeological evidence of early tool using, plus studies of the use of body language in human communication (see Chapter 15) may suggest the pathway to vocalization.

Human Cognitive Ability. Children, whatever their parents' language, do not have to be urged to learn to speak, nor do they have to be taught any basic linguistic rules, such as correct word order. They seem to pick up automatically both the desire

---

sign language a language in which hand and body gestures, instead of sounds, are used to express meaning

for speech and the rules necessary to make their speech intelligible to others. Moreover, no matter how difficult or simple the language, all children learn to speak at about the same time. This suggests that the capacity for language acquisition is innate in human beings (Chomsky 1972; see also George 1989; Locke 1993). A child learning English seems to know instinctively that "Mama go bye-bye" makes sense, whereas "bye-bye go Mama" does not. Children learning to speak other languages are similarly endowed.

To explain these findings, some influential linguists have proposed the hypothesis that human beings possess a natural grammatical ability, or **universal grammar,** programmed in their brains from birth, so that at the deepest mental levels, the structure of all languages is the same. The most prominent of such theorists is Noam Chomsky, whose controversial ideas converge with the interpretive stance we call *cognitive anthropology* (Chapter 3). Cognitive anthropologists argue that the human brain contains "mental structures," fixed patterns of learning and thinking, so the minds of human beings everywhere conform to the same patterns.

Sign Languages.   About one in a thousand babies is born deaf or nearly so, which makes learning a spoken language very difficult. Indeed, children who are unable to hear a language find it almost impossible to speak it naturally, since normal speech depends, to a great extent, on repeating what one hears. Deaf or hearing-impaired children can be trained to understand the speech of others through lipreading, but they can never understand as well as a person who can hear, because 75 percent of spoken English words cannot be accurately lip-read (Fromkin and Rodman 1988:383). Sign languages, through which deaf people communicate using hand and body gestures instead of sounds, help to solve this problem. They are fully developed languages that, like spoken languages, allow their users to understand and create unlimited numbers of new sentences. Also like spoken languages, sign languages are grammatical, are sys-

tematic, and change over time (Fromkin and Rodman 1988:383). Since they do not require the ability to produce and hear sounds, they add weight to the notion that language learning depends on a biologically determined cognitive ability.

The most common sign language used in North America is American Sign Language (ASL) (Figure 5.1), which includes not just words but also grammatical rules like those that structure spoken languages. The formal units of ASL, which correspond to the sounds of spoken languages, are called **primes.** Primes transmit their meaning in one of a number of ways, including the configuration of the hand and the motion of the hand(s) toward or away from the body (Fromkin and Rodman 1988:384).

Other behaviors observed in the deaf also bolster the hypothesis that language is innate in human beings. Deaf children of deaf parents, when exposed to sign language, learn it in stages that parallel those by which children who can hear learn

Like spoken languages, sign languages allow their users to express an unlimited number of ideas, but they rely on hand and body gestures instead of sounds to convey meaning. Heather Whitestone, crowned Miss America in 1994, uses sign language to say "I love you" to her fans.

---

universal grammar a hypothetical grammatical ability inherent in all human beings from birth

prime a formal unit of American Sign Language, corresponding to a sound in a spoken language

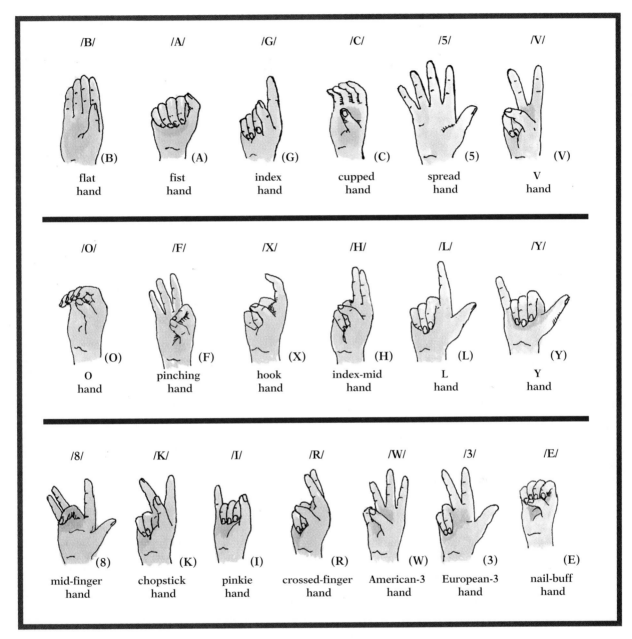

Figure 5.1

Primes, the individual signs that make up American Sign Language (ASL), correspond to the individual sounds of spoken languages. Above are the hand configurations corresponding to ASL's primes in order of the frequency with which they are used. Source: Fromkin and Rodman 1988:385.

spoken language. Deaf children often sign themselves to sleep, just as children who can hear talk themselves to sleep, and they sign to their dolls and stuffed animals. Sometimes sign language users make gestural errors identical to slips of the tongue in spoken language. "Finger fumbles" amuse signers just as slips of the tongue amuse speakers (Fromkin and Rodman 1988:384–388).

• Ask Yourself •

In English, if someone is rushed we say, "Where's the fire?" In Latin, you would say "Ubi ignis est?" This translates into English as "Where fire is?"—hardly a grammatical utterance. If linguistic rules are really innate, how would you explain differences in word order between languages?

Writing

Notations and Calendars.   **Writing** is the graphic or visual representation of language, using lines or other strokes on a two-dimensional surface, in media ranging from rock carving to laser printing. Writing cannot have been invented quickly. It must have been preceded by many different attempts by prehistoric human beings to map, demonstrate, illustrate, or record things.

Until the 1960s, it was widely assumed that the earliest attempts at writing had been made sometime after the beginnings of agriculture, less than 10,000 years ago. In 1964, however, science writer Alexander Marshack made a novel suggestion: that engraved markings on pieces of bone and antler found in European archaeological sites (see Figure 14.1 on page 348), some of them as much as 35,000 years old, were really graphic representations of ideas, and thus ancestors of writing. Archaeologists had previously assumed that these markings were either decorations or grooves cut to improve one's grip on pieces of bone used as handles for tools. Bucking the tide of archaeological opinion, Marshack (1972) embarked on a quest for evidence in support of his hypothesis about prehistoric notations.

Much of Marshack's argument rested on techniques borrowed from the police laboratory. Using a microscope, he photographed otherwise invisible features on a number of engraved bones. Just as a gun leaves distinctive marks on bullets fired from its barrel, so each different stone tool used in carving a piece of bone leaves its own distinctive "signature." Through his microscope, Marshack observed repeatedly that the markings on a given piece of bone would all be made with different implements. He reasoned that if the markings had served merely as decorations or to "rough up" the bones to improve their grip, all the markings on a given bone would have been cut with a single tool. However, as many as 24 different tools had been used to make a single set of marks. This implied that the marks were cut on different occasions, which would be characteristic of record keeping.

On some of the artifacts Marshack studied, a long series of vertical lines was inscribed—usually 29, 30, or 31 in a row. Marshack believes these represent successive nights on which the moon was visible—in other words, a lunar month. To gatherers-and-hunters, the moon in its regular succession of phases was a sort of calendar in the sky, but people required graphic assistance to keep track of this calendar. The engraved artifacts seemed to have served the purpose nicely. Notational systems closely resembling the European Ice Age devices were used until recently in parts of Australia, Siberia, and Africa, which lends support to Marshack's ideas.

Today, although many anthropologists agree with Marshack that prehistoric people could and did make graphic representations, the first attempt at writing remains undocumented. Perhaps someone's need to communicate her physical presence at a particular place by leaving marks on a rock or tree were the first "written" symbols, or perhaps a fisherman remembered a particularly plentiful catch by means of a tally stick onto which notches were carved. Maybe a hunter sought to provide his fellows with directions to where game animals were feeding by representing—on the dirt of the forest floor, with a pointed stick—the streams, swamps, and rock outcroppings they would need to pass. We will never know, but what is now clear from the work of Marshack and others is that by the last Ice Age, long before the development of agriculture, our ancestors were communicating with one another not only with speech but also with graphic symbols.

• Ask Yourself •

Imagine yourself in a world without calendars or timekeeping devices of any sort. What events would you most want to keep track of? How important to you would it be to know how many days had elapsed since the last full moon?

---

writing the graphic or visual representation of a language

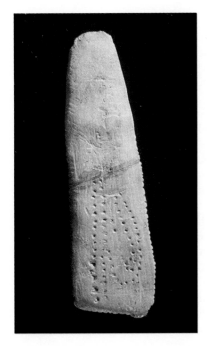 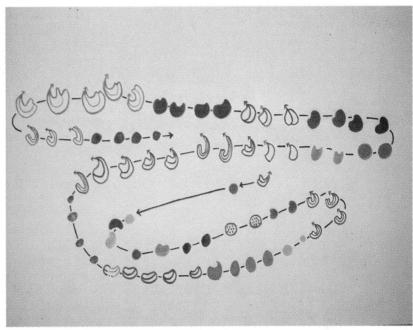

Before writing, people must have tried many ways of representing their ideas graphically. Science writer Alexander Marshack believes this piece of bone, which was found in a rock shelter in France and may be as much as 30,000 years old, is an ancient calendar. According to Marshack, the markings on the bone depict the cycles of the moon over a period of two and a half months.

True Writing. Some 10,500 years ago, Middle Eastern farmers, landowners, and traders began keeping records of crop sales and real estate transactions using little clay tokens of different shapes such as spheres, cones, and disks, sometimes marked with lines or indentations. Each token represented a particular object or a certain quantity, and by lining up several tokens one could symbolically convey notions such as "5 sheep" or "18 hectares of land."

Like the origins of graphic representations, the origins of true writing are also problematic. One specialist in the prehistoric uses of clay, Denise Schmandt-Besserat (1992), suggests that true writing evolved directly from the shapes produced when such tokens were pressed into wet clay. According to her, clay tablets found at Uruk, an ancient town in present-day Iraq, represent an evolutionary stage in a system of recording that had been in use in the Middle East since the first stages of the transition from a gatherer-and-hunter way of life to a more settled, agricultural life. She suggests that this new way of life required a record-keeping system.

Four principal stages marked the evolution of writing, according to Schmandt-Besserat (1992). The first occurred about 10,500 years ago, when tokens of specific shapes were used to represent items, such as bread, sheep, and clothes, that were traded among villages. These tokens seem to have served as invoices or bills of lading. Thus, a herder selling ten sheep to someone in another village might give a middleman transporting the shipment a sealed pouch containing 10 tokens representing sheep—or perhaps one "sheep" token and one token representing the quantity 10. This document would have guaranteed the accuracy of the shipment when "read" by the buyer.

The second stage began about 5500 years ago, with the enclosure of tokens in hollow clay spheres. The personal seal of the seller was pressed into the fresh, wet clay on the outside of each sphere. The clay subsequently hardened, so the sphere had to be broken open on delivery, revealing the tokens inside.

The third stage, following closely upon the second, began when people found that the need to break open the clay spheres to check the record, perhaps during shipment, could be avoided if a

The characters that made up cuneiform writing, which spread throughout the Middle East some 5000 ago, were impressed into wet clay with a pointed stick. Impressing was better than inscribing, because inscribing—rather like snowplowing—gouged out curls of clay that tended to obscure the details of the symbol being inscribed.

duplicate record was made by pressing each token on the outside of the sphere while the clay was still wet. The characteristic shape of each token *inside* the sphere was thus recorded on its shell. Intact spheres have been found and opened, and the tokens inside them have corresponded exactly to the impressions on the outside. Schmandt-Besserat suggests that these marks may be considered to be the crucial link between the old system of recording in three dimensions and writing.

---

pictograph a simple pictorial representation of an object

cuneiform ancient writing consisting of an arrangement of tiny wedge-shaped dents impressed into wet clay

descriptive linguistics the branch of linguistics that seeks to describe the features of languages

The final stage occurred when the system of impressions became generally understood, about 5200 years ago. The tokens themselves then became unnecessary, and full-fledged writing appeared. Instead of tokens, a pointed stick was used to inscribe the same symbols into clay. Schmandt-Besserat argues that new words, for which there had never been tokens, were subsequently added. Many of them were obviously **pictographs**—simple pictorial representations of the objects they stood for. A rising sun, for example, stood for "day."

Schmandt-Besserat's ideas are controversial, but it does seem clear that ancient pictographic writing evolved into the more stylized **cuneiform,** in which an arrangement of tiny wedge-shaped dents impressed into wet clay produced a version of the earlier pictogram. Five thousand years ago, cuneiform writing quickly spread throughout the Middle East, making possible more complicated and codified systems of commerce, law, religion, history, literature, and science.

• Understanding Languages •

Descriptive Linguistics

The total number of languages spoken by human beings, past and present, is estimated to be about 5000—more or less depending on what is considered to be a distinct language (Wurm 1991:1). Of these languages, many, particularly those spoken in the developing world, have only recently been put into written form, and hundreds of languages have never been written down. Thus anthropological linguists sometimes find themselves having to learn a spoken language that has no written form. When this happens, the linguist must analyze the language, primarily so that he or she can learn it for fieldwork purposes but also so that the language can be taught to and learned by others. All the sounds of which the language is made up must be isolated; the precise meanings of all these sounds must be identified; the vocabulary of the language must be listed; and its grammatical rules must be defined. Later, the language must be put into written form, using the alphabet of some written language.

Descriptive linguistics is the branch of linguistics that aims to identify, describe, and analyze the components of languages. When a language is unwritten, this is a difficult undertaking. Imagine that you are an ethnographer who has just encountered a group of people whose language

Anthropological linguists are trained to describe and analyze little-known languages, some of them unwritten. In the village of Kailga in the New Guinea highlands, linguistic fieldworker Alan Rumsey (right, with fern headdress) studies one of the 45 distinct languages spoken in Papua New Guinea.

has never been written down and who do not speak or write *your* language. With the use of gestures—smiles, waves, nods—you manage to communicate your friendly intentions. The people respond cheerfully, inviting you with gestures to sit down with them and make yourself comfortable. A babble of unintelligible sounds surrounds you, not one of which is meaningful. Soon refreshments are fetched, and someone presents you with a strange-looking drink, accompanied by a brief remark. To you, the words sound like this:

ME-KAHM-KEH-SHOW-MAH-EEN-RA-DAS-TEE-BAH-SHEED[1]

You do not know what the utterance means, although in the context of the situation it probably has something to do with being offered a drink. Moreover, you can count 11 different sounds making up this utterance, but you have no idea how many individual words these 11 sounds represent, or what their meanings might be. You do not even know whether they constitute a complete sentence or merely a phrase.

The people point repeatedly at you using the two syllables SHOW-MAH, so you infer that these two syllables together might translate into the English word "you." But you already know that languages are made up of a lot more than their vocabularies, and even if you were able to divide the utterance into the individual words that make it up, and to translate those individual words, you do not know the grammatical rules according to which the words are arranged. In English, after all, the phrase "Steve loves Laura" is not the same as the phrase "Laura loves Steve." In our language and many others, word order is everything—and the rules governing word order are only a small fraction of the many rules required to speak and understand a language.

Phonology. Where would a descriptive linguist facing such a situation begin? An important part of descriptive linguistics is understanding the various sounds used in a language and the way these can be combined into meaningful words, phrases, and sentences. The first task, then, is to identify all the meaningful sounds used in the language under study—all the sounds that can make a difference in meaning. It is not the case that *every* sound used in a language makes a difference in meaning. In English, for example, the sounds that the letters *t*

---

[1] This example is not, of course, taken from one of the world's still-unwritten languages. If it were, it would not be written here. The example is from Farsi, a language spoken by millions of Middle Easterners.

and *th* make are meaningful sounds. They can change *tan* to *than*. But in other languages there may be no meaningful distinction between these two sounds. The smallest meaningful unit of sound in a language is called a **phoneme.** These minimal linguistic units serve to differentiate the meanings of words. The study of the phonemes in a language is called **phonology.**

A descriptive linguist begins the study of a previously unwritten language by making a list of all the phonemes in the language. These are unlikely to be the same sounds that make up English. Some of them correspond to individual letters with which the linguist is familiar; in the example above, there is an *s* sound, for instance, and a *b* sound. Some of them correspond not to letters but to combinations of letters. Even in the English language, phonemes and letters do not correspond on a one-to-one basis. The letter *t* is a phoneme, and so is the letter *p*. These phonemes are responsible for the different meanings of the words *tan* and *pan*. But the two-letter combination *th* is also a phoneme, since *tan* clearly does not mean the same thing as *than*.

Morphology. After having identified all the sounds that together make up the new language, the descriptive linguist next identifies the larger combinations of sounds that mean something in the language. The smallest combination of sounds that has some meaning in a language is called a **morpheme,** and studying morphemes is termed **morphology.** As phonemes may correspond to individual letters, so morphemes may correspond to individual words, but not always. In English, even a single letter—for example, the letter *s*—can change the meaning of a word. *Hat* is not the same as *hats,* so the English word *hats* is made up of not one but two morphemes, *HAT* plus *S*. Languages vary widely in the number of morphemes their words contain. In English, most words contain only one or two, but in some languages, many morphemes can be strung together to form a single word.

Using phonology and morphology, a discriptive linguist would be able to divide ME-KAHM-KEH-SHOW-MAH-EEN-RA-DAS-TEE-BAH-SHEED into six individual words:

MEKAHM KEH SHOWMAH EENRA DASTEE BASHID.

Syntax. Besides the phonology and the morphology of a language, the descriptive linguist is concerned with **syntax,** the rules governing the way the morphemes can be arranged in order to make sense. He or she must learn what meaningful beginning-morphemes (**prefixes**) and ending-morphemes (**suffixes**) can be attached in what way to what kinds of words; how to **conjugate** the language's verbs—that is, to change the verbs to reflect different tenses, persons, moods, and so on—and how to **decline** its nouns—to change them to reflect particular cases, numbers, or genders. It might take months of study for a descriptive linguist to understand that:

MEKAHM is a form of the verb meaning "to want," and consists of two morphemes: the verb stem, MEK-, and a morpheme indicating the first person singular in the present continuous tense, -AHM. It means "I am wanting."

KEH means "that," in the (English-language) sense of introducing a subordinate clause rather than serving as a demonstrative pronoun. Two phonemes make it up—the gutteral sound you have chosen to represent with the English letter *k*, plus a short-*e* sound. The first of these two phonemes sometimes sounds like a *k* and sometimes more like a hard *g*, but although these two sounds are different phonemes in English (changing "kill" to "gill," for instance), they are only one phoneme in the language under study.

SHOWMAH, as the descriptive linguist might have guessed on the first day of fieldwork, means "you."

EENRA is translated by two English words, "this" and "thing," but in the language under study it is only one word, meaning "this thing."

---

phoneme (phonology) the smallest meaningful unit of sound in a language

morpheme (morphology) the smallest combination of sounds that has meaning in a language

syntax the rules governing the way morphemes can be arranged in order to make sense

prefix a morpheme that is added at the front of a word to alter its meaning

suffix a morpheme that is added to the end of a word to alter its meaning

conjugate to change a verb to reflect different tenses, persons, and moods

decline to change a noun to reflect case, number, or gender

Table 5.1
A Phonetic Alphabet for American English Pronunciation

Consonants					Vowels			
p^h	pill	t^h	till	k^h	kill	i	beet	I	bit
p	spill	t	still	k	skill	e	bait	ε	bet
b	bill	d	dill	g	gill	u	boot	U	foot
m	mill	n	nil	r	ring	o	boat	O	bought
f	feel	D	rider	h	high	æ	bat	a	pot
v	veal	s	seal	?	bottle	ʌ	but	∂	sofa
θ	thigh	z	zeal	l	leaf	aj	bite	aw	bout
Ō	thy	č	chill	r	reef	oj	boy		
š	shill	ǰ	Jill	j	you				
ž	azure	ʍ	which	w	witch				

The English language is represented by more phonemic symbols than it has letters because one letter can represent several different sounds. Above are the phonemes of English as it is pronounced in America, with examples of how each sound is used in an actual word.

Source: Fromkin and Rodman 1988:57.

DASTEE and BASHID are the two parts of a compound verb. One is a form of the word for "have," and the other expresses the subjunctive mood. Together the two words mean "you should have."

Now the descriptive linguist is finally able to translate the phrase on page 101. The individual who presented the drink was saying: "I-want-that-you-this-thing-should-have"—or, loosely translated, "Here, have a (drink)."

One difficulty in writing down phonemes is that a phoneme and the letter used to represent it when transcribed may not always match. The words *heed* and *head* both have the letter *e* as their second letter, but their pronunciation is different. To avoid the possibility of making a mistake, linguists have developed a system of phonemic symbols, each of which represents one sound only. The most popular system of phonemic symbols is one proposed by the International Phonetic Association (IPA). Table 5.1 shows the phonemic symbols for the consonants and vowels of American English.

Paralanguage. In addition to phonemes, morphemes, and syntax, human speech also makes use of voice effects. These include pitch (the relative

• Ask Yourself •

An immigrant from China was recently fired from his job in the United States because his employer felt his accent did not present a good image for the company. In North America, British accents are generally considered charming, but some others are not. Do you speak English with an accent? If so, has this ever caused you problems? Do you find any particular accent more or less attractive than any other?

lowness or highness of the voice, determined by the frequency at which the voice box resonates), softness or loudness, speed, and other vocal qualities, which may be used singly or in various combinations to convey meaning. The collective term for these features of language is **paralanguage.** To appreciate how efficiently paralanguage can convey meaning, imagine an angry parent disciplining a naughty child; the parent's tone says as much as his or her actual words.

paralanguage the use of voice effects to convey meaning

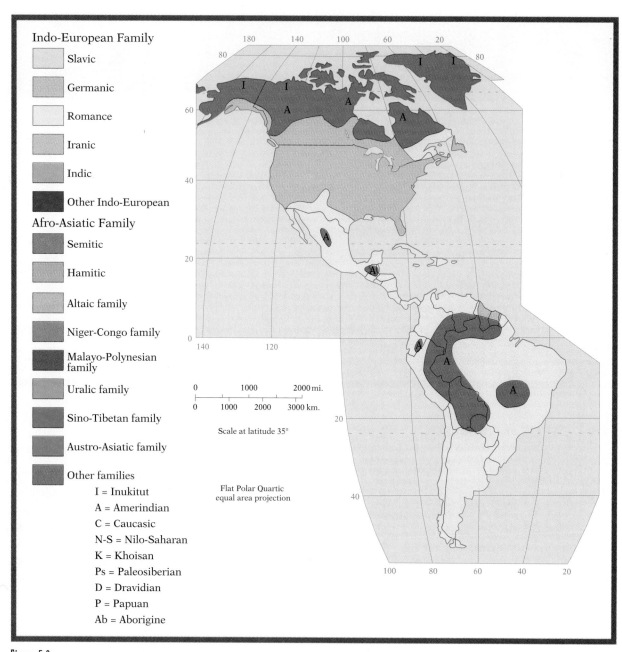

Indo-European Family
- Slavic
- Germanic
- Romance
- Iranic
- Indic
- Other Indo-European

Afro-Asiatic Family
- Semitic
- Hamitic
- Altaic family
- Niger-Congo family
- Malayo-Polynesian family
- Uralic family
- Sino-Tibetan family
- Austro-Asiatic family
- Other families
  - I = Inukitut
  - A = Amerindian
  - C = Caucasic
  - N-S = Nilo-Saharan
  - K = Khoisan
  - Ps = Paleosiberian
  - D = Dravidian
  - P = Papuan
  - Ab = Aborigine

0   1000   2000 mi.
0   1000   2000   3000 km.

Scale at latitude 35°

Flat Polar Quartic
equal area projection

Figure 5.2

The Distribution of the Major Language Families in the World. Source: Jordan et al. 1994.

Consider how the meaning of a sentence changes when the intonation is changed:

He's coming, isn't he

If this is said in a way that the speaker's voice falls on the second *he*, the utterance is probably intended as a flat statement, with which the speaker expects the listener to agree. However, if the words are spo-

ken so the second *he* is uttered with a rising tone, the meaning changes. In this case, the speaker is in doubt about the validity of the statement, and is making a request for information (Crystal 1975:165–166).

One important focus of contemporary paralinguists is the ways in which paralanguage affects communications between the sexes, a subject discussed later in this chapter (see Gender and

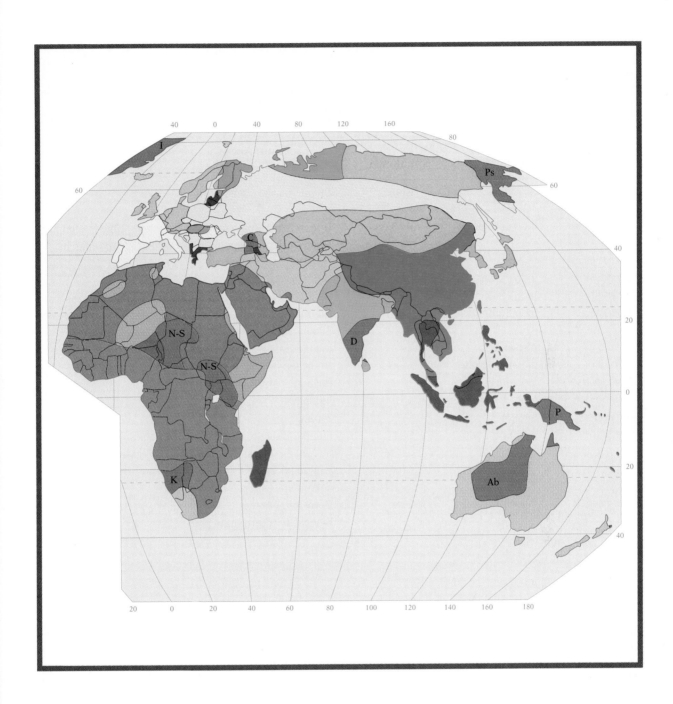

Language, below). Another is the overlap between paralanguage and body language—the nonverbal ways human beings convey ideas, feelings, and intentions through bodily movements and facial expressions, unconscious or conscious (see Chapter 15). Paralanguage manifests itself differently depending on who is speaking, what language is being used, and the context of the conversation, but it is a feature of all spoken languages.

Historical Linguistics

Historical linguistics approaches the study of language diachronically, rather than synchronically as descriptive linguistics does. Historical linguists are

---

historical linguistics the branch of linguistics that studies the histories of languages, both living and dead, and the relationships between languages and dialects

Table 5.2
The Leading Languages (Those with Over 100 Million Total Speakers)

Language	Family	Millions of Speakers	Main Areas Where Spoken
Han Chinese (Mandarin)	Sino-Tibetan	864	China, Taiwan, Singapore
English	Indo-European	443	British Isles, Anglo-America, Australia, New Zealand, South Africa, Philippines, former British colonies in tropical Asia and Africa
Hindi	Indo-European	352	Northern India
Spanish	Indo-European	341	Spain, Latin America, southwestern United States
Russian	Indo-European	293	Russia, Kazakhstan, parts of Ukraine and other former Soviet republics
Arabic	Afro-Asiatic	197	Middle East, North Africa
Bengali	Indo-European	184	Bangladesh, eastern India
Portuguese	Indo-European	173	Portugal, Brazil, southern Africa
Indonesian	Malayo-Polynesian	142	Indonesia
Japanese	Altaic	125	Japan
French	Indo-European	121	France, Belgium, Switzerland, Québec, New Brunswick, and as a language of the educated elite (and official language) in most former French and Belgian colonies
German	Indo-European	118	Germany, Austria, Switzerland, Luxembourg, eastern France, northern Italy

Source: World Almanac, 1991.

interested in the histories of the world's living, or currently used, languages (see Figure 5.2) and in the decipherment of dead, or obsolete, languages. They are also interested in the past and present relationships among languages (one reason why this subfield of anthropology is sometimes called **comparative linguistics**), and relationships among **dialects**—varieties of a language based on region, occupation, or class.

Of the world's total of 5000 or so languages, less than 300 of which have over a million speakers (see Table 5.2), hundreds are now extinct (Wurm 1991). One of the greatest challenges to historical linguists is trying to construct **protolanguages,** the putative ancestors of known languages. Searching for a protolanguage is often a speculative undertaking, since such a language lacks any spoken or written examples. Thus, the protolanguage that is re-created rep-

---

comparative linguistics an alternate term for historical linguistics

dialect a variety of a language resulting from the speaker's region, occupation, or class

protolanguage a hypothetical language thought to be the ancestor of a known language

Table 5.3
Basic English Core Vocabulary

1	I	26	root	51	breasts	76	rain
2	you	27	bark	52	heart	77	stone
3	we	28	skin	53	liver	78	sand
4	this	29	flesh	54	drink	79	earth
5	that	30	blood	55	eat	80	cloud
6	who	31	bone	56	bite	81	smoke
7	what	32	grease	57	see	82	fire
8	not	33	egg	58	hear	83	ash
9	all	34	horn	59	know	84	burn
10	many	35	tail	60	sleep	85	path
11	one	36	feather	61	die	86	mountain
12	two	37	hair	62	kill	87	red
13	big	38	head	63	swim	88	green
14	long	39	ear	64	fly	89	yellow
15	small	40	eye	65	walk	90	white
16	woman	41	nose	66	come	91	black
17	man	42	mouth	67	lie	92	night
18	person	43	tooth	68	sit	93	hot
19	fish	44	tongue	69	stand	94	cold
20	bird	45	claw	70	give	95	full
21	dog	46	foot	71	say	96	new
22	louse	47	knee	72	sun	97	good
23	tree	48	hand	73	moon	98	round
24	seed	49	belly	74	star	99	dry
25	leaf	50	neck	75	water	100	name

Source: Renfrew 1987:114.

resents more of a hypothesis than a certainty. But the historical linguist is aided in this seemingly impossible task by two facts. First, in any language there is a **core vocabulary,** made up of basic words (see Table 5.3). These include words for parts of the body, objects in the natural environment, and the numbers below ten. In any language, there are about the same number of them. Some linguists think core words change very slowly because they are essential for social interaction; and when they do change, they appear to change in fairly systematic, predictable ways.

Reconstructing a "lost" language begins with a search among early written languages from the same general area of the world for **cognates,** words historically derived from the same source. In practice, this means finding words in different languages that are similar in appearance and meaning.

core vocabulary the most basic words of any language

cognate a word (or language) historically derived from the same source as another word or language

The Farsi word for brother, for instance, is *barodar*, which is quite similar to the English word *brother*. The two words are cognates.

In any two languages, there will be a certain number of overlapping or nearly overlapping words, since a small percentage of every language's words are replications of the sounds these words are intended to convey. Bees the world around, for instance, say "buzz." But there are other, genuine cognates among languages. These are apt to be core words, slow to change. Once core words are identified, the systematic process by which the ancient core words came into existence can be mapped, and their antecedents inferred. For example, the English word *hand* has cognates in German (*hand*), Dutch (*hand*), Swedish (*hand*), Danish (*haand*), and the now-extinct Gothic language (*handus*) (Ruhlen 1987:6). From these cognates, the historical linguist can infer a common ancestral form in the lost language called Proto-Germanic. By collecting the ancestral forms of words in use today, historical linguists can attempt to reconstruct a protolanguage.

The work of linguist Joseph Greenberg, a specialist in Native American languages, illustrates how historical linguists trace the spread of languages. American archaeologists have long thought that the first Native Americans came from Asia, more than 10,000 years ago, by trekking across a bridge of land that once connected Siberia with Alaska. But it was not known whether this migration happened just once or repeatedly, and where the migrants originated. Greenberg, who began his study of Native American languages in 1954, collected lists of words from many New World languages over a period of years, compared their cognates, and hypothesized that there were only three separate American protolanguages: Eskimo-Aleut, Na-Dene, and Amerind. The geographical locations where people speak the languages derived from these three basic families suggest that three separate migrations took place from Asia into the New World (Ruhlen 1987:10).

Greenberg and other linguists discovered a small but significant number of "global cognates," or word similarities between languages spoken in different parts of the world and thought to be totally unrelated to each other. This hints at the possibility that all the languages in the world may ultimately be derived from a single protolanguage (Ruhlen 1987:10).

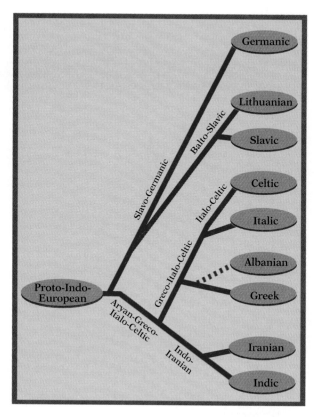

Figure 5.3

Almost all of the European languages of the present time have as a common root, Proto-Indo-European, which may have been spoken in Anatolia about 8500 years ago. Source: Renfrew 1989:110.

Archaeologist Colin Renfrew recently studied the process by which languages spread and became increasingly differentiated in Europe. As long ago as 1860, the German linguist August Schleicher hypothesized that most of the European languages (with the exceptions of Hungarian, Basque, Estonian, and Finnish) diverged like the branches of a tree from an ancestral language called proto-Indo-European (Figure 5.3). However, a lack of data prevented any plausible explanation as to where proto-Indo-European may have originated, what processes led to its spread, or over what period of time its successive transformations into current languages, such as English, German, French, Italian, and Spanish, occurred (Renfrew 1989:110).

Renfrew (1989) attempted to resolve these questions by linking language and agriculture. He noted

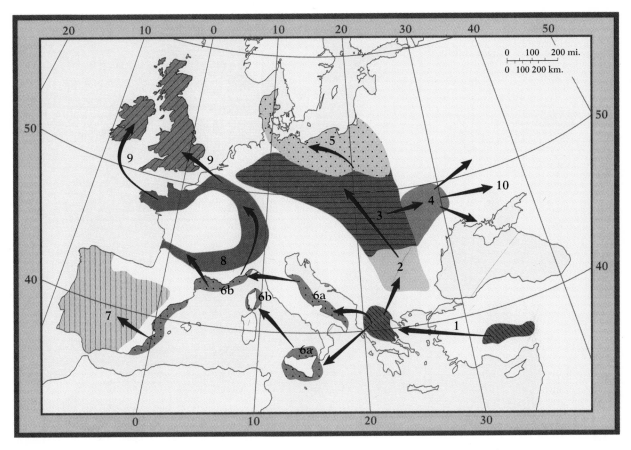

Figure 5.4

The succession of language transformations hypothesized by Colin Renfrew as a parallel to the diffusion of agriculture. Each transformation is indicated by a number. Source: Renfrew 1989.

that about 8500 years ago, agriculture began to spread from Anatolia, in what is today Turkey, to other parts of Europe, due to increasing population pressure. Anatolian farmers, taking the language now called proto-Indo-European with them, first moved into central Greece, later spreading westward and northward from there (Figure 5.4). During the time a group of farmers and their descendants remained in one region, their language, now isolated from the original proto-Indo-European, gradually became transformed into a new one. With the passage of time, the agriculture introduced by these migrants again led to population increases, so some of their descendants migrated in their turn, taking the new languages with them. This process continued exceedingly

slowly—on average, maybe less than a mile a year—until most of Europe had been colonized by farmers. Renfrew estimated that it may have taken 1500 years for the farmers, with their many languages derived from proto-Indo-European, to spread to northern Europe (Figure 5.5).

As the work of Greenberg, Renfrew, and other linguists shows, languages change even as cultures do, and usually through the same mechanisms (see Chapter 16); indeed, linguistic change is a kind of culture change. The process usually happens in one of two basic ways: either two groups of people speaking different languages are brought into contact with one another (by conquest, colonialism, or migration, for example), or members of a group of people speaking one language are separated from

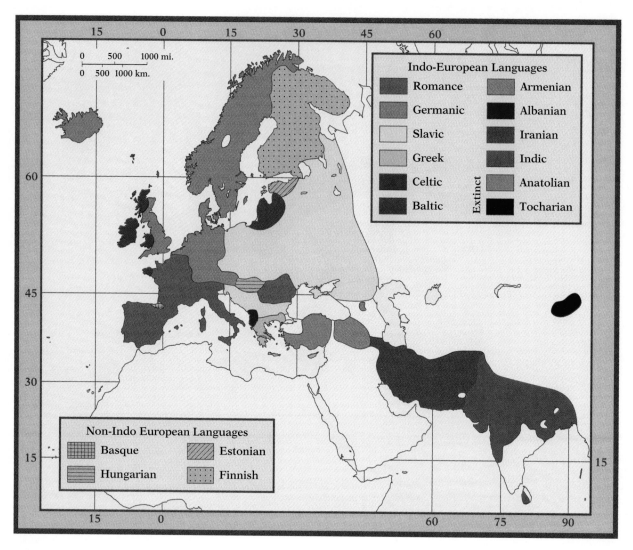

Figure 5.5

The Indo-European languages cover a region stretching from Iceland in the northwest to northeastern India in the southeast. Source: Renfrew 1989:108.

• Ask Yourself •

Have you ever listened to a college professor or other professional person using a specialized vocabulary, and said to yourself, "He's not even speaking my language!" If you eventually become involved in the speaker's professional arena, you will one day be using this strange vocabulary too. This is an example of how new terms are introduced into and spread throughout a language.

one another, either geographically or socially (for instance, by socioeconomic differences), eventually developing unique ways of speaking. Either way, the result is linguistic change, as new words, different spellings, syntactical differences, and even new grammatical rules become standard.

Dialects change in the same way as languages, and because the dialectic differences used by English-speakers in different parts of the United States are more familiar to us than linguistic differences elsewhere, they provide our examples. In the northern states, the cooking surface of a stove is

The Anthropologist at Work

William Labov

Linguistic research has sometimes contributed to solutions for social problems. Education, advertising, medicine, and the law have all benefited from the work of anthropological linguists.

In 1984, a threat to bomb a Pan American Airlines plane at the Los Angeles airport was recorded on tape. A New York man was arrested for the crime, and put on trial. After analyzing the tape, linguist William Labov (1988: 170–181), called as a witness, concluded that the threat had been uttered not by a New Yorker, but by a native New Englander. The California jurors who listened to the tape could not distinguish between New York and New England accents, but by comparing the vowels of the defendant with those of the real bomber, Labov was able to convince the judge the defendant could not have made the call. Despite the circumstantial evidence against him, "the clarity and objectivity of the linguistic evidence" was compelling (Labov 1988:180). The accused was acquitted.

---

usually called a *burner,* while in southern states it is an *eye.* In the middle Atlantic states, a long sandwich is called a *hero,* while in New England it is called a *grinder.* Depending on location, a drink made of milk and ice cream may be called a *milkshake, cabinet,* or *frappe.* But such differences may be the product of another kind of linguistic separation as well; members of different ethnic, socioeconomic, religious, or occupational groups may literally not speak the same language. At the end of this chapter we provide an example of linguistic divergence based on ethnicity and socioeconomic status: the use of Black Vernacular English (BVE).

A once-promising technique for historical linguists, **glottochronology,** was popularized by Morris Swadesh in the 1960s. This was a method for pinpointing the time at which two languages branched off from a common ancestor, thus becoming **sibling languages.** The technique was based on two assumptions. The first was that in every language, some words fade from use and are replaced with new words, whereas others remain in use. Second, the "fading" of core words takes place at a constant rate. Thus, two languages identical in vocabulary at the time their speakers go their separate ways will become increasingly different as time goes on, through word loss and innovation (Renfrew 1987:114–119). The greater the difference between two related languages, the greater the time separating them from their common ancestor.

Promising as it seemed, this method has now been recognized as flawed in several respects. Most damagingly, there is no reason to assume that languages lose words at a constant rate. Social factors, such as whether a community is literate or not, certainly influence vocabulary. As Colin Renfrew (1987:117) has remarked, "Glottochronology in its simple assumptions is just too good to be true."

• Sociolinguistics •

Language is a principal vehicle by means of which people express their thoughts, beliefs, interests, and

---

glottochronology a method for establishing the approximate time at which two languages branched off from a common ancestor

sibling language one of two or more languages that branched off from a common ancestral language

Writing and reading create psychological distance between senders and receivers of words, but speaking and listening bring them physically and psychologically close. As she recounts a tale from Africa's rich oral tradition, Nongenile Masithathu Zenani, a master storyteller of South Africa's Xhosa people (see map on page 353), uses her whole body to entertain and educate her audience.

feelings. But can a language, in addition to performing this function, actually *affect* the thoughts, beliefs, interests and feelings of its speakers, encouraging them to think in certain ways, limiting their imaginations in some ways and expanding them in others, and channeling their intellectual and emotional lives in certain directions? **Sociolinguistics,** a branch of linguistics that focuses on the relationship between language and society, suggests some answers.

From Nonliteracy to Literacy

Some authorities contend that introducing writing into a nonliterate society alters not only the ways

in which people absorb, retain, and transmit information, but also the ways in which they think and arrange their social relationships (Goody 1981; Ong 1982). Thus, in certain important ways (though not in every way), literate people may express themselves and view their world differently from nonliterates. This argument is based in part on studies of poets and storytellers in present-

---

sociolinguistics a branch of linguistics that focuses on the relationship between language and society

• Ask Yourself •

Try to imagine living in a community where no one knows how to read or write, and there is no electronic means of communication. How would this affect your studies? Your job? Your social life?

Anthropology and the Environment

Language and Subsistence

Language is more than a means of communication; it is also a practical tool that enables groups of human beings to thrive in particular environments. Unsurprisingly, therefore, we find that languages reflect the environmental features that most affect their speakers' way of life, and particularly the way they make their living. For example, while English contains only one word for *camel*, the languages of Middle Eastern camel-herding people contain many terms denoting various kinds of camels and the harnesses, saddles, and other trappings that accompany camel herding as a way of life. The wide variety of terms from which camel herders can choose helps them to communicate with one another about a vital matter—their livelihood—more efficiently and precisely than would be possible using the English language. Likewise, the vocabularies of the Native American people of the Northwest Coast of North America, whose ancestors depended heavily on fishing, contain a large number of terms for fish and fishing equipment. The ancestors of many English-speakers were sheep farmers, and English—although most English speakers are unaware of it—contains many words for "sheep." Only a few of them—lamb, ewe, ram—are familiar to most English speakers today, but in the north of England where sheep are economically important, local people speak of *tups, wethers, gimmer hoggs,* and *shearlings.*

The Spanish language evolved from a proto-Indo-European language spoken in Castile, a region of Spain characterized by a rough, mountainous landscape. Reflecting this environment, the Spanish language contains a large number of terms specifying distinctive features of this landscape, as Table 5.4 shows. Creating a vocabulary of terms to distinguish among different types of mountains and hills was a useful linguistic adaptation to life in this rugged environment.

---

day, nonliterate societies and in part on the analysis of the poetry of the great Greek bard, Homer, whose rich oral legacy was written down only after his death. Linguistic scholars have discovered that oral texts are often shaped by their nonliterate contexts. Once literacy is introduced into a society and spoken texts begin to be written down, the stories and poems of the society change radically.

The transition from an oral society to one in which most individuals are literate appears to provoke certain radical changes in culture. Literate people, for example, tend not to view their world as a unified system of categories or explain it in myth, as do many nonliterate people. As literacy develops, formerly nonliterate people reorder their world into fragmented subsystems, in which economics, art, religion, kinship, and politics are seen as separate matters instead of parts of one unified system. This is the kind of view Westerners have created. The philosopher Walter Ong (1982) proposes that the use of an alphabet (a limited series of characters that can be arranged meaningfully only in certain ways) transformed the consciousness of Westerners, who reconstructed their traditional view of the world to make it consistent with the way in which they organized their written language.

Literacy has features that contrast markedly with those of nonliteracy. Literacy stresses the *content* of a linguistic transaction (a tale, poem, or message); nonliteracy places greater emphasis on

Table 5.4
Some Spanish Words Describing Mountains and Hills

Spanish Word	English Meaning
candelas	Literally "candles"; a collection of *peñas*
ceja	Steep-sided breaks or escarpment separating two plains of different elevation
cejita	A low escarpment
cerrillo or *cerrito*	A small *cerro;* a hill
cerro	A single eminence, intermediate in size between English *hill* and *mountain*
chiquito	Literally "small," describing minor secondary fringing elevations at the base of and parallel to a *sierra* or *cordillera*
cordillera	A mass of mountains, as distinguished from a single mountain summit
cuchilla	Literally "knife"; the comblike secondary crests that project at right angles from the sides of a *sierra*
cumbre	The highest elevation or peak within a *sierra* or *cordillera;* a summit
eminencia	A mountainous or hilly protuberance
loma	A hill in the midst of a plain
lomita	A small hill in the midst of a plain
mesa	Literally "table"; a flat-topped eminence
montaña	Equivalent to English *mountain*
pelado	A barren, treeless mountain
pelon	A bare conical eminence
peloncilla	A small *pelon*
peña	A needlelike eminence
picacho	A peaked or pointed eminence
pico	A summit point, English *peak*
sandia	Literally "watermelon"; an oblong, rounded eminence
sierra	An elongated mountain mass with a serrated crest
teta	A solitary, conical mountain in the shape of a woman's breast
tinaja	A solitary, hemispherical mountain shaped like an inverted bowl

Source: Hill 1896:292–297.

the *style* in which it is presented. Literacy also increases the psychological distance between the sender and the receiver of a linguistic transaction, often granting anonymity to the receiver (the reader). Listeners in a nonliterate culture are physically close to the sender, and this affects what the sender will say and the way he or she will say it. Finally, the use of print turns words into texts that are tangible things, existing on flat surfaces at arm's reach, in sharp contrast with the intangible intimacy of the world of sound that envelops the teller of tales in a nonliterate society. In some degree, in other words, the form of language affects human perception.

The Sapir-Whorf Hypothesis

The best-known attempt to demonstrate a relationship between language and perception is called the **Sapir-Whorf hypothesis** (sometimes the **Whorfian hypothesis**), after two linguists, teacher and student, who worked together on the idea that the language we learn as members of our society not only reflects our view of the world and makes it possible for us to express it, but actually structures the way we perceive the world. Edward Sapir (1884–1934) first proposed that the "language habits" of a group of people inform their perception of reality. Later, Benjamin Whorf (1897–1941) expanded on the idea. Speakers of different languages, according to Sapir and Whorf, actually see the world quite differently.

How is this possible? A language, Sapir and Whorf pointed out, consists of a great deal more than a long list of words, each standing for some particular object or concept and directly translatable into another language. If all that we had to work with, linguistically, were lists of words, we could communicate with each other only in a rudimentary way. There would be many concepts we would be unable to express: past, future, or hypothetical action, for example, or the idea of subject and object—which person or thing is acting and which is being acted on. So in addition to its list of words, every language has a set of rules, called its **grammar**.[2] Grammar regulates the order in which words should be spoken so that they make sense, designates what prefixes or suffixes should be added to words to convey precise meanings, and incorporates other guidelines for speakers. Using correct grammar, speakers can convey the idea of action taking place in the future, or of hypothetical action that *might* take place. They can make it clear what or whom is an actor and what or whom is being acted on, or suggest possession or emphasis.

Sapir and Whorf hypothesized that both our words and our grammar shape the way we see reality. Facts, objects, people, and events can be classified in many different ways. In English, for example, we refer to all our cousins by the same term, *cousin*. But this term includes a wide variety of people, of both sexes and from both sides of the family. Other languages lump together relatives that English separates, and separate relatives English lumps together.

The word for *mother's sister's daughter* may be different from the word for *father's sister's daughter*, both *cousins* in English, or the word for *mother's sister's daughter* may be the same as the word for *sister*. Such verbal classifications are important. As we shall see in Chapter 9, in some cultures certain cousins are considered potential spouses, but in others they are prohibited as spouses. The use of terms such as *cousin* and *sister* reflects these practices.

Whorf's ideas came in part from his study of the language of the Hopi of the American Southwest. In the Hopi language, the past, present, and future tenses, as we use them in English, do not exist. Instead, Hopi speakers distinguish two different states of existence into which all events fit: the state of being, in terms of which the Hopi discuss things that have actually existed in the past or actually exist now, and the (potential) state of becoming, in terms of which they discuss things that will or might happen in the future. According to Whorf, the Hopi view of time likewise differs noticeably from ours. We view time as a linear progression, he argued, because our language uses different tenses for verbs. The Hopi, because their language lacks these tenses, do not (Carroll 1956).

There has been some anthropological support for the Sapir-Whorf hypothesis. Basing her work on Malinowski's data from the Trobriands (see map on page 19), Dorothy Lee (1985) argued that English and Trobriand speakers have different worldviews because their languages are ordered by different grammars. Our worldview is ordered *lineally*. Whenever possible, we impose lines on the world around us: we *draw* conclusions, *trace* relationships, and envision the present as having *developed* from the past. We think, in other words, in terms of causality, movement, and progress. Trobrianders see things differently. Rather than being lineally arranged, their world is based on the idea of eternal, self-contained patterns of objects, actions, and events. Since there is no past or present, one thing does not cause another. An action

---

[2] *Grammar* differs from *universal grammar*, defined previously.

Sapir-Whorf hypothesis (Whorfian hypothesis) the idea that the way in which the members of a society order their world is conditioned by their language

grammar the rules governing word order, prefixes and suffixes, and other aspects of a language.

may be completed, but this doesn't mean it is over; "it may (still) be present or timeless" (Lee 1985:114). A yam, to the Trobrianders, is a yam, period. It does not *become* overripe. An overripe yam is another thing altogether. Events do not lead to other events; they form elements in patterned wholes. Tenses do not exist in the Trobriand language, which also lacks words to express causal relationships.

If we were to describe what is going on when we plant a coconut, we would probably use a time line and assume that specific actions produce specific results: "first we do action A, then we do action B, which causes event C to happen." Here is a translation of a Trobriand description of what happens when a coconut is planted; strings of words with hyphens between them represent single words in the Trobriand language:

> Thou-approach-there coconut thou-bring-here-we plant-coconut thou-go-thou-plant our coconut. This-here it-emerge sprout. We-push-away this other coconut-husk-fiber together sprout it-sit together root.

The Trobrianders do not make lineal connections between the various steps involved in planting a coconut, nor do they draw a causal relationship between the planting and the subsequent sprouting. Although this lack of a sense of action and reaction may seem peculiar, Lee discerns a good fit between the Trobrianders' language and their worldview. The Trobrianders understand what continuity is, but *progress* as speakers of English use the term is not important to them (or at least not in Malinowski's day). Value, in the Trobriand view of the world, lies in the sameness of things, in repeated

• Ask Yourself •

The vocabulary of a language reflects the interests and pursuits of the people who speak it. Thus, the "world" languages, such as English and Russian, incorporate numerous scientific and technological terms. What words might be found in languages spoken in nonliterate societies that are not found in the "world" languages?

patterns. What is good is that which is the same as it was in the past. As Whorf claimed for the Hopi language, the Trobriand language makes the past, present, and future one and the same, and the Trobrianders' use of language reflects this attitude.

The Sapir-Whorf hypothesis is attractive to some anthropologists for its cultural relativism, but it has not won universal acceptance, partly because tests carried out to verify it have not always succeeded (Polomé 1990:462). Still, there does not seem to be much doubt that language influences the view a community has of the world it lives in and, as the Zimmermans discovered (Malcolm 1981), is intimately connected with other aspects of culture. In fact, words may not even be the most important aspect of a language. When we speak, we are doing more than simply trying to make a listener understand what we think and feel. We are also trying to define our relationship with the listener, to identify ourselves as a member of some social group, or to persuade the listener to accept some point of view. Like us, the speakers of other languages use words to convey a host of deeper cultural messages—perhaps to reinforce gender or class distinctions between people, for example, or to identify themselves with a particular social group or ideology.

A good cross-cultural example of the intimate link between language and culture can be found in the variable ways in which color terms are used. Because people in different societies use color terms for different purposes, their languages express the idea of color in different ways. Some languages use many words to represent colors; some use few. Others—for example, the language of the Nuba, cattle herders of the Sudan, in Africa (see map on page 379)—have no term at all meaning "color." This made it confusing for the ethnographer of the Nuba, James Faris, to discuss color with them. Once when Faris asked about the color of palm leaves, he was given a word he later learned means "crisp."

The Nuba combine all the colors for which Westerners have separate words into only four terms, which correspond roughly to the English words black, white, red, and yellow (Faris 1972:59). The Nuba term for black covers dark red, brown, purple, and blue. White is used for very light colors—pale blue, pale green, pink, and grey. Red suggests not only the various shades of what English speakers would describe as red but pink and orange as well; and yellow refers to what we would call green, greenish yellow, yellow, and blue-green. Possibly the Nuba (and other people whose languages contain relatively few color terms) do not see and distinguish shades of color in the same manner as other people (Ember 1978), although when they need to they can describe the colors of objects accurately by using their four basic color terms together with other descriptive terms meaning, for instance, "dark" or "light." It seems more likely that this aspect of Nuba language is a reflection of Nuba culture: making fine distinctions between different colors is not particularly important in the technologically simple life of the Nuba.

Gender and Language

Sociolinguistics has found an important place in contemporary studies of gender (Todd and Fisher 1988), since there can be significant differences in the ways in which women and men use language. In an important though much-criticized book on language use in the United States, *Language and Woman's Place* (1975), feminist Robin Lakoff used the term *women's language* for two things: (a) the language American women customarily use, and (b) the language used in American society to describe women. Both, Lakoff believes, can deprive a woman of her identity as a person.

The "polite" style of speech that American females are supposedly taught to use may encourage them to express uncertainty rather than decisiveness. In the following example, (A) may be either a man or woman, and (B) is a woman:

(A) When will dinner be ready?

(B) Oh . . . around six o'clock . . . ?

Some linguists believe that American women are taught a different, more "polite" style of speech than men, which makes them seem uncertain and indecisive. In this conversation, the man at left does appear to have the upper hand, although age, position, or other factors besides gender may be the reason.

Using the paralanguage Lakoff believes typical of American women, (B) responds to the question using a rising intonation, indicated by the question mark. This suggests to Lakoff (1975:17) that the woman is seeking confirmation from (A), even though she is the person who has the requested information. (B) is placing herself in the position of requiring confirmation, even approval, from (A). She sounds unsure of herself, as if she were saying "Six o'clock, if that's okay with you." Lakoff argued that one result of this "polite" speech will be that (B) will be thought of as someone who cannot be taken seriously or trusted with any real responsibility, since "she can't make up her mind" and "isn't sure of

herself." In short, her speech pattern is taken to reflect something about her character and abilities. Lakoff concluded that if (B) were a man, he would be much more likely to reply with something like:

(B) Six o'clock, and you'd better be here!

Certain American linguistic conventions, Lakoff (1975:23) believes, may subtly denigrate women. For example, in a sentence in which either the word *woman* or the word *lady* might be used, the choice of *lady* may trivialize the subject under discussion. Lakoff describes a newspaper article that referred to its female subject as a "lady atheist." Using *lady* in this context, Lakoff thinks, reduces the woman's position to that of a scatterbrained eccentric, some-one not to be taken seriously.

The hypothesis that American women speak more tentatively than men because they seek affirmation has been effectively challenged on two grounds: first, that Lakoff (1975) failed to support it with hard data, and second, that the hypothesis was grounded in feminist ideology, which caused Lakoff to assume an existing (but never demonstrated) link between a particular way of speaking and the absence of female assertiveness. Far from regarding this style of speaking as "weak," others see it as an attractive way of expressing oneself (Hamilton et al. 1991:104). Moreover, Lakoff ignores ethnographic evidence from Canada, the United Kingdom, and Australia, where some men habitually end sentences on a rising note (Cameron et al. 1989:75–76). The meanings of linguistic forms can be understood only if we also consider other factors, including the roles being played by participants in an interaction, the objectives of the interaction, and participants' status relative to one another and to the social context in which the interaction takes place (Cameron et al. 1989:91–92). Gender is at best only one factor.

Psychological anthropology provides an alternative interpretation of "women's language." Carol Gilligan hypothesizes that middle-class American girls are enculturated differently from boys. While girls are urged to maintain ties with their families (particularly their mothers), boys are encouraged to sever these ties. Because of these differences in enculturation, women choose a different form of speech, a form in which they can express empathy: identification with the feelings and interests of others (Boe 1987). The lack of solid evidence that females have greater empathy than males weakens this hypothesis also, but it is an intriguing one all the same, since it encourages anthropological linguists to look for possible connections between language and children's enculturation in different societies.

Pidgins and Creoles

Sociolinguists are also interested in the social contexts in which new languages are created.

pidgin a language in which the syntax and vocabulary of two other languages are simplified and combined

A sign in St. Lucia, West Indies, guides visitors in two languages, English and the local creole. The contributions of both French and English to St. Lucian creole are evident: "plas," deriving from the identical French and English word "place," is pronounced as in French; "wichach" is related to the English word "research"; and "foklo" is creole for the English "folklore." The word order is French.

Composite languages called *pidgins* and *creoles* provide examples of how languages come into being (Holm 1989).

When two people wish to communicate but neither knows the other's native tongue, they may use elements from both tongues, or even a third. In a **pidgin** language, the syntax and vocabulary of the "lender" language are greatly simplified. Prepositions may be omitted, and tenses may be limited to the present. For example, if you were a member of one language community and wanted to comfort a person of another language community who had injured his leg, instead of declaring in your own language "Your leg will get well again," you might say, in pigdin, "Bimeby [by and by] leg belong you he-all-right gain [again]." Or, to ask at a hardware store for a pan in which to cook bread, you might say: "Me like-im saucepan belong cook-im bread" (Hudson 1980:64).

Since pidgin languages tend to evolve from people's practical need to communicate, usually for purposes of commerce, they are sometimes called *trade languages*. One famous pidgin language, from which the examples above are taken, is Neo-Melanesian Pidgin, or Tok Pisin (from *tok* meaning "talk," and *pisin* meaning "pidgin"). This has become the standard language of trade and administration in New Guinea (see maps on pages 166, 198, and 385), where many dozens of different languages are spoken. Using Tok Pisin, speakers of all these different languages can communicate. The use of Tok Pisin in preference to other local languages can also convey subtle social messages; in one village in New Guinea, the use of Tok Pisin carries with it the idea that the speaker is literate, Christian, and engaged in modern commercial enterprise (Kulik 1992). Perhaps not surprisingly, the young people of the village in question speak only Tok Pisin. The previous local language, now used only by the elderly, is dying out.

Although a pidgin language tends to be something of a "minimum language," pidgins do not lack rules of syntax. They have syntactical rules, and linguists consider them real languages.

Should a pidgin language evolve to the point where it actually becomes the mother tongue of a community, it is called a **creole** (Bickerton 1983). Creolization might occur, for example, in a setting in which husbands and wives, each with different native tongues, speak pidgin at home. Their children learn pidgin as their only and therefore native language, so for them, their parents' pidgin has become their creole. This happened on a large scale among African slaves brought to the New World. Residents of several formerly slave-holding islands in the West Indies speak a creole language (locally called *patois*, although this term is used for creoles and dialects outside the West Indies as well) that combines English and French (the languages of the former slave owners). In West Indian patois, the sentence "Now we're going to discuss patois" becomes "A pwesent nous parlee about patois," thus combining French and English elements. Today, there are more speakers of creole languages such as West Indian patois than of pidgin languages: 10 to 17 million, compared with between 6 and 12 million (Hudson 1980:66).

When a speaker switches from one language or dialect to another depending on his or her audience, this is called **code switching** (Heller 1988). People in some parts of the world do this easily and continually. The choice of which language to use is carefully, if sometimes unconsciously, calculated to reflect social realities such as the self-identity of the speaker or the relationship between speaker and listener (Myers-Scotton 1993). Being able to speak more than one language with equal, or roughly equal, competence is called **bilingualism.** When a person from Kenya, east Africa, codeswitches between English and the local language, Kiswahili, she may consciously or unconsciously want to convey to her listener that she is both African and well-educated. In English-speaking Caribbean countries, native-born people are skillful codeswitchers. Routinely speaking creole when conversing informally at home, they speak English, their official language and the one taught in schools, while they are at work.

Social Status, Personality, and Language

Language can establish differences in social status between people, express such differences—and even influence the personality of speakers. The languages spoken in Indonesia, a former Dutch colony, provide an example. Until the end of the nineteenth century, the Dutch colonialists used their power to restrain local people from speaking Dutch. As one local observer commented, "European languages . . . are carefully excluded from . . . all the native schools, from an apprehension . . . that such knowledge might possibly prove too dangerous a weapon in the hands of the natives" (quoted in Krauss 1994:381). Instead, Indonesians were obliged to speak one of the hundreds of languages spoken by local ethnic groups, or Malay, a trade language.

During the Dutch colonial period, a man named

---

creole a pidgin language that has become the mother tongue of a community

code switching switching from one language or dialect into another language or dialect

bilingualism being able to speak more than one language with equal, or roughly equal, competence

Raden Saleh (1811–1880) lived on Indonesia's main island, Java. In childhood Saleh had learned to speak his native Javanese as well as Malay. Later, as an adult, he traveled in Europe (which was unusual for an Indonesian of the time), and learned several European languages. Recently, a series of letters written by Saleh has been studied by Werner Krauss. Some, written in Malay, were to a Dutch colonial official in the Netherlands; others, in German, were to a German duke. In his Malay-language letters, Saleh comes across as a stereotypical nineteenth-century Javanese person addressing a European: his words seem defensive, lacking in

self-assurance, "simple and child-like" (Krauss 1994:384). But a completely different personality appears in the letters composed in the German language. These portray Saleh as a "cosmopolitan dandy and artist, intellectually and emotionally . . . mature, a man responsible for his own destiny" (Krauss 1994:384).

Why the striking difference between the two "personalities"? Krauss finds the explanation in the context of contemporary Dutch-Indonesian relationships of status and power. Because Malay was a trade language, used for commercial purposes rather than to spread knowledge or support personal growth, it was depreciated by Dutch and Indonesians alike. Learning this language of "submission and obsequiousness" as a child caused Saleh to assimilate these attitudes (Krauss 1994:388). By contrast, German, a language spoken by sophisticated Europeans, conveyed high prestige on its speakers. In learning German as an adult in Germany, Saleh acquired the self-confident personality of one speaking a high-status language.

Black Vernacular English

The term **vernacular** denotes the standard language or dialect of a population. **Black Vernacular English (BVE)** is a dialect of English, thought by linguists to contain remnants of the African languages once used by slaves, which is spoken by black youths involved in the street culture of the inner cities of the United States (Labov 1984:xiii; Lee 1994). Black Vernacular English differs from *Black English*, a term that refers to the entire range of linguistic forms used by black people in the United States—from the creole language called **gullah,** spoken in coastal South Carolina, to the most formal literary style (Labov 1984:xii). There are a number of reasons for the persistence of BVE in American cities, among them the increasing isolation of inner-city blacks from middle-class American culture, speakers' desire to assert their cultural distinction by using an "in-group" code, and the stigma attached to using "proper" English in some inner-city settings (Lee 1994:1). In its syntax, phonology, and vocabulary, BVE differs so much from the forms of English spoken by white, middle-class Americans that some have considered it

---

vernacular the standard language or dialect of a population

Black Vernacular English (BVE) a dialect of English spoken by black youths in the inner cities of the United States

gullah a creole language spoken by black residents of coastal South Carolina

unacceptable in the context of American society, and have tried to discourage its use.

Labov (1984) has described some of the distinctive properties of BVE. For example, the form of the verb *to be* used in standard American English is omitted in certain constructions ("He a teacher"; "he happy"; "he with them"). The position of negatives is sometimes inverted ("Ain't nobody gon' hit you"). And the word *it* is sometimes used as a substitute for *there* ("It ain't nothin' happenin'").

Until the 1970s, when studies of BVE began to be published, such deviations from standard American English were believed by many authorities to be evidence that BVE was merely an inferior form of English. Black students who expressed themselves in BVE and who failed to understand questions put to them by their teachers in standard American English were regarded as less capable of learning than their white peers. A middle-class white teacher hearing a student say, "I don't want none" or "they hers" would sometimes consider the student to be suffering from "verbal deprivation" rather than as speaking a legitimate dialect of English.

Recent research has suggested that BVE may be considered a legitimate form of English. Its syntax, phonology, and other linguistic features make up a linguistic system well suited for communication. Today, some teachers in American inner-city schools believe their goal should be to encourage black students to retain their skills at using BVE, the dialect they need to function in their home environment, and at the same time enable them to acquire the standard dialect of American English that they need to succeed in the wider society. Some now teach standard English as a second language (Lee 1994:1).

Conclusion

Like the Wild Boy of Aveyron (Chapter 2), who was unable to communicate with other human beings or participate in human society, those who are not born into a cultural setting cannot behave in a way we consider really human. Without language, culture—the most distinctive hallmark of human beings—is impossible. It could not exist, much less

develop or be transmitted to others. Nothing contributes more to making human beings human than language.

Not only is language a unique human ability; it is also a compelling human need. Human beings, it seems, *must* communicate—must put their feelings into forms that enable others to understand them. This is the most important way human beings have of coming together, of creating society. The social institutions described in later chapters, such as marriage and political organizations, could not have come into being without language.

Summary

- Some form of communication, using vocalizations, gestures, or a combination of the two, is thought to have evolved among our hominid ancestors. No one knows when spoken language developed, although it is certain that by the time anatomically modern human beings emerged some 35,000 years ago, they could speak.

- The first attempt at writing is likewise undocumented, but some prehistoric people made graphic representations that may have been the ancestors of writing.

- Studies of the way children learn language and the use of sign languages suggest that a biologically determined cognitive ability underlies human linguistic ability.

- Language can be studied from several perspectives, synchronic and diachronic. These perspectives include analyzing the individual sounds, vocabulary, and grammar of specific languages, written or unwritten; studying the history and development of a language; discovering how human beings learn languages; examining how language influences human thought and culture; and examining the ways human beings use language as an instrument of interaction.

- Descriptive linguistics involves the study of the sounds and sound combinations that make up a given language and the ways in which these can be arranged so as to be meaningful.

- Historical linguistics deals with the history of the world's languages—how they developed, how they have changed through time, and how they are related to one another.

- Sociolinguistics focuses on the ways in which language affects, and is affected by, thought and culture. Sociolinguists study how nonliteracy and literacy influence culture; how language structures the way human beings perceive the world (an idea called the Sapir-Whorf hypothesis); how language reflects gender attitudes; how composite languages called *pidgins* and *creoles* develop; and how dialects of standard English, such as Black Vernacular English, are used.

- Culture could not exist without language.

Key Terms

bilingualism
Black Vernacular English (BVE)
code switchng
cognate
comparative linguistics
conjugate
core vocabulary
creole
cuneiform
decline
descriptive linguistics
dialect
glottochronology
grammar
gullah
historical linguistics
hominids
morpheme (morphology)
paralanguage
phoneme (phonology)
pictograph
pidgin
prefix
prime
protolanguage
Sapir-Whorf hypothesis (Whorfian hypothesis)
sibling language
sign language
sociolinguistics
suffix
syntax
universal grammar
vernacular
writing

Suggested Readings

Crystal, David. 1980. *A First Dictionary of Linguistics and Phonetics.* Boulder, CO: Westview Press. Many anthropologists find the linguistic branch of their discipline confusing because of its large technical vocabulary. This dictionary presents an admirable solution to their problem. Its clarity and comprehensiveness make it indispensable to anyone wishing a command of linguistic terms, and we have relied on it heavily in this chapter.

Darnell, Regna. 1990. *Edward Sapir: Linguist, Anthropologist, Humanist.* Berkeley: University of California Press. A biography of the famous linguist whose studies of Native American languages helped to establish the subfields of historical and descriptive linguistics.

Giglioli, Pier Paolo (ed.). 1986 (orig. 1972). *Language and Social Context.* Harmondsworth, Middlesex, U.K.: Penguin Books. Fifteen articles, each by a different linguistic authority, give cross-cultural treatment to three topics: face-to-face interaction; the relationship among language, social structure, and cultural traits; and the relationship among language, conflict, and social change.

Graddol, David, and **Joan Swann.** 1989. *Gender Voices.* Oxford: Basil Blackwell. A well-reasoned cross-cultural comparison of how language and gender influence each other without the ideological bias that usually skews such studies.

Hall, Clifford, and **Paul Byers.** 1992. *Ambiguous Harmony: Family Talk in America.* Norwood, NJ: Ablex. By dissecting just 15 minutes of "ordinary talk" among members of an American family, the authors of this entertaining and readable book provide a valuable illustration of the close connection between language and culture.

Lyons, John. 1981. *Noam Chomsky.* New York: Viking. The famous linguist's own books and articles tend to be a bit weighty for nonlinguists. Lyons's review of Noam Chomsky's work will make his interesting hypothesis clearer to students.

Renfrew, Colin. 1987. *Archaeology and Language: The Puzzle of Indo-European Origins.* Cambridge: Cambridge University Press. A fascinating and readable example of how linguistic analysis is used to trace population movements.

Steedman, Carolyn, et al. (eds.) 1985. *Language, Gender and Childhood.* London: Routledge and Kegan Paul. A collection of eight essays on the ways in which language is central to the positions of women and girls in society, and how such positions have come about.

Trudgill, Peter. 1983 (orig. 1974). *Sociolinguistics: An Introduction to Language and Society* (rev. ed.). Harmondsworth, Middlesex, U.K.: Penguin Books. Demonstrates how gender, class, and religion create differences within as well as between languages. The book also discusses the influence of language on the way people think and on the cultural traits they have created.

Introduction

"Tennessee," panhandling on a busy downtown Los Angeles street corner, tells any passerby who will listen that he is trying to collect money to buy a bus

ticket back home to the state that gave him his name (Corwin 1984:3). His friend "Tom" asserts proudly that he has not looked for steady work in years; occasionally he unloads trucks to make a few dollars, but he prefers just to hang out. Tennessee and Tom are members of a group of homeless men whose base of operations is a Los Angeles park. By begging, scrounging, eating some of their meals free at local churches, wearing used clothing, and protecting themselves from the elements with newspapers, cardboard boxes, sheets of plastic, and an occasional night in a city-run shelter, these homeless men not only survive but also claim to be enjoying life.

Many of the homeless in America's cities are victims of the economy, unable to find the steady work they need to obtain permanent homes and reliable sources of food, clothing, and other necessities of life. Some are alcoholics (see Spradley 1970), some have AIDS or other diseases, some are mentally ill. But others, like Tennessee and Tom, are apparently content with their unusual way of life. Determinedly self-reliant, they have deliberately chosen their hand-to-mouth existence. Their strategy for procuring the things they want and need is quite different from that of most Americans, but it seems to work for them.

Many homeless people in the United States want permanent homes and steady jobs, but others claim they have developed a satisfactory strategy for procuring the things they want and need. In Washington, D.C., a homeless man passes the White House, pushing his "household" in a shopping cart.

This chapter is about the different ways in which people obtain the necessities of life, and how different natural environments, technologies, social relationships, activities, and ways of thinking all come together to produce different kinds of cultures. We call the complex of technologies, activities, and ideas that together add up to a particular way of making a living within a particular environment an **adaptation** to that environment.

• Collecting Versus Producing •

The term **subsistence** refers to all of the ways in which people get the basics they need to live—food and drink, clothing, shelter, security, and warmth. There are two main subsistence methods, collection and production: people can collect things that have already been provided by nature, or they can produce the things they need. Some win their subsistence by combining the two.

Subsistence based entirely on the collection of necessities from the natural environment, which once characterized all human life, is by far the older of the two ways of making a living, having been practiced for over 2 million years. The adaptation of Tennessee and Tom, who collect rather than produce the things they need to survive, may seem similar to this way of life, but there is a major difference: instead of collecting from the natural environment, they rely on the productive efforts of others. Collecting subsistence necessities from the natural environment is extremely rare today.

Subsistence based on producing food and other necessities is a relatively recent human adaptation. This way of life began at different times in different places, so no precise date can be given. But all over the world, the drama unfolded in much the same way: after thousands of generations of collecting, people began to manipulate their natural environment to make it more productive. The first steps must have been simple: since some berry bushes produce more berries after a forest fire, perhaps someone set a fire intentionally in order to have more berries to pick; or perhaps someone noticed that wild rice plants produced more rice when they were not surrounded by other plants, and removed the competing plants from places where wild rice grew. Over many generations, human beings increasingly tried to shape the environment to their own needs. Eventually, probably after thousands of years, they domesticated both plants and animals for food and other uses (Figure 6.1).

The change from collecting to producing was thus a gradual process rather than a single event. Producing did not become widespread anywhere in the world until some ten thousand years ago. Subsequently, more and more wild plants and animals were domesticated, and eventually people developed the expertise to decide for themselves just where various species would reproduce and how much reproduction would take place. The impact of producing on human life and culture was so revolutionary that the shift from a lifestyle based on collection to one based on production is called the **Neolithic** ("new stone") **revolution** after the kinds of stone tools people were making at the time.

Plant domestication encouraged the establishment of villages and towns, because farmers generally need to live in permanent proximity to their crops in order to tend, protect, and harvest them. When people began living in settled communities, their way of adapting to their environment became more complex. Some produced no subsistence necessities at all, instead producing goods or services that they could exchange for the things they needed. This kind of specialization remains with us today.

The nineteenth-century cultural evolutionists correctly identified a general trend in human history from collecting (by **gathering and hunting**) to simple methods of production (such as growing crops and rearing animals by simple methods) to

---

adaptation a complex of ideas, activities, and technologies that add up to a particular way of making a living

subsistence all the ways in which people get the things they need to subsist

Neolithic revolution the shift in human subsistence from collecting to producing subsistence needs

gathering and hunting the nonproducing method of subsistence

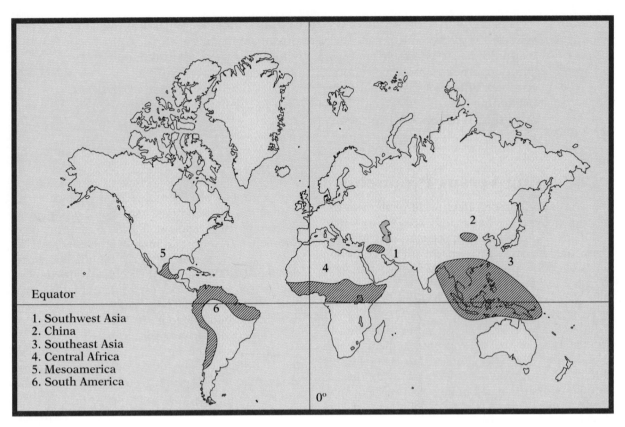

Figure 6.1

Probable Locations of Early Plant and Animal Domestication.

more complex methods of production (such as mechanized agriculture and industrialism). There are many variations on these ways of life, but they all fit under one of the two basic subsistence methods: collecting or producing. Some subsistence activities fit under either one. Shellfishing, for instance, can be considered either collecting or—if shellfish are being encouraged to reproduce in certain places and then are harvested like crops—simple food producing.

Not every society has moved from one subsistence method to the next, much less at the same rate, so over the last ten thousand years many different adaptations have existed simultaneously. This remains true today. Nor do clear-cut dividing lines separate one way of life from another; members of a single society can gather food, hunt game, and grow crops. But to make our description clearer, we shall discuss contemporary people's major adaptations as if they were distinct from one another, addressing such questions as what societies practice each adaptation now and in what environments, what methods contemporary people use to get the things they need, how the work of getting these things is shared, and (most important) what it would be like to live in a society that bases its livelihood on a given adaptation.

• Collecting: Gatherers • and Hunters

Out of a current world population of more than 5 billion people, only an estimated 250,000, or about $\frac{1}{20,000}$ of the world's total, currently rely on gathering and hunting. Despite their rarity, however, gatherers and hunters are of exceptional interest to anthropologists, for three reasons. First, theirs is by far the oldest adaptation; indeed, for most of human history, it was the only one. People have been gatherers and hunters for so long that 98 percent of the direct ancestors of every person on this earth pursued this way of life. Second, during the almost inconceivably long period of time in which all people were gatherers and hunters, they established some basic behavior patterns that are still with us today, such as family units, cooperation in food procurement, and commodity exchange. To understand why people behave as they do today, it is helpful to look at our gatherer-and-hunter roots. Third, the small number of gatherers and hunters is rapidly dwindling. There were many more of them in the last century than now, but even in the nineteenth century, anthropologists could see that if they did not study gatherers and hunters promptly and thoroughly, the opportunity would be forever lost.

In the past, most gatherers and hunters lived in temperate surroundings, but over the years they have disappeared from their traditional homelands. Some moved and some adopted another way of life, but most became extinct. In every case the reason

was competition from other people who practiced a different adaptation. Today the world's remaining gatherers and hunters live in inhospitable, marginal environments, such as the Arctic, deserts, and forests, in which subsistence is at best uncertain.

The absence of contemporary gatherers and hunters from the temperate zone makes it difficult for us to know how earlier gatherers and hunters lived in such environments, although archaeology can help. More than fifteen thousand years ago, the ancestors of today's Europeans lived a gathering and hunting way of life, sheltering themselves in the mouths of caves in what is now continental Europe. Based on evidence from sites in France and Spain (see Figure 14.1 on page 348), archaeologists have discovered that environmental conditions in western Europe were much more hospitable than the term *Ice Age* suggests. Vast grasslands were home to herds of reindeer, horses, and cattle, whose bones litter Ice Age sites. The remains of bear, deer, and wild pigs show that prehistoric people also exploited forests, where they

Of the world's population of over 5 billion people, only about a quarter of a million rely solely on gathering and hunting to get the things they want and need. In the Kalihari desert of Botswana, Africa, a San gatherer and hunter digs for edible roots.

In gatherer-and-hunter bands, men do the big-game hunting. This activity may not provide as much food as the gathering done by women, but it can strengthen social bonds. A nineteenth-century painting shows Native American Hidatsa hunters working together to kill buffalo.

probably gathered nuts, fruits, and other plant foods as well. (The remains of these foods do not often survive for archaeologists to recover.) Cave paintings of leaping salmon show that streams were also a source of food (Pfeiffer 1982:61–62). In short, some Ice Age environments, far from being marginal, offered gatherers and hunters a wide range of plant and animal life to exploit. From this comfortable subsistence base, they were able to develop a rich and long-lived culture of technological sophistication and artistic accomplishment.

All gatherers and hunters share certain features. First, since they must move from time to time in search of food (often with the seasons), they live in temporary camps. They can accumulate little beyond the clothes on their backs, tools, and perhaps a few ornaments, since they must carry any possessions with them when they move. Thus, indi-

vidual ownership of property, common among more settled people, is not well established among gatherers and hunters, and the few objects they do have are apt to be temporary rather than permanent possessions. They make their tools and shelters when and where required, and when these things have served their functions, they are abandoned, to be replaced when needed. Food, too, is generally collected when required; storing it would tie the group to one place.[1]

Second, gatherers and hunters live in small social units of 25 to 50 people practicing the same subsistence strategy and related to one another by kinship or marriage. The size of such a group, which

---

[1] Exceptions occur. For example, certain Inuit people, arctic gatherers and hunters, store food in frozen caches.

anthropologists call a **band,** is apt to fluctuate considerably, as births, deaths, and marriages add or subtract members or as resource scarcities or conflicts cause members to split up. Ultimately, however, the size of a band is limited by the **carrying capacity** of its environment—the maximum number of people who can live indefinitely within a given area at a given level of technology (Zubrow 1975:15).

Third, gatherers and hunters allocate tasks according to sex and age. Women usually gather fruits, nuts, seeds, and berries, and sometimes small animals, shellfish, eggs, or insects as well. This work provides most of the group's calories (Dahlberg 1981). Women also prepare the meals. Despite women's major contribution to subsistence, however, their work is not usually as highly valued as men's work. Adult men hunt, providing the group with much of its animal protein, although hunting is usually less a contributor to the food supply than it is a way for males to enhance their individual prestige or strengthen social bonds through collective effort. One efficient method of hunting is the drive, in which adult males (and occasionally females as well) join forces to goad their prey into waiting traps, using fires or shouts or beating the bushes

Females sometimes hunt small game, but it is rare for them to hunt big animals. Big-game hunting is dangerous, and societies with few members need to protect their females from danger, since it is they who produce the children that perpetuate the group. Even if most of a small group's males were to die in hunting accidents, those remaining could father many children. But should too many of a small group's females die, the few remaining females, giving birth at the average rate of less than one child per year, would be unable to ensure the continued existence of the group. Perhaps another reason why females rarely hunt big game is that this activity is incompatible with looking after children. There are, however, exceptions. Among the Agta of the northern Philippines, some women fish and hunt wild pigs alongside men (Estioko-Griffin and Griffin 1993:206).

Most bands are characterized by egalitarianism. This does not mean that everyone is equal, but rather that everyone of the same sex and age has roughly the same standing in society. Among middle-aged men, for example, there is no boss who can command his fellows because of his superior social status, education, or wealth. Perhaps because

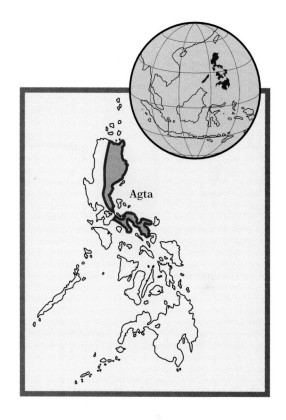

property cannot be accumulated, no one can be "richer" or "better" than the next person. Then, too, since a person's job is usually the same as that of everyone else of the same age and sex, no superior positions exist for the ambitious to seek. Thus, the only major differences in social position are those based on sex or age; older persons are usually accorded more respect than younger ones, and their opinions carry more weight. Women may have a somewhat higher status in bands than in other types of societies; decisions affecting the group are usually arrived at by consensus, and women have a say. They may even wield a good deal of influence. Agta women, who provide their families with both gathered and hunted resources, "have

band a group of gatherers and hunters; alternatively, a particular kind of political organization (see Chapter 12)

carrying capacity the maximum number of people who can live indefinitely within a given area at a given level of technology

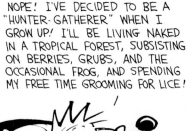

© *CALVIN & HOBBES copyright 1993 Watterson. Distributed by Universal Press Syndicate.*
Reprinted by permission. All rights reserved.

considerable authority in decision making in the family and in residential groups" (Estioko-Griffin and Griffin 1993:206).

Warfare is relatively uncommon among gatherers and hunters, for several reasons. Property, a major cause of conflict in some societies, is far less important in bands than in most other types of society. Bands or their members do not "own" land, for example. Instead, members of different bands acknowledge one another's rights to exploit any area. Peaceful relations are also encouraged by the fact that band members typically marry members of other such groups, so people in one band are likely to have relatives in others. This is not to say that conflict never arises between gatherer-and-hunter groups, but when it does, it is more likely to be resolved by the disputing parties' moving further apart than by fighting

Anthropologists used to assume that all gatherers and hunters lived in a condition of want. A wandering lifestyle and a lack of material goods seemed to suggest an impoverished existence and a constant struggle to survive. But recent studies have shown that some prehistoric gatherers and hunters, particularly those who occupied hospitable environments, may have enjoyed a comfortable lifestyle (Sahlins 1974). In many parts of the temperate zone, nature provided food, water, and the materials for shelter and clothing in sufficient abundance to have made it probably unnecessary for people to work more than a few hours a day. Even some gatherers and hunters today seem to have plenty of time free from the necessity of searching for food. If affluence is defined as having everything one wants and needs, then—as anthropologist Marshall Sahlins (1974) points out—gatherers and hunters are "the original affluent society." Still, the majority of today's gatherers and hunters are hardly affluent, because of the marginal environments they have been shunted into by people of more powerful societies. Many must work hard merely to survive. The Inuit (see Chapters 1, 12, 14, and 16) are a striking example.

• Ask Yourself •

Do you agree with Sahlins's definition of affluence? As a college student, what goods or other resources would you need to consider yourself affluent?

• Simple Production Methods •

How Production Began

Why, where, when, and how the production of subsistence necessities began is unclear. Human beings may have domesticated plants and animals as early as the end of the last Ice Age, which would make "cave people" the world's first producers. This could have begun when a gatherer realized that there were ways in which she could alter the natural environment to encourage the growth of certain plants. Selective burning, weeding, pruning, and transplanting are all effective, nonagricultural ways to produce food crops (Bender 1975). Or perhaps gathering and hunting people began transplanting and cultivating flowers for the pleasure of their appearance and smell, and subsequently discovered how to grow crops for more practical reasons (Smith 1975). Playing with pets may have provided the knowledge necessary for animal domestication (Smith 1975). Worsening climatic conditions, such as a long drought, may have forced some gatherers and hunters to develop other ways of getting food, or perhaps some bands grew to exceed the carrying capacity of their local environments, prompting their members to experiment with ways to feed more people. These are only hypotheses; the origins of domestication remain a mystery.

Archaeologists have found evidence to suggest that domestication occurred in at least three and perhaps as many as six different areas of the world, and at different times (Figure 6.1). Wheat and barley, for instance, as well as goats and pigs, originated in present-day Iraq and Iran (see map on page 396) some ten thousand years ago. In Central America, people grew corn, beans, peanuts, avocadoes, sweet potatoes, and tobacco as early as nine thousand years ago. And approximately six thousand years ago, in places that are now parts of China and Thailand, people first domesticated rice and soybeans. Because of pronounced environmental differences among these regions of the world, anthropologists have not been able to agree on any one model explaining how domestication occurred (Flannery 1973), and we are still "far from a complete understanding of the transition" to food production (Pryor 1986:892).

The various ways of life based on simple methods of production share two significant characteristics: they are small scale, and they do not include the use of machinery. Beyond these similarities, however, there are considerable differences between the two major types of simple production: horticulture and pastoralism.

Horticulturalists

The impact of the Neolithic revolution on human life can hardly be overestimated. With domes-

ticated plants and animals, human beings were no longer totally reliant on natural resources. Yet simple gardening, or **horticulture**, meant that human beings had to give up many of the advantages of the gatherer-and-hunter way of life—among them some mobility, egalitarianism, and leisure time.

Horticulturalists use hand-held tools, such as stone or metal hoes or wooden digging sticks, to plant seeds in holes dug in the ground. They care for the resulting crops without chemical fertilizers, complex irrigation systems, or farm machinery. Nor do they use animals or plows to help in planting and harvesting. Their domesticated animals are usually only small food animals like chickens or pigs. This technologically simple way of life has endured for ten thousand years, and still exists today in many parts of South America, Africa, and Asia, and elsewhere.

The most widespread horticultural technique goes by three different names: **swidden, slash-and-burn,** or **shifting cultivation.** Gardeners clear a patch of forest land by cutting down any large trees and slashing away the undergrowth. After allowing the remaining tangle of branches and weeds to dry, they set fire to it. Often the horticulturalists leave the charred tree trunks where they have fallen and plant corn, yams, manioc, coconuts, or other crops among the debris. As untidy as a plot such as this looks, it can be remarkably productive, since the ash from the burned vegetation provides a natural fertilizer for the soil. The gardeners harvest their crops at different times, so there are always some plants in the soil.

After the ground has been prepared and the crops planted, the gardeners' chores consist of weeding and protecting the growing crops from animals. In general, though, swidden cultivation involves relatively little work between planting and harvesting. After several years, the nutrients in the soil become depleted and underbrush begins to take over. At this point, the horticulturalists abandon the plot, shifting their efforts to a newly burned area. After allowing the plot to lie undisturbed for a time so fresh nutrients in the

---

horticulture a method of subsistence based on growing crops with simple tools and technologies

swidden, slash-and-burn, or **shifting cultivation** a form of horticulture in which a plot of land is cultivated for some years and then abandoned in favor of a new one

Using hand-held tools, horticulturalists clear forest land for planting by felling trees and burning away undergrowth. They then plant their crops among the fallen tree trunks. In Mexico, Mayas fell a tree while burning brush from their horticultural plot.

form of rotting plant life can restore fertility to the soil, the cultivators may return to begin the cycle all over again.

Unlike gatherers and hunters, horticulturalists usually live in permanent or semipermanent villages, since they need to stay close to their crops. But like gatherers and hunters, they tend to live very near their relatives. This is because gardening is more successful when there are a number of people to share the work. Thus large kinship groups (Chapter 9), which are often land-owning corporations and work units as well, are common among horticulturalists.

For the amount of energy put into horticulture, many more calories' worth of food are produced than can be gathered and hunted with the same amount of effort. Horticulture is thus a more efficient way of getting food than gathering and hunting, so communities of horticulturalists can be larger than gatherer-and-hunter bands. However, it takes more people to clear garden plots, guard and weed them, and harvest and store crops than it takes to forage for nuts or stalk and kill an animal. So at

the same time that it requires a larger population, the horticultural way of life also makes a larger community possible. Horticulturalists' villages may contain as many as several hundred people.

While sex and age largely determine jobs among gatherers and hunters, many horticultural societies offer some degree of occupational specialization, allocating jobs not only on the basis of sex and age but also according to individual talent, interests, and family heritage. In these societies, if a person is particularly adept at textile weaving or if her mother was a weaver, it is likely she will be a weaver too. One job that usually falls to women in horticultural societies is gardening, and in some of these societies they do most of it. They may even own the land on which crops are grown. Perhaps for this reason, the position of women is, on the average, higher in horticultural than in gatherer-and-hunter societies (see Quinn 1977:199). However, women rarely assume leadership positions, and in horticultural societies in which women do not control resources, they are

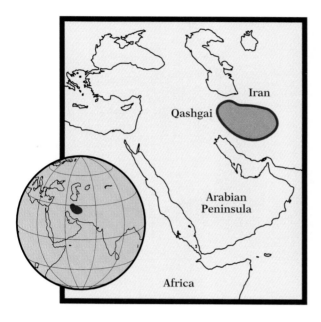

• Ask Yourself •

During their long semiannual migration, Qashgai women use umbrellas to protect themselves from the sun. When they encounter strangers, they lower the umbrellas to shield themselves from view. Do you think this behavior can be related to the concept of the evil eye (Chapter 2)? How would an ethnographer, female or male, best approach these women?

raising crops. The Qashgai of Iran, for instance, raise sheep, goats, and camels in an arid climate, and the Evenks of Siberia herd reindeer in a very cold one.

Because the needs of their herds must be accommodated, and because their herds sometimes cannot find food in one location all year round, many pastoralists practice **transhumance,** a way of life in which people move their homes and herds from one grazing area to another, depending on the season. In the spring, for example, the Qashgai move their animals from the

apt to be dominated, politically, socially, and economically, by men.

Warfare, which we noted above is uncommon among gatherers and hunters, is more frequent among horticulturalists. The violence may be small-scale, but can reap a severe toll in lives. Horticulturalists, unlike gatherers and hunters, control property, such as land, crops, and houses. Individuals and groups typically distinguish themselves according to the amount of property they control, with leaders (usually male) having more wealth and power than other people. These societies are thus usually less egalitarian than gatherer and hunter societies, a feature of horticultural societies that can provoke envy, hostility, or conflict. Increased population density, too, can lead to conflict if it causes resource insufficiencies.

Pastoralists

Pastoralists depend for their subsistence mainly on herds of animals that provide meat and milk and sometimes transportation, wool, or hides. Today, most pastoralists are found in regions unsuitable for

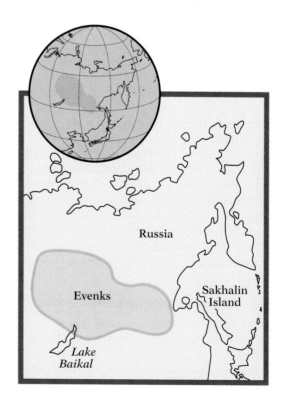

pastoralists those who practice a method of subsistence based on herd animals

transhumance a pastoral way of life in which people move with their herds according to the seasons

The pastoralist Qashgai, who herd sheep, goats, and camels in south-central Iran, set up temporary herding camps each time they move their animals to new grazing land. Families live in large black tents made from goat hair.

warm lowlands where they have spent the winter to the cooler slopes of the Zagros Mountains, where fertile summer pastures can be found (Beck 1980). In the fall, they move back to the lowlands. Other pastoralists, called **nomads,** are on the move year-round to provide their animals with adequate grazing.

Pastoralists live in **herding camps,** temporary places of residence where families that herd and travel together live in tents or other simple shelters. Usually, camp members are related by blood or marriage to individuals in other camps in the same region; and although they may separate to find suitable grazing for their animals, they typically join together for mass migrations. During migrations, everything the pastoralists own—tents, clothing, food, pots and pans, weaving looms, and religious

articles—is loaded onto the backs of animals. Babies, the sick, and the elderly ride, but everyone else walks, prodding the herds along on trips that may last several weeks and cover hundreds of miles.

A pastoralist household is apt to be relatively large. A married couple and their offspring commonly share their shelter with other family members, perhaps unmarried siblings of the wife or husband, or a widowed aunt. Although individual households may be large, camps are usually small, consisting of only a few related families. However, the number of pastoralists who consider themselves members of the same ethnic group may be enormous. The hillsides of southwestern Iran are peppered with herding camps, each numbering only six or eight tents but adding up to many thousands of people who consider themselves Qashgai.

Like gatherers and hunters, pastoralists usually allocate daily work by sex and age rather than skill or preference. Tending herd animals takes great muscular strength, so it is men, not women, who control the most important resource in these societies. Men may also hunt or farm part time. Women perform household tasks, such as preparing food, gathering wood for fuel, caring for babies, and

---

nomads pastoralists who travel constantly throughout the year, within a large area, to provide their animals with grazing land

herding camp the pastoralist residence, consisting of the temporary homes of families that herd and travel together

In pastoralist societies, jobs tend to be allocated by sex, with men caring for herd animals and women performing household tasks. Near Shiraz, Iran, a Qashgai woman gathers wood to fuel her camp stove.

weaving rugs. Whereas men are identified with animals, females are associated with domestic life.

Far from being self-sufficient, pastoralists are part of the larger economy of the area in which they move, and they maintain strong ties with local nonpastoralists. Their mobile way of life does not permit them to collect or manufacture all of their subsistence necessities, so they must trade their wares—cheese, rugs, or whatever else they produce—with settled people living near their camps or with merchants who serve as middlemen. Thus a pastoralist may travel with a load of wool or cheese to the urban shop of a merchant who stocks household goods, and trade his wares for the things he and his family need (see chapter-opening photo, Chapter 7, page 150).

Over the course of history, pastoralists have tended to be warlike. The aggressive Mongols of ancient Central Asia, for instance, were pastoralists. From the cultural materialist perspective, one reason might be that the livelihood of pastoralists depends on the availability of adequate grazing lands for their animals. Land is worth fighting for.

Pastoralist societies are not as egalitarian as those of gatherers and hunters, but neither are they usually highly stratified. There is often a leader who makes important decisions in consultation with other men. But this leader is not a political specialist; he is a herder like every other man.

• Complex, Contemporary • Production Methods

Peasants

In the Middle East, China, Africa, South America, India, and some parts of Europe, farmers called *peasants* (see Chapter 1) plow fields and thresh grain with the help of animals rather than machines. Their adaptation, based on **nonmechanized agriculture,** differs from horticulture in that not all the work of cultivation is done by hand. Instead, peasants use wooden or metal plows and threshers pulled by horses, donkeys, or water buffaloes. Their cultivated lands may be irrigated by water pumped from wells, drained from tanks, or diverted from streams and run

nonmechanized agriculture agriculture using wooden or metal plows, pulled by animals

Anthropology and the Environment

Living Off the Land: The Tetum Horticultural Cycle

The Tetum people of Indonesia are classic horticulturalists whose yearly cycle of plant cultivation begins with the rainy season in the fall (Hicks 1988). The sky becomes cloudy in Indonesia in October, and early November brings downpours that last for hours, changing the tawny covering of grass and trees that blanketed the island during the dry season to green foliage. As the rains begin, Tetum families hurry to their swidden plots, eager to thrust their digging sticks into the damp soil. The women and girls do the actual planting, dropping corn, yam, and vegetable seeds into shallow holes. A family usually seeds a garden in about two days, camping out at night in a crude lean-to near the garden. When the job is done, the planters move on to another plot. Most families have two or three. As soon as the planting is finished, the planters return to their villages.

By mid-December, the rains are at their heaviest, and the corn is already 3 feet high. Tetum families take refuge from the soggy weather in the dry comfort of their village homes. The women weave cloth, make pottery, and plait mats from dried palm leaves. Men talk politics and make gardening tools. Social gatherings are rare, for whenever a brief dry spell occurs families hurry out to weed their gardens rather than to socialize. When February arrives, bringing some dry days, families harvest their corn. The planting was women's work, but men and women join together for this chore, which must be done quickly before the rains arrive. In March, rain returns in force, and rice is planted, followed in April by a second corn crop. The Tetum venture out of their houses only to weed, protect their fast-growing crops from birds, and harvest a few vegetables. But social activities pick up in June, as the dry season approaches. Weddings, parties, cockfights, and visits from distant relatives are interrupted only by the harvesting of corn and rice. Children join adults in the cheerful job of threshing the harvest with their feet.

By September, with the harvesting over, men tramp to their gardens to burn the stubble and weeds that

---

through man-made channels. They may enrich the soil with chemical fertilizers purchased in a nearby town, or fertilize their crops with dung from their domestic animals. In the past, some nonmechanized agriculturalists formed independent chiefdoms (see Chapter 12, page 296), but today this adaptation exists only in the context of the nation-state. Because people who practice this way of life have frequent contact with people in towns and cities, they are geographically and economically less isolated than gatherers and hunters or horticulturalists.

What Are Peasants? Anthropologists find it difficult to agree on what peasants have in common because the details of their adaptation, their social relations, and their economic and political lives can vary considerably from region to region and culture to culture. This great variety is not surprising since there are literally millions, perhaps even billions, of peasants around the world today.

One authority, Raymond Firth (1950:503), adopts as the defining characteristic of peasants the scale of production rather than the product. "Many a peasant farmer," writes Firth, "is also a fisherman or craftsman by turns, as his seasonal cycle or his cash needs influence him." Most anthropologists, however, would probably side with another authority, Robert Redfield (1956:26), who restricts the term *peasant* to agricultural people. Peasant authorities agree that most peasants share a particular set of features, including nonmechanized agriculture and an economic and social relationship

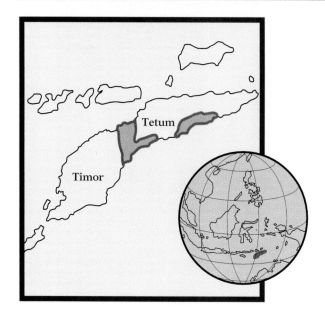

September burn-off into the soil with their digging sticks, repairing fences, and rebuilding lean-tos. By the end of the month they have returned to their villages to wait for the rain to signal the start of another year's cycle.

In Indonesia, after the rainy season has yielded to the dry, Tetum horticulturalists harvest their corn and rice. Young people help thresh the rice harvest by stamping on the grain with their feet.

have accumulated over the year. Since they do not want to miss any of the fun going on back home, they spend little time looking after their fires, and sometimes their garden lean-tos are destroyed. Soon it is October again, and families prepare their gardens for another wet season by mixing the ashes left by the

with those who are not peasants but who live in the same area and share the same general cultural tradition.

Perhaps the feature that most helps us to understand peasants is their relationship to larger, more powerful cultural traditions. Peasants are always found in the context of a wider, literate culture, which Redfield (1956) terms a **Great Tradition.**[2] Usually peasants speak the same language as other members of their Great Tradition, partake in its artistic genres, rec-

ognize its history as their own, tell its myths, sing its songs, and honor its culture heroes. If a nation-state is Muslim, for example, its peasants are Muslims too. Thus peasants can be viewed as less sophisticated, more impoverished, smaller-scale, rural reflectors of a Great Tradition rather than as the bearers of their own distinctive culture.

Like horticulturalists, peasants grow most of their own food, make their own clothes, build their own houses, fashion their own farm tools, and rely on their own skills to satisfy other subsistence

[2] Because they are found in literate societies, peasants cannot be considered nonliterate. Many, however, are illiterate (see Chapter 1 for definitions of these terms).

Great Tradition the wider, literate culture in which peasants exist

The subsistence adaptation of most peasants is nonmechanized agriculture, in which animals are used to pull wood or metal plows and threshers. Near Isfahan, Iran, a peasant threshes wheat with a wooden sled.

needs. But they are by no means independent. Despite producing most of what they need and performing their own labor, they exist within the confines of a national culture, and thus are subject to their nation's laws, involved in its markets, obliged to pay taxes, and eligible to be drafted into the armed forces.

At the same time, however, peasants may be isolated, to one degree or another, from the mainstream of national political, economic, and social life. Some—those who cannot read and do not own radios or television sets—are uninformed about what is going on nationally or internationally. Others—those who read newspapers, listen to the radio, or watch television—know what is happening nationally and internationally. But it is rare for peasants to become involved in national-level political life or even to organize themselves to present their views and causes to the outside world. In some cases this is because they are overburdened with more immediate concerns; in others, it is because they have been exploited for so long by their economic and political superiors that they fail to recognize their potential power. This could be considerable in situations in which the peasants produce food for their urban countrymen. But it is difficult to generalize about peasants, for their political situation differs widely depending on the nation-state in which they live.

Peasants grow food mainly to support their own households, but they also produce surpluses to sell for cash or, if they do not own their land, to use as rent. As recently as the first half of this century in Iran (see map on page 396), for example, wealthy landowners owned vast farms that were divided into plots farmed by peasants. A peasant sharecropper could keep only one-fifth of the produce from his plot of land (Jacobs 1966:137). Meanwhile, the landowner, the owner of the irrigation system that watered the plot, the owner of the ox that was used to plow it, and the supplier of the seed each took a fifth also. Since the landowner usually owned the irrigation system and provided the seed, he got 60 percent, the ox owner 20 percent, and the peasant 20 percent—sometimes scarcely enough to feed his family. This traditional system has largely disappeared in Iran because of government-mandated land reforms, but it is still the case that peasants in

The Anthropologist at Work

Kaj Århem

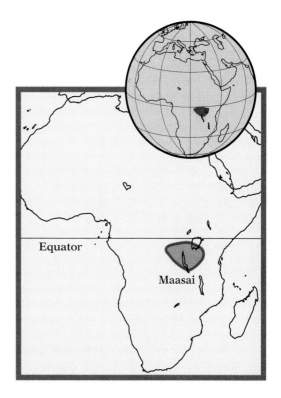

The Ngorongoro Conservation Area in northern Tanzania, East Africa, is a natural and cultural legacy for the entire world (Århem 1985:12ff). Its wildlife is among the most plentiful of any region on our planet, and Olduvai Gorge, where physical anthropologists found human fossils that changed our understanding of human evolution, is located there. The Ngorongoro Conservation Area is also home to about fifteen thousand cattle-herding Maasai pastoralists.

The government's Ngorongoro Conservation Area Authority (NCAA), which manages the region, has two major policy concerns: environmental conservation and the economic development of local communities—two aims that concern many other governments and development agencies as well. Many of these organizations assume that pastoralism and environmental conservation are incompatible.

In 1980, the NCAA hired Swedish anthropologist Kaj Århem to explore the relationship between pastoralism and the environment in the Ngorongoro Conservation Area. Århem visited the area to collect data on local land use, settlement patterns, population trends, and living conditions. He studied the Maasai not only synchronically but also diachronically, examining statistical data collected by earlier researchers. Combining findings obtained from both approaches, Århem discovered that, in contrast to the assumptions of the NCAA, the land use system of the Maasai was both environmentally sound and economically rational. Even though they ranged widely, Maasai cattle were controlled, thus reducing pressure on natural resources. The Maasai social system proved to be a resource of great development potential, because it included an elaborate system of rights that regulated access to specific grazing areas and water sources.

Århem found the Maasai had a "profound knowledge of the semi-arid savanna environment they called home" (Århem 1985:102–103). His applied anthropological work resulted in reports to the NCAA showing that environmental conservation and the subsistence needs of Maasai pastoralists could be integrated into a comprehensive development strategy that would also be environmentally sound.

regions such as Latin America, India, and the Middle East sometimes find themselves in situations ripe for exploitation by landowners and national governments.

The Worldview of Peasants. Because of their ethnic variety and geographical spread, it is hard to generalize about how peasants view the world, but we do find some features shared by most. They tend to identify strongly with their land, their families, and the ethic of hard work (Redfield 1956:112). Some tend to view the world as a place in which there are not enough good things—wealth, happiness, good health—to go around, a view termed the **image of the limited good** (Foster 1965, 1972; Gregory 1975; Kennedy 1966; Piker 1966). Inherent in this view is the idea that if one person accumulates more than his or her share of goods, another will have less than a full share. This notion can make peasants jealously protective of what they have, suspicious in their relationships with others, and wary of change—attitudes that are reinforced by the self-sufficiency of peasant families.

Many peasant groups have a history of domination by other groups. Latin American peasants, for example, were for many generations under the direct domination of Spanish or Portuguese landlords. In part because of their historically subordinate economic, political, and social relationships with others, some peasants appear, to nonpeasants, to be passive or fatalistic. Long denied opportunities to advance themselves, they seem to think they are powerless to change things. Their religious beliefs sometimes encourage them to think that whatever happens is the will of God.

Kinds of Peasants. The best-known authority on peasants is probably Eric Wolf (1955, 1957,

Among peasants, it is customary for all able family members, including children, to contribute to the family's subsistence. In rural Guatemala, a Mayan peasant child labors homeward under a heavy load of firewood.

1966), who distinguishes between two categories of peasant groups: **closed peasant societies** and **open peasant societies.** This distinction is useful for understanding the differences between the traditional peasants of the past and those of modern times, many of whose lives are no longer as isolated or as traditional as those of their ancestors.

• Ask Yourself •

Peasants depend on their own children for labor, so families tend to be large, and children may have little formal education. The need of peasants for extra hands to help with the farming is in direct conflict with the aims of national governments that wish to limit population size and educate children. Do you see any way in which national-level policymakers could resolve these conflicting aims?

---

image of the limited good the view that the world is a place in which there are not enough good things to go around

closed peasant society a type of peasant society characterized by production for household use, old-fashioned technology, isolation from mainstream city life, and resistance to change

open peasant society a type of peasant society characterized by substantial participation in a national or international economy

Closed peasant groups are more likely than open peasant groups to incorporate the characteristics of peasant communities we have outlined above. In a closed peasant society, outsiders are unwelcome and the membership of the community is clearly defined. Crops feed families and pay the rent. Little if anything is left over for sale, which keeps peasants in closed societies relatively isolated from the mainstream of city life. Their technology is old-fashioned, and they resist change. Relative to urban members of their Great Tradition, they live in poverty and what Wolf (1966) calls "defensive ignorance"—that is, they remain uneducated in order to protect their traditional way of life. Finally, their culture discourages the accumulation and display of wealth; those who manage to accumulate some wealth are pressured to return to the economic level of everyone else by sharing with relatives or by spending their accumulations on community events. The model for this closed form of peasantry was developed from ethnographic research carried out in peasant villages in Mexico by Robert Redfield and Eric Wolf, but closed peasantries occur in other parts of the world as well, such as Spain (Gilmore 1980:6).

The open type of peasantry, according to Wolf (1966), arose in response to the increasing demand around the world for crops that could readily be sold for cash, a product of the rise of capitalism. An open peasant society is therefore geared to a national or international economy, and the peasants may sell half or more of what they produce rather than using it all to feed themselves or pay rent, as in closed peasant societies. The coffee growers of Latin America, familiar from television advertising, grow coffee not mainly for themselves but for outsiders. Open peasant communities own their land and sometimes borrow money, although on a small scale. They are much more integrated into the larger society than closed peasants, and they may welcome changes from the outside. They expect success, and are thus more tolerant of accumulating wealth and displaying it than are peasants in closed societies.

Evolutionary anthropologists have observed that, in general, status differences between the sexes become greater as societies move from the gatherer-and-hunter type to horticulture to nonmechanized agriculture to nation-states. Thus, we might expect to find quite pronounced gender asymmetry in peas-

The status of women in peasant societies tends to be relatively low, perhaps because peasant women typically work in the domestic sphere rather than outside it. Here, a northern Indian peasant woman prepares cakes of cattle dung to be used as fuel for her family's cookstove.

ant societies, and in fact the status of women in these societies, in terms of social, economic, and political influence, is virtually always lower than that of men. A number of explanations have been proposed (Mukhopadhyay and Higgins 1988). One feminist anthropologist, Christine Ward Gailey (1987), suggests that economies based on money may encourage status differences based on sex. Although members of both sexes are producers in peasant societies, the goods women produce—mainly food and clothing for their families—are not cash-producing, while the goods produced by men—such as agricultural surpluses—are. Thus, Gailey claims, women's work is devalued in these societies.

Urban Dwellers

The world is becoming increasingly urban. In 1950, only two cities, London and New York, had populations over 8 million; today there are 20 of these huge cities, 14 of them in developing countries. At present, the total urban population of the developing countries is an estimated 1.3 billion people—more than the total populations of Europe, Japan, and North America combined. At a growth rate of 50 million new urbanites every year, due both to natural increases in resident populations and immigration from rural areas, over half the people in the developing world will live in cities by the year 2020 (Bradford and Gwynne 1995:13).

Living in cities forces people to develop indirect and complex means of obtaining food and satisfying other needs. We will say relatively little about the adaptation on which modern urbanization rests—large-scale, mechanized agriculture (agribusiness) combined with industrial production—because anthropologists usually consider the holistic study of large-scale societies at this level of technological complexity to be more within the scope of sociology than anthropology. Still, increasingly since World War II, anthropologists have turned their attention to cities, focusing their ethnographic research on subpopulations such as street gang members, corporate executives, or prison inmates, and developing a new specialty called *urban anthropology* (see Chapter 1). Among its practitioners, two topics, urban migration and poverty, are attracting considerable anthropological attention.

Urban Migration.   Increasingly over the last 150 years or so, peasants have been forced from their land by overpopulation, natural disasters, or war-

fare, or have been seduced by the promise of greater economic opportunities in cities. Urban migration was encouraged by the nineteenth-century Industrial Revolution and the rapid pace of technological development in the twentieth century. With more efficient farm machinery and more intensive agricultural production, it takes fewer farmers to feed the world's nonfarmers; thus, increasing numbers of peasants have been unable to sustain themselves economically. In search of an alternate adaptation, they have flocked to cities in huge numbers. What has happened in Peru is fairly typical. In 1940, the country's agricultural interior was home to 65 percent of the population, and the coast, where the major cities are located, held less than 30 percent. Today, more than half the people of Peru live in its few coastal cities, many of them in slums, whereas fewer than 40 percent live in the interior (CNP 1984).

Most immigrants from peasant communities to cities fail to raise their standard of living, at least initially. As occupants, by necessity rather than choice, of marginal, "peri-urban" land, they may have less (and less healthy) food, smaller living quarters, poorer sanitation, and poorer health than they did in their rural homelands. Jobs are difficult to find because the immigrants have little or no training for urban work. To ease their poverty, most try out new professions requiring little experience or training. Many become souvenir peddlers, taxi drivers, shoeshine boys, gardeners, or maids.

In addition to being more economically impoverished, urban dwellers' lives are not, in general, as socially rich as those of peasant villagers. Anthropological research has shown that when peasants move to cities, family ties are apt to loosen, religion to decline in importance, and interpersonal relationships to become increasingly superficial. In the impersonal atmosphere of a city, former peasants may feel isolated, sometimes so much so that not even clubs or new business relationships can help. Yet the social isolation of urban migrants has an adaptive aspect. Oscar Lewis (1966b) argues that in urban slums, where essential resources are scarce, permanent relationships such as marriage can be a handicap. Being able to break off relationships easily improves a person's chances of survival.

For some urban immigrants, poverty and social isolation can precipitate a sense of hopelessness that prevents them from seizing whatever political, economic, and educational opportunities

In search of a better way of life, peasants have flocked to the cities of the Third World, but often their dreams of better jobs and more money are frustrated. In Comas, a shantytown in Peru, a dwelling is constructed from straw matting.

may exist. Others, however, develop innovative mechanisms to help them cope with their situation. In many cities, immigrants have banded together to form self-help groups called **voluntary associations**—political, recreational, religious, or occupational organizations through which individuals cooperate to achieve specific goals. In Nigeria, for example, urban immigrants from different ethnic groups have created voluntary associations called *tribal unions,* modeled on traditional, rural mutual aid groups (Little 1982:192). These provide social activity, financial support for jobless members, and help in times of illness or death (178–179). As they become urban laborers, traders, or police officers, formerly rural Nigerians discover that tribal unions help ameliorate the harshness of city life.

Recent migrants to the Peruvian coastal city of Lima typify the problems and prospects of urban migrants (Stein 1985). Extreme poverty is nearly universal among them; many live in slums, where their housing may consist of straw matting, an abandoned automobile, or a sewer pipe, and where there are no sanitary facilities, electricity, or clean water. Traditional customs have died slowly, and many migrants remain wedded to traditional ideas. When they get sick, for example, some continue to visit a traditional curer rather than a doctor (despite the fact that access to modern medical attention is available and free). They also retain the traditional idea of family labor; in little sweatshops all over Lima, family members, including children, work together to produce small articles for sale on the streets.

voluntary association a self-help group

As elsewhere, self-help organizations have sprung up in Lima's immigrant neighborhoods. In one neighborhood, migrant families banded together to bring electricity into their homes by ingeniously (if illegally) tapping into power lines in neighboring communities. They had no running water, so they organized a water delivery service. Trucks now bring water to the entrance of the community, and residents carry it home in pots and jugs. They also organized themselves to achieve political and economic goals. Each city block elected a representative to a neighborhood board of directors, which presents issues of community concern to local authorities. And recently, a group of young mothers formed a collective to combat malnutrition in children. The group collects money from residents to buy inexpensive powdered milk in bulk for the community's children.

Urban Poverty. A universally acceptable definition of poverty, one that does not rest on standards that apply only to some cultures, is almost impossible to provide. Most Westerners would probably describe poverty as the lack of certain material things—money, nice clothes, a car, a comfortable place to live. Yet many non-Westerners who lack these things cannot be termed impoverished, since they have other things that are more valuable to them. Earlier we saw that some gatherers and hunters, who lack virtually every material commodity Westerners value, might even be termed affluent, if by affluence is meant having everything one wants and needs. Similarly, poverty is sometimes defined in terms of U.S. dollars or the equivalent, and every country in the world has been categorized by the World Bank (a branch of the United Nations) as low-, middle-, or high-income based on how much of the country's gross national product (GNP) each individual represents.[3] Translated into U.S. dollars, the GNP per person in a low-income country is $635 or less (World Bank 1993:234). However, many people around the world conduct at least part of their lives without using money. Some grow their own food; others barter for goods and services (see Chapter 7). Thus, using dollars to categorize either individuals or whole nations as rich or poor, while

helpful in some contexts, is inadequate in others, and in some cases may be ethnocentric as well.

Thus, poverty cannot be adequately defined, cross-culturally, as the lack either of particular material objects or of money. Instead it must be defined in terms of whatever is needed for adequate living in a particular cultural context. If, whatever their cultural setting, people lack any of the things they consider necessities in the context of their individual setting—and especially if they also lack the means to obtain these—then they can be considered impoverished. Poverty is a state of want rather than of scarcity.

Both rural and urban people can be impoverished, but urban poverty is more apt to include undernutrition, impermanent residence, unstable sexual relationships, and feelings of deprivation and despair. On the basis of his fieldwork in Mexico, Puerto Rico, and New York, Oscar Lewis (1961, 1966a, 1966b), coined the expression **culture of poverty** for the ideas and behavior poor people in some capitalist societies develop as they adapt to urban circumstances. Among the characteristics of the culture of poverty are a lack of involvement in the institutions of the wider society (except for the armed services, courts, prisons, and welfare organizations); financial circumstances that include a shortage of cash, lack of savings, borrowing, and pawning; inadequate education and virtual illiteracy; mistrust of the police and government; social relationships that include early experience with sex, widespread illegitimacy, wife abandonment, and mother-centered families; and a lack of privacy (Lewis 1966b:xliii–xliv).

Patrick Moynihan (1965), who wrote about poor American blacks, agrees with Oscar Lewis that their culture is essentially different from that of the well-off. It is not, Moynihan claims, a "failed" white culture, but a genuine culture in its own right, transmitted from generation to generation. But the idea that there is a distinct culture of poverty has been criticized by Charles Valentine (1968), among others. While agreeing that poor people develop attitudes that enable them to adapt to their situation, Valentine suggests that in the United States no substantial differences separate the culture of poor

---

[3] A country's GNP is the value of all the goods and services the country produces in a year.

culture of poverty the ideas and behavior of poor people in some capitalist societies

people from that of others. He claims that the poor fail to live up to the values of the wealthy mainly because they lack the same educational opportunities. This means that the jobs available to the children of richer families are closed to the poor.

Elliot Liebow (1967), another authority on urban dwellers, carried out field research on the street corners of a Washington, D.C., ghetto. Like Valentine, Liebow argues that one reason poor urban blacks in the United States develop patterns of behavior distinct from those of the broader American culture is that they lack the educational opportunities available to wealthier Americans. Liebow writes of men able and willing to work, who cannot earn enough money to support themselves and their families. Their chances of securing regular employment are good only if they are prepared to work for less money than they can live on. The few good jobs available are difficult to obtain, and insecure when they are obtained. Construction work is desirable because it pays better than many other jobs, but it is uncertain due to the weather, seasonality, and business ups and downs. In addition, many of the highest-paying construction jobs are beyond the physical capacities of some men. Liebow adds that the wages for certain jobs are kept artificially low because employers assume that workers will make up the difference between their wages and their minimum financial requirements by stealing. Without education to prepare them for personally satisfying jobs, and without jobs that provide enough money to support themselves and their families, urban blacks are forced to develop their own culture.

Thus, there are at least two different views of urban poverty. The first is that the urban poor develop their own unique adaptation, fundamentally different from the larger society's way of doing things. The second is that the urban poor share many values with members of the larger society around them; their adaptation is different only because they lack the education and income to conform. Urban anthropologists have not yet come to agreement on which view is correct, but recent research in several cities in the United States suggests a possible approach to a solution. As working-class residents move away from impoverished city neighborhoods, they leave behind only the poorest and most socially isolated residents. Their neighborhoods then decay rapidly, and the behavior and culture of those who remain, which had not previously been the standard behavior and culture for the neighborhood, become standard and even spread to neighboring communities (Wilkerson 1987). It may be that the "culture of poverty" develops as a response to the success of some poor urban dwellers in overcoming it.

Conclusion

Among the factors influencing the way the members of a society live are the natural environment (climate, terrain, and available natural resources), the level of technology available to the group (including not only a society's productive capacities but also its level of economic and political development), tradition (including the society's organization, customs, and system of values), the society's interaction with other societies, and its population size (in turn affected by its fertility rate, health status, and family ideals).

The argument that a single factor accounts, either solely or largely, for a particular adaptation is a form of determinism. (Those who view the environment as not just affecting but as actually determining cultural features, for instance, are called *environmental determinists.*) Although various determinist explanations have been proposed to explain human adaptations, they are too simplistic. The adaptations discussed in this chapter have been brought about by combinations of the factors discussed here, and probably others as well.

• Ask Yourself •

In this chapter, we have tried to give you a feel for a variety of different lifestyles. Did any of them ring a bell with you, or is your own lifestyle very different from all of them? If you had to choose one, which adaptation described here would best suit you?

Summary

- An adaptation is a complex of technologies, activities and ideas that combine to form a particular way of making a living within a particular environment.

- *Subsistence* refers to the various ways in which human beings obtain the necessities of life. All human beings pursue one of two subsistence methods: collecting things that have already been provided by nature, or producing the things they need.

- Collecting, the subsistence method gatherers and hunters use, is by far the older of the two methods, but today only a few gatherers and hunters remain. Producing necessities is far more common.

- Simple production methods include horticulture and pastoralism, while complex methods include the peasant and urban adaptations.

- Horticulture, which has been practiced for ten thousand years, is simple gardening using hand-held tools. The most widespread horticultural technique—swidden gardening, also called slash-and-burn or shifting cultivation—both permits and requires a larger community than gathering and hunting.

- Pastoralism is based on herding. Pastoralists are either transhumant (taking their animals to different pastures on a seasonal basis) or nomadic (moving their animals constantly in search of pasturage).

- The peasant adaptation is generally characterized by a household-based economy set in the context of a larger economic system; a worldview that focuses on family and community; the idea of limited good; and, sometimes, elements of conservatism and passivity.

- Peasant communities may be categorized as either closed or open, depending on how much of what they produce is for household use versus for sale in an external market. A closed peasantry is the more traditional type; an open peasantry, the more modern.

- Urban immigrants often have similar characteristics no matter where they live: poverty, the retention of certain peasantlike attitudes and values, and general feelings of helplessness. Some are prevented by these handicaps from bettering their lot, but others are able to help themselves by forming voluntary self-help associations.

- Poor urban dwellers' "culture of poverty" is characterized by a lack of involvement in many of the institutions of the wider society and by impermanent social relationships. There is continuing debate about whether or not it should be considered a distinct culture.

Key Terms

adaptation
band
carrying capacity
closed peasant society
culture of poverty
gathering and hunting
Great Tradition
herding camp
horticulture
image of the limited good
Neolithic revolution
nomads
nonmechanized agriculture
open peasant society
pastoralists
subsistence
swidden, slash-and-burn, or shifting cultivation
transhumance
voluntary association

Suggested Readings

Auel, Jean M. 1980. *The Clan of the Cave Bear.* New York: Crown. A best-selling novel about "cave" people. The main character is a woman whose many adventures, inventions, and feats require a considerable stretch of the imagination to be believed, but the book nevertheless presents an accurate portrait of the late Ice Age gatherer-and-hunter way of life.

Dragadze, Tamara. 1988. *Rural Families in Soviet Georgia.* New York: Routledge. Among the many excellent studies available on peasants, this short book describing a traditional Russian village is particularly interesting since less is known about Russian peasants than others.

Howells, William H. 1985 (1977). Requiem for a Lost People. In David E. K. Hunter and Phillip Whitten (eds.), *Anthropology: Contemporary Perspectives* (4th ed.), pp. 259–263. Boston: Little, Brown. A particularly moving account of the extermination of a gatherer-and-hunter group.

Mullings, Leith (ed.). 1987. *Cities of the United States: Studies in Urban Anthropology.* New York: Columbia University Press. A nonspecialist's introduction to urban research in the United States. Topics include wage labor, welfare, unemployment, kinship among city dwellers of lower socioeconomic status, and minority education.

Rigby, Peter. 1985. *Persistent Pastoralists: Nomadic Societies in Transition.* Totowa, NJ: Biblio Distribution Center. A discussion of rural development and management in the context of the economic conditions found among East African pastoralists, including the Maasai.

Introduction

No doubt you have heard about Peter

Minuet, the Dutchman who traded a few

beads and other small articles worth about

$24 to some Native Americans in 1626 and

received what was eventually to become Manhattan Island in return. Depending on your point of view, this moneyless transaction was either the world's best deal or its worst swindle.

In moneyless transactions, called **barter,** goods as well as services are exchanged without the use of money. Barter probably dates back to the earliest human societies and is still common today, not only in traditional societies but also in the West. A California woman wallpapers a room in someone else's house in exchange for hypnotism treatments for her husband, who is trying to give up smoking. Another woman, who loves gardening, weeds and hoes a stranger's yard in exchange for driving lessons for her teenage daughter. A restaurant owner in Austin, Texas, trades meals for a roll of carpeting. In Nova Scotia, a lobster fisherman builds a rowboat for an Irish-moss collector in exchange for help in hauling in his lobster traps. And a major airline based in New York trades airlines tickets for new tires for its aircraft (*Mother Earth News* 1984:108; *Ms.* 1982:70; *Nation's Business* 1985:18; Sweet 1980:86).

In the case of the Native Americans of Manhattan, bartering land for beads made a great deal of sense. Cash was of no value to them, but beads were highly desirable. Since today most North Americans use cash, why does barter thrive in our society? Some people barter because they need things they do not have enough cash to purchase. Others feel they get more for less through bartering. Still others barter to avoid paying sales or income taxes. Barter is especially attractive in recessions since people can get what they want and need without having to spend money. It can be a most rational economic activity.

Economic activity? In Western societies the word *economic* means "having to do with money," but in economic anthropology the term does not necessarily imply the use of money. This chapter discusses the different kinds of economic behavior, some of it moneyless, in different societies.

• Economics Versus • Economic Anthropology

The anthropological approach to economic behavior differs from that of economists. This is because economics as a formal academic discipline was developed by Westerners, and its concepts are based on Western economic behaviors such as maximizing profits, minimizing expenditures, investing, and acquiring surpluses. From a cross-cultural point of view, the Western model is ethnocentric, and may thus be ill suited for explaining what motivates individuals in non-Western societies. Material gain or the idea of accumulating savings may be less important to non-Westerners than to Westerners, for example, and profits may take the form of prestige rather than material goods. The concepts of formal economics have not therefore proven especially useful for understanding economic behavior in non-Western societies.

• Ask Yourself •

Have you ever taken part in a moneyless transaction? If so, why? Were you offering goods or services for barter? How did you find someone with whom to barter? Were you satisfied with your end of the transaction?

---

barter economic transactions in which goods and services are swapped without the use of money

Copyright © Drawing by John O'Brien, The New Yorker Magazine, Inc.

Both anthropologists and economists view the **economy** of a society, whether small or large scale, nonindustrialized or industrialized, as all the ways in which the society's members attempt to fulfill their wants and needs. Any behavior directed toward the fulfillment of wants and needs is economic behavior. But if "the economy" is easy to define in both disciplines, "wants and needs" are less so, for two reasons. First, although anthropologists agree with economists that wants and needs can be things (*goods,* in economic terms) or work (*services*), wants and needs can also include what economists might consider ephemeral actions, such as songs or rituals, as well as other intangibles, such as love or respect. Second, apart from the basic necessities of life such as food, clothing, and shelter, wants and needs vary greatly among societies. Cash, of no use whatsoever to the Native Americans of Manhattan, is of universal value in contemporary North American society. Purple-rimmed clamshells, which contemporary North Americans bypass on the beach without a glance, were once highly prized by Native Americans.

Since wants and needs vary so much, people satisfy them in many different ways, but in any case choices must be made. You weigh what resources are available to you and in what quantity; you choose from among the different goals that you desire and that your resources can gain for you; then you decide what resources, and in what quantity, you wish to expend to achieve what goals.

The resources people use to fulfill their wants and needs are called **means.** These can be either material or nonmaterial: money, labor, raw materials, tools, time, energy, and will are all means. Formal economic theory assumes that means are always limited, or "scarce," but this does not seem to hold true for all societies. The goals achieved by expending resources are called **ends.** These, too, can be material or nonmaterial: food, shelter,

---

economy in the most general sense, all the ways in which the members of a society satisfy their wants and needs

means all the material and nonmaterial resources people use to fulfill their wants and needs

ends the goals achieved by expending resources

Barter, the exchange of goods or services without the use of money, dates back to the earliest human societies and continues to be practiced today. On a highway near Kiev in the Ukraine, where vodka is plentiful but gas is in short supply, a stranded motorist offers to barter one for the other.

honor, and political influence are all ends that can be attained by using various means. Formal economic theory holds that the way people expend means to achieve ends is rational and predictable, an assumption many anthropologists dispute.

Many economic anthropologists doubt that the economic behavior of people in nonindustrial societies can be fully understood in terms of the rational allocation of scarce means toward the achievement of specific ends calculated to satisfy wants and needs. Trobriand yam gardeners (see map on page 19) work to fulfill the wants and needs of their families, but they are also motivated by their desire to follow local marriage customs by giving gifts of yams to their married sisters (Weiner 1988:91–92). Such behavior is difficult to account for under formal economic theory. Understanding Trobriand economic behavior requires placing this behavior within the holistic context of Trobriand values and institutions, a context in which the mutual obligations of certain women and men are of economic importance.

Land ownership among gatherers and hunters provides an example of how anthropology has challenged long-established ideas about economic behavior. Nineteenth-century cultural evolutionists believed that gatherers and hunters had no concept of private land ownership; the land belonged to everyone. They further believed that the idea of private land ownership evolved only when horticulture (see Chapter 6) made it possible to live permanently in one place. But anthropological research has shown that horticulture, permanent residence, and land ownership are not necessarily partners. Archaeologists working in coastal southern New England, the Middle East, Africa, and elsewhere have proven that in the past, if their local environment was rich enough in subsistence necessities to make nomadism unnecessary, gatherers and hunters settled down in one place.[1] Meanwhile, ethnographers have shown that the presence or absence of the idea of land ownership is independent of either permanent residence or horticulture.

We now know that resource distribution and defensibility are probably more important than either horticulture or permanent residence in developing notions about landowning. Where the natural environment provides abundant, predictable, nonmobile resources (beds of oysters would be an

---

[1] Gatherers and hunters today live in marginal areas unsuitable for sedentary life, so information about the adaptation of gatherers and hunters to beneficent environments (see Chapter 6) must come from archaeology.

example), gatherers and hunters may "own" land even though they are not horticulturalists. But where resources are scanty, fluctuating, or highly mobile (an overhunted herd of deer, for example), gatherers-and-hunters may need access to very large tracts of land to meet their subsistence needs, and neither private ownership nor residence in one place may be feasible. So the general correlation of gathering-and-hunting economies with communal rather than exclusive (individual or group) rights to land is considerably influenced by local ecological conditions.

In short, anthropologists have shown that different societies, as they attempt to provide for the survival and well-being of their members, may develop different economic behaviors; different institutions to direct, control, and maintain their economies; and different economic priorities. At first these may not appear constant, predictable, or even rational to the Western economist, but in the light of cultural relativism they can be seen to make sense.

• Production, Distribution, • and Consumption

Economic behavior, whatever its subsistence base (see Chapter 6), involves three separate activities: people produce things, they distribute them, and they use or consume them (see Figure 7.1). These activities and the behavior accompanying them are interrelated, and comprise all **economic systems.**

Production

Production occurs when members of a society convert natural resources into things people want and need. A service, such as a rainmaking ritual or a psychiatric consultation, is as much a product as an arrowhead or a jet plane. Whatever the product, production takes place within a particular social context and involves particular human abilities, ideas, and traditions. Therefore, production is not simply economic behavior; in a broader sense, it is cultural. Indeed, production is so essential a feature of culture that the social philosopher Karl Marx regarded it as basic to all societies—a viewpoint that has greatly influenced many anthropologists. The cultural aspects of production—the human abilities, ideas, and traditions involved—rather than the products themselves, are what anthropologists find most interesting.

• Ask Yourself •

In her medical practice in upscale Beverly Hills, a successful obstetrician provides health care for rich women. One day a week, she provides prenatal care and delivers babies, without pay, at a clinic in a poor neighborhood in nearby Los Angeles. Is this rational economic behavior? An unknown percentage of the women she treats at the clinic are infected with AIDS, and there is a small but real chance that the doctor will become infected too. Does this danger alter your opinion about whether her behavior is rational?

Among the variables affecting production are natural resources; technology, including tools and production methods; the customs that govern the organization of labor; and productive aims and priorities. Aims and priorities may be the most important and are the most difficult to determine.

Effects of the Natural Environment. The natural environment provides the raw materials necessary for production. Some cultural materialists argue that the environment is the major factor in production. Suppose you are an economic anthropologist trying to understand a society's system of production. For the sake of simplicity, let us assume it is a technologically simple society. You might start by determining whether the society's natural environment is an exploitable one with plenty of natural resources, or a more limited one with scanty, widely separated, or nonrenewable resources. You would try to discover which resources are available all year around (for instance, flint for tools); which are seasonally renewable (like berries or hibernating animals); which would naturally recur if depleted by humans (such as herds of game animals); and which could not renew themselves if used up (like veins of copper ore). You would discover that some depleted resources would renew

---

economic system the interrelated production, distribution, and consumption of goods and services in a society

production transforming natural resources into things people want and need

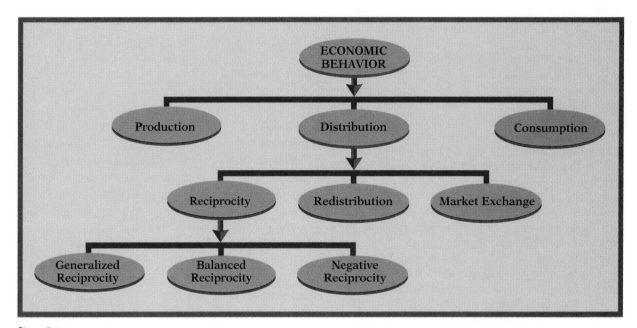

Figure 7.1
One Approach to the Study of Economic Behavior.

themselves rapidly (beds of shellfish, for instance), whereas others (such as groves of trees) would recover only after a period of many years.

After you documented the availability of local raw materials, you would explore the people's handling of their resources, determining whether the ones they depend on can be controlled or increased by domestication, whether they conserve their resources and how, and whether they can stay in one place and manage their resources by gardening or herding or have to move to where resources are located. You would also ask people how they obtained resources that their local environment lacked.

After you had identified all of the resources available and understood how they were managed, your understanding of the effects of the natural environment would still not be complete. You would also want to learn about the beliefs and values revealed by the people's choices of what resources to exploit. What is considered a resource in one society might not be considered one in another. North Americans do not eat horses and dogs, even though they are aware that these animals are edible and are exploited as a source of food by people in other societies. As important as the natural environment and its resources are, therefore, they alone cannot explain economic behavior.

Technology and Production.   Technology includes all the information, expertise, equipment, and traditions that members of a society can draw on to produce what they require to satisfy their needs and wants. A society's level of technological expertise not only influences the ways in which things are produced but also restricts what the society can produce and in what quantities.

Continuing with your effort to understand economic production in a nonindustrial society, you might next examine its technology. First taking the synchronic point of view, you would determine what the people actually *do* with the raw materials their environment provides—how they use natural objects (like stones, pieces of wood, or lumps of clay) or natural forces (like running water, wind, or steam). They may use them in the same form in which nature provides them. A fist-sized stone, picked up from the ground and thrown at an enemy, is being used in its natural form; so is a hot spring in which someone is taking a bath. Simply moving nature's products might make them useful— for example, piling up stones to make a wall. So might reducing natural resources or changing their shape—chipping away at a chunk of stone to fashion a sharply pointed tool, for instance. Or raw materials might be combined, as in making a canoe from wood, bark, and pine pitch; or transformed, as

What is considered a resource in one society may not be so considered in another. In China's Yunnan Province, a man prepares dog meat for a feast.

in shaping a piece of clay into a pot and hardening it in a fire.

Next, to examine production diachronically, you would search for signs that technological changes were occurring or that some aspects of the society's technological capacity were remaining relatively stable. Such observations would be easier if you could draw on a written history of the society or an archaeological study of its past.

Perhaps the society you are investigating is a prehistoric one. In this case, your information about the people's level of technological development must come from archaeology. Cultural evolutionists point out that technologies generally evolve through time in the direction of greater complexity and efficiency. Chipped stone arrowheads, for example, were used for hunting and warfare long before metal arrowheads—more efficient, but more difficult to produce—were made. Certain objects (like metal arrowheads) can therefore imply certain technologies, such as metalworking. Scholars interested in prehistoric societies can often get a good idea of technological change by observing how ancient pots change from one level to the next in stratified archaeological sites. They often find that people became more skillful at making pots over time.

Production and the Organization of Labor. Your society's technological capacity would directly affect the organization of work needing to be done. Some societies, as we saw in Chapter 6, allocate jobs according to sex and age, but other criteria can also be used, including skill, personal preference, and family tradition.

Since the society you are studying is a technologically simple one, its members are more likely to reduce or combine natural resources than to transform them. Usually, this means that individuals rather than groups do the producing and that individuals generally carry out the same activities involved in production as other people of the same sex and about the same age. You would find little or no differentiation among people on the basis of who does what—no bosses, no employees, no unskilled as opposed to skilled laborers. This distribution of tasks encourages social equality, since there is little reason to view one person as different from or superior to others. If this was a society of gatherers and hunters, you would probably find each female gatherer making her own baskets for collecting wild plant foods.

More complex technologies require different social organizations. Eric Wolf, influenced by the work of Karl Marx, has usefully modified some ideas originally proposed by Marx about how people organize themselves for production. Marx suggested that there are several different kinds of production (he called them "modes of production"), distinguishable from one another by the different

Craft specialization, common in food-producing societies, is determined partly by sex. Among the Makassai of Timor, weaving is women's work. Traditional techniques and designs are passed down from mother to daughter in certain families only.

kinds of social relationships existing among the producers. Wolf (1982:75) identifies three, although there are others as well. In the **kin-oriented mode of production,** common in many technologically simpler societies, labor is organized on the basis of descent (see Chapter 9) and marriage (Chapter 10). For example, household members in a nonmechanized farming society may cooperate to perform tasks too big for individuals to perform themselves.

More complex technological capacities, involving knowledge or techniques that may be difficult or time-consuming to learn, may produce craft special-

kin-oriented mode of production a system of production in which labor is organized according to descent and marriage

tributary mode of production a system of production in which producers must pay tribute to people who control the things needed for production in order to gain access to them

ists who pursue a single task full time while their basic wants and needs are provided for by others. Age and sex, modified by talent and inclination, generally determine who learns a particular craft. Such specialization is undeveloped among gatherers and hunters; it is much more common in food-producing societies. An example is provided by the Makassai people of Timor, for whom weaving is a craft that passes from mother to daughter in certain families. If you are a full-time weaver, canoe builder, pottery-maker, or blacksmith, you cannot be a hunter or a farmer, too. Someone else must provide your food. In societies with craft specialists, the possibilities for social distinctions already exist, so these societies are apt to have some sort of a ranking system.

Sometimes, to gain access to the things they need for production, producers in nonegalitarian societies must pay tribute to higher-ranking individuals who control these things, politically or militarily. Wolf (1982) calls this a **tributary mode of production.**

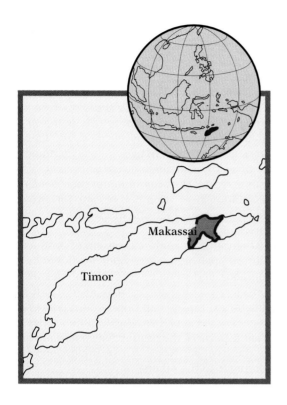

Makassai

Timor

Another, still more complex level of technological capacity may require the cooperation of so many laborers working on the same project that managers are needed to organize their work. Here, individuals are differentiated from one another on the basis of who does what. Some people are lowly laborers, others are higher-ranking supervisors, and still others control the resources needed for production. The pyramids in Egypt could not have been built in an egalitarian society. Too many different and technically difficult jobs were involved, from stone quarrying to engineering to project management.

Wolf's (1982) third mode, the **capitalist mode of production,** occurs when **capital** (resources not used up during production, such as factories) is controlled by nonlaboring, decision-making people called capitalists, and other people (workers, who do not own capital) sell their labor to the capitalists to make a living.

If your society were a prehistoric one, archaeological objects could provide clues to social organization. Since technology is interconnected with social organization, archaeologists can sometimes infer what sort of social organization an extinct culture had by determining the kind of technology it

used. Arrowheads made of chipped stone, so often found at archaeological sites once occupied by gatherers and hunters, provide a clue to how their makers may have organized themselves. Because these artifacts almost always differ somewhat from one another, archaeologists conclude that their makers did not mass-produce them; each person made his or her own. The inference that the artifacts were not made by specialists leads us to the supposition that the makers may have been social equals, which in turn implies an egalitarian kind of social organization, as is found in gatherer-and-hunter bands (see Chapter 6; bands are also discussed in Chapter 12). However, although certain kinds of technology are compatible with certain kinds of social and political organization, this association is not invariable enough to support technological determinism, the view that a society's level of technology determines either its system of production or its sociopolitical organization.

Productive Aims and Values. An anthropological study of production must also include an examination of the economic values of the society under study, such as the worth its members attribute to the goods, services, and nonmaterial things they produce. The basic material necessities of life are, of course, highly valued in all societies, but beyond these basics much of what is considered valuable is culture-bound, or culturally defined.

One factor influencing the value of various commodities is availability. Easy access to a commodity or service and a plentiful supply tend to reduce its value, and vice versa. In North America, cashew nuts are in great demand among members of the cocktail-party circuit, who are willing to pay a relatively stiff price for them. But in rural Iran, where cashew orchards yield nuts in abundance, enormous burlap sacks of them are found in every bazaar, and a handful costs the local equivalent of a few pennies. Cashew nuts are a staple ingredient in Persian cooking, rather than an expensive gourmet item. Availability accounts for the contrast in value.

capitalist mode of production a system of production in which capital is controlled by capitalists, and workers, denied access to ownership of capital, must sell their labor to the capitalists in order to make a living

capital resources not consumed in the process of production

A plentiful supply of a commodity reduces its value. In North America, cashew and pistachio nuts are sold in small, expensive packages, but in a town in southwestern Iran, where cashew and pistachio nuts grow locally and in abundant supply, a shopper ignores big sacks of very affordable nuts.

Industrialized societies tend to value the overproduction of goods so that surpluses are maintained. Surpluses are more likely to be valued in a society in which labor is specialized. With task specialization, a society can increase its production, because dividing production into specialized tasks performed by different workers is more efficient than assigning all of the steps to a single individual,

distribution the way in which goods and services are allotted in a society

reciprocity mutual exchange of gifts or services

especially when production involves many steps. To manufacture a jet plane, some workers rivet while others install wiring.

It should be noted, however, that what constitutes a surplus depends on definition. Simpler societies may also overproduce. In those political organizations known as chiefdoms (Chapter 12), for example, overproduction is encouraged. Families may produce a surplus of agricultural commodities to pay taxes to local chiefs who reciprocate by giving public feasts, thus maintaining their leader-follower relationships. Another reason for overproduction is to create a failsafe mechanism to combat the threat of famine.

In attempting to analyze a system of production, the natural environment, technology, the organization of labor, and value are not the only features to be considered. Other forces may also play a part. Capital, for example, is an important aspect of production in some societies. But in all societies, the different aspects of the productive system are holistically intertwined. None can be understood without reference to the others.

Distribution

Distribution refers to the ways in which people allocate the goods and services they produce. The economist Karl Polanyi (1971) identified three ways in which products could be distributed among a society's members: reciprocity, redistribution, and market exchange.

Reciprocity. Gifts, as anyone who has ever given or received a birthday present knows, come with strings attached: both giver or receiver feel the gift should be reciprocated. Likewise, a person who accepts a service or favor from another feels a sense of obligation to pay this back. Gift giving creates a bond between giver and receiver, a bond that is likely to be extended into the future with additional mutual giving and receiving.

Mutually obligatory behavior occurs in all societies. The French anthropologist Marcel Mauss (1990) claimed in 1922 that mutual gift giving is the most ancient way of distributing products within a social group, and it remains the only method of distribution used in some nonindustrial societies. Mauss thought the human compulsion for mutual giving and receiving, or **reciprocity,** underlies much of human behavior in every society. It comes in three different forms: generalized reciprocity, balanced reciprocity, and negative reciprocity

Where reciprocity is generalized, those who have subsistence necessities share with others without the expectation of any immediate return. In Togiak, Alaska, Native American Yupik women fillet red salmon for distribution beyond their immediate families.

(Sahlins 1968). Each can occur in any kind of society, and all three may be found together in the same society.

Generalized Reciprocity. In Western culture as well as in others, people sometimes give gifts without expecting an immediate return or even any obvious return. However, a seemingly altruistic gift is frequently given in the expectation that sooner or later it will be reciprocated. The kind of gift in which no immediate return is expected but in which both giver and recipient anticipate an eventual balance is called **generalized reciprocity.** It is related to a person's position in society. Those who can give are expected to; those who cannot give are not.

To use a familiar example, nuclear family members in Western society who give one another presents at Christmas usually expect gifts in return. We do not demand that our gifts be immediately balanced by gifts of identical value; most American parents receive a lot of finger paintings in return for the expensive toys they give their young children. But eventually, children grow up, and they may wind up giving their parents, now on reduced retirement incomes, gifts that are equal to or greater in value than those they received as children.

Generalized reciprocity is typical of gatherer-and-hunter economies. Successful food seekers share the food they have collected with their neighbors without expecting an immediate return. Not only are they paying off their outstanding debts of food, they are also investing in a form of "social security" against the time when they may be too old or too ill to forage. Usually no tally of the gifts given and received is kept, and in some of these societies a generous giver is not permitted to boast about his or her contributions. The Semai of Malaya actually forbid the recipient of a gift from expressing gratitude, for to do so would imply that he or she must have calculated its value (Dentan 1979).

In the harsh desert country of southern Africa, the !Kung people eke out a living by hunting small antelopes, birds, rats, snakes, reptiles, and insects and by gathering wild fruits, seeds, roots, and nuts. They are unable to accumulate surpluses for the day when their luck in finding food runs out. Some four thousand !Kung practice this way of life today, in large part because of their effective system of generalized reciprocity.

Richard Lee (1969:58), who carried out field research among the !Kung, describes how each morning up to 16 of the 20 or so members of a typical !Kung band leave camp for a day's gathering and hunting. In the evening, they return with whatever food they have been able to find, and the entire band shares the total supply of food available. The next morning, the gathering-and-hunting party may be made up of different individuals, who when they return in the evening similarly distribute their spoils among every member of the band. Who went or who stayed behind on either or both days does not

generalized reciprocity gift giving with the expectation that sooner or later this act will be reciprocated

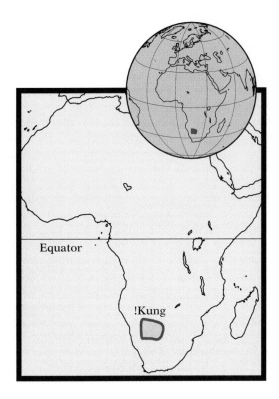

matter; every member of the band has the right to a share of whatever food is brought into camp, for in time each adult in the band will have brought in food for the others. Thus the balance of giving and receiving among the !Kung may be unequal in the short run, but it evens out over many days and weeks.

Balanced Reciprocity. **Balanced reciprocity** most often occurs between social equals who are not closely related. Like generalized reciprocity, this form can occur in any kind of society; but as an economically significant kind of behavior, it typically occurs in technologically simple, small-scale societies with political organizations such as the tribe or chiefdom (see Chapter 12) rather than in large-scale societies with the "state" kind of political organization.

---

balanced reciprocity the immediate (or fairly prompt) return of goods equal in value to what has been given

silent barter a kind of barter in which the trading partners never meet each other face to face

Like generalized reciprocity, balanced reciprocity is also based on one's place in society, but in contrast to generalized reciprocity, it involves the immediate (or fairly prompt) return of goods equal in value to what has been given. When giver and receiver are social equals and a gift is not reciprocated, or not reciprocated with a gift of the same value, both parties may feel embarrassed. Both expect that eventually an equitable balance of gifts will be achieved; otherwise the gift-giving relationship will break down.

One form of balanced reciprocity that occurs in some non-Western societies, including that of the !Kung, is **silent barter.** Like the examples of modern-day, Western barter described at the beginning of this chapter, silent barter involves the direct exchange of goods without the use of money. But silent barter is atypical, in that the trading partners never meet each other face to face. Instead, each group of traders leaves its goods to be traded at a pre-arranged place. Later, the group's trading partners come along, and if they like what they see, they take the proffered goods and leave their goods in return. Silent barter is a convenient method of exchange between hostile communities.

In Chapter 3, we described the Trobriand Islanders' kula ring, a ritual exchange of shell necklaces and armbands (see Figure 3.2 on page 53). This example of balanced reciprocity was first described by Bronislaw Malinowski, and later reinterpreted by several other anthropologists from their own theoretical perspectives. You will recall that in the kula, each gift of a shell ornament required the receiver to reciprocate promptly with a countergift of another shell ornament of equal or greater value. Thus, armbands and necklaces circulated endlessly around the kula ring, often winding up in the same hands that had given them away years ago.

These objects were not currency that the islanders could use to buy whatever they wanted; they were exchanged only for each other. But even though they lacked any practical value, their symbolic value was considerable. To be presented with one of these items was to gain prestige, and to give one symbolized a donor's generosity and increased his reputation. So eager were the Trobrianders to win prestige and fame that they regularly embarked on dangerous trading expeditions to distant islands, laden with necklaces and armbands to give away. As part of their ritual interaction, traders from different islands (who might otherwise have been hostile toward one another) were obliged to treat one another with great courtesy, each man seeing to the comfort and safety of his trading partners whenever they were in his home territory.

What was really going on here? Were the islanders really so eager to gain prestige that they were willing to befriend potential enemies and risk their lives on dangerous ocean voyages? Marvin Harris (1993:242–243), drawing on the work of Reo Fortune (1989:206–210), has attempted to explain the logic of the kula ring from a cultural materialist perspective. He points out that another, quite different kind of trading, for food and other practical commodities, was going on at the same time. Residents of naturally well-endowed islands were able to trade their agricultural surpluses to residents of less fertile islands, which specialized in the mass production of nonedible necessities such as pottery and canoes. Long before Malinowski's visit to the Trobriands, interisland trading partnerships between certain men and particular villages had developed, with food being exchanged on a regular basis for artifacts. Balanced reciprocity made possible a network of relationships that welded the entire group of islands into a single economic unit.

A somewhat different explanation suggests that the kula ring placed people in a position in which they could trade with one another for such economic necessities as yams, coconuts, canoes, pottery, and fishing nets. In contrast to the symbolic exchanges of armbands and necklaces, trading for essential goods involved a lot of haggling. Were it not for the former, the islanders might well have been too fearful of their neighbors on other islands to attempt any kind of economic relationship (Fortune 1989). The importance, in economic systems, of social factors—such as the Trobrianders' exchange of ritual objects in pursuit of prestige—reminds us that human beings are rarely so overwhelmed by economic interests as to neglect social ones. "Economic man," a creature whose motivations are economic to the virtual exclusion of social or psychological impulses, is merely an ideal.

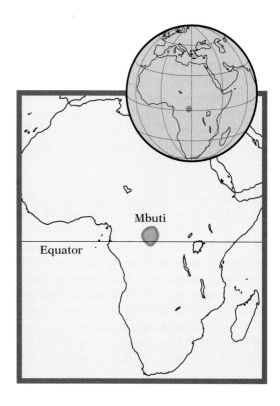

Negative Reciprocity. **Negative reciprocity** characterizes exchanges between strangers or even enemies (Sahlins 1968). Each partner tries to get the better of the other, and their behavior varies from energetic haggling to outright theft. The Mbuti of Africa, for example, exchange meat and personal services for other kinds of food and for goods produced by their neighbors, whom the

Mbuti strongly dislike (Turnbull 1965). When performing services for these neighbors, the Mbuti work as little as possible, and their neighbors counter with resentful threats intended to increase the Mbutis' productivity.

Redistribution. One way of allocating goods, called **redistribution,** is to designate one individual or group to collect goods and then parcel them out among the members of a society. This form of distribution is common in our own society as well as in certain small-scale societies. In Western society, for example, the heads of individual households may pool the earnings of their productive members

---

negative reciprocity an economic interaction between hostile parties in which each partner tries to get the better of the other

redistribution a way of distributing goods in which the goods are gathered into the possession of a particular individual or group and then parceled out among the members of a society (ordinarily the parents) and then redistribute these earnings among all the members of the household, whether productive or not.

Redistribution also occurs between households. In North America, as we are all well aware, state and national governments collect taxes from working people's salaries and then redistribute what has been collected to other members of society based on presumed need. Although it may take the form of money—a welfare payment to an individual, perhaps, or a grant from the National Endowment for the Humanities to a struggling theater group— redistribution may also be in the form of services or goods.

Redistribution can be regarded as a **leveling mechanism,** a cultural device according to which individuals are obligated to distribute their material wealth so that no one can accumulate more than anyone else. Among gatherers and hunters, we generally find little accumulation of material wealth among individuals or groups; simple technologies and a nomadic lifestyle do not lend themselves to owning things. When a gatherer and hunter does come into possession of something valuable—some meat, for example—it is shared of necessity; neither its possession nor its redistribution convey status. Where residence is sedentary, however, property can be stored without the inconvenience of transporting it. In agricultural and industrial societies, therefore, the accumulation of wealth is usually regarded as highly desirable, and the possession of wealth creates or reinforces social inequalities. But in some of these societies in which the unequal distribution of property is possible, having more wealth than others is culturally forbidden, and individuals or groups whose material resources have increased may be obliged to spread their wealth, usually converted into food or gifts, among other members of society. Giving wealth away maintains or even increases the prestige and influence of such a person, at the same time as economically reducing him to the level of the less wealthy members of the community.

In some of the world's nonindustrialized societies, the agent of redistribution was in traditional times a political leader called a chief (see Chapter 12). As we noted earlier when discusing surplus accumulation, a chief, like a Western business tycoon, was often a person who made a career of accumulating wealth. But here the similarity ends, for a chief would then distribute his wealth to his followers in return for their continued support.

Malinowski (1965:46–47) remarks that tradition entitled a Trobriand chief to receive great quantities of tribute, much of it in the form of food (especially yams), from villagers in the district in which he wielded authority. In addition, the chief was (theoretically) the owner of all the coconut trees and pigs in his district, which meant he could claim a portion of the coconuts from each tree and a piece of meat from each pig that was butchered. He thus accumulated supplies of yams, coconuts, and meat far beyond what he and his immediate family could use. But instead of storing these goods for the future or trading them away for his own advantage, the Trobriand chief was obligated by custom to redistribute his accumulated wealth.

Eventually, most of the chief's wealth would be returned to his villagers in the form of payments for a variety of public services. A Trobriand chief could order canoes, houses, and yam storerooms to be constructed; wars to be waged; wooden sculptures to be carved; kula expeditions to be organized; and village magicians to perform their magic. But he had to pay for all of these services. In effect, Trobriand villagers were consuming the products of their own labor, but their wealth first had to pass through the hands of their overlord, whose authority was thereby recognized and reinforced. Malinowski (1965) notes that it was this process of concentration and redistribution of wealth that made the chief's wealth an instrument of political power in Trobriand society.

Market Exchange.   In common usage, the term *market* refers to the physical site where goods are exchanged. **Market exchange** is something more abstract, a form of exchange in which transactions are impersonal rather than based on one's position in society, on kinship, or on political relationships. Unrestricted participation by any and all members of a society is a common feature of market exchange. Because everyone is free to offer goods

---

leveling mechanism any of various cultural devices or rules according to which individuals are obligated to redistribute their material wealth, so that no one can accumulate more than anyone else

market exchange the kind of exchange in which transactions are impersonal rather than based on descent, marriage, social position, or political relationships

*In some societies, the exchange of goods is based on kinship or political status, but in a "market"
economy all of a society's members are free to exchange items of value. In a market town in the
highlands of Guatemala, people from outlying villages gather at an open-air market to buy and
sell pottery.*

for exchange in any quantity and to accumulate
things in any quantity, shifts in supply and demand
are common. These shifts govern the value, and
hence the **price**—the worth, expressed in the form
of some conventional medium of exchange—of the
available goods and services. In market exchange,
prices are established for whatever is being
exchanged. Because each person is theoretically
free to sell and buy in any quantity, market
exchange is sometimes called *free-market exchange*,
but the concept is more ideal than real. In actuality,
market exchange is usually subject to political regulations, including trade barriers, customs regulations, price controls, and rationing, so it is not
really "free."

Market exchange is mostly found in states (see
Chapter 12), because it is possible only in societies
with dense populations that can produce food efficiently enough to support large numbers of people.
For market exchange to develop, the food supply

must be so abundant and dependable that most
members of society can abandon subsistence activities and specialize in other areas of production.

Market exchange usually involves **money**—
objects accepted as tokens of specific amounts of
worth. Paper bills and metal coins serve as most of
the Western world's exchange media, but in non-
Western societies money can be shells, blocks of
salt, or other objects.

The term *money* has many shades of meaning.
Western money must be acceptable as a medium of
exchange to everyone concerned and able to be used

---

price the worth, expressed in the form of some agreed-on
medium of exchange, of goods and services

money objects accepted by a society's members as tokens of
specific amounts of worth

to purchase the entire range of goods and services available. Money that fulfills these criteria is known more specifically as **general-purpose money.** Money also has to be physically durable, sufficiently portable to be moved from one trading transaction to another, capable of being divided into small units, and liquid enough to be easily exchangeable for other things. And money must have the same purpose and value for everyone—blind to social or political or religious or economic differences among its users. The American dollar, the Swiss franc, and the British pound are all forms of general-purpose money.

If we limit the term *money* to objects having these attributes, it is exceedingly rare in technologically simple, nonliterate societies. But if we loosen the definition somewhat, money is not nearly so rare, for the idea of using certain objects to represent stipulated amounts of value is widespread. The major difference between general-purpose money and the other kind, **special-purpose money,** is that the latter is not comprehensive: it cannot purchase an entire range of goods and services but only specified items. One kind of special-purpose money, used in New Guinea, consists of shells strung together in units about as long as a man's outstretched arms. With this shell money, villagers can buy only pigs, nothing else.

Another example comes from Rossel Island, which lies near New Guinea. The Rossel Islanders place a high value on shells, but unlike the Trobrianders' shells, Rossel Island shells can be viewed as a kind of special-purpose money since they serve as a medium of exchange and a standard of value rather than simply as ornaments for display or prestige (Armstrong 1967).[2]

The people of Rossel Island have 22 different kinds of shells, which they divide into three classes. The first class contains shell types 1 to 10; the second class, types 11 to 17; and the third class, types 18 to 22. To buy certain goods, one needs a shell of a certain number. A large house costs a number 20 shell. One cannot pay for a house with two number 10 shells, for they are not thought of as being equal to a single number 20 shell. Thus the shells of Rossel Island are not convertible, as Western money is.

A Rossel Islander who borrows a number 1 shell must repay with a number 2. A person who borrows

New Guinea

Rossel Island

a number 2 shell must repay with a number 3, and so on, through shell type number 9. But an islander who borrows a number 10 shell cannot be compelled to return a number 11, for the series 1 to 10 has more generality than the other two series. Finally, the total number of shells used as money numbers no more than one thousand, a feature that severely reduces the money's usefulness.

George Dalton (1968) suggests that anthropologists might find it useful to classify economies according to the importance they accord to market exchange. He proposes three categories of economic system: (1) economies without markets; (2) economies with **peripheral markets,** or markets of relatively little economic importance in which only

---

general-purpose money objects of value that can be used to purchase anything available for purchase

special-purpose money objects of value that can be used to purchase only specific goods and services

peripheral market a market of relatively little economic importance, in which only objects, as opposed to land or labor, are bought and sold

---

[2] Armstrong, an economist, carried out only two months' fieldwork on Rossel Island. Since he was unable to do much participant observation, his findings have been challenged.

On Rossel Island, shells—like money in Western society—serve as a medium of exchange and a standard of value. However, these shells can be used to purchase only some of the goods and services available on the island. Thus, they must be considered special-purpose rather than general-purpose money.

objects, as opposed to land or labor, are bought and sold; and (3) economies dominated by markets.

Although many kinds of goods can be exchanged in an economic system lacking market exchange, usually by reciprocity and redistribution, land and labor are not among them. Instead, these important commodities are allocated among individuals by descent, the relationship of marriage, and social group membership. Reciprocity and redistribution also characterize economies with peripheral markets, but in this second kind of economy there is in addition a narrow range of things that are exchanged according to market principles. Still, most people do not get the bulk of their income from sales in the market, and land and labor are not bought and sold; kinship and social position govern most exchanges, and as on Rossel Island, special-purpose money may be used. The third type of economy, dominated by market exchange, is typical of state-organized societies, with or without peasant communities. Land and services as well as goods can be freely bought and sold, and few economic transactions depend on rights and duties derived from descent or affinity.

Consumption

Consumption refers to all the ways in which the goods, services, and nonmaterial things produced within a society are used. Far from merely satisfying basic wants and needs, consumption in most societies has a wide range of purposes, one of the most important of which is to symbolize social prestige. In Western society, one drives a Rolls Royce not only for transportation from one place to another—a bicycle might do just as well for that—but also to demonstrate that one is wealthy enough to buy such an expensive car. In some societies, consumption as a mark of status is a potent device for establishing political influence, as we see below in the case of the Kwakiutl.

The link between production and consumption has proven particularly instructive to economic anthropologists. In gatherer-and-hunter societies, this link is direct. Since each family accumulates food and other necessities for itself, gatherers and hunters have no need for an institutionalized redistributive system in which goods are amassed by one person or organization and then distributed to the needy. A person able to acquire a surplus distributes it directly among the less fortunate, without fanfare, much less a bid for power. In more complex societies, in contrast, the link between production and consumption is much less immediate. In the Trobriand Islands, as we saw, products moved from producer to consumer through the chief, whose job was to redistribute them. This was no mere economic service. The chief's power was directly tied to the wealth he collected from and redistributed to his people. In any society, the more remote the connection between production and eventual consumption, the more likely it is that consumption has functions that go beyond the satisfaction of immediate needs.

Consumption for prestige was a central value of traditional Native Americans of the Northwest Coast, who developed it to a high art. A village chief would give a huge feast for another chief, from a neighboring village, with whom he had some political dispute. All the villagers under the sway of both chiefs would be invited. This **potlatch,** as it was called, represented a way for the host to win the political support of both sets of villagers. The feast

consumption all the ways in which the goods, services, and nonmaterial things produced within a society are used

potlatch among Native Americans of the Northwest coast, a form of institutionalized consumption consisting of a huge party given by a chief for a rival chief and for all the villagers under the sway of both chiefs

In traditional times, potlatch hosts impressed their guests with gifts such as carved wooden household utensils, blankets, food, and containers of fish oil. Today the potlatch continues, but potlatch goods are more apt to consist of plastic wares. This photo shows distribution of potlatch goods at the 1983 potlatch given by T'lakwagila (William T. Cranmer) in Albert Bay, British Columbia. © Photo by Vicki Jensen.

required months of preparation, followed by days of feasting, gift-giving, dancing, and storytelling.

A potlatch host's primary concern was to increase his own prestige relative to his rival's, and to this end he would throw the most massive, most elaborate potlatch possible, sometimes bankrupting himself in the process, to demonstrate that his wealth and generosity were superior to those of his rival. He would shower his guests with food and gifts—artworks, blankets, fish oil, and household utensils such as carved wooden boxes and spoons. Although potlatch customs differed somewhat among the various Northwest Coast groups, most chiefs would stop at nothing to impress their guests with their wealth and generosity. In one kind of potlatch, the **destructive potlatch** of the Kwakiutl (see map on page 18), hosts went so far as actually to destroy their most valued possessions in front of their guests, feeding bonfires with fish oil and furniture, burning houses and canoes, and even slaughtering slaves. They were sending their chiefly rivals the message that they were so wealthy they could afford to indulge in wanton waste.[3]

---

[3] Different interpretations of the potlatch depend on the particular interests of different analysts. Franz Boas (1966) first identified these lavish parties as a means by which village chiefs could increase their influence, and our description of the potlatch follows that of Boas. The "destructive potlatch" may actually be an aberration from the more traditional form, possibly resulting from such factors as the decimation of local populations.

Potlatch guests, for their part, would grumble about their hosts' stinginess, pretend to find the food unsatisfactory, and determinedly refuse to be impressed by the display of wealth around them. All the while, they would be carefully estimating the value of the goods being given away or destroyed and comparing the generosity of their host with that of his rival.

Sooner or later, to counter his host's bid for prestige, a chief for whom a potlatch had been given would have to reciprocate with a potlatch that equaled—or better yet, exceeded—that of his rival. At this counter-potlatch, the former chiefly guest would strive to display, give away, or destroy more and superior artifacts and to distribute more abundant and tastier food than his rival. This competition would continue until one chief was too impoverished to continue, whereupon both communities would regard the survivor as the winner of whatever dispute had prompted the rivalry.

Like the kula, the potlatch can be explained from several perspectives. Some anthropologists consider it a mechanism for redistribution, pointing out that chiefs amassed food by encouraging villagers to

destructive potlatch a variety of potlatch in which Kwakiutl hosts destroyed their most valued possessions

produce surpluses, later redistributing these surpluses to the producers at potlatches. Others have interpreted the potlatch as a powerful political symbol: villagers' acceptance of their chief's gifts symbolized their subordination to him, even as these same gifts symbolized his authority over them. Still others point out that potlatches helped ensure against occasional famines, which could occur even along the resource-rich Northwest Coast. Chiefs would give potlatches when they were wealthiest, which was when their local natural resources were most abundant. But sometimes their guests were from areas that were experiencing temporary food shortages, so food and goods provided in the course of one village's potlatch may have helped the residents of another cope in hard times. In this way, shortages and abundances balanced out over the years, with both villages benefiting from their competition in the potlatch (Piddock 1965).

• Economic Development •

The term **economic development** refers to a variety of strategies designed to increase the capacities of national economic systems to improve human welfare. Although any country can of course develop economically, the term is most often applied to "developing" countries. There is no agreement on what a developing country is, but living standards are usually lower than in "industrialized" countries; per capita income tends to be relatively low; the rate of population increase is usually relatively high, meaning that the **dependency ratio** (the number of people in the workforce versus those who are too young or elderly to work) is unfavorable; and modern industry and international trade may be just commencing. Most (but not all) developing countries are located in the Southern Hemisphere, and many have histories of colonialism.

The goal of economic development is to satisfy such basic human needs as food, shelter, and health care by stimulating economic growth, redistributing income more equitably, and reducing poverty. More specific aims vary from country to country, but they usually include raising a country's gross national product (GNP) and per capita income; developing its industrial base; increasing productivity; accumulating capital; and improving social services, usually by increasing allocations to public programs such as health, agriculture, public works (road building, for example), and education.

There is no best way to go about achieving these goals, for the histories, traditions, natural resources, and political systems of developing countries vary greatly. Many have chosen to develop modern economies, but political instability, international conditions, tradition, or class structure have inhibited others. Successful economic development also depends on what kind of economy is desired. Socialist economies are centrally planned and controlled, while capitalist economies rely more on market exchange than on central controls.

Given such great variety, it is not surprising that individuals, nations, and international aid agencies have often disagreed about how best to achieve economic development. Different personal, political, religious, and ethnic beliefs and values may be difficult to reconcile. Many developing countries, for example, have had sharp declines in their death rates because of modern medicine but no corresponding declines in their birthrates, so population growth is rapid (see Figure 7.2). This can be highly detrimental to economic development: a rapidly growing labor force, for example, may result in widespread unemployment. A specialist in development given the job of solving this problem in a particular developing country might suggest that the government adopt an official policy of two children per family and impose tax penalties for noncompliance. Or she might encourage an international aid organization to distribute free family-planning services and contraceptives. Or he might urge sexual abstinence. Which solution was favored would depend on whether the specialist was a government official in the country, a policymaker for an international aid organization, or a religious leader.

Some anthropologists apply their specialized knowledge to promote economic development. An early example of this kind of applied anthropology, begun in 1952, was the famous Cornell-Peru Project, nicknamed the Vicos Project. Vicos was a *hacienda*, a huge farm worked by peasants, located in an Andean valley in Peru (see map on page 171). Like many other haciendas, it was owned by absentee landlords. The peasants who farmed the land were tenants who contributed three days of labor each week to their landlords in exchange for a

---

economic development strategies for improving national economies based on the assumption that they will lead to improvements in human welfare

dependency ratio the number of people in a nation's workforce compared with the number who are too young or too old to work

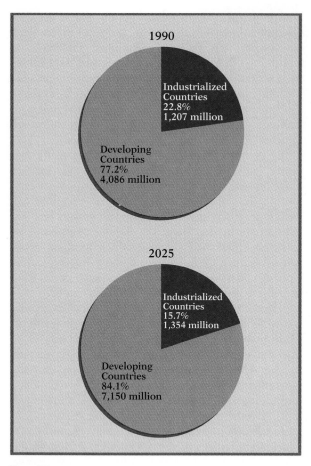

Figure 7.2

The Increasing Population of the World. Rapid population growth is a major problem for developing countries because it slows economic development, but unless present trends are reversed, these countries will see huge population increases over the next generation. By the year 2025, world population may top 8 billion people, more than 80 percent of them in developing countries. Source: United Nations Population Division.

house, a small garden plot, and some domestic animals. This arrangement was not a satisfactory one for the 1700 or so peasants of Vicos. Their plots were small, their crops frequently failed, and often they were unable to feed themselves and their families adequately. Continually in debt to their landlords, they had few prospects for a better life.

Anthropologist Allan Holmberg thought the Vicos peasants should have a higher standard of living, become more involved in decisions affecting the hacienda, and eventually be economically independent. Hoping to demonstrate that anthropologi-

• Ask Yourself •

In the past, peasants in a certain developing country grew enough food for their own families and sold their surpluses for a little cash. Today, because of economic development and the urbanization and industrialization that accompany it, these peasants live in cities and work in factories. Along with more cash, they now have all the pressures and health problems of urban life. In your opinion, are they any better off?

cal research and economic development could improve their lives, he created the Vicos Project with the help of Peruvian colleagues (Mangin 1979:65). His strategy was participant intervention. He would not simply participate in the project, as a fieldworker engaged in testing a hypothesis would do, but would also intervene in the peasants' lives to help bring about what he regarded as desirable changes. His approach was holistic, incorporating not just economic but also social and cultural improvements—better education, better health care, and increased community participation in decision making. Holmberg planned to transfer control of the hacienda gradually to members of the community as their health and education improved and their self-esteem, sense of community, and economic decision-making abilities grew.

After the hacienda's lease was turned over to Cornell and the Peruvian Indian Institute, the peasants were given improved varieties of seed, fertilizers, and insecticides to use on the owners' land. Success was apparent, but the peasants lacked money to buy the supplies with which they could similarly improve the yields of their own small gardens. So a government-sponsored cooperative credit program was established, supervised by anthropologists and other specialists on the project team.

In keeping with Holmberg's holistic approach, the team encouraged other initiatives as well. Education and school hot-lunch programs were begun. A model garden was planted to demonstrate better methods of growing vegetables, and sewing machine training was offered so the peasants could make their own clothes. These lessons not only taught skills but also gave the peasants a sense of participation in what was going on around them, the opportunity to gain new respect as

The Vicos Project, an economic development project aimed at improving the lives of peasant sharecroppers on a huge Peruvian hacienda, or farm, raised the standard of living of these peasants, who eventually purchased the hacienda. Above, Vicos peasants make bricks.

possessors of modern skills, and a way to increase their families' incomes (Doughty 1987:456). In addition, the peasants were encouraged to assemble frequently for discussions. As a result of these meetings, they began to place increasing trust in one another and to seek cooperative solutions to common problems.

The community prospered, and in 1962 the tenant farmers purchased the hacienda from its owners (Mangin 1979:66). By the late 1970s, the peasants were better fed, better housed, and far better educated than they had ever been under the old system. And their standard of living had risen above that of peasants on neighboring haciendas.

The Vicos Project did not escape criticism. Some critics pointed out that neighboring communities also improved their lot somewhat, without help from any project. Others felt that Cornell and the Peruvian government had exaggerated their own contributions and played down those of the people themselves. Still others claimed that

Anthropology and the Environment

Economic Development and Environmental Degradation in Armenia

For many years, landlocked Armenia, part of the former Soviet Union, suffered massive environmental damage as a result of intensive economic development. Armenia became part of the Soviet Union in 1921, and over the next 50 years, as it played a growing part in the nation's centrally planned economy, its industrial output multiplied 146-fold (Hekimian 1995:49 ff.). Its many factories produced chemicals, metals, construction materials, and later computers, semiconductors, and laser technology. But these factories also produced deadly air and water pollution. As a result, the average life expectancy of Armenians fell as health problems—from heart and lung diseases to birth defects and infertility—increased. For many years, the government-controlled press denied the disastrous effects of the pollution, and Armenians did not feel free to protest their region's industrialization and its links to their worsening health.

The Yerevan basin, where Armenia's capital is located and over half its population lives, was particularly hard hit. In this region, home to over 60 percent of Armenia's industry, carbon monoxide from car exhaust fumes, sulfur dioxide from the fuel burned at electric power plants, and soot and ash from factories spewed into the atmosphere. The Medzamor nuclear power plant in the capital city of Yerevan leaked radiation. In early 1990, when the air quality of the Yerevan basin was analyzed, it was found to exceed the maximum permissible concentrations of pollutants by several times (Hekimian 1995:52). Armenia, and Yerevan in particular, had the highest incidence of four kinds of cancer of any of the former Soviet Republics (Hekimian 1995:51).

With the coming of glasnost and the breakup of the Soviet Union, Armenians began to feel freer to form environmental protection groups and to bring environmental issues to public attention, and soon the pressure on the government to do something became intense. Armenia declared its independence in September 1991, and a new government,

---

the Vicos experiment was unique and therefore could not be replicated in other parts of the world. Although controversy over the project's value remains (Doughty 1987; Mangin 1979), the fact is that after the peasants bought their hacienda, their incomes, literacy rate, and standard of living continued to rise.

As an experiment in economic development and applied anthropology, the Vicos Project was the first holistically designed community development and land reform program that succeeded in improving the life-style, sense of self-worth, and rights of impoverished peasants (Doughty 1987:458–459). In a more general way, Vicos showed that in certain circumstances anthropologists have the theory, knowledge, and methods required to make significant contributions toward the resolution of apparently intractable problems of cultural development.

The Vicos Project may have been successful, but other economic development projects have been less so. Recently, for example, the U.S. Agency for International Development (USAID) attempted to promote economic growth in Casiguran (see map on page 174), a poor, rural farming village in the Philippines. Most of the farmland in the village contained coconut trees and root crops, important in the local diet. The project's planners believed that by introducing new crops and livestock aimed at local markets—coffee and pineapples, goats and cows—poor farmers' agricultural output and household

headed by a democratically elected, non-Communist president, took some immediate steps to reduce environmental pollution. The Medzamor nuclear power plant, constructed in the same way as Chernobyl and situated on an earthquake-prone fault line, was shut down. A chloroprene plant, a copper smelter, an aluminum plant, and a chemical factory were also closed. These measures helped to reduce the amount of pollution spilling into the air and water, but worsened the new nation's already severe economic problems. Thousands of workers lost their jobs. Energy rationing was imposed, which reduced industrial productivity and led to further unemployment.

Further economic development in Armenia is unlikely if the country's environmental problems are not corrected. However, cleaning up the environment would cause further economic hardship. People in Yerevan are more immediately affected by energy rationing and escalating food prices than the possibility of a Chernobyl-type environmental disaster. They are pressing the government to reopen the nuclear power plant, which could supply the country with much of the electricity it needs to get the economy back on its feet. Today, Armenia badly needs inexpensive yet effective environmental clean-up programs (Hekimian 1995:57). Sadly,

because of continuing economic crisis and political strife, the environmental agenda, once a high priority for the new government, has been relegated to the back burner.

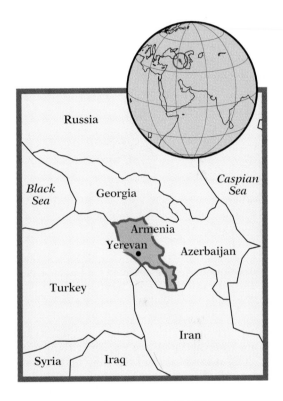

incomes would increase and local economic inequalities would thereby be reduced.

Thus, a number of poor households were chosen to participate in the project, the farmers were "educated" about the advantages of agricultural intensification, and the new species were introduced. But after two years, most farmers had seen no significant increase in either agricultural production or household income (Clatts 1991:270). The project's planners had failed to take into account how much labor, land, and capital poor farmers would be willing to invest and what new products the local market could absorb. Moreover, the planners failed to recognize the critical role women played in the agricultural economy, so they

did not teach the new agricultural technologies to the appropriate producers. Even worse than its failure to produce economic growth was the fact that the project aroused hostility by intensifying the same economic inequalities it had been devised to reduce. Designed to help the poorest farmers, the project actually increased the power of the existing political elite.

Failed efforts such as this encourage some anthropologists to oppose the very idea of economic development. Prominent among them is Arturo Escobar (1991), who points out that even though development anthropologists are more responsive to the traditional values of a "developing" community than nonanthropologists might

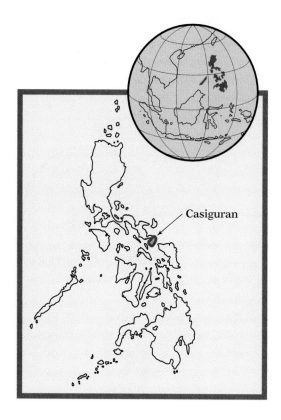

Casiguran

should be admitted and used for improving people's lives as well as for furthering scientific knowledge (van Willigen 1986:30). There is no consensus between those anthropologists who work for development agencies and those who are hostile to development work.

• Ask Yourself •

Some advocates of economic development like to see money, technical assistance, roads, hospitals, or goods freely given to needy developing countries with no strings attached. Others argue that simply giving things to these nations will not promote sustainable development in the long run but will only encourage dependency. In a debate, which side of this controversy would you be more comfortable defending?

• Business Anthropology •

In Western society, businesses are essentially economic organizations, with both the organizations themselves and the individuals in them dedicated to making as much money as possible in the most efficient way. But businesses are also *social* organizations, each of which has its unique culture (Young 1986). Like all social groups, businesses are made up of people of both sexes and a wide range of ages, who play different roles, occupy different positions in the group, and behave in different ways while at work. In fact, relationships among a company's employees often extend well beyond the office or factory. Many corporations have their own health clubs, after-hours get-togethers, and sports teams, and co-workers are often joined together outside the workplace by friendship or even marriage (Young 1986).

be, they are nevertheless usually acting on behalf of some international agency; thus their view of what is best for a community may be the agency's rather than that of the local people. Others who criticize anthropologists' involvement in economic development projects note that scientific and development goals are sometimes at odds (van Willigen 1986:30). Ethnographers testing a hypothesis do not deliberately affect the behavior of the people among whom they carry out research, but anthropologists involved in development projects usually adopt an explicit commitment to bringing about change.

Development anthropology's defenders, among them the Vicos Project's Allan Holmberg, might respond that all ethnographic research influences the community being studied, and this inevitability

Just as anthropologists carry out fieldwork in nonliterate, peasant, and urban societies, they also apply ethnographic research methods to businesses, both Western and non-Western. The kind of anthropology undertaken by anthropologists who study workers and workplaces is called **business anthropology**. This is an applied field; most business anthropologists either work for corporations or act as consultants to management. It is not a new field, having begun as early as 1932 with a study of

---

business anthropology work undertaken by anthropologists who study workers and workplaces, and act as consultants to management

The Anthropologist at Work

Elizabeth Briody

The management of General Motors, a multinational industrial giant, noticed that some employees, on returning to the United States from long-term overseas assignments, had more trouble readjusting than others. Business anthropologist Elizabeth Briody, employed by the company's Research Laboratories in Warren, Michigan, spent three years analyzing this problem. She discovered that employees who worked for a division of GM that had both foreign and domestic branches usually adjusted comfortably upon their return, whereas employees of divisions that had only domestic branches often did not. Through interviews, Briody discovered the reason: workers returning to domestic divisions felt that their co-workers in the United States had little appreciation for their overseas work. They had difficulty readjusting because they were upset at being thought of as having contributed little to their home branch (Dunkel 1992:12).

---

productivity at a General Electric manufacturing plant. But business anthropology has expanded as a field only since the early 1980s.

One reason a company might hire a business anthropologist might be to carry out a **cultural audit,** a study of discrepancies between the way the company should ideally conduct its business and what really happens (Weber 1986:43). The business anthropologist interviews both workers and managers, sometimes from the position of employee, to discover what problems the workers face and how management might improve its performance.

Business anthropologists also function as market consultants, helping companies design and produce the products that will sell best. They interview consumers, discover their likes and dislikes, determine what values motivate the purchase and consumption of particular products, and try to predict what changes in a company's products or marketing strategy might entice buyers. Market segmentation by sex, age, social class, ethnic group, and subculture

---

cultural audit in business anthropology, a study of discrepancies between the ideal and actual conduct of business within a company

Some anthropologists use their training in anthropology to help private businesses to be more profitable. At a car dealership in Massachusetts, business anthropologist Kristina Cannon-Benventre reviews customer service procedures with the service manager. Her advice has helped the firm to win customer loyalty and repeat business.

are all of interest to business anthropologists (Burkhalter 1986:116).

Some business anthropologists work internationally, assisting corporations that conduct business abroad to interact smoothly with people of different cultures. The anthropologist informs managers about the ways in which business is usually conducted in specific cultures and suggests ways to match products with local potential customers (Burkhalter 1986:118). Managers of North American companies rarely know much about the customs of non-Western cultures—and ignorance can be expensive. One company with international ambitions, trying to sell sneakers in the Middle East, embossed a symbol representing Allah, the God of Islam, on the sole of each shoe—a dreadful blasphemy that any Middle Eastern ethnographer could have warned against (Varisco 1992).

Conclusion

Economic anthropologists regard economic behavior as thoroughly embedded in society (Plattner 1989:3–4), meaning that if we are to understand a society's economy, we must view the society holistically. We cannot separate economic behavior from political, religious, or kinship behavior or, indeed, from any other aspect of the society's culture. Thus, for example, "The reason that the United States stopped buying sugar from Cuba in the 1960s was political, not economic; retail activity peaks in late December for religious, not economic, reasons; and the fact that marijuana is one of the larger cash crops in California is of social as much as economic importance" (Plattner 1989: 4).

But if economic behavior cannot be understood apart from other aspects of behavior, the reverse is also true. A culture cannot be understood without an understanding of its economic system.

Summary

- Economic anthropology is the study of how societies allocate their resources (means) to achieve their wants and needs (ends).

- The concepts underlying the formal academic discipline of economics are based on Western economic behaviors, so economic theory cannot

fully explain economic behavior in non-Western societies.

- For both economists and economic anthropologists, economic behavior consists of production, distribution, and consumption. Together, these add up to a society's economic system. Beyond this, however, economic anthropology rests on a cross-cultural, rather than a Western, view of economic behavior.

- Production, the transformation of resources into things people can use, is affected by what resources the environment provides, the technology available, the organization of the producers' labor, and their cultural values.

- Distribution—allocating products to those who need or want them—can involve moneyless giving and receiving (reciprocity—generalized, balanced, or negative); the pooling and disbursement of commodities, also moneyless (redistribution); or a market system, in which transactions are impersonal and negotiated with money.

- Consumption refers to all the ways in which the goods, services, and nonmaterial things produced within a society are used, for purposes including the satisfaction of basic wants and needs, symbolizing social prestige, or establishing political clout.

- The term *economic development* refers to a variety of strategies designed to increase the capacities of national economic systems to improve human welfare.

- Although some economic development projects have successfully improved people's lives, others have not, and anthropologists continue to debate whether they should be involved in these subjective, nonscientific endeavors.

- Anthropologists are increasingly using their expertise to help businesses improve their efficiency, a form of applied anthropology called *business anthropology*.

- Business anthropologists analyze the internal operations of companies, sometimes carrying out cultural audits; survey the market potential for products; and advise companies that conduct business abroad how they might interact more smoothly with customers and workers of different cultures.

Key Terms

balanced reciprocity
barter
business anthropology
capital
capitalist mode of production
consumption
cultural audit
dependency ratio
destructive potlatch
distribution
economic development
economic system
economy
ends
generalized reciprocity
general-purpose money
kin-oriented mode of production
leveling mechanism
market exchange
means
money
negative reciprocity
peripheral market
potlatch
price
production
reciprocity
redistribution
silent barter
special-purpose money
tributary mode of production

Suggested Readings

Leach, Jerry W., and Edmund Leach. 1983. *The Kula: New Perspectives on Massim Exchange.* Cambridge: Cambridge University Press. A thought-provoking collection of articles, remarkable for its comprehensive treatment of the kula. Provides new insights into the ideas and behavior associated with the kula as practiced by societies other than the Trobrianders.

Plattner, Stuart. (ed.). 1989. *Economic Anthropology.* Stanford: Stanford University Press. Twelve scholars discuss a wide range of economic topics in the context of gatherer-and-hunter, horticultural, peasant, and urban societies. An essay on the roles women play in economic institutions is particularly interesting.

Sackmann, Sonja A. 1991. *Cultural Knowledge in Organizations: Exploring the Collective Mind.* Newbury Park, CA: Sage. This contribution to our understanding of business anthropology shows how insights gained in cognitive anthropology can be applied to modern businesses.

Sahlins, Marshall. 1972. *Stone Age Economics.* New York: Aldine. A collection of essays about the economics of technologically simple societies. The first, "The Original Affluent Society," has been widely quoted and reprinted.

Introduction

In 1953, many Americans were shocked

when a former marine named George

Jorgensen announced publicly that he had

just undergone surgery that had changed

him from a man into a woman (Masters, Johnson, and Kolodny 1985:285–287). At Jorgensen's request, Danish doctors had removed his external sex organs and had surgically created artificial female genitalia in their place. Synthetic hormones had already begun to stimulate growth of the patient's breasts and decrease muscularity. Photographed in a dress, nylons, and a blonde wig to launch a new career as a nightclub performer, Jorgensen announced that hereafter he—now she—would be known as Christine.

The real marvel of Jorgensen's transformation from man to woman was the sophistication of the new surgical and hormonal techniques that had allowed doctors to perform this successful sex change, but in the newspapers of the day, medical achievement took a back seat to sensationalism. Besides the details of the surgery itself, what fascinated most Americans about the case was that a man would want to become a woman in the first place. Jorgensen claimed, to general amazement, that despite his external appearance he had never felt comfortable in a man's body. Even as a child, he was sure he had been destined to be a woman.

Jorgensen was a **transsexual,** the term for individuals who decide to adopt the social position of the sex opposite to their anatomical one, whether or not they have had sex-change surgery. (The term is often used incorrectly to mean a person who has both male and female physical characteristics; the correct term for such an individual is **hermaphrodite.**) Although the Jorgensen case astounded and titillated many conservative Americans, transsexuals—as we shall see later in this chapter—are often readily accepted, even revered, in other cultures.

The human desire for sexual activity is a biological universal. However, cross-cultural data on sexual attitudes and practices, compared with other kinds of anthropological data, are quite rare and sometimes unreliable because ethnographers have often brought their own sexual reticence or biases with them into the field. More important, attitudes toward sexuality, sexual statuses, and sex practices are extremely variable cross-culturally. This makes human sexuality an exceptionally promising field for anthropology, but in fact anthropologists are only now becoming aware of the research possibilities in this field (Davis and Whitten 1987:88). Individual cultures have certainly received attention, and ethnographic data on sex are numerous enough, but there have been few attempts to coordinate these isolated research findings (88).

To maintain social order, every society has developed rules by which people's desire for sex is directed and controlled. But these rules vary widely. In determining which individuals make acceptable sex partners and which do not, one's choice is almost unlimited in some societies, whereas in others there are precise rules—so specific that a woman might well be limited in her choice of a husband to a cousin on her father's side of the family (see Chapter 10). Sexual intercourse between males

---

transsexual an individual who adopts the social role of the sex opposite to his or her anatomical one

hermaphrodite an individual who has both male and female physical characteristics

Transsexuals—people who adopt the social position of the sex opposite to their anatomical one—are readily accepted in some cultures and viewed as oddities in others. Transsexual George Jorgensen underwent sex-change surgery and became Christine Jorgensen, above.

• Sex and Gender •

In all societies the difference between males and females is the most fundamental of all distinctions between people (age differences, discussed in Chapter 11, run a close second), and ideas and expectations about the differences between the sexes form the basis of standards around which much of social life is organized. However, the male-female dichotomy is not clear-cut. "Maleness" and "femaleness," as well as the behaviors that are supposedly male or female, are qualities and expectations largely determined by culture rather than by biology. Anthropologists have therefore found it useful, when analyzing sexual behavior cross-culturally, to distinguish between the *biological* aspects of human sexuality (all those aspects that are chromosomally determined) and its *cultural* aspects (all those aspects that are culturally determined).

The terms *sex* and *gender* are frequently used to make the distinction. There is as yet no consensus among anthropologists regarding the precise meanings of these terms (Gilmore and Gwynne 1985:3), but the word **sex** usually refers to the biological category into which a person is born—male or female. Sex is dictated by chromosomal and anatomical characteristics and is usually permanent. The term **gender** refers to the learned aspects of sexuality, and includes sexual orientation (as revealed by one's choice of a sex partner) and sex roles (the behaviors associated, in a given society, with females or males). Culture seems to be even more important than biological differences in determining the sex roles people play. A person's **gender identity**—his or her self-identification as male or female—does not necessarily coincide with his or her sex as defined by anatomy (Money and Ehrhardt 1977).

and females is recognized as necessary for creating new life in almost every society (a few, as noted below, have prohibited even this expression of sexuality), but in some societies, sex for other purposes is discouraged or even feared. Homosexuality is discouraged for some, whereas in others, it is actively encouraged, and in still others it is a matter of no concern. This chapter surveys the diverse ways in which people in different cultures express their sexuality.

---

sex the biological category into which a person is born, male or female, as determined by chromosomal and anatomical characteristics

gender learned maleness or femaleness, as reflected in sexual orientation and sex roles

gender identity an individual's self-identification as male or female

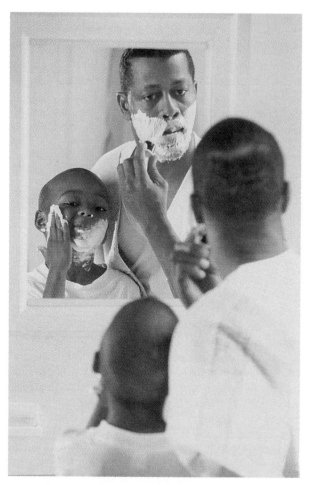

Learning to play the social role associated with one's sex begins early in life. Imitating his father helps an American boy establish his gender identity—his self-identification as male.

The most critical period in determining gender identity is from 18 months to 3 or 4 years. If gender is to be reassigned after this period, the psychological development of the child may be hampered, and after the onset of puberty, gender identity is too well established in most human beings to be changed (Money and Ehrhardt 1977:4, 179).

• Ask Yourself •

Among your acquaintances, does a female who displays characteristics usually associated with males encounter disapproval? How about a male who acts like a female? If you answered yes, which sex do you think meets with more disapproval?

Most societies classify infants as either male or female at birth, and assign social roles accordingly. Learning to identify oneself as a member of a particular sex and to behave in a manner appropriate to that sex is part of enculturation (Chapter 2), and it begins almost immediately. In North America, for instance, gender identification begins the first time a baby boy's father tussles with him gently and addresses him as "tough guy." Observing how his parents behave is perhaps the most important way he formulates his gender identity. He watches his father to see what he should do to be male, and he observes his mother to see what he must *not* do to be male. The opposite, of course, is true for girls.

In Chapter 5 (see page 118), we mentioned the work of feminist anthropologist Carol Gilligan (1982), who suggests that middle-class American girls are enculturated differently from boys: they are encouraged to maintain close ties with their families, particularly their mothers, while boys are not. This, according to Gilligan, produces adult females who value social continuity and accommodation, and adult males who value independence and aggressiveness. This general notion finds support cross-culturally. Nancy Chodorow (1974) has shown that in some societies, boys must reject feminine qualities and identification with their mothers to become men. Among the Shavante of Brazil, for example, boys must leave their homes and reside in a special house, where they are taught behavior appropriate to males in their society. Girls, in contrast, continue their early relationship with their mothers as they become women. In his fieldwork among the Tetum (see map on page 139), David Hicks discovered that Tetum females were associated with the idea of bringing two parties together, while men were associated with separating them. A woman assumes the role of priest at a wedding, when wife givers and wife takers come together. At a death ritual, a man, by drawing his sword, performs the task of driving the soul of the deceased from the community of the living.

The Shakers, who numbered in the thousands early in the nineteenth century, abstained from sex, believing it to be evil. Because they produced no successors, the sect virtually disappeared. A nineteenth-century lithograph shows Shakers performing the dance that gave them their name.

• Attitudes Toward Sexual • Expression

Negative Versus Positive Attitudes

Although sex is universal, not every society views it as a positive contribution to social life. Sex can be invested with negative, even evil, connotations, and powerful efforts may be made to suppress it.

One example is the Shakers, a small group of English Quakers who left their church and country to immigrate to upstate New York in the late eighteenth century.[1] Two of the Shakers's most important principles, both arising from the belief that sex is evil and corrupting, were to avoid sexual relations and marriage (they also promoted pacifism, the communal ownership of property, seclusion from

---

[1] The sect's name reflects its manner of worship; Shakers would sing, dance, and tremble as they felt themselves filled with spiritual power.

• Ask Yourself •

In January 1993, more women entered the U.S. Congress than ever before. In your opinion, will these women be guided by distinctively feminine values as they grapple with difficult political decisions and seek to increase their influence as individual politicians? If so, do you expect this to change anything about the way the country is run?

the outside world, sexual equality, and abstinence from liquor and tobacco). By the early nineteenth century, the Shakers had recruited some six thousand members, but because they abstained completely from sex, they of course produced no successors. As time passed, and fewer and fewer people agreed that sex was ungodly and could be dispensed with, the Shakers gradually declined in numbers, and today the sect has all but disappeared.

While few societies disapprove of sex to the extent that the Shakers did, cross-culturally there is a wide range of attitudes toward sexual behavior.[2] The Thonga of Africa believe that sexual activity can adversely affect both nature and humans. Some people, particularly married couples, are considered sexually "hot," and hence dangerous. By having sex too often, "hot" people are likely to upset the fragile balance of nature and injure people who are elderly or sick (Frayser 1985:1). In Uttar Pradesh, India, some people believe that sex should be reserved for reproduction only, not for pleasure. The Manus of New Guinea, like the Shakers, consider sexual intercourse to be evil and shameful (1–2). In former times, the Bella Coola of the Pacific Northwest believed that sex weakened people and should therefore be avoided by those wishing to be successful at enterprises like hunting. Bella Coola men refrained from sex for four days before a hunt.

Other cultures share the Bella Coola belief that sex can strip individuals, especially men, of their vitality. Societies with such beliefs often limit sexual activity before tasks requiring skill, strength, or energy. Consider the findings of anthropologist W. Arens, who as a college student traveled by chartered bus to a football game with his university's team. Two players, noticing that there were some unoccupied seats, asked the coach if their girlfriends could ride to the game with them. "Absolutely not," the coach responded—but it would be all right if the girls joined their boyfriends for the ride *home*. Years later, interested in the cross-cultural analysis of symbolic behavior, Arens (1981) recalled this incident while studying the customs of professional football players in the United States. At training camps, players are often isolated from women; even married players must live at the camp, apart from their wives, and may visit them only if there is no game or practice the next day. Professional football games are often played on Sundays, and players routinely spend Saturday nights with one another rather than with their wives. This custom defies the scientific finding that sex before physical exertion can be beneficial because it promotes relaxation, but it shows that some Westerners, too, believe that sex strips a man of his strength.

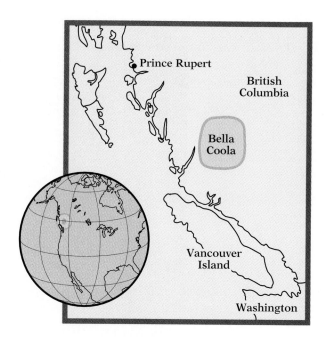

Most people in Western society consider sex to be a positive aspect of life under some circumstances (for instance, when viewed as an expression of love between a wife and husband) and a negative one in others (for instance, when it transfers a venereal disease from one person to another), although until relatively recently sex outside of marriage in mainstream Western society was severely disapproved of (D'Emilio and Freedman 1988; Flandrin 1991). Most Christian churches regarded premarital and extramarital sex (see below) as immoral; but an even more powerful reason for the long-lasting prohibition against it was probably the disastrous social and economic consequences of unwed motherhood. In the course of only a few decades, however, public attitudes toward sexual activity changed so radically that the change has been termed a *sexual revolution*. Varieties of sexual behavior once considered immoral or even criminal have come to be tolerated or even viewed as normal.

This dramatic change actually began well over half a century ago, in the 1920s, when young, middle-class Americans began to dance to a new, black-inspired kind of music called jazz, watch Hollywood sex sirens perform in the movies, read the widely publicized works of sexual theorists such as Sigmund Freud and Havelock Ellis, and "scoff . . . at the sexual prudery" of earlier years (D'Emilio and Freedman 1988:241). World War II, during which

---

[2] For many of the examples in this chapter, we rely on Suzanne Frayser's useful book *Varieties of Sexual Experience: An Anthropological Perspective on Human Sexuality* (New Haven, CT: HRAF Press, 1985).

huge numbers of American women took factory jobs once held by men who had been drafted into the armed services, liberated both men and women from traditional social expectations (Margolis 1984). In the early 1960s, the introduction of "the pill" provided additional leverage for changing America's attitude toward sex. Women in particular, freed from the threat of unwanted pregnancy, now had even greater opportunities to enjoy their sexuality. Their increasing sexual liberation was closely intertwined with the feminist movement of the late 1960s and 1970s. The fact that they now paid no more of a penalty than men for sexual activity contributed to women's increasing social equality.

Then, beginning in the early 1980s, AIDS (acquired immune deficiency syndrome) began to exert a profound effect on sexual behavior, at least wherever the causes and consequences of this disease were understood. In the West (as elsewhere), other sexually transmitted diseases (**STD**s), such as gonorrhea and syphilis, had been common, sometimes epidemic, for years. Their existence no doubt had had some moderating effect on sexual behavior, but these diseases were either curable or controllable, which diminished their impact on behavior. AIDS, however, is fatal, and as its incidence increased dramatically through the 1980s and into the 1990s, sexual behavior changed accordingly (D'Emilio and Freedman 1988:357). Although AIDS did not curtail the casual attitude of many Westerners toward sex, it did affect the amount and kind of sexual activity in which people engaged. In other words, AIDS slowed the pace of the sexual revolution. It remains to be seen whether a medical victory over this disease will result in a return to the unbridled sexual activity of the 1970s.

Despite AIDS and other STDs, most members of modern, industrialized, Western societies view sexual relations as desirable. They have sex for pleasure as well as procreation, and they consider this activity to be both enjoyable and healthy. In North America, sex for pleasure and for physical and mental well-being is viewed as so desirable that advertisers of products from cars to household cleansers continually promote their wares by associating them with sexually attractive individuals. In response, Americans lavish millions of dollars a year to increase their sex appeal by buying these products.

Children and Sexual Expression

Scientific evidence has established that children are capable of virtually every type of sexual expression found in adults, including erections and orgasms (Ford and Beach 1951:197; Masters, Johnson, and Kolodny 1985:200). Cross-culturally, however, there is as much variety in people's attitudes toward sexual activity among children as toward adult sexuality. These attitudes range from outright denial of childhood sexuality, to prohibition, condemnation, disinterest, amusement, pride, or even encouragement (see Masters, Johnson, and Kolodny 1985:623).

A few cultures do not accept the view that children have sexual urges (Ford and Beach 1951:180), an attitude that was to a great extent true of Western society until Sigmund Freud's research suggested otherwise. And in some societies, children's sexuality is acknowledged but repressed. The Kwoma of New Guinea punish boys so severely for masturbating that they learn not to touch their genitals even while urinating. In most of these restrictive societies, adults maintain a conspiracy of silence about sex while children are present, and children are not allowed to see adults indulging in sex. As in Western society, they may be told fanciful tales about where babies come from, and, as a result, may remain ignorant of the many culturally determined aspects of sex until they are married. There is, however, no evidence to suggest that the normal biological urges of these children are actually repressed (183).

In still other societies, childhood sexuality is actively encouraged. The Trobriand and Alorese Islanders, introduced in earlier chapters, allow their children to masturbate freely and to engage in sex play with other children. And in a few other societies, adults not only encourage childhood sexuality but actually participate in it. Parents among the Siriono of Bolivia, for instance, fondle their children sexually (Ford and Beach 1951:188), although some say they are merely soothing them (Masters, Johnson, and Kolodny 1985:632). Societies with liberal attitudes toward childhood sexual activity tend to be the ones in which children are permitted to observe adults engaging in sex. Alorese children, for instance, are familiar with all of the details of adult sexual intercourse by the time they are five years old (Ford and Beach 1951:189).

STD sexually transmitted disease

Siriono

We can regard these restrictive and permissive societies as representing polar extremes regarding attitudes toward children and sex. Most societies lie between these two poles.

Premarital, Extramarital, and Postmarital Sex

Some societies forbid premarital sex entirely, but many more either permit or encourage it. In fact, the idea that young people should not have sex before marriage is quite unusual, cross-culturally. Western society is one of only a few in which premarital sexual activity short of intercourse is common among the unmarried as a way of preserving virginity and/or avoiding pregnancy (Masters, Johnson, and Kolodny 1985:627).

The Maasai of East Africa (see map on page 141) provide an example of a society in which premarital sex is encouraged. After rituals marking the end of boyhood, young Maasai males leave the villages

• Ask Yourself •

Can you think of any reasons why members of a society would want to prevent young children from learning about sex? If you become a parent, how will you handle this subject with your children?

where they were born and go to live in remote camps called *kraals*. For the next 10 or 15 years, which a young man spends as a warrior, the kraal is his home. Here, older warriors teach him how to fight and to raid other tribes' herds of cattle. The warriors cannot marry, but they are permitted to have sex with young women who live with them in the kraal. Such liaisons are not expected to lead to marriage. A girl who gets pregnant returns to her village, where she marries. She is not stigmatized for having had premarital sex nor for having become pregnant, because the Maasai welcome children—and anyway, at one time or another the majority of Maasai females have sexual relations with the warriors in the kraal. When his period as a warrior comes to an end, a man returns to his village, marries, and assumes the rights and duties of a husband and father (Saibull 1981; Saitoti 1988).

In contrast, there are various societies around the Mediterranean where girls must remain virgins until they marry or else suffer public shame and greatly reduced chances of marriage. Since marriage is the "overriding criterion for a fulfilling life" for females in this region (Brandes 1985:113), parents vigorously protect the chastity of their unmarried daughters. In the town of Monteros, Spain, for instance, the "main prerequisite to marriage for women . . . is virginity" (118). Since potential husbands believe that premarital sex for females (but not for males) is somehow defiling, an unmarried woman's chances of marrying are much reduced if she loses her virginity, but a virtuous daughter can readily find a husband. Parents in Monteros tell their daughters, "Good linen, preserved in a trunk, can readily be sold" (118).

Two ideas about premarital sex are encountered worldwide, although not universally. The first, called the **double standard,** is the notion that the rules governing sexual behavior should be different for males and females living in the same society. Of a sample of 61 societies compared by Frayser (1985:203), 18 percent sanctioned premarital sexual activity for males but not for females. In contrast, not a single society permitted females to engage in premarital sex while forbidding the same

double standard the notion that within a single society the rules governing sexual behavior should be different for males and females

In Kenya, unmarried Maasai men live in remote cattle camps called kraals. Here they have sexual relationships, not expected to lead to marriage, with young Maasai women. Above, Maasai youths and their girlfriends clasp hands.

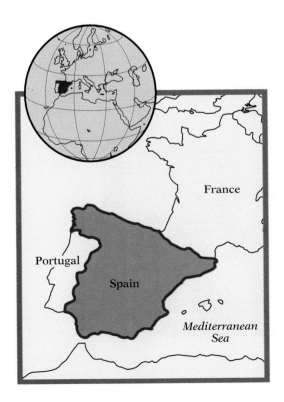

behavior to males. Cross-culturally, then, the double standard is strongly biased in favor of male premarital sex. Frayser adds, however, that in 82 percent of the societies she sampled, no double standard exists. In these societies, members of both sexes must either avoid premarital sex, or else both males and females are allowed to indulge themselves.

The second idea, often found where premarital sex is permitted, is that the females involved must not become pregnant (Frayser 1985:204). Premarital sex is permissible for enjoyment but not for reproduction. Sexual relationships are, in other words, classified as physical rather than social. One might assume that this restriction would characterize modern societies with access to reliable birth control methods, but it applies in nonindustrial societies as well. Typically, if a girl becomes pregnant the pregnancy must be terminated through abortion or the child must be killed. Alternatively, by marrying its father the girl may be permitted to transform a physical relationship between two individuals into the social relationship of marriage.

In no society does marriage always satisfy every human sexual urge; everywhere, incompatibility, illness, or absence are sometimes inevitable (Masters, Johnson, and Kolodny 1985:634).

Extramarital sex (or adultery), meaning sexual relationships involving at least one person who is married but not to the current sex partner, is understandably quite common cross-culturally, and is by no means universally condemned. Indeed, the number of societies that condone extramarital sex, usually under specific circumstances, is relatively high; in one study of 139 societies, 39 percent permitted or approved of adultery (Ford and Beach 1951:113). Among the Toda of India, for example, both married men and married women are allowed to have extramarital relationships, and the language of these people does not include a word for adultery.

Where extramarital sex is permitted, the choice of partner may be limited—typically to a brother or sister of the husband or wife. The Siriono (see map on page 186) permit a husband to have extramarital sex with his wife's sisters or his brothers' wives or even these women's sisters (Ford and Beach

1951:114) but not with women outside of these categories.

The variability in human sexual behavior is again revealed in differences among cultures in the disapproval or prohibition of extramarital sexual activity, more commonly by women. In the study of 139 societies just cited, 61 percent forbid married women to have sex with men other than their husbands (Ford and Beach 1951:115). Far fewer societies restrict married men in this way (the double standard again). But even in societies in which married men are free to have sex with women other than their wives, these relationships may be hard to form because, married or not, all males are competing for the same women. Therefore, although in theory a double standard exists, in actual practice it may be somewhat unusual for a man to be able to "take advantage of his theoretical liberties" (115).

Recent research into American sexual behavior has shown that marriage is such a powerful social institution in this culture that more than 80 percent of women and 65–85 percent of men of every age claim that they have had no sexual relationships with anyone other than their spouses during marriage (Michael et al. 1994:105). The "marriage effect" is "so dramatic" that it does not matter if the couple married in their teens or not until their 30s, after having lived with several other partners.

• Ask Yourself •

What is your personal feeling about premarital sex? Does knowing that in other societies premarital sex is encouraged modify your attitude in any way?

In some societies, widows are expected to wear black clothes and are forbidden to remarry or engage in postmarital sex. Widows in Osijek, Yugoslavia, mourn the deaths of their Croatian husbands, victims of civil war.

The outlawed Indian custom of sati, in which a wife immolates herself on her husband's funeral pyre, is still practiced occasionally in rural India. In this collage, photographs of a Hindu wife, Roop Kunwar, who committed sati, and her husband, Maal Singh, have been incorporated into an idealized depiction of Roop's self-sacrifice.

Few anthropologists have studied postmarital sex—sexual activity among people who are widowed or divorced but have not remarried (Masters, Johnson, and Kolodny 1985:634). One reason may be that there is relatively little postmarital sex to study. In many societies, a widowed or divorced person is expected to remarry immediately, often (in societies in which more than one spouse is permitted) to a cousin or to the husband or wife of a sibling. (This custom is called either the *levirate* or the *sororate,* depending on the sex of the widowed or divorced person; see Chapter 10.) Other societies forbid bereaved spouses, especially widows, to engage in postmarital sex or to remarry.

In a few societies, widows' lives are considered to be over, either figuratively or literally. Some Indian Hindus, for example, once thought a woman whose husband died should die as well, by throwing herself onto the funeral bonfire in which the body of her husband was being cremated. Such

self-sacrifice, they believed, would guarantee a heavenly reunion for the couple. The practice was outlawed in 1829, but customs are often slow to change, and this one, called *sati,* is still practiced occasionally in rural India. As recently as 1987, in a small village in northwestern India, Maal Singh, a married man of only 24, died of gastroenteritis (Tully 1991:210 ff.). At his cremation, his young widow, Roop Kunwar, 18, either voluntarily placed herself on her husband's bonfire or was forced to do so by her father-in-law and other relatives. She burned to death. Shortly thereafter, Roop's father-in-law and 15-year-old brother-in-law were arrested on charges of murder and abetting a suicide. The death of Roop Kunwar unleashed the fury of Indian feminists, who felt that the young woman's death symbolized the ongoing subjugation of Indian women. But devout Hindus by the thousands came to worship at the place where Roop Kunwar died, showing that even today there is widespread respect for a Hindu woman who loses her life in the name of conjugal obligation.

In modern Western culture, it is assumed that people who have once been married, particularly relatively young people, will continue to have sexual relations, and there is general tolerance of postmarital sexual activity (Masters, Johnson, and Kolodny 1985:635). Even though there is little stigma attached either to remaining single after having been married or to having postmarital sexual relations, most divorced or widowed people in our society, unless they are very elderly, eventually remarry.

• Sexual Statuses •

Is There a Gender Hierarchy?

Generally speaking, throughout Western history men have enjoyed more privileges, greater respect, and higher social status than women (Lerner 1986). The same is also true in many other societies. Societies in which males dominate females are called *patriarchies.*

Feminist anthropologists disagree about the causes of patriarchy (Mukhopadhyay and Higgins 1988). Some suggest that it stems from the contrast between the two worlds, or domains, in which individuals live—the domestic (or private or household) domain and the public domain. Activity in the **public domain** conveys more status and authority than activity in the **domestic domain.** Women's activities frequently center about the domestic domain, and men are more active in the public domain.

The concept of two separate spheres of activity helps to put women's relative social status into perspective, and can be linked to other cultural variables such as subsistence strategies, descent systems, and residence patterns, to form a broader, more holistic view of cultures. Some horticultural societies, for example, require women to perform most of the actual work of gardening; that is, they play relatively important economic roles outside (as well as inside) their homes. In these societies, women's status tends to be relatively high. Not surprisingly, in some of these societies family names and some important kinds of property tend to be inherited in the female line, and husbands must often leave their father's homes upon marriage and go to live in or near the homes of their fathers-in-law. Property inheritance and postmarital residence are both good indicators of women's relatively high status. In most agricultural societies, in contrast, the public domain is dominated by men because harnessing big farm animals to plows and digging irrigation channels is heavy work performed mainly by men. Women in such societies tend to be more confined to the domestic domain, and these societies are often characterized by relatively low status for women and by family names and property passing down the male line, and wives having to live with or near their fathers-in-law.

Recently, feminist anthropologists have introduced the concept of **gender hierarchy** into the continuing discussion about patriarchy. The term "refers to the association of what is culturally considered to be maleness ... with social power" (Gailey 1987:x). Females may partake in this hierarchy, but only by adopting the values and behavior appropriate to males. In a gender hierarchy, in other words, there is a difference in status between "maleness" and "femaleness" rather than between specific males and females. Virtually always, maleness is more highly valued.

The concept of gender hierarchy may help us to understand how strong female leaders can be present in societies in which men are generally dominant. Among the Lovedu of Africa, women traditionally served as chiefs (Friedl 1985:228), and it could hardly be said that former British Prime Minister Margaret Thatcher, the "Iron Lady," did not command respect. Yet modern feminists point out that even in Lovedu and British societies, women are, in general, dominated by men.

Late twentieth-century women have shown that there are few activities, beyond biologically determined ones such as breastfeeding, that can be carried out by members of one sex only, yet in most

---

public domain the social sphere that centers on the wider social world outside of the home and is associated with political and economic activity above the household level

domestic (private, household) domain the social sphere that centers on the home and is associated with such activities as child rearing and food preparation for household consumption

gender hierarchy a ranking of cultural notions of maleness and femaleness, as opposed to a ranking of individual males and females

In many societies, there is a clear distinction between women's and men's jobs. Weaving is a common task for women all over the world. Near Quetzeltenango in the highlands of Guatemala, a Maya woman works at a hand loom.

societies men occupy the most important places in public life (if not in the household arena). One cultural-materialist explanation might be that the sex that controls the production and distribution of most of a society's material goods will dominate. Men everywhere tend to control their societies' material wealth, and this seems to determine the relative statuses of men and women and their different roles (Friedl 1984, 1985). But instead of explaining why so many societies consider men superior to women, this observation simply prompts another question. Why is it that men rather than women so often control the production and distribution of a society's material wealth? The answer may lie in the way jobs have historically been assigned according to sex.

The Sexual Division of Labor

The more technologically simple a society, the more likely it is that jobs will be allocated according to sex (Chapter 6). In gathering-and-hunting societies, for instance, males and females have clear-cut roles that seldom overlap. Having collected a great deal of data from nonindustrialized societies, anthropolo-

gists now generally agree that biological differences between the sexes represent the starting point for the rather rigid division of tasks observed in most societies, especially in nonindustrialized settings.[3]

In a cross-cultural study of the division of labor that included 186 societies, Murdock and Provost (1973) discovered that 14 subsistence activities were exclusively allocated to men in every society. These jobs included hunting, mining, boatbuilding, metalworking, and lumbering. Nine other occupations were allocated to men in most of the societies, but in some were assigned predominantly or even exclusively to women. These included tilling fields, building houses, caring for and butchering large domestic animals, fishing, and rope making. In all 185 societies, there were no subsistence activities assigned exclusively to women, and only

---

[3] Earlier we pointed out that many basic human behaviors were established during the long period of time in which prehistoric peoples were gatherers and hunters or simple agriculturalists. This suggests that studying the division of labor in nonindustrialized societies can help us understand contemporary Western society. This assumption—that nonindustrialized people can shed light on our present situation—is common in anthropology.

9—including collecting fuel and water, gathering vegetable foods, cooking, spinning, and laundering—that were usually allocated to women. The 50 remaining occupations—including planting and harvesting crops, milking animals, preserving meat and fish, making clothing and leather goods, basket weaving, and pottery making—were performed by men, women, or members of either sex.

Why do societies commonly associate certain jobs only with males? Our partial list suggests that "male" jobs are those that require a greater degree of physical strength, concentration, endurance, and risk, and are performed publicly. But many women have muscles, concentration, and endurance, and are not opposed to taking risks or working in public. For example, in parts of the developing world women daily trudge for miles with enormous loads of firewood or water balanced on their heads, without apparent exhaustion. In one interesting study of women's strength, scientists recruited a group of rural African women to carry heavy loads on their heads while walking on a treadmill (*New York Times* March 11, 1986). Since oxygen use accurately reflects energy use, the researchers monitored the amounts of oxygen required to carry loads of various sizes. To their surprise, the women were able to carry loads weighing up to 20 percent of their body weight without any increase in their use of oxygen, which meant that loads of this size did not result in any increased expenditure of energy. Carrying an astonishing 70 percent of their body weight increased the women's oxygen use by only half. In contrast, males carrying backpacks equaling 20 percent of their body weight increased their oxygen use by 13 percent, and when they carried loads of 70 percent of their weight, their oxygen use nearly doubled.

To explain why the women could carry heavy loads so much more efficiently than men, the scientists speculated that perhaps carrying weight on their heads over many years produces some anatomical change in women that allows them greater energy efficiency, or maybe the way they walk minimizes the up-and-down movement of their loads. Either way, the experiment showed that women's strength and endurance sometimes outstrips men's.

There is, however, one vitally important activity that only females can perform: nursing infants (White et al. 1975; Burton, Brudner, and White 1977; see also Maher 1992). In societies in which there is no alternative to breastfeeding (as well as those in which alternatives exist but women nevertheless choose to nurse their babies), women may breastfeed for many months and even years. If their babies are to survive, these women *must* take the major responsibility for their care. Child care is a time-consuming job that if well done, strictly limits the type and number of other tasks a woman can undertake at the same time. It eliminates any job that requires intense concentration (such as hunting), since babysitters cannot turn their backs on young children, even for a moment. Jobs that would expose children in the care of the workers to physical danger, such as metalworking, must also be avoided. So women are rarely assigned jobs that involve intense concentration or danger, or for that matter, long-distance travel, sharp tools, or potentially dangerous animals. Instead, they are allotted jobs that are consistent with looking after young children, and, as our list shows, these tend *not* to be the jobs in which the resources or products of society are controlled or distributed. Thus, women generally do not have access to the power that controlling and distributing resources conveys.

Supporters of this cultural-materialist hypothesis further assume that societies, like individuals, are efficient, and that they therefore consistently minimize the time and effort it takes to train people to perform various jobs. For this reason most individuals—including most women who are beyond their childbearing and babysitting years—tend to keep on performing the same jobs throughout their lives rather than retraining for "male" jobs.

Since so often women *must* do the tasks necessary for and consistent with child rearing, the occupations remaining to be done by males are usually those that do not involve child care. Men in nonindustrialized societies rarely care for children, even in those few societies in which women are important politically or economically (Frayser 1985:93–94). Cross-cultural comparisons show that older girls, women whose children have grown up, or women who have no children of their own look after young children far more commonly than men. Feeding and caring for young children are virtual female monopolies, and this has a profound effect on the division of labor in nonindustrial societies. Frayser's conclusions agree with those of White and his colleagues (1975). Labor is divided on the basis of sex so that the subsistence activities on which a society depends will be performed in the most efficient way. If a society is to operate as effectively as possible, certain sexual distinctions and restrictions must be made.

In parts of the developing world, women routinely carry heavy loads on their heads as part of their everyday chores. As village women in Rajasthan, northwestern India, carry pots of water home from a well, they pass men whose work, by comparison, seems less physically demanding.

Feminist anthropologist Ernestine Friedl (1984: 135) notes that women's relative power is the most limited in societies in which women neither provide the bulk of the subsistence necessities nor have much of a hand in the distribution and exchange of valued goods and services outside of the household, or "extradomestically." When women make a major contribution to the food supply and personally take part in its extradomestic distribution, their personal autonomy and influence over others tends to be greater.

The point is aptly illustrated by the sheepherding Sarakatsani of northern Greece. As they do in other Mediterranean societies, men dominate women among the Sarakatsani (Campbell 1964), and the division of labor is strongly associated with local gender-specific beliefs and ideas. Men must display impatience, pride, courage, and masculinity. In contrast, the essential feminine virtues are reticence, patience, fearfulness, humility, and, most important, a sense of shame for being a woman. These ideas help to dictate which jobs are appropriate for men and women.

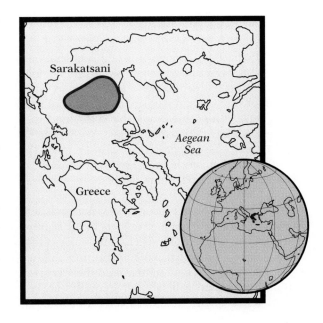

If Friedl's argument is valid, one could hypothe-size that Sarakatsani women probably contribute relatively little to the food supply and play limited roles, if any, in the distribution of resources outside the family. This is in fact the case. Although in an emergency someone of either sex may carry out almost any task, women's work is mainly domestic work: women look after children, cook, make woolen clothes and blankets, cut firewood, raise chickens, carry water, search the mountain slopes for wild foods, and grow vegetables in small gardens. Men spend most of their time caring for flocks of sheep and making and selling products derived from sheep. They also manage their household finances, engage in local politics, arrange marriages for their children, and protect their wives and daughters from insult and assault. The strong dominance of Sarakatsani men over women is apparently a result of these work arrangements.

The Question of Warfare

Warfare is almost universally a male pursuit. Even in the few societies in which women participate in combat, men are generally considered to be better combatants. The reason why has prompted much discussion, but two explanations in particular have attracted anthropologists' interest. The first relies on the hypothesis that males are more naturally aggressive than women and that warfare is primarily an expression of this instinct. The principal male sex hormone (testosterone), it has been hypothesized, seems to predispose males to a somewhat higher level of aggression than females (Konner 1982).

The second argument (see Friedl 1984:135; Frayser 1985:97–98) follows from the fact that only women can bear children and see them through infancy. If a society sent some of its women to war—presumably its youthful women, at the peak of their fighting strength—some would be killed, and thus their reproductive contribution lost, with possibly catastrophic consequences for the society. The potential number of children any one woman can bear is limited to a maximum of about one per year. A man, however, can father many children per year. Thus the loss of men in warfare would not be as serious, in terms of the continued existence of the group, as the loss of women. The specialization of occupations that mandates that women care for children while men fight—so common around the world—is thus perhaps not as "natural" as it seems. It may be a cultural response calculated to avoid extinction.

• Varieties of Sexual • Behavior

There is great variety in the kinds of sexual behavior, both public and private, that are acceptable in different societies. Some societies allow both males and females considerable liberty to express themselves sexually. Others demand restraint—sometimes of the members of both sexes, sometimes of males or females only, sometimes of people of certain social groups or ages. In most societies, sexual behavior that causes physical or psychological harm (rape or child molestation, for example) is prohibited, although there are some exceptions to this generalization. Rape in the course of warfare has been common throughout human history, and rape as an act of social control of women occurs in some societies, including Western society. Sexual practices that may offend some people yet not cause harm to those who engage in them, such as masturbation or homosexuality, are somewhat less widely restricted, although even here tremendous variation among societies occurs.

Masturbation

There is relatively little anthropological information on sexual self-stimulation, although the available data seem to suggest that the range of attitudes is as wide in this area of sexual activity as in any other (Masters, Johnson, and Kolodny 1985:627). Around the world, masturbation seems to be more common among children and adolescents, in whom it is generally tolerated, than among adults, in whom it is generally considered a less desirable form of sexual activity, for both males and females, than sex with a partner (Ford and Beach 1951:156–157; Masters, Johnson, and Kolodny 1985:627). In some societies, masturbation may be considered defiling or, in the case of males, emasculating; in others, it signifies the inability to attract a sex partner. For adolescents, however, it is considered a "natural and normal activity" in many societies that disapprove of the practice among adults (Ford and Beach 1951:157).

Until about the middle of this century, masturbation was discouraged in Western society because of the mistaken belief that it could cause such harmful conditions as sterility, fatigue, misshapen genitals, memory loss, pimples, or insanity (Masters, Johnson, and Kolodny 1985:359–360). We now know that no physical damage results from masturbation, but every one of a group of American males questioned in a recent study said he believed that if it were practiced "excessively," mental illness would result (Offir 1982:190). Nevertheless, 92 percent of American men and 54 percent of American women masturbate occasionally or frequently (Ford and Beach 1951:153–154). Such figures show that masturbation is a statistically normal kind of sexual behavior and, most authorities now contend, a "legitimate type of sexual activity" (Masters, Johnson, and Kolodny 1985:360).

Homosexuality

Although our ethnographic data on homosexuality are relatively scarce (Carrier 1980:101), the desire of some people, both male and female, to have sexual relations with members of their own sex seems to be common worldwide. In fact, homosexual intercourse seems to be the "most important alternative form of sexual expression utilized by people . . . around the world" (118).

Ford and Beach (1951:130) report that in a sample of 76 societies for which information on homosexuality exists, 63 percent regard homosexual activities between adults as normal and socially acceptable. In only 27 percent of these societies is it considered rare or kept secret. For some societies—classical Greece is an example (Dover 1989)—homosexuality is or was socially accepted.

The horticultural Etoro people of New Guinea (see maps on pages 166, 198, and 385) have an intense distaste for sex between males and females (Kelly 1976). Men avoid women as much as possible, for they believe each male has a limited quantity of "life force" within him, and some of it is lost each time he has sex. Men are reluctant to have sex with women for reasons other than reproduction, and the birth of a baby is taken as evidence of a great sacrifice on the part of its father, whose life is believed to have been shortened by the sex act. Etoro women who encourage their husbands to have sex with them may be regarded as witches. Given the belief that intercourse between the sexes is dangerous, it is not surprising that Etoro customs prohibit sex between men and women for more than two hundred days out of the year. Homosexual relations, however, are condoned by the Etoro. Infant boys are thought to be

Homosexuality is found all over the world, with a majority of societies viewing it as socially acceptable. In San Francisco, a gay couple celebrates after officially registering their partnership at City Hall.

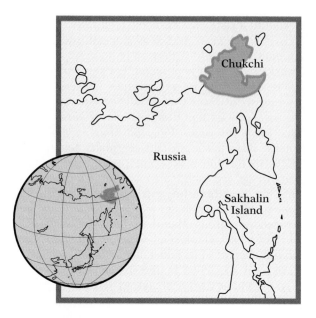

or in addition to being a private matter (Carrier 1980:103). In Siberia, for example, Chukchi men could become powerful religious figures (called shamans; see Chapter 13) by assuming the gender role of women (Lewis 1989). These transformed "women" were permitted to marry other men, and they engaged in homosexual intercourse with their husbands. Because they were thought capable of contacting the spirits and curing the sick, Chukchi shamans enjoyed high prestige. Women, too, could become shamans, as long as they adopted the gender of males. In this role they could marry (biological) males. Similarly, in Africa, some Lango men dressed as women, simulated menstruation, and married other men (Ford and Beach 1951:131).

In contrast, in 27 percent of the societies in Ford and Beach's (1951:129–130) study, homosexuality is reported to be absent, rare, or secret. In these societies, homosexuals are typically punished or ridiculed.

Homosexuality appears to be no more or no less common in North America than elsewhere. Data from recent research in North America suggest that more people find others of the same sex sexually attractive than actually engage in homosexual acts (see Table 8.1), and that males engage in—or at least report—more homosexual activity than females.

born without any of the vital "life force," and they must acquire it to grow into men. They do so by engaging in homosexual relations. Their society places no prohibitions on these activities.

In numerous societies, including some Native American, Polynesian, Asian, and African societies, homosexual behavior is institutionalized instead of

Table 8.1
Homosexuality in America: Percentages of Study Participants Reporting Homosexual Behavior

	Males	Females
Claim to be attracted to members of the same sex	6%	4%
Had sexual relations with member of same sex in past year	2%	Less than 2%
Had sexual relations with member of same sex after age 18	Slightly over 5%	4%
Had sexual relations with member of same sex at any age after puberty	9%	Slightly over 4%
Classify self as homosexual or bisexual	2.8%	1.4%

Source: Michael et al. 1994:174–175.

Because in the past the majority of Americans regarded homosexuality as abnormal and therefore offensive, most such relationships were, until recently, conducted privately rather than publicly. But the recent efforts of gay activists to promote the view that homosexuality is normal, and thus should not be seen as shameful, are helping to change our society's traditional view of homosexuals.

• Ask Yourself •

Try to identify the community of people you feel most a part of. This might be your extended family, high school friends, dorm mates, fellow sorority or fraternity members, or teammates. How is homosexuality viewed within this community? Does your personal view of homosexuality differ from that of this group?

Transsexuality and Transvestism

Cross-cultural comparisons of gender identity reveal that some cultures permit biological females to identify themselves as cultural males, and vice versa. As we saw earlier, people who adopt the social role opposite to their biological inheritance, as Christine Jorgensen did, are called transsexuals. People who are sexually stimulated by wearing clothing appropriate to the opposite sex—in other words, males who enjoy dressing like females and females who like to dress like males—are called **transvestites (cross-dressers).**

Not all transvestites are transsexuals, and not all transsexuals are cross-dressers. Transsexuality and transvestism occur everywhere, and in some cultures are considered normal behavior. They may even be institutionalized. **Berdaches,** transvestite and apparently transsexual men who felt they had been prompted in visions to behave like women, were found in some Native American societies (Callender and Kochems 1983; Williams 1986).[4] Berdaches had many of the same rights and duties as women. They were permitted to dress, style their hair, and speak like women and to cook, do needle-work, and carry out other female activities. The Mohave of California allowed biological females to

Berdaches—transvestite and apparently transsexual men found in some Native American societies—wore women's clothes and carried out women's activities. Zuni berdache We'wha wears a woman's ceremonial costume.

adopt male gender and biological males to adopt female gender (Martin and Voorhies 1975:96–99). When a Mohave person adopted the social role opposite to his or her biological sex, a ceremony was performed. The person would change names and put on the clothing appropriate to the new

transvestite (cross-dresser) a man who dresses like a woman or a woman who dresses like a man

berdache in some midwestern and western Native American societies, a transvestite and perhaps also transsexual male who was prompted by visions to dress and behave like a woman

---

[4] Carrier (1980:106) points out that there is much ambiguity in the anthropological use of the term *berdache,* which has been used as a synonym for *homosexual, hermaphrodite, transvestite,* and *effeminate male.*

gender. So thorough was the transition that the persons involved could marry someone of the same sex because they now had a different gender. Institutionalized cross-dressing occurs today in northwestern India, where males called **hijadas** (also spelled *hijras*) cross-dress, beg for charity, and dance and sing at ceremonies as women (Nanda 1990).

Conclusion

Human sexuality, as noted at the beginning of this chapter, is an ideal subject for cross-cultural analysis because sexuality is universal but the ways in which it is expressed vary widely from culture to culture. For many years, however, the collection of anthropological data on sex and gender was hampered by Westerners' own conservative attitudes toward the subject. In particular, there was little fieldwork focusing on sexuality in women, since such a large proportion of anthropologists were men (Masters, Johnson, and Kolodny 1985:621). Also, sexual activities that were considered abnormal or immoral in Western society were seldom investigated in the field—and when they were, bias was often involved. In discussing homosexuality with informants in New Guinea in the mid-1930s, one anthropologist asked respondents whether they had "ever been subjected to an unnatural practice" (Carrier 1980:101–102). The informants, of course, may not have viewed their homosexual or other sexual practices as unnatural, so the data collected may well have been distorted.

Realizing that our cross-cultural understanding of sexuality was totally inadequate, Gilbert Herdt and Robert Stoller, an anthropologist and a psychoanalyst, decided to pool their expertise in a study of non-Western sexuality. Herdt had carried out fieldwork among the Sambia of New Guinea, and in 1979 he returned to New Guinea with Stoller. The collaborators' goal was to thrust the study of sex more centrally into ethnology (Herdt and Stoller 1986:vii–viii). Their primary research method was not participant observation but interviews, and their perspective was psychological. Women as well as men were interviewed, and the result is perhaps the most exhaustive account of sexuality in a non-Western culture that has yet been attempted.

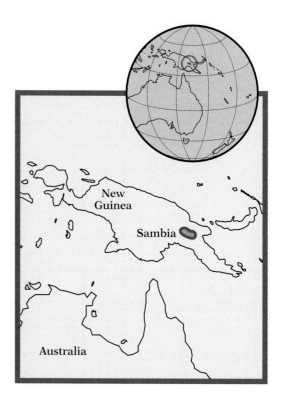

Thanks to our own culture's changing attitudes toward sex, modern ethnographers are less inhibited than their predecessors from seeking data on the subject. Today, as the work of Herdt and Stoller (1986) shows, any question may be put to a willing informant. As a result, we are starting to learn a great deal about what it means to be a woman or a man and about the sexual behaviors of both. What anthropologists have found in their cross-cultural work on sexuality is that there seem to be no "natural," "normal," or "right" sexual behaviors or attitudes. Instead, the whole spectrum, from prohibitive to conservative to indifferent to permissive, can be found among the world's populations.

Summary

- The desire for sexual activity is biological, but its expression and regulation are cultural.

- The term *sex* refers to biological maleness or femaleness; *gender* refers to cultural notions of maleness or femaleness.

- A person's gender identification—his or her sexual orientation and sex role—need not coincide with sex as defined by anatomy.

---

hijada (*hijra*) in northwestern India, a man who cross-dresses, begs for charity, and entertains like a woman at ceremonies

- Some anthropologists claim that male and female children in America are socialized differently; girls are encouraged to maintain social relationships, while boys are encouraged to reject such ties in favor of independence.

- Attitudes toward sexuality vary widely: some societies view sex as negative or evil, whereas others consider it a positive aspect of life.

- The range of attitudes toward premarital sex, postmarital sex, extramarital sex, and sexual activity among children varies widely from society to society.

- Western society's formerly conservative attitude toward sex has loosened considerably over the last 30 years due to many factors, including the growing empowerment of American women.

- Cross-culturally, men often dominate women. Some anthropologists interpret this in the context of public and domestic domains, and link it with such elements of culture as subsistence strategies, descent, and residence.

- A cultural-materialist explanation for male dominance is that whoever controls the production and distribution of the material goods produced by a society is in a position of dominance.

- In the sexual division of labor, women often must take the major responsibility for the care of children. Jobs that allow women to take care of children tend not to be the ones in which the resources or products of society are controlled or distributed.

- Men rather than women usually wage warfare, perhaps because of the biological fact that only women can bear children and societies do not want to put their child-bearers at risk.

- Masturbation, homosexuality, transsexuality, and transvestism are common cross-culturally. They are considered abnormal in some cultures, and normal (even institutionalized) in others.

Key Terms

berdache
domestic (private, household) domain
double standard
gender

gender hierarchy
gender identity
hermaphrodite
hijada (*hijra*)
public domain
sex
STD
transsexual
transvestite (cross-dresser)

Suggested Readings

Ardener, Shirley. (ed.). 1993 (1978). *Defining Females: The Nature of Women in Society*. New York: St. Martin's Press. A collection of articles that view the role of women in a cross-cultural light. It includes discussions of taboos, virginity, education, and birth.

Gilmore, David D. 1990. *Manhood in the Making: Cultural Concepts of Masculinity*. New Haven: Yale University Press. From a psychological perspective, Gilmore examines what it takes to be a man in various societies. Although most societies stress aggressiveness, stoicism, and sexuality, no archetypical male exists. Gilmore concludes that masculinity is learned rather than inherent.

Herdt, Gilbert H. 1987. *The Sambia: Ritual and Gender in New Guinea*. New York: Holt, Rinehart & Winston. A fieldwork study about the use of ritual homosexuality to train warriors among the Sambia. Herdt describes how Sambia culture helps to form gender identity and to stimulate the display of sexuality in a variety of social situations.

Miller, Barbara Diane. (ed.). 1993. *Sex and Gender Hierarchies*. New York: Cambridge University Press. An up-to-date inquiry into the gender hierarchy, a topic that has inspired vigorous debate.

Morgen, Sandra. (ed.). 1989. *Gender and Anthropology: Critical Reviews for Research and Teaching*. Washington, DC: American Anthropological Association. Intended to help college professors bring cross-cultural findings on women into their teaching and research, this edited collection begins with a history of feminist scholarship that shows no single "feminist school" of anthropology exists.

Morris, Jan. 1974. *Conundrum*. New York: New American Library. This autobiography by the well-known English travel writer Jan (formerly James) Morris chronicles the tragedy and joy of the author's psychological and physical transformation from man to woman.

Saitoti, Ole Tepilit. 1988 (1986). *The Worlds of a Maasai Warrior*. Berkeley: University of California Press. A remarkable autobiography by a Maasai man, which includes an intimate account of his experiences as a warrior. Among the topics he discusses are his circumcision and his relationships with young women.

Introduction

UNSOLVED MYSTERY: WHO'LL GET THE RICHES HOWARD HUGHES LEFT BEHIND?

Newspaper Headline, 1976

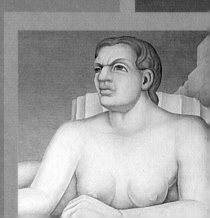

When the industrial tycoon Howard Hughes died in April 1976, he left behind what was described as "the second largest accumulation of riches ever piled up by a single American citizen"—something over $2 billion. But Hughes, an eccentric, reclusive figure in his later years, had left neither a clearly authentic will nor any immediate family to whom his wealth should obviously go—no wife, no children, no grandchildren, no sisters or brothers. His closest known relatives at the time of his death were an 85-year-old aunt and several cousins.

Under the laws of the state of Texas, where Hughes lived, a portion of the estate of an individual who dies without leaving a will may be claimed by any relative of the deceased, no matter how remote. After the U.S. government takes its share, the estate is divided among all claimants according to family ties. Suddenly, **descent** (a relationship defined by a connection to an ancestor through a series of parent-child links) became of overwhelming concern to a number of people who believed they had a legitimate claim to part of Howard Hughes's vast fortune. By August 1976, four months after his death, some 33 Hughes "wills" had surfaced, bequeathing millions to "relatives" Howard Hughes didn't even know he had. Eventually a total of 22 legitimate Hughes relatives were found.

Descent was important in the Hughes case because a great deal of money was at stake, but for most North Americans—whose culture incorporates the Judeo-Christian idea that every person is a worthy individual in his or her own right, not just a member of a particular family—descent is relatively unimportant. In many other societies, people are greatly concerned with family ties, not only because they might inherit something of value but also because their occupations, social status, and choice of spouse are more strongly influenced by the families to which they belong, and the ancestors from whom they trace their descent, than by their character or accomplishments.

In those societies in which descent affects social position, individuals are acutely aware of the names, accomplishments, kinship relationships, and social status of their ancestors, for these are what determine one's place in society. An individual born into a noble family, for example, is, by virtue of descent, automatically a member of the nobility, and as such is entitled to certain privileges denied to commoners. Among Westerners, in contrast, family ties among the living are important, but who is related to whom or descended from what ancestor does not concern us greatly on a day-to-day basis. Most of us would find it difficult to name our eight great-grandparents, much less our more remote ancestors.

Descent involves relatives by birth, or "blood" relatives, in contrast to relatives by marriage (see Chapter 10). Blood relatives are also known as **consanguines (consanguinal kin),** because they are related

---

descent a relationship defined by a connection to an ancestor through a series of parent-child links

consanguines (consanguinal kin) individuals related by ties of consanguinity

Can you name all eight of your great-grandparents? Can you name any of *their* parents?

by **consanguinity,** a relationship based on the tie between parents and children that also includes more distant relatives. As noted in Chapter 4, the complete set of such relationships for any single individual forms that person's genealogy. In every society, these relationships pass (or, as anthropologists say, "descend") from one generation to the next, following certain rules.

This chapter examines, from a cross-cultural perspective, how descent contributes to social identity; how it fits together synchronically with other aspects of culture such as rights and duties, inheritance, religion, marriage, political authority, and residence; and how it influences individuals' attitudes and behavior.

In many non-Western societies, family ties are of greater importance than they are in North America. A young Korean shows off part of his family tree, which extends back to the sixth century and occupies five thick volumes.

enable us to display relationships between relatives more conveniently than is possible with verbal description alone.

Figure 9.1 contains triangles, circles, squares, vertical lines, extended "equals" signs, horizontal brackets, and a variety of letters. Combined, these symbols represent the family relationships of a particular figure, the person from whose perspective the diagram has been constructed. In any kinship diagram, this person is called **ego,** and ego is always represented by whichever triangle, circle, or square is darkened. In Figure 9.1, ego is the darkened triangle at the bottom of the diagram, and each of the other shapes represent people who stand in particular relationships to ego. For instance, there is a triangle labeled *father,* but this person is *father* only with respect to ego. From the perspectives of other individuals represented in the diagram, this person may be a brother, uncle, husband, or other male relative. Because a kinship diagram is always constructed from the perspective of a single person, it follows that there cannot be two or more egos in the same diagram.

Using only a few different symbols, we can easily diagram most kinship relationships. Triangles stand for males, circles stand for females, and squares are used when gender is irrelevant for purposes of the diagram. In this particular diagram, ego is male, but we could just as easily have constructed the diagram from the point of view of a female or an ego whose sex is irrelevant.

• Kinship Diagrams •

Anthropologists use kinship diagrams to help describe and explain descent. These diagrams

consanguinity a relationship based on the tie between parents and children that also includes more distant relatives

ego the individual from whose perspective a kinship diagram is drawn

The Anthropologist at Work

Mormon Genealogists

An example of how kinship is integrated with religion is provided by the members of the Church of Jesus Christ of the Latter Day Saints, better known as Mormons. Mormons believe that to enter the kingdom of heaven after death, one must have been baptized a Mormon. Thus no one born before 1830, when the Mormon church was founded, can gain entrance to heaven unless he or she is baptized by proxy. Following the advice of their founder to "seek after your dead," Mormon genealogists have embarked on a monumentally ambitious project to collect the names and relationships of the dead all over the world in order to identify their ancestors and to perform for them, by proxy, the ordinances that will ensure their entry into the "Celestial Kingdom." Since all Mormons have non-Mormon ancestors, these genealogists aim for no less than a complete compilation of the names and lines of descent of every member of the human species for whom some record exists—an estimated 6 or 7 billion people (Shoumatoff 1985).

In the 1960s, by tunneling 700 feet into a granite mountain in Utah, the Mormons constructed six huge bombproof vaults for the storage of genealogical records. In one of these is already stored, on microfilm, over a billion names, a prodigious proportion of what the Mormons hope will eventually be a complete archive of human genealogy, "wherein the name and vital records of every man and woman born on earth is collected, indexed, computerized, and, ultimately, baptized into the . . . family of saints" (Stewart 1980:8).

To make its compilation of names and genealogies as thorough as possible, the Mormon Genealogical Society is laboriously searching through old birth and death records, family histories, church rosters, marriage license applications, land sale documents, and censuses in 44 countries, both Western and non-Western, around the globe. Realistically, the genealogists have little hope that they will eventually record the name of everyone who ever lived, since so many people lived and died before the time of recorded history, but they do expect to ferret out records for most of the people who lived between 1500 and 1900, eventually adding the names and records of all twentieth-century people. Whenever possible, they will augment this stupendous list with ancient records, oral or written, extending deep into the past. Some Chinese clan histories, for example, go back to 1000 B.C. (Stewart 1980:8).

By now, the Mormons "have done enough genealogy to realize that everybody, in the end, is kin" (Shoumatoff 1985:13). The stunning fact of the matter is that there is no human being now alive anywhere on this earth who is more distantly related to any other human being than the degree of fiftieth cousin. "The

---

To keep kinship diagrams uncluttered, triangles, circles and squares may represent not just one individual but a whole category of relative. In other words, every individual related to ego in the same way is represented by the same triangle, circle, or square. In Figure 9.1, for example, there is a circle representing ego's "father's sister" (a person English speakers call "aunt"). If ego's father has several sisters, all of them—unless there is some special reason for distinguishing them—are represented by this one circle, because each aunt stands in exactly the same relationship to ego.

The other commonly used symbols in kinship diagrams—vertical lines, extended "equals" signs,

Following the advice of their church's founder to "seek after your dead," Mormons are searching through documents all over the world in an attempt to collect the names and genealogies of every- one who has ever lived. They do their genealogical research in bomb proof laboratories dug into a mountain in Utah.

'family of man' which has been posited by many religions and philosophies . . . actually exists" (244).

The Mormon genealogists pursue their quest largely for religious reasons, but the amassing of names has other useful functions as well. Genetic researchers, for example, have used the work of the Mormons to learn more about hereditary diseases, and lawyers have resorted to the records stored in the Mormons' "mountain of names" to settle legal claims (Shoumatoff 1985:280–281). But perhaps the most important function of the Mormon genealogists' work is to satisfy, for the many individuals who consult it, what some people believe is a "basic human need for kinship" (14).

horizontal brackets, and slashes—represent rela- tionships or events rather than categories of relatives. A vertical line stands for descent. In Figure 9.1, lines of descent link individuals in three generations. An extended equals sign stands for the tie created by marriage. A horizontal bracket stands for the relationship between siblings: the figure shows that ego has a sister, represented by a circle connected to ego's triangle by a bracket. A slash through a triangle, circle, or square indicates the individual represented is dead, as is the case in Figure 9.1 of ego's wife. Finally, a slash through an equals sign shows that a marriage has ended in divorce, as happened between the couple at the top

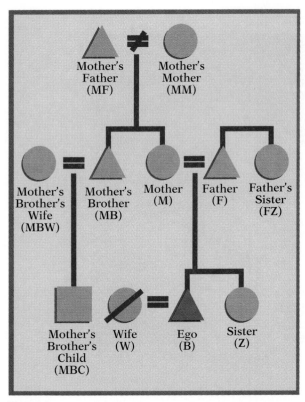

Figure 9.1

Kinship Diagram. In a typical kinship diagram, ego is the point of reference from which we define all relatives. With triangles, circles, vertical lines, horizontal lines, extended "equals" signs, and abbreviations, we have the basic tools to reduce a tangle of complex kinship connections to a relatively simple diagram.

of the diagram (ego's mother's father and mother's mother).

While *categories* of individuals and their relationships are represented by signs, *individuals* are identified in kinship diagrams by letters. Some are represented by the first letters of their kinship terms; others are represented by two or more letters, combinations of the letters that stand for the basic kinship terms. Some possibilities are

F = father,   FF = father's   father   (or   paternal grandfather)
M = mother,   MM = mother's   mother,   MF = mother's father

D = daughter,   DD = daughter's   daughter   (or granddaughter)
S = son, SS = son's son (or grandson)
FB = father's   brother,   FBC = father's   brother's child
MB = mother's brother, MBC = mother's brother's child
C = child
H = husband, W = wife

Since the terms *son* and *sister* both begin with the letter *S*, the letter *Z* is used to designate sisters, while *S* denotes sons. Thus

FZ = father's sister
FZS = father's sister's son

and so on.

Figure 9.1 shows some of ego's relatives. We can see from the diagram that ego has one or more sisters, but no brothers. His mother has at least one male sibling (MB), and his father has at least one female sibling (FZ). Ego's mother's brother is married, and MB and his wife (MBW) have a child (MBC)—represented by a square, since we do not wish to be specific about this child's sex. Ego's grandparents on his mother's side—MF and MM—are shown on the top line of the diagram.

In kinship diagrams, an "uncle" is typically specified precisely as either FB (father's brother) or MB (mother's brother). A cousin could be many different people: FBD, FBS, FZD, FZS, MBD, MBS, MZD, or MZS. We avoid terms like *uncle, aunt,* and *cousin* because they can refer to any one of several different people. *Cousin,* for example, can be either a male or female, and related to ego through either parent. Moreover, a person who stands in the relationship of cousin to ego in the context of Western society might not be considered a cousin if ego were a member of a different society, despite the fact that the genealogical relationship between ego and this person is identical in both cases.

In North America, we usually use kinship terms such as *cousin* without worrying about their imprecision, but in many cultures precision is essential, since distinctions among kinship terms can reflect differences in how rights and duties are allocated. To take the usages of such cultures into account, anthropologists distinguish between two basic types of cousins (Figure 9.2). **Parallel cousins** are children of siblings of the same sex. Ego's mother's sister's child (either male or female) is ego's parallel cousin, because ego's mother and her sister are sib-

parallel cousin children of siblings of the same sex

Drawing by R. Chast; © 1988 The New Yorker Magazine, Inc.

lings of the same sex. Ego's father's brother's child is also ego's parallel cousin, because ego's father and his brother are of the same sex. **Cross cousins** are children of siblings of the opposite sex. Ego's mother's brother's child (either male or female) is ego's cross cousin, because ego's mother and her brother are of the opposite sex. Ego's father's sister's child is also ego's cross cousin, since ego's father and his sister are opposite-sex siblings.

Cousins linked to ego through M (for example, ego's mother's brother's child) are ego's **matrilateral cousins,** and those linked to ego through F (e.g., ego's father's sister's child) are **patrilateral cousins.**

Thus, although English kinship terminology groups them indiscriminately under the broad term *cousin*, anthropological usage accords each type of cousin its own special term: matrilateral cross cousin, matrilateral parallel cousin, patrilateral cross cousin, or patrilateral parallel cousin. Distinguishing among

cross cousin children of siblings of the opposite sex

matrilateral cousin cousin on the mother's side

patrilateral cousin cousin on the father's side

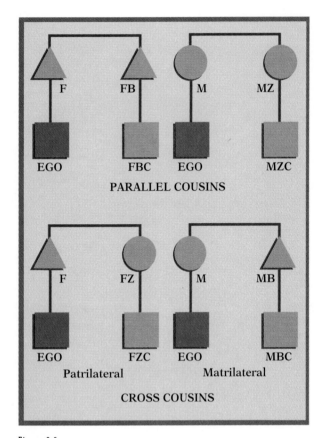

Figure 9.2
Parallel and Cross Cousins

these cousins is not important for the allocation of rights and duties in Western society, but in certain non-Western societies it is very important indeed, for certain cousins are considered to be ideal potential marriage partners for ego, while others are absolutely prohibited (see Chapter 10).

Some anthropologists use a different convention for representing individuals in kinship diagrams. Instead of using the first letter of the word for each relative, they use the first two letters. Thus, father is Fa, mother is Mo, and daughter is Da. Other rela-

tives are represented by a combination of these symbols: father's sister is FaSi, and mother's brother is MoBr.

• Families •

In the stereotypical (and idealized) Western view, a family consists, at a minimum, of a father, a mother, and their unmarried children. Today, however, the majority of "families," in both North America and the rest of the world, take some other form. To be as inclusive as possible of these many alternative forms, we may define a **family** as two or more individuals who consider themselves related, who are economically interdependent, and who share the responsibility for rearing any children in their group. This definition is expansive enough to include not only individuals who are related by blood or marriage, but also those unrelated in either of these ways but who nevertheless consider themselves related (a homosexual couple, for instance, or an adult and an adopted child). Members of a family usually live together, but since this is not always the case, our definition of the family does not include common residence as a criterion.

The various functions of the family may include attending to the physical, psychological, economic, linguistic, and social needs of infants and children, and providing adults with the resources they need to cope with the problems of daily life. These resources include psychological benefits such as security and a feeling of being loved.

Family Types

Anthropologists use distinct terms for the different forms a family can take. A **nuclear (or elementary or simple) family** is a unit consisting of a father, a mother, and unmarried children. Many people belong to two nuclear families: the one into which they were born or adopted and the one they created by having or adopting children. In some societies, a man may be married to more than one wife at the same time, and a woman may have more than one husband at same time (see Chapter 10). Such unions are best considered as two or more nuclear families sharing one member in common, rather than as a single nuclear family.

In most societies, the nuclear family has essential economic, sexual, psychological, child-rearing, and legal functions to fulfill. These functions could

---

family two or more individuals who consider themselves related, who are economically interdependent, and who share the responsibility for rearing any children in their group

nuclear (elementary, simple) family a social unit consisting of a father, a mother, and unmarried children

"I guess we'd be considered a family. We're living together, we love each other, and we haven't eaten the children yet."

Drawing by S. Gross; © 1993 The New Yorker Magazine, Inc.

The popular TV show "Rosanne" portrays a nuclear family, consisting of a married couple and their children. This family type has long been viewed as the ideal in Western culture, but it is becoming less and less common.

relatives it may include. One's extended family might include the members of the family one was born into, together with the married children of this family, and the families those married children created through their marriages. Or an extended family might consist of two brothers, their wives, and their children.

The nuclear family is virtually universal, but some exceptions do occur. Among the Nayar of southwest India in traditional times, a family "was in no sense a legal, residential . . . productive, or distributive group" (Gough 1962:363). A husband/father did not live with his wife and children, did not eat regularly with them, and did not work with or for them, nor did he customarily distribute goods to his children. Instead, he lived with or near his sisters, and his children and wife resided with the wife's brother, who provided for them. Thus the Nayar residential group comprised children, their mother, and the mother's brother.

be managed by other institutions, but the family provides a very convenient way of combining them.

An **extended family** is a larger family group, more variable than the nuclear family in terms of the

---

extended family a larger family group than the nuclear, whose membership is more variable

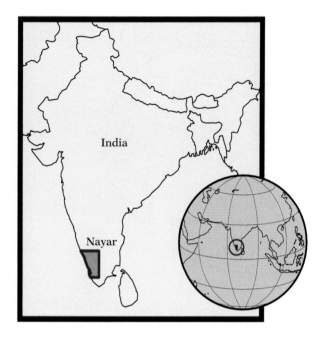

Another variation on the family unit is found in Israel, where some people live in **kibbutzim** (sing. form: **kibbutz**), agricultural collectives whose main features include communal living, collective ownership of all property, and communal child rearing (Lavi 1990). The nuclear family, as defined above, does not exist in the kibbutz, any more than it does among the Nayar. A wife and husband do not form an economic unit. Instead, each works for the kibbutz as a whole. Women cook, sew, launder, and carry out other domestic chores not only for their husbands but also for the whole kibbutz. Men grow agricultural produce for everyone, not just for their wives and children. Children live apart from their parents, eat together, and are supervised by nurses, visiting their parents for a few hours every day.

Western "Family Values"

Many Westerners value the traditional nuclear family as the ideal social unit. During the 1992 presidential campaign, for example, the Vice President of the United States, Dan Quayle, repeatedly promoted the virtues of the "traditional" nuclear fam-

---

kibbutz an agricultural collective in Israel whose main features include communal living, collective ownership of all property, and the communal raising of children

ily. To emphasize his point, he condemned the TV sitcom "Murphy Brown" for portraying a family headed by a single parent—a woman who had chosen unwed motherhood. Quayle may not have approved of single-parent families, but U.S. government figures show that they are becoming increasingly common. In 1991, only 26 percent of all U.S. households consisted of married couples with children, in contrast to 40 percent in 1970. The number of families headed by single, never-married women increased at an annual rate of almost 15 percent during the 1970s. It dropped to just under 10 percent between 1980 and 1991, but female-headed households still constitute the fastest-growing type of family in the United States. In 1992, single mothers—never-married, separated, divorced, or widowed—headed about 24 percent of families with children; single fathers headed about 3 percent (Applebaum and Chambliss 1995).

The marriage rate, too, has decreased. Fewer Americans married in 1991 than in any year since 1965. One explanation links marriage with economics: perhaps more marriages are postponed when the national economy is weak. Another explanation may be that many modern American women either choose to have jobs outside their homes or have to have them for economic reasons, yet at the same time many wish to be mothers. Since both activities are time-consuming, some women try alternative ways of sequencing babies and careers. Some marry,

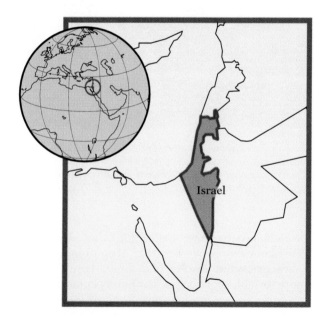

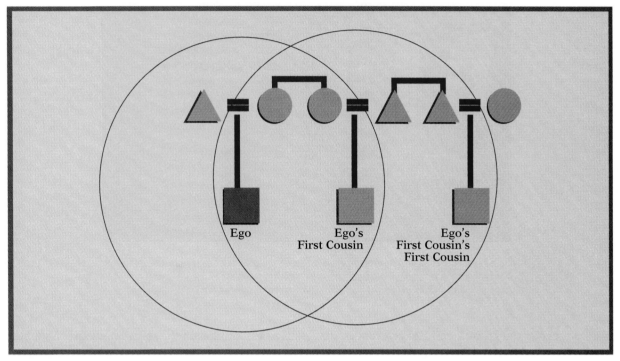

Figure 9.3

Partial Kindreds. Not every member of ego's kindred has the same ancestors; only siblings of ego have the same ancestors and hence belong to the same kindred as ego (after Fox 1983: 165).

then have babies, then start careers; others establish careers first, then marry, then have children. Others, like Murphy Brown, choose careers and babies prior to or without marriage (Barringer 1992).

Family Property

Family ties may grant certain rights over the property of relatives, especially in non-Western societies. *Property* sometimes means tangible property such as houses, fields, buffaloes, or, as in the case of Howard Hughes, $2 billion. But the property regulated by descent may also consist of intangible wealth.

In Western societies, intangible property regulated by descent may include the right to use a family surname or eligibility for membership in a certain social class, both of which pass to children through their parents. In non-Western societies, other rights, such as the right to run for a certain political office or to wear certain ornaments, can be regulated by descent. Descent may also impose certain duties on relatives, duties that may again involve both types of property. The obligation to help a relative build a house involves something

tangible, while the obligation to refrain from speaking in the presence of a superior is intangible.

Kindreds

Even larger than the extended family is the circle of relatives known as the **kindred,** a group of individuals who all have at least one living relative, ego, in common (Figure 9.3). Ego's kindred consists of all relatives, on both M's and F's side, to whom ego considers himself or herself related. Potentially, this group of people could be enormous, but in practice each individual limits the number of relatives from whom mutual rights and obligations are expected by forgetting about, or not keeping in touch with, the more distant ones.

Kindreds are "ego-focused" groups—that is, their members do not have a common ancestor;

---

kindred a group of relatives who all have at least ego in common

In Borneo, members of a number of Iban extended families live together in a single long-house. Each occupant is related to every other occupant, either by consanguinity or marriage. Thus, every occupant lives with numerous members of his or her kindred.

instead, ego is the group's point of reference. The members of ego's kindred are not all related to one another. Ego's kindred may include cousins on M's side and cousins on F's side, but the kindreds of these individuals may not include each other. Apart from ego's siblings, therefore, ego does not share exactly the same kindred with anyone else. Because kindreds are personal groupings, they cannot have any legal, economic, or political function outside of the perspective of ego. Ego's children do not inherit membership in ego's kindred; they have their *own* personal kindreds. Ego's kindred is ego's alone, so when ego dies, this kindred becomes extinct.

The Iban of the island of Borneo in Indonesia provide an example of how kindreds function. These people live in large houses, called longhouses, each containing from 30 to 350 inhabitants (Fox 1983:160). Extended families occupy separate apartments in this building, with as many as 50 extended families in the same longhouse. Members of the extended families are related to each other either by consanguinity or marriage, so that any given individual has many members of his or her kindred living in the same building.

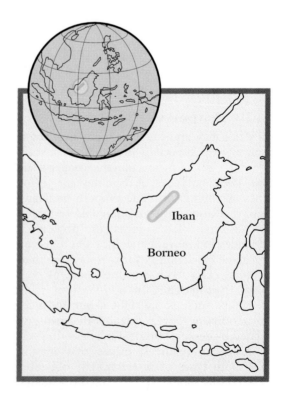

• Ask Yourself •

List and count the members of your kindred. Does this group contain all your first cousins, or have you lost touch with some of them—due to divorce, perhaps, or geographical separation? Does it contain more distant relatives?

The many people living together in an Iban long-house do not form an economic group, yet in the past, large groups of Iban men pursued common economic goals, joining together on large-scale trading and head-hunting expeditions. They managed to field such numerous forces by exploiting the only kinship group of any size they had, the kindred. An Iban man's personal kindred might include his father, father's brother, mother's brother, son, brother, and other consanguines up to and including his first and second cousins, from whom he had the right to demand help and to whom he had the duty to reciprocate when they needed his help. But a single kindred rarely had enough members to help a man with a full-scale trading or raiding venture. More were needed. So the consanguines of ego's consanguines would be called upon. Each member of ego's kindred had his *own* kindred, and could call upon its members to join forces with the original ego's kindred. Each new recruit, in turn, recruited members of *his* kindred to join the expedition, and so on. In this way, more and more men were drawn into the network until eventually there were enough to carry out the task, be it trading or head-hunting. If the venture succeeded, each participant shared in the spoils.

• Descent Groups •

Every society has some system of descent. For many, although not Western society, the most prominent expression of this system is the **descent group,** a group of consanguines, male and female, who believe they can trace their relationship to one another back to a common ancestor who founded their group. Descent groups can be of enormous influence in the lives of their members, especially in some non-Western societies in which persons not belonging to such a group are denied full legal recognition. Before examining the different forms descent groups may take, we shall first describe some of the features most of them share.

The Corporate Nature of Descent Groups

A descent group is a corporate group—a body that, under local law or custom, is recognized as representing all its members, and that is endowed by society with certain rights and duties. Unlike the kindred, descent groups continue in existence from generation to generation even as their members are

born and die. Diagramatically, a descent group is apt to resemble a pyramid, for as the number of descending generations increases, so, too, does the number of relatives in each generation. The members of descent groups often control resources or own property in common, and cooperate in such activities as building houses, cultivating gardens, and protecting common political interests.

Descent Groups and Residence

Often the adult members of the same sex in a descent group have the same pattern of residence. Either they are all localized (meaning they live with or near one another) or they are all dispersed. There is an advantage to having a descent group that is localized. If descent is through males, men are kept together on their ancestral lands, always at hand to prevent men of other descent groups from moving in and exploiting their territory's natural resources. And such a group is more cohesive than one whose members are scattered, since its members can easily be assembled in an emergency—a natural disaster or a social upheaval, such as an attack by another descent group. The advantages of localized groups when descent is through females are not so great, since it is not usually females but males who manage land, fight, and hold political office. However, localized females do provide benefits to their descent groups. They may, for instance, be jointly responsible for continuing the traditions of their groups.

Descent Groups and Exogamy

Exogamy is the social rule that one must marry someone from *outside* one's own group, however that group is defined. The Western extended family is an exogamous unit, since family members must seek spouses from families other than their own. (In contrast to exogamy, *endogamy* is the practice of marrying a spouse chosen from *within* one's own group. Endogamy is discussed in the next chapter.)

Descent groups are often exogamous. When this is the case, their members may not marry one another, but must find their spouses outside the group. Sexual relations between group members constitute incest,

---

descent group a group made up of individuals who trace their descent to a common ancestor

exogamy the social rule that one must marry someone from outside one's own group, however that group is defined

even though in large descent groups some members will be only very distantly related. But descent groups vary widely concerning the rigor with which their members conform to the ideal of exogamy.

Clans and Lineages

The two major types of descent groups are clans and lineages. A **clan** is a descent group whose members believe themselves descended from (or in some special way related to) the same founding ancestor, male or female. The founder may have lived so long ago that a member's precise genealogical tie to this ancestor, who may be referred to as the clan's **culture hero,** cannot be calculated. Often, the founder is a mythological being or animal who defies biological credibility as the literal founder of a human group. Or the founder may be an inanimate object, such as the sun or a lake.

If a clan's founder is believed to have been a plant or animal, that item is often the clan's **totem,** or special symbol. Clan members are usually forbidden to harvest that particular plant or kill that animal for food or other purposes, although the members of other clans in the same society may do so. Should you belong to the Eel Clan, for example, the eel would be your totem, and you would be forbidden to kill or eat an eel, although members of your society's Sun Clan could do so.

Among the intangible property a clan may own is the right to tell an **origin myth** describing how the clan was founded. In detailing how the clan came into existence and setting forth the social features that make it distinct from other clans, this myth may be highly imaginative. But an origin myth is not just a local entertainment. It may also serve as a local constitution, justifying the rights and privileges claimed by present-day members of the clan. Many such myths are fine specimens of oral literature (see Chapter 14).

Lineages consist of consanguines who can trace genealogical links through known ancestors to a genuine human ancestor, who may have lived many generations before. The size of a lineage is limited by the depth of its genealogical ties. Clans, because they do not depend on actual genealogical links, can go back many generations more. In some societies, lineages are linked together into clans. Figure 9.4 shows the internal division of the Eel Clan of the Tetum people of Indonesia (see map on page 139).

The Eel Clan consists of three lineages, each of which has certain rights and duties. The lineage called Bua Laran owns most of the Eel Clan's political and economic property, including the office of clan head, and Kailulik owns much of its religious property, including the office of clan priest. Baria Laran, which owns smaller amounts of property, supplies deputies for each of the two leaders. Since the Eel Clan is exogamous, strictly speaking no Eel person can marry another, although if the individuals in question belong to different lineages within the clan, marriage may be tolerated. But there is no question about lineage exogamy. Consanguines from the same lineage are always forbidden to marry.

Members of the three lineages believe that their clan was founded by a creature who was half eel and half man, while each lineage was founded by a real, historical person. The story of how this happened is related in "The Origin Myth of the Tetum."

---

clan (patriclan, matriclan) a descent group whose members believe they are descended from (or in some special way related to) the same founding ancestor or ancestress

culture hero a mythological being, animal, or inanimate object thought to be associated with the origins of a clan

totem a plant, animal, or object from which members of a clan are believed to have descended, or which plays some central role in its history

origin myth a story describing the origins of some feature of the physical environment, of a society, or of a culture; often describes the appearance of a clan's culture hero and how the clan was founded

lineage (patrilineage, matrilineage) a descent group made up of consanguines who can trace their precise genealogical links, through known ancestors, to a founding ancestor

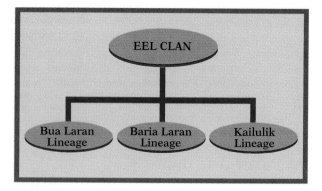

Figure 9.4

Tetum Eel Clan. Many important political and religious functions within the Eel Clan are divided among the three lineages shown here, but all males and females within each of these lineages are members of the same clan.

Aboriginal Australian societies are famous for their totems, plants or animals that represent clans. Here an Australian group whose totem is the kangaroo performs the Dance of the Two Kangaroos.

The Origin Myth of the Tetum

Seven Tetum brothers went traveling in a strange land. One day at midday, the six oldest commanded the youngest to collect water from a nearby stream, but when the youth arrived at the stream he saw an eel muddying the water. He returned to his brothers empty-handed, and told them what he had seen. The brothers accused him of lying, and ordered him to go back for water, but again he found the water so dirty, thanks to the continued thrashing of the eel, that he returned to his brothers without any. This time the eldest brother, armed with a chopper, accompanied the youngest brother back to the stream, where he lifted the eel from the water and hacked it to pieces.

They carried the pieces back to camp, where the older brothers ordered the youngest to cook the meat while they went for a stroll. After they had left, the butchered eel, much to the youngest brother's astonishment, began to speak. "By sunset," it predicted, "you, too, will be an eel." The

youth ran to find his older brothers, but by the time they all got back to the camp the eel was silent. Again the older brothers accused the youngest of lying, and continued their stroll. Twice more the eel repeated its prediction to the youngest brother, and twice more the skeptical older brothers scorned the youth. Finally, the brothers sat down to a meal of rice and eel meat—but the youngest discovered that *his* meat was still raw.

Their meal finished, the seven went to the spring to bathe. When it was time to leave the water, the elder brothers climbed out onto the bank. But the youngest was unable to follow them, for—although his head remained human—his body had been transformed into that of an eel. From the water he shouted to his brothers, "Today I told you what I had seen and heard, but you wouldn't believe me. Now look at what has happened! But do not feel sorry for me. I want you to go and buy a pig and some rice, and cook them." The startled brothers did as they were instructed. After they had cooked the food, the youngest brother continued giving orders: "Never shall you or any of your descendants eat the meat of eels! Never allow any of your descendants to bathe in this spring again!" Then, after teaching them some songs and dances, the youngest brother struck his head against a rock and was transformed completely into an eel. Thus did he leave the world of humanity.

The six surviving brothers divided up their property, split up into two groups of three, and set off in opposite directions. The eldest brother eventually left his two brothers, and established his own home. In the course of time he married and fathered three sons, each of whom founded one of the lineages of the Eel Clan. Henceforth, each lineage would partake of clan privileges and fulfill clan responsibilities in its own way.

• Rules of Descent •

There are three common forms of descent: patriliny, matriliny, and cognation.

Patriliny

Patriliny (patrilineal descent) is a system of descent in which males provide the links by which property descends to the next generation. The male and female consanguines in a patrilineal system are termed **agnates (patrikin).** Agnates trace their descent from a common male ancestor. Since ties of descent in a patrilineal system are with one's father's consanguines only, not one's mother's, if you were a female in a society with patrilineal descent you could inherit property from your father, but could not pass on to your children any property that was considered to belong to your father's descent group.

As an example of how a system of patriliny works, consider the way in which family names are traditionally passed along in Western society. Children inherit them from their fathers, but even though the right to use a name descends to daughters and sons

alike, only sons pass it to *their* children. We can say, therefore, that family names (if nothing else) in Western society descend patrilineally.

Other societies transfer not only family names by patrilineal descent, but also other property, tangible or intangible. Examples might include the right to live in a certain place after marriage, to own a house there, to succeed to a certain political or religious office when the previous generation's incumbent dies, to perform certain rituals, and to recite certain myths. In some societies, the right to belong to a certain patrilineal descent group, or **patrigroup** (a generic term that covers both clans and lineages), is considered the most desirable right of all. Inheritable duties for members of patrilineal descent groups might include helping one's agnates in agricultural work, defending the patrigroup's land and livestock when these are threatened by rival patrigroups, and helping to maintain the patrigroup's prestige in local affairs.

Figure 9.5 shows a very small patrigroup. If we extended the descent lines to cover more genera-

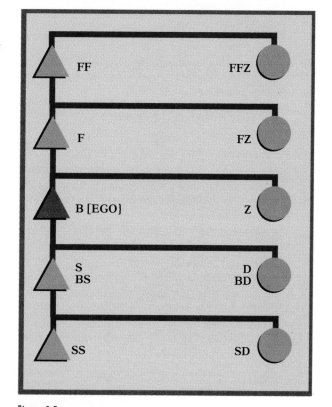

Figure 9.5

A Patrigroup. In patrigroups, the descending ties are all through males, but note how females are "hooked" onto the patriline.

---

patriliny (patrilineal descent) a system of descent in which males provide the links by which property descends to the next generation

agnates (patrikin) consanguines who trace their descent from a common male ancestor

patrigroup a patrilineal descent group, whether patriclan or patrilineage

tions, we would have a small lineage, and if we went back much further we might finish up with a clan. But to avoid complications, we limit the group to five generations only. Imagine you are ego. (Note: Ego's triangle in Figure 9.5 is labeled B for brother, since ego and his brothers are represented by that one triangle.) The group includes all male and female agnates directly connected to you through your father (F), his father (FF), and so on—that is, each male in a direct line back to the founder of the group. It also includes each male descended from you (since you are male) and your male agnates: your son (S), your brother's son (BS), and your son's son (SS). Finally, it includes each of your female agnates in every generation, from your father's father's sister (FFZ) to your son's daughter (SD).

The advantages to patrilineal systems of descent groups that are localized was noted earlier. When male agnates continue to live in the same community after marriage, they are able to prevent other descent groups from moving in and exploiting their patrigroup's territory and resources. Localized descent groups are particularly common where patrigroups own valuable property. A wife resides with her husband after marriage, while a husband continues to live where he was born and where his father, brothers, and other agnates of his patrigroup live. This form of residence after marriage is called **patrilocal residence,** and it often occurs with patriliny.

Women may seem devalued in patrisystems, but this is not necessarily so. In patrisystems, sisters and daughters are patrigroup insiders, and for a man to marry a woman from his own patrigroup would violate the rule of exogamy. Thus, if male babies are to be born to ensure the continuance of a patrigroup into the next generation, each man must find a wife from another patrigroup—hence the importance of women for the men of a patrigroup. Without wives and mothers there would be no patrigroup.

The Nuer of Africa provide an example. By residing patrilocally after they marry, male Nuer agnates form localized patrigroups. This means brothers and male cousins are always on hand to look after their patrigroups' local resources, consisting largely of cattle. The sisters of these men, when they marry, go to live with their respective husbands. Nuer women are thus the *nonlocalized* agnates of their patrigroups. Although these female agnates are dispersed around the territories of their respective husbands' patrigroups, this does not create any

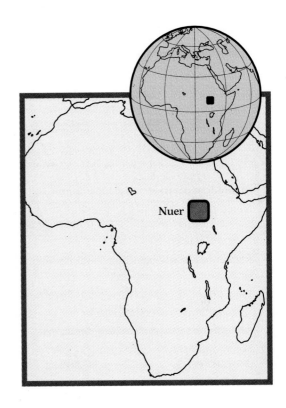

problem for Nuer society, since the line of descent runs not through them but through their brothers.

Matriliny

In a system of **matriliny (matrilineal descent),** which is much less common than patriliny, females, not males, provide the links by which property, tangible or intangible, descends to the next generation.

In Figure 9.6, ego is shown as male to make the contrast with patriliny clearer. If you were this male consanguine in a **matrigroup** (whether matriclan or matrilineage), your group would consist of all females and males linked to you by matrilineal

---

patrilocal residence residence for a husband near or with his father after marriage

matriliny (matrilineal descent) a system of descent in which females provide the links by which property descends to the next generation

matrigroup a matrilineal descent group, whether matriclan or matrilineage

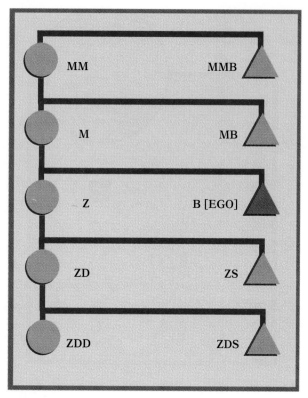

Figure 9.6

A Matrigroup. In matrigroups, the descending ties are all through females, but note how males are "hooked" onto the matriline.

descent through your mother (M), her mother (MM), her mother's mother (MMM), and so on— that is, each female in a consanguinal line back to the group's female founder. Your matrigroup would also include all females descended from your sister and your other female relatives, such as your sister's daughter (ZD) and your sister's daughter's daughter (ZDD). As is also true of the patrilineal diagram, these descent lines can be extended through many generations.

In matrisystems, males and females alike inherit tangible and intangible property from their mothers, but only females can pass down this property to

matrikin (uterine kin) consanguines who trace their descent from a common female ancestor

matriarchy a society dominated by females politically and economically

patriarchy a society politically and economically dominated by males

the next generation. A male may be free to bequeath personal property to his own children, but he cannot do so with property that is considered to belong to his matrigroup. It is his sisters who provide the links by which his matrigroup's property passes to the next generation.

Thus, as a male in a matrisystem, you would not be the legal caretaker of your own children, but rather of your *sister's* children. Whatever your feelings towards your children and whatever the contribution you make to their upbringing, your legal interests lie with your sister's children. It is *their* future (not your own children's) that you work to secure, for your sister's children (unlike your own) are members of your descent group, and will eventually come into their inheritance from you and this group. Your own children will not inherit your estate because they are members of another matrigroup, their mother's. If, for example, you occupy a political office that descends matrilineally, it is one of your *sisters'* sons who has the right to succeed you. If your own son is to inherit an office, he must inherit it from his mother's (your wife's) side of the family.

With certain reservations, much of what we said about patrigroups also applies to matrigroups. Consanguines in matrigroups are called **matrikin (uterine kin).** Matrikin are consanguines who trace their descent from a common female ancestor, and they include males as well as females, as Figure 9.6 shows. The origin myths of matrigroups tell of female founding ancestors, and totems and food prohibitions form part of the complex of rights and duties binding members of matrigroups to each other.

Yet matriliny cannot be regarded as the mirror image of patriliny, because in every society about which we have good ethnographic data, males and females are unequal, with males rather than females generally dominating political and economic life. Women may exert decisive influence in the domestic sphere, and a few individual women, like Indira Gandhi or Margaret Thatcher, may become important figures in public life, but overall the distribution of political and economic influence in any society heavily favors males. Indeed, we have no evidence that any **matriarchy,** a society in which women dominate men politically and economically, has ever existed (Rosaldo and Lamphere 1974:3). All societies fall somewhere between strong **patriarchy** (political and economic domination by men) on the one end of the scale and the egalitarian midpoint between matriarchy and patriarchy on the other.

Clans are descent groups whose members believe they are all related to the same founder. Often, as among the Nuer of Africa, clan members live near each other after they marry. Here, Nuer clansmen—brothers and male cousins—work together to make leather thongs.

The result for matriliny of this bias is that while mothers in matrilineal societies provide the *links* between female matrikin of different generations, they generally are not involved in the executive management of the property that passes down the matriline—because they are women. Mothers, for instance, cannot transmit their matrigroup's property to their children, so patriliny and matriliny are not mere opposites in this regard; nor do women occupy whatever political offices their matrigroup controls. Instead, it is their brothers, their *male* matrikin, who exercise these responsibilities. Hence the great importance, in matrisystems, of the relationship between mothers' brothers and sisters' sons. If ego is male, he inherits property from his mother's brother (not his father), and when he dies, his property passes to his sister's son (not his son). His son inherits property from *his* mother's brother.

Matriliny sounds much more complicated to Westerners than patriliny, perhaps because—

although ours is not a patrilineal society—we have the traditional transfer of surnames as an example of patrilineality in action. There are no such examples of matrilineality in Western society. For many Westerners, it is a conceptual struggle to envision descent through females in conjunction with the control of wealth and the exertion of authority by the male siblings of females.

Matrigroups and patrigroups regard sisters and wives differently. Because in a matrigroup a man's heirs are his sister's children, not those of his wife and himself, it is his *sister*, not his wife, who gives birth to the children whose existence enables his matrigroup to continue into the next generation. A man's sister is therefore more important to the continuance of his matrigroup than is his wife. In a society with patrigroups, in contrast, a man's sister (after she has married) bears children for her husband's patrigroup; it is the man's *wife* who provides children for his patrigroup. This helps explain why,

Anthropology and the Environment

Deforestation in Uganda

Each year, 17 million hectares of the earth's forests—an area the size of Austria—are destroyed by farming, lumbering, and firewood collection (Brown 1991). The effects of this loss are felt not only globally, as the number of plant and animal species inhabiting the planet continues to dwindle and the cleansing effects of forests on the air and water are lost, but also locally. Throughout the world, growing numbers of indigenous people live in places where the once-plentiful forest resources on which they depend for their lives and livelihoods are becoming ever scarcer.

In the southwestern part of Uganda, East Africa, where 95 percent of the people are subsistence farmers, local communities have traditionally relied heavily on forest products for necessities such as house beams and firewood (Mukolwe et al. 1995:134 ff.). The area contains rich, dense tropical forests, characterized by extraordinary biodiversity, but over the last 50 years these forests have dwindled as more and more forested land has been cleared for farming. Between 1954 and 1991, the size of southwestern Uganda's Bwindi Impenetrable Forest declined by 27 percent, from 400 square kilometers to 321.

The main reason for the loss of forested land has been population growth, due partly to immigration but mainly to the region's high fertility rate—an average of 7.8 children per mother in 1989 (Kaijuka et al. 1989). In the 20 years between 1971 and 1991, population density increased from 132 to 201 people per square kilometer; in some communities, it is now as high as 500, and the region's population is projected to double in the next 26 years (Mukolwe et al. 1995:134). The area's high fertility rate can be attributed to aspects of the local culture, including the value traditionally placed on early marriage and large families.

What have southwestern Ugandan farmers done in the face of increasing population pressure on their local environment? Their main response has been to clear more land, in order to ensure that each generation has enough to survive (Mukolwe et al. 1995:135). In southwestern Uganda, as in many African communities, families must farm in order to survive. Under the local inheritance rules, when a farmer dies, his land is distributed equally among his sons. They, in turn, use their shares of land to support their own families, and upon their deaths bequeathe it to *their* sons. Within a generation or two,

in societies with matrigroups, bonds between brother and sister may be stronger than those between husband and wife, and also why, in societies with patrigroups, the opposite is true.

Yet another difference between patrigroups and matrigroups is residence after marriage. If you are an adult female member of a society with matri-groups, you may spend your whole life living with or near your close female matrikin—your mother, her sisters, and your own sisters. Your father and any of your brothers who are not yet married will live with you. When you marry, your husband will leave his home and come to live with you and your matrigroup. Since he is in effect living near your mother, this form of postmarital residence is called **matrilocal residence.**

The Zuni (see map on page 14) provide an example of matrilineal descent accompanied by a

---

matrilocal residence residence for a husband near or with his wife's parents

a plot of land that once sustained one family must now provide food for several, and through the years the plots of land on which families depend become smaller and smaller. Eventually, sons inherit pieces of property too small to sustain their families, forcing them to clear additional land for cultivation.

The Government of Uganda has regulated the clearing of land and cutting of trees in areas such as Bwindi Impenetrable Forest for some years, but the regulations have not been stringently enforced. In 1991, Bwindi Forest became a national park, and enforcement was increased, but local residents continued to harvest forest resources out of necessity. In a survey, 26 percent admitted that they had cut timber from Bwindi Forest with which to build homes. Some also admitted cutting firewood in the forest. Given the government ban, such activities are probably more extensive than the survey revealed. Most of the people surveyed (62 percent) said they understood the value of natural resources conservation in theory, but even more (70 percent) considered their own needs more important (Mukolwe et al. 1995:139).

No culturally and environmentally acceptable solution to the problem of deforestation in southwestern Uganda has been found. However, the government of Uganda, in cooperation with the international aid organization CARE, is working with local community groups on several important issues, including environmental conservation, more efficient agricultural practices, and health care. The idea is that if southwestern Ugandans' environmental awareness is heightened, their agricultural yields are increased, and they have improved access to health care, their population growth rate may slow, and the forests of southwestern Uganda may not be doomed to extinction.

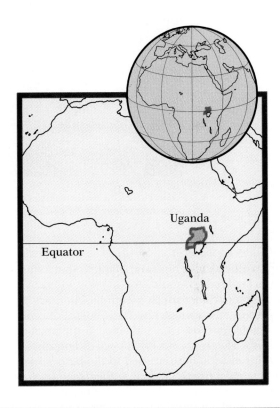

matrilocal rule of residence. Today these pueblo-dwellers, while preserving much of their cultural heritage, are integrated into modern North American culture. In traditional times, however, a Zuni man divided his loyalties between two women, his sister and his wife. When he married, he left his parents' household and moved to his wife's (Benedict 1989:75–76), where he lived with his wife, her sisters (unmarried and married), the husbands of his wife's married sisters, his wife's unmarried brothers (her married brothers having moved out to live in *their* wives' households), his wife's father (who years before would have left his parents' home to come to live with his wife), and his mother-in-law. The house in which this group lived belonged to the women, who also owned the household's supplies of corn and certain heirlooms, and had the responsibility of protecting the secrets of their clan from members of other clans—including their husbands. The status of Zuni husbands, especially new husbands, was thus relatively low. Only gradually, as his children

Although males as well as females are matrigroup members, the core of a matrigroup consists of women of different generations bound together by consanguineal ties. Above, three generations of matrilineal Navajo women.

grew older, did a husband acquire some standing in his wife's household.

In economic matters, a Zuni husband was a contributing member of his wife's household, but for religious purposes he remained a member of his sister's. He grew corn for his wife's household, not for his sister's, but returned to the latter's house to officiate at rituals. A man's allegiance as brother carried more weight than his allegiance as husband because of his importance in his sister's home as the performer of her household's rituals. This conflict of loyalties brought about frequent divorces. An ex-husband would return to his sister's house, leaving his children (who, of course, belonged to his wife's matrigroup, not his) with his ex-wife. A Zuni woman had no similar conflict of interest. The only family to which she owed allegiance was her own household, which was one of many that made up her matrigroup.

avunculocal residence the residence pattern by which male ego resides with his mother's brother

Matrilocal residence does not accompany matriliny in all matrisystems. In some matrilineal societies, a male resides with his mother's brother, a custom known as **avunculocal residence.** This is a more efficient way than matrilocal residence of keeping matrilineal property under the control of the men who have a stake in it. If widely practiced in a society, avunculocal residence also tends to keep brothers together after they have married because, unlike matrilocal residence, wives must come to live with their husbands, not vice versa. Among the matrilineal Tsimshian, neighbors of the Kwakiutl, children of both sexes spend their early years living with their parents. A daughter remains with her parents until she marries, when she goes to live with her husband. A son, however, usually leaves his father's household sometime between the ages of 8 and 14 to live with his mother's brother. One result of avunculocal residence is that a core of males, related matrilineally, is established as a local group. Since it is these males who control their matrilineage's property, their common residence makes it easier for them to protect it than if they lived dispersed in matrilocal fashion like Zuni husbands (Vaughan 1984:60–61).

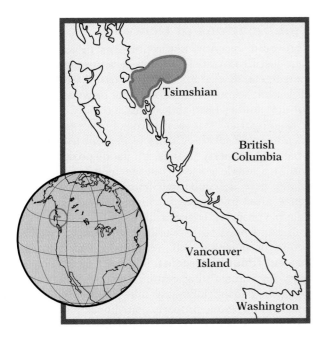

Cognation

A society like that of the Nuer or the Trobrianders, which reckons descent through either males or females but not both, is said to have a rule of **unilineal descent.** But most societies reckon descent through *both* males and females. This practice is known as **cognation** or **cognatic descent,** and is the most common descent system in the world. It is easily understood by Westerners since it is the system that prevails in the West, although we do not have cognatic descent groups, as some societies do.

In cognatic descent, an individual of either sex can transmit property in any form to individuals of either sex in the next generation, and individuals are in principle equally related to their mothers' and their fathers' families. The rights and duties that may be transmitted in this unrestricted fashion are the same as those transmitted under patriliny or matriliny, but descent groups created by cognation are nevertheless decidedly different from those formed by patrilineal or matrilineal descent.

First, the number of individuals ego is considered to be related to as a member of a cognatic descent group is potentially much larger than the number of ego's relatives in a matrilineal or patrilineal descent system, since ego is a consanguine of both M's and F's kin. As we have seen, in patrilineal and matrilineal systems, individuals automatically belong to either their father's descent

group *or* their mother's, but cannot be a member of more than one.

Second, cognatic descent groups overlap; ego belongs to several of them at the same time. Since theoretically ego can trace descent back to each of the ancestors of both parents, the number of cognatic descent groups of which he or she is potentially a member is equal to the number of ancestors. Going back only as far as ego's grandparents gives ego four ancestors (FF, FM, MF, MM). If ego's society happens to have cognatic descent groups and these four grandparents each belong to a different one, then ego will belong to all four. This can bring about conflicts when it comes to rights and loyalties, because ego's rights and duties overlap as his or her descent groups overlap. Consider residence, for example; with which descent group should ego reside? No one descent group in a cognatic system has a stronger claim on ego's presence than any other, and a group that decided to keep its members together could do so only by depriving other groups of potential members.

Another problem involves a common duty of descent group members: to avenge the mistreatment of fellow consanguines (Fox 1983:150). Suppose ego's society has four cognatic descent groups, and ego belongs to all four. If a man from one descent group kills a consanguine of ego's from one of the other descent groups, which descent group does ego support?

Such problems can be solved. Some cognatic systems allow individuals to choose the descent group with which they want to affiliate. When an individual can choose to join either F's side of the family or M's, this is called **ambilineal descent.** Although ties with the side not selected may still be recognized, whatever economic and political resources the chosen descent group owns are made available to the individual.

Just as cognation permits individual choice regarding descent, so it encourages a variety of residence

---

unilineal descent a line of descent that runs through either males or females but not both

cognation (cognatic descent) a form of descent reckoned through both males and females

ambilineal descent the kind of descent in which one may choose to join either one's father's or mother's side of the family

choices, as Western society illustrates. If they have not already established a home before marriage, Western newlyweds try to find one in a location separate from those of their families, an arrangement termed **neolocal** ("new place") **residence.** The independence of couples from their parents and parents-in-law is adaptive in a mobile society in which jobs change and people often have to move.

When couples are permitted to choose whether to live with the husband's relatives or the wife's, this is called **ambilocal residence.** In our society, this is usually only temporary; but in other societies, the arrangement may last for a longer time or even be permanent (e.g., the Iban). Although more restricted than neolocal residence, ambilocal residence offers more freedom of choice than the other residence arrangements discussed. The couple moves in accordance with the relative advantages offered by residing with one or the other set of relatives.

Some North American newlyweds must live with relatives for economic reasons, but most consider neolocal residence—a home separate from both their families—far preferable, even when they must do without the usual household amenities.

neolocal residence residence for a married couple in a location separate from the residences of their families

ambilocal residence the residence pattern by which couples choose whether to live with the husband's relatives or the wife's

bilineal descent (double descent) a combination of patriliny and matriliny

Combinations of Descent

Until quite recently, anthropologists thought they were justified in labeling entire societies patrilineal, matrilineal, or cognatic, on the basis of which rule of descent seemed to predominate. However, cross-cultural studies have shown that a society does not have to restrict itself to one type of descent system. It can exploit all three rules of descent to allocate whatever property it has at its disposal. Thus, within a single society, lineage membership and names may descend matrilineally; rights to residence after marriage, patrilineally; and rights to tangible property, cognatically.

In some parts of the world, there occurs a combination of patriliny and matriliny called **bilineal descent (double descent).** It assigns the responsibility for transmitting certain types of inheritable property patrilineally and other, quite different, types of inheritable property matrilineally. The Yako provide an example. These West Africans have exogamous patriclans and matriclans, which are localized and divided into lineages (Forde 1961). Males of a lineage live together, their wives forsaking their childhood homes to live with them. A man's rights to a house, land, and protection lie in his patriclan and patrilineage. When he dies, his land and house descend to his sons. However, property that is moveable—for example, money and livestock—is inherited matrilineally. In other words, at a man's death his land and house become the property of his sons, and his money and cattle go to his sister's sons.

• Kinship Terminologies •

English-speakers use English-language *kinship terms* (or *relationship terms*)—such as *father, mother, brother, sister, son, daughter, aunt, uncle, cousin, nephew, niece,* and *grandchild*—to denote relatives. All societies use such terms for classifying relatives. In some cases, a kin term groups several or many individuals together as members of a single relationship category; the English kin term *cousin,* a catch-all term into which a number of ego's relatives (male or female, father's side or mother's side) fit, is an example. In other cases, a kinship term distinguishes between persons; in English, *father* distinguishes one man from all others. In non-Western societies and in languages other than English, the classification may be quite different. Instead of the general term *cousin,* there may be different kin terms that distinguish among different kinds of cousins. Or a single kin term may group the relatives we call *father* and *father's brother* into a single category.

Some societies classify certain relatives together (or "equate" them) because the relatives occupy the same social status or carry out much the same social role. Other relatives are distinguished from one another rather than equated because they occupy different social statuses or carry out different social roles. For example, in some societies a man is encouraged to marry his mother's brother's daughter (MBD). We sometimes find in such societies that the term for MBD is the same as the term for wife (W): MBD = W. (Note that if a man marries his MBD, this is a matrilateral cross cousin marriage.) For the Ema of Timor (see map on page 139), the preferred marriage for a man is with his MBD, and—not surprisingly—the Ema word for MBD is the same as the word for W (Hicks 1990:76).[1]

A **kinship** (or **relationship**) **terminology**—the complete set of kinship terms by which relatives are known—is thus one way in which a culture imposes order on the social world of relatives. As children become enculturated, they learn that different kinship terms are associated with the sort of treatment they can expect to receive from relatives—as well, of course, as how they should behave toward these relatives as they become older and more socially responsible.

Six kinds of kinship terminology have attracted the most anthropological interest. Individually, they are labeled the Hawaiian, Eskimo, Omaha, Crow, Iroquois, and Sudanese systems,[2] but they are grouped into three broad categories:

- nonlineal terminologies: Hawaiian and Eskimo
- lineal terminologies: Omaha, Crow, and Iroquois
- descriptive terminology: Sudanese

Nonlineal terminologies are often found, logically enough, in societies in which descent is cognatic rather than unilineal. In the Hawaiian and Eskimo terminological systems, ego does not distinguish relatives on F's side of the family from those on M's. Thus in both of these systems ego calls MZ and FZ by the same term, a term meaning "aunt." (If this sounds familiar, it is because most Westerners use the Eskimo system.) Calling these two women by the same term suggests that, from the point of view of ego, both sides of the family are equally important (or unimportant)—legally, economically, or politically. Similarly, in these two systems ego calls a cross cousin by the same term as a parallel cousin.

In lineal terminologies, which are commonly found in societies that have lineal descent, ego distinguishes between parallel cousins and cross cousins and between certain relatives on F's side of the family and on M's. Lineal terminologies are sometimes called **bifurcate merging terminologies** because certain relatives are separated (or bifurcated) from one another by being referred to by different terms, while others are merged into a single term. For example, F and FB might be "merged," and both thus referred to by the same term, because these two men belong to the same line of descent. At the same time, MB might be "bifurcated" from F and FB by the use of a different term for MB, because he belongs to a line of descent different from F and FB. Similarly, MZ might be classified with M, in which case ego would refer to both women by the same term but would use a different term for FZ. It follows logically that in lineal terminologies ego refers to parallel cousins and siblings by the same term, but uses a different term for cross cousins.

Descriptive terminologies "describe" individuals by assigning them terms that are used only for them (or others in the same exact genealogical positions), thus distinguishing between relatives in a highly specific way. In English, the term *sister* is a descriptive term; it is used to denote one kind of

---

[1] The correspondence between kinship terminologies and forms of descent system is not inevitable or evident in every society. Thus, societies with the same marriage preference as the Ema may use two different words for MBD and W.

[2] These categories are conventional in cultural anthropology today; however, it should be noted that their usefulness has been questioned by some anthropologists.

kinship (relationship) terminology the complete set of terms by which relatives are known

bifurcate merging terminology a terminology in which F and FB are known by the same term, whereas MB is known by a different term; and where M and MZ are known by the same term, whereas FZ is known by a different term

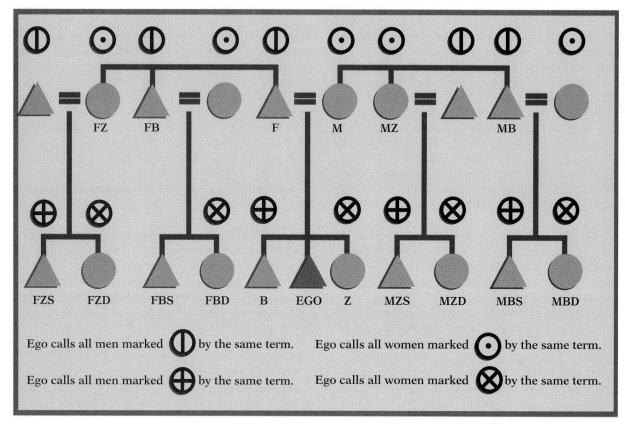

Figure 9.7

Hawaiian Terminology. This nonlineal terminology uses the least number of terms of any kinship terminology; in each generation, there is one term for males and another for females.

relative and no other. Merging is less important than bifurcation in descriptive terminologies.

Hawaiian

The **Hawaiian terminology** is the simplest of all kinship terminologies, since it uses the fewest terms (Figure 9.7). Although the Hawaiians provided its name, other societies use it also. In each generation

there are only two kin terms: one for males and one for females. Thus—taking the generation above ego as an example—ego refers to F, FB, and MB by a single term. The same is true for M, MZ, and FZ. In ego's own generation, male cousins are classified with brothers, and female cousins with sisters. The same principle is true for ego's children's generation. Nephews are referred to by the same term as sons, and nieces by the same term as daughters.

Eskimo[3]

In the **Eskimo terminology** (Figure 9.8), ego refers to nuclear family members (in English: *father,*

Hawaiian terminology a terminology found in many cognatic societies, in which all relatives of the same sex in the same generation are included under the same term

Eskimo terminology a terminology found in many cognatic societies, in which members of the nuclear family are distinguished from all other relatives

---

[3]This kinship terminological system continues to be referred to as the *Eskimo* system, even though some of the people for whom it is named now call themselves Inuit.

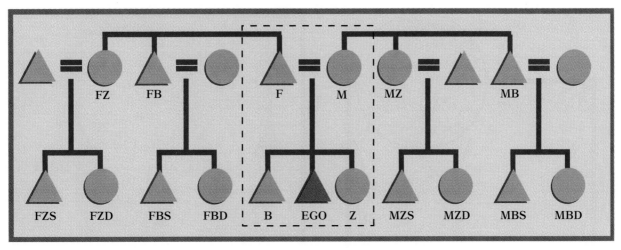

Figure 9.8

Eskimo Terminology. In this nonlineal *terminology, one calls members of one's nuclear family by terms that are given to no other relatives outside of this kinship unit. Thus, the terms given to parents differ from those used for uncles and aunts, sibling terms differ from cousin terms, and terms for children differ from those for nephews and nieces. But one does not distinguish cross cousins from parallel cousins.*

mother, brother, and *sister*) by terms used for no other relatives outside this kinship unit. Thus, the terms used to refer to parents differ from those used to refer to aunts and uncles, the terms that refer to siblings differ from cousin terms, and terms for children differ from those for nieces and nephews. However, as in the Hawaiian system, ego does not distinguish cross cousins from parallel cousins, referring to each by a single term. The system thus verbally distinguishes members of the nuclear family from other relatives, so it is not consistent with the existence of lineal descent groups. It is, however, consistent with cognation, and as cognation is the most common descent system in the world, so the

Eskimo terminology is the most common terminology. In addition to the Inuit, most North Americans and members of other industrialized societies use it. So do members of societies as different from each other as the gathering-and-hunting !Kung of Africa and the pastoralist Sarakatsani of Greece.

Omaha

The **Omaha terminology** is a lineal terminology named after a Native American group of the Great Plains, and is usually associated with patrilineal descent (Figure 9.9). In effect, certain terms are extended across two or more generations in the same patrilineal line. Thus ego uses a single kin term to refer to MB, MBS, and MBSS. Similarly, ego's M is referred to by the same term as MBD, and FZC is referred to by the same term as ZC. Why would a society develop this kind of terminological system? It may happen because of patrilocality, the mode of residence that commonly accompanies

---

• Ask Yourself •

In many societies, including Western society, people who are not really kin are sometimes addressed using kinship terms. Do you always use kin terms literally, or do you sometimes extend them to include persons who are not really related to you? For example, are all the women you call "aunt" really your aunts?

Omaha terminology a bifurcate merging terminology sometimes accompanying patrilineal descent in which, among other identifications, MB = MBS = MBSS

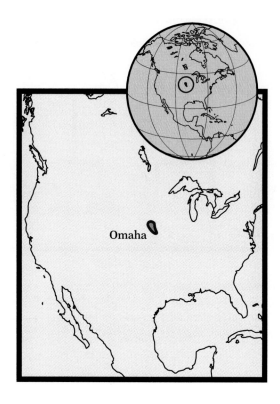

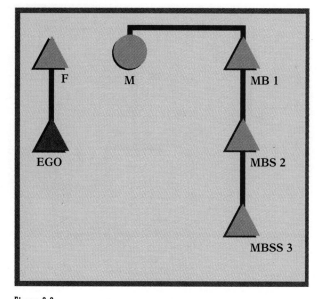

Figure 9.9

Omaha Terminology. In this lineal *terminology, one extends some terms across two or more generations in the patrilineal line. Thus, one calls one's mother's brother, his son, and his son's son by the same term, one's mother by the same term as mother's brother's daughter, and one's father's sister's child by the same term as sister's child.*

patriliny. With patrilocality, ego's mother's consanguines may not be living near ego, so there may be little practical need to distinguish between members of different generations in patrigroups other than ego's own.

Crow

Another Native American society, the Crow, gives its name to this second lineal terminology (Figure 9.10), which, like the Omaha system, may also be associated with unilineal descent. Also like the Omaha system, the **Crow terminology** extends some terms across two or more generations. But because it usually accompanies matrilineal rather than patrilineal descent, the extensions occur in matrilines rather than patrilines. Thus (recalling that in matriliny, ego is a member of M's lineage but

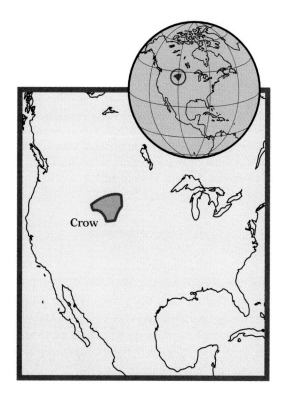

Crow terminology a bifurcate merging terminology sometimes accompanying matrilineal descent in which, among other identifications, FZ = FZD

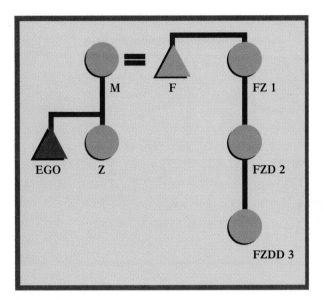

Figure 9.10

Crow Terminology. In this lineal *terminology, one extends some terms across two or more generations in the same matrilineal line. Thus, one calls one's father and father's sister's son by the same term, and father's sister and father's sister's daughter by another.*

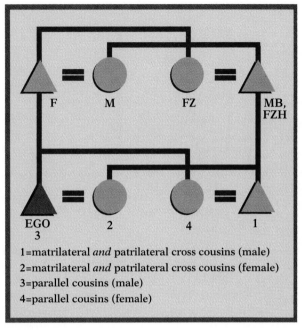

1=matrilateral *and* patrilateral cross cousins (male)
2=matrilateral *and* patrilateral cross cousins (female)
3=parallel cousins (male)
4=parallel cousins (female)

Figure 9.11

Iroquois Terminology. In this lineal *terminology, which occurs with both patrilineal and matrilineal descent, one calls both cross cousins by the same term. Sometimes this is the same term as that for spouse, suggesting that cross cousins are preferred as husbands or wives. One may not marry a parallel cousin, and to signal this difference between the two kinds of cousin, a parallel cousin is called by a different term from a cross cousin.*

not F's), ego refers to F and FZS—two members of a matrilineage other than ego's—by the same term. But separate terms are given to MZ and MZD, two members of ego's own lineage. Thus in the Crow system, ego does not necessarily distinguish between members in different generations of matrigroups other than his or her own (F = FZS; FZ = FZD), but does distinguish between members in different generations of his or her own matrigroup, because it is the members of this matrigroup (M, Z, ZC) who are most important, not the members of other matrigroups.

Iroquois

The **Iroquois terminology,** the third lineal system (Figure 9.11), is named after the Iroquois people of upper New York State, and, like the Omaha and

---

Iroquois terminology a bifurcate terminology associated with unilineal descent in which the matrilateral cross cousin and patrilateral cross cousin are known by the same term, which may sometimes be the same term as spouse

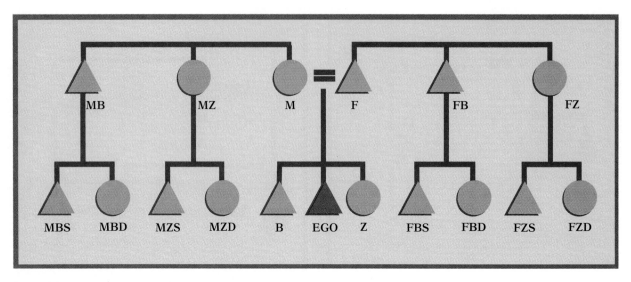

Figure 9.12

Sudanese Terminology. In this descriptive *terminology, one does not merge relatives into a single term; instead, they are separated. Thus, one calls one's father, father's brother, mother's brother, mother's sister, father's sister, siblings, and cousins by distinctive terms.*

cousins on both sides are preferred as husbands or wives. But parallel cousins are forbidden as marriage partners, and to signal the important difference between the two kinds of cousins, ego refers to a parallel cousin by a different term from a cross cousin. This system occurs in many parts of the world, especially the tropical forest region of South America and among the gatherers and hunters of Australia. It is nonexistent in Europe, and very rare in Africa.

Sudanese

Although not considered a lineal terminology because it lacks certain of the distinctions and equations between relatives found in lineal terminologies, the **Sudanese terminology** may be found in societies that have lineal descent (Figure 9.12). However, unlike the Omaha, Crow, and

Crow systems, is often associated with unilineal descent. However, it occurs in societies that have either patrilineal or matrilineal descent. Ego's cross cousins on both sides of the family, M's and F's, are referred to by the same term. Sometimes the same term is used for spouse, suggesting that cross

Sudanese (descriptive) terminology a terminology often associated with unilineal descent, with separate terms for F, FB, MB, MZ, FZ, siblings, and cousins

Iroquois terminologies, it assigns individual terms to relatives such as ego's F, FB, MB, MZ, FZ, siblings, and cousins. There is no merging here; this terminology separates relatives in a highly specific way. For this reason it is sometimes called a *descriptive terminology;* each relative is associated with a special term that "describes" only that relative. The system may be used in societies in which the different relatives each have different political, economic, or social parts to play in the community.

Conclusion

For personal, social, legal, economic, and political reasons, human beings organize themselves into groups based on actual or imagined ties of kinship. In the West, where genealogical ties result not in membership in descent groups but in loosely organized, self-defined kindreds, such groups have little direct effect on their members' daily lives. But for most people, even Westerners, consanguinal ties are fundamental to self-identity. As the genealogical writer Alex Shoumatoff (1985:13–14) says, "The family . . . provides the most intense, intimate, and permanent relationships most of us will have; and this is not likely to change."

Summary

- As a minimum, a family is a group of two or more people who consider themselves related, who are economically interdependent, and who share the responsibility for rearing any children in their group.

- Families can take several forms, including single-parent families, nuclear families, extended families, and kindreds.

- However defined, families help individuals cope with their physical, psychological, economic, linguistic, and social needs.

- Descent—relationships defined by connections to ancestors through parent-child links—establishes people's social identities while specifying their mutual rights and duties and creating legal, economic, political, religious, and personal bonds among them.

- Descent involves "blood" relatives (in contrast to relatives by marriage). Blood relatives are called *consanguines* and are related to each other by consanguinity, a relationship based on the tie between parents and children but also including more distant relatives.

- The complete set of consanguinal ties for any single individual is that person's "genealogy."

- There are three major types of descent system: patriliny, matriliny, and cognation.

- In patriliny, one reckons descent through one's father's line; in matriliny, through one's mother's line; and in cognation, through both parents' lines.

- Anthropologists use kinship diagrams to portray descent systems graphically.

- The three descent systems yield three different forms of descent groups: patrilineal, matrilineal, and cognatic.

- Features associated with patrigroups and matrigroups include a corporate nature, a residential pattern based on sex, the principle of exogamy, and a clan or lineage organization (or both).

- In general, males dominate females, politically and economically. This means that males wield political and economic power in patrilineal systems, but females do not enjoy corresponding influence in matrilineal societies.

- Patriliny is often associated with patrilocal residence, while matriliny is often associated with matrilocal residence, although some matrisystems favor avunculocal residence.

- Descent groups created by cognation are called cognatic descent groups. Cognation is much more widespread throughout the world than either patriliny or matriliny, and is a more flexible form of descent. Cognatic descent groups overlap; a person can belong to several at the same time.

- In ambilineal descent, one can choose whether to join one's father's or mother's side of the family.

- Bilineal descent, a rare type, brings together patriliny and matriliny, but each mode of descent is given a different task to perform.

- Kinship terms are important for anthropologists because they reveal how societies classify relatives and how they may allocate social positions. They also offer clues about whether cognation, patriliny, or matriliny prevails, and may suggest the relative importance or unimportance of the father's or mother's side of the family.

- There are six kinship terminologies: the Hawaiian, Eskimo, Omaha, Crow, Iroquois, and Sudanese.

- The Hawaiian and Eskimo systems often accompany cognatic descent, while the others typically accompany unilineal descent.

kindred
kinship (relationship) terminology
lineage (patrilineage, matrilineage)
matriarchy
matrigroup
matrikin (uterine kin)
matrilateral cousin
matriliny (matrilineal descent)
matrilocal residence
neolocal residence
nuclear (elementary, simple) family
Omaha terminology
origin myth
parallel cousin
patriarchy
patrigroup
patrilateral cousin
patriliny (patrilineal descent)
patrilocal residence
Sudanese (descriptive) terminology
totem
unilineal descent

Key Terms

agnates (patrikin)
ambilineal descent
ambilocal residence
avunculocal residence
bifurcate merging terminology
bilineal descent (double descent)
clan (patriclan, matriclan)
cognation (cognatic descent)
consanguines (consanguinal kin)
consanguinity
cross cousin
Crow terminology
culture hero
descent
descent group
ego
Eskimo terminology
exogamy
extended family
family
Hawaiian terminology
Iroquois terminology
kibbutz

Suggested Readings

Bohannan, Paul, and John Middleton (eds.). 1968. *Readings in Kinship and Social Organization.* Garden City, NY: Natural History Press. A collection of wide-ranging, often classic, essays. Many are useful for understanding marriage as well as descent.

Coontz, Stephanie. 1992. *The Way We Never Were: American Families and the Nostalgia Trap.* New York: Basic Books. A sociologist argues that America has known many different family forms, yet none has ever adequately addressed universal problems such as poverty, child abuse, or gender inequality.

Gailey, Christine Ward. 1987. *Kinship to Kingship: Gender Hierarchy and State Formation in the Tongan Islands.* Austin: University of Texas Press. A feminist perspective on the differing influences exerted by men and women on the South Pacific Tonga islands. Gailey casts her net wide, describing male and female influences on many aspects of Tongan culture, from economic exchanges to marriage to disputes about who should fill political offices. This is a distinctly holistic study of descent.

Graburn, Nelson (ed.). 1971. *Readings in Kinship and Social Structure.* New York: Harper & Row. A collection of some of the classic papers on descent and marriage. Indispensible for comparing the views of a number of anthropologists.

Hicks, David. 1988. *Tetum Ghosts and Kin*. Prospect Heights, IL: Waveland Press. Reissue (original 1976). A synchronic study showing how descent is integrated with marriage, ecology, and religion in a technologically simple society.

Keesing, Roger. 1975. *Kin Groups and Social Structure*. New York: Holt, Rinehart and Winston. An introduction to descent and marriage, from a clearly written structural-functionalist perspective.

Introduction

BROTHER AND SISTER GUILTY OF

MARRYING INCESTUOUSLY

Newsday, August 2, 1979, p. 13

It was the kind of headline guaranteed to attract public attention, and curious readers pored through the accompanying article for details of a bizarre episode that had recently occurred in Massachusetts. Shortly after his birth some 20 years earlier, readers learned, a baby named David had been separated from his sister, Victoria, then 2 years old. Given up by their mother for adoption, the two children had been sent to opposite ends of Massachusetts, where each was raised by foster parents. When she reached adulthood, Victoria longed to meet the brother she barely remembered. By researching old birth records, she was at last able to locate him, and in the spring of 1979, when she was 24 and her brother 22, she arranged to meet him at his foster parents' home.

Later, Victoria was to tell a judge, "It was love at first sight." Obviously her brother felt the same way, for a short time later the two siblings, mentioning their blood relationship to no one, were married in Andover, Massachusetts, by a justice of the peace. With different last names and different addresses, there was nothing to suggest that the two were really brother and sister.

Victoria and her brother David, given up for adoption as children, were raised apart. Reunited as young adults, they fell in love and were married. When their illegal marriage was discovered, a judge ordered them to end their incestuous relationship—an unenforceable ruling.

The state of Massachusetts was alerted to the unusual union it had sanctioned when the bride's adoptive mother discovered the facts of her daughter's marriage and notified authorities. David and Victoria were ordered to appear in court, where they claimed total ignorance of the law against incestuous marriages. They had heard, Victoria admitted, that children born of incestuous unions were liable to be abnormal in some way, but "we had decided before we got married . . . that Dave would get a vasectomy."

Under Massachusetts law, incestuous marriages are automatically void, and incest carries a maximum penalty of 20 years in jail. But Massachusetts was lenient with the young couple. The judge sentenced them to 2 years' probation and ordered both to undergo counseling. They were permitted to continue living together as unmarried housemates on the condition that they end their incestuous relationship. How that edict could be enforced, though, was what their probation officer called "the thousand-dollar question."

The case of Victoria and David provides an illustration of the limits society places on who can marry whom. North American society is not alone in imposing such limitations; rules governing marital eligibility, while they vary from culture to culture, are found in every culture. This chapter examines the virtually universal institution of marriage: its functions, the criteria used to define appropriate marriage partners in different societies, the different kinds of marriages, and divorce.

• The Functions of Marriage •

As a minimum, **marriage** is a socially sanctioned contract establishing the domestic and civic rights and duties of the people (usually one male and one female, but not always) who enter into it. It may, of course, be many other things as well. Our definition is very broad in order to make it applicable cross-culturally.

In Western culture, one of the ingredients of marriage is romantic love, that intense and sexual attraction in which the lover idealizes the object of attraction and expects this feeling to last (Jankowiak and Fisher 1992:149). In many societies, whether a married pair are in love with each other or not is relatively unimportant; a more important consideration is the relationship between the families of the couple. In the Middle Ages (fifth to fifteenth centuries), this view typified Western culture: Europeans regarded romantic love as generally unattainable in marriage and an inadequate justification for it. Romantic love was a rarified sentiment reserved for someone unattainable—someone already married to another, someone belonging to a different social class, or someone who had died.

Sometimes romantic love is even regarded as potentially dangerous to society, on the assumption that those caught in its spell refuse to allow the expectations of others to intrude on their happiness. Lovers are known for turning in on themselves and possibly neglecting the world of rights and obligations outside their little island of self-absorption. A relationship of this kind does nothing to further the interests of the lovers' families or their societies. Understandably, then, romantic love has often been ignored or discouraged as a basis for marriage.

Although not all cultures exalt romantic love as Western culture does, two anthropologists recently conducted a cross-cultural study that suggested it is nevertheless common in most cultures (Jankowiak and Fisher 1992:149), even though it may be expressed in different ways and

---

marriage a socially sanctioned contract spelling out the domestic and civic rights and duties of the people who enter into it

may not be considered as necessary for, or even desirable in, marriage. To determine whether romantic love existed in a particular culture, the anthropologists studied informants' claims about their feelings of love, ethnographers' statements that the concept of love was present, and elopements resulting from mutual affection. They also examined folktales, love songs, and other art forms.

One source the anthropologists consulted was a series of ethnographic interviews with Nisa, a woman of the !Kung gatherer-and-hunter society (see map on page 162).[1] Nisa recognized a clear difference between two kinds of love: the "companionship" she shared with her husband and the more exciting romantic love she enjoyed with her lover. She described her relationship with her husband as "rich, warm, and secure," while her relationship with her lover was "passionate and exciting, although often fleeting and undependable" (Jankowiak and Fisher 1992:152).

The anthropologists reported that romantic love occurred in 147 out of the 166 cultures they studied. Given the fact that anthropology is only now beginning to focus on the subject, the apparent absence of romantic love in the remaining 19 cultures may be due to a lack of relevant data. If so, romantic love may be a human universal.

Findings from physical anthropology are consistent with this possibility. Anthropologist Helen Fisher (1992) suggests that romantic love evolved some 4 or 5 million years ago, when human beings began to walk upright and carry their food to places where it was safe to eat. Mothers carrying infants would have found this difficult without a partner, so a basic change in reproductive strategies took place: male-female bonding. With the evolution of bonding came changes in body chemistry that stimulated and sustained bonding by producing feelings of infatuation and attachment, the ingredients of romantic love. To this day, humans' romantic feelings are regulated biochemically. Thus, Fisher suggests, whatever their culture, all human beings have the capacity for romantic love.

Romantic love seems to occur in almost all societies, although it is not always considered a necessary ingredient of marriage. Clockwise, Indonesian, Nigerian, Native American, and Yugoslavian couples show that the face of love is similar everywhere.

The permanent bonding of lovers cannot, however, be regarded as a function of marriage, cross-culturally. The major functions of marriage worldwide are to form new family units, to define the reciprocal rights and responsibilities of married people, to create alliances between the families of married couples, and to spell out how the productive efforts of a couple and the goods and services produced within their marriage should be apportioned for their mutual benefit.

Establish New Nuclear Families

Chapter 9 introduced the concept of exogamy, the requirement that individuals choose their spouses from families (however broadly or narrowly this term might be defined) other than their own. Joining two representatives of different families usually (but not always) creates a new family for the mutual benefit of its members—not just the

---

[1] In the spoken language of the !Kung, there are a number of sounds that do not occur in English. One of them is a soft explosive noise, called a "click," that sounds something like a cross between a "k" and an "l" and is made in the throat. The exclamation point in front of the word "!Kung" (and other words expressed in English but derived from this and other African "click" languages) indicates that this word begins with a "click" rather than with any sound that can be represented using the English alphabet.

husband and wife but also any children who may be born to or adopted by them. The new grouping typically provides each member with such basic needs as food and shelter; a socially approved role; and, in the case of children, protection, nurture, and enculturation.

Specify Rights and Responsibilities

Marriage customs are extremely diverse, but in every society the institution defines certain rights and responsibilities for married people, and often for their families as well. At a minimum, marriage establishes that a husband is the legal father of children born to his wife, and that she is the legal mother of his if she produces them; that the husband and wife each have a sexual monopoly over the other (unless the husband has more than one wife or the wife has more than one husband, in which case a spouse shares sexual rights with several cospouses); that the couple have either partial or monopolistic rights to the fruits of each other's labor; that each has partial or total rights over property belonging to the other; and that a joint fund of property is established for the benefit of the children of the marriage (Leach 1963:107–108).

Such rights and responsibilities are common to most kinds of marriage, and they contribute to the solution of such universal problems as establishing who can have sex with whom, who is to care for offspring, and how work and the products it generates are to be allocated between husband and wife.

Create Alliances

Marriage not only establishes a married couple's rights and responsibilities to each other and to their children; in many non-Western societies, it also creates alliances among the relatives of the married couple. While the term *marriage* refers specifically to the relationship of the couple, **affinity** refers to all the relationships a marriage engenders, not only between the married pair but also among the relatives of both. Individuals brought into relationship with one another through the marriage of a relative are called **affines.** The affines belonging to a group that reared a woman who has become the bride of a man in another group are termed *wife-givers,* and the affines belonging to a group that has taken a woman as the bride of one of its members are termed *wife-takers.* The ties among affines, called **affinal alliances,** can serve various subsistence, political, legal, economic, and social functions, to the benefit of everyone involved in the alliance. In some societies, affines have an obligation to help one another with tasks requiring a group—for example, building a house or campaigning for a political office.

One common affinal obligation in non-Western societies is to provide affines with subsistence necessities; for example, gifts of food might be required at the time of a marriage, birth, or death, or on other occasions. The custom can be highly functional. If one affinal group has suffered a poor harvest but its partner group living in another region has not, gifts of food may sustain the impoverished group over its period of famine. Affines may also be required to perform ritual services for one another, as among the Rindi. In this eastern Indonesian society, wife-givers are considered the source of life and spiritual well-being. A man with a long-term illness may move into the house of one of his clan's wife-givers, place himself symbolically under the spiritual protection of the ancestor of this wife-giver, and stay there until he recovers (Forth 1981:292). By contrast, wife-takers are associated with death. If someone dies away from home, "his clan's wife-takers may be called upon to transport the corpse" (291). These customs show how descent, marriage, and religion come together in a thoroughly holistic way in Rindi society.

Another common obligation of affines is mutual defense. In times past, if you were a Tetum man and your clan was attacked by another clan, not only would you be compelled to join in the defense effort; your affines, too, would be expected to offer assistance (Hicks 1990). If you refused, they would

---

• Ask Yourself •

What are the usual reasons for elopement in Western society? What are some of its social and emotional consequences for the married couple?

affinity relationships created by marriage

affines relatives by marriage

affinal alliance ties between affines

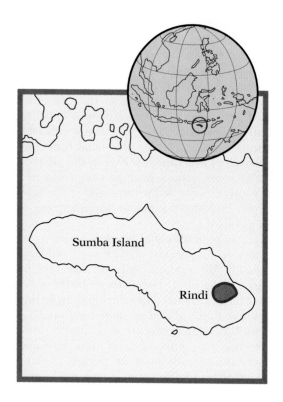

ethnic group rather than Jordanians, a preference that reinforces their ethnic identity.

Affinal alliances can be so important a component of culture that when they break down, as may occur with modernization, the consequences can be as extreme as they are unexpected. In the New Guinea highlands before contact with the outside world, marriages created affinal links between trading groups. Stone ax heads were made by groups living where suitable stones were available, and interregional trade saw to their distribution. In the process, intergroup marriages were contracted, which created affinal ties that made trade easier between groups. After steel axes were introduced from the West, however, local production of stone ones ceased. As trade declined, so did the opportunity to contract marriages and create affinal ties between groups. Eventually, as older people died and fewer intergroup marriages were arranged, the network of affinal ties decayed, and conflict and full-scale warfare increased (Podolefsky 1984:85).

Allocate Goods and Services

In many societies, including Western society, marriage may involve the transfer of goods and services among affines, either at the time of marriage or later (Goody and Tambiah 1973). The terms *bridewealth, bride-service,* and *dowry* are used to

not come to *your* aid when you and your clan were attacked.

Affinal alliances require regulations that spell out how suitable marriages can be brought about. The rule of exogamy, of course, requires descent group members to choose spouses from groups other than their own, thus bringing two groups into alliance. But in many cases a society will not want its members to choose spouses from groups so distant or so alien that useful affinal alliances cannot be formed. So, in addition to rules of exogamy, many societies have rules of **endogamy:** spouses must be chosen from *within* a certain group. Usually the endogamous group within which one is encouraged to find one's spouse is relatively large, such as a religious or ethnic group. Indeed, one reason for endogamy is to preserve a religious or ethnic tradition. Many people living in Jordan, for instance, identify themselves as Palestinian rather than Jordanian, and are encouraged to choose spouses from within the Palestinian

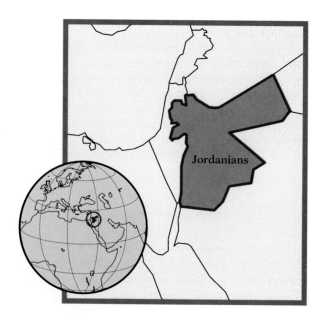

endogamy the custom in which one's spouse must be chosen from within one's own group

For the Tetum of Indonesia, burying the dead is a job that can be carried out only by the affines of the dead person. Here one of the female affines of a deceased person dresses another in preparation for a burial ritual.

distinguish among the goods and services thus distributed.

Bridewealth. **Bridewealth (bride-price)** is property transferred from a groom's family to the bride's on the occasion of a marriage. Animals, money, houses, jewelry, or clothing—virtually anything considered of value in a society—can constitute bridewealth. The number and quality of items may depend on the wealth of the groom's family, their

prestige relative to that of their new affines, and the social importance of the particular marriage.

Westerners sometimes react ethnocentrically to the idea of bridewealth, interpreting it as payment for a woman who is being "sold." However, among

---

bridewealth (bride-price) property transferred from a groom's family to his bride's at marriage

those who give or receive bridewealth, the custom enhances the repute of both sexes. A married woman's prestige among her peers may be influenced by the size of the bridewealth her husband gave for her, and having proved himself wealthy enough to pay a large bridewealth may add to the prestige of a husband. This does not mean that women in societies in which bridewealth is given enjoy equal status with men; often they do not. Yet bridewealth is a custom that both women and men may support. Some years ago in Zimbabwe, southern Africa, a law was enacted that was intended to give women equal rights. Among other things, it states that a woman can decide for herself whether her prospective husband must pay bridewealth. Given the choice, many Zimbabwean women "continue to view [bridewealth] as a symbol of worth and dignity in a male-dominated society" (*New York Times* 3/27/86:A17).

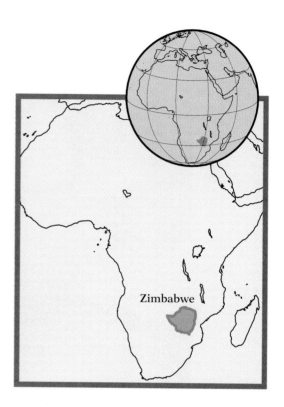

Bridewealth—property presented to a bride's family by a groom's family when a marriage takes place—consists of money or other goods considered valuable in a society. In Tanzania, East Africa, bridewealth cattle are driven from a Gogo groom's home to that of his bride. Cattle and Kinship Among the Gogo: A Semi-pastoral Society of Central Tanzania. *Copyright © 1969 by Cornell University. Used by permission of the publisher, Cornell University Press.*

Generally speaking, the more rights a groom's family gets as the result of a marriage, the larger the bridewealth. This is especially true in patrisystems, in which the most important right a groom's family obtains is the right to claim as members of its own group any children the wife may bear. Also common in patrisystems is the right to expect the bride to live with her new husband and his relatives, rather than vice versa. This custom, patrilocal residence (see Chapter 9), ensures that the groom need not live with his in-laws in an alien place, where he may have few privileges. Following from this right is that of the groom's family to the fruits of the new wife's labor. From her wedding day onward, the bride is a contributing member of her husband's household, not the household into which she was born. If the bridewealth is not paid, these rights are not secured and the marriage may be declared void.

Even though bridewealth is more common in patrilineal societies, it may also occur with matriliny. But in matrilineal societies, the children a married couple produce belong to the wife's descent group, not the husband's. Since the marriage benefits the husband's group less, the bridewealth is usually smaller.

Narrowly defined, a dowry is gifts a bride's family presents to a groom's at the time of a marriage. In northwestern India, to mark the wedding of a member of the nobility, the male consanguines of the bride arrive at the groom's home carrying platters of money.

Bride-service. **Bride-service** occurs when a son-in-law works for his father-in-law to compensate him for the loss of his daughter's services. Sometimes the son-in-law's labor is for a limited period of time, perhaps until his wife gives birth to their first child. Sometimes it lasts until the older man dies.

Dowry. Narrowly defined, a **dowry** is the goods given by a bride's family to the family of her groom. As such, the custom is quite rare. More broadly, a dowry consists of the goods—jewelry, money, household items, animals, or other valuables—a bride brings with her to her marriage. Once widely practiced in both Asia and Europe, this custom may have originated where land could be inherited only by sons, and thus was a way for parents to include their daughters as beneficiaries of their wealth.

In India, dowries have been declared illegal, in part because of a tendency of some families to view the birth of a daughter as an unwelcome financial burden and to treat girls accordingly. Yet a dowry is still a part of many Indian marriages. Especially among the poor, it may pay for the wedding itself rather than enrich the groom's family or purchase household necessities for the couple.

• Marriage Partners: • Preferred and Prohibited

Sex and marriage are very different, but in most societies, sex is assumed to be an essential ingredient of marriage, and individuals who are permitted to have sex with each other are generally also allowed to marry. Thus, appropriate marriage partners are

• Ask Yourself •

Can you think of other functions of marriage, as it is understood in the West, that make it particularly adaptive within the context of Western society?

---

bride-service an arrangement in which a son-in-law is obliged to work for his father-in-law as a way of compensating the father-in-law for the loss of his daughter's services

dowry goods given by a bride's family to the family of her groom

• Ask Yourself •

What purpose does the custom of gift-giving at marriage serve in Western culture?

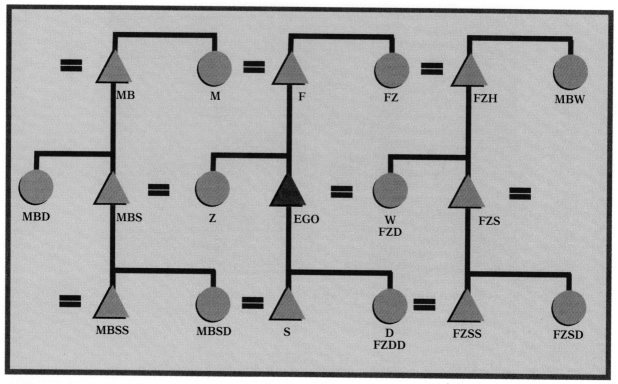

Figure 10.1

Patrilateral Cross Cousin Marriage. In patrilateral cross cousin marriage, a man marries his father's sister's daughter and a woman marries her mother's brother's son.

usually permitted to be sex partners as well. All societies regulate these matters, sometimes by prohibiting certain marriages (as in the case of David and Victoria) and sometimes by encouraging or even mandating certain marriages. However, the rules defining permitted and prohibited sex and marriage partners vary widely from culture to culture. In some societies, sex or marriage between biological first cousins is considered wrong and is discouraged or even legally prevented; in others, marriage between first cousins is encouraged as the ideal, or preferred, marriage.

Preferred Marriages

Earlier we pointed out that affinal relationships among the relatives of a married couple may be more important socially than the personal relationship between the married pair. Members of societies in which strong affinal alliances are important often experience intense social pressure to marry a certain person or a person from a particular category. In some cases—traditional China, for instance—an individual would have no choice at all; he or she might as an infant have been betrothed to a particular person.

In societies in which marriages between certain relatives are advocated, the preferred spouse is commonly a first cousin, which means that the bride and groom have a set of grandparents in common. One reason for such a marriage is to continue the existing ties between the bride's family (wife-givers) and the groom's (wife-takers).

Cross Cousin Marriage. Chapter 9 distinguished between two kinds of cross cousins, patrilateral (on the father's side) and matrilateral (on the mother's side). In some societies with preferred marriage

---

cross cousin marriage a marriage between two cross cousins

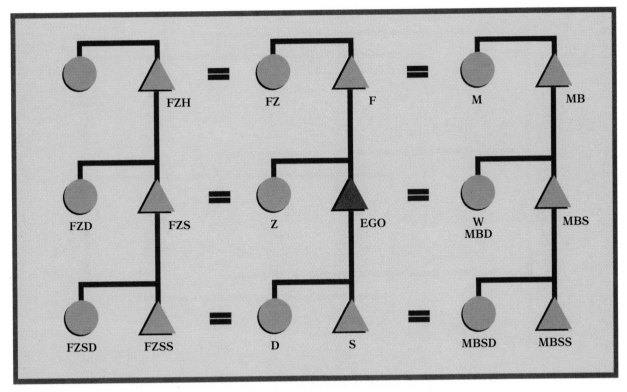

Figure 10.2

Matrilateral Cross Cousin Marriage. In matrilateral cross cousin marriage, a man marries his mother's brother's daughter and a woman her father's sister's son.

rules, individuals are strongly encouraged to marry one kind of cross cousin or the other.

In **patrilateral cross cousin marriage** (Figure 10.1), a man is required or at least encouraged to marry his father's sister's daughter, and a woman is required or encouraged to marry her mother's brother's son. As though to express this preference, societies with this form of marriage may use the Crow kinship terminology (see Chapter 9, page 228), in which parallel cousins and cross cousins are distinguished from each other, and the kinship term used for the cross cousin who is the preferred marriage partner is often the same as the term for spouse. Thus a man calls his father's sister's daughter by the term *wife*, and a woman calls her mother's brother's son by the term *husband*.

Similarly, in societies that practice **matrilateral cross cousin marriage** (Figure 10.2), in which a man is required or encouraged to marry his mother's brother's daughter and a woman is required or encouraged to marry her father's sister's son, this preference is often revealed in the use of the Omaha kinship terminology (see Chapter 9, page 227). Again, the cross cousins are distinguished from each other, and the kinship term used for the cross cousin who is the preferred marriage partner is often the same term as that for spouse.

What happens if the preferred marriage partner does not exist or is unavailable—for example, if a man is supposed to marry his mother's brother's

---

patrilateral cross cousin marriage a man's marriage to his father's sister's daughter or a woman's marriage to her mother's brother's son

matrilateral cross cousin marriage a man's marriage to his mother's brother's daughter or a woman's marriage to her father's sister's son

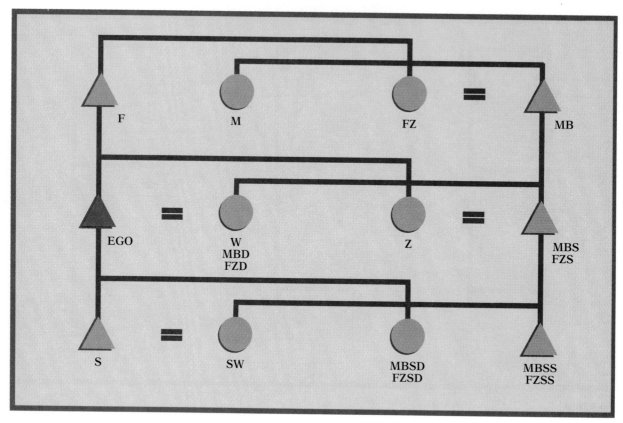

Figure 10.3

Bilateral Exchange. In bilateral exchange, men of different families or descent groups exchange their "sisters" (either biological sisters or other female relatives classified as sisters) as brides.

daughter but his mother's brother does not have a daughter? In that case, an eligible substitute is found.[2]

Patrilateral cross cousin marriage as practiced by the Trobriand Islanders (see map on page 19) shows just how flexible the notion of a preferred spouse can be. The preferred marriage for a Trobriand man is with his father's sister's daughter, a woman he calls by the kinship term *tabugu* (Malinowski 1962:534). But while this is the ideal, it is not often the actual practice (Weiner 1976:185). Although a male Trobriander *says* he would prefer his father's sister's daughter as a marriage partner,

census material shows that his actual choice is likely to be a more distantly related woman of his father's clan, perhaps a second or third patrilateral cousin. In either case, he often ends up marrying into the same clan his mother did. In fact, *every* woman in this clan is considered *tabugu*. Thus, it seems that the preference among Trobrianders is really for a certain *category* of women, *tabugu* women, rather than for a particular individual.

Bilateral Exchange. A third type of preferred marriage is **bilateral exchange** (Figure 10.3), in which men of different nuclear families or descent

<hr>

[2] The same problem occurs in Western society when tradition dictates that a specific relative perform a specific role, and it is usually solved in the same way. The father of a bride, for example, is expected to "give her away" at her wedding. If, however, he cannot be present, another relative—the bride's brother, perhaps, or an uncle—is usually chosen to fill in.

bilateral exchange a form of cross cousin marriage in which the men of two nuclear families or descent groups, related to one another as cross cousins, exchange women in marriage; sometimes called *direct exchange*

groups, related to one another as cross cousins, exchange their "sisters" as brides (though not all at the same time, of course). In this context, the word *sisters* includes not only biological sisters but, more widely, a range of female relatives that one group of men may "give" to another. Because, in effect, men of two groups are exchanging "sisters" directly for "sisters," this institution is sometimes referred to as *direct exchange*. In bilateral exchange, if you were a woman, you might marry a person who is both your mother's brother's son and your father's sister's son. If you were a man, you might marry a person who is both your mother's brother's daughter and your father's sister's daughter. This preference may be suggested by the use of the Iroquois kinship terminology. In bilateral exchange both categories of cross cousin—preferred as marriage partners—are typically known by the same term as that for spouse.

Parallel Cousin Marriage. As with cross cousin marriage, there are two kinds of **parallel cousin marriage**: matrilateral and patrilateral. In **matrilateral parallel cousin marriage** (Figure 10.4), a man is required or encouraged to marry his mother's sister's daughter, and a woman is required or encouraged to marry her mother's sister's son. In **patrilateral parallel cousin marriage** (Figure 10.5), a man is required or encouraged to marry his father's brother's daughter, and a woman is required or encouraged to marry her father's brother's son.

The adaptive function of parallel cousin marriage is demonstrated by some Muslim groups living in the Middle East. In the past, the subsistence strategy of these patrilineal people was nomadic pastoralism (see Chapter 6). Herds of animals were owned by patrilineages. Two brothers, by arranging for their respective offspring to enter into a patrilateral parallel cousin marriage, could keep their wealth together, in the form of herds of animals. If one of their offspring were to marry a person from

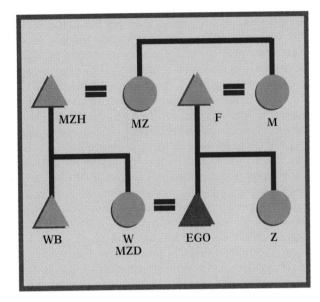

Figure 10.4

Matrilateral Parallel Cousin Marriage. In matrilateral parallel cousin marriage, a man marries his mother's sister's daughter and a woman marries her mother's sister's son.

another patrilineage, the family's property might have to be divided up.

Arranged Marriages

Arranged marriages are not uncommon in societies in which affinal alliances have important social

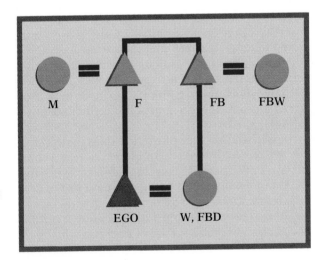

Figure 10.5

Patrilateral Parallel Cousin Marriage. In patrilateral parallel cousin marriage, a man marries his father's brother's daughter and a woman marries her father's brother's son.

---

parallel cousin marriage a marriage between two parallel cousins

matrilateral parallel cousin marriage a man's marriage to his mother's sister's daughter or a woman's marriage to her mother's sister's son

patrilateral parallel cousin marriage a man's marriage to his father's brother's daughter or a woman's marriage to her father's brother's son

implications. If you were a member of such a society, your marriage would so directly involve your relatives that they would be very interested in your future spouse and very concerned about the social position and wealth of your future affines. Indeed, they would have every right to help you choose your spouse. Your affection for your spouse, or the fact that the two of you took the first steps toward marriage by yourselves, might be a consideration, but your marriage would be too important socially to allow your personal feelings to control the future. The opinions of your senior relatives and your future spouse's senior relatives, not your own, would be paramount, and these relatives would finalize, if not actually arrange, the match.

In the many societies around the world where marriages are arranged for individuals who do not love each other, the hazards threatened by this often-unreliable sentiment are avoided. The cost is personal freedom, but the result may be a satisfying marriage with considerable benefit to the families of the two spouses.

Free-Choice Marriages

Societies without explicitly preferred marriage rules are more common than those with them. In most societies—including Western, peasant, and nonliterate societies, from North Americans to Middle Easterners to Inuit to !Kung San—factors other than genealogical connections determine the choice of spouse. These include personal attraction, social status, or wealth (Lévi-Strauss 1969:xxiii). The diversity of the societies in which there is no preferred marriage partner, and their wide geographical distribution, suggests that, in functional and cultural-evolutionary terms, the greater flexibility brought about by not limiting spouses to a preferred kinship category must offer certain adaptive advantages.

Despite the absence of explicit rules, however, a society may still make its preferences felt. Young people in Western society are familiar with the kinds of pressure family or friends may exert to persuade one to marry "appropriately." Subtly or not so subtly, one may be urged to marry into a certain social class, or pick a spouse of a certain religion or one who is well educated.

incest taboo the prohibition of sex between relatives

TIMES MATRIMONIALS

TALL, very fair, beautiful convented Engineer, Doctor, professionally qualified girl from cultured family for 6'1" / 38, only son Brahmin Engineer extremely handsome dynamic personality teetotaller simple habits working   parents India, boy visiting India March. Girl's beauty main consideration. Photo first instance. Write

♥ **WANTED** convent educated beautiful girl preferably Punjabi Brahmin for very smart boy in service 26 / 167 / 5000 hailing from very respectable world fame   family. Only son. No dowry. Girl only consideration. Please apply

WANTED for extremely good looking well versed in domestic affairs upto age of 40 yrs. for a divorced Senior I.A.S. Officer aged about 50 years   No dowry. Simple and early marrige. Write

BEAUTIFUL bride graduate or above preferred for only son of   Officer practising Law owns house telephone. No dowry. Write with horoscope and photo.

In many societies around the world, marriages are arranged by the relatives of individuals who do not know each other. In New Delhi, India, the parents of unmarried men and women seek alliances for their children through newspaper ads.

Prohibited Marriages

David and Victoria's story was newsworthy because sex between members of the same family is considered incestuous in Western society (even though an estimated 10 to 14 percent of American children under 18 have been involved in incestuous acts). Incest between siblings is thought to be the most common type, but father-daughter incest is the most often reported (Shepher 1983). The prohibition against incest is normally restricted to members of the nuclear family, although some countries, states, or religions also prohibit marriages between first cousins. But in societies with descent groups, this prohibition can apply to sex or marriage between more distantly related members of the same descent group. Anthropologists call the prohibition of sex between close relatives the **incest taboo.**

Incest seems to be so commonly disapproved of throughout the world that this taboo comes close to being universal. A number of explanations have been proposed for this widespread disapproval, among them the social, cooperation, psychoanalytic, genetic, and instinct explanations.

The Social Explanation. Malinowski (1927:251) and others have asserted that, were incest permitted within the nuclear family, competition for sex among family members would bring about such mutual hostility that families would be destroyed. According to the **social explanation,** the incest taboo arose to prevent this from happening. Some anthropologists counter this argument by suggesting that although competition between father and son for the mother, and between mother and daughter for the father, would certainly disrupt the simple family, sibling incest need not do so.

The Cooperation Explanation. To survive in the demanding environment of prehistoric times, Tylor (1889) and later Lévi-Strauss (1969) argued, nuclear families were forced to cooperate. To encourage cooperation, early human beings developed nuclear family exogamy, which forced members of one family to look for spouses in others. The resulting marriage ties bonded otherwise independent families into societies. Early human beings had a choice, as Tylor put it, between "marrying out and dying out." Unfortunately, there are two logical problems with this **cooperation explanation.** First, there are other ways of fostering cooperation between nuclear families—ways that some societies have actually put into practice, such as the exchange of labor or gifts. And second, the "marry out or die out" idea does not explain why members of a nuclear family are forbidden to *have sex* with each other. It explains only why they are forbidden to *marry* each other.

---

social explanation an explanation for the incest taboo that suggests it arose to prevent family disintegration

cooperation explanation an explanation for the incest taboo that emphasizes the social advantages that come from obliging members of the same family to marry outside of it

psychoanalytic explanation an explanation for the incest taboo that suggests its origin lies in an attempt to control the unconscious desire of children to have sex with the parent of the opposite sex

genetic explanation an explanation for the incest taboo that emphasizes the genetic advantages of marrying outside the family

The Psychoanalytic Explanation. Freud (1918) argued that every boy subconsciously longs to have sex with his mother—an urge Freud labeled the Oedipus complex, after a tragic figure in Greek drama who unwittingly married his own mother. Thus, a son, according to Freud, cannot help but be jealous of and hostile toward his father. Fearing that his father might retaliate against him, the son unconsciously represses his sexual urges. But they continue to haunt him, resulting in feelings of horror at the very thought of having sex with his mother. Freud believed a similar urge and repressive reaction, which he termed the Electra complex (after another figure in Greek drama, who killed her mother), are felt by a daughter toward her father. One weakness of this **psychoanalytical explanation** is that the members of some societies apparently feel no horror about incest whatsoever. Needham (1974:66) reports that the Kodi of Indonesia claim to know of individuals who sleep with close relatives, but no one much cares.

Recent research has suggested that a more promising solution to the incest problem probably lies not in any of these three formulations but rather in explanations based either on genetics or instinct.

The Genetic Explanation. Victoria and David claimed to have heard that the offspring of closely related parents are more likely to suffer biological defects than other children. This belief underlies the **genetic explanation** for the incest taboo: incest is forbidden because societies recognize the potential for impaired offspring. Research has demonstrated that over generations reproductive vigor is lost among animal populations that inbreed, whereas outbreeding promotes genetic diversity, which promotes the ability of a species to adapt to changes in the physical environment. Advocates of this explanation argue that in a society that has no incest prohibition, a high proportion of children will be born impaired. In prehistoric times, when societies were small and the lives of their members precarious, societies with many impaired members were less able to compete successfully with rival societies that had rules against incest and were thus producing more robust individuals. Natural selection took care of the rest. Societies permitting incest gradually died out, unable to compete successfully for resources against stronger societies, while those in which incest was prohibited thrived. Hence, the argument goes, today (as far as we can tell) all societies have an incest taboo.

Some critics of this explanation have noted that inbreeding is not necessarily harmful to a species. Inbreeding will rapidly increase undesirable biological traits, but desirable ones will also be intensified. Since undesirable traits develop relatively quickly where inbreeding is not prohibited, the genes associated with these traits will be rapidly eliminated from the population. The controversy has not been resolved.

The Instinct Explanation.   Edward Westermarck (1922:192–194), in what may be called the **instinct explanation,** argued that the incest taboo was not so much a rule for preventing individuals from committing incest as it was a cultural reflection of the natural aversion people feel toward sex with persons who have lived closely together, either as siblings or as parent and child. Once established, this aversion might result in moral disapproval and institutionalized prohibition (1922:198, 203–204). But how does this feeling of aversion arise? Anthropologist Paul B. Roscoe (1994) has recently sought to resolve the problem Westermarck left unsolved. According to Roscoe, research on neurophysiological processes in the human brain has shown that sex and physical aggression are very closely linked, and that human beings thus experience sex as a form of aggression. But aggression is incompatible with the powerful affections that arise when persons live closely together as siblings or as parent and child, and it is this incompatibility that creates the feeling of aversion to sex between them.

• Types of Marriage •

Given two sexes, there are four theoretical possibilities for marriage: one man and one woman might be married to each other, one man might be married to two or more women at the same time, one woman might be married to two or more men at the same time, or several men and several women might be married to one another simultaneously. Ethnographic fieldwork has shown that each of these possibilities exists.

----

instinct explanation an explanation for the incest taboo suggesting that members of the same family instinctively find one another sexually unappealing

monogamy the marriage of one husband and one wife

A new kind of marriage has emerged in twentieth-century Western society: serial monogamy—consecutive monogamous marriages to a number of different spouses. Above, actress Elizabeth Taylor, who had previously married Nicky Hilton, Michael Wilding, Mike Todd, Eddie Fisher, Richard Burton (twice), and John Warner, with her most recent husband, Larry Fortensky.

Monogamy

Today, in most of the industrialized world, a person is permitted to have only one spouse at a time, a form of marriage called **monogamy.** It is easily the most common kind of marriage found around the world, perhaps because in most societies the number of adult males and females tends to be approximately equal. Another reason why monogamy is so common may be that having more than one spouse at a time may entail considerable initial outlay (in the form of bridewealth, for example), which many people cannot afford. This economic explanation is countered, however, by the fact that multiple spouses may convey later economic advantages.

Monogamy may be the only legal form of marriage in Western society, but as divorce and remar-

"Look, I'm not talking about a lifetime commitment. I'm talking about marriage."

Drawing by Maslin; © 1995 The New Yorker Magazine, Inc.

riage become increasingly common, a novel form of Western marriage has emerged, **serial monogamy,** defined as consecutive monogamous marriages to a number of different spouses. The actress Elizabeth Taylor Hilton Wilding Todd Fisher Burton Burton Warner Fortensky may be the Western world's best-known exemplar of serial monogamy.

Polygamy

Another form of marriage, one common in many parts of the non-Western world, is **polygamy,** in which a person has more than one spouse at the same time.

Polygyny. One form of polygamy is **polygyny,** in which a man has two or more wives at the same time. In Islamic countries, for instance, a man may legally have up to four wives at a time, a moderate number compared with what was acceptable in the past among the Tsimshian of the Northwest Coast (see map on page 223). Tsimshian chiefs could have as many as 20 wives (Rosman and Rubel 1986:16).

From the point of view of the women involved, polygyny may offer some advantages. The first is economic. A household in which several women are working together produces more than one in which one woman is working alone. Since the husband may reap the rewards of his wives' labor, their work, whether in his fields or among his herds, may make him richer than a monogamous man; if the wives together produce a large number of offspring, the children, too, may contribute to his household's output. The household may also benefit from the husband's many affines. Some Trobriand chiefs practiced polygyny on a grand scale, their major income coming from annual marriage contributions consisting of goods and services owed them by the brothers of their wives (Malinowski 1962:130–132). One chief had five dozen wives, giving him considerable economic influence.

Women's second benefit in polygynous marriages is social. Co-wives may value one another's company and relish the prestige that comes from

---

serial monogamy consecutive monogamous marriages to a number of different spouses

polygamy a form of marriage in which a person has more than one spouse at the same time.

polygyny marriage between a husband and more than one wife

Anthropology and the Environment

Marriage, Family Size, and Resources in Mali

Wherever population growth outstrips the capacity of the environment to supply the resources needed by more and more people, sexual behavior and environmental concerns intersect. The problem of environmental degradation due to population growth may be especially acute in societies in which the possibility of long-term resource depletion is offset by deeply ingrained cultural preferences for large families.

In rural Mali, West Africa, 7 children is seen as the ideal family size (Kak and Signer 1995:77), and motherhood is considered to be women's most important role. Girls sometimes marry at age 13 or 14; most marry around the age of 16 and widows are urged to remarry quickly, so virtually all women are married. Family size and child spacing are usually not openly discussed by husbands and wives; instead, men—traditionally dominant in this polygynous Moslem society—make the decisions on these matters. The average woman bears 6.7 children (Kak and Signer 1995:77), and the population is currently growing at about 3 percent per year. If this rate of growth were to continue, the environmental impact would be significant, but through the mid-1970s Malians believed that their country was big enough,

and had enough natural resources, to absorb a larger population (van de Walle and Maiga 1991:84).

Malian women expect and want to bear many children, but because the infant mortality rate is extremely high, they prefer to space their pregnancies two or three years apart so their babies will have a better chance to survive. Yet most do not know about modern contraceptives. Traditionally, a new mother postpones her next pregnancy by breastfeeding or by abstaining from sex for up to three years. She may also rely for contraception on wearing a *tafo*, a belt made of animal skin and cotton that has been blessed by a traditional healer (Kak and Signer 1993:12).

The district of Katibougou, in Western Mali, is a poor agricultural area where droughts frequently make subsistence farming—a major economic activity—difficult. A few years ago, a Malian midwife, aware that the local environment was neither rich nor reliable enough to provide the necessities of life to a steadily growing population indefinitely, designed an experimental project to bring modern family planning methods to the attention of the Katibougou villagers. Because the notion of a small family is unacceptable in Mali, the midwife decided to promote family planning not as a means of limit-

being married to a man who can afford more than one wife. When fields must be hoed, water carried, and animals milked, more help is available. Children, too, benefit socially from this arrangement, often forming close relationships with each

of their fathers' co-wives. And a child may have half-brothers and half-sisters of about the same age to play with.

Polygyny is also an efficient way for a society to provide for its widowed or otherwise single women. They become co-wives, perhaps little begrudging this status since their only alternative may be living alone, which may be undesirable. If the women involved are sisters, this arrangement—known as **sororal polygyny**—can be particularly attractive.

---

sororal polygyny the custom in which two or more of a polygynous man's wives are sisters

ing family size, but as a way to improve the chances of infant survival and achieve the cultural norm of long birth spacing.

Her project, with support from an international aid agency, took a number of innovative steps. First, in recognition that Malian men had great influence on contraceptive choices, male as well as female health workers were trained to educate villagers about how family planning could improve child spacing and help them achieve their desired family size. Traditional gender roles discouraged men and women from communicating about sex, so the female health workers worked with the community's women and the male workers with the men. Gradually, as they learned more about the health and economic advantages of birth spacing, men became less resistant to the idea of family planning. The project also integrated family planning services with other kinds of health care, so that at a single clinic villagers could get contraceptive information and supplies, prenatal and postnatal care, immunizations, malaria prevention, and other basic medical care. Another innovative measure was to provide the health workers with bicycles so they could get out into the community to visit clients. And the project initiated several income-generating activities, such as a cereal grinding business, a women's textile cooperative, and a ferry service to provide transportation across the Niger River, in order to provide both the health workers and family planning acceptors with some income.

After five years, the use of modern family planning methods in Katibougou district had grown from virtually none to almost 58 percent of married couples. Villagers who decided to use modern contraceptives said they mainly wanted to improve child survival, but they also cited increased economic productivity and quality of life improvements as side benefits of family planning. They also reported increased communication about family planning between men and women, which may in the long run enable women to play a more active role in deciding matters related to their own fertility. Today, the project's clinic, still the only health facility serving Katibougou district, offers an integrated family planning and health program—including educational sessions on environmental health matters such as safe drinking water—in a format that has been very successful in increasing its clients' acceptance of family planning services (Kak and Signer 1995).

Within a society that values early marriage, polygyny, and large families, the Katibougou project has found a way to promote modern family planning methods as an effective way of enhancing child survival and hence the quality of life, while at the same time respecting clients' cultural norms. The project is now serving as a model for family planning service delivery elsewhere in Mali, having been replicated by the government in other areas of the country. Thus, in the long run, it may help to mitigate the environmental consequences of unchecked population growth in Mali.

In rural Iran, one of the authors of this book (Gwynne) visited a family that included an elderly Moslem husband and his two wives, sisters who were originally married to two different men. When the husband of the elder sister died, she became the second wife of her younger sister's husband. The two women obviously liked each other's company, jointly cooking and serving a meal to their guest, laughing with each other at private jokes, and joining together to tease their husband.

However, polygyny—perhaps especially when it is not sororal—sometimes creates jealousy among co-wives, which not even separate residences can reduce. And in urban settings, polygyny has been cited as a cause of neglect of children because husbands often lack the economic wherewithal to provide for two or more separate households (Coles and Mack 1991:81).

In the United States, polygyny was introduced into the Mormon church in 1843 and became official

Polygyny, a kind of marriage in which a man has two or more wives at the same time, is permitted in many societies. The 40 wives of Kenyan husband Danja Akuku have borne him a total of 349 children

Mormon policy in 1852. Declared illegal under U.S. law in 1887, the practice still survives among some traditional Mormons, despite the fact that the church now excommunicates polygynists. In 1983, Royston Potter, a Mormon who was illegally married to three women at once, contended that the law prohibiting plural marriage violated his constitutional right to religious freedom, but a federal judge ruled against him. In a more recent case, the state of Montana decided to turn a blind eye to polygyny, with the result that in tiny Pinesdale, Montana, a man can apparently have as many wives as he wants (*New York Times* 9/18/87:A18).

polyandry marriage between a wife and more than one husband

fraternal polyandry the custom whereby two or more of a polyandrous woman's husbands are brothers

Polyandry.   Much rarer than either monogamy or polygyny is **polyandry,** marriage in which a woman has more than one husband. It occurs in Africa and the Americas, but one area in particular—the region around the Himalayas—is famous for polyandry.

Sometimes, the husbands who share a wife are brothers, a form of marriage known as **fraternal polyandry.** This kind of polyandry accounts for a higher proportion of polyandrous marriages than sororal polygyny does for polygynous unions. Cultural materialists claim that fraternal polyandry prevails when it offers some economic advantage to the people involved. In mountainous Tibet, for instance, productive farmland is scarce, yet much of the population depends on farming. If a farmer with a small plot of land and several sons divided his land among his sons, none of them would end up with a plot big enough to support a family

Himalayan societies are famous for polyandry, a form of marriage in which a woman has more than one husband at the same time. A Tibetan wife with her two husbands.

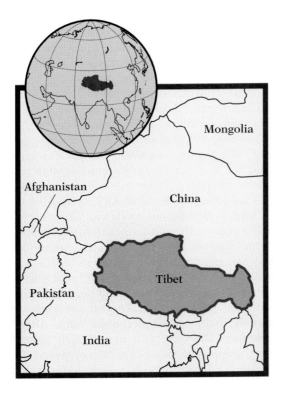

(Goldstein 1987). Were all the farmer's sons married to the same woman, however, there would be no need to partition the property into insufficient plots, for the brothers could live and work on it together and bequeath it jointly to their sons. Also, the number of claimants to the land would be reduced because one woman—even one with several husbands—can produce fewer children in a lifetime than several women can.

Factors other than the scarcity of land (a problem that can be resolved in various ways) may encourage polyandry. In traditional times, the Nayar of south India were professional warriors, which meant that men were often away from home fighting as mercenaries. Death was a constant risk. Polyandry helped reduce the danger that Nayar descent groups would become extinct (Gough 1962).

Group Marriage.   A fourth, extremely rare, form of marriage involves two or more men and two or more women simultaneously. Anthropologists report

Aweikoma

this kind of marriage, called **group marriage,** in only a few non-Western cultures, such as the Aweikoma of southern Brazil (Henry 1964). In this society, a marriage might begin with a monogamous or polygynous union. In time, another man or woman or two might be added; meanwhile, some spouses might leave or die. The Aweikoma household was thus a large, flexible unit to which spouses could be added or deleted for a variety of reasons (37).

The living arrangements of members of North American "hippie" communes of the 1960s might also be considered group marriages, in that sexual and economic bonds existed among two or more women and two or more men simultaneously. Few such arrangements proved long-lasting or particu-

• Ask Yourself •

How do you feel about communal living arrangements in which sex with anyone is possible? What advantages and disadvantages would be open to the members of such a group? Can you envision yourself as part of such a group?

group marriage a form of marriage involving two or more men and two or more women as marriage partners at the same time

larly rewarding for their participants. Many disintegrated as tensions developed over responsibilities for the children who were born or the need to earn a living.

The communes of the 1960s were not original to this rebellious period; similar arrangements had existed previously. In the nineteenth century, some 50 idealistic men and women established a commune called the Oneida Community in upstate New York (Klaw 1993). They believed that romantic love between individual males and females would result in sexual possessiveness, which would reduce cooperation among the group's members. So they pledged themselves to one another in a literal group marriage. Unlike their twentieth-century successors, the Oneida Community achieved economic success after its members began producing a line of silverware, which despite the commune's demise is still popular today. The commune lasted about 30 years, disbanding when its leader died without leaving an adequately prepared successor. Many former members soon established conventional, monogamous marriages. Despite their avowed commitment to "free love," it seems the commune's members had long previously organized themselves into monogamous pairs.

Other Marriage Customs

The manner in which marriage takes place varies from a complete lack of formality (the bride may simply move in with the groom and the two are henceforth considered married) to a long, complicated ritual that unfolds over many days.

Marriage among the Trobriand Islanders (see map on page 19) exemplifies the lack of formality that characterizes marriage in some societies. Unmarried Trobrianders enjoy considerable sexual freedom, as long as they are discreet. A woman enters her lover's house after dark, spends the night with him, and slips out at dawn. When a couple decide to marry, they announce this decision by sitting together on the veranda of the young man's house one morning, rather than parting in secret (Weiner 1988:77). Local gossips are quick to note this interesting development, and news of it quickly reaches the girl's mother, who—if she approves—brings the pair a meal of cooked yams. After the couple share this meal, they are officially married.

On the island of Timor (see map on page 139), in contrast, the Tetum stage an elaborate ceremony in which as many of the groom's and bride's patrikin as can attend appear at the bride's house, dressed in their best clothes. The bride and groom sit together on a mat woven of dried palm leaves, the same mat they will later sleep on. They hold hands as the bride's mother, acting as priestess for an event of great cosmological, economic, political, legal, and religious significance, prays at length to the ancestral ghosts of both families for the bride's fertility and the compatibility of their respective lineages. She is believed to bring together for their mutual benefit not only the couple, but also their lineages, including both human members and ancestral ghosts.

Westerners have a variety of wedding ceremonies from which to choose. A simple civil wedding in an official's office, attended only by bride, groom, and a few witnesses, suits some couples. Others favor a more elaborate setting and ceremony, often introducing religion as a central component. In Britain, when a member of the royal family marries, the event is a state affair, with hundreds of foreign governments represented. But no matter where a wedding takes place, it is usually celebrated with food, music, and dancing.

Among the many marriage customs described in the anthropological literature are bride-capture, ghost marriage, the levirate, and the sororate. Of these, the levirate and sororate are the most widely encountered.

Levirate and Sororate. These similar marriage customs, widespread around the world, underscore the importance of marriage as a way of creating ties between families. In many societies, when a husband or wife dies and leaves a spouse behind, the survivor automatically becomes the husband or wife of a sibling of the deceased. This custom is referred to by one of two different terms, depending on whether the survivor is female or male. In the **levirate,** a widow marries her dead husband's brother; in the **sororate,** a widower marries his dead wife's sister. Since in either case the original married

couple's two groups of affines typically maintain their affinal relationship, these institutions not only support widowed individuals, they also function as devices by which affinal alliances are maintained.

Bride-capture. In some societies, including contemporary ones, a man may win his bride by carrying her off forcibly. Often, however, such **bride-capture (bride-theft)** is more of a ritual than a literal abduction, and serves to symbolize social values while cementing family alliances.

In rural Crete, an island in the Aegean Sea, near Greece, males are expected to be independent, innovative, aggressive, and smart, while females are expected to be the passive, chaste objects of male competition. Cretan bride-theft symbolizes these values (Herzfeld 1985). A Cretan man who has his heart set on marrying a particular woman asks her father for her hand in marriage, either in person or through agnates acting as his intermediaries. Sometimes the father agrees to the match, on the condition that the suitor prove himself by a daring act such as stealing some sheep (28). But the father may also refuse, perhaps because he feels his daughter is too young or because he hopes for a better match. If the suitor is a self-respecting young man, his response to this refusal is to abduct the woman, often with the help of his male agnates. The bride may know of, and approve, the impending abduction (23). Thus she is hardly surprised should her suitor, his brothers, and his cousins "entice" her into a car and drive off with her.

A successful abduction changes the attitude of the prospective bride's father. "Since the suitor has proved himself, and has also compromised the bride to the point where no other self-respecting village male would . . . make her his bride, his failure to marry her would seriously compromise her natal family" (Herzfeld 1985:29). The father must now make certain the marriage takes place, for he can no longer guarantee his daughter's sexual innocence.

Cretans are unconcerned about the prewedding hostility that the father's initial rejection of the

• Ask Yourself •

Can you think of additional adaptive advantages of the levirate and sororate? What is your own feeling about a widower who marries his dead wife's sister? How about a divorced man who marries his ex-wife's sister?

levirate the custom in which a widow marries her dead husband's brother

sororate the custom in which a widower marries his dead wife's sister

bride-capture (bride-theft) the forcible and frequently symbolic carrying off of a bride

suitor causes between the families of the groom and bride. On the contrary, "only those who are worthy of one's rivalry are also worthy of friendship" (Herzfeld 1985:42). Once a man has proven his social worth by successfully capturing his bride, the two families resolve their differences (43), converting their enmity, through respect, into a "cooperative and positively valued relationship" (42).

Ghost Marriage. In societies with patrilineal descent groups, the continued existence of these groups depends on their male members producing offspring. Here, the functions of marriage and descent converge. Marriage provides a man with his wife, who produces the children who ensure the continued existence of his descent group. But what if a male should die unmarried or before his wife produces heirs? The Nuer of the Sudan (see map on page 217) ensure that a man's name will continue into the next generation through **ghost marriage,** an institution involving the belief that ghosts are capable of fathering children. Should a Nuer male die before he has married, his agnates find a woman willing to marry his ghost. After the "wedding," a brother of the dead man sleeps with the wife, whose future offspring will bear the dead man's name. If the deceased was already married but his wife had not yet produced a son, the widow is also expected to sleep with her brother-in-law, and the Nuer assume future offspring were sired by the dead husband's ghost. If the husband has no brothers or the widow does not have sex with them, the children of any man she lives with are considered to be the children of the dead husband (Evans-Pritchard 1956:163–164).

• Divorce •

Divorce is not as universal a feature of human culture as marriage, but it is nevertheless legally permissible in most societies (although in some it is prohibited by religion). There are as many variations in divorce practices as there are in marriage customs, and not surprisingly, they reflect society's prevailing social, economic, and political priorities. Where descent groups are of paramount importance, for example, divorce may be difficult

to obtain or even unknown. In China, where divorce was traditionally prohibited, one of a wife's duties was providing children for her husband's patrilineage—too important a duty to permit her to leave him (Freedman 1967, 1970). But where marriage is viewed relatively casually, divorce is a straightforward matter. An Islamic Minangkabau man in western Sumatra has merely to utter the words "I divorce you" three times to divorce his wife (Bachtiar 1967:367). Minangkabau wives, by the way, do not enjoy the same right to easy divorce that their husbands do.

The larger-scale and more technologically sophisticated a society, the weaker its ties of marriage, for several reasons. First, in large-scale societies, especially mobile ones like Western society, individuals continually meet new people of the opposite sex. Second, people are likely to live longer in technologically advanced societies, and longevity sometimes leads to marital discontent. Third, many of the functions of marriage in large-scale, technologically sophisticated societies are fulfilled by other institutions. A married person's economic support, for example, does not depend on cooperation with a spouse when both spouses earn paychecks outside their joint household and can continue to do so even if they part.

The grievances that provide grounds for divorce vary greatly. Adultery is sufficient cause in some Western cultures, but elsewhere it may not even merit punishment. In still other societies, it is not

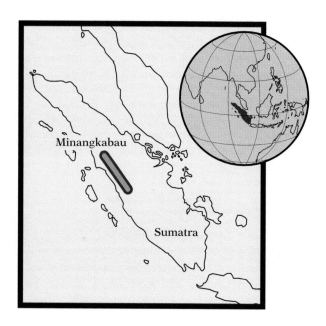

---

ghost marriage the custom in which the ghost of a man who has died "marries" and is considered able to father a child

merely divorce but death that awaits the adulterer. Among the Sarakatsani, pastoralists of mountainous Greece (see map on page 193), the worst thing a wife can do is to have sex with another man. According to the Sarakatsani worldview, adultery challenges the authority of a husband, attacks the moral unity of the family, and dishonors it. Adultery is so serious an offense that a husband who encounters his wife making love with another man must kill both of them (Campbell 1964:152).

There is a great deal of sexual inequality in this matter worldwide. Surveying 139 societies, Ford and Beach (1951) discovered that in 61 percent, husbands were allowed extramarital affairs though the same licence was prohibited to their wives. But the range of human behavior in this area is very broad indeed. Extramarital sex may be permitted, or even encouraged, for economic or political reasons. Among the Aleuts of the northern Pacific, for example, wife-lending was practiced to help men cement friendships (Frayser 1985:210).

Beating a spouse, most often a wife, constitutes justification for divorce in many societies, Western and non-western, although this is not invariable. Among peasant farmers in Ecuador, wife-beating is accepted as a normal part of marriage. Parents transfer farmland, scarce in this mountainous country, to their daughters at marriage, but men must wait until both their parents die to inherit farmland. As a result, a wife's inherited land is the only real property a newly married couple has. But Ecuadorians consider men superior to women and insist that they dominate (McKee 1992:150–151). Men begin marriage as economic inferiors because of their wives' ownership of land, which inevitably creates tension between them. If a husband feels that other villagers view him as a "loser," especially in economic matters, he may take out his frustrations on his wife to prove his manhood and publicly demonstrate his superiority. Provided it is not too extreme, his behavior is condoned by others since the "potential for abuse and wife-beating is built into the . . . cultural system" (151).

Conclusion

Marriage as defined in this chapter is a virtually universal institution. Its near universality might be accounted for by the fact that marriage effectively satisfies so many human needs. It provides a way to house and feed people; it efficiently apportions their labor and property; it fulfills their need for sex, companionship, and love; it helps to prevent sexual jealousy and conflicts; it forges alliances between groups; it nurtures and enculturates children.

Yet other institutions also fulfill these functions. To take Western society as an example, people can be housed and fed in college dormitories, hotels, prisons, or homeless shelters; their labor can be regulated by laws and by supply and demand within a free-market system; property can be allotted by gift-giving, inheritance, and taxation; children can be reared by extended kin or in orphanages and educated in schools; and sex can take place as easily outside of marriage as within it. The fact that other institutions can accomplish what marriage accomplishes perhaps suggests that marriage is universal not because the functions it performs are unique but because it most efficiently satisfies the most human needs.

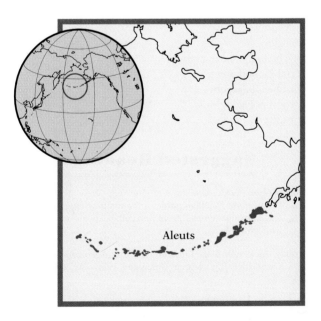

Aleuts

Summary

- Marriage, a virtually universal institution, is a socially sanctioned contract, usually between one man and one woman.

- The functions of marriage typically include establishing new nuclear families, spelling out the reciprocal rights and responsibilities of married pairs, creating alliances between families, and sometimes allocating goods and services through bridewealth, bride-service, or dowry.

- Societies regulate sex and marriage, some by creating rules that require or encourage certain unions (preferred marriages of several different kinds), and some by creating rules that forbid certain unions (prohibited marriages).

- For many societies the choice of spouse depends on such factors as race, religion, or social status.

- In societies in which the rights and duties that bind affines are so crucial that marriage cannot be left to romantic choice, marriages are arranged.

- Every society incorporates rules about who can have sex with and marry whom, but there is great variety regarding which relationships are considered incestuous and which are not.

- In some societies, sex or marriage with a biological first cousin is forbidden as incestuous, but in others, sex and marriage with a first cousin are encouraged.

- Explanations that have been put forward to explain the alleged universality of the incest taboo include the social, cooperation, psychoanalytic, genetic, and instinct explanations.

- Marriage to one spouse at a time is termed *monogamy;* marriage to two or more spouses at the same time is termed *polygamy.*

- A woman's marriage to more than one man at the same time is called *polyandry,* and a man's marriage to more than one woman at the same time is called *polygyny.*

- The most common types of marriage are monogamy and polygyny; rare types are polyandry and group marriage, in which several men and several women are married to one another.

- Other marital institutions include bride-capture, ghost marriage, the levirate, the sororate, and a wide range of wedding customs.

- Divorce is not as universal a feature of human culture as marriage, but is nevertheless permissible in most societies.

Key Terms

affinal alliance
affines
affinity
bilateral exchange
bride-capture (bride-theft)
bride-service
bridewealth (bride-price)
cooperation explanation
cross cousin marriage
dowry
endogamy
fraternal polyandry
genetic explanation
ghost marriage
group marriage
incest taboo
instinct explanation
levirate
marriage
matrilateral cross cousin marriage
matrilateral parallel cousin marriage
monogamy
parallel cousin marriage
patrilateral cross cousin marriage
patrilateral parallel cousin marriage
polyandry
polygamy
polygyny
psychoanalytic explanation
serial monogamy
social explanation
sororal polygyny
sororate

Suggested Readings

Fox, Robin. 1983. *Kinship and Marriage.* New York: Viking Penguin. An excellent guide to the main systems of descent and marriage, written from an ecological/cultural materialist perspective.

Goody, Jack, and S. J. Tambiah. 1973. *Bridewealth and Dowry.* Cambridge: Cambridge University Press. An informative discussion of bridewealth; dowry; and more broadly, property rights in Africa, Eurasia, and South Asia.

Needham, Rodney (ed.). 1971. *Rethinking Kinship and Marriage*. ASA Monographs 11. London: Tavistock Publications. Eleven articles on fundamental aspects of descent and marriage by various anthropologists. Needham's own two contributions are the best summaries of kinship and marriage, and of their histories, that have yet been published.

Spain, David H. 1987. The Westermarck-Freud Incest-Theory Debate: An Evaluation and Reformulation. *Current Anthropologist* 28(5):623–645. An attempt to combine the instinct and psychoanalytic explanations of incest, with commentaries by several anthropologists.

Chapter 11 Groups

Introduction

According to the admissions catalog of a big midwestern university, the on-campus living and social arrangements for undergraduates included about a dozen

fraternities—more or less depending on how many of these all-male clubs had, at any given time, been placed on probation by the dean for infringements of academic or social rules. The admissions catalog conveyed the impression that these fraternities were very much alike. Each was governed by a democratically elected president, vice president, financial officer, and social affairs director. Each listed, among its reasons for existence, brotherhood, academic excellence, and worthy charitable goals. Each professed democratic ideals and pledged full cooperation with the university's goals and regulations as well as ongoing involvement in campus projects and issues. The catalog also gave the impression that although only about a third of the male undergraduates on campus actually belonged to a fraternity, becoming a member was simply a matter of deciding which one you liked best.

So it came as a surprise to some male freshmen to discover that what the catalog suggested about fraternities did not reflect the actual situation at all. In reality, these organizations were not alike. Instead, they were ranked, in the minds of everybody on campus, from best to worst. One fraternity had a high proportion of athletes and was widely acknowledged to be the most prestigious. Another, also high-ranking, contributed more than its share of officers to the student government and other campus organizations. Lower down in the ranking scheme was a fraternity considered to be made up of rich students with preppy tastes, and somewhere below that was one known for its wild parties and frequent confrontations with the campus security force. There was even a bottom-of-the-heap fraternity that consisted, in the view of most students, of members unacceptable to the other fraternities.

Even as the fraternities themselves were unequal in social status, applicants to the fraternities, too, quickly assumed different positions in a ranking system. Long before the end of the rush period, when students interested in joining fraternities made this choice known, a rigid "pecking order" of freshman applicants had developed. This peck-

• Ask Yourself •

Do you think fraternities and sororities improve the college experience? If your college or university has fraternities and sororities, are you a member of one? If so, why, and if not, why not? If your institution has no fraternities or sororities, would you like to have them? Why or why not?

ing order reflected the perceptions of those involved in the selection process—freshmen hopefuls and upperclass fraternity members alike—about the relative desirability of various freshmen as fraternity brothers. It was based on the applicants' personalities, physical appearance and style of dress, participation in campus clubs and sports teams, and behavior at rush functions.

Chapters 9 and 10 described how the institutions of descent and marriage serve to classify individuals as members of particular groups. But many other kinds of groups exist besides those created by descent and marriage. Each group is defined by what it is that brings its members together and what these members have in common. Their sex and age, relative social standing, and common interests are some of the attributes that bring North American students together into sororities or fraternities. In other societies these same attributes—plus occupation, ethnicity, and so on—may create groups. This chapter describes some of the ways in which the members of different societies are grouped, as well as some of the cross-culturally important customs and institutions created by groups.

Distinguishing among individuals or groups according to their socially defined attributes is called **social classification,** and it is a human universal. The number of people grouped together may be small (e.g., the members of a nuclear family) or huge (e.g., ethnic Ukranians in the United States, a group tied together by common traditions and language). Like most of the things human beings do, classifying, or "pigeonholing," people serves a number of useful purposes. Simple identification is among the most important; when a person is classified as a member of a particular group, or a group is ranked relative to other groups, both the similarities and differences between that person or group and others are immediately known. But social classification serves other purposes as well. It may be used to allocate rights and duties on the basis of the category occupied, provide group members with mutual support, aid in social solidarity, or prevent discord.

A system of social classification may merely differentiate between individuals or groups viewed as social equals, or it may convey notions of superiority and inferiority. When the occupants of various pigeonholes in a system of social classification are viewed as unequal to one another, the result is **social stratification (social ranking).** In this case, people or groups are distinguished from one another and also hierarchically ordered. Like all classification systems, stratification systems may be formal and large-scale (like the hierarchical arrangement of ethnic groups in societies with many such groups) or informal and individual (like the stratification of students in a grade-school classroom, in which every student knows just how the others—sports heros, geniuses, dimwits, jokesters, daredevils, bullies—stand relative to one another). When people are classified hierarchically, like the layers of a many-tiered cake, their different positions are called **ranks.** A society that is divided up hierarchically is referred to as a *stratified* or *ranked* society.

---

social classification a systematic way of distinguishing among individuals or groups according to their different socially defined attributes

social stratification (social ranking) a system of social classification in which various statuses are viewed as unequal to one another

rank a position in a hierarchical system of social classification

• Status, Role, and Prestige •

Individuals and groups occupying pigeonholes in a system of social classification often find that certain attitudes and types of behavior are expected from them. They also find others' reactions toward them to be fairly consistent. This raises two questions: how do occupants of particular pigeonholes in social classification systems know how to behave in relation to the occupants of other pigeonholes and society at large, and how does society ensure the appropriate behavior by the occupants of these pigeonholes? The interactions among individuals, groups, and society at large can be analyzed using the concepts of status, role, and prestige.

The anthropological term for what we have referred to as a pigeonhole is **status,** a term used in two ways in English. Status may refer to one of several interrelated positions in a social structure, or it may denote prestige. We restrict our use of the word to the first sense: status is the place an individual occupies in a social structure. Every status is characterized by certain attitudes and expectations, and when interacting with one's fellows, one is actively expressing the attitudes and expectations associated with one's status. When the attitudes linked with a given status and the behavior that expresses these attitudes are combined, the complex they form is known as a **role.** The difference between status and role may be expressed in the following way: an individual or group occupies a status, but plays a role.

Sometimes the occupant of a status fails to play the role society expects. Status and role are so closely linked that when this happens the offender may be forced to relinquish his or her status. The role associated with the status of president of the United States involves obeying the Constitution. In the early 1970s, Richard Nixon failed to fulfill society's expectations for this role when he withheld information from Congress concerning the Watergate burglary. Subsequently, he lost his status as president.

Prestige involves social reputation and depends on people's evaluation of a status. It is thus a more subjective concept than either status or role. The higher the value placed on a status, the higher its prestige. Depending on the society, wealth, power, social origins, education, occupation, dress, ornaments, religion, or personal achievement may make some statuses more prestigious than others.

Members of a society do not always agree on what qualities determine high or low prestige. In societies undergoing Westernization, the values that have long supported the superiority of the traditional aristocracy, such as descent, wealth, or race, may become increasingly irrelevant to members of the lower classes, for whom new criteria for evaluating prestige emerge, such as education, white-collar employment, or Western styles of dress. Determinants of prestige can change rapidly. In the late 1970s in Iran, Western clothes, goods, and music conveyed high prestige, particularly among the young. Almost overnight, however, these tokens of prestige were displaced by others: a traditional Muslim life-style, extreme forms of Muslim religious expression, and anti-Western sentiment.

Anthropologists studying social classification try to isolate the factors that determine prestige. Among the fraternity members described at the

---

status the place an individual occupies in the social structure

role a combination of the attitudes associated with a given status and the behavior that expresses them

prestige social reputation based on a subjective evaluation of social statuses relative to one another

Prestige depends on people's subjective evaluation of the status of others. In Tokyo, Japan, a visiting businessman, at left with briefcase, greets his host. The visitor's slightly lower bow shows that in this particular context he is inferior to his host.

beginning of this chapter, good looks, a "cool" demeanor, and athletic ability were among the qualities contributing to high prestige, but in the broader context of North American society, wealth probably supersedes any of these as the major component of prestige. Among the Makassai of Timor (see map on page 159), in contrast, an impoverished member of a noble patrigroup enjoys much greater prestige than someone who owns dozens of buffaloes or rice fields, but who belongs to a commoner patrigroup.

• Social Stratification •

The sociologist Max Weber (1947:424–429; 1971:250–264), one of the first scholars to establish possible connections among power, prestige, and unequal access to resources, suggested that social inequality tends to develop in a society when

1. People have unequal access to whatever is considered valuable: natural resources, labor, money, or—especially in non-Western societies—intangibles such as ritual knowledge.

2. People are entitled to different degrees of prestige, depending on criteria such as descent, wealth, or race, or, more recently, education or westernization.

3. Some people enjoy more power, either physical or ideological (based on ideas or charisma), than others.

Such differences are both causes and characteristics of stratified societies.

Class

Inequality often presents itself in the form of social **classes.** These occur in many kinds of societies, from technologically simple to modern, and were described by Karl Marx as groups created and defined by economic production (see Chapter 7). In modern societies, production involves unequal control over what Marx called the "factors of production," resources that include land, labor, and capital. Classes are distinguished by their different relationships to these factors. Those who exert the greatest control over resources belong to the upper

classes; those whose control is limited or lacking altogether belong to the lower classes. Defined in this way, classes are more than just occupational groupings. The owners of a bookstore and a shoe-store are members of the same class, while the salespeople employed in both of these establishments belong to a different class.

Marx's definition of class as an economic phenomenon assumes that in creating their own wealth, the high-ranking classes will exploit the labor of the low-ranking classes. Marx also suggested that conflict between different classes, which has been going on throughout human history, is inevitable.

Some people recognize themselves as members of particular classes, holding common ideas and working together toward common goals (Fallers 1977). Others, equally identifiable as members of classes according to Marx's definition, do not. Social scientists have long argued about whether class consciousness, people's self-identification as class members, should be used as a criterion in defining class. Marx himself offered no answer.

In societies stratified by class, the lower classes often suffer while the upper classes prosper from their misery. But class distinctions do not always benefit only the upper classes. In Peru, pronounced distinctions have long existed between a small, wealthy, white upper class of European ancestry and much larger classes of middle-income and poor people of Native American or mixed Native American and white ancestry. Especially in the past, the prosperous whites controlled the country's formal institutions (including the government, the church, and the schools), and often exploited the lower classes economically. At the same time, however, they provided employment, education, and health care to poorer Peruvians. Until the middle of this century, the poor benefited from—indeed came to depend on—this system of vertical patron-client relationships. When in need, they looked up the social ladder, seeking help from charities and other organizations created by the upper class (Stein 1985). Although the system has disintegrated in recent years as Peru has become increasingly industrialized, for many years it had some benefits for members of both classes.

In the nineteenth century, class stratification exerted considerable influence traditionally among the Maloh, an agricultural people of Borneo, and its functions were readily apparent. The Maloh were stratified into three social ranks: aristocrats, commoners, and slaves (King 1985:14). These classes

---

class a group defined by the amount of control it exerts over factors of production

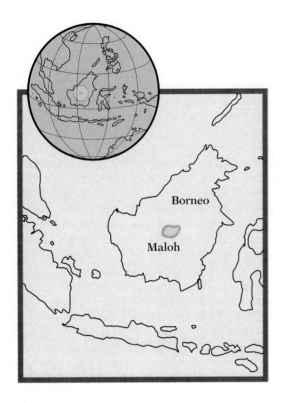

• Ask Yourself •

In the context of North American society at large, what social class do you think you belong to—lower, middle, or upper? What attributes, your own or your family's, identify you as a member of this class? To which class would you assign the following well-known people: O. J. Simpson, Newt Gingrich, Donald Trump, Madonna?

more attention or deference—in the press, say, or in a public setting such as a restaurant—than a night watchman. In some societies, certain occupations are regarded as being so lowly or degrading that only those of inferior social rank undertake them. Likewise, prestigious jobs may be performed only by members of a superior rank.

Traditional Hindu society in India, divided into four **varnas** ("colors"), illustrates this custom. The priestly (or Brahman) varna had the highest prestige. It was followed, in descending order, by the warrior varna (Ksatriya); merchants and cultivators (Vaisya); and craftsmen, laborers, and servants (Sudra). Traditionally, beneath all four varnas were a group of people so inferior they were considered outside this ranking system altogether: the untouchables. Well-defined sets of rights, duties, and rules of conduct set the individual varnas apart from each other and the untouchables. How a Hindu person should behave, what treatment he or she could expect, and what his or her social responsibilities were depended on which group the person had been born into (Tyler 1973:77).

Within each varna were numerous **castes,** hereditary social groups identified with special rights, duties, and prohibitions, each occupying a permanent place in a hierarchy of similar groups and each associated with a distinctive occupation. These castes shared several well-defined features. Caste members inherited their membership patrilineally,

filled different positions in the process of production. The aristocrats controlled labor (the work of slaves as well as compulsory service from commoners); they had rights to more and better land than commoners; they accumulated agricultural surpluses and trading profits; and they translated part of these benefits into permanent forms of wealth, such as ritual objects. Commoners controlled their own land and labor, although from time to time they were obliged to work for aristocrats and pay tribute to them. Slaves worked for their aristocratic owners rather than for themselves, and could be exchanged for goods or used as sacrificial victims in rituals. Some slaves farmed independently, but they had no rights to land, and the products of their labor belonged to their masters. Because their classes were traditionally based on unequal rights over resources used for production, the Maloh are a classic example of a class-stratified society as defined by Marx.

Caste

In complex societies, jobs are often ranked according to the prestige granted to those who perform them. In North American society, no one is surprised when a member of the U.S. Senate is given

varna one of four traditional divisions of Hindu Indian society

caste a hereditary social group associated with a particular occupation; bound by distinctive rights, duties, and prohibitions; and occupying a permanent place in a hierarchy of similar groups

So lowly that they were considered to be outside the traditional Indian caste system altogether, untouchables were historically the poorest of Indians. In a small village in the Indian state of Bihar, these untouchables, residentially segregated from other Indians, still live in poverty.

and were members for life. Castes were endogamous; members were required to marry someone from the same caste, although from a different patrilineage. Each caste occupied a permanent position in an overall hierarchy of castes, with each (except for those at the top and bottom) ranked as superior to as well as inferior to at least one other. An Indian village might contain residents belonging to a number of castes, each associated with one of the four varnas. Untouchables belonged to no caste.

If you had been a member of a caste in traditional India, only you and other members of your caste would have had the right to perform the traditional services "owned" by your caste. Indeed, you would have had virtually no choice about whether

to perform these services or not; your occupation would have been the one to which membership in your particular caste entitled you, not the one that would earn you the most money or make the best use of your talents. If you were a member of the Washerman caste, you would be a washerman, and only you and your fellow washermen could have made clothing ritually clean. Anyone, of course, might physically have been able to launder clothing, but for Hindu society "ritually clean" meant that the washing had been done by an individual of the stipulated caste. Likewise, you would have had to be a member of the Astrologer caste to read horoscopes, or a Barber to cut hair. You could not have accepted food from, or have had sex with, a person of any caste that ranked below yours. Finally—as is often true of members of descent groups, too—you would probably have been prohibited from eating certain foods forbidden to members of your caste.

Specialists in Indian culture disagree about whether the caste system should be considered predominantly an economic or a religious institution. From an economic perspective, castes were occupational in nature, but the hierarchical ordering of castes was reinforced by a religious concept. At the core of Hinduism lies the notion of personal purity and pollution. One way these were determined was by one's varna; Brahmans were purer than Sudras, and this kind of purity or pollution was unchangeable. But a person could also be polluted by normal biological functions—eating, excretion, sex, childbirth, or death—and such pollution was thought to be contagious. Thus, for example, sexual relations between individuals of unequal rank were considered highly polluting for the higher-ranked partner. This is where the economic specialization of the caste system and the Hindu religion merged: the ranking of castes was based on the degree of purity or pollution associated with the job traditionally performed by members of a given caste.

Like traditional Hindus, Westerners also recognize formal occupational groups, which in the West are called labor unions. There are, of course, fundamental differences between castes and labor unions. Membership in a union is not hereditary, nor are unions hierarchically arranged. However, in both kinds of group, membership is associated with a particular job. In both the West and India, eligibility for a certain specialized category of job—bricklaying, for instance, or pipe fitting—requires that a person be a member of the proper group.

Systems of social classification neither work perfectly nor remain unchanged, and the caste system is no exception. Over the last half-century, the system has been considerably weakened, first by Western influences and then by Indian law. The Indian government has tried to raise the status of members of low-ranking castes by encouraging them to change the occupations allocated to them by tradition, and this has allowed many Indians to break out of the system.

In his account of life in the southern Indian village of Gopalpur, Alan R. Beals (1980:82–83) describes how missionaries converted many members of the village's lower castes to Christianity, a religion in which everyone is believed equal in the sight of God. Among those converted were some members of the lowly Chamar, or Leather Workers, caste, whose job it was to dispose of the carcasses of animals that had died in the village. One day, Beals writes, a water buffalo died in Gopalpur, but the Chamars refused to remove it on the grounds that they had rejected traditional ways and were no longer members of the Chamar caste. So the buffalo's corpse lay rotting in its stall. Eventually, no longer able to bear the stench (made all the worse by the fierce Indian heat), an angry committee of villagers belonging to other castes tied the animal's legs together, thrust a pole through them, and carted the carcass to the edge of the village. Only a generation before, this could not have happened, for non-Chamars would never have polluted themselves by performing such a defiling job.

Like Beals, William and Charlotte Wiser, who studied social relations in the Indian village of Karimpur between 1930 and 1960, found that much had changed when they returned in 1970. "There are fewer caste restrictions than there used to be," claimed villagers, although they added that castes were still endogamous and that most of Karimpur's Hindus were still uncomfortable with the idea of accepting food from a member of a lower-ranking caste. But the villagers added, "these rules . . . have not interfered with our personal relationships with each other. [We have] friends in other castes and we think nothing of it. Friendship is more important than caste, anyhow" (Wiser and Wiser 1971:225).

In the two decades since the Wisers' return to Karimpur, the caste system has continued to decline in importance for many Indians. Yet because the system continues to be functional, it persists, especially in rural India, despite the fact that discrimination by caste has been declared illegal. Some Indian Hindus continue to identify themselves as caste members, and those who do are aware of their position and function in the hierarchy and of what behavior is expected of them, both within their own caste and in relation to members of other castes. This "provides a sense of security . . . if a man moves into a strange environment, he identif[ies] himself with his own caste group, where he feels secure and at ease" (Wiser and Wiser 1971:259–260). The system has another important function, too. By forcing people into dependence on one another's specialized services, it promotes their interaction and encourages cooperation among the groups to which they belong, thereby increasing the integration of the entire society.

Slavery

In a caste system, however polluting the occupation and however inferior the caste, at least people owned their own labor. A slave, however, is in a radically different position. Slaves do not own their labor. On the contrary, they are themselves owned by other people.

Slavery has taken a number of different forms. War captives and their descendants formed a class of slaves in some societies; in others, slaves were a commodity that could be bought and sold. The rights granted to a slave varied, too. In ancient Greece, a slave could marry a free person, but in the stratified society of the southern United States before the Civil War, slaves were not allowed even to marry each other, because they were not permitted to engage in legal contracts. Still, slaves in the South often lived together as husband and wife throughout their adult lives, forming nuclear families that remained tightly knit until they were separated at the auction block (Henretta 1987:415).

About 4 million blacks lived as slaves in the American South in 1860. The institution served mainly economic purposes: plantation owners could not have gotten nonslave laborers to work at the pace or with the discipline they commanded from slaves, and such laborers would have had to be paid. Despite the expense involved in purchasing and maintaining slaves, slavery was much more economical for the whites than wage labor. In addition, it allowed slave owners, most of whom were

Slaves in the American South, barred from marrying, often lived together as husband and wife until they were separated at the auction block. An 1861 print shows members of a slave family being sold at auction.

planters, to enforce a strict organization of labor. Work was specialized, and slaves could be severely disciplined if they failed to measure up to their owners' demands. The owner or his assistant, the overseer (usually a white man), divided his workers into "gangs," which were assigned certain jobs depending on the season. The overseers and their subordinates, slaves themselves, used the threat of the whip to force gangs into tight, coordinated units for plowing, hoeing, and picking crops (Henretta 1987:411).

After slavery had become established, the notion that slaves deserved their status helped to maintain the institution. Both planters and the politicians they voted into power claimed that blacks were an inferior race, unsuited for freedom and in need of rigorous social control by whites. They also noted that slavery liberated whites from the most degrading types of work. Southerners thus regarded slavery as guaranteeing equality and freedom for whites, and argued that the institution actually served to protect the highest values of the United States (Henretta 1987:414). As with the Hindu caste system, ideology justified and reinforced the economic system.

Apartheid

Stratification, as we noted, tends to come about when the things a society values are distributed unequally among its members. It is only a short step from this kind of inequality to the belief that some people are naturally inferior to others. This belief underlies **apartheid** ("apartness"), an official policy of the (white) government of South Africa from 1948 until 1991. The intent of apartheid was to maintain the social superiority of white people, and under its provisions the overwhelming majority of all South Africans, those with dark skins, were physically, politically, and

---

apartheid a former policy of the government of South Africa, under which nonwhite South Africans were physically, politically, and economically segregated from the white minority

Until its abolition in 1991, the official South African government policy of apartheid segregated nonwhites physically, politically, and economically from whites. In 1985, children played in the black township of Khayelitsha.

economically segregated from the white-skinned minority. Whites were separated from nonwhites under apartheid, while nonwhites (black Africans, Asians, and people of mixed race) were also separated from one another. They were prohibited from living or working in certain areas reserved for whites, from staying overnight in public accommodations, and from using public facilities. Whites and nonwhites were educated separately and to different standards, and nonwhites were not represented in government. Until the 1980s, nonwhites were required to carry identity cards authorizing their presence in white neighborhoods.

Apartheid was legally abolished in South Africa as a result of a number of factors, including the increasing self-awareness of nonwhite South Africans; their access to the media; the work of the once-outlawed African National Congress (ANC), which represented the interests of blacks; demonstrations and strikes; international sanctions; and finally, reforms instituted by the government of the (then) South African President, F. W. de Klerk. In 1994, South Africa held its first all-race election, which the ANC candidate, Nelson Mandela, won by a wide margin. Still, residential and educational segregation and unequal access to resources remain facts of life in South Africa.

• Ask Yourself •

How many differences can you identify between the official South African policy of apartheid and the ways in which blacks were treated in the United States after the Civil War but prior to the civil rights movement of the 1960s? What about now?

• Age Groups •

Age sometimes creates social groups that cut across other distinctions, such as political affiliations or religious convictions. A Cub Scout troop, this year's debutantes, the local Young Republicans Club, and the senior citizens' bowling league are North American examples of social classification by age. In each case a particular interest combines with age to unite members of the group, but common interest is not necessary for the classification of people by age. In some societies, people who are otherwise separate or even opposed to one another are brought together solely by age. Two common applications of age as a principle for social classification are the age grade and the age set.

Social groups called age groups, *created solely on the basis of age, are common in many societies. In North American society, groups similar to age groups exist, but age group members, like these Atlanta debutantes, usually share some common interest as well.*

Age Grades

An **age grade** is a period of life through which an individual passes as he or she grows older. We recognize the existence of age grades in our own society, calling them *infancy, childhood, adolescence,* and so on. But our categories are vague compared with the age grades of some other societies.

Age grades are fixed. No matter what the age grades are actually called, a person living an average life span must pass first through infancy, then childhood, then adolescence, followed by young adulthood, middle age, and ultimately old age. It is the maturing individual who moves; the age grades remain static as the individual passes through them. We may thus conceptualize a system of age grades as a sort of immovable backdrop before which individuals pass as they grow older.

Like a school grade in North American society, each age grade provides its members with a context in which they can learn the information and behavior appropriate to their age. Moreover, each age grade is associated with certain rights and duties: an individual in a particular age grade is expected to behave in certain ways and to conform to certain rules. This is as true in our own society as it is in others: an infant is not held to the same standards of hygiene as its parents, nor do we expect middle-aged people to act like adolescents, or grant adolescents the same rights as adults. Adolescents cannot vote or legally drink at bars; middle-aged people can.

Age Sets

Age sets, especially common in East Africa and South America, are groups of individuals of about the same age who move, as a group, through successive age grades. (This movement is often marked by "rites of passage," which are discussed

---

age grade a period of life through which an individual passes as he or she grows older

age set a group of individuals of about the same age who move as a group through successive age grades

The Shavante combine age grades and age sets. Above, boys leaving the age grade of childhood and entering the bachelor age grade are initiated into one of eight cyclical age sets.

in Chapter 13, page 335.) Unlike age grades, which are fixed, age sets can be thought of as moving forward through time.

In societies with age sets, a person normally becomes a member of one of these groups when still a young child or around puberty. The other members of the same age set, who may or may not all be of the same sex, will be of roughly the same age. Usually age sets have names. If you were in an age set called the Lions, you and the other Lions would remain together as Lions while you got older. Age sets can thus be envisioned as individual steps on a constantly moving escalator, with the members of a given age set remaining on one step as the step moves forward through time. Membership in an age set does not convey particular rights and duties (like the right of adult age-grade members to drink in bars), but does foster a sense of common identity with other members, just as being in a gang does for some American teenagers. This sense of identity is an important function of age sets.

The type of age-set system just described is known as a **lineal age set.** Each age set maintains its individual identity through time, from its members' childhood to their old age. When all the members have died, the set becomes extinct. The Maasai of East Africa, for example, classify all males born during the same four-year span as members of a particular lineal age set (see map on page 141). If, instead of a lineal system, a society has a **cyclical age set** system, an age set need not become extinct when its members die. Instead, its name is taken up by children who are just entering the age-set system, those in the lowest age grade. If the age set is called Lions, the new Lions repeat the path traced out several generations earlier by older Lions, until they in their turn have passed through each of the age grades from infancy to old age. Then the Lions set begins its next cycle with the age grade of infancy.

Age grades and age sets may coexist, a combination resulting in certain important functions, among them social identification, enculturation, mutual support, and protection. As members of an age grade and age set, individuals are efficiently enculturated as a group (a major function of age grades) and also form bonds of loyalty and affection with their age mates (an important function of age sets).

lineal age set a system in which an age set ceases to exist when all of its members have died

cyclical age set a system in which an age set is continually recycled

this entitlement, and indeed, given the perpetual warring state of Shavante villages—at least in the 1960s, when their ethnographer, David Maybury-Lewis, worked among them—they travel at their peril.

A summary of the three principal differences between age grades and age sets emphasizes the following features: first, a person's age grade changes as she or he grows older, but once installed in an age set that person remains in it for life. At age 7 an individual occupies the age grade of childhood, and at 70 he or she occupies the age grade of old age, but once a Lion, always a Lion. Second (and following from this first difference), age grades are immovable, whereas age sets move through time. Finally, unlike age grades, age sets are not associated with distinctive duties, rights, types of behavior, or attitudes.

• Ask Yourself •

Do you belong to any social group based primarily on age? If so, were you ineligible for membership in this group before you reached a certain age? When you are a few years older, will you again be ineligible for membership? Besides age, what are the qualifications for membership?

The two thousand or so Shavante of central Brazil provide an example. The Shavante are scattered among about a dozen villages, some of which lie many miles apart and are politically independent. Counteracting the divisive nature of this political organization are interlocking age grades and cyclical age sets that cut right across Shavante villages because the same age grades and age sets occur in each. Adolescents from every village thus belong to the same age grade, and each age set has members in every village.

The Shavante have four age grades for males: children, bachelors, young men, and mature men (Maybury-Lewis 1974), each with distinctive rights and duties. Interlocking with these age grades is a cyclical system of eight age sets (Figure 11.1). A male becomes a member of an age set at the end of childhood as he becomes a bachelor, and his membership links him to other Shavante bachelors in his own village as well as in every other village. When he enters the age grade of young men he becomes entitled to hospitality and protection from his age-set fellows in any Shavante village to which he might travel. Males of no other age grade have

• Ethnic Groups •

Chapter 1 introduced ethnic groups: groups whose members share cultural traditions and values and a common language, and who distinguish themselves from other groups (and are so distinguished by others) (Barth 1981:199–200). The term is often limited to **minorities,** groups that are smaller than the dominant group in their society.[1] The composition of an ethnic group can be heterogeneous: as with other kinds of groups, different life-styles or different levels of income or education may distinguish individuals within the same ethnic group from one another.

There may be many ethnic groups in one country or even in one city. The island nation of Madagascar, for example (see maps on pages 331 and 416), has

---

minority an ethnic group typically numerically smaller than the dominant group in its society

[1] Some social scientists use the term *minority* even in societies where the "minority" is numerically larger than the dominant ethnic group. This is true of South Africa, where blacks outnumber whites but are still sometimes referred to as a minority group.

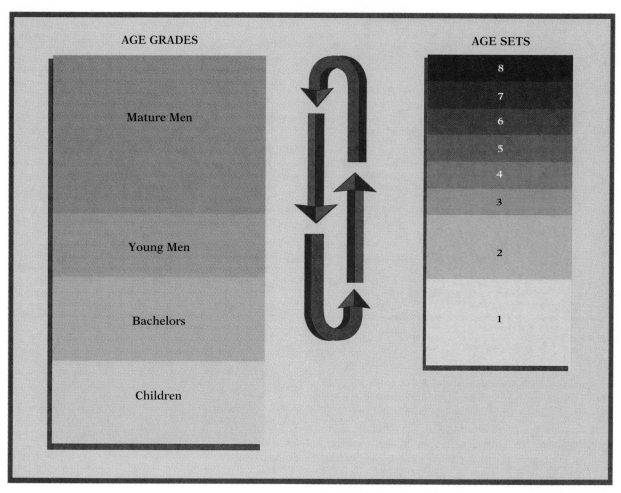

AGE GRADES

Mature Men

Young Men

Bachelors

Children

AGE SETS

8
7
6
5
4
3
2
1

Figure 11.1

Shavante Age Grades and Sets. The interlocking system of Shavante age grades and age sets helps enculturate and integrate this society's members.

some 18 different ethnic groups. New York City has even more. Because of their many ethnic groups, these societies can be termed **polyethnic.** In such societies, ethnicity is a means of social classification. People use it to anticipate, to evaluate, and—sometimes—to try to understand the behavior of others.

In addition to ethnic groups, the term *ethnicity,* the identification of individuals with particular ethnic groups, was also discussed in Chapter 1. Members of ethnic groups may be proud of their ethnicity, and may signal this feeling and express

their mutual solidarity by behaving in a distinctive manner, living near one another, attending special functions, performing rituals traditional to their group, or wearing distinctive clothing that sets them apart. But ethnicity can attract discrimination against members of ethnic groups, especially for urban ethnic minorities.

The concept of ethnicity has proven useful to domestic government agencies and international organizations trying to assist ethnic minorities in polyethnic societies to advance themselves. Rather than treating the inhabitants of a developing country as culturally homogeneous, for instance, most international aid agencies now try to take into account the values, institutions, and customs of

polyethnic made up of different ethnic groups

Ethnic group members may demonstrate their feelings of pride in, and solidarity with, their group by wearing particular articles of clothing. In Iran, a Kurdish woman with henna-reddened hair wears the traditional costume of her group.

• Ask Yourself •

Do you identify yourself as a member of a particular ethnic group? Why or why not? If your ethnic heritage is dual (e.g., German Jewish mother, Italian Catholic father), with which ethnic group do you identify more strongly? Why?

various ethnic groups, targeting relief or aid to their particular needs.

• Common-Interest Groups •

The discussion of urban migrants in Chapter 6 included the term *voluntary association,* which we

defined as a mutual-aid society, usually formed for relatively well-defined, practical reasons. We described a typical voluntary association, a group of young mothers in an immigrant neighborhood in Lima, Peru, who formed a collective to combat malnutrition in their children by buying powdered milk in bulk.

Voluntary associations are one kind of **common-interest group,** a group defined not by descent, residence, affinity, sex, class, or age but by common needs and concerns. Although they occur in nonliterate and peasant societies, such groups are more frequently found in urban societies.

The functions of common-interest groups in North American society are varied. Some, like bridge clubs, garden clubs, or barbershop quartets, exist mainly to entertain their members. Some, like Little League teams, encourage athletic prowess and promote team spirit. Some, like the Girl Scouts, Boy Scouts, or Future Farmers of America, stress education and character building. Some, like Rotary Clubs or the Red Cross, exist largely for charitable purposes. Some, like doctors' or secretaries' professional associations, are related to jobs. Others, like the League of Women Voters, are political. And still others, called **ethnic associations,** are based on common ethnicity. Common-interest groups in non-Western societies fulfill these same functions.

One kind of common-interest group is based on sex. Because both women and men find advantages in participating in activities that relieve them of the cultural roles assigned them on the basis of sex, some of these groups are exclusively female or exclusively male. Others, although they exist for the benefit of one sex, may have members of both.

Women's Groups

Cross-culturally, women's groups seem to be less common than men's. One reason may be that women's child-rearing and domestic chores keep them at home, so they have less opportunity than men to organize their own groups. Or it may be that restricting women to the home, particularly

common-interest group a group defined by the common needs and concerns of its members

ethnic association a common-interest group based on ethnicity

The Anthropologist at Work

Zhusheng Wang

China, the most populous country in the world, has 56 officially recognized ethnic groups (see Figure 11.2). The largest, the Han, includes over 90 percent of the nation's people, but even among the other 55 ethnic groups, together totaling almost 70 million people, a few groups are very large, numbering as many as 10 million people. Others contain only a few thousand.

One midsized Chinese ethnic group is the Jingpo (also called the Kachin), consisting of more than half a million people who live on both sides of the mountainous border between China and neighboring Burma (see Figure 11.2). Until recently, relatively little was known about the 100,000 or so Jingpo on the Chinese side, because the area had been closed to the outside world since the Communists assumed power in China in 1949.

The Communists launched an ambitious nationwide program to modernize China's "underdeveloped" people, integrate them culturally with the rest of the country, and convert them to socialism. The first step was to identify and count China's ethnic minorities. Led by Communist party committees, teams of researchers traveled to minority areas all over China. Once the government officially recognized a minority, it worked to bring the group into what it considered the country's economic and cultural mainstream. It was a difficult task; minority groups often inhabited inaccessible areas and resisted some of the changes the government wished to impose, for they considered their traditional culture to be the very essence of their identity.

By 1984, the government had somewhat relaxed its largely unsuccessful efforts to institute reforms among minorities, and economic development was progressing, if slowly. That year, a Chinese scholar at the Yunnan Nationalities Research Institute, Zhusheng Wang, joined a team of social scientists sent to assess the progress of economic, social, and cultural change among the Jingpo (Wang 1991). The researchers found that sluggish economic development in the region where the Jingpo lived could be attributed to ineffective government policies. These policies themselves resulted from the central government's ignorance of Jingpo culture and its failure to acknowledge the ethnic distinctiveness of the Jingpo people.

Wang went back to southwest China in 1988–1989, this time as a graduate student in anthropology at an American university. Working in the Jingpo village of Dazhai, he recorded information on the people's systems of kinship and marriage, their politics, and their beliefs and rituals. He also documented the changes, initiated by the Communist government, that had been imposed on the village. Wang found the residents of Dazhai eager for economic development and modernization but at the same time insistent on preserving their ethnic identity. The road to change in Dazhai, he concluded, will be a long, rough one.

Figure 11.2

Ethnic Minorities in China. Unshaded areas are Han Chinese, the host culture; the Jingpo are represented by the number 6. Adapted and simplified from Timothy J. Carter et al., "The Peoples of China," map supplement in National Geographic Magazine *158 (July 1980). Source: Jordan et al. 1994: 331.*

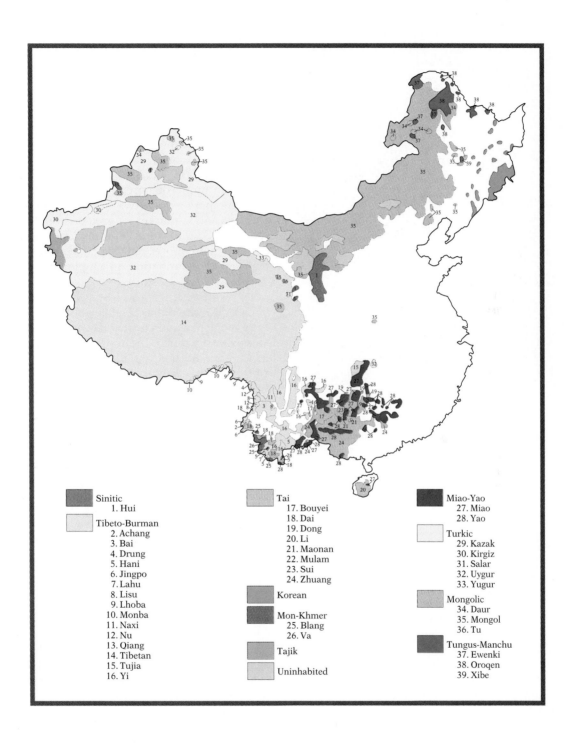

Sinitic
1. Hui

Tibeto-Burman
2. Achang
3. Bai
4. Drung
5. Hani
6. Jingpo
7. Lahu
8. Lisu
9. Lhoba
10. Monba
11. Naxi
12. Nu
13. Qiang
14. Tibetan
15. Tujia
16. Yi

Tai
17. Bouyei
18. Dai
19. Dong
20. Li
21. Maonan
22. Mulam
23. Sui
24. Zhuang

Korean

Mon-Khmer
25. Blang
26. Va

Tajik

Uninhabited

Miao-Yao
27. Miao
28. Yao

Turkic
29. Kazak
30. Kirgiz
31. Salar
32. Uygur
33. Yugur

Mongolic
34. Daur
35. Mongol
36. Tu

Tungus-Manchu
37. Ewenki
38. Oroqen
39. Xibe

Both women and men sometimes need a break from the constant companionship of the opposite sex, an idea institutionalized in women's and men's common interest groups. Above, women in Brooklyn, New York, meet weekly for quilting and companionship.

in small-scale societies with extended families, creates domestic groups of related women, so women need not organize groups outside of the family to enjoy the company of other women. It may even be that—because in the past most ethnographers were males who had relatively little opportunity to glimpse women's side of society— women's groups are more common than we suppose. Although they may be fewer in number, however, women's groups exist in most societies and serve multiple functions, from self-help to charitable purposes to recreation.

In the 1960s, North American newspapers still advertised female and male jobs in separate columns; airlines hired stewardesses but not stewards, and fired stewardesses who got married. Some states even prohibited women from waiting on tables at night. By the middle of the decade, however, many American women were question-

ing the roles society had traditionally allotted to them. In 1966 the National Organization for Women (NOW) was founded. Seldom has a common-interest group grown so rapidly and to such size. Over the next 25 years, as hundreds of thousands of American women (and even some men) joined its ranks, the group raised both women's and men's awareness about gender inequities in American life and, through its advocacy of women's rights, helped bring about radical changes in numerous areas of public life. Thanks in large part to NOW, women entered the American labor market in greater numbers than ever before and joined professions previously closed to them; moreover, they weakened the force of sexual discrimination in employment and in access to credit (Gross 1992:16).

One consequence of the North American women's movement has been heightened awareness of the incidence and consequences of physical violence against women. In the 1960s, rape crisis centers were established, and in the 1970s their success inspired the establishment of shelters where women beaten by their husbands or boyfriends could seek protection (Hoffman 1992:25).

From this informal beginning as a loose coalition of emergency shelters, a battered women's movement has evolved, with the goal of combating domestic violence. Women in Duluth, Minnesota, for example, developed a model program for battered women designed to ensure that police, prosecutors, judges, and probation officers conveyed the message that the legal system will not tolerate domestic violence. In addition to providing safe havens for battered women, police officers are now required to arrest violent husbands or boyfriends regardless of whether their victims want them to, and men who assault women must receive treatment as well as punishment. One member of the Duluth battered women's group estimates that in Duluth alone at least five women are alive today who would otherwise have been killed (Hoffman 1992:25). The program has been widely imitated throughout the United States.

A similar program has recently begun in La Paz, Bolivia, where about a quarter of the population are Native Americans called the Aymara. In the culture of the Aymara, a woman is the property of her husband, and wife-beating is a test of manhood. Because husbands are viewed as kings, their right to beat their wives is protected, sometimes by the wives themselves. But increasingly Aymara women

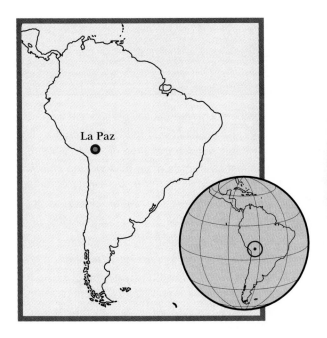

In the culture of the Aymara of Bolivia, a man's right to beat his wife has long been accepted, but recently Aymara wives have begun to organize to protect themselves from such abuse. Above, an Aymara beating victim seeks treatment at a government-sponsored shelter for battered women.

are "trying to organize and . . . assert their rights," according to an American sociologist in La Paz (Nash 1992). "These women have networks, organizations, and a lot of solidarity. They are trying to help each other." The Bolivian government's Office of Battered Women has recently opened a halfway house where abused women can receive treatment and respite.

Caribbean women have for decades been joining voluntary associations to improve their welfare (Ellis 1986:14). Today, the Caribbean Women's Association (CARIWA), a regional umbrella organization made up of nongovernmental women's groups, has a membership of more than 500 women's groups representing 12 Caribbean countries. Although all of these groups are dedicated to improving the economic and social well-being of women (154), they have widely varying goals, from consciousness raising to preventing rape to increasing agricultural production.

Like their Bolivian counterparts, Caribbean women, too, are raising their voices against violence—sometimes literally, through the medium of calypso, a kind of music popular throughout the Caribbean region. Calypso is famous for its lively, African-inspired beat and clever lyrics, which frequently offer pointed social or political commentary. Accompanied by a steel band, a good calypso singer never loses an opportunity to promote a

politician, advocate a cause, or poke fun at a cultural institution.

Traditionally, calypso songs were written and sung by men, and in the past they often reflected Caribbean society's tolerance of men's macho behavior (Reyes 1986:120). Caribbean women were sometimes portrayed in calypso songs as scheming, promiscuous, or money-crazy (119). The lyrics of a calypso hit of some years ago advised men,

> Every now and then, knock them down
> They love you long, and they love you strong.

Recently, however, women have begun to compose and sing calypsos themselves, and to use them to promote women's causes. One popular song takes men to task for violence against women:

> If I does not leave now
> Is licks in the morning
> In the evening.
> I telling you flat
> I done wit' dat.

Attitudes are often slow to change, and those reflected in men's calypso verses are no exception, but it appears that Caribbean women themselves are successfully exploiting this traditional West Indian art form to protest ill treatment and lobby for a less sexist society.

Anthropology and the Environment

Women and Water in Kenya

Water covers nearly three-quarters of the earth's surface, but only 3 percent of it is fresh, and most of that amount is frozen in the polar ice caps, buried underground, or otherwise inaccessible for human use. Thus fresh, clean water accounts for less than 1 percent of the total water on earth (Miller 1994:336), and the supply is constantly decreasing due to pollution by human beings. Today over one-fifth of the world's population—1.2 billion people, most of them in developing countries—do not have adequate access to the clean water they need for drinking, bathing, cooking, laundering, disposing of wastes, or irrigating crops. Yet adequate amounts of clean water are essential for human life.

Especially in developing countries, women are primarily responsible for obtaining the fresh water their families need. Many do not have running water at home, so they must walk to a well, stand in line for a turn at the hand pump, draw water to the surface, and carry it home in heavy jars or cans (see picture on page 193). At home, women are the managers of the water they have procured, since they are the family members who are usually responsible for cooking, dishwashing, and laundry. When supplies of fresh water are scarce or located at great distances from homes, it is women who pay the greatest price, and when new wells are dug that bring clean water closer to their homes, they are the primary beneficiaries.

Kwale, a poor, rural district on the coast of Kenya, East Africa, with a rapidly growing population, lies in an area of seasonal droughts. By the mid-1970s, the wells in Kwale no longer provided sufficient quantities of clean water reliably all year round (Mwangola 1995). To supply her family with fresh water, a village woman, carrying heavy water containers, would have to walk two or more miles to a slippery-sided, dangerous well—even further, when local wells dried up (Mwangola 1995). Depending on family size, some women had to make this round trip as many as eight times a day. When water was available, it was often tainted, causing a wide variety of illnesses; 80 percent of all illnesses in developing countries can be attributed to unsafe water and poor sanitation (WASH 1992:2). There was an urgent need for new, reliable sources of clean water.

Men's Groups

In some societies, men join together to set themselves apart from women, sometimes (as we saw in Chapter 8, page 186) because contact with women is thought to weaken them. The Etoro of New Guinea believe that each male has a limited quantity of "life force," some of which he loses each time he has sex with a woman. Beliefs of this kind encourage the segregation of males from females, and New Guinea is famous for its men's associations.

Other men's groups exist for different reasons. **Military associations,** common to many traditional and modern societies, are groups of males who have fought or may fight together. In some societies, military associations are combined with age grades. Among the Shavante, for instance, the role of warrior belongs to the mature men's age

military association a group of males who have fought or may fight together

In 1975, Kenya's National Council for Women, made up of some 40 small women's groups, took on the challenging task of increasing rural Kenyan women's access to adequate supplies of safe water. Funded under a United Nations project intended to benefit women in poor countries, this effort became known as the Kenya Water for Health Organization (KWAHO). The women who managed the project realized that making safe water more accessible to local families was not just a matter of digging boreholes and installing hand pumps. Any new water sources would need to take local people's problems and priorities specifically into account. Right from the beginning, therefore, KWAHO solicited the involvement of the intended beneficiaries of fresh water supplies. Village women were asked to identify their water-related needs, select those locations for new wells that would best suit the most community members, choose the kind of hardware they felt would be easiest to maintain and repair, collect funds, and actually help to install their new hand pumps. Each community was urged to develop its own plan of action. The overall goal was for local people, many of them women, eventually to take over full responsibility for the operation and maintenance of their new water sources.

The Kwale project began in 1984, targeting about 50,000 people in 50 villages. Dangerous, old wells were boarded up, the government drilled 100 new boreholes, and, with the help of KWAHO, community members installed new hand pumps. The results were dramatic: "a 50 percent reduction in the number of cases of diarrhea and vomiting in the villages with new, safe sources; less illness of other kinds; far less walking; and greater ease in drawing water to the surface" (Mwangola 1995:89). Eventually, the villages of Kwale district took full charge of their new wells, maintaining, cleaning and repairing the pumps and handling all the necessary finances. The Kwale pilot project was so successful that it was expanded to cover the whole district, with a population of some 700,000 people (Mwangola 1995:89).

The Kenya Water for Health Organization is an example of what women's self-help groups are accomplishing in many developing countries. Today KWAHO—with a staff of nearly 200 water engineers; anthropologists; public health and information specialists; teachers; agricultural and health workers; representatives of women's, church, and educational groups; and other specialists—performs many tasks: prospecting for water, undertaking socioeconomic surveys, conducting educational workshops, training community leaders, promoting low-cost water pumps, and handling public relations. It is estimated that so far, more than one million Kenyans have been served by KWAHO.

grade. In other societies, military associations exist without age grades, although in any society men who go to war together are likely to be members of the same generation.

Military associations formed an important part of the culture of the Native Americans of the Great Plains of North America. Able-bodied Cheyenne men (see map on page 284) belonged to military associations with names like Fox, Hoof Rattle, Shield, Bowstring, and Northern Crazy Dogs (Hoebel 1978:40–42). When he felt he was ready to

• Ask Yourself •

Do you belong to a group that is composed exclusively of males or females? If so, do group members ever display negative feelings about members of the opposite sex? Why or why not? If you do not belong to any group based on sex, would you be interested in joining one? Why or why not?

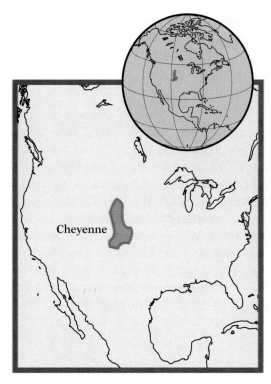

go to war, a Cheyenne boy joined whichever group he wished, often choosing the one to which his father or an older brother belonged. In addition to going to war against other Plains groups, Cheyenne military associations policed tribal ceremonies and hunts and worked with the tribal council to make and enforce laws.

The prestige of a military association fluctuated, but there was no permanent hierarchy; these groups were organized internally in the same way and carried out the same activities. Only dress, dances, and songs distinguished them. Some, however, did have female members: the virgin daughters of tribal chiefs, who served as maids of honor. These young women joined the warriors in rituals and sat in the midst of the circle of war chiefs during council meetings. If a maid of honor lost her virginity before she married, this brought her association's warriors bad luck.

Conclusion

Societies consist of various social groups defined by such criteria as sex, descent, marriage, relative social standing, age, occupation, ethnicity, or common interest—or in most cases, combinations of two or more of these criteria. The groups may intersect with one another, forming a multidimensional matrix so complex that every individual in the society can be fitted in somewhere. A person in North America might be a member of a particular family, a women's field hockey team, NOW, Students Against Drunk Driving, Delta Gamma sorority, the Democratic party, and the Presbyterian church, all at the same time. Every group in which you, as an individual in a society, claim membership, or to which you are assigned membership by society, affects not only how others perceive you but also how you view yourself, what you think, how you feel about yourself, and how you behave. Without groups to identify, distinguish among, and influence the ideas and direct the behavior of individuals, there could be no society.

Summary

- Social classification, or distinguishing among people according to their different socially defined attributes, is a universal feature of human societies.

- Social classification can be based on age, occupation, descent, sex, social standing, common interests, ethnicity, or other criteria.

- Social classification can serve a number of purposes, including identification, allocating rights and duties, mutual aid, social solidarity, and preventing conflict.

- Some systems of social classification distinguish between individuals or groups viewed as social equals, whereas others convey notions of superiority or inferiority.

- When people are regarded as unequal to one another, the result is termed *social stratification,* and the different layers into which society is thus stratified are called *ranks*.

- Social stratification is based on differences in status, role, and prestige.

- A status is a place in the social structure, carrying with it society's expectations of a certain kind of behavior.

- A role involves the behaviors associated with a particular status.

- Prestige is relative repute, a more subjective concept based on factors including wealth, power, social origins, education, occupation, dress, body ornaments, religion, and personal achievement.

- Some stratified societies divide people into groups (called classes) defined by economic production.

- Stratification may take the form of a caste system, as in Indian society, with a hierarchy based on occupation and notions of religious purity.

- Other social institutions found in stratified societies are slavery (under which the members of one class—slaves—do not even own their own labor) and apartheid (under which South African nonwhites and whites were segregated from each other to promote and maintain the superior position of whites).

- Some societies use age to create social groups, two widespread examples being age grades and age sets.

- An age grade is a period of life through which an individual passes as he or she grows older, while an age set (which can be either lineal or cyclical) is a group of individuals of about the same age who mature together.

- Some societies have both age grades and age sets, which may be combined.

- In polyethnic communities, ethnic group membership is a useful means of social classification since it enables community residents to anticipate, evaluate, and try to understand the behavior of others.

- Common-interest groups, such as the voluntary associations often found among urban immigrants, are based on members' common needs and concerns.

- Women's groups occur in various parts of the world, but do not seem to be as common as men's groups.

- Some men's groups exist to keep males apart from females, while others have more pragmatic goals.

Key Terms

age grade
age set
apartheid

caste
class
common-interest group
cyclical age set
ethnic association
lineal age set
military association
minority
polyethnic
prestige
rank
role
social classification
social stratification (social ranking)
status
varna

Suggested Readings

Bernardi, Bernardo. 1985. *Age Class Systems: Social Institutions and Polities Based on Age* (David I. Kertzer, trans.). Cambridge: Cambridge University Press. An outstanding introduction to age systems, including discussions of the Shavante and Maasai.

Bradfield, Richard Maitland. 1973. *A Natural History of Associations: A Study in the Meaning of Community*, Vols. I and II. New York: International University Press. The Nuer, Trobrianders, and Hopi are among many cultures whose associations are discussed in these volumes. The author includes an extended discussion of ecology and social organization.

di Leonardo, Micaela. 1984. *The Varieties of Ethnic Experience: Kinship, Class, and Gender Among California Italian-Americans*. Ithaca, NY: Cornell University Press. The social conditions of Italian-American families in the San Francisco Bay area are the focus of this detailed ethnographic study of one of the most prominent minority groups in the United States.

Hanson, Jeffery H. 1988. Age-set Theory and Plains Indian Age-grading: A Critical Review and Revision. *American Ethnologist* 15:349–364. Like the Shavante and Maasai, many Native American groups also had age systems. Hanson attempts to explain the presence of age systems among Native Americans of the Great Plains by correlating them with warfare and horses, among other variables.

Raheja, Gloria Goodwin. 1988. India: Caste, Kingship, and Dominance Reconsidered. In *Annual Review of Anthropology* 17:497–522 (Bernard J. Siegel, Alan R. Beals, and Stephen A. Tyler, eds.). Palo Alto, CA: Annual Reviews. A student who wants a brief yet comprehensive overview of this topic will find this an extremely useful introduction.

Introduction

In Everett, Washington, in the summer of 1994, two 17-year-olds, while robbing a pizza delivery man of $40, clubbed the man so severely with a baseball bat that they

inflicted multiple skull fractures and permanently impaired his vision and hearing (Egan 1994:A12; anon. 1994:6). Adrian Guthrie and Simon Roberts, both Native Americans and members of the Tlingit ethnic group of the Northwest Coast of North America, were soon caught, brought to court, and convicted. But before they were sentenced, a Tlingit advocate appeared to argue that imposing a sentence in keeping with traditional Tlingit law might prove a more effective way to punish and rehabilitate the two young men than sending them to prison. The most fitting punishment, he suggested to the judge, would be the ancient Tlingit custom of banishment.

Judge James Allendoerfer agreed that invoking Tlingit law would be appropriate under the circumstances, and turned the two young men over to the elders of their ethnic group with the understanding that they would be sentenced to an 18-month period of exile to one of the remote, deserted islands off the Northwest coast. There they would live without modern conveniences, and as part of their punishment would be obliged to cut and notch logs that would be sent to Everett for the construction of a new house for their victim. Their exile would give them time to reflect on the seriousness of the injuries that they had caused their victim, and to recover their inner peace.

When news that this "traditional" Tlingit sentence might be imposed was made public, Tlingit elders expressed surprise, asserting that banishment had never been a traditional part of Tlingit customary law. They realized, however, that their ethnic group and its ancient legal system had been placed in an embarrassing position as the result of the massive publicity the case had received in the national and international press. They therefore accepted responsibility for imposing a sentence for a criminal act without legal precedent within their culture, but that had somehow been thrust into the domain of Tlingit custom and law. Some Tlingit welcomed the opportunity to resurrect and implement aspects of their ancient legal tradition. "For too long now," said one elder through a translator, "white people have trampled . . . our words, our culture, our tradition. We must reactivate the Tlingit . . . courts, traditions, and culture" (anon. 1994:6).

So the Tlingit elders put the sentence of banishment into effect, and Guthrie and Roberts headed into exile. But the state of Washington did not relinquish its authority in the case. Judge Allendoerfer reserved the right to examine the two young men after their 18-month exile to determine whether or not the unique punishment had rehabilitated them. Apparently it did not, for in the summer of 1995, he sentenced them to jail.

The Tlingit incident illustrates the importance of social control—whether within large-scale, state-level societies or small-scale, traditional chiefdoms, whether maintained through established sanctions or through punishments newly devised to suit particular offenses. In any society, laws that must be observed, penalties that punish their infraction, and procedures that can be called upon to judge guilt or innocence, impose sentences, and provide recompense form a holistic system of social control, without which no form of society could be maintained.

To be effective, however, a system of social control must be accompanied by the socially mandated authority and power to ensure that it functions smoothly. Allocating to some of society's members the authority and power to regulate the behavior of others by setting common goals, changing them, enforcing them, and preventing and resolving conflict is termed **politics.** By definition, politics exists in every human society, and all societies have some kind of **political organization (political system)**—some mechanism, formal or informal, for establishing and maintaining social control. This chapter takes a cross-cultural look at the various ways in which systems of politics and social control are organized and function.

• Political Leadership •

Power and Authority

If individual members of a society were free to set their own agendas and behave as they liked, there could be no society, only anarchy. Every society, therefore, designates certain individuals (and often groups as well), by formal or informal means, to exercise leadership and control over others: to establish and maintain the society's priorities (sometimes called policies); to prevent, limit, or

resolve conflicts between individuals or groups; to dissuade or punish those who challenge the social order; and to direct change. These individuals or groups assume or are granted power and authority denied to others.

Power is the capacity to control the behavior of others, using such means as education, persuasion, force or threat of force, punishment, or reward (Galbraith 1983). It may be based on physical strength, wealth, or efficient organization. Or it may be based on superior knowledge; in some societies, only certain people—priests or hereditary rulers, for instance—are allowed access to certain kinds of information. In still other cases, personal power is based on something much less tangible: **charisma,** a term which comes from a Greek word meaning "divine gift." Sociologist Max Weber (1963:48), who identified charisma as an important source of power in society, saw it as the very essence of leadership: a quality that makes charismatic people so dynamic, so compelling, that they naturally command agreement, inspire loyalty, and generate enthusiasm among their fellows.

Authority is the socially granted right to exercise power. Ordinarily it is conveyed to an individual through an **office**—a position in which a certain kind and amount of authority is inherent and which exists independently of its occupant at any given time. Theoretically, authority can exist without power, although it would be useless (e.g., a "lame-duck" president); and power can, of course, be exercised without authority. But for social order, both are needed.

• Ask Yourself •

We all know of charismatic public figures, but do you know any charismatic individuals personally? Have you ever followed someone's lead mainly because of the force of that individual's personality?

politics the process of regulating the behavior of members of a group

political organization (political system) a mechanism, formal or informal, for establishing and maintaining social control

power the capacity to control the behavior of others, using means such as education, persuasion, coercion, punishment, or reward

charisma personal magnetism capable of inspiring agreement, loyalty, and enthusiasm

authority the socially granted right to exercise power

office a position in which a certain kind and amount of authority is inherent, and that exists independently of its occupant at any given time

Power is the capacity to control others, while authority is the socially granted right to use power. Both are needed to maintain social order. During a robbery in California, a gunman with power but without authority makes his getaway.

Where does authority come from? It may be either inherited or earned. Inherited or **ascribed authority** is not a standard feature of North American political organization, yet it is very common around the world. The English throne, which

ascribed authority authority that is inherited rather than earned

achieved authority authority that is earned

Prince Charles will one day inherit from his mother, Queen Elizabeth, will give him ascribed authority. **Achieved authority,** in contrast, is earned. The office of U.S. senator, for example, is won by securing a greater number of votes than one's competitors for the same office, and conveys achieved authority on its incumbent. Achieved authority is an idea familiar not only to North Americans but also to members of many other societies, Western and non-Western. Like U.S. senators, village leaders among the Shavante of Brazil (see map on page 275) achieve their authority through a combination of hard work, skill, ambition, and luck.

Sometimes ascribed and achieved authority exist side by side in the same political organization.

Ascribed authority is inherited, while achieved authority is earned. Among the Ashanti of Ghana (see map on page 363), chiefly authority is ascribed; the former leader of the Ashanti, shown above sitting on his throne, inherited his office matrilineally.

Among the Tetum (see map on page 139), the office of village headman is inherited patrilineally, but a potential headman will inherit the office from his deceased father only if local villagers consider him just, ethical, and knowledgeable about tradition. Otherwise, another man—but one who is also related patrilineally to the former incumbent—will be installed as the new headman.

Politicians

In Western societies, successful politicians must appear to be intelligent, well informed, honest, and hard-working, and it doesn't hurt to be good-looking and have plenty of charisma. But these attributes do not define the successful politician in all societies. Cross-culturally, no single set of attributes results in political success; indeed, behavior that might go a long way toward ensuring success in one setting is almost guaranteed to result in failure in another. In some societies, marrying another wife or two would give a male politician more prestige, more followers, and thus more political influence, but certainly not in North American society. Politicians the world over must adapt themselves to particular political contexts.

A comparison of political leaders in Tetum and Shavante society demonstrates the wide variability in the qualities that can make (or break) a politician. Among the Tetum, political offices are "owned" by patrigroups. The heads of these patrigroups wield influence more because of the authority vested in the office of patrigroup head than because of their leadership abilities. True, a leader needs certain qualities to be successful, but intelligence, dedication, and charisma—highly valued in some political systems—are not especially admired. Instead, the Tetum admire a man who has a thorough knowledge of his group's myths and how they can be applied in legal cases, patience and wisdom in negotiating disputes between members of his patrigroup, honesty, reliability, and the capacity to win the respect of his followers.

Rarely is this combination of attributes found in a single Tetum leader. Yet because inherited offices are traditional, a former patrigroup head's eldest son who exhibits only some of these qualities, and is not considered a weakling, is almost always asked to fill his father's shoes. Provided he does not abuse his office, he will be permitted to remain in it until he dies or leaves it voluntarily. Such is the respect given ascribed leadership that even a totally incompetent fellow sometimes holds office, although the real authority is exercised by men of his patrigroup acting on his behalf. This is because the Tetum distinguish between office and officeholder. The former endures and is respected always; the latter dies and is replaced, and may or may not be respected.

The Shavante, unlike the Tetum, are divided into **factions**—informal, mutually contentious political action groups that exist within larger units, such as political parties or villages. A typical Shavante village of 100 to 300 people is divided into two or three competing factions (Maybury-Lewis 1974). The individual considered to be the most effective politician in a faction is its leader. He does not inherit his position (in fact, the Shavante have no political offices), nor is he elected by other members of the faction; he is chosen by consensus. He owes his position entirely to his personal qualities, and retains it only as long as he can maintain these qualities. When old age or ill health blunt his political skills or charisma, his personal hold over his faction weakens until a new and more dynamic person impresses its members as being more capable of leadership. At this point, the members of the faction switch allegiance.

The qualities that impress the Shavante enough to make them follow one politician rather than another are quite different from those the Tetum admire. Shavante demand that their leaders be truculent, assertive, and athletic. They must be successful hunters and display great oratorical skill. They must have no hesitation about killing political rivals if necessary, although the Shavante have more respect for a leader who uses persuasion than for one who is so weak that he has to resort to killing those whom he cannot sway verbally. The Tetum may tolerate a leader who is incompetent, but the Shavante follow only a leader who is dominant among men.

• Ask Yourself •

Apart from the issues a politician may support, what are the personal qualities you admire in someone who is running for or holds a political office?

faction an informal, adversarial political group existing within a larger unit, such as a political party or village

The smallest-scale and least complex kind of political organization, the band, is most often found among gatherers and hunters. At their camp in Australia, members of an aborigine band cook a sea turtle caught by one of their number.

• Types of Political • Organizations

Different kinds of societies have different kinds of political organizations. To help make sense of the differences as well as the similarities among political organizations, Elman R. Service (1971) has classified them into four categories: bands,[1] tribes, chiefdoms, and states (see Table 12.1, page 302).

Each of these four political organizations developed in the ancient past, and each is associated with a particular way of making a living (see Chapter 6). Three of them can still be found today, although one—the band—is exceedingly rare. Independent chiefdoms no longer exist. The band type of political organization is associated with the gathering-and-hunting life-style, and the tribe with horticulture or pastoralism. The chiefdoms that

existed in the past were based on extensive nonmechanized cultivation, and were in many cases societies in the process of becoming states, which helps to explain their absence today. States, of course, are common today; Chapter 6 introduced the life-style of peasants and urban dwellers, two groups that exist within modern states.

The categories *band, tribe, chiefdom,* and *state* are ideal ones to which many exceptions can be found, but they help us to understand politics in two important ways. First, when societies are viewed from the synchronic perspective, these categories permit us to see how political organizations are integrated holistically with other factors affecting social life, such as descent systems and forms of subsistence. Second, because they can be arranged according to their increasing complexity, the categories are also useful diachronically. Although it is not difficult to find exceptions, we can see a general trend, from bands to tribes to chiefdoms to states, toward increasing size and increasingly complex subsistence strategies and economic arrangements.

[1] The term *band* was defined in Chapter 6 as a group of gatherers and hunters. The same term is used for the kind of political organization characteristic of gatherer-and-hunter groups.

Bands

As noted in Chapter 6, the band, the smallest-scale and least complex kind of political organization, is most often found among gatherers and hunters. A typical band contains only 25 to 50 people, most of whom are closely related to one another by blood or marriage. Political offices are nonexistent in bands, so no one individual can achieve official authority over others. Adults of the same sex and approximately the same age enjoy roughly the same prestige, making bands the most egalitarian of all political organizations. Rights to private property are unusual: ordinarily, any property—a spear, for instance—may be taken up and used by anyone. The distribution of goods is through generalized reciprocity (Chapter 7); successful gatherers and hunters share their spoils with everyone in the band, including those whose search for food has been fruitless and those who made no effort to find food. Land, too, belongs to the group.

With no one in authority, band members make political decisions informally, by consensus. When some activity must be performed in common, band members unite behind the person who most inspires their personal confidence, and then only for a clearly defined period of time. On a deer hunt, the most experienced hunter becomes the leader, the others following his orders only for the hunt's duration. Should the hunters decide to stay home and perform a ritual the next day, a different person—someone especially knowledgeable about ritual matters—organizes and leads the ritual. In contrast to the authority exercised in other categories of political organization, authority over a band is temporary and weak.

The band type of political organization and cognation, the descent system most typical of bands (Chapter 9), fit together well. Cognatic descent encourages both locational and social mobility. In bad times when food is hard to find, cognatic bands can split up easily, with nuclear families going their own way for a time or perhaps moving in for awhile with relatives in other bands who have better access to food. Under such circumstances, having ties to both one's mother's and father's relatives is useful.[2] The band type of political organization, informal and leaderless, accommodates the frequent splintering and reforming of groups.

An example of the band type of political organization in operation is provided by the Inuit of Angmagssalik, on the coast of Greenland near the North Pole (see map on page 17). This is such a harsh region that the band formerly living there had to alternate between two subsistence strategies to survive (Mauss 1979). In winter, band members relied for their survival on seal hunting. Nuclear families, which had traveled alone during the summer, would unite to form a large extended family and move into a stone longhouse on the seashore. Each had a leader, a man who gained his authority by demonstrating his maturity, hunting skill, wealth, and prowess as a magician. His was thus the achieved type of authority. His duties included distributing seal meat after a hunt, receiving strangers, and allotting seats for rituals in the longhouse. But his authority was limited. He was not permitted to issue orders, and the adult members of the extended family collectively owned the longhouse and everything in it. Any game he or another hunter might capture was shared among all longhouse residents.

At the beginning of summer, the Angmagssalik band would break up into nuclear families, which would then scatter across eastern Greenland to hunt animals that were themselves widely dispersed. Artifacts and food now belonged to the individual nuclear families. Each had a leader whose authority was of the ascribed type, deriving from his position as senior male in his nuclear family rather than from any personal qualities. The ascribed authority of the nuclear family head carried more weight than did the achieved authority of the winter headman.

Tribes

A **tribe** consists of a few hundred to several thousand people who distinguish themselves from other

---

tribe a political organization often occurring among horticulturalists or herders, whose members identify themselves as distinct from members of other groups based on their common heritage, and often common ancestry

[2] Flexibility and mobility are also useful in larger-scale societies with greater task specialization. In Western society, for example, people tend to change jobs and move a number of times throughout their lives. For them, a descent system that does not tie them strongly to their kin is adaptive. As noted in Chapter 9, Western society, like band society, is cognatic.

When a tribe depends upon horticulture for its subsistence, the tribespeople usually live in semipermanent or permanent villages like this one in Xishuan, China. Horticulture provides food reliably and abundantly enough to permit tribes to number in the hundreds or even the thousands.

groups based on their common heritage, and often common ancestry as well. Typically, tribespeople are horticulturalists or pastoralists whose method of subsistence provides food more reliably and abundantly than gathering and hunting, so tribes can be more populous than bands, and their settlements can be more concentrated. Even as horticulture and pastoralism permit larger groups, they also make larger groups necessary, since both activities require cooperative labor. It takes many hands to clear a forest for planting or to move a herd of camels from one grazing area to another.

Horticultural tribespeople tend to live in permanent or semipermanent villages. Because these are relatively large, a variety of groups—descent groups, political factions, military associations (Chapter 11)—can develop. Descent groups are especially important to tribal people, since descent is a convenient way to organize cooperative labor. Sometimes descent groups or other groups cross-cut a number of tribal villages, knitting local communities into a much larger society. This cannot happen among ever-shifting bands.

As in bands, tribal authority is "noncentralized": it is not concentrated in a single office or person, but spread among several or many roles and leaders. The various groups and factions have their leaders, but their leadership is attained informally, and typically no especially rich or powerful individual heads the whole tribe. Instead, the leaders of the various factions and other groups come together into a temporary coalition when necessary—in the face of a threat from the outside, for instance. Alliances are constantly being formed and broken.

Sometimes an informal leader emerges to settle conflicts among members or integrate a tribe's various groups in the face of an outside threat. This leader has no official mandate and occupies no formal office; his authority derives from his ability to

Political leaders called "big men" win their positions through charisma, eloquence, strength, political skill, and generosity. In the Western Highlands of New Guinea, a big man can be recognized by the wealth of ornaments he displays.

On New Guinea and neighboring Melanesian islands (see maps on pages 166, 198, and 385), political leaders who are charismatic, eloquent, physically powerful, politically skilled, and generous may achieve recognition as **big men.** They exhibit many of the characteristics of tribal leaders in other societies. A big man does not occupy an office; his power depends on the influence he exerts over his personal following. His generosity is particularly important, for making loans and gifts to supporters and potential supporters is essential for gaining leadership (Lederman 1990).

The Qashgai, pastoralists of western Iran who were first introduced in Chapter 6 (see map on page 135), provide an example of the tribal type of political organization. The Qashgai, who migrate between upland and lowland areas in a continual search for pastures to feed their extensive flocks of sheep and goats, are divided into more than 50 individual tribes. A few of these tribes are huge, containing many descent groups and several thousand families; others are much smaller, some with as few as five or six families. The families, nuclear or extended, live in large, open-sided black tents made of goat hair, with an average of about 10 people per tent (Beck 1980). Those who share a tent form an independent, cooperative economic unit.

In the winter, the Qashgai, in groups consisting of 30 to 100 tents, set up their herding camps on land leased from settled people or owned by the tribespeople in common, near the southwestern Iranian city of Shiraz where the winter weather is relatively mild. In the spring, at the Iranian New Year, a long migration begins. Now the Qashgai, on foot or horseback, with camels and donkeys to carry their necessities, make their way northwestward through the foothills and into the uplands of the Zagros mountains, pasturing their flocks along the way. The trip may cover close to 400 miles and take four to six weeks. After spending the summer in the cool mountains, the Qashgai migrate slowly back to their warmer winter quarters.

The political structure of Qashgai tribes is noncentralized. Each tribe is divided into clans, and

coerce and persuade people to support him. The active support of many people is very important to a leader in a tribal society—their joint labor provides food and their loyalty gives him his influence. Hence he is usually a person who has a large retinue of people around him, many political supporters, and possibly many wives, through whom he has connections with many lineages. Having emerged to wield influence over others, this temporary leader will be respected, and his advice taken, for as long as his charisma lasts. When his charisma wanes, another leader will take his place.

big man in Melanesia, a politician whose power depends on the influence he exerts over his followers rather than on a political office each clan is divided into sections headed by an elder male (called a "white beard"). This leader is not elected, but chosen informally on the basis of his natural abilities as a leader. A council of white beards makes the important decisions that affect the migrating unit, such as when to migrate and when to pitch or strike the tents. In this way, every member of every Qashgai family has an indirect say in decision making.

Chiefdoms

Chiefdoms, which we describe in the present tense even though they no longer exist in their classic form, are relatively complex political organizations that control sedentary populations numbering in the thousands (Earle 1989:84). Their subsistence base is almost always extensive, nonmechanized cultivation, which is usually necessary to guarantee the regular and abundant supplies of food an organization as complex as a chiefdom requires.[3]

In most chiefdoms, authority is centralized in the person of a chief, who oversees and coordinates various lower-level political units from his position at the political center of society. This officeholder's authority may be ascribed; his chieftaincy, for instance, may be inherited patrilineally or matrilineally. Or it may be achieved: he may be elected on the basis of personal qualities. Or the office of chief may be obtained partly as a result of ascription and partly as a result of achievement, as among the Tetum. In any case, a chieftaincy is usually a permanent office.

Social classes, almost nonexistent in bands and only weakly developed in tribes, are much more common in chiefdoms, which therefore cannot be described as egalitarian. These societies may be divided into classes such as royalty, aristocrats, commoners, and slaves. Usually the higher classes—royalty and aristocrats—control the political offices, from chief down to the lowest official, and no one outside these elite classes can aspire to office.

A chief protects his people from external enemies; coordinates his subjects' labor; resolves disputes; and collects, stores, and redistributes much of his society's wealth. In some chiefdoms, he per-

A Tetum chief inherits his office patrilineally, but needs wisdom, patience, honesty, reliability and the respect of his followers to be successful. On the island of Timor, a Tetum chief shows off his badges of office.

sonally symbolizes the health and well-being of the society, so much so that should he become sick his subjects may fear for the welfare of the chiefdom. Some chiefs are even considered by their subjects to be divine (Feeley-Harnick 1985).

The chiefdom of the Azande of Central Africa (see map on page 51), like other chiefdoms that once thrived in Central and West Africa, was so complex that its ruler is referred to in the ethnographic literature as a king rather than a chief, and his underlings as princes. In the early years of this century, these sedentary, nonmechanized cultiva-

---

[3] There are a few exceptions, including the gatherers and hunters of the Northwest Coast, whose food supply was prodigious enough to support this complex form of political organization.

chiefdom a relatively complex political organization controlling a large, sedentary population

tors were divided into many "kingdoms." Each kingdom was subdivided into provinces, whose administrative structure mirrored that of the kingdom. Provinces were led by princes, usually sons of a king: Both offices were ascribed and transmitted patrilineally (Evans-Pritchard 1971). Kings and princes acted as supreme judges in courts of law in their own domains, and the king was also commander-in-chief of the forces of his kingdom, responsible for public order, communications, and intelligence for his realm. He did not interfere with the internal administration of any province except the one he lived in, unless a province rebelled or its leader proved too incompetent to govern. The king would then intervene quickly and violently (Evans-Pritchard 1971).

The king lived in the large, central province, and regarded the princes as his representatives in the outlying provinces. Since they enclosed his own province, those of the princes formed a buffer zone that protected the king's territory from attacks by other kings. Broad paths led from the king's headquarters to those of the princes, and along them tribute from the princes passed to the king. In their turn, the princes received tribute from their own subjects. Thus, millet, groundnuts, sweet potatoes, chickens, and beer passed continually from the level of the lowliest subject through the princes to the king. But much of the wealth that subjects gave their rulers in the form of tribute was returned to them as meals, since a king or prince was obligated to provide hospitality to his subjects when they visited (Evans-Pritchard 1971).

An Azande king could have many wives, and the more he had, the greater the labor force available for his gardens and the more food his household could produce. The more food, the greater his hospitality and the larger the number of his followers; the larger his following, the greater his prestige and authority; the greater his prestige and authority, the greater the wealth he received, in the form of fines, fees, gifts, tribute, and the labor of his subjects (Evans-Pritchard 1971).

Chiefdoms like that of the Azande were huge political organizations, their populations numbering in the tens of thousands. Although the descendants of these populations still live in Africa, African chiefdoms, like those in other parts of the world, no longer exist as independent political entities. All have been absorbed into states.

States

A **state** is a large, complex, autonomous political unit that includes many communities and, usually, hundreds of thousands of people (see Figure 12.1). It has a centralized **government**—a formal organization through which the political process is carried out—with authority and power to conscript labor, make and enforce regulations, collect taxes, and create and maintain institutions to support itself. The territory covered by a state has well-established boundaries, and its people enjoy rights of citizenship, though these rights may not necessarily be the same for everyone. To obtain the huge and reliable supply of food needed to sustain the population of a state, technologically complex agricultural methods must be used, such as irrigation, terracing, and animal or machine power.

Kinship frequently conveys authority in other types of political organizations, but authority in states is based on the **law.** This term has been the subject of considerable debate in political anthropology, and various definitions have been proposed. Some are based on what constitutes law in Western societies, and are therefore culture-specific. Thus, for Radcliffe-Brown (1965:212), law is "social control through the systematic application of the force of politically organized society." Edward E. Evans-Pritchard (1940:162) sees law as existing where there is some "authority with power to . . . enforce a verdict." By either of these definitions, societies that lack "force" or the "power to enforce a verdict" would have to be considered as having no laws. But even gatherer-and-hunter societies, where authority (when it exists) is noncentralized and temporary, have agreed-upon regulations that have evolved through time and to which people are expected to conform. Thus, a more expansive definition, one that ignores the somewhat ethnocentric criterion of enforcement,

---

state a large, complex, autonomous political unit, consisting of many communities and large numbers of people under a centralized government that can conscript labor, make and enforce laws, collect taxes, and create and maintain institutions to support itself

government a formal organization through which the political process is carried out

law an institutionalized body of rules, created over time and ratified by a society or its leaders

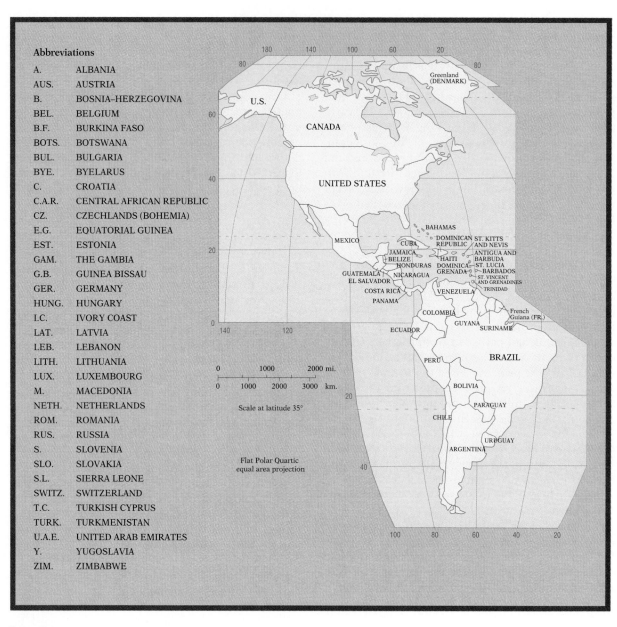

Abbreviations

A.	ALBANIA
AUS.	AUSTRIA
B.	BOSNIA–HERZEGOVINA
BEL.	BELGIUM
B.F.	BURKINA FASO
BOTS.	BOTSWANA
BUL.	BULGARIA
BYE.	BYELARUS
C.	CROATIA
C.A.R.	CENTRAL AFRICAN REPUBLIC
CZ.	CZECHLANDS (BOHEMIA)
E.G.	EQUATORIAL GUINEA
EST.	ESTONIA
GAM.	THE GAMBIA
G.B.	GUINEA BISSAU
GER.	GERMANY
HUNG.	HUNGARY
I.C.	IVORY COAST
LAT.	LATVIA
LEB.	LEBANON
LITH.	LITHUANIA
LUX.	LUXEMBOURG
M.	MACEDONIA
NETH.	NETHERLANDS
ROM.	ROMANIA
RUS.	RUSSIA
S.	SLOVENIA
SLO.	SLOVAKIA
S.L.	SIERRA LEONE
SWITZ.	SWITZERLAND
T.C.	TURKISH CYPRUS
TURK.	TURKMENISTAN
U.A.E.	UNITED ARAB EMIRATES
Y.	YUGOSLAVIA
ZIM.	ZIMBABWE

Figure 12.1

The Independent States of the World. Source: Jordan et al. 1994:136–137.

is needed to accommodate societies that do not fit the Western model.

For our purposes, law may be defined as a body of rules that were created over time, are institutionalized (acknowledged societywide or even internationally), and have been ratified by a society or its leaders. These laws permit the state to create and control complex bureaucracies such as armed services, a civilian police force, and a department of taxation, which give the state great power over individuals, their behavior, time, labor, money, and sometimes even their minds.

States have often sought to extend their territories by encroaching on the boundaries of neighboring bands, tribes, chiefdoms, or less powerful states. Colonial ambitions of this kind have been common in the West, especially among those states that have come to the fore in the last 500 years.

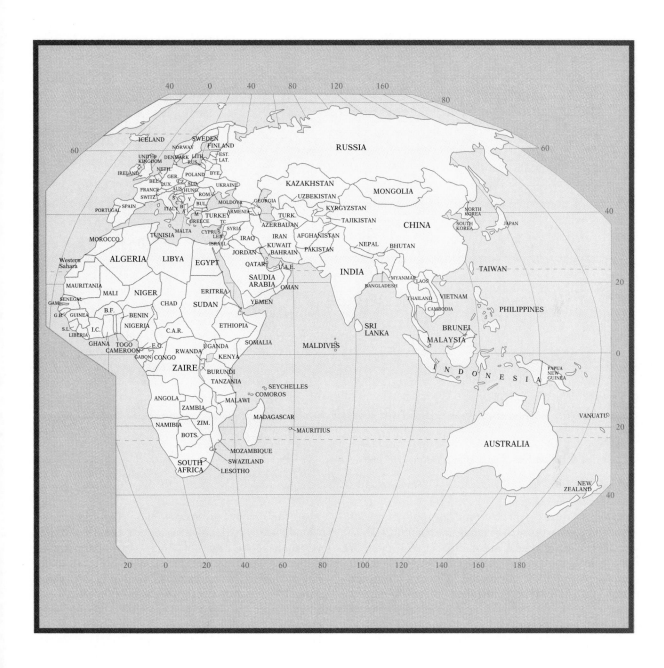

The first states arose, apparently independently, beginning in the fourth millennium B.C. (see Figure 12.2): Babylonian and Sumerian (in Mesopotamia, now Iraq), Egyptian (Nile Valley), Mayan and Aztec (Mesoamerica), Incan (Peru), Shang (China), and possibly Harappan (Indus Valley, now Pakistan[4]). A number of theories have been proposed to explain their emergence. One is based on the concept of the **hydraulic society,** a society in which crops are watered not just by rainfall but by a sophisticated water management system that includes irrigation, drainage, and flood control (Wittfogel 1957). Such

---

[4] Archaeologists are unsure whether or not the term *state* should be applied to the political organization of Harappan civilization.

hydraulic society a society in which crops are irrigated by a complex system of water management

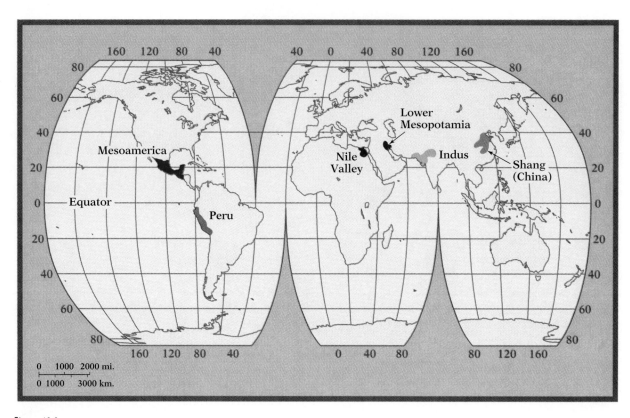

Figure 12.2
The Location of the Earliest States. Source: Hayden 1993:363.

a system requires a more complex organization of labor than agriculture that relies upon rainfall does, and this in turn affects other aspects of society. A huge number of workers must be supervised, so managers must be appointed. Once a complex water control system is installed, these managers must agree on how the water is to be distributed and how disputes between water-users will be handled. To attain this managerial control, bureaucracies evolve. Sometimes the bureaucrats operating the system become extremely powerful.

Oriental Despotism a kind of political system, highly developed in ancient China, in which some individuals achieved power by controlling water and labor

In the past, anthropologist Karl Wittfogel argued, some hydraulic systems worked so well, over such a long time, that huge, dense populations developed, which required ever more bureaucrats to control them. The bureaucrats' authority increased so much that eventually those who authorized access to water and managed the labor force were able to concentrate political power in their own hands, giving rise to a highly stratified political organization. When some individuals managed to manipulate their way into positions of great power, despotism resulted. Since this kind of system appears to have reached an extreme form in China's Yellow River Valley, Wittfogel termed the phenomenon **Oriental Despotism.**

The Aztec state, first known to Westerners in 1519, was begun by people who entered the Valley of Mexico about A.D. 1200. By the early fifteenth century, only 300 years later, the Aztecs

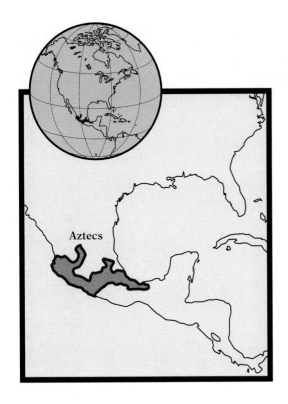

had expanded their realm from the Pacific Ocean to the Gulf of Mexico. Their capital, the ruins of which today lie underneath Mexico City, was called Tenochtitlan.

Aztec society recognized five classes: a royal class, which provided the Aztec ruler; a small class of nobles; a large middle class; a small lower class; and a slave class. Only royalty and nobles shared in the booty that flowed into Tenochtitlan from conquered neighboring states, although middle-class men whose service to the state was exceptional were sometimes elevated by the king into the nobility. Slaves and members of the lower class had no power and owned no land, but carried out the bulk of the agricultural work. Most were unskilled laborers, barely able to support their own families.

Since water management contributed to its agricultural success, the Aztec state is classified by anthropologists as a hydraulic society. Corn and other crops were planted and tended by hand on plots made by cutting water plants from the surfaces of rivers and lakes (an unusual method; in most early states, plows and draft animals were used in cultivation). These plants were piled up in thick layers to make floating "islands," anchored in place by willows planted along the edges of the canals that ran between them. Long dikes controlled flooding and assured access to neighboring fresh-water lagoons. This was a sophisticated kind of crop-raising indeed.

One problem with Wittfogel's thesis is that there doesn't have to be any connection between complex hydraulic systems and states. The Romans had a complex bureaucracy without a sophisticated water control system, and the Makassai of Timor (see map on page 159) have a complex water control system, including irrigated agricultural terraces, but no state system. An alternative hypothesis (Carneiro 1970, 1978) covers such cases. Three factors, according to Carneiro, operate jointly to foster state formation: physical limitation or "circumscription" (environmental or social), increasing population, and warfare. Narrow valleys, arid areas, oases, or small islands are examples of environmental circumscription; political units cannot expand geographically in such places. Social circumscription—when neighbors prevent a population from emigrating, for example—can also prevent expansion.

When gatherers and hunters become horticulturalists, Carneiro argues, population increases. But their geographical expansion may be prevented by environmental or social circumscription. Since land is scarce, conflicts arise and war erupts. The losers, unable to flee, are forced to submit to the victors, who demand tribute. To pay it, the losers intensify their production, employing new techniques and working harder. Their villages grow, eventually uniting to form chiefdoms. In time, one chiefdom conquers others, and a state is formed. Like the Wittfogel hypothesis, Carneiro's thesis has not escaped criticism, since there are examples of population increase within circumscribed environments that did not lead to state formation.

Ronald Cohen and Elman R. Service (1978:32) see state formation as the result of the attempts of political leaders to obtain and hold power by organizing public works, redistributing wealth, and forming armies for their followers' benefit. Yet

Table 12.1
Types of Political Organizations and Typically Associated Features

Type of Political Organization	Size and Complexity	Major Subsistence Strategy	Economy	Social Structure	Descent	Political System
Band	Smallest, least complex; 25 to 50 people	Gathering and hunting	Generalized reciprocity	Generally egalitarian	Cognatic	Noncentralized; no offices; temporary leaders; political decisions made informally, by consensus; few rights to personal property
Tribe	Larger, more complex than bands; few hundred to several thousand members	Horticulture; pastoralism	Balanced reciprocity	Personal inequality; weakly developed social classes	Lineal or cognatic	Noncentralized; offices rare; leadership attained informally; factions possible; warfare common
Chiefdom	Larger, more complex than tribes; population may number in the thousands	Nonmechanized agriculture	Balanced reciprocity; redistribution	Distinct social classes	Lineal or cognatic	Centralized authority; chief is officeholder; political decisions made formally
State	Largest, most complex political organization; tens of thousands to millions of members	Large-scale, technologically complex agriculture; industrial production	Market exchange; money	Highly stratified	Cognatic	Centralized government; authority based on law; rights of citizenship; complex bureaucracies

another explanation stresses the state-forming effects of long-distance trade (Polanyi et al. 1957). Each of these approaches—Wittfogel's, Carneiro's, Cohen and Service's, and Polanyi's—gives us insights into how states may have originated, but none can be used to explain every case of state formation.

Some feminist anthropologists have tried to show that as states arise, women's authority and status decrease and a gender hierarchy (Chapter 8) emerges. They argue that in "kinship societies"—bands, tribes, and chiefdoms, in which descent and marriage help determine access to positions of influence, authority, and power—women hold a greater share of these positions than they do in states, political organizations in which kinship usually has much less impact.

Christine Ward Gailey (1987:264) uses the Polynesian chiefdom of Tonga, where women tradi-

tionally wielded considerable influence, as a case study to make this point. In Gailey's view, as westernization transformed the Tongan chiefdom into a state, activities over which women exercised control, such as births and marriages, fell increasingly under the domination of civil authorities representing the newly emerging state. At the same time, as the economy became more dependent on cash, goods traditionally produced by women lost their value to Tongans, and women's labor itself became devalued. Arguing on the opposite side of this hypothesis are other feminists who do not believe that the rise of the state necessarily brings about the subjugation of women (Silverblatt 1988:444–448).

• Conflict Containment • and Resolution

The boundaries of acceptable behavior—what is permissible to do, say, or even think or look like—vary widely from society to society. In fact, these boundaries are not always the same for everyone in a given society. Boundaries that are institutionalized are called laws; those that are informal are termed **norms.** Sometimes norms and laws are grounded in religion or mythology; in technologically simpler societies, people often say that their ancestors taught them how to behave.

Norms and laws protect the social order, without which societies could not exist. Still, they are often ignored or violated, and the result may be conflict—the disruption of the social order. Nonconformity with norms and laws takes many different shapes, ranging from victimless crimes (like using illegal drugs) to personal attacks (such as rape, theft, or murder) to political terrorism to

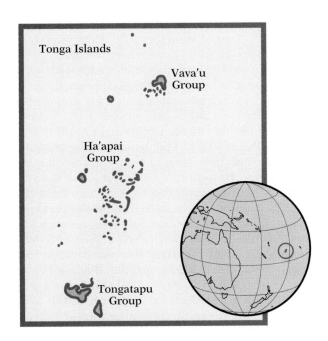

• Ask Yourself •

Jews and Christians believe that their most important rules, the Ten Commandments, were given to them by God through the prophet Moses. Do you think this is true? If not, where do you think these social rules came from?

norm an informal rule for behavior

larger-scale civil rebellions to wholesale revolutions and international disputes. To prevent, contain, or resolve such conflicts, societies have ways of encouraging and enforcing conformity with norms and laws, and discouraging and punishing nonconformity. Some of these means are orderly (a North American legal trial, for example); others (like civil war) reflect a breakdown of the social order.

Orderly Means

Councils and Committees.   Councils and committees are advisory groups found in many different kinds of societies. We have briefly mentioned **councils** among the Shavante, Tetum, and Qashgai. They meet in public and are usually made up of informally appointed elders. **Committees** differ from councils in that they meet privately (Bailey 1965:20). Moreover, whereas councils are typical of simpler political organizations, committees are more characteristic of states. But the two kinds of groups can and often do coexist within the same political organization. When this occurs, councils are superior to committees, whose tasks and powers are delegated to them by councils.

Councils tend to be consensus-seeking bodies, while committees are more likely to achieve agreement by voting (although either kind of body may reach decisions in either way). Consensus seeking is typical of small social groups whose members have frequent personal interaction. Once a council or committee increases to more than about 50 members, decision by consensus is no longer possible. Voting is typical of larger groups whose members do not see much of one another in daily life and who owe their main allegiance not to other group members but to people (perhaps many millions) outside the council or committee. Members may in fact represent these

outside people, as is the case with the U.S. Congress (Bailey 1965).

In the village of Pentrediwaith, Wales, everyone knows everyone else. The villagers recognize that disputes would disrupt their community, so they go to great lengths to avoid them. A common tactic is to duck any uncomfortable issues; for example, a villager will not refuse an unreasonable request outright, but may never get around to fulfilling it (Frankenberg 1957). Still, conflicts do arise in Pentrediwaith from time to time, and the villagers handle them by forming committees to discuss and resolve them by compromise and consensus. To protect committee members who propose controversial motions, the minutes of these meetings are not recorded in any detail. Sometimes outsiders from England are brought into committees and maneuvered into bringing up topics that need to be discussed but are so controversial that the villagers do not wish to be associated with them. In this way, the blame for any resulting unpleasantness falls on outsiders rather than on villagers.

Committee members are anxious to work out compromises, knowing that if a decision is not a compromise it will not be carried out. Frankenberg (1957:94, 138) tells of an instance in which a committee in Pentrediwaith refused to seek consensus, insisting instead on taking a vote to reach a majority decision. The secretary of the commit-

---

council an advisory group, typical of simpler political organizations, that is usually informally appointed, meets in public, and resolves conflicts by consensus

committee an advisory group, most common in states, that meets in private and usually achieves agreement by voting

Councils, advisory groups composed of informally appointed elders, meet in public and achieve resolutions to local problems by consensus. In Botswana, Africa, Tswana council members welcome a foreign dignitary to their outdoor meeting

tee, who was in the losing minority, "forgot" to write up the minutes, and the decision was never implemented. In Pentrediwaith, consensus not only dampens disputes, it resolves them, too (Bailey 1965:8).

Sanctions. A **sanction** is a reaction by society to approved or disapproved behavior (Radcliffe-Brown 1965:205). Reactions to approved behavior are called *positive sanctions;* reactions to disapproved behavior are called *negative sanctions.* The Nobel Prize and a round of applause are both positive sanctions; the death penalty, a $50 fine, and unflattering gossip are negative sanctions. We can now point out an additional difference between (institutionalized) laws and (informal) norms: laws are always backed up by sanctions; norms often are not.

Just as sanctions can be either positive or negative, so each kind can be either diffused or orga-

nized (see Figure 12.3). **Diffused sanctions** are spontaneous expressions of either approval or disapproval. Either way, they are informal and noninstitutionalized. A round of applause and unflattering gossip are both diffused sanctions, one positive, the other negative. **Organized sanctions,**

---

sanction a positive or negative reaction by society to approved behavior (positive sanction) or disapproved behavior (negative sanction)

diffused sanction a spontaneous expression of either approval or disapproval

organized sanction a formalized and institutionalized expression of approval or disapproval

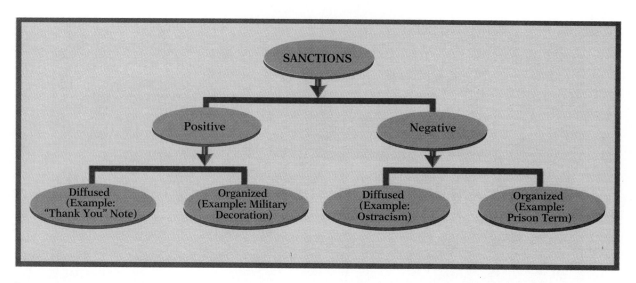

Figure 12.3

Types and Examples of Sanctions.

in contrast, are formalized and institutionalized, like the Nobel Prize or the death penalty.

Thus, *diffused positive sanctions* are informal gestures of approval. Teachers who care for their students and who go out of their way to help them master and enjoy a course may receive thank-you notes at the end of the semester; these are diffused positive sanctions. *Diffused negative sanctions*, in contrast, are informal punishments. Often they are verbal: an offender may be criticized, ridiculed, or even completely shunned, a severe negative sanction known as **ostracism.** *Organized positive sanctions* are formal gestures of approval—military or civilian decorations, for example—given to individuals who have done something admirable. *Organized negative sanctions* are formal punishments, such as a spell in prison, administered to rule-breakers or those who have neglected to fulfill their social obligations. Generally the most clearly defined of sanctions, these differ from diffused

ostracism a diffused sanction in which the offender is shunned

court a group of people with the authority to hear the cases of disputants and their witnesses, to determine innocence or guilt, and to decide on punishment

The Nobel Prize, a formal gesture of approval given to people who have done something admirable, is an example of an organized sanction. Here Nelson Mandela (left) and Frederik de Klerk (right), present and former prime minister of South Africa, receive their Nobel Prizes for peace, at Oslo, Norway, in December 1993.

negative sanctions in that they have the weight of society behind them.

Who is responsible for deciding what sanctions to apply and under what circumstances? In most societies, one or more people have the right and duty to sit in judgment of their fellows and decide what, if any, sanctions should be imposed. Depending on the society, such authority might be vested in the head of a simple family or a lineage, a village chief, a group of tribal elders, a king or emperor, or a jury.

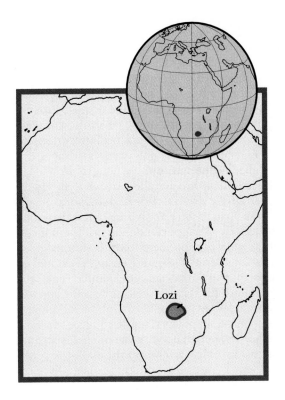

• Ask Yourself •

Have you ever been sanctioned, positively or negatively, by a group of which you are a part? What did the sanction consist of? Was it diffused or organized? What was your reaction?

Courts and Judges. In many societies, the identification of wrongdoers, the decision to punish them or not, and the method of punishment to be used are duties of a **court,** a group of people with the authority to hear the cases of disputants and their witnesses, to determine innocence or guilt, and to decide on punishment (Gulliver 1969:24). A court's members are not directly involved in the dispute. The head of a court is usually a judge, who acts on behalf of the community or a higher political authority. In societies with centralized political systems, the judge is typically backed up by the weight of the entire political system, because his office is a political position.

In Central Africa, a judge of the Lozi chiefdom relies in his decision making on a concept familiar to Westerners: that of the reasonable man (Gluckman 1969:367–371). The Lozi judge asks himself whether an accused person behaved reasonably and in conformity with custom. If the offense involves an action that the defendant committed in his capacity as a father, for instance, the judge compares the defendant's behavior against Lozi norms for paternal behavior. Standards of accepted behavior are familiar to each Lozi indi-

• Ask Yourself •

Have you ever been responsible for deciding on someone's guilt or innocence or served as a mediator in a dispute? If so, what evidence did you consider in making your judgment?

vidual, and deviants know that if they are brought to court they will be judged according to their degree of conformity to these standards. Fear of the court serves as a sanction against deviant behavior—even behavior that does not actually break the law.

Sometimes, instead of being vested in the person of a judge, the authority to sit in judgment may be combined with the other functions of a lineage head, ritual leader, village headman, senior kinsman, or other influential person (Gulliver 1969:25). When a dispute occurs, such a person may be pressed into temporary service as a **mediator**—a third party, neutral to the dispute, charged with negotiating a settlement. In contrast to judges in centralized political systems, mediators may be little more than spokespersons for public opinion, summing up the consensus on the disputed matter (Gulliver 1969:25). Sometimes, when the contending parties agree to accept the mediator's decision as final and binding, the process of settling a dispute is called **adjudication.**

Some conflicts are handled in what might be termed *informal courts.* When a dispute occurs among the Arusha of East Africa, each disputant recruits a body of supporters and with them meets peacefully with his opponent and his supporters to negotiate a settlement. Supporters are recruited on the basis of patrilineal descent, similar age, and neighborhood. Each party seeks to win the support of influential men, such as members of lineage councils. These supporters, neither judges nor neutral mediators, negotiate with the other disputant's supporters to reach a compromise. Social pressures of every kind are brought to bear by each party on the other, and if an agreement is to be reached at all, each must give ground and accept a compromise. Enforcement is rarely a problem since both sides accept the compromise as the best solution available under the circumstances (Gulliver 1969:26).

Another alternative is for an entire community to act as its own court, with community consensus deciding the verdict. The Central Inuit (see map on page 17) require the disputants in a wife-stealing argument to confront each other in a public song contest (Hoebel 1964:93–99). Before the whole community, each disputant sings songs ridiculing the other. The man who manages to sing the wittiest, most satirical song receives the most applause from the assembled group and is judged the winner by community consensus.

Determining Innocence or Guilt.   Whether a court exists or not, determining the innocence or guilt of accused individuals is basic to the enforcement of rules and norms. Evidence of either is required, but what kind of evidence is acceptable and who should assess its merits vary widely among societies. In the North American system, a judge, jury, or both analyze the conflicting claims of both parties in a dispute, determine the facts of the matter, and proclaim guilt or innocence. If the accused is found guilty, a judge then imposes a penalty as determined by law. In other societies, other methods may be used to establish the facts, determine guilt or innocence, and specify penalties.

In societies other than our own, **divination** is sometimes used to determine innocence or guilt. In a divination, performed by a ritual specialist called a **diviner,** something that will happen in the future is foretold, or something that happened in the past is revealed (divined) with the help of supernatural agents.

Another method of determining guilt or innocence is the **conditional curse,** a verbal formula containing a conditional phrase, something like "If I'm lying, may lightening strike me dead!" This is similar to the oath required of witnesses in North American courts, which obliges them to tell the truth "so help me God."

Mere words, however, are not a sufficient guarantee of the truth everywhere, as shown by the **trial by ordeal,** a physical test of the accused for the purpose of revealing the truth. In Europe, in the Middle Ages, the hands and feet of an accused witch were bound together, and she (or more rarely he) was tossed into a stream. Water symbolized purity, so if the accused sank to the bottom, it was believed she was free of witchcraft since the water had accepted her. If she floated, it was believed that the water had rejected her because she was tainted by witchcraft.

mediator a person who is neutral to a dispute and charged with negotiating its settlement

adjudication the process by which a dispute is settled after the disputants agree that a mediator's decision will be binding

divination a ritual designed to foretell the future or interpret the past, with the help of supernatural agents

diviner a person who performs a divination ritual

conditional curse a verbal formula, containing a conditional phrase, designed to establish innocence or guilt

trial by ordeal a physical test of an accused person for the purpose of revealing the truth

Disorderly Means

Unfortunately, disputes are not always resolved in orderly fashion. Resolution within the prevailing system of laws and norms may not be sought, may be sought but not achieved, or may be achieved only to break down in the face of renewed hostility.

In a divination ritual, a past or future event is "divined" with help from supernatural agents. In Mali, a Dogon diviner (left) studies the paw prints of foxes as he attempts to foretell the future.

In the case of disputes between individuals, society may require the disputants, and only them, to resolve their differences in a physical contest—a spear fight, for example, or a boxing match. When groups rather than individuals are involved, the result may be feuds or wars.

Feuds. A **feud** is a prolonged but usually intermittent hostile relationship between two groups. Especially typical of tribes, feuding often occurs between two descent groups or factions. The way feuds are carried out differs among societies, but feuds share three important characteristics (Pospisil 1974:3). First, despite the way the word is commonly used, feuds involve not individuals but groups, for whom injury to even one member is considered injury to all. Second, feuds are physical. Violence, even killing, is believed to be justified for either of two reasons: revenge on enemies or glory for one's own group. Typically, the violence follows a pattern: injury, reprisal, and counterreprisal. Thus, once begun, feuds tend to continue, perhaps

for generations. And third, feuding takes place within societies rather than between them, so feuding groups share the same cultural values, institutions, and expectations and observe the same set of rules (Pospisil 1974:4).

Feuding is found more often in tribes than in bands, chiefdoms, or states because tribes are large enough to be divided up into special-interest groups but still small enough to be organized on the basis of kinship rather than some overarching principle of law. But feuding can occur even in states, including Western ones. It is most common where formal educational or religious institutions are absent or weak, or where the government exerts little authority.

This was the case in the late nineteenth century in the isolated, mountainous area of the United States where West Virginia borders Kentucky. The region's residents—many of them farmers, hunters, and illegal moonshiners by occupation—largely ignored civil authority. Their children rarely attended school, so illiteracy was high. Religion had no more influence on most people's behavior than government or education. Nuclear families tended to be large, with a dozen or more children, and extended families enormous. Family ties were strong, but boys grew up pursuing solitary activities such as hunting and fishing, "often . . . untem-

---

feud a prolonged but usually intermittent hostile relationship between two groups

Societies sometimes require or permit disputants to resolve their differences in one-on-one contests. In July 1804, U.S. Vice President Aaron Burr shot and killed his political opponent, Alexander Hamilton, former Secretary of the Treasury, in a duel provoked by the political rivalry of the two men.

pered by strong parental or social discipline" (Rice 1978). In this political, economic, and social setting erupted the longest-running and most notorious of the late nineteenth-century Appalachian feuds: the feud between the Hatfields and the McCoys.

No one knows just what started the feud. It seems to have been rooted in everyday conflicts of the time: different opinions on the Civil War, political arguments, minor theft. The first killing, in 1865, followed an earlier exchange of gunfire, a couple of pig-stealing episodes, and some vandalism. A brief Romeo-and-Juliet episode involving a Hatfield and a McCoy, strongly opposed by both families, increased the enmity, and home-brewed liquor contributed to hot tempers on both sides. After a Hatfield was acquitted of pig-stealing charges, the McCoys refused to accept the decision of the court and "resorted to the law that might makes right" (Rice 1978:16). Soon afterward, a Hatfield was murdered. In the decades that followed, the feud escalated. Members of the two extended families, increasingly active politically, won friends in official positions and even filled some of these positions themselves, but frequently they took matters into their own hands, ignoring the law. In the 1880s, threats, fights, beatings, arson, and murder were frequent occurrences.

Eventually, however, as the century came to an end, better education and technological development drew the Appalachian mountain area increasingly into the American cultural mainstream. At the same time, it became more and more difficult to take the law into one's own hands and get away with it; local customs gave way in the face of more strictly enforced state and national legal and political processes. Sometime during the early years of the twentieth century, the famous Hatfield-McCoy feud fizzled out.

Warfare. Two important features distinguish wars from feuds. First, warfare is conducted on a level above that of the local community; warring groups are usually either relatively large-scale elements within a single nation (civil war) or whole nations (international war). The second difference lies in the relationship between the antagonistic parties. In a feud, the participating groups are part of the same relatively small-scale social system—for instance, antagonistic lineages within the same tribe. (If we consider the nineteenth-century Appalachian community of much-intermarried, white, western European immigrant farmers a "tribe," this is the situation in which the Hatfields and the McCoys found themselves.) In warfare, although the disputants may be covered by the same broad cultural umbrella (as were the combatants in the American Civil War), at a lower level they represent quite distinct political or social or economic organizations. This may be why they fight.

Modern wars are of three kinds—world wars, more geographically confined wars (which may nevertheless, like the Vietnam or Persian Gulf conflicts, include extraregional superpowers among the combatants), and smaller-scale, intraregional conflicts such as the recent civil war in Bosnia. Although there are obvious differences among them, their causes are similar. Values such as honor, freedom, or religious principles may be the avowed reasons for fighting, but social and economic inequalities between the combatants—the lack of territory, unevenly distributed natural resources, unequal influence in a larger political arena, unequal access to regional or world markets—are more likely to be the real causes. In the recent war between Iran and Iraq, young men on both sides went willingly to their deaths in the name of religion, even though this war was not so much about the ideological differences between two branches of Islam as it was about the region's underground oil riches.

*In what may be America's most famous feud, the Hatfields and the McCoys—extended families
living in Appalachia in the late nineteenth century—threatened, fought, and killed each other
over a period of four decades. Here, Hatfield men pose with their guns in 1899.*

How do anthropologists explain warfare? Many hypotheses have been suggested, but no consensus has been reached (see Ferguson and Farragher 1988). Some scholars claim that warfare is motivated by people's involuntary reactions to environmental, economic, or cultural forces (Robarchek 1989). One ecological argument suggests that warfare prevents population growth that would lead to the overexploitation and deterioration of resources (Vayda 1961:347). Yet there are many examples in human history in which populations have increased, causing natural resources to deteriorate, but war has not erupted (Hallpike 1973:457). A deterministic view of this kind implies that people are the helpless pawns of irresistible forces.

Functionalists have argued that warfare strengthens the internal solidarity of groups that engage in it. But it does not follow that the entire society of which a warring group is a part is also strengthened. In fact, many societies punish members who risk plunging their particular groups into war. Among the Konso of Ethiopia (Northeast Africa), if a man steals a goat from a man of another town, the elders of the thief's town, far from feeling obliged to support the thief (thereby, as the functionalists would insist, strengthening the solidarity of their town), force him to pay compensation (Hallpike 1973:460).

People are not "passive machines pushed this way and that by ecological, biological, sociological, or even cultural determinants" (Robarchek 1989:903–904). At least some of the time, they make decisions among clear options and constraints in pursuit of a variety of goals. Another explanation for warfare, which we might call the pragmatic explanation, seems to fit this view and also the realities of human history. Its most eloquent spokesper-

• Ask Yourself •

Can you think of possible causes of warfare in addition to the ones mentioned above?

The Anthropologist at Work

Elizabeth S. Grobsmith

The system of social control found in Western society often involves the incarceration of criminals, not only to punish them for their misdeeds and prevent them from committing additional crimes, but also to prepare them for their eventual return to society. But not all prisoners are alike; they vary by sex, age, educational level, socioeconomic status, religion, and ethnic group affiliation. As prison officials attempt to accord prisoners the humane treatment and rehabilitative services that are important principles of the modern Western penal system, they are often faced with the need to understand the many different cultures of their charges.

Over the last 20 years, Elizabeth S. Grobsmith, a professor of anthropology at the University of Nebraska-Lincoln who also works as a consultant in applied anthropology, has been helping the Nebraska Department of Correctional Services to better understand the culture of the state's Native American prisoners, who represent about 4 percent of Nebraska's prison population (Grobsmith 1992). Grobsmith's work with Native American prisoners began in 1975, when the U.S. District Court in Nebraska decreed that they must be allowed to maintain their traditional culture, including their religious practices, while in prison.

Nebraska's Native American prisoners were eager to practice their religion behind bars, but their traditional rituals, involving what seemed to their jailers to be unusual and therefore suspicious paraphernalia and practices, caused tension between inmates and guards. When the Native Americans wished to unwrap their Sacred Pipe and its accompanying religious articles according to special procedures dictated by custom, this challenged the normal inspection procedures for items prisoners are allowed to use. Healing ceremonies carried out by Native American ritual specialists from outside the prison sometimes required a totally darkened room and the use of scalpels or blades. Guards confused the smell of the sage, cedar, and sweetgrass burned during religious rituals and private prayers with marijuana. Prisoners, for their part, were offended by their jailers' suspicions and accusations, which sometimes worsened the situation. Rather than submitting to drug tests they found humiliating, for example, they would refuse to be tested, thus appearing guilty.

---

son, C. R. Hallpike (1973:459), rejects deterministic explanations of warfare. The desire for power, prestige, material wealth, and sex, and the envy of those who have them, are among the most powerful forces in human nature, Hallpike writes. To attain such goals, and to keep others from attaining them, is sufficient reason for warfare. "The human race has evolved few more definitive means of proving one's superiority over an enemy than by battering him to death . . . , burning his habitation, ravaging his crops, and raping his wife" (459).

Warfare has changed through the ages and is now more technologically complex and more destructive of both property and human life than ever before. Moreover, it has developed from an activity involving only a few of a society's members (e.g., members of a military association) to one that can involve hundreds of thousands of professional combatants and millions of noncombatants. Various modern-day measures to contain warfare either have failed, like the League of Nations, or have still to prove themselves, like the United Nations.

Conclusion

This chapter presents a cultural-evolutionary model of political organizations that assumes a general

Grobsmith found that the problem of cross-cultural communication between Native American prisoners and jailers had several dimensions. Most prison officials and guards had received no education in Native American culture, and were therefore unfamiliar with Native American beliefs and practices. Native American inmates found it difficult to explain to the authorities the beliefs underlying their practices. As a specialist in Native American culture, Grobsmith was able to interpret the meaning of Native American customs for prison authorities, and convince them of the traditional legitimacy of such customs.

More broadly, Grobsmith found that the data about prisoners collected by the Nebraska correctional system were generally inadequate to design effective and humane policies and programs for prisoners. Her work demonstrated that calling on the expertise of an anthropologist at the time prisoners first enter the penal system upgrades the quality of the data authorities collect about them, which in the long run enables corrections officers to provide inmates with more effective services. The State of Nebraska, for example, estimated that about 40 percent of Native American prisoners were dependent on drugs and alcohol, and offered treatment programs for these prisoners. But in interviews with over half of Nebraska's Native American prison population, Grobsmith discovered that every one of them admitted to drug or alcohol dependency. Without expanded treatment programs built around reliable data, the likelihood of prisoner rehabilitation was slim; Grobsmith pointed out that "the consequence of ignoring Native American prisoners' needs is the ultimate return of most . . . to incarceration" (Grobsmith 1992:7). But armed with better data, prison authorities were now able to justify requests to the state for additional resources to develop treatment programs.

Grobsmith was also called upon to interpret Native American prisoners' beliefs and attitudes involving their families. One inmate wished to attend the funeral of his grandfather, but prison authorities routinely prohibit prisoners from attending funerals of anyone but "immediate" family members. Grandparents were therefore excluded—until the anthropologist explained that the Native Americans' system of descent made such kin more "immediate" than was the case in the European kinship system.

"Native Americans are only one of a number of ethnically diverse groups within the prison population that could benefit from the work of anthropologists," says Grobsmith (5). Her 20 years of experience working with Native American prisoners have led her to conclude that "opportunities abound for the application of anthropological methods, techniques, and data in addressing issues relative to incarceration" (5).

trend toward bigger populations and increasingly complex ways of life between the first and the last of the four types of organizations described. Increasing complexity, however, is not the same as progress, and the two may not necessarily coincide. As we noted in Chapter 3, neo-evolutionists favor the term *process* to refer to what happens to cultures through time, since the word does not imply progress or, for that matter, any change at all. With these two notions in mind, let us take a brief look at modern, state-level political organization.

In every society, political power is unequally distributed; it rests largely in the hands of certain people who impose order, define and pursue society's goals, punish disobedience, direct change, and sometimes (depending on the size of the society) oversee bureaucracies made up of lesser officeholders. How do societies determine which individuals get to wield political power? Although room exists for some wrangling over leadership in every kind of society, the more complex the political organization, the more difficult it is for any given individual to be an important player on the political stage. In bands, experienced male heads of households typically get to be leaders, although other adults have their say in these highly egalitarian political organizations. In tribes and chiefdoms, many adults are ineligible for leadership for reasons of descent, sex, or class, and among those who are eligible there may be much jockeying for influence, power, wealth, and followers. Relatively few individuals wind up with real political power. The same was true in early state-level political organizations: only some people were eligible for political roles.

Today, in many state-level societies, every adult member is, in principle, eligible to participate in politics, and even to become a leader. But many states have populations too large to permit more than a small proportion of their members to play any direct part in politics, much less to become leaders. Instead, states may claim to have instituted "representative" governments. They may further claim that representatives are selected democratically.

This kind of system is more ideal than real. In representative governments, who is represented, and how, varies. So does the process of "democratic" selection of leaders. Modern states commonly prevent certain categories of people from participating in politics: South Africa before 1991 is an example. In India today, it is the avowed intent of one political party to exclude Moslems, who constitute 10 percent of the nation's population, from the political process. Even in the United States, young adults whom society considers old enough to be pressed into military service to benefit the state but who are still under the age of 21 are excluded from candidacy for office. These examples make it clear that even though there is a demonstrable cultural evolutionary tendency for political organizations to become bigger and more complex through time, there is no corresponding tendency for these organizations to become more representative or more equitable. No kind of society has yet developed a political system in which everyone is assured a chance to participate—except, perhaps, the band.

Summary

- *Politics* refers to the ways in which societies regulate the behavior of their members.

- Political organizations have leaders who set priorities; prevent, limit, or resolve conflicts; punish those who threaten the social order; and direct change.

- *Power* is the capacity to control the behavior of others, and may be based on physical strength, wealth, organization, knowledge, charisma, or a combination of these.

- *Authority*, which may be either ascribed or achieved, is the socially granted right to exercise power, and is usually conveyed to an individual through an office that exists independently of its occupant.

- Political leaders must have both power and authority.

- Elman R. Service has described four types of political organizations: bands, tribes, chiefdoms, and states. From the first to the fourth, they are characterized by increasingly complex subsistence strategies, larger size, and increasingly complex economic arrangements.

- The band is most common among gatherers and hunters, among whom power and authority are noncentralized and allocated on an informal, temporary basis.

- In tribes, which are characteristic of horticultural and pastoralist societies, power and authority are also noncentralized.

- In now-extinct chiefdoms, which were usually based on extensive cultivation, power and authority (either achieved or ascribed) were centralized in chiefs.

- States, the largest and most complex political organizations, are based on technologically sophisticated agriculture and have centralized governments with the authority and power to conscript labor, make and enforce laws, collect taxes, and create and maintain institutions to support themselves.

- The boundaries of acceptable behavior, which vary widely from society to society, may be either informal, in which case they are called *norms*, or formally recognized, in which case they are called *laws*.

- Authority in states is based on laws.

- One explanation for the emergence of states is that of Wittfogel, which is based on the idea that man-made water-control systems encourage the development of powerful bureaucracies in which political power becomes concentrated.

- A rival explanation is that of Carneiro, who considers environmental or social circumstances as jointly encouraging state formation.

- A third explanation is that of Cohen and Service, who think state formation results from the attempts made by political leaders to obtain and hold power by organizing public works, redistributing wealth, and forming armies.

- A fourth explanation is offered by Polyani, who stresses the effects of long-distance trade on state formation.

- None of these explanations can explain every case of state formation.

- To prevent, contain, or resolve conflicts, societies have ways, orderly or otherwise, of encouraging and enforcing conformity with norms and laws, and discouraging and sometimes punishing nonconformity.

- Orderly methods of social control include dispute-resolving councils and committees; sanctions, either positive or negative, diffused or organized; courts; and divination.

- Disorderly methods of social control include feuds and wars: world wars, regional wars, and smaller-scale, intraregional conflicts.

- Some anthropologists claim that warfare is motivated by people's responses to environmental, economic, or cultural forces; others emphasize war's function as a cohesive mechanism; still others explain war in terms of the universal human desire for power, prestige, material wealth, or revenge.

Key Terms

achieved authority
adjudication
ascribed authority
authority
big man
charisma
chiefdom
committee
conditional curse
council
court
diffused sanction
divination
diviner
faction
feud
government

hydraulic society
law
mediator
norm
office
organized sanction
Oriental Despotism
ostracism
political organization (political system)
politics
power
sanction
state
trial by ordeal
tribe

Suggested Readings

Bailey, F. G. 1991. *The Prevalence of Deceit.* Ithaca, NY: Cornell University Press. A study of how truth can be relative in political contexts, and how power can depend on the ability of politicians to deceive their supporters. This well-written book illuminates the tactics and antics of those who would rule us.

Chagnon, Napoleon. 1992. *Yanomamo* (4th ed.). New York: Harcourt Brace Jovanovich. A graphic account of the causes and consequences of warfare among South American forest dwellers.

Conley, John M., and William M. O'Barr. 1990. *Rules Versus Relationships: The Ethnography of Legal Discourse.* Chicago: University of Chicago Press. This book deals with law in the American legal system, and contains a wealth of information on how the law actually works at the grassroots level.

Gledhill, John, Barbara Bender, and Mogens Trolle Larsen (eds.). 1988. *State and Society.* London: Unwin Hyman. Scholars from different disciplines examine social hierarchies and political centralization in case studies that include chiefdoms and states. West Africa, Hawaii, the Valley of Mexico, and ancient Egypt are a few of the examples given.

Roberts, Simon. 1979. *Order and Dispute: An Introduction to Legal Anthropology.* New York: St. Martin's Press. A useful introduction to basic topics in the anthropology of social control. Examples include gatherer-and-hunter and pastoralist societies as well as states.

Starr, June, and Jane F. Collier (eds.). 1989. *History and Power in the Study of Law: New Directions in Legal Anthropology.* Ithaca: Cornell University Press. A collection of case studies on topics ranging from the invention of legal ideas to the language of public executions in Norway to constitution making in Islamic Iran to the American love of litigation.

Introduction

Be it enacted by the General Assembly of the State of Tennessee, that it shall be unlawful for any teacher in any of the universities, normals and all other public

schools of the State . . . to teach any theory that denies the story of the divine creation of man as taught in the Bible, and to teach instead that man has descended from a lower order of animals. (Quoted in Weinberg 1957:174–175)

People who believe that their religion's doctrines are all literally true are called *fundamentalists*. In 1925, Christian fundamentalists cheered when Tennessee passed a law requiring public schools to teach students, as truth, the account of the creation of human beings as presented in the Bible. They regarded the alternative theory—that human beings did not suddenly appear on earth in modern form but had evolved from earlier, apelike creatures—as antireligion, despite the fact that the theory of evolution was supported by a growing body of fossil evidence. In their successful efforts to incorporate their views into state law, they had been assisted by a famous politician and orator, William Jennings Bryan, himself an archfundamentalist.

Dismayed by Tennessee's new law, a 24-year-old evolutionist and high school biology teacher, John T. Scopes, together with some friends, hatched a plot to test its legality. Their plan called for Scopes to defy the law by teaching evolution openly in his Dayton, Tennessee, classroom. Scopes was promptly reported to the local authorities, arrested, and brought to trial.

The prosecution was spearheaded by fundamentalist Bryan himself. Opposing him and leading Scopes's defense was a renowned trial lawyer, Clarence Darrow. The jury chosen to sit in judgment on Scopes consisted of 12 males, 11 of whom were Christians and regular church-goers (6 Baptists, 4 Methodists, and a member of the Disciples of Christ). Judge John T. Raulston presided.

Darrow opened the proceedings by roundly challenging the new law. He then asked the court's permission to put scientists who specialized in evolution on the witness stand, but Judge Raulston refused to allow such testimony. So, in a surprise countermove, Darrow requested permission to put an expert on the Bible on the stand—none other than Bryan, the prosecution's own attorney. The subsequent interchange between Darrow and Bryan provided an instructive, if at times irreverent, illustration of the impact of strong religious belief on people's ideas, emotions, and behavior (Weinberg 1957:209–227).

Darrow: Did you ever read a book on primitive man? Like Tylor's *Primitive Culture*, or Boas, or any of the great authorities?

Bryan: I don't think I ever read the ones you have mentioned.

Darrow: Have you read any?

Bryan: Well, I have read a little from time to time. But I didn't pursue it, because I didn't know I was to be called as a witness.

Darrow: You have never in all your life made any attempt to find out about the other peoples of the earth—how old their civilizations are—how long they had existed on the earth, have you?

Bryan: No, sir; I have been so well satisfied with the Christian religion that I have spent no time trying to find arguments against it.

DARROW: Were you afraid you might find some?. . .

BRYAN: Your honor, I think I can shorten this testimony. The only purpose Mr. Darrow has is to slur at the Bible. . . .

DARROW: I object to that.

BRYAN: (continuing) . . . to slur at it, and while it will require time, I am willing to take it.

DARROW (angrily): I object . . . I am examining you on your fool ideas that no intelligent Christian on earth believes. (A few cheers; prolonged boos.)

The beliefs and opinions expressed so vehemently at the Scopes trial were significant not only to those present in Dayton in the hot summer of 1925, but to all Americans, because religion is embedded in the very fabric of every society. The Scopes trial provides this chapter with its theme: that religious belief, behavior, and emotion are social as well as individual phenomena. In fact, in most technologically simpler societies, religion permeates every aspect of social life, from marriage to politics to trade, and actually helps to maintain the social order.

In a 1925 legal test of the Tennessee law that schoolchildren be taught the Bible's version of the Creation, defense attorney Clarence Darrow, in a court session held outdoors due to hot weather, mercilessly grilled prosecuting attorney and Bible expert William Jennings Bryan on the witness stand. Bryan's Christian fundamentalism did his cause no good.

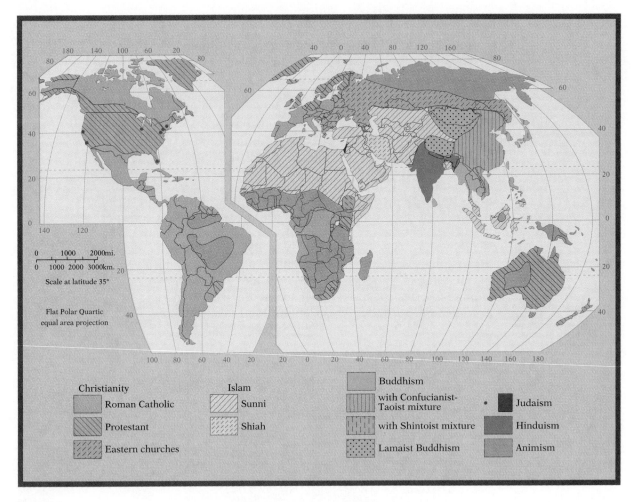

Figure 13.1

Distribution of the World's Major Religions. Source: Jordan et al. 1994: 214.

• Elements of Religion •

"Religion is the belief in Spiritual Beings" (Tylor 1873:424). This was one of the first definitions of religion, and its simplicity, along with its emphasis on belief, has made it a long-time favorite with anthropologists. Around the world, people who share a religion also share certain beliefs about spiritual beings, the origins of human beings, the meaning of life and death, and what happens to people after they die.

The religious beliefs of some major (or world) religions, such as Hinduism, Islam, Judaism, and Christianity (see Figure 13.1), are organized into consistent doctrines, but this is not true of all reli-

gions. Ethnographers sometimes report asking questions about religion in small-scale societies and finding that no one seems able to put the ideas current in the society together into any coherent format. Perhaps even more frustrating for the Westerner is the tendency for informants to contradict one another, and sometimes even themselves, when attempting to describe the attributes of the spirits they believe in, the nature of life after death, or the origin of the world.

The traditional beliefs of some Native Americans demonstrate this kind of flexibility. The Crow religion (see map on page 228), for instance, imposes no concrete doctrines, does not mandate any generally accepted rules of conduct, and does not oblige

Table 13.1
Some Approaches to Understanding Religion

Approach	Some Leading Advocates
Intellectual	Edward Tylor, James George Frazer
Emotional	Robert Lowie, Bronislaw Malinowski, Sigmund Freud
Sociological	Emile Durkheim, A. R. Radcliffe-Brown

its followers to accept a fixed set of beliefs about the nature of the universe (Lowie 1970:30). No Crow individual would be denounced as a heretic because he or she rejected the current theory of creation, and in the absence of an official dogma on the subject there is nothing to prevent a variety of versions.

Whether religious beliefs are organized into a set of doctrines or are only loosely formulated, they are often associated with a code of moral behavior. For example, the Koran, the sacred book of Islam, contains many beliefs that taken together give the followers of Islam a guide for living a morally good life.

Religious beliefs are also associated with **rituals:** behaviors that use symbols to communicate meaning in repetitive, stereotypical ways. Not all rituals are religious; kneeling in a mosque (a religious act) and nodding one's head to signify agreement (a non-religious act) are both rituals. Some rituals are very simple, consisting of a single symbolic act (kneeling and nodding are examples); others are complex, consisting of a combination of symbols of many kinds (including actions, words, sounds, colors, and even scents) that have some special meaning and are repeated at specific times. A religious wedding is an example of a ritual in this broader sense.

Religious beliefs are frequently associated with **myths,** timeless stories that describe the origin of something—the world, a natural phenomenon, or

---

ritual stereotyped, repetitive behavior, either religious or nonreligious, that uses symbols to communicate meaning

myth a story describing the origins of the world, some natural phenomenon, or some aspect of culture, which contains at least one physically or humanly impossible event or situation

some aspect of culture such as a particular custom or idea—and "confront us with at least one event or situation which is physically or humanly impossible" (Needham 1978:59). Some rituals are the dramatic reenactment of myths. Among the Tetum (see map on page 139), the ritual performed at the birth of a child reenacts the birth of the first Tetum people from the "womb" of the earth goddess.

Anthropologists interested in religion (see Table 13.1) have noted that it has the capacity to inspire awe, fear, love, hatred, ecstasy, and other emotions among its followers. Basing his definition of religion on fieldwork among the Crow, Robert Lowie (1970:xvi) emphasized its emotional content, defining religion as a "sense of the Extraordinary, Mysterious, or Supernatural." Victor Turner (1967) also stressed the importance of emotion—specifically, the emotional impact of symbols, such as the milk tree—on believers (see Chapter 2, Figure 2.1). But other aspects of life also stir up emotions—politics, works of art, love—so religion cannot be defined solely in emotional terms.

Emile Durkheim (1965), in seeking to define religion, first drew attention to the importance of the distinction between the terms *sacred* and *profane*. *Sacred,* he said, defined things set apart from ordinary life; *profane* described ordinary, secular things. This distinction made, Durkheim went on to define religion as "a unified system of beliefs and practices relative to sacred things . . . which unite into one single moral community, called a Church, all those who [follow] them" (62). The definition highlighted Durkheim's belief that religion is communal in nature; members of a society acquire their religious beliefs, rituals, and even to some extent their emotional reactions to these as a result of enculturation. Because religious ideas express the very

On the island of Flores in eastern Indonesia, men from different villages slash at each other with buffalo-hide whips in a ritual performed so that local spirits will make crops fertile. If blood is drawn, villagers believe a good rice harvest will follow.

nature of the society in which they are embedded, they are necessarily valid for their particular societies. In tacit acknowledgment of the important anthropological concept of cultural relativism, Durkheim wrote, "There are no religions which are false. All are true in their own fashion; all answer, though in different ways, to the given conditions of human existence" (15).

Since religion is a social phenomenon, the values, ideas, and patterns of behavior evident in other areas of a society's culture appear also in its religion. For example, the pastoralist Nuer of Africa (see map on page 217) are divided into clans, which are in turn divided into lineages. These lineages are divided into smaller units, which themselves are divided into even smaller subunits. At the bottom of

• Ask Yourself •

Do you think of yourself as religious? If so, do you practice your religion? How? In a world where there are so many religions, can we ever be sure which is the "true" one? Do you think it matters whether your own religion, if you practice one, is "true" or "false"?

this complicated social hierarchy is the individual. Not surprisingly, Nuer ideas about spirits correspond exactly to this social structure (Evans-Pritchard 1974:117–119). The tribe, the largest social unit, is identified with the supreme Nuer god. Descending through the structural hierarchy, each Nuer clan has its own major spirit, inferior to this supreme god; each lineage has its own spirit, inferior to the clan spirit; and so on. Finally, each Nuer individual has a spirit, or soul, which occupies the lowest ranking in the hierarchy of spirits.

Durkheim went further with the notion that religion reflects other aspects of culture. He asserted that in effect, society is a god because it possesses godlike properties: it has absolute power over its members, gives them a feeling of perpetual dependence, and is the object of great respect. Religious beliefs, Durkheim concluded, are actually the ideas by which believers explain the nature of their society.

The Bible, the Western world's major religious text, illustrates Durkheim's hypothesis that religion draws its ideas and images from the larger fund of ideas and images current in society. In societies where males tend to be dominant over females, politically and economically, gods are generally represented as male, and traditional Western society is no exception. The Bible incorporates and reflects Christians' and Jews' notions about gender, and affirms the traditional dominance of the male sex in their cultures. The Biblical god is definitely male.

Western society is more gender-sensitive today than it was in the past, so it was perhaps inevitable that attempts would be made to bring the Bible into line with modern attitudes about gender (Austin 1983). One such effort yielded a revised translation of Bible readings commissioned in 1983 by the United States National Council of Churches. In it, God is referred to as both the "father" and "mother" of "humankind," which seems quite logical to those who view God as sexually neutral. What is surprising, however, is that Jesus—who in the New Testament is indisputably a man—is also sexually

neutral. An earlier version of the gospel of John, for instance, contains this passage: "For God so loved the world that He gave His only Son, that whoever believes in Him should not perish, but have eternal life." The sexually neutered version reads, "For God so loved the world that God gave God's only Child, that whoever believes in that Child should not perish, but have eternal life." When criticized for this awkward language, which blatantly obliterates the sex of a historical figure, the translators defended themselves by pointing out that they resorted to sexual neutralization only in those passages that refer to Jesus as the messiah. When Jesus is referred to as a historical person, masculine pronouns are maintained.

• Origins of Religion •

Archaeological Clues

It is not known how religion first began, although archaeology provides some clues about when. Some archaeologists interpret materials found at sites dating as far back as 70,000 years ago as evidence of religious belief. Later, some 30,000 years ago, the Upper Palaeolithic Cro-Magnon people of western Europe (see Figure 14.1, page 348) seem to have been expressing religious feelings when they carved and painted bones, stones, and the walls of caves. The survival of these gatherers and hunters required that females reproduce abundantly and that hunting be successful. Both fertility and successful hunting are prominent themes in Cro-Magnon art. Statuettes called "Venus figurines" represent women with pregnant bellies and huge breasts; cave paintings include apparently pregnant animals and others with spears lodged in their bodies. Perhaps the hunters believed they could influence events by creating the image of a pregnant woman or animal or by portraying the killing of an animal, thus prompting life to imitate art. This requires a belief in agencies beyond the merely human.

Psychological Hypotheses

Beyond these archaeological clues to the origins of religion, scholars have proposed various psychological hypotheses to explain how religion began. In the nineteenth century, Edward Tylor (1873) noticed that a belief in unseen beings was a common feature of religions. Perhaps, he suggested, this belief arose in prehistoric times because people

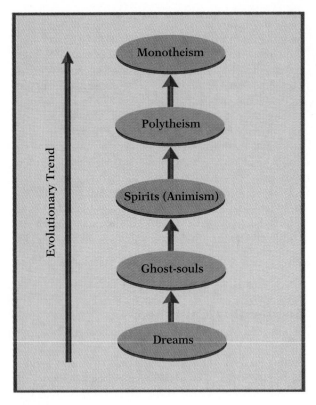

Figure 13.2
Edward Tylor's Ghost-soul Hypothesis.

known to have died are often encountered in dreams. The ancestors of modern human beings, according to Tylor, reasoned that there must be some part of them that exists outside of their visible, tangible bodies and continues to live after the death of the body. If people had such "ghost-souls," perhaps trees or bodies of water or even the stars had them too. Early ideas about these nonphysical manifestations of physical entities evolved with the passage of time, in Tylor's view, into beliefs in nonphysical beings—spirits—that could exist quite independently of physical entities (see Figure 13.2).

Tylor gave the name **animism** to the belief that invisible beings inhabit the bodies of animals, plants, and inanimate objects. Animism was, he

animism the belief that souls or spirits inhabit animals, plants, or inanimate objects

polytheism the belief in the existence of many gods

monotheism the belief that there is only one god

claimed, the first religion. To win favors from ghost-souls or spirits, people began offering sacrifices to them, and thus were religious rituals born. As time passed, people conjured up increasingly powerful spirits, and **polytheism**—the belief in the existence of many gods—evolved. Polytheism in turn evolved into **monotheism,** the belief that there is only one god. For Tylor, the modern notion of God was an extension of notions of ghost-souls and spirits.

Monotheism, of course, characterized the religion of Tylor's own society, Christianity. Tylor's view that monotheism was the result of a long evolutionary process was typical of many nineteenth-century anthropologists. It was ethnocentric since it implied that monotheism is somehow the logical end product of a process in which simpler beliefs were gradually replaced by more complex ones. Actually, there is no reason to think that monotheism is a more developed or more complex form of religion than beliefs in ghost-souls, spirits, or multiple gods.

Another possible origin for religion has already been suggested: the human desire for control over events in a world where things often seem to occur randomly. The Cro-Magnon cave dwellers may have been expressing this need when they painted their pictures of speared game animals. Similarly, someone who places a crucifix on the dashboard of a car believes, somewhere deep inside, that the crucifix can have some beneficial effect on what happens to the car and its occupants.

Yet another explanation for how religion may have begun stresses the emotions. Sigmund Freud proposed that a common human emotion, guilt, was the wellspring of religion. To illustrate the point, he relied on a variation of the Oedipus myth (see the discussion of incest in Chapter 10). Freud conjured up a scenario that he thought might have taken place in primeval times, when the predecessors of modern human beings supposedly lived in a group led by an elder male, who kept all the females in the group for his own pleasure. Eventually this man's frustrated sons revolted, killing him and eating his body in a cannibalistic orgy. Later, overcome by pangs of guilt, the sons elevated their slain father to the status of a hero. In the fullness of time, the dead elder's status was raised still higher, until he eventually became a god.

This tale suggests today's Christian eucharist or mass, a ritual in which a priest or minister and congregation commemorate the death of Jesus and then symbolically consume his flesh and blood. The parallel between Freud's story and this symbolic behavior is striking; but whether or not Freud was influenced by Christianity, he got his anthropology all wrong. No evidence exists to suggest that any religion originated in this way, but Freud's stress on the emotional component of religion is consistent with that of certain anthropologists, such as Robert Lowie, for whom the essence of religion was a feeling of high emotion.

Another psychological explanation for the existence of religion lies in human beings' need to understand how and why things happen. Inexplicable things disturb us, and religion helps us to make sense of them. The need for understanding has by no means been eclipsed by the scientific discoveries of recent decades; although we now understand how the earth revolves around the sun, how diseases are transmitted, and how babies are conceived, mysteries concerning the human condition still exist, and we are still trying to understand them. A parent devastated by a child's death may be comforted by believing that the death was somehow a part of God's plan.

An example of human beings' "need to know" comes from the island of Java, in Indonesia (see map on page 120). While the anthropologist Clifford Geertz (1966:16) was doing fieldwork in a Javanese village, a large toadstool of peculiar shape sprouted from the ground in a remarkably short time. So unusual was this phenomenon that people came from miles around to marvel at its strange and sudden appearance. Their fascination did not lie in the importance of toadstools in Javanese culture, for toadstools have no special significance in Java. Its odd shape and speedy growth were solely responsible for all the clamor it caused. The toadstool failed to fit into the usual Javanese categories for ordering things, thus challenging the islanders' ability to understand their world and raising the disagreeable possibility that their beliefs about nature were somehow inadequate.

So the villagers felt compelled to come up with some explanation. Several could have been proposed—that the toadstool was a fake, that it had been transplanted from somewhere else, that it was the result of unusually heavy rain. Rather than select a "scientific" explanation, however, the villagers settled on a religious one: they decided that the toadstool had been created by spirits. Although

Religion may be a response to our desire for control in a world where events often seem to happen randomly. On the dashboard of his car, a devout Hindu places marigold petals and incense before pictures of two Hindu gods in the belief that the gods, thus honored, will protect both car and driver.

Revitalization movements, typically under the leadership of charismatic figures, tend to emerge when people are socially and economically deprived. One such movement ended in tragedy in 1978, when members of the People's Temple in Jonestown, Guyana, followed their charismatic leader, Jim Jones, to death by suicide.

• Ask Yourself •

Do you wear a religious symbol or carry a lucky charm? Do you ever knock on wood, hold your breath when passing a cemetery, or avoid walking under a ladder? Why or why not?

based on faith rather than evidence, their explanation gave them comfort and satisfaction.

Ethnographic Evidence

Anthropologists may not know how the first religions originated, but ethnographic data show how

revitalization movement a popular movement for radical change, led by a charismatic figure and usually prompted by social, economic, or political upheaval

religions have evolved in more recent times. Over the last several centuries, many small-scale societies have undergone social, economic, and political upheavals, often as a result of contact with other cultures. Under these circumstances, new religious beliefs and practices, or variations on old ones, have sometimes emerged (Wallace 1985). These **revitalization movements** often take the form of popular movements for radical social change. They have political in addition to religious implications, and are often inspired by charismatic figures of the kind discussed in a political context in Chapter 12.

The "Handsome Lake" religion of the Iroquois of upper New York State (see map on page 229) is a telling example (Kehoe 1989:113–127). During the Revolutionary War, the Iroquois had supported the British, and after the American victory they had been dispersed in reservations as white settlers took over their lands. By about 1800, the Iroquois

In Melanesia, followers of millenarian movements called cargo cults believe that certain ritual acts will ensure the eventual arrival of longed-for Western goods. On the island of Tanna, cargo cult members drill with bamboo "rifles" in preparation for the day when their cargo will arrive.

were suffering under wretched social and economic conditions, and alcoholism was taking a heavy toll. In this context, Handsome Lake, an Iroquois chief, claimed to have experienced visions in which spirits warned him that the Iroquois would be destroyed unless they changed their

millenarian movement a response made by a deprived community, characterized by anticipating a time when its hopes will be fulfilled

cargo cult a popular movement for social change in Melanesia, whose followers believe that certain rituals will bring ships loaded with valuable cargo

ways. Forcefully preaching this message to his people, the charismatic Handsome Lake succeeded not only in initiating radical economic changes—traditional Iroquois farming methods were replaced by European methods, for example—but also in founding a new religion based on traditional Iroquois beliefs and rituals.

One well-known kind of revitalization movement is the **millenarian movement,** a response made by a community to a situation of deprivation. The society's members anticipate and prepare for a coming period in which their hearts' desires will be fulfilled. Such movements have sprung up from time to time in Melanesia, where they are called **cargo cults.** The first one seems to have developed among troubled tribespeople in eastern New Guinea (see maps on pages 166, 198, and 385), where early in the twentieth century a charismatic visionary convinced his followers that the spirits of their dead ancestors would soon return to them in ships loaded with valuable cargo, and would eradicate the European invaders. In later years, Melanesians came to believe that certain rituals would make weapons, cars, food, and other Western goods—similar to those which they had seen in the possession of American troops during World War II—appear as ships' cargo.

Revitalization movements—even those attended by some success, such as the Handsome Lake religion—are usually self-limiting because they are based on unrealistic expectations. When people realize that the new order they seek is not just around the corner, that their revered leader lacks the power to fulfill his claims, and that the cargo will never arrive, the movement collapses.

• Ask Yourself •

What parallels can be drawn between the revitalization movements described above and fundamentalist Christian sects in the United States, whose leaders exhort us on television to behave in certain ways in order to be saved? Would you call David Koresh's Branch Davidian cult a revitalization movement?

• Religious Practitioners and • Their Social Contexts

Most religions have someone to lead, guide, inspire, or interpret religious beliefs and expressions for others. The role of the religious specialist varies among religions, but three categories of religious specialist are especially noteworthy because of the important roles they play in their societies: shamans, prophets, and priests.

Shamans

The term **shaman,** borrowed from the vocabulary of a Siberian group, the Evenks (see map on page 135), can be translated as "one who is excited or moved." Shamans (also popularly known, especially in the movies, as "medicine men" or "witch doctors") are powerful, charismatic, religious figures, who are believed to have been chosen by the spirits to function as intermediaries between the world of spirits and human beings (Lewis 1986:88–92). Shamans may be men or women; in some societies, they are transvestites. Cross-culturally, most appear able to hallucinate or to enter trances, sometimes with the use of drugs and sometimes as a result of natural ability. They may enter trance states in order to be "possessed" by spirits whom they have invited into their bodies, or to "leave" their bodies to visit spirits in the next world. Usually, before a shaman can practice "controlled" spirit possession, he or she must suffer the "uncontrolled" invasions of such beings. This traumatic experience, so overwhelming that a shaman who has successfully endured it is sometimes said to have died and been reborn, qualifies the shaman to cure others of physical or mental illness.

Trickery may also be one of the talents of a successful "master of the spirits." Like professional magicians in Western society, some shamans are ventriloquists; others practice sleight of hand. In many societies, shamans are called on to perform the "sucking cure," in which they claim to suck evil out of the body of someone who is ill. In reality, the evil that is sucked out may be something like a splinter of wood that the shaman has tucked into his cheek before beginning the cure.

Successful shamanism involves the shrewd manipulation of both information and props. However uncontrolled shamanistic behavior might seem at times, shamans must keep their wits about them to convince their clients that they know what they are doing. The strangeness of shamans' behavior has encouraged some anthropologists to suggest that shamanism functions as a socially acceptable way for mentally ill people to resolve their problems, either by tuning out or acting out. In reality, however, people who are mentally ill lack the self-control to be good shamans.

---

shaman a religious figure, believed to be chosen by spirits, who functions as an intermediary between the world of spirits and human beings

Shamans, charismatic religious figures believed to be chosen by spirits, serve as intermediaries between the spirit world and the world of the living. During a shamanistic performance in Korea, a female shaman shows by entering a trance that she has been possessed by a spirit.

Prophets

We have seen that when a society undergoes rapid social change its religion is likely to be affected. At such times, people may feel disillusioned, disenchanted, or dissatisfied, and their conservative, established religion may be incapable of changing to accommodate their new needs. Under these circumstances, which may be associated with revitalization, a **prophet**—a charismatic leader, usually male, who offers solutions in times of extreme social unrest—may emerge. A prophet is typically a person who has undergone some intense spiritual experience: perhaps a spirit has shown him new truths and new ways of behaving, or urged him to return to traditional ways. As a result of this experience, the prophet usually feels he has a mission to fulfill among his fellows, and if he is convincing he may develop a following. In this way, prophets sometimes bring new religions into being.

---

prophet a charismatic leader who emerges after some intense spiritual experience

The charismatic prophets who emerged among the Native Americans of the Great Plains during the last decades of the nineteenth century are illustrative. At the time, Plains groups were undergoing considerable cultural deprivation. Their vast bison herds had been all but wiped out, and their crops had repeatedly failed. White people had seized their land and herded them onto reservations. Alcoholism, measles, and whooping cough, introduced by the whites, had killed thousands. The relentless westbound expansion of white pioneers had left massacres and broken peace treaties in its wake, and Native Americans were growing increasingly frustrated and desperate.

In this context, a series of charismatic Native American prophets emerged, predicting that—if people would only follow them—the whites would be wiped out, the bison would return, Native American lands would be recovered, sickness and death would disappear, dead kinsmen would be restored to life, and everlasting prosperity and happiness would reign (Kehoe 1989). All that was needed to bring about the millennium was that people have faith, pray, and repeatedly perform a ritual

Ghost dancing among the Sioux led to heightened tensions between these Native Americans and U.S. military authorities charged with keeping the peace, and eventually to the massacre of the Sioux in 1890 by U.S. Army troops at Wounded Knee, South Dakota. Above, Sioux victims of this massacre are buried in a mass grave.

called the Ghost Dance, a performance in which ancestral ghosts were thought to take part.[1] Since such promises offered the Native Americans their only hope, ghost dancing was widely practiced, but to no avail.

The Jesus of the Christian religion, a man who broke away from religious orthodoxy during a time of social upheaval, is another example of a prophet. Jesus persuaded people to give up their ways of life and livelihoods and become his life-long disciples, in the process inspiring a religion that provided answers to many people's perplexities. After his death, the church he founded continued under the noncharismatic leadership of one of his followers, Peter, and eventually became an institution.

Priests

Unlike prophets, who emerge when the social order is changing rapidly, **priests** tend to have a well-established place in society. They are most often found in agricultural or technologically complex societies in which religion is practiced on a larger scale and more publicly than elsewhere.

Like the shaman or prophet, the priest is a religious specialist who mediates between human beings and spirits, but here the similarity ends. The priest does not become a religious figure by entering trances or attracting a devoted following in times of social stress, but rather by learning doctrines and rituals from other, older priests. Personality and personal experience are much less relevant for priests than they are for shamans and

---

[1] The Ghost Dance was widely performed by members of a number of different Plains ethnic groups. Because it was so widespread, the U.S. government viewed it as a potential threat to regional stability, and commissioned anthropologist James Mooney to study the institution—an early instance of applied anthropology (see Chapter 1).

priest a religious specialist whose authority comes from the office he or she occupies

prophets; instead, priests are officeholders whose authority is drawn from their official position.

• Religious Beliefs and • Rituals

Beliefs

Gods. Westerners are familiar with the concept of a supreme being who created the universe and everything in it. Not all societies conceive of such a god, and among those societies that do, a wide variety of attributes is associated with the god. This kind of god may be masculine or feminine, and may reign alone or share his or her power with other gods.

The idea of an all-powerful earth goddess or earth mother appears in the religious thought of the ancient Babylonians, Sumerians, Assyrians, and Greeks, to name only a few peoples with such beliefs. A modern-day example is found in the religion of the Tetum (see map on page 139), for whom the female earth goddess is contrasted with another, masculine, god who dwells in the sky. Humanity was created, say the Tetum, after the sky god had sex with the earth goddess. The sky god then retreated to his celestial home, and has since played no part in human affairs. The earth goddess, however, has been worshiped ever since the first human beings emerged from holes in the ground (the goddess's body). The spirits and demons that occasionally haunt people's lives are thought of as being different forms of this goddess.

Other Supernaturals. In many religions there is a supernatural world inhabited by the souls of the dead, souls that have become transformed by time into ancestral ghosts, demons, and nature spirits.

• Ask Yourself •

In the popular book *The Exorcist*, later made into a movie, an evil spirit takes possession of a young girl. The spirit is eventually expelled by exorcism, a rarely performed ritual of the Catholic church. Do you believe people can be possessed by spirits? If so, can exorcism expel spirits?

In the belief system of the !Kung San (see map on page 162), for example, the universe is inhabited by a high god, a lesser god, and a host of minor animal spirits that bring good luck and misfortune, success and failure. The principal figures in this assemblage, though, are the souls of recently deceased !Kung, who not long ago were the parents, kin, and friends of the living (Lee 1984:103). Now they hover near villages, and when serious misfortune strikes, the !Kung believe that these souls have caused it.

Because ancestors are so important to members of patrisystems or matrisystems, a belief in ancestral ghosts often accompanies these systems. Typically, ancestral ghosts are active in the affairs of the living, and they may provide positive or negative sanctions. Among the Bara of southern Madagascar, for instance, ancestral ghosts and their living lineage agnates form a single religious congregation in which the living worship the dead (Huntington 1988:33). The ghosts control the behavior of their living agnates by threatening to inflict sickness if they disobey local laws. To avoid these sanctions, the living sacrifice cows as offerings to their dead agnates.

Life After Death. In most belief systems, some aspect of the deceased person—mind, soul, or even body—remains alive somewhere, but apart from this commonality, religious beliefs are extremely varied concerning life after death. The Shavante (see map on page 275), for instance, have invented

Anthropology and the Environment

The Water Temples of Bali

On the island of Bali in Indonesia, the major agricultural crop for the country's many subsistence farmers is rice. Grown in irrigated fields and, in the most productive areas of Bali, harvested twice a year, this crop demands constant attention, not only agriculturally—it must be carefully watered and fertilized—but, Balinese farmers believe, ritually as well (Lansing 1983; Hicks 1995).

The cycle of rice cultivation in Bali begins when flood gates on dams located along natural streams and artificial canals are raised, and water floods rice fields below. Bali's streams and canals interconnect with one another and then run down valleys and across rice fields for many miles, so the water they contain sometimes irrigates fields spread over hundreds of square miles. The irrigated fields remain under water for most of the growing period, the farmers gradually decreasing the level of the water until by harvest time the fields have become dry. After the harvest, the fields are allowed to remain dry, and wild grasses spring up. Later, the farmers plow these grasses into the soil, and a new growing cycle begins.

Rice can be planted in nearly any month of the year in Bali, and supplies of water are usually adequate to support two crops of rice per farmer per year—provided farmers cooperate in their use of water. If all of them planted and harvested their rice at the same time, there would not be enough water to go around. So groups of farmers stagger their rice cultivation according to an elaborate plan. At any given time, some fields are flooded and others are dry, which helps to ensure a constant and sufficient supply of water for all.

Water figures prominently in the Balinese religion, a form of Hinduism, as well as in agriculture. Distributed throughout the country are "water temples," holy places where spirits and human beings are believed to come together in a balance that is essential for life, prosperity, and fertility in agriculture. Here, holy water, sanctified by priests, is used to purify both human beings and rice crops. The network of water temples also plays a major role in the management of water supplies for agricultural purposes. From the level of the smallest neighborhood (where several farmers' fields stand adjacent to one anoth-

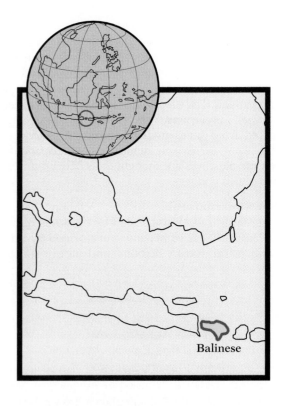

Balinese

On the island of Bali in Indonesia, water resources management combined with religious belief have produced this luxuriant rice crop, waiting to be dedicated to the goddess Dewi Sri before being harvested.

er) to districts (composed of several neighborhoods) to whole regions (composed of many districts), farmers are brought into one huge pan-Balinese system of water management through the rituals performed and the agricultural decisions made at the water temples.

The yearly allocation of water for rice irrigation begins at a pair of water temples located near the sacred Lake Batur. It is at these temples that the rice growing and water management schedules for the entire island are coordinated. Brahman priests from the two temples bless water drawn from the sacred lake, and together with regional leaders, decide on the schedule according to which water will be distributed across the entire island of Bali for the coming year.

The schedule is passed along to the priests of temples located at the headwaters of major valleys. Once a year these priests perform rituals commemorating their temples' foundings. Taking care to specify different times for each area, the priests decide when dur-

ing the forthcoming year temple rituals may be performed in the districts that lie below. Then, at the appointed time, the priests of the district temples sacrifice offerings—meat, drink, and flower petals—to the rice goddess, Dewi Sri, at the same time opening the floodgates under their temples' control. This system of scheduling continues down to the neighborhood level, where several farmers share a canal in common. This neighborhood group collectively plants, harvests, and offers sacrifices to Dewi Sri at tiny shrines located in the fields.

At each level, then—region, territory, and neighborhood—Balinese rice fields are flooded in a sequence that is fair and convenient to all. By using religious rituals to stagger the schedule of rice cultivation, the supply of water for irrigation is never exhausted by any one group. The water temple system demonstrates how religious beliefs can have a significant effect on the way human beings interact with and manage their natural environment.

a colorful afterworld, which souls of the dead reach only after a long and perilous journey as far to the east as it is possible to travel (Maybury-Lewis 1974:289). On its way, a soul is guided by ancestral ghosts who have gone before it and who attempt to protect it from danger, for should a person's soul be killed before reaching the community of the dead, it would be obliterated forever, and if it got lost, it might wander forever between the worlds of the living and the dead. Once in the world of the dead, though, the soul has entered a place of abundance, where life is easy and souls spend their time singing and dancing. The souls of evil people never reach this hoped-for village of the dead.

Rituals

Rituals, religious and nonreligious, are a universal feature of social life. North Americans engage in religious rituals to cleanse people of sin (such as confession in the Catholic church), secular rituals to bring people together (such as Thanksgiving dinner), political rituals to sway public opinion (such as baby-kissing by candidates), and many more. Other societies have curing rituals to restore health, agricultural rituals to make crops grow, fertility rituals to cause pregnancy, and death rituals to ensure the entry of the departed into the afterworld.

Several hypotheses have been suggested to explain why rituals are cultural universals. The functionalist Malinowski (1954) hypothesized that—faced with death or some other grave threat—people use rituals to control their anxiety. Individuals never possess every scrap of knowledge required to overcome life's challenges, Malinowski argued, and nonliterate people, especially, lack the technology needed to feel secure when faced with danger. Malinowski's Trobriand Islanders (see map on page 19), who made perilous sea voyages in open canoes, performed rituals before setting out as a way to reduce the tension between their feelings of helplessness and the safety they would like to secure. Performing rituals brought about the same feeling of security they would have achieved with a greater knowledge of weather forecasting or superior navigational techniques. Trobrianders did not perform rituals before sailing in safe lagoons.

Another explanation, offered by Rodney Needham (1985:177), is that human beings perform rituals simply because they are programmed by their very natures to do so. "Considered in its most characteristic features, [ritual] is a kind of activity—like speech or dancing—that man as a ceremonial animal happens naturally to perform."

Among the most common forms of religious ritual are sacrifices, rites of passage, and rituals of propitiation.

Sacrifices.   A **sacrifice** is an offering made to a spiritual being. The same term is also used for the sacrificial ritual itself. The person or group making the offering has some specific goal in mind, such as ensuring a productive agricultural season or appeasing the anger of an offended god. The most dramatic kind of sacrifice, of course, is the sacrifice of a human being. It would be difficult to find an American elementary school student who did not know that the Aztecs of preconquest Mexico (see map on page 301) made gruesome human sacrifices to their bloodthirsty gods, which were as likely to be carried out on the streets as in temples (Clendinnen 1991). Townspeople would deliver victims to the place of sacrifice, dispatch and then dismember them. Why this mass slaughter? Divine hunger may have been one reason. The Aztecs believed that humans had to pay debts, regularly and in human blood, to the earth, whose fruits they had enjoyed. Only sacrifice could fully extinguish these debts, by enabling the gods of the earth to feed on the bodies of human beings as human beings had fed on them (Clendinnen 1991:74–75). But whether it is a human life, a sum of money, or merely a small portion of food that is being offered, the give-and-take nature of a sacrifice bridges the gap between giver and receiver. The sacrifice creates a relationship, just as gift-giving establishes bonds of reciprocity (see Chapter 7). The individual making the sacrifice hopes that the spirit who receives it will feel obligated to help.

Rites of Passage.   Status is of great importance in most societies (see Chapter 11), and the transition of an individual from one social status to another is often marked by a special, usually public, ritual. Transitions of this kind are called **rites of passage** (see Figure 13.3). The movement of an individual

---

sacrifice an offering made to a spirit; the term also denotes the ritual itself

rite of passage a ritual performed at a period of transition in the life cycle

The Aztecs of preconquest Mexico sacrificed human beings to their gods. In a contemporary illustration, an Aztec priest, standing before a temple, cuts the heart from one victim while another lies at the foot of the temple steps.

• Ask Yourself •

What moral difference, if any, do you see between priests' ritual sacrifice of human beings to feed hungry gods and Serbs' slaughter of their Muslim neighbors in Bosnia to bring about "ethnic cleansing"?

from one age grade to another, like that of Shavante bachelors as they officially become young men (Chapter 11), is frequent cause for a rite of passage. The term was coined by the Belgian anthropologist Arnold Van Gennep (1961), who observed a remarkable similarity among such rituals, no matter where they occur.

Another common occasion for these rituals of transition is marriage, when individuals leave the unmarried state and enter the state of marriage. Such a move changes the place of both individuals in society; their rights and privileges, duties and responsibilities are dramatically altered. Society no longer grants them the right to date members of the opposite sex in public, for example, but now each enjoys the right of exclusive sexual access to the other. The role change is so important that many societies mark it with a public statement of the altered condition—a ritual during which

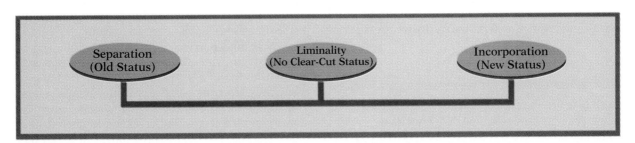

Figure 13.3
Three Stages in a Rite of Passage.

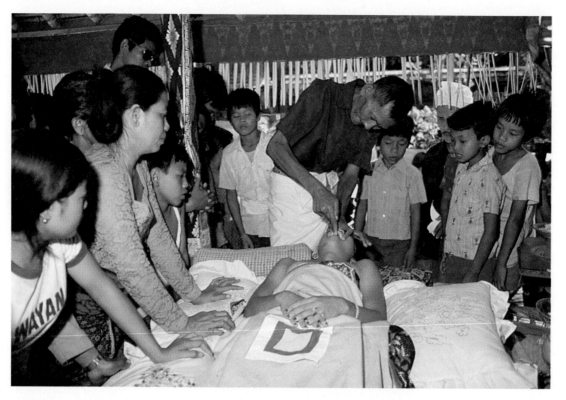

In all societies, birth, marriage, and death are recognized as important social transitions. Some societies also mark puberty with a ritual. Here, an adolescent in Bali (see map on page 332) undergoes a traditional tooth-filing ritual thought to enhance beauty and to prevent her from being denied entrance into the spirit world.

society can see the individuals involved as clearly removed from their prior positions and just as clearly repositioned in their new ones. The status of the kin surrounding the individual in transition may also change: when a man dies, his wife becomes a widow; when a woman dies, her husband becomes a widower; when both parents die, a child becomes an orphan.

Important social transitions for members of all societies occur at birth, puberty, marriage, and death, and van Gennep observed that the rites of

passage performed at these times have a distinctive structure. They consist of three separate stages: separation, liminality, and incorporation (Figure 13.3). By moving through each stage in order, an individual leaves his or her original status in society, is temporarily isolated from society in some way, and then enters his or her new status.

The **separation** stage of a rite of passage conveys the idea of severance from the old status. (In the traditional Western wedding, for example, the bride is symbolically separated from the rest of society behind her veil.) This stage is followed by **liminality,** in which individuals find themselves in a "neither here nor there" position, half way—physically, psychologically, or both—between their old status and the one they will soon occupy. (To continue with the wedding example: at the altar the bride is physically positioned between her father, representing the life she is about to leave,

separation first stage of a rite of passage, in which an individual is separated from an established status

liminality second stage of a rite of passage, in which an individual has no established status

and her husband-to-be, symbol of the new life she is about to enter.) The final stage, **incorporation,** often involves a meal or a dance in which the person for whom the ritual has been held rejoins society in a new role. (At a wedding, the joyful exit of the bride and groom, arm in arm, through a crowd of beaming family and friends symbolizes their reintegration, each in a new state, into society.)

The death ritual of the Tetum (see map on page 139) is a rite of passage like the Western wedding, and incorporates the same elements. When a Tetum man breathes his last, his hair is immediately cut, his nails are pared, and his clothing is stripped from his body—three acts that symbolize his separation from life. At the same time, hair and fingernails are clipped from his close kin, whom the Tetum call "the people of death" because of their close association with the deceased. These activities signify that the intimate ties between the dead man and his relatives are now severed. The corpse is then carried to a special "death house" on the edge of the hamlet, further symbolizing for the dead man's relatives and neighbors his separation from the everyday human world of Tetum society. The body lies in the death house for almost three days before being carried to the local cemetery. During this liminal period, the deceased is between the human world and the world of the dead, neither at home nor in his grave, neither alive among his relatives and neighbors nor buried in the ground among his ancestral ghosts. On the third day after death, the corpse is lowered into its grave, signifying the former villager's incorporation into the world of the dead. After the burial, the "people of death" share a meal with their village neighbors, an act that reintegrates the dead man's kin into Tetum society.

Rituals of Propitiation. A **ritual of propitiation** is intended to appease the spirits. Such a ritual is performed in the fall by the Inuit of Baffin Island (see map on page 17), when the goddess Sedna is believed ready to provide plenty of food if the community has observed her laws over the previous year (Hutchinson 1977). The Inuit gather around three shamans whose mission is to visit Sedna in her underwater home. Sending their souls into the underworld is considered the shamans' greatest feat. By this spiritual descent, they attempt to please their powerful goddess so they may live untroubled by famine, bad weather, and sickness. The shamans begin chanting, and soon their souls leave their bodies to descend to Sedna's house.

There they ask her if the forthcoming year will bring health and plenty of food. Sedna then rebukes them for disobeying her laws but assures them that if they mend their ways she will grant them their desires. The souls of the shamans then return home with the good news—but also with Sedna's admonishment that in the future they must observe the laws.

• Magic •

Religious rituals usually involve spiritual beings, and if some beneficial result is desired it is usually they, not the person performing the ritual, who are thought of as able to bring about this outcome. **Magic,** in contrast to religious ritual, is designed to bring about some desired practical result without the intervention of spirits. A magician attempts to take direct control over some part of nature or of other people. Magic may occur either in association with religion—sometimes the two even occur in the same ritual—or independently of it.

This distinction between magic and religion was made in 1890 by James Frazer (1966:55–59, 65–69), who considered magic to have more in common with science than with religion. Instead of relying on spirits to grant what people wish, Frazer wrote, the magician attempts, like the scientist, to manipulate the laws of nature to achieve the desired result. From the Western point of view, the difference is that the laws of nature on which the scientist bases his or her actions are valid, while those on which the magician's actions are based are not. However, from the point of view of those who believe in magic, the laws of nature and those governing magic rituals are equally valid.

The interconnections among magic, religion, and science so fascinated Frazer (1966) that—true

---

incorporation final stage of a rite of passage, in which an individual is integrated into a new status in society

ritual of propitiation a ritual intended to appease a spirit

magic a ritual intended to bring about some desired practical result without the intervention of spirits

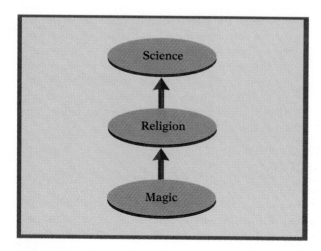

Figure 13.4

James George Frazer's Three Stages of Human Intellectual Development.

to the Victorian tradition of seeking origins within the philosophical framework of cultural evolution—he proposed a hypothesis to explain how the three were diachronically linked (see Figure 13.4). In their intellectual evolution, Frazer wrote, people first entered a stage of magic, seeking to manipulate objects and events without the help of spirits. When their efforts inevitably failed, they turned in hope to spirits to provide them with the things they desired, and the age of religion was born. Much later, skeptical individuals realized that religion could not provide all the answers they needed. Thus was born the age of science, in which Frazer saw himself and his fellow Victorians.

Frazer went on to distinguish between two types of magic (1966:12–14). To perform **imitative** (or homeopathic) **magic,** one imitates the desired

imitative magic a ritual that imitates the result desired

contagious magic magic based on the idea that even after they have been separated, things once in contact can influence each other

good magic magic performed to achieve ends that society considers beneficial

sorcery bad magic, performed to achieve ends society regards as evil

effect, and it happens. The Azande (see map on page 51) prick the stalks of bananas with the teeth of crocodiles, hoping that the fruits will be as abundant as crocodiles' teeth (Evans-Pritchard 1985:450). To perform **contagious magic,** one obtains some object that was once in contact with someone—perhaps a tooth or an article of clothing—and does something to it in the belief that this action will affect the person with whom the object was once in contact. Cross-culturally, it is common for the hair clippings or nail parings removed from an individual as part of the separation phase of a rite of passage to be carefully hidden lest some enemy get hold of them and burn them in a ritual of contagious magic designed to injure those from whom they were cut.

Good magic is carried out to achieve ends that society considers beneficial. A ritual to ensure safety at sea is good magic. "Bad magic," also called **sorcery,** is carried out to achieve ends that society regards as evil. A ritual to cause an innocent neighbor to sicken and die is an example of sorcery.

A belief in the efficacy of magic is found in many societies—and not just technologically simpler ones. Interestingly, it often seems to work. Sometimes this can be attributed to coincidence; one performs a magical ritual to restore one's sick mother to good health, and sure enough, she improves. Auto-suggestion, too, may be involved: a patient who believes he or she will be restored to good health often is.

To test Malinowski's hypothesis that people use magic in situations of uncertainty, George Gmelch (1985:231–235), an anthropologist and former professional baseball player, drew on his personal experiences of the game. Among baseball's three essential skills—pitching, hitting, and fielding—it is pitching that involves the greatest degree of uncertainty. "The pitcher," noted Gmelch, "is the player least able to control the outcome of his own efforts." His best pitch may be hit for a home run; his worst may be hit directly into a teammate's glove. It is not uncommon for a pitcher to perform well and lose or to perform badly and win. He is dependent on the proficiency of his teammates, the ineptness of the opposing team, "and the supernatural (luck)."

Gmelch (1985), observing baseball pitchers, discovered a whole series of rituals, taboos, and "sacred" objects that together form a complex of "pitcher" magic. Rituals include tugging one's cap between pitches, touching the rosin bag after each bad pitch, and smoothing the dirt on the field. "Many baseball fans have observed this behavior, never realizing that it may be as important to the pitcher as throwing the ball," wrote Gmelch. One common taboo involves the words "no-hitter." A pitcher who hears these words while a no-hitter is in progress believes that the no-hitter will be lost. Pitchers may also view articles of clothing as "sacred" objects. While playing for Spokane, pitcher Alan Foster forgot his baseball shoes on a road trip, and borrowed a pair from a teammate. That night he pitched a no-hitter. Later, he bought the shoes from his teammate, and they became his most prized possession.

With ethnographic data such as these, Gmelch demonstrated that Malinowski was correct. In baseball, magic is most prevalent in situations of chance and uncertainty. The uncertainty involved in pitching helps to explain the elaborate magical beliefs and rituals that accompany this activity, whereas fielders' high success rate in fielding, which involves much less chance, offers the best explanation for the absence of magic in this activity.

• Witchcraft •

Witchcraft, like magic, is a close relative of religion, especially the religions of technologically simpler societies. It is the belief that certain individuals, called witches, can injure others by psychic means. Everyone knows that evil exists, but it is a difficult concept to understand, especially when bad things happen to people who are "good" within the context of their societies. Personifying evil as a witch represents one common way of explaining the existence of evil in the world. Where witchcraft is believed to exist, misfortune occurs not because people deserve it, and not just randomly, but because witches cause it to happen. Edward Evans-Pritchard (1985:18), the ethnographer of the Azande (see map on page 51), described how pervasive witchcraft is in the daily lives of these people.

> If blight seizes the groundnut crop, it is witchcraft; if the bush is vainly scoured for game, it is witchcraft; if termites do not rise when their swarming is due, and a cold, useless night is spent in waiting for the flight, it is witchcraft; if a prince is cold and distant with his subjects, it is witchcraft; if a magic rite fails to achieve its purpose, it is witchcraft; if, in fact, any failure or

People who believe in witchcraft explain misfortune by saying witches cause it to happen. Among the Azande of central Africa, individuals who believe they have been attacked by witches sometimes consult a "witch doctor" to discover who is bewitching them.

> misfortune falls upon anyone at any time and in relation to any of the manifold activities of his life, it may be due to witchcraft.

Most Westerners' instinctive reaction to such explanations is to reject them as foolishness. But in both technologically simple societies and those familiar with modern science, there are times when no satisfying, empirically based explanation for an unfortunate event can be found, and the belief that witches cause misfortune is no more unreasonable than attributing it to "bad luck." An

---

witchcraft the belief that certain individuals, called witches, can injure others by psychic means

In both Western and non-Western societies in which people believe in witchcraft, witches are far more often female than male. Here, a "classic" European witch—an elderly female clad in a robe and pointed hat—flies through the air on a broomstick.

map on page 55), 13 were women. In fifteenth-century Essex, England, most witches were women (MacFarlane 1990:230). Historian H. C. Erik Midelfort (1972) discovered that in sixteenth- and seventeenth-century southwest Germany the overwhelming majority of accused witches were women. According to Malinowski (1954), most Trobriand witches were women, and the flying witches feared by all sailors were always female. While witches among the Azande and some other African societies are as likely to be male as female, many other African groups, such as the Nupe, Tallensi, Yoruba, and Luvale, heavily stress the feminine nature of witchcraft. Not to be outdone, the Balinese have created as one of their most profound terrors the great female witch Rangda.

Why should women be particularly associated with evil? In addressing this question, scholars have exploited several of the perspectives introduced in this book. Structural-functionalists, for example, point out that in most societies women, relative to men, are deprived of political and economic power. Attributing occult power to women "compensates" them for a lack of legitimate power.

One historian, seeking to account for the gender bias in witchcraft accusations in colonial New England, has taken a psychological approach (Demos 1983). He bases his argument on a study of infant development by Dorothy Dinnerstein (1990), who attempted to discover the origins of antifemale attitudes in Europe and North America. Dinnerstein begins by noting that no matter what its sex, an infant's first experiences are entirely of and with its mother. It is she who creates the baby's sense of security and provides milk, caresses, and soothing noises. Inevitably, however, she also withholds these delights. She can never gratify her infant's needs all the time, nor satisfy its every craving. In the developing mind of the infant, therefore, the mother becomes ambiguous, both loving and rejecting.

The developing infant also becomes aware that it is dependent on its mother for its very existence, and has no choice but to acknowledge her power over its life. At the same time, the infant finds it impossible to fully separate itself psychologically from its mother, or to place her into a neat pigeonhole in a system of personal classification. As the infant becomes a child, it projects its mother's "unclassifiability" onto all women. Eventually, both males and females invest the female sex with what Dinnerstein calls the "magically formidable" qualities of all mothers: ambiguity, power, malevolence,

Azande who trips over a stump and cuts his toe knows, just as anyone else would, that the wound was caused by the foot hitting the stump (Evans-Pritchard 1985). But why, they ask, did the man fail to spot the danger? They consider several possible reasons, such as carelessness, stupidity, a failure to observe the proper taboos, or a failure to pay sufficient attention to one's ancestors. But if these can be ruled out, the Azande believe the accident may have been caused by witchcraft. A Westerner in the same situation might fall back on bad luck.

Women are labeled witches far more often than men. This was as true in colonial America and historic Europe as it is in many parts of the non-Western world today. In 1692, of 19 witches hanged on Witches' Hill in Salem, Massachusetts (see

and mysteriousness—the exact attributes of the New England witch.

The New Englanders' disinclination to stereotype males as witches can also be explained by Dinnerstein's analysis. By the time an infant realizes the existence of what has up until then been a marginal figure, its father, it will have already passed the earlier critical stage of growing self-awareness and will have grown completely accustomed to itself as an independent being. Secure in this feeling, the infant can classify the second person in its young life as a being much like itself. The father figure is not perceived as at all ambiguous or mysterious, nor are there any unpleasant experiences to cast a shadow on him.

Structural anthropologists might seek a more global explanation for the association between women and witches. They might remind us that there is a worldwide mental association of femaleness with the negative (or evil) side of experience, and of maleness with the positive (or good) side. Witches are evil, and so are primarily identified with females. What of those few societies that regard males as equally likely, or even more likely, to be witches? In such societies, ecological or cultural or social factors might outweigh these universal mental associations.

Since the 1960s, North America and England have witnessed the emergence of a movement whose followers, although they sometimes call themselves witches, usually refer to themselves as neopagans. Neopagans see themselves not as practitioners of rituals designed to inflict harm on others but as revivers of pagan beliefs and practices from the time of the pre-Christian religion called **wicca** or, more recently, **neopaganism.** Feminism and harmony with nature are strong features of modern-day neopaganism, as is a desire to seek ways of curing sickness other than those offered within the context of the typical physician-patient relationship in contemporary Western medicine (Orion 1995).

Conclusion

Religion provides an order essential to both the individual and society, serves as an outlet for human emotions, acts as an agent of change, comforts people and brings them together socially, and satisfies the universal human need to explain the meaning of life and human misfortune.

• Ask Yourself •

Neopagans contend that Western women were traditionally attended by female midwives when they gave birth, until the male-dominated medical profession seized control of this crucial process and made it unnecessarily complicated and expensive. Do you think Americans give doctors too much control over their health care? Do you view the medical profession as male-dominated?

Perhaps the greatest of all human misfortunes is death. Men and women may avoid other trials—sickness, accidents, social failures—for a long time, hoping their run of luck continues unabated, but their intellects oblige them to accept the inevitability of death. They know for certain that whether death befalls tomorrow or in 60 years' time, it is an inevitable part of life, so it may be this certainty that prompts humanity's endless speculation about what, if anything, follows death.

Such universal interest suggests how earlier human beings might have come to imagine the existence of some kind of life after the death of the body, and why many contemporary people continue to believe in an afterlife. There is no evidence to suggest that modern-day people are ceasing to think about death and its possible aftermath, or that twentieth-century science is succeeding in explaining this mystery to their complete satisfaction. So human beings continue responding to what might almost be called a religious instinct. One way to interpret the universality of religion, therefore, is to view it as an attempt to deny the dismal possibility of our own permanent extinction.

Summary

- Religion may be defined as a belief in spiritual beings.

wicca a pre-Christian European religion

neopaganism a modern revival of a pre-Christian religion

- Religion involves beliefs, rituals, and emotions that often contribute to social coherence, especially in technologically simpler societies.

- The earliest indications of religious belief date to the Middle and Upper Palaeolithic periods.

- Tylor's hypothesis for how and why religion began is based on the notion of spirits encountered in dreams and trances.

- Freud's hypothesis is based on people's supposed guilty feelings and their consequent elevation of father figures to the status of gods.

- Durkheim's hypothesis stresses the nature of religion as a force for maintaining social order.

- Religious change in the form of revitalization movements of various kinds, such as cargo cults, seems to be a product of social, economic, and political upheaval.

- In most religions, specialists—shamans, prophets, and priests—lead, guide, inspire, or interpret religious belief.

- Shamans, most frequently found in small-scale societies, are thought to experience direct contact with spirits, often by entering trance states.

- Prophets—charismatic leaders who seem to have answers to people's problems—are apt to emerge when society is changing rapidly.

- Priests, in contrast to both shamans and prophets, are officeholders who depend not on personal charisma, talent, or social stress so much as on traditional doctrines and rituals taught to them by older priests.

- Religious beliefs include believing in gods, spirits, souls, and life after death.

- Religious beliefs may be justified in myths and expressed in a variety of rituals such as sacrifices, rites of passage, and rituals of propitiation.

- Magic is a ritual intended to bring about some desired practical result without the intervention of supernatural agents.

- Witchcraft provides a way of accounting for unfortunate happenings when other explanations fail.

- Women are labeled witches far more often than men, a phenomenon that may be examined from the structural-functionalist, psychological, and structuralist points of view.

- The relationship of gender to witchcraft is evident in the rise of neopaganism, which has a strong feminist component, in North America and Britain.

- It may be the certainty of death, and the horror of the idea of permanent extinction, that is responsible for the universality of religion.

Key Terms

animism
cargo cult
contagious magic
good magic
imitative magic
incorporation
liminality
magic
millenarian movement
monotheism
myth
neopaganism
polytheism
priest
prophet
revitalization movement
rite of passage
ritual
ritual of propitiation
sacrifice
separation
shaman
sorcery
wicca
witchcraft

Suggested Readings

Atkinson, Clarissa W., Constance H. Buchanan, and Margaret R. Miles (eds.). 1985. *Immaculate and Powerful: The Female in Sacred Image and Social Reality.* Boston: Beacon Press. Hinduism, Buddhism, and Catholicism are among the religions included in these 11 studies of how religious symbols represent women in different cultures.

Atkinson, Jane Monnig. 1992 (1989). *The Art and Politics of Wana Shamanship*. Berkeley: University of California Press. An ethnographic study of shamans in an eastern Indonesian society that treats the capacity of shamans to bring about cures, their role as mediators between the human and spirit worlds, and shamanistic ritual performances.

Bynum, Caroline Walker, Stevan Harrell, and Paula Richman. 1986. *Gender and Religion: On the Complexity of Symbols*. Boston: Beacon Press. A series of articles on how women use religious symbols differently from men in Buddhism and various other religions.

Lehman, Arthur C., and James E. Myers (eds.). 1989. *Magic, Witchcraft, and Religion: An Anthropological Study of the Supernatural* (2nd ed.). Mountain View, CA: Mayfield. Fifty articles covering a wide range of topics, including witchcraft, cargo cults, shamanism, ritual, and the Bible. Some contributions are classics in the field of religious anthropology; others, equally good, are less well known but deserve a careful reading.

Obeyesekere, Gananath. 1981. *Medusa's Hair: An Essay on Personal Symbols and Religious Experience*. Chicago: University of Chicago Press. This book contains a series of case studies based on interviews with religious practitioners in Sri Lanka, most of whom are women. Linking the ideas of Sigmund Freud and Max Weber, the author shows how symbols created by individuals are transformed into symbols accepted by communities. Emotion, belief, ritual, and society are brought into a single system.

Russell, Jeffrey B. 1980. *A History of Witchcraft: Sorcerers, Heretics, and Pagans*. London: Thames & Hudson. The most informative introduction yet to witchcraft. Russell surveys the gender bias against women in some detail.

Introduction

On the streets of the South Bronx in New York City, they were known as the Bombers. Depending on your point of view, they were either juvenile delinquents who

expressed their social rebelliousness by spray-painting graffiti on city subway cars and other public property, or gifted young artists stifled by an environment that failed to provide outlets for their creative urges. The Bombers' big, energetic, cartoon-like paintings—full of sweeping strokes, overlapping images, clashing colors, and personal names— expressed the young painters' confusion, anger, need for attention, and sense of alienation from their society.

Until recently, the Bombers were being accused (and frequently convicted) of vandalism. Now, thanks to a new city youth program, nine former graffiti painters have become legitimate artists, under a contract in which they have agreed not to deface property in exchange for free art supplies and work space. Trading their spray cans for paintbrushes and canvases has proven lucrative for several of the young artists, who have discovered that their subway-style graffiti has artistic merit, at least for some art lovers. At a recent exhibition, their works of art, which included traditional landscapes as well as pop-art style graffiti graphics, sold for as much as $200 each, and several of the artists have received commissions for future works (*New York Times* 1987b).

Few aspects of culture challenge the anthropologist's commitment to cultural relativism as much as the broad area of human endeavor popularly called *art*. One problem is that the Western way of conceptualizing topics distinguishes between art and non-art. Westerners often feel they can tell what is artistic and what is not, but in many other cultures there is no such rigid distinction, and Western ethnographers sometimes find themselves studying non-Western objects and behaviors that take them far beyond the realm of what they would ordinarily call art (Hardin 1988:36). One expert has gone so far as to argue that the category *art* does not exist outside of Western ideas (Anderson 1992).

Thus, it is difficult to propose a universally acceptable definition of art. Given that the category of objects and behaviors Westerners call art is itself an artifact of Western culture, we prefer to use the term *expressive culture* for the wide range of objects and behaviors discussed in this chapter. Where the term *art* appears, it is used to denote specific categories of expressive culture.

Expressive culture concerns aesthetics, a sense of what is beautiful (Coote and Shelton 1992). Aesthetic experience is highly subjective and individual, of course, but in addition, it reflects cultural values. Accordingly, we define **expressive culture** as the purposeful arrangement of forms, colors, sounds, language, and/or body movements in ways that have meaning and/or are aesthetically appealing not only to those who do the arranging but also, in most cases, to other members of their culture as well.

Various categories of expressive culture—painting, drawing, sculpture, music, literature, drama, or dance, to name only a few—play central roles in every human society. Although not every society exploits every category, the universality of expressive behavior suggests that the urge to produce meaningful or pleasing creations is innate. And while the creative impulse may initially be an individual matter, culture plays a crucial part in artistic creation by determining which artistic media and styles individuals in a particular society or ethnic group will adopt as their modes of artistic expression, and by suggesting what artistic themes will be pursued. As the Bombers' graffiti shows, expressive culture is often at one with the beliefs, ideas, institutions, and behaviors of the social groups in which it

---

expressive culture the purposeful arrangement of forms, colors, sounds, language, and/or body movements in ways that have meaning and/or are aesthetically appealing to those who do the arranging, and usually to others as well

is created—a culturally patterned reflection of society itself. This is what makes it so interesting to anthropologists.

These two observations—that human beings have a strong natural impulse to express themselves artistically, and that what they create is culturally patterned—provide this chapter with its main themes.

• Forms of Expressive Culture •

This chapter focuses on four of the many categories of expressive culture created by human beings: (1) the plastic and graphic arts, such as sculpture and painting; (2) language, in both its spoken and written forms, when used as an artistic medium; (3) music; and (4) dance, an art form that combines several artistic media.

The Plastic and Graphic Arts

Plastic art is three-dimensional art in which objects are created by modeling or molding a variety of materials, including wood, metal, clay, bone, ivory, and stone. Carving, sculpture, baskets, and pottery are all forms of plastic art. **Graphic art,** in contrast, is art that is rendered on a two-dimensional surface, whether that surface is paper, a piece of canvas stretched across a wooden frame, or the rough stone wall of a cave. Drawing, painting, and stone-incising are all forms of graphic art.

The Origins of Plastic and Graphic Art. No one knows who first had the idea of creating something that had no practical value (or at least was not created primarily for practical purposes) but was nevertheless worth the effort of its creation because it was aesthetically pleasing, meaningful, or both. Archaeologists have discovered, however, that by Upper Palaeolithic times, plastic and graphic art was an important aspect of human life and culture.

The earliest plastic and graphic art seems to have been created in western Europe (Figure 14.1),

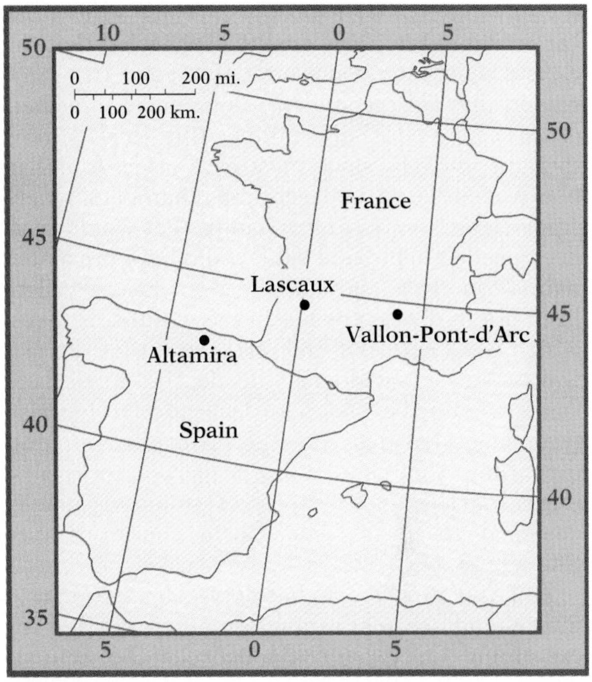

Figure 14.1

Three Great Cave Painting Sites in Europe: Altamira, Lascaux, and Vallon-Pont-d'Arc.

where as long as 30,000 years ago gatherers and hunters stroked colored pigments, obtained from rocks, on the walls of caves, using brushes made from grass or feathers. More rarely, these artists sculpted three-dimensional clay images. Their most common artistic theme was wild animals, which is hardly surprising since they lived in a wilderness in which human beings were far outnumbered by wild cattle and horses, reindeer, ibex, and mammoths. The first works of art often show great artistic sophistication and technical skill. Cave artists frequently made use of the natural unevenness of a rough cave wall to suggest the taut muscles of a charging bison or reindeer, and they understood the use of shading to suggest depth.

From an anthropological point of view, perhaps

---

plastic art sculpture and other three-dimensional forms of art

graphic art two-dimensional forms of art such as painting or drawing

• Ask Yourself •

Do you have a favorite way of expressing yourself through art?

the most interesting aspect of cave art is the motivation behind it. Early analysts suggested that the cave dwellers created works of art for the same reason that college students hang posters in their dorm rooms: for decoration. But this is now thought unlikely, since most cave art is found in poorly ventilated underground chambers where smoke from the fires or oil lamps that would have been needed to provide light would have prevented habitation. It is more likely that cave dwellers lived not in the depths but in the mouths of caves, which were better lit and airier, and that the artworks they created deep inside the earth held some meaning beyond mere decoration. It has also been suggested that some prehistoric cave paintings, those that show animals pierced by spears, might have been examples of imitative magic, designed to ensure success in the hunt (see Chapter 13, page 323).

One way in which archaeologists have sought to understand the motivation behind cave art is by examining the relationship between the animals drawn and the diets of the people who created the art (Rice and Paterson 1985). There is no simple correlation between the number of bones of particular animals found in Upper Palaeolithic sites and how frequently the same animals appear in artwork. In general, larger species, such as wild cattle, are overportrayed relative to the number of their bones found, and smaller ones, such as deer, are underportrayed. This suggests that the cave artists portrayed either the animals they preferred (presumably the meatier species) or the ones they most feared. To test this hypothesis, archaeologists identified the meatiest species by studying average animal weights, and the most fearsome by rating each animal on the amount of danger involved in hunting it. They discovered that *both* the meatier and the more dangerous species were consistently overportrayed in cave art, relative to the number of bones found. It is clear that "the art is related to the importance of hunting" for the cave artists (Rice and Paterson 1985:98).

Similarities in Plastic and Graphic Folk Art. **Folk art,** the art produced by traditional societies, is often termed *primitive*, not because it is necessarily simple, either in conception or execution, but

folk art the art produced by traditional societies

• Ask Yourself •

Can you think of examples of purposeful, as opposed to merely decorative, graphic or plastic art in Western society?

because it is produced in a technologically simple context. Both the ideas expressed and the techniques used in folk art may be highly sophisticated. Although these ideas and techniques vary through time and from culture to culture, the art of small-scale, traditional societies, especially those little affected by Westernization, is apt to share certain similarities. For example, the pottery of America's prehistoric Pueblo people, with its striking black-and-white painted geometric decoration, is almost indistinguishable from the pottery made in the ancient town of Shahr-i Sokhta in Iran (see Figure 14.2), yet these two cultures were located on different sides of the globe and were separated from each other by 3000 years.

Scholars interested in the anthropology of art have often asked why the people of different cultures, widely separated from one another in time and space, would produce works of art that were so similar. Part of the explanation can be found in the artistic media used and the limited number of ways in which those media can be manipulated. The same media tend to be available to people living the same life-style, even if they are separated in time and space. The Pueblo people and the people of Shahr-i Sokhta were both simple horticulturalists. Most such people know very well that clay can be found in the ground, that it can be molded into various shapes, and that baking objects molded of clay will make them permanently hard and waterproof. One practical application for this knowledge is making clay containers for food and drink. Thus it is not surprising that clay pots, formed and fired in very similar ways, were used (and are still being used) in many horticultural societies.

If a particular medium (in this case, clay) suggests a particular artistic form, it also suggests a certain artistic style. The decorations on the pottery made by the Pueblo people and the people of Shahr-i Sokhta are nearly identical. Both societies favored angular designs, consisting of straight lines, triangles, and filled areas, in the same two colors, black and white. Anthropologists can suggest at least two

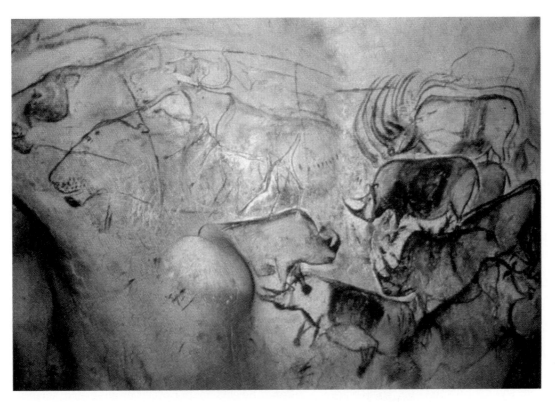

The 1994 discovery of over 300 magnificent Palaeolithic paintings at Vallon-Pont-d'Arc, Ardeche, southern France, shows the first panthers ever to be discovered in cave art, and many rhinos—animals that were rarely hunted. The paintings may have had something to do with magical beliefs.

Figure 14.2

People living the same life-style, even when widely separated in time and space, often use the same artistic media in the same ways. A pot created before 2000 B.C. by the people of ancient Shahr-i Sokhta in Iran (left) is similar to one created around A.D. 1100 by the Pueblo people of the American Southwest (right).

The Anthropologist at Work

Mary Strong

When Mary Strong was working toward her Master's degree in anthropology at New York University in 1973–1974, she could not help noticing that the walls of buildings on the Lower East Side of Manhattan were often adorned with colorful murals painted by local young people. Impressed by the talent that had produced the murals and a painter herself, Strong inquired if she could join in, and the young painters consented. Her participation, coupled with her interest in murals as a medium through which ethnic identity can be expressed in urban neighborhoods, led to two decades of involvement in urban wall painting; a doctorate in anthropology from Temple University, where she specialized in the anthropology of art; and membership on the board that administers the New York's City Arts Workshop, a nonprofit organization that promotes projects to strengthen the sense of ethnic identity in poor city neighborhoods.

Strong believes that "anthropology should give back immediately the results of ethnographic work." Thus, in addition to studying the meaning of New York's wall paintings and their relevance to the social context that inspires them, she continues to exercise her own skills as a painter. Mainly, however, she serves as a mural organizer, talking to young artists about their artistic goals, helping them fashion pleasing designs, and encouraging them to search for inspiration in the local library—an institution unfamiliar to some of them.

Before work on a planned mural can begin, Strong must do some strenuous politicking, since neighbor-hood residents, including the leaders of local gangs, must agree to the project. Murals must also be acceptable to every ethnic group in what are normally multiethnic neighborhoods, and this, too, entails negotiations. In general, neighborhood residents are very supportive. Local businesspeople are often so eager for neighborhood beautification that they supply the brushes, paints, and buckets, and local construction companies sometimes agree to loan the necessary scaffolding. In some neighborhoods, enthusiasm runs so high that residents help the artists and the anthro-pologist clean up the garbage that accumulates during the work in progress.

A recent mural project coordinated by Strong and a colleague, Mayrah Brown, was sponsored by the Crown Heights Youth Collective, an African American group in Brooklyn, New York. Crown Heights is an eth-nically mixed neighborhood that includes Orthodox Jews, African Americans, and Latinos. In early 1992, the neighborhood was shattered by violence following an automobile accident in which a young Jew was struck by a car driven by an African American. To help restore some measure of peace between the two eth-nic groups, the Crown Heights Youth Collective planned a mural entitled "Peace" (see picture). With Strong's help, the painters decided to incorporate designs chosen from the world of nature, plus the reli-gious symbols of all the ethnic groups in the locality. The mural, some 100 feet long and 8 feet high, took 20 painters about 2 months to complete. When it was finished, local politicians and community leaders joined with neighborhood residents to celebrate.

---

reasons for the striking similarity between the dec-orated pottery of the two societies. First, in simple horticultural settings black and white paints are easily made from ash and powdered bone. Second, designs composed of straight lines can easily be made by hand, but curved designs are very difficult to paint on pottery without the use of a potter's wheel.

Mary Strong's applied anthropological work in Crown Heights and elsewhere in the New York metropolitan area has resulted in a number of practical benefits. The young people involved are gaining confidence in their abilities as artists. Other local people, impressed by the murals, are sprucing up their neighborhoods by picking up trash and planting flowers in pots. But perhaps the most beneficial outcome of Strong's work is that it has helped residents of multiethnic neighborhoods to realize how important it is for members of different groups to be tolerant of and communicate with one another. Their collaboration in these striking works of art has provided local young people with a model for developing the kind of immediate and long-term mutual respect that Strong teaches.

In Crown Heights, New York City, a mural painter from the Crown Heights Youth Collective (background), working on a mural entitled "Peace," is joined in his efforts by two passersby. Mary Strong's applied anthropological work in Crown Heights has helped members of this multiethnic community to collaborate with one another through the creation of colorful works of art.

Another explanation for cross-cultural artistic similarities follows from the possible existence of so-called "mental universals," discussed in Chapter 3. Indeed, the hypothesis that mental universals exist was proposed precisely because expressive culture in so many societies includes similar patterns and themes in myths, rituals, plastic art, and graphic art. According to this hypothesis, straight-lined black-and-white designs on simple clay pots are found all over the world because such designs are mental universals, and thus hold some natural attraction for all human beings.

Verbal Art

As long as people have been communicating with words, they have manipulated language—sometimes alone, sometimes in combination with other sounds (such as music) or body movements (as in drama)—to create pleasurable or meaningful works of art. In Western societies, art in the form of words—poetry, fiction, essays—is usually read from a printed page, and thus experienced silently. But in nonliterate societies, art in the form of words is **oral art,** spoken (or sometimes sung) aloud. Even in some small-scale societies whose language is now written, art in the form of words is still primarily oral.

In traditional settings, oral art consists of stories, songs, poems, riddles, sayings, and other traditional verbal expressions collectively referred to as *folklore*. Often, the verbal expressions of disparate cultures exhibit remarkable similarities. For instance, the "trickster"—a playful folk figure often portrayed as a young, small, or weak cultural outsider who regularly outwits older, larger, or more powerful characters thanks to his cleverness and humor—appears in the oral art of cultures all over the world.

The formal study of folklore grew out of nineteenth-century scholars' interest in the verbal art of European peasants. Later, when ethnographers began collecting data from traditional societies outside Europe, the term came to be applied to their oral literature as well. Today, folklore and cultural anthropology overlap so much in the area of expressive culture that folklorist Alan Dundes, today's leading authority on traditional verbal narrative, is a faculty member in a department of cultural anthropology.

The audience for a Western book consists of an unrelated group of individuals separately reading something composed by an author they have in most cases never met. The audience for a work of oral art, in contrast, consists of socially related individuals who not only listen together to a work of oral art, but may also become an important part of it. The oral artist (in contrast to the author of a book) becomes a performer. He or she is in direct, continuing contact with individuals who, by their instant reaction to the performance, stimulate and sometimes even guide the artist into composing what they wish to hear. The audience thus enters into the act of creation.

The audience for a work of oral art may consist of members of a particular group, perhaps a lineage or age set or people of a certain social rank, and the theme, content, and purpose of the oral narrative to which they listen may change to fit the social context in which it is recited. The words may also change from recitation to recitation as the mood of the audience changes. And a story told to children will be told differently to adults. Because of this flexibility in content, there is no single, accurate version of an oral narrative.

The importance of the audience to the oral artist is vividly illustrated by South African storyteller Nongenile Masithathu Zenani, whose picture appears on page 112. Mrs. Zenani is a teller of traditional Xhosa tales whose art is simultaneously innovative and imitative (Zenani 1992). Basing her narratives on centuries-old traditional Xhosa stories already well known to her audiences, she embellishes on these stories, using new similes, new metaphors, and new gestures to keep them fresh and interesting. Thus, while the basic outline of a given tale may be familiar to her listeners and its outcome predictable, every telling of it is new, and commands not only the rapt attention but also the emotional involvement of its listeners.

Mrs. Zenani learned her craft the way all Xhosa storytellers do—by listening intently, over the course of a lifetime, to stories told by others. Now elderly, she still listens to other storytellers, always willing to improve her own performances by incorporating effective new stylistic devices and interesting details into her own repertoire. In this way, Mrs. Zenani's performances combine the best features of all the oral performances she has ever heard.

As she begins a narrative, the tall, regal Mrs. Zenani seems almost disdainful of her audience, pulling a red cape about her and proceeding with her story despite the chatter of those around her. Absorbed in her own words, she alternately grimaces, frowns, and smiles, varying the pitch, intensity, and speed of her voice and using precise, controlled movements of her hands and body to illustrate and punctuate her tale. Soon the faces of her listeners show that they have

---

oral art art in the form of spoken words

become psychologically immersed in the performance. Mrs. Zenani's natural verbal ability, powers of observation, and formidable memory work together to produce original verbal masterpieces that reflect not only her personality but Xhosa culture as well.

Oral narratives like Mrs. Zenani's may be categorized as myths, legends, or folktales. The criteria used to define these categories of oral art overlap somewhat, so that a narrative that one anthropologist would classify as a *folktale* might be termed a *legend* by a colleague. Still, these classifications can help highlight themes that make one kind of narrative different from another.

Myths. In Chapter 13, myths were defined as timeless stories that explain origins: of the world, societies, natural phenomena, or particular rituals. Other common mythological themes include the origins of fire, animals, the sexual differences between women and men, incest, agriculture, and death. The central character in a myth is often a culture hero, a larger-than-life individual who lived in the distant past, and myths always include some event that is humanly impossible. Clan myths, for example, may describe how a fabulous creature founded the group. Every culture tells such stories, although in some they are taken more literally than in others.

The myth that is perhaps the most famous in Western society describes the origins of humanity and of the differences between male and female—the story of Adam and Eve. The myth of the founding of the Eel clan of the Tetum (see Chapter 9) is an example of an origin myth from a non-Western society. Both of these myths are religious narratives, describing improbable events that occurred in some long-ago distant mythological time, in order to provide explanations for things that are important in the contemporary world. The story of Adam and Eve explains, among other things, how evil entered the world, while the Eel story explains how certain Tetum rituals originated.

In societies like Tetum society, where myths help to account for the existence of particular rituals, rituals may physically reenact the events related in a myth. Not every myth, however, is associated with a corresponding ritual: the Western myth of Adam and Eve, for example, has no ritual counterpart.

For over four decades, structural anthropologist Claude Lévi-Strauss has been the world's best-

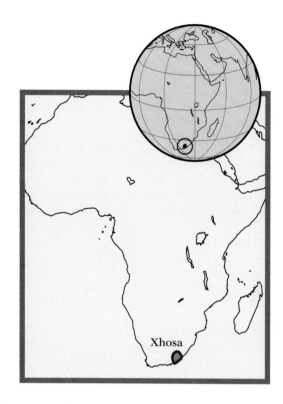

Xhosa

known authority on myths. Beginning in the 1950s with an innovative interpretation of the Oedipus myth, Lévi-Strauss has revived anthropology's interest in the subject and has brought it to the attention of a wide academic audience. Lévi-Strauss's methods for analyzing myths are complicated, and even experts in this field are sometimes baffled by his procedures, but at least two of his suggestions have elicited much interest. First, Lévi-Strauss insists that *all* versions of a myth must be taken into account before the meaning of the myth can be understood. It is fruitless, he claims, to try to establish which version of a myth is the "true" one—a quest beloved by earlier generations of scholars. Second, Lévi-Strauss claims that insights into the meaning of a myth can be gained by searching through it for oppositions and analogies such as male/female, culture/nature, and right/left.[1] Once he has unraveled the meaning of a given myth by considering all its versions and the oppositions they contain, Lévi-Strauss seeks to place it in its cultural context and to draw holistic conclusions about the culture that produced it.

---

[1] In Chapter 3, we saw that opposition is an important tool of structural anthropology.

Legends. **Legends** are narratives that tell of events set in specific places in the real world, at times less remote than the mythological past. Their chief characters are real human beings rather than gods, godlike humans, or animals, and they often focus on historic events: victories in battle, great migrations, or the heroic deeds of ancient chiefs or kings. Many legends incorporate some kernel of historical truth that has been embellished upon over the generations. The story of George Washington's boyhood encounter with the cherry tree, a tale invented long after Washington's time, might be considered an American legend.

Folktales. **Folktales** are stories about the adventures of animals, human beings, or both. Legends may be based on or even confused with reality, but folktales are acknowledged to be fiction. One country blessed with an abundance of folktales is Russia, and it was a Russian scholar, Vladimir Propp (1988), who pioneered the structural analysis of folktales in his book *Morphology of the Folktale*, originally published in Russian in 1928.

A familiar kind of folktale is the **fable,** a folktale that instructs those who hear or read it in some important moral lesson. Because they are instructive, fables may serve as tools for educating young people in their culture's attitudes, values, and standards. Aesop's *Fables*, perhaps the most famous collection of fables in Western literature, includes a tale, "The Tortoise and the Hare," that tells how a slow-moving but determined tortoise plods its way to victory in a race against a much speedier but overly confident and frequently sidetracked rabbit. Its message is that persistence yields success. Compare this familiar story to the Tetum fable "The Monkey and the Shark," which teaches the value of cooperation among patrikin.

> Once upon a time, Monkey and Shark jointly owned a garden, which Monkey selfishly wanted all for himself. He craftily suggested he and Shark, a sea creature, run a footrace, with the garden as the prize. Shark realized he was no match for speedy Monkey, so the night before the race, he dove down to his home in the sea to have a chat with his three brothers, and together they devised a plan for outwitting Monkey. The next morning, as the race began, Monkey dashed into the lead, but when he turned the first corner of the racetrack, there was Shark, plodding

According to an American legend, the young George Washington once cut down an ornamental cherry tree with an ax. Confronted by his angry father, he immediately confessed, for even as a child this future personification of our national integrity could not tell a lie. His father, legend has it, was so impressed by George's honesty that he forgave the boy immediately.

> slowly along ahead of him. Amazed he had not seen Shark pass him, Monkey did not realize that the runner ahead of him was really one of Shark's look-alike brothers. Determined to win, Monkey overtook his rival and sped off, leaving the first Shark brother behind. Whipping around the next turn, however, Monkey again could scarcely believe his eyes, for Shark was once more ahead of him. Monkey surged forward more furiously than ever, once more gaining the lead, but as the finish line came into view, there was Shark just crossing it. "The garden is mine now, Monkey," said Shark. "Your selfishness has caused you to lose everything. From now on, I'll cooperate only with my true brothers."

---

legend a narrative that describes events set in a specific place in the real world, at a time less remote than the mythological past

folktale a fictional story about the adventures of animals or of animals and human beings

fable a category of folktale that teaches some important moral lesson

• Ask Yourself •

The Tetum folktale "The Monkey and the Shark" bears a close resemblance to the Western fable "The Tortoise and the Hare." What similarities and differences do you detect in their themes?

Music

Music is a form of expressive culture whose medium consists of sounds, patterned in different rhythmic combinations. The elements of music are tones, percussion, and rhythm. A **tone** is a sound that has a certain duration, quality, and (most important) a certain highness or lowness, determined by the frequency of its sound vibrations (a tone's highness or lowness is called its **pitch**). **Percussion** consists of toneless sounds made by striking something. When a series of consecutive tones of various pitches are assembled in coherent sequence, the result is a melody. Music is made up of patterned combinations of tones (usually assembled into melodies), toneless percussive sounds, and rhythms. These patterned combinations differ among societies, and studying them within a given cultural context or cross-culturally is called **ethnomusicology.**

The sounds out of which human beings make music can be produced in two different ways. First, the human body can be used as a sound-producing instrument. The human voice can produce an enormous range of different tones, and percussive sounds can be made by clapping the hands, stamping the feet, or slapping the thighs. All of these sounds are elements of music encountered cross-culturally. Second, music can be produced by instruments, which range in complexity and musical potential from simple rattles made from dried gourds to technologically complex electric organs and sound synthesizers.

Defined as a form of expressive culture consisting of patterned sounds, music is found in every society. Moreover, even though music (like language) was until recently an ephemeral art—meaning that works of musical art disappeared as soon as they were performed—music (like oral art) prob-

ably played an important part in prehistoric cultures, too. The evidence lies not only in the fact that every culture known today creates music; there are also archaeological hints distributed worldwide: ancient instruments such as whistles, flutes, drums, rattles, and **bullroarers** (elongated pieces of bone or other materials, which when attached to cords and whirled about the head produce an eerie, prolonged tone).

Like other forms of expressive culture, music is culturally patterned, and therefore differs widely among societies. Westerners, having been introduced to the music of their own cultural tradition as part of the childhood enculturation process, usually find Western music most appealing. Conversely, they may find Asian music unappealing, because it separates tones from one another differently from Western music. In the fixed set of tones (or **scale**) on which Western music is based, each tone is separated from its nearest neighbor according to how many more or fewer vibrations it comprises. Divided from one another in this way, the tones on which Western music is based make up an **octave,** a set of eight primary tones. To the Western ear, music based on the octave sounds "correct" and pleasing. But in Japan, where the set of tones on which traditional music is based does not conform to the octave, Western music may sound unmusical. The two very different kinds of music are, however, equally pleasing to listeners in the context of their own cultures.

In every society, music is an important part of social life. In North American society, for instance, it almost always accompanies parties, weddings,

---

tone a sound of distinct duration, quality, and pitch

pitch the highness or lowness of a musical sound, largely determined by the frequency of its sound vibration

percussion toneless sounds made by striking something

ethnomusicology the study of music in its cultural context, either in a single society or cross-culturally

bullroarer an elongated piece of bone or other material, which when whirled about on a cord produces a tone

scale a fixed set of tones on which music is based

octave a set of eight primary tones

On the island of Bali in Indonesia, orchestras called gamelans, *made up mostly of drums and xylophones, play traditional music which many Westerners find unmelodic. Here, members of a* gamelan *orchestra play at a Balinese funeral.*

and funerals. On the island of Bali (see map on page 332) and in other parts of Indonesia, music is a traditional accompaniment for oral literature as well. There, orchestras called **gamelans** provide music for the repeated enactment of local legends, as important a part of Balinese social life as the yearly Christmas holiday is to some Westerners. A gamelan may contain up to 75 instruments played by as many as 30 musicians (Sumarsam 1995). Most of the sounds come from bronze and wooden xylophones shaped like discs or cylinders and from bulbous, hollow bowls beaten with hammers. The tonal system employed by a gamelan is made up of scales divided into intervals different from those in Western music. The resulting music is soft, mellow, and liquid, though perhaps unmelodic to many Western ears.

Sometimes, traditional and Western-influenced artistic forms—musical or other—are combined to produce a new, unified artistic tradition. The two original forms must be close enough to each other to be joined into a single tradition. In the Caribbean, for example, Western and African music have combined to produce a new musical category called *reggae,* which is pleasing within the context of both musical traditions. The blending of two or more cultural traditions into a single new one is called **syncretism.** Since Western music is quite different from, say, Native North American music, syncretism is much less likely to occur between these two musical categories than between two more similar ones. A Native American child may learn to play the clarinet at school while learning traditional Native American music at home. Since no blending is possible, the child must keep the two types of music separate for different occasions.

gamelan an Indonesian orchestra containing as many as 75 different instruments

syncretism the blending of two or more cultural traditions into a single new one

Dance

In Western as in other societies, there are a number of categories of artistic expression in which not one but several artistic media—form, color, sound, language, and/or body movement—are arranged in pleasurable or meaningful ways. Drama, for example, combines language with body movement. Opera, perhaps the most elaborate of the Western combined art forms, arranges all five media into what for some is pure pleasure and for others a sensory overload.

One combined art form is dance, which unites body movement with music or, in some societies, only with percussive sound. Dance is almost universal, but its purpose varies. Depending on the society, it may express social solidarity, religious feelings, or political convictions, or may be performed purely for pleasure.

Consider the dance called *bar'a*, which is performed on religious holidays, at weddings, and on other festive occasions by tribal people in the Middle Eastern country of Yemen. Accompanied by the beat of drums, bar'a dancers, always men, perform closely together in an open circle, moving forward and backward with a variety of hops, knee bends, and turns while brandishing daggers in their right hands (Adra 1985:70). One dancer, the leader, directs the movements and timing of the others, who try to remain in step with the beat of the drums. The basic bar'a dance step is not in itself complicated, but maintaining close coordination between dancers and drummers is tricky, and with many dancers crowded together, each wielding a dagger, a misstep can result in injury.

Following Bateson's (1972:10) hypothesis that "the patterning of a work of art can provide information on the underlying value system of the culture in which it is produced," anthropologist Najwa Adra went to Yemen in the late 1970s to study the bar'a dance. She discovered that the dance is a metaphor for Yemeni tribesmen's concept of tribalness. By performing the bar'a, dancers are symbolizing, for participants and spectators alike, "the coherence of the tribe, its ability to function cooperatively, and the strength and endurance of its members." Adra (1985:75) concluded that "the dance and other arts can be a valuable source of information on the motivating value system of the culture that produces them."

In 1990, the political situation in Yemen changed dramatically with the unification of North and South Yemen, never previously under one rule, into a single country. One effect of this unification has been the increasing importance to Yemenis of the concept of nationhood. Urbanites have taken up tribal symbols as part of the national attempt to

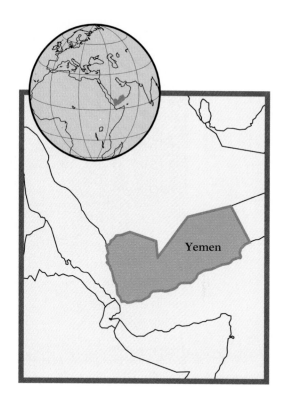

forge a new Yemeni identity. People who are not of tribal origin genealogically are now wearing tribal dress, eating tribal foods, and carrying tribal daggers. The bar'a dance, not surprisingly, has changed too. Once a localized, rural art form, it is now increasingly popular in cities. Once performed by tribesmen, it is now danced by nontribal Yemenis. Suddenly, bar'a has became not a tribal but a Yemeni art form (Adra 1992).

In some settings, the combination of sound, movement, and religious belief that make up a dance proves so potent that dancers fall into trance states (Shaara and Strathern 1992; Ward 1989; Winkleman 1986). The brain waves of dancers in a trance are patterned much like those of epileptics just before a seizure. It seems likely, therefore, that not only a dancer's state of consciousness but also his or her physiological state is altered during a dance-induced trance.

A particularly dramatic example comes from Bali, Indonesia (see map on page 332), where religious rituals often incorporate dancing. One such ritual reenacts a violent knife fight between the power of fear, represented by an elaborately costumed witch dancer, and the power of life, repre-

A dance called bar'a *is performed on festive occasions by men in the Middle Eastern country of Yemen. In al-Ahjur in rural Yemen, bar'a dancers, accompanied by drums, symbolize their tribe's ability to function cooperatively by circling energetically while brandishing traditional tribal daggers.*

sented by several dancers dressed up as a dragon. During the dance, in which body movement and persistent, rhythmic drumming converge to create a highly emotionally charged atmosphere, the dancers—each wielding a long knife called a *kriss*—fall into trances. Holding their krisses so that the sharp points press against their chests, the dancers whirl wildly about in time to the beat of the drums. Remarkably, no one gets hurt; overly violent dancers are gently restrained by onlookers, and their knives are taken away. At the end of the ritual, the onlookers help the performers to emerge from the trance state with fragrant incense and a sprinkling of holy water.

Despite the lack of scientific studies, anthropologists and other students of the dance have repeatedly observed that a combination of certain stimuli often produces a trance. In the ritual Balinese witch-killing dance just described, these stimuli include rhythmic drumming, rapid breathing resulting from exertion, dizziness produced by whirling around, and perhaps self-hypnotic suggestion. In other rituals performed in other societies, inhaled smoke or some other narcotic, flickering light, and self-inflicted deprivations (such as fasting

before dancing) may also play a part in inducing a trance. Whatever the physical changes these stimuli produce, the result is the same. Dancers "tune out," hallucinate, experience muscular spasms or actual seizures, and sometimes faint. Later, they often report having had a religious vision or an out-of-body sensation, or having been possessed.

• Functions of Expressive • Culture

If the main function of expressive culture is the individual creation of something new, meaningful, or pleasurable, it also has a number of important social functions. Through expressive culture, ideas can be conveyed, social institutions symbolized, values portrayed in concrete form, and order imposed on the external world—and perhaps on the internal world of the mind as well.

Reflecting a Society's View of the World

A society's expressive culture can mirror its general perception of the world. Norman Rockwell's hugely popular and very American mid-twentieth-century paintings, for instance, portray the comfortable, rural, child-oriented, patriotic, optimistic, God-fearing America that Americans believed they had secured through their contribution to the Allied victory in World War II.

Another example of this same phenomenon comes from West Africa, an area of the world that has produced some of the world's most varied, prolific, and sophisticated art, most notably in the form of wood carvings. Using a structural approach, anthropologist James Fernandez (1971) analyzed the wooden sculptures of the Fang people of Gabon and Cameroon, and found that these works of art reflect, to a remarkable degree, the Fang view of the world. The Fang envision the world as a series of complementary oppositions, of which the most common are right/left, northeast/southwest, and male/female. In each pair, one of the partners (e.g., male) balances its complementary but opposed partner (e.g., female), which sets up an even tension between the two. To the Fang way of thinking, this tension imparts vitality and balance.

In a reflection of this preference for harmonic tension between complementary opposites, numerous features of Fang social life are similarly arranged into pairs of complementary oppositions. Fang villages consist of two rows of huts facing each other; a village consisting of only one row of houses is considered neither pleasing nor functional. Indeed, a collection of buildings like this is not regarded as a real village at all (Fernandez 1971:366–367). Similarly, in the men's council house, two rows of benches face each other, and from these opposed benches, the parties to disputes face each other on equal footing.

Fang woodcarvings of human figures and faces are very much a part of the society in which they are produced. Since Fang people say that balance and vitality give them pleasure, we would expect them to feel that objects reflecting these qualities are beautiful. Fang artists strive to express balance and vitality

In addition to their aesthetic appeal, works of art can symbolize social institutions and depict values. Norman Rockwell's painting of children gathered around their teacher in an old-fashioned country schoolhouse expresses the simple, rural values many Americans cherish. Printed by permission of The Norman Rockwell Family Trust. Copyright © 1946 The Norman Rockwell Family Trust. A Country School by Norman Rockwell, 1946.

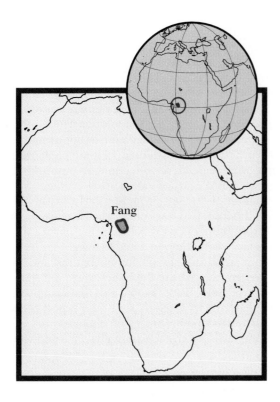

Before they begin work, Alaska's Inuit stone carvers carefully study pieces of stone to determine what kind of spirit they conceal. They then carve works of art of great aesthetic and, today, commercial appeal. In a government-sponsored art studio, Inuit craftsman Tagoonarak works on a stone swan.

in their carved figures' arms, legs, and ears—all parts of these figures that are in complementary opposition to each other. When the Fang compare wooden statues of their ancestors for their artistic merits, these are the qualities they find most desirable.

Unlike the Fang, the Inuit of Alaska live in a natural environment so harsh that it might be supposed they lack the time, materials, or energy for artistic creativity. Nevertheless, the Inuit produce stone carvings of considerable sensitivity and widespread appeal. Like the woodcarving of the Fang, stonecarving of the Inuit (see map on page 17) reflects the worldview of its creators. One elderly Inuit stonecarver, Tagoonarak, produces particularly powerful and aesthetically pleasing work—elegant carvings of animals, birds, fish, or sometimes human figures (Malcolm 1979:A13). These reflect the traditional Inuit life of gathering and hunting that Tagoonarak remembers from his childhood. When he carves an animal, shape and bulk are more important than details, which are often merely scratched in. Human beings, engaged in everyday tasks, are never smiling, but are often leaning forward as if bearing some heavy burden

or perhaps countering a strong wind. Tagoonarak's work conveys the essence of life in a demanding and hostile natural environment.

Affirming Social Organization and Group Solidarity

The Native American groups of the Northwest Coast were stratified into many different social ranks, whose members were much concerned with questions of relative status and prestige. Their potlatches (see Chapter 7, page 167; see also the map on page 18) involved the exchange, and sometimes even the destruction, of material goods by rival chiefs for the purpose of increasing their prestige. Many of the objects exchanged or destroyed at potlatches were works of art—painted wooden chests, conical hats, woven blankets—all elaborately and distinctively decorated. The most prized objects of all were "coppers," large, shield-like copper plaques considered to be the highest form of wealth and owned only by men who had given extraordinary potlatches. Since chiefs' prestige could best be increased if they showed disdain for their wealth, behaving as if much more were available, chiefs sometimes destroyed great quantities of coppers and other art objects during potlatches.

Not surprisingly, much of the traditional art of the Northwest Coast, which was created in a variety of media and remains among the most distinctive of any society, symbolized and confirmed its owners' social rank, status, and prestige. The most spectacular art objects were totem poles—tall, elaborately carved cedar tree trunks that rose, sometimes to a height of 60 feet, beside chiefs' houses (Stewart 1993). They bore carved images of beavers, frogs, hawks, eagles, and wolves, as well as thunderbirds and other imaginary beings. Perched atop a pole would often be a human figure wearing a hat. A series of rings around this hat represented successful potlatches given by the chief who owned the house: the more rings, the greater the chief's prestige. Totem poles were dramatic visual reminders of the hierarchical structure of Northwest Coast society.

Expressive culture can also bring about social solidarity, the comforting sense of individuals that they are accepted members of a single social group. Iranian girls knotting carpet threads on the same loom, a group of tourists standing in awe before Michaelangelo's famous David, the congregation of an American church singing an Easter hymn, Nuba men applying paint and ash to one another's faces, American moviegoers watching a James Cameron film—all are brought solidly, if temporarily, into social relationships with their fellows through an artistic medium.

Influencing Events

Art can be a potent agent for culture change (see Chapter 16), not only reflecting but also affecting what happens in the world. This is particularly true of Western art, which is more apt to express nonconformist or countercultural ideas and values than the traditional art of small-scale societies. By challenging prevailing ideas and values and encouraging audiences to reorient their ways of looking at the world, Western painters, writers, sculptors, dancers, dramatists, and musicians have helped to bring about social changes ever since the

The art of Native Americans of the Northwest Coast reflected their intense concern with status and prestige. Each ring around a hat at the top of a totem pole represented a successful potlatch given by a particular chief, a visual reminder of the chief's prestige.

Renaissance. Art that generates new ideas and values is called **revolutionary art.**

Western art is more revolutionary than the art of other societies because the social context in which Western art is created encourages artists to produce works of originality and individuality, to explore their society's beliefs, and to challenge its institutions. Possibly, too, the continual replacement of

---

revolutionary art art that generates new ideas and values

Rock stars often champion individuality and self-indulgence, which counter more traditional Western values such as conformity and self-discipline. Truth or Dare *(1991), a documentary film about Madonna, shows this hardworking performer taking life easy, and downplays the effort that goes into actually producing rock music.*

older Western artistic styles with newer ones is "an evolutionary paradigm . . . related to [Western] patterns of politics, war, and a theory of history" (Pasztory 1989:37). In other words, Westerners' general outlook on life, which incorporates expectations of continuous evolutionary change (biological, social, and historical), may be reflected in continuous artistic change.

A classic example of Western revolutionary art is Western rock music of the 1950s and 1960s. When it first burst on the musical scene in mid-century North America, rock music flew in the face of some firmly ingrained ideas about personal behavior and morality. The activities, ideas, and values its lyrics championed, as well as the way of life its artists seemed to espouse, were frowned on under the widely accepted model of moral rectitude and personal success current at the time. According to this model, conformity, self-denial,

self-discipline, and teamwork were highly valued. Because of its apparent call for self-indulgence and individuality, rock was viewed by many as dangerously immoral—an image that its performers, true revolutionary artists, skillfully perpetuated. Rock music had its intended effect: by the post-Vietnam 1970s, some of the values it celebrated, such as unfettered sexual expression or the freedom to "do one's own thing," had won broad acceptance in Western culture.

In nonliterate societies, the potential of art to encourage change tends to be more limited, because individual creativity and stylistic innovation, with their implicit or explicit challenge to existing value systems, are usually not so highly prized. **Conservative art** is often preferred in these societies. Artists typically seek to maintain the existing order rather than to overthrow it and replace it with a new one.

This is not to say that traditional, non-Western artists never try to influence what happens in the world. To the contrary, as we noted in a discussion of imitative magic in Chapter 13, in non-Western societies works of art are often created with the express

conservative art art that sustains the existing social order

purpose of affecting or changing things. However, these are apt to be particular, immediate events rather than fundamental alterations in value systems. An artist might create carvings or paintings, for instance, specifically to help ensure success in hunting.

Expressing Political Themes

Expressive culture can also have profound political significance, challenging ideas and values, symbolizing political institutions, or adding weight to political causes. In societies with centralized political organizations (chiefdoms and states), it can serve as potent propaganda, confirming and strengthening the authority of leaders. Under Hitler, Germany's Third Reich created a government arts institution, the Reichs-kulturkammer, to oversee the work of German painters, sculptors, and architects. At its height, this institution supported as many as 23,000 German artists, encouraging them, through their works of art, to idealize German family life in paintings of pastoral scenes and to legitimize and glorify German military efforts in statues of intrepid German warriors (Adam 1992).

In the area of West Africa that is now Ghana, the king of the Ashanti, a confederacy of African cities that united about 1701, owns numerous works of art, many made of solid gold. By possessing these objects, the Ashanti king (see picture on page 290) demonstrates that he is the most powerful individual in his kingdom. Each successive Ashanti king inherits from his predecessor a variety of ritual objects symbolizing his supremacy in the confederacy.

Of these objects, the Golden Stool is the most sacred (Fraser 1972). This boxlike container, which houses the soul of the nation and symbolizes the union of cities, is believed by the Ashanti to have fallen from heaven, at the bidding of the head priest, into the first Ashanti king's lap. Before he called the Golden Stool down from heaven, however, the head priest demanded that various other

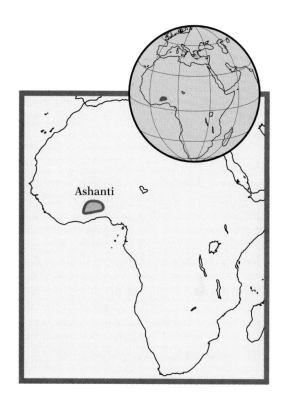

symbols of the individual cities, which consisted of other stools, shields, and swords, be surrendered to him. These he buried in a riverbed, so no art object in the new nation could claim a longer history than the Golden Stool and hence be considered superior to it. This action also disposed of the powerful symbols of the former independence of the cities. To ensure that all the newly unified cities accepted the Golden Stool as the symbol of their single king, the priest commanded that locks of hair, nail parings, and rings belonging to the most important chiefs be collected and put inside it.

These events occurred nearly 300 years ago, but the Golden Stool of the Ashanti continues to retain its powerful symbolism. Credited with supernatural powers, the stool must never be allowed to touch the bare ground, and when displayed in public, always rests on a silver-plated throne. The Golden Stool must be fed at regular intervals, for were it to suffer hunger, it might sicken and die, and with it the soul of the Ashanti nation.[2]

• Ask Yourself •

Recently, a self-described New York artist produced an unusual "work of art": he arranged for three nude couples to caress and kiss each other in public. When asked whether this was really art, he replied, "It's art because I'm an artist and I say it's art." Do you agree?

---

[2] The story of how the Golden Stool arrived from heaven is, of course, an origin myth explaining how the single nation of the Ashanti came to be.

Sometimes members of a society invent an artistic "tradition" by claiming that certain symbols, ideas, or customs, actually of recent origin, are traditional parts of their culture. This phenomenon is called **invented tradition** (Hobsbawm and Ranger 1992). For example, a clan might invent or embroider upon an origin myth to justify its current political aims.

Transmitting Culture

Various forms of expressive culture, as we noted earlier, may function as learning tools through which information is transmitted. Both the Tetum folktale about the Monkey and the Shark, recounted earlier in this chapter, and Aesop's fable of the Tortoise and the Hare incorporate moral lessons important in the context of their respective societies. Likewise, the Mahabharata, a long epic poem told repeatedly over the last 2000 years in India, contains an Indian history lesson. For literate Indians, the lessons of the Mahabharata, which recounts the struggles for dynastic succession in an ancient kingdom, have long been transmitted in written form, but to this day they continue to be passed along by word of mouth in rural Indian villages, where nonliterate storytellers can recite and sing passages from the Mahabharata for hours on end (Weisman 1987:C17). Today, Indians buy tape cassettes of this work of oral art, listening to them as avidly as some Western rock fans listen to R.E.M. Indian children read colorful comic-book versions describing the fabulous adventures of the superheros of the poem, much as Western children read about Mighty Morphin Power Rangers, and adults and children alike watch Mahabharata TV serials with the same enthusiasm that some Westerners watch "Melrose Place." The Mahabharata represents one way in which the lessons and values of the Indian past are made accessible to present generations.

Expressing Gender Relationships

Affirming the relationship of males and females in a society is another way in which expressive culture becomes social commentary. Alan Dundes

(1989:152ff.) has analyzed an eastern European folktale, told (or sometimes sung) in several variations in peasant communities in Hungary, Bulgaria, Romania, Greece, Albania, and Serbia. "The Building of Skadar" recounts an attempt by a group of men, sometimes described as brothers, to build a castle, bridge, or monastery. Because of a supernatural spell, whatever the builders manage to erect during the course of a day is magically undone at night. In a dream, the builders learn that the spell can be broken if the first woman to arrive at the site the next day is walled up in the foundation. The men agree not to inform their wives, who daily bring their husbands' lunches, so that the victim may be selected by fate. However, all the men but one break this agreement.

The next day, the wife of the one worker who honored his promise arrives at the construction site carrying food for her husband, and learns that she is to be entombed. In some versions of the tale, she is tricked into entering the unfinished building when her husband throws his wedding ring into the foundation and then asks her to retrieve it. When she tries to do so, the builders wall her up. In some versions, she begs the men to leave a small opening, "a window at her breasts," so that she may suckle her infant son.

How are we to interpret this sad tale? The story, Dundes (1989) suggests, is a symbolic expression of women's traditional role in this part of eastern Europe. Beginning, as a structural anthropologist

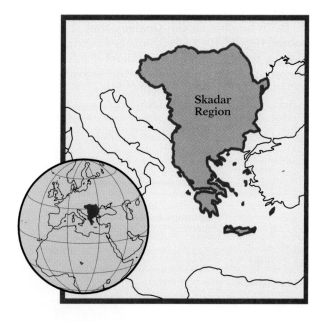

---

invented tradition symbols, ideas, or customs that members of a society claim as traditional parts of their culture but that in reality are of more recent origin

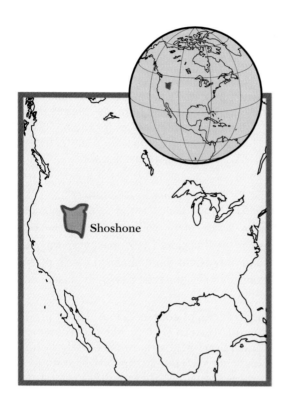

incorporates the notion that women must pay for the offenses of men. Seeking support for his analysis in the local ethnography, Dundes found that brides in Serbia live within their husband's households and have little or no status until they produce offspring, preferably male. Local wedding songs commonly include images of marriage as death.

The art of other societies may express a more harmonious relationship between the sexes. The Shoshone Indian Sun Dance has been described as a beautiful symbol of the cooperation between males and females in a society in which subsistence work is divided between women who gather food and men who hunt. The song that accompanies the Sun Dance is begun by a male, whose opening phrase is repeated by other men accompanying themselves on drums. After this repetition of the opening phrase, women join the singing. Midway through the final repetition, the men stop singing and drumming and the women finish the song (Vander 1989:7).

• Ethics and Folk Art •

The Yolngu, a small-scale, clan-based society of Northeast Arnhem Land, Australia, produce intricate

would, by searching for oppositions and analogies, Dundes notes that in eastern Europe, men work outside the home whereas women work inside: thus, men are to women as outside is to inside. In this story about the relationship between men and women in marriage and the impact of marriage on women's lives, women must be sacrificed so that men can accomplish their work. For a woman, marriage is like being locked up until death. This aspect of gender relations is symbolized by the husband's dropping his wedding ring into the construction site, for it is in pursuit of a wedding ring that the wife enters her tomb. In versions of the story in which the wife retains a window on the outside world so that she may feed her son, Dundes suggests, the message is that the welfare of a male child is the only reason not to shut a woman away completely.

The treachery of the men who warn their wives not to be the first on the scene, Dundes adds, again evokes eastern European notions of male-female opposition. The trusting man who places his faith in his fellow men causes not his own death but the death of a female. The wife is walled up not because of any fault of her own but because of the perfidy of men. Eastern European culture, Dundes concludes,

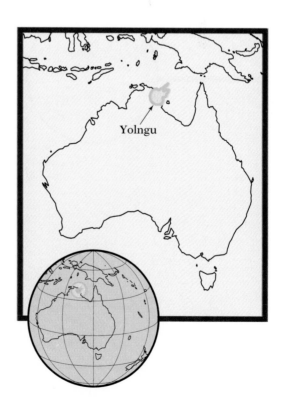

paintings on bark. These paintings, highly symbolic and very significant to the Yolngu, portray natural objects—animals, birds, human figures, rivers, trees, clouds—and often include intricately patterned fields of fine, crosshatched lines. Most represent either mythological events involving the ancestors of the Yolngu or topographical features, although the distinction between the two is not always clear-cut, since the Yolngu see the natural features of their world as "a continuing manifestation of ancestral events" (Morphy 1991:218).

The Maori of New Zealand, another small-scale society whose religion involves reverence for their ancestors, produce a very different kind of art. When someone dies, the Maori preserve the head of the deceased, decorating it with elaborate tattoos and revering it as a religious object. The decorated Maori heads are similar to the bark paintings of the Yolngu in that both incorporate and express traditional religious beliefs.

Prior to European contact, objects such as the Yolngu bark paintings and Maori heads were intended solely for, and were confined to, the societies that produced them. In the postcontact period, however, Westerners repeatedly "discov-ered" the intriguing and often beautiful objects produced in non-Western societies, and learned to appreciate them as works of art. In time, as more and more such objects found their way into Western hands, there arose a considerable demand for them in the West, and in many cases Westerners were willing to pay high prices for them.

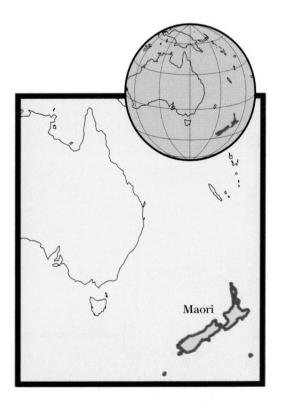

Maori

• Ask Yourself •

How would you feel if your great-grandmother's remains were unearthed in an archaeological excavation and displayed in a museum? Do you feel the same way about the international sale of ancient Egyptian mummies and their display in museums?

The problem, of course, is that the art produced in any non-Western society, like the Yolngu paintings and Maori heads, is often closely bound up with its belief system—so much so that many non-Westerners consider their works of art to be sacred. This raises an interesting ethical issue: are Westerners justified in collecting and displaying what is considered sacred in its original context—and are non-Westerners justified in selling it? Sellers and buyers have mixed opinions, and so do anthropologists. On the one hand, art is an integral part of a society's culture, so that removing a work of art from its cultural context eliminates its capacity to contribute to the culture that created it. On the other hand, since works of folk art are apt to be created from wood, cloth, fibers, and other perishable materials that decay rapidly in the environment where they were created, collecting objects that would otherwise perish and preserving them in museums or even private collections may prevent the loss of objects of great ethnographic as well as artistic value.

No consensus on this controversy has yet emerged (MacClancy 1990; Price 1990), and the members of the small-scale societies involved have themselves adopted widely differing positions. When a London auction house recently announced that it had acquired a sacred Maori head and was planning to sell it, the Maori people objected, and, through the National Maori Council, began legal moves to stop the sale. The Council was supported by England's Royal Anthropological Institute (RAI), which took the position that selling such objects

Traditional artists in Australia paint animals, birds, human figures, and natural objects on bark, both for their own rituals and for sale to Western museums, galleries, and private collectors.

When an auction house in London made plans to sell the preserved, tattooed head of an ancestor of the Maori of New Zealand as an art object, the Maori, for whom such heads have religious meaning, objected. During the debate that ensued, a cartoon showing a Maori head tattooed with the symbol for the British pound appeared in a London newspaper.

was unethical when it was not condoned by members of the society in which a work of art originated—and the Maori had made it abundantly clear that they objected strongly (Benthall 1988:1; *Anthropology Today* 1988). The sale was canceled. The Yolngu, however, have taken a different tack: they now produce some bark paintings for their own rituals, and others, containing different meanings, for sale to Westerners. As a result, Yolngu art has become incorporated into the postcolonial Australian market economy and indeed the world market economy. It can now be found in art galleries not only in Australia but also around the world (Morphy 1991:2).

One argument in support of external sales of culturally meaningful objects is the potential loss of non-Western artistic traditions if small-scale societies were to ban such sales. Earlier in this chapter we described the Inuit stone carver Tagoonarak. Over the last 25 years, Tagoonarak's world has changed dramatically because of the enormous, and not universally welcomed, impact of external changes on traditional Inuit life. Cigarettes, alcohol, television, and computers have entered the people's lives. Children have drifted away from traditional Inuit customs, and even the elderly find it difficult to continue their old traditions amid the confusion of conflicting values and disrupted patterns of behavior. A younger generation of Inuit, unfamiliar with traditional ways, is largely uninterested in carving stone for traditional purposes. When the elderly carvers like Tagoonarak are gone, the production of traditional Inuit art may come to an end (Malcolm 1979:A13)—unless younger Inuit can accommodate this art to the social changes inevitably taking place around them.

Conclusion

Although both Western art and art created in nonliterate societies are vehicles for the expression of cultural ideas and values, an important contrast can be drawn between them. In Western societies, artistic efforts are often set apart from other occupations. Works of art are most likely to be created by individuals such as ballet dancers, movie producers, rock stars, novelists, sculptors, painters, and opera singers whose main role in the economic system is to produce artistic creations. Moreover, Western art is apt to be self-justifying rather than a means to some practical end. It is appreciated, enjoyed, and understood for itself rather than as a method of achieving a particular, immediate goal.

In nonliterate societies, we also find specialists who produce works of art—basket-weavers or pottery-makers, for example—but their art is not as self-justifying; it often has some practical purpose beyond its aesthetic appeal. And in nonliterate societies we are much more likely to find artists whose creations are inspired by motivations beyond personal artistic expression, and whose art is thus a by-product of broader cultural goals. A Hopi shaman creates a sand painting because this is part of a curing ritual, and an African storyteller recounts legends to educate candidates in tribal lore for an initiation ceremony. Non-Western art, in short, is more likely than Western art to be closely integrated with economic production, religion, politics, the law, descent, and other aspects of social life.

"What you're doing is art, too—everything we do is art!"

Drawing by Drucker; © 1993 The New Yorker Magazine, Inc.

Summary

- Expressive culture, a human universal, constitutes all the ways people purposefully manipulate certain media (including form, color, sound, language, and body movement) into arrangements that are pleasurable, meaningful, or both.

- The forms, extent, and significance of expressive culture are not uniform across societies: rather, these are determined by the cultures of which they are a part, and by the particular artistic media that cultures have available to them.

- In any culture, the available artistic media are limited, both in number and potential. This may help explain why works of art from societies widely separated from one another in space or time may look so much alike.

- If cognitive anthropologists are correct about the existence of mental universals, these might also help to explain artistic similarities among cultures.

- Among the most common forms of art are the plastic and graphic arts, verbal art (such as legends, folktales, and myths), music, and dance.

- The functions of art include mirroring a society's view of the world, affirming a particular social organization and people's sense of social solidarity, influencing future events, expressing political ideas, transmitting culture, and expressing gender relationships.

- Most small-scale societies today are a product of both traditional and recent Western influences, and over time their art has changed to reflect this.

- Sometimes, traditional and Western-influenced artistic forms combine to produce a new, unified artistic tradition. This is called *syncretism*.

- The artistic traditions of some non-Western societies are threatened with extinction. Westerners' interests in these traditions may help to preserve them, but at the same time these interests raise ethical concerns.

- In Western societies, art is likely to be created for its own sake rather than to achieve some practical goal, and artistic efforts are often set apart from other occupations. In non-Western societies, in contrast, art often has some practical purpose beyond its aesthetic appeal, and is more likely than Western art to be integrated with other aspects of social life.

Key Terms

bullroarer
conservative art
ethnomusicology
expressive culture
fable
folk art
folktale
gamelan
graphic art
invented tradition
legend
octave
oral art
percussion
pitch
plastic art
revolutionary art
scale
syncretism
tone

Suggested Readings

Anderson, Richard L. 1992. *Art in Small-Scale Societies* (2nd ed.). Englewood Cliffs, NJ: Prentice-Hall. A comprehensive overview of the visual art of nonliterate societies, which provides an authoritative introduction to its meaning, creation, and creators.

Brunvand, Jan Harold. 1981. *The Vanishing Hitchhiker: American Urban Legends and Their Meanings*. New York: W. W. Norton. Stories about grandmothers' runaway corpses, batter-fried rats, and other oddities are reproduced here as modern American folktales.

Corbin, George A. 1988. *Native Arts of North America, Africa, and the South Pacific*. New York: Harper & Row. Magnificent photographs accompany this introduction to the plastic and graphic arts of the peoples of New Guinea, the Inuit, the Ashanti, the Trobrianders, the Australian aborigines, and the Maori, whose artistic efforts include masks, body decoration, sculptures, and shields.

Myers, Helen (ed.). 1992. *Ethnomusicology: An Introduction. The Norton/Grove Handbooks in Music*. New York: W. W. Norton. An excellent collection of essays dealing with almost every aspect of ethnomusicology, including gender and music, dance, and a vast number of other topics of interest to contemporary anthropology.

Rosman, Abraham, and Paula G. Rubel. 1990. Structural Patterning in Kwakiutl Art and Ritual. *Man* 25:620–640. By means of a structural analysis, the authors show that the art of the Kwakiutl of the Northwest Coast expresses certain religious ideas.

Introduction

The professor in a big introductory course

in anthropology at a state university often

illustrated his lectures with ethnographic

films. Most of these films portrayed events

in the lives of people living in small-scale societies in faraway parts of the world. Over the course of the semester, students in the class saw Inuit hunters celebrating a successful seal hunt with drumming, dancing, and singing; a group of Middle Eastern nomads walking hundreds of miles to take their sheep to new pastures; Balinese dancers performing a religious drama to the eerie accompaniment of strange-looking stringed instruments; and opposing groups of Pacific islanders, wearing elaborate feather headdresses, fighting each other with homemade spears. The reaction of the students to these films was mixed. Some viewers were intrigued, others were bored, and still others admitted that at times they were shocked or even repelled. In general, however, the students were more struck by the strangeness of what they saw on the screen than by similarities between the filmed scenes and events in their own lives.

One day, toward the end of the semester, the professor dimmed the lecture hall lights for yet another film. This one, like several of the others, began with a darkened screen and the heavy thump of distant drumming, and some students groaned inwardly at the thought of having to sit through what they anticipated would be another strange, incomprehensible, or even repellent dance, drama, sacrifice, or other ritual. As the screen slowly brightened, shadowy human figures became visible—moving shapes with flapping clothing and grotesque, voluminous hairdos. Smoke swirled around the silhouetted figures, who bounced up and down rhythmically to the faint but steady beat of the drums.

As the sound track gradually grew louder and musical tones surfaced above the percussive thumping, the students began to listen more intently, for they thought they recognized something familiar. Soon the screen brightened, and they began to laugh, for this footage, far from showing a primitive rite filmed in some remote land, had been filmed at a popular nightclub near the campus, and the mysterious figures gyrating rhythmically to the music were none other than the students themselves.

In their physical appearance, human beings, unlike all other living things, are much more than just the products of particular sets of genes. True, each person inherits a genetic legacy that very largely determines the gross body form in which he or she must remain for life. But beyond what is biologically determined, one of the important ways in which human beings are fundamentally different from all other organisms on earth is that only they constantly and purposefully alter their outward appearance. (We use the term *purposefully* to distinguish people from other animals, such as chameleons or weasels, that change their outward appearance in automatic response to specific external stimuli.) Our bodies are like painters' canvases on which different cultural and personal beliefs, attitudes, ideals, and preferences are presented to the world through particular kinds of dress, jewelry, cosmetics, or hairdos; through other forms of body alteration or adornment, like piercing, scarring, or tattooing; and through body movements such as gestures, postures, and facial expressions.

In Chapter 14, we discussed expressive culture, pointing out that in every society aesthetic expression has both individual functions (creating something new, personally meaningful, or pleasurable) and social functions (expressing ideas and values, symbolizing social institutions). This chapter is also about aesthetic expression, but here we focus on the human body as a vehicle for expressive culture, providing a cross-cultural view of what people do with and to their bodies in order to express a variety of cultural messages. The chapter investigates some of the ways in which people alter, adorn, or modify their bodies; how body movements convey different messages in different cultural settings; and how attitudes toward the body—what is acceptable, what is forbidden, what is ugly, what is beautiful—vary from culture to culture. By examining what motivates people to choose particular forms of body expression and how these forms fit holistically into their cultural contexts, the chapter illustrates what can be learned about a culture from studying its people's physical appearance.

• Body Adornment •

We use the term *body adornment* to refer to the voluntary and reversible (as opposed to permanent) changes people make to the outward appearance of their bodies. These changes include wearing clothing and jewelry, using cosmetics (which in many societies are applied to the body as well as to the face), and styling and coloring the hair.

Clothing

Human beings almost completely lack the external physical protection from the natural environment that other animals possess, such as tough hides, hard shells, layers of feathers, or thick coats of fur. Even people living in tropical climates, where no insulation against cold weather is needed, must protect their bodies from the sun, rain, stinging insects, thorny vegetation, or rough surfaces. No doubt for this reason, the vast majority of people wear clothes. The native people of Australia, called the Aborigines, were an exception; most were reportedly naked when first contacted by Westerners. But (as far as we know) for practical reasons, few societies in the past, and none today, completely lack a tradition of clothing the body.

Garments protect their wearers, but have another, equally important, function as well: to convey messages, both about individual clothes wearers and about the culture or subculture of which they are a part (Barnes and Eicher 1992; Kaiser 1990). One of these is the message of sexual identity. Few societies depend totally on anatomical differences to distinguish males from females. In most, different styles of clothing confirm the differences between the two sexes. Contemporary Western society is unusual in that certain items of casual wear, such as jeans, T-shirts, and jogging shoes, are considered appropriate for both males and females. In India, women wear saris, men wear dhotis—never the reverse.

Wearing clothes seems not to depend on any innate human sense of modesty, for there is no universal agreement about which parts of the body should be kept hidden from view. In many (but by no means all) societies, the sexual organs, especially those of adults, are kept covered, but in other societies they are intentionally exposed. Sometimes clothing both covers and accentuates simultaneously; Western women's bras and Pacific men's penis sheaths both conceal and emphasize parts of the body. Depending on the society, other parts of the body—the hair, the lower part of the face, the ankles, the female midsection (to name just a few)—are either well hidden or intentionally exposed to public view.

Another message clothes convey is self-identity. If you were shown close-up photographs of the faces—and only the faces—of two young males, you might be able to determine their approximate ages, ethnic origins, states of health, and moods, but you would have trouble determining which was the face of a punk rocker and which a preppy. Whole-body photographs of the same two males, however—one in a metal-studded leather jacket, combat boots, and spiked hairdo; the other in an oxford-cloth shirt, madras slacks, deck shoes, and

• Ask Yourself •

American football uniforms have heavily padded shoulders and codpieces to provide protection for their wearers. These same uniform features, of course, also accentuate players' size and masculinity. Is this intentional or not? Do other kinds of Western sports uniforms intentionally emphasize players' size, strength, or other attributes?

Although adults' sexual organs are kept hidden by clothing in most societies, in some they are intentionally exposed or accentuated. In Irian Jaya, Indonesia, a Dani man (see map on page 385) wears a traditional penis sheath.

short, slicked-down hair—would give you a great deal of information about the different interests and values of these two individuals, provided the cultural context was one with which you were familiar.

The interests and values expressed by the appearances of these two individuals are not merely personal. Clothing reflects cultural as well as personal beliefs and ideals, and it is the cultural rather than the personal aspects of clothing that most interest anthropologists. What can we learn about the worldview of a given society from the

purdah the physical seclusion of women, a custom common in the Middle East

way its members dress? In what values do the society's members collectively believe? What can clothes tell us about who is socially, politically, or economically dominant in the society and who is not? About the relationships between the sexes in the society and the attitudes of members of one sex toward members of the other? About the people's sense of national or ethnic identity, their conservative or liberal inclinations, even their religious beliefs?

Head coverings are a good example of the range of ideas that can be transmitted by a single item of clothing. The custom of covering the head, and sometimes the face as well, with a piece of cloth is widespread among females in Middle Eastern societies. Women wear headcloths ranging in size from small kerchiefs to large, enveloping semicircles of cloth that cover the entire body, including the head and sometimes much of the face. These veils are the external expression of deeply rooted Middle Eastern customs and collective ideas (Fernea and Fernea 1987), some of which find their origins in the Muslim religion.

The Middle Eastern custom of veiling originated in the time of the prophet Muhammad (A.D. 570–632), founder of Islam, as an outward symbol of religious identity. Muhammad's wives, so the story goes, were once mistaken for slaves—a grievous insult. To avoid future confusion, female followers of Muhammad began to wear veils (Fernea and Fernea 1987:106). But if its first cultural message was one of religious identity, veiling soon began to send a message about social status as well. Because it obstructed both movement and vision, the veil made performing certain tasks very difficult. A poor woman obliged to labor in the fields could not wear one. Thus, wearing this garment soon began to suggest a privileged life-style and high social status. This notion remains widely held today.

Veiling delivers other cultural messages too. Many Middle Easterners believe that females have strong sexual appetites and that their sexual behavior reflects directly on the honor of their families. For some, a family's honor rests in part on controlling women's sexuality (Lindholm and Lindholm 1985:234). To protect women from sexual temptation, and males from the uncontrollable lust of dangerous women who might ruin their good names, the physical seclusion of women, a custom known as **purdah,** has been practiced

In some cultures, women traditionally wear garments that hide both their faces and bodies. Faces may be shielded by light fabric through which women can see enough to get about, heavier fabric in which eye holes have been cut, or full masks of leather or even metal. In the Hadramaut region of South Yemen (see map on page 357), a woman wears her culture's traditional garb.

since the time of Muhammad. Houses may be surrounded by high walls, and women may spend their entire lives virtually imprisoned behind them. Wrapping a woman in a garment that conceals her body from public view is another reflection of the same idea. Today, a Middle Eastern woman wearing a veil on a public street is signaling "hands off!" A man who approaches a veiled woman invites serious trouble, for he is shaming both the woman and her family. This does not mean that a woman wearing a veil is necessarily repressed, inhibited, or even ultraconservative.

A modern Muslim woman's veil may conceal a T-shirt, jeans, and sneakers.

Another cultural notion associated with veiling is modesty. Among the Bedouin, Arabic-speaking nomads of the Middle East, modesty is an essential component of personal honor and respectability (Abu-Lughod 1986, 1987). The honorable person keeps his or her distance from members of the opposite sex (except for close relatives); casts the eyes shyly downward; moves with formality; and refrains from eating, smoking, talking, or laughing in certain social situations. Young, unmarried women show that they are modest and respectable by wearing kerchiefs on their heads. Married women wear black headcloths that can be drawn protectively across the face when they are in the presence of certain men, such as in-laws. To display one's modesty in this way is a matter of pride for the Bedouin, who consider this behavior "a sign of respect for the social and moral system" (1987:29).

These examples show that in the Middle East, the cultural meanings attached to wearing a veil (or not wearing one) are many. Depending on where and in what style it is being worn, the veil can symbolize a woman's faith, the idea of protection (both from danger and from temptation), the notion of women as temptresses who must not be allowed to distract men, status and wealth, and personal modesty. And although we have been discussing the veil as an article of female apparel, among the Tuareg, camel pastoralists of North Africa, men wear veils because lips are considered obscene.

Westerners, too, convey messages with their clothing. In church, a woman's hat or kerchief is a mark of her religious faith; at a party, her expensive beaded dress suggests her wealth and thus her social status. Her white bridal gown symbolizes her purity, and her bridal veil her modesty. When she wears a bikini she does so not to express faith, wealth, social

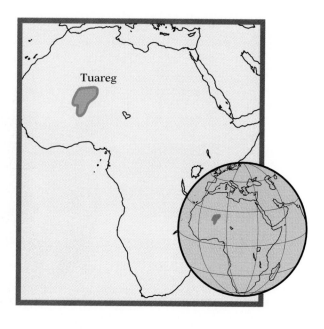

status, purity, or modesty but rather to show off her attractive body. Her message is one of good health, self-discipline, self-esteem, and interest in attracting the attention of the opposite sex.

• Ask Yourself •

How do you feel about our society's custom of veiling brides? What cultural message(s) do you think a bridal veil conveys? If you marry, will a veil be part of your wedding?

Jewelry

In North American culture, rings and other kinds of jewelry often convey specific messages. A graduate's high school or college ring denotes both educational status and institutional affiliation; a married person's wedding ring reveals his or her marital status; and a football player's Superbowl ring testifies to his athletic prowess, not to mention his membership in a very exclusive athletic group. Men's lapel pins and tie tacks are another class of jewelry often intended to signal professional, religious, political, or social affiliations or to reflect their wearers' interests in particular sports or hob-

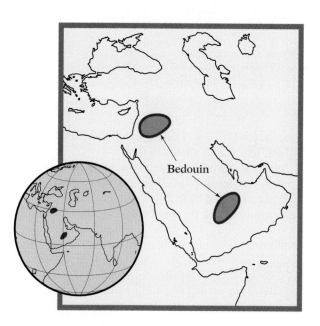

When introduced in 1945, this kind of bathing suit was considered nothing short of atomic, so it was named after Bikini Atoll, an atomic bomb test site. But Roman women were wearing similar garments as early as A.D. 300. In the hunting lodge of emperor Maximilian Herculius are found mosaics of goddesses, heroes, jungle animals—and bikini-clad women (Swindells 1987:23).

bies. Other items of jewelry worn in our society deliver less intentional or even unconscious messages. A woman's sparkling diamond cocktail ring may suggest wealth and thus social status, but she may claim she wears it only as an ornament.

Jewelry reflects status, group membership, or personal interests in other societies, too. When a young Zulu woman falls in love, she makes a beaded necklace resembling a close-fitting collar with a flat panel attached, which she gives to her boyfriend. Depending on the colors and patterns of the beads, this necklace can convey a host of different romantic messages. A combination of pink and white beads in a certain pattern, for instance, might mean "you are poor ... but I love you" (Dubin 1987:134). Some Zulu men wear multiple necklaces, each a gift from a different girlfriend. Together they prove their wearers' attractiveness to the opposite sex: the more necklaces, the more girlfriends. A married man's necklaces may show how many wives he has. With other items of beaded jewelry—belts, bracelets, and anklets—young Zulu women let the world know whether they are romantically involved with someone or still available, the same message that engagement rings impart in our own society.

In addition to proclaiming social, educational, or marital status, group affiliation, or personal interests, jewelry is sometimes worn for good luck or to protect its wearer from harm. In North America, jewelry bearing religious symbols is common, and many wearers refuse to remove such jewelry for fear of bad luck.

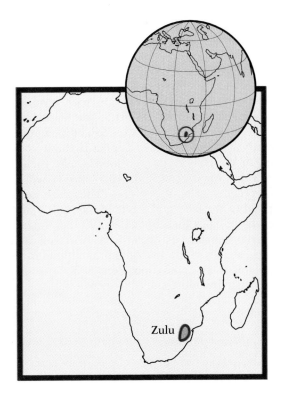

Zulu women give their boyfriends beaded collars with flat panels that convey different romantic messages, depending on the colors and patterns used. Near Durban, South Africa, a young Zulu man's neck ornament signals his romantic involvement.

Cosmetics

Another way in which people adorn their bodies is by temporarily decorating their skin with **cosmetics,** the general term for preparations designed to improve the appearance of the body, or part of it, by directly but temporarily applying them to the skin. In Western society, cosmetics take the form of various mass-produced, petroleum-based, colored creams, oils, or powders. These are usually applied to the face, and are much more frequently used by females than by males. In other societies, the term *cosmetics* may refer to body as well as face paints, usually made by combining animal or vegetable oils with colored powders made from naturally occurring minerals.

The extent to which cosmetics are used in human societies, from the remote jungles of South America to the high-fashion capitals of western Europe, suggests that the notion of adorning or enhancing the surface of the body, like the idea of covering it with clothing, comes close to being a human universal. There are differences of placement, emphasis, and extent among various traditions of cosmetic use, but the reasons for wearing cosmetics are similar.

In every society with a cosmetic tradition, including Western society, one reason bodies are decorated is to enhance them—to make them appear more perfectly in accord with society's ideals of beauty (although, as we shall see at the end of this chapter, what is considered attractive varies widely from society to society). But in some societies, the use of cosmetics quite consciously provides other benefits as well. Cosmetics may protect people from harm, express their social status, or identify them as members of particular classes or families. Benefits of this kind are probably part

---

cosmetics preparations designed to improve the appearance of the body, or part of it, by directly but temporarily applying them to the skin

The Anthropologist at Work

Anthropology and the Fashion Industry

The high-fashion industry is thriving in the United States, Europe, and most recently Japan. We know of no anthropologists working in this industry, but why not? Since clothing is so expressive of its wearers' beliefs, attitudes, and ideals, an anthropologist could contribute greatly to the design and marketing of clothes.

Consider, as an example, the current fashion among many young, Western males for expensive, thick-soled, high-topped athletic shoes, usually worn with laces undone. What is the basis of the enormous appeal of this kind of footwear among a particular group of people? Do such shoes convey messages of athleticism,

wealth, nonchalance, or all of these, or something else altogether? Understanding what admirable personal qualities or social allegiances are suggested by particular elements of dress would enable one to design other kinds of clothing, accessories, or footwear that would also appeal to members of the same group.

A college graduate with a thorough understanding of the kinds of cultural or personal messages that elements of dress can convey, and also of how attitudes about revealing or concealing certain parts of the body are changing in Western society, might prove to be an able designer and seller of clothes. If you are considering a career in the world of fashion, perhaps you can think of ways that majoring in anthropology might make you uniquely employable.

---

of the reason behind Western cosmetic use also, although Western cosmetics users may not be aware of it.

If Westerners differ little from members of other societies in their primary motivations for applying cosmetics, they do differ from some in the relatively modest extent to which they decorate themselves. Cosmetic use in some societies is so extensive it would make the heavy-handed application of cosmetics to a female American screen star by a Hollywood makeup artist seem moderate.

A well-turned-out Nuba male from Kordofan Province in the Sudan of northern Africa is literally painted from head to foot. Among the Nuba, body painting begins in infancy, when a baby's scalp is decorated with either red or yellow paint, depending on its family membership (Faris 1972:30). Thereafter, body painting is used to suggest one's social and physical status as well as to beautify, and it becomes more and more complex with advancing age. A young Nuba boy, for example, wears simple, inconspicuous, red and greyish white decorations on

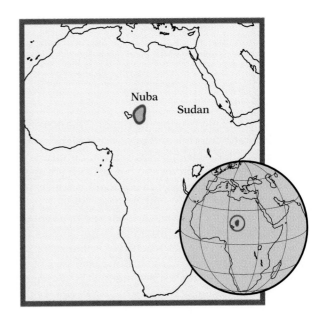

Cosmetics are universally used to beautify people, protect them from harm, express their social status, or identify them as members of particular groups. In Liberia, a Bassa girl being initiated into the Sande, an all-female secret society, is covered with a chalky white clay.

his scalp, gradually earning the right to use increasingly elaborate, colorful, and extensive designs as he matures (38). Each change of age and status means a new kind of decoration for the boy, as with advancing years he earns the right to use more products in a wider range of colors and designs. (Westerners, too, sometimes use cosmetics as an age marker, as when an American girl is forbidden by her parents to wear lipstick until she has reached a certain age.)

The scalp, face, chest, back, arms, and legs of a young adult Nuba male may literally be covered with colorful designs (Faris 1972:18–19, 62), both purely decorative (straight and curved lines, dots,

triangles, crosshatching) and representational (animals, airplanes, lightening, stars—even English words, which may or may not be intelligible to the Nuba). Often these designs are asymmetrically placed on the face or body and are strikingly modern looking. They may take up to an hour to apply and may be redone daily.

Decorating the body as well as the face with cosmetics is by no means limited to rural or small-scale societies. Some modern, urban girls and women in North Africa, the Middle East, and South Asia decorate their skin with henna, an orange-red dye made from leaves (see photo, page 82). Urban Moroccan women, for example, may be decorated on suitable occasions with fine lines and dots forming intricate designs. These are typically applied to the hands and feet, which then look as if they are clad in lace gloves or stockings. Henna is applied at a "henna party," to which the girl or woman to be decorated invites her friends, a professional henna artist, and sometimes professional musicians or other entertainers. During the long and careful process of decorating, the guests eat, sing songs, tell jokes, and dance around the woman being decorated (Messina 1988).

• Ask Yourself •

Compared with females, North American males use cosmetics only rarely. How do you feel about cosmetic use among males? What message is a man who uses a bronzing lotion sending? A man who uses eye shadow?

Moroccan women who use henna say they apply it for a variety of reasons. A girl or woman may be decorated in preparation for a religious festival or her wedding, to cheer her up in late pregnancy, to soften her skin, to prevent spirits called *jinni* from causing illness or misfortune, or to calm her nerves. Whatever the reason, applying henna is cause for celebration; a henna party provides a "lively departure" from formal Islamic expectations of proper female behavior (Messina 1988:46). People from different regions admire different designs, and styles of decoration change constantly, but the designs themselves have no explicit meanings.

Hairdressing

As the most easily manipulated feature of the human body, hair may be the feature most fre-

In many societies, the act of cutting the hair symbolizes relinquishing personal power. In what has become a traditional rite of passage in the U.S. military, new Marines are shorn of their hair as their training begins.

quently exploited for self-expression. Furthermore, hair—like fingernails—continues to grow throughout life, which for some cultures suggests that it has life and power of its own, even as individuals do. In such cultures, hair may be imbued with special symbolic significance or mystical qualities. For the Rindi of Sumba, in Indonesia (see map on page 240), the combination of life and power suggests the fertility of crops or of human beings. In one Rindi ritual, hair is clipped from the front of men's heads or from the back of women's to ensure the fertility of rice crops (Forth 1981:167–168). The clippings are discarded like useless rice chaff, which is similarly thrown away. The hair that remains on the head symbolizes rice that has been harvested and that, of course, feeds the Rindi villagers. The idea behind the ritual is that by getting rid of what is useless and retaining what is essential, the rice crop next season will also be maintained.

Cross-culturally, clippings of hair commonly symbolize the individual from which they have been taken. Moreover, hair can be seen as a sort of extension of the human body, a notion that adds to its usefulness as a symbol for the individual or even the entire society. Thus, we find that in many societies the act of cutting the hair is a symbol for surrendering power, as in the Biblical story of Samson.

Hair may also symbolize the possibilities for sex, the prohibition of sex, or merely the control of unrestrained sex. For the Rindi, hair worn long symbolizes unrestrained sexuality and fertility, whereas hair fastened into a topknot or bun symbolizes restrained sexuality and controlled fertility. The people in this society demonstrate their control over sexual behavior either by cutting their hair, which suggests an absolute restriction, or by binding it, which suggests sexual restraint (Forth 1981:159).

In Chapter 3, we mentioned a study in psychological anthropology by Gananath Obeyesekere (1984:33–51), who called upon the symbolism associated with hair to demonstrate links between culture and personality in Sri Lanka (see map on page 60). Obeyesekere detected an association between the long, dirty locks of matted hair worn by priestesses of a Hindu-Buddhist cult and snakes, and a further association of snakes with anxiety about castration (see photo, page 60). His study demonstrated, among other things, that the physical properties of hair make it highly suitable for expressing an individual's ritual or social status.

The symbolism associated with hair is familiar to Westerners. A little boy's first trip to the barber to have his baby curls shorn is an important event to

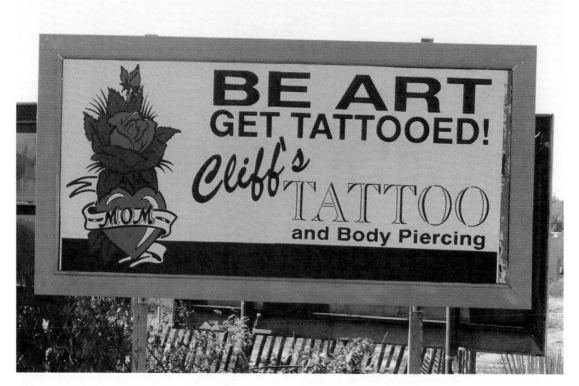

The members of many societies alter or adorn their bodies to express cultural or personal values, beliefs, and preferences. A sign in a suburb of New York City suggests the possibility of the body as a medium for aesthetic expression.

some Western families. The toddler's parents snap photographs, and bystanders exclaim what a "big boy" he has suddenly become. An 11-year-old girl who cuts off her braids is announcing that she feels ready for adulthood. Hair fashions—different choices regarding cut, color, and curl—identify both male and female teenagers as belonging to one or another social or ethnic group, as being bold or shy, or as conforming to traditional values or rejecting them. Advertising for hair-coloring products exhorts middle-aged men and women to "wash away that grey" in order to project youth and vitality. In Western society as in others, hair conveys a wide range of cultural messages.

cicatrization a form of scarification in which the skin is repeatedly punctured in an intricate pattern

• Body Alteration •

Altering the outward appearance of the body by making permanent, irreversible changes to it is widely practiced in Western as well as non-Western societies. In the West, tattooing the skin and piercing the ears are customs of long standing; inserting metal rings or other objects through the fleshy parts of the nose, brow, navel, or other parts of the body—customs long practiced elsewhere—are relatively new to Westerners. Members of certain non-Western cultures also pierce the septum of the nose to insert a piece of bone or shell; solder a tall stack of iron rings around the neck, thus elongating it; or practice **cicatrization**—repeatedly puncturing the skin in an intricate pattern to produce permanent, decorative scarring. Westerners may think of these kinds of body alteration as deformation or mutilation rather than decoration, but they are not fundamentally different from ear piercing or tattooing.

Sometimes both sexual and social status are symbolized by a single bodily alteration or artifact. Among the Kayapó of Brazil, a lip disc called a labret symbolizes masculine strength, maturity, and leadership.

Any of these practices may be undertaken for purely decorative purposes, to express religious beliefs, to achieve imagined health benefits, or as elements in rites of passage.

Labrets

Labrets or lip plugs, objects typically made of wood or bone that are inserted into the flesh of the lower lip, are found in many places around the world, including East Africa and South America. They vary considerably in shape and size. A small version is usually inserted in childhood, and may be increased in size as the individual matures, reflecting changes in his or her social status.

Among the Kayapó of Brazil, a young man who has become a father for the first time is seen as having officially passed from boyhood to manhood (T.S. Turner 1987). This passage from one social status to another is symbolized by a permanent physical change: the small plug that was inserted through the flesh of his lower lip when the new father was himself an infant is replaced by a much larger, saucerlike plate, which may reach a diameter of 4 inches.

The insertion of the new labret is painful, although perhaps no more so than the insertion and periodic tightening of dental braces in Western

Kayapó

labret a plug inserted through the flesh of the lower lip

society, which many Westerners consider quite bearable given the perceived aesthetic benefits of orthodontia. The benefits of the lip disc are equally worthwhile for the Kayapó. Once a father, a Kayapó male is entitled to speak his mind on matters of concern to his village. In fact he must, if he is to earn the respect of other villagers, for silence is not considered a virtue. Verbally assertive, mature males, and they alone, command the political respect that permits them to preside over village life. The lip disc thus symbolizes not only fatherhood but also a male's status as a mature, strong, verbally aggressive village leader. Sexual and social status are combined in this single symbolic artifact. Kayapó women are not permitted to wear labrets because of their strong symbolic association with fatherhood and manhood (T. S. Turner 1987).

Scarification

The personal artistic tradition of the Nuba (see map on page 379), whose body painting we described earlier in this chapter, also includes **scarification:** creating designs on the body by the intentional wounding and subsequent healing and scarring of the skin. (Cicatrization, mentioned above, is one form of scarification.) A young Nuba girl's body is decorated with its first scars at the onset of puberty, usually when she is 9 or 10 (Faris 1972:32). The skin on the abdomen is repeatedly hooked with a sharp thorn, pulled away from the body, and sliced with a small metal knife. Later, when the girl begins to menstruate, this first series of scars is complemented by a second, extending from beneath her breasts to her back and covering her torso. Finally, after she has given birth and has weaned her first child, she is again scarred, this time over the rest of her back, neck, the backs of her arms, buttocks, and the backs of her legs.

The scarification procedure is painful, and although Nuba girls try to remain stoic, some lose consciousness from the pain and loss of blood. Yet the perceived benefits of scarification outweigh its painful penalties. The Nuba see scarification primarily as a "beauty treatment" (Faris 1972:36), but it is also a symbol of sexual status, proclaiming that a female has begun to develop sexually, is sexually mature and thus marriageable, or has become a

---

scarification designs made by the intentional wounding and subsequent healing and scarring of the skin

mutilation any irreversible alteration of a healthy human body

mother. Nuba boys are not decorated with body scars, though both males and females are scarred above the eyes and on the temples. Again, this is done mainly for the sake of beauty, but the Nuba also believe that facial scars will improve one's vision and prevent headaches.

Mutilation

Pain is carried to greater extremes in societies that practice actual **mutilation** of the body. Mutilation is the irreversible alteration or removal of any healthy part of the body, and it is common cross-culturally, although the reasons behind it vary. In the name of God, Middle Eastern Muslims may sever the hands of those found guilty of theft. Some Westerners, too, remove healthy tissues in the name of religion, routinely circumcising infant boys for religious reasons. Circumcision, in the West and elsewhere, is also practiced for perceived health or cosmetic benefits. The removal of other healthy tissues for cosmetic reasons now constitutes a substantial Western medical specialty, whose practitioners are increasingly performing surgeries such as liposuction (removal of fat from under the skin), breast reduction, and rhinoplasty (the surgical restructuring of the nose) to improve their patients' appearance.

Some small-scale societies, past and present, incorporate similar practices. The cave art of Europeans of the Upper Palaeolithic period (see Figure 14.1, page 348), whose paintings of animals we described in Chapter 14, includes images of mutilated human hands, made by placing a hand firmly against a cave wall and then blowing a mouthful of paint at it to produce a smudgy, haloed outline. Caves in northern Spain contain images of hands missing all their fingers; other hand images lack a single digit, or a fingertip or two. While an artist could conceivably produce such a painting by bending under one or more fingers of a healthy hand at the second joint, the Upper Palaeolithic mutilated hand images were clearly made using real hands, since it is impossible to fold under one's fingertips at the first joint and still produce an image as sharp as those in the cave paintings.

Archaeologists do not know why the gatherers and hunters of northern Spain intentionally mutilated themselves. Perhaps removing fingers or fingertips was intended to appease the ghosts of long-dead ancestors, or to punish miscreants—like the removal of hands in the Middle East today. Deformed hands may even have been considered beautiful, as are the small, straight noses of

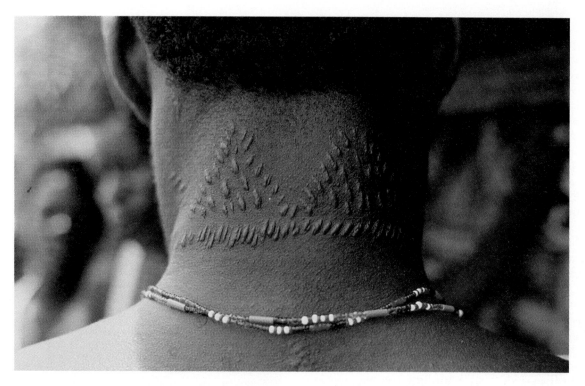

Scarification is a general term for designs made by intentionally wounding the skin, while cicatrization refers specifically to repeatedly puncturing the skin to produce a permanent decorative pattern. Here, a Tofinnu man in Benin, Africa, enhances his cicatrization with a colorful necklace.

Westerners who have had bone and flesh removed by plastic surgeons. It has even been suggested that the deformities were unintentional; they may have resulted from frostbite, infection in cuts acquired during stone toolmaking, or some crippling disease. Unintentional or not, the Upper Palaeolithic hunters deliberately left a record of their deformities.

In a modern-day echo of this Ice Age practice, the culture of the Dani of western New Guinea incorporates a similar custom. The religion of the Dani is a form of ancestor worship. When a Dani villager is killed by an enemy from a neighboring village, the ancestral ghosts of the victim's community require that the death be avenged by killing an enemy in retribution. In addition, the ancestors demand the performance of a ritual involving the severing of a fingertip from a young female relative of the victim (Heider 1979:124–126). This ritual, a rite of passage for the deceased, may require that as many as three young girls, between about 3 and 6 years old, sacrifice a finger joint. Some Dani girls undergo the ritual for more than one dead relative. The mutilation is performed by a ritual

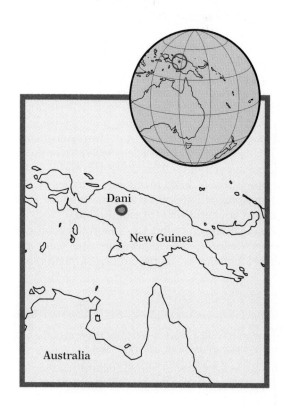

specialist, who first ties a string tightly around the upper arm of the chosen girl. He numbs her fingers by striking them hard against a rock, then severs one or two fingers at the first joint with a blow from a stone ax. Someone quickly bandages the girl's wounds with leaves, and afterward she sits quietly for the rest of the day, probably in a state of shock, holding her bloody hand upright so healing can begin.

In other circumstances, the Dani are eager to avoid causing pain to children, which suggests the great importance of the reason behind hand mutilation—to lessen the anger of their long-dead ancestors, now ghosts. The girl's pain is apparently thought of as a sacrificial offering to these phantoms. Going beyond the Dani's own explanation, a structural-functional interpretation of this custom might suggest that mutilation is a symbolic way of integrating Dani females into the otherwise all-male intertribal cycle of killing and revenge. Whatever the reason behind the practice, the result is that many Dani women go through life with mutilated hands. Apparently, however, they perform household tasks with little trouble, and knit and weave with great skill.

Earlier we mentioned another form of mutilation, circumcision, cross-culturally much more common than the severing of fingers or hands. In contemporary Western societies, only males are circumcized, but a procedure to alter the external genitalia was performed on females in the United States and Europe up until Victorian times, usually as a medical treatment for masturbation (see Masson 1986). Circumcision is still performed on females in some non-Western societies (see photo on page 83), although not to "cure" masturbation (Abdalla 1982; Lightfoot-Klein 1989). Over much of Africa, in parts of the Muslim world, and elsewhere, circumcision of both males and females is a customary part of rites of passage marking the official entry of boys and girls into adulthood.

Female circumcision can involve several different procedures, which fall into two main types. **Clitoridectomy** is the partial or complete removal

of the clitoris and sometimes the labia minora as well. **Infibulation** includes clitoridectomy, but refers more specifically to the process of stitching together the two sides of the vaginal opening (the term comes from the custom of the ancient Romans of fastening a pin, or fibula, through the labia majora to prevent women from committing adultery). Unlike male circumcision, these procedures can have a profound negative effect on a female's sexual responsiveness.

More important for our purposes than the details of the physical procedures performed is an undersanding of their cultural explanations. Circumcision of both males and females may be carried out to promote physical or psychological

Among the Dani, fingers from the hands of young girls are sacrificed to the spirits of the dead. Here, a Dani girl (center), her hand wrapped in banana leaves, recovers from her sacrifice.

---

clitoridectomy the partial or complete removal of the clitoris and sometimes the labia minora as well

infibulation the process of stitching together the two sides of the vaginal opening

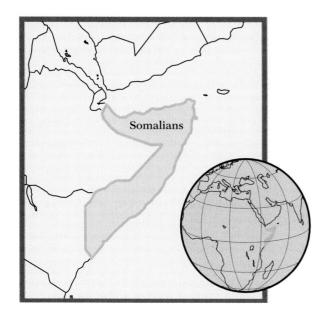

health, as a mark of social status, or to make a symbolic statement about sexual identity and the different roles of men and women. In circumcising males, for instance, people may say they are removing the female aspect, and in circumcising females they may say they are removing the male part.

Among some Somalians in Northeast Africa, girls are customarily infibulated between the ages of 6 and 12. While older women gather around to restrain the girl and offer advice and encouragement, a female specialist performs the operation with a razor. No antiseptics or anaesthetics are used to protect the girl from infection or pain (Abdalla 1982:18). Somalians give several reasons why female circumcision is performed. First, it is a rite of passage that, in the Somali view, transforms a girl into a marriageable woman—a desirable social status. Second, virginity is highly valued in Somali society, and infibulation provides visual proof that an unmarried female is a virgin (52). The smaller the entrance to a bride's vagina, the greater her reputation, the higher her value in the marriage market, and the more honorable her family (20).

As is true of the circumscision of infant males in North America, causing pain to children, wherever it occurs, is done for reasons of tradition, religious belief, and status—reasons considered powerful enough to justify both pain and the possibility of unintended, adverse health consequences. Recently, some Western parents and pediatricians have rejected male circumcision on the grounds that its possible health benefits are outweighed by the pain it causes and the potential risk of bleeding or infection it entails, but the practice is deeply ingrained among Americans, and some 60 percent of American male infants are still routinely circumcised (Lindsey 1988). Health and hygiene are the explanations generally given to justify this mutilation in North America, but religious tradition is the justification for Jews, and many non-Jewish parents approve of circumcision for their infant sons because they think most other boys are circumcised and they do not want their sons to be embarrassed in the locker room later on in life. The force of custom is very strong.

• Body Language •

Movements of the body and face are among the ways in which human beings communicate with others (Vargas 1986). **Body language** (**kinesics**) consists of nonverbal ways of conveying ideas, feelings, and intentions through body movements and facial expressions. Unlike body adornment and alteration, body language may be unintentional or even unconscious. It includes universal facial gestures such as smiling or frowning, completely reflexive movements such as the involuntary enlargement of the pupils of the eyes when a person see something attractive, and conscious movements such as squaring the shoulders before entering a roomful of people.

Whether involuntary or controllable, body language can send many kinds of messages. Imagine the different postures, gestures, and facial expressions of the following: someone who is violently angry and ready to fight, someone who is grief-stricken after receiving devastating news, someone who feels obliged to listen to a dull lecture, and someone who has just caught a touchdown pass or pitched a no-hitter. These examples illustrate the extent to which body language mirrors intentions, feelings, or states of mind.

The body language that conveys the most basic human emotions—anger, grief, boredom, joy—is similar all over the world. However, body language that can be controlled, as opposed to involuntary

---

body language (kinesics) nonverbal communication through body movements or facial expressions

actions that cannot, may have one meaning in one culture and an entirely different meaning in another. In parts of Latin America, tapping the head with a forefinger means "I'm thinking," but in North America it can mean "you're crazy." The "A-OK" gesture of circled thumb and index finger, familiar to North Americans, is considered vulgar in Brazil. In Finland, people who fold their arms are thought to be arrogant, but in Fiji, the same gesture signals disrespect (Axtell 1985:43–47). In traditional Tibet, a low-status person, upon encountering a higher-status person on the street, sticks his tongue out at his superior as a symbol of respect. Controllable body language, like verbal language, is a product of culture rather than nature.

Differences in the body language employed by males and females can sometimes reveal much about gender relations in a society. Consider, for example, a recent study of the body language of Western office workers, female and male (McKee 1990). Researchers videotaped bank employees, and then analyzed their body language to discover "whether men speak a language women don't—the language of power."

> The answer, it seems, is yes. [The] film clips show men . . . stretching like lazy lions, stalking majestically about to define their space, and pawing their female counterparts patronizingly in displays of dominance. The women, on the other hand—even those of equal rank to the male managers—huddle together like sheep . . . or hover in doe-like deference to the species they plainly perceive as . . . superior. . . . The men confer like a war council—upright, arrogant, with bold gestures—while the women, even if they're talking business, appear to gossip in girlish camaraderie.

The researchers noted that some women in positions of power, such as former British Prime Minister Margaret Thatcher, change their style of moving and speaking to reflect their new status. Men, they prophesied, will have to "start learning the submissive body language of subordinates as more lionesses begin to prowl the business jungle."

Sexual messages that are conveyed bodily illustrate the combination of involuntary and controllable behaviors that make up body language. Whatever their culture, children learn the body language appropriate to members of their sex, mostly without being aware they are learning it. Little girls

imitate their mothers or older females; little boys imitate their fathers or older males. (In the West, this imitation is often based on the behavior of characters on television or in the movies in addition to or instead of family members.) However, the nonverbal ways of communicating that are learned in this fashion vary widely from one culture to another.

Western adults often use their bodies to signal sexual interest (Hall and Hall 1987). A woman may lower her chin, glance briefly upward at a man, and look away, or she may look directly at him, narrowing her eyes and slightly parting her lips. Either way, her eyes will seem brighter than usual because her pupils are dilated, an unconscious physiological response to her feelings. She is likely to make what students of animal behavior call "preening gestures": touching the back of her hair, straightening her back, crossing her legs if she is seated. She may place her hand on her thigh or stroke the inside of her wrist as she talks, showing the palm of her hand. A man, to attract a particular woman, may place his hands in his pockets or hook his thumbs through his belt, movements that raise and square his shoulders, making them look larger. When he catches her eye, he may hold her glance a little longer than is usual in our society. If he receives an encouraging smile, he may move toward her, standing within her "personal space" (the space beyond which casual conversation always takes place in our culture), and engage in playful talk. His preening gestures may include straightening his tie or cuffs or smoothing his hair (88).

The body language with which both males and females in Western culture signal sexual interest is thus partly conscious and intentional and partly unconscious and unintentional. Either way, it is usually relatively easily deciphered by members of the same culture who are of the opposite sex. However, the body language with which Westerners are familiar may be misinterpreted by members of other cultures, and vice versa. In Latin America, people engaged in ordinary conversation typically stand closer to each other than do people in North America, so the relative lack of personal space between two people who are speaking to each other does not in itself signal sexual interest.

• Attitudes Toward the Body •

Attitudes toward the body include concepts of what is beautiful versus what is ugly, what is healthy ver-

Body language is a combination of intentional and involuntary behaviors. To signal sexual interest, a woman may intentionally narrow her eyes, part her lips, and touch her hair, while her pupils dilate in an unconscious physiological response to her feelings.

sus what is unfit, what is sexy versus what is not, and what suggests high moral character versus low. Opinions on these matters differ from society to society. To the Classic Maya, who lived in Mexico, Guatemala, and Belize about a thousand years ago, flat, elongated heads, achieved by pressing children's heads between boards, were considered beautiful. In traditional China, short female feet were considered so desirable that the feet of upper-class girls were tightly bound so they would not grow normally but remain forever child-sized. In North America, the slimness of women's feet, rather than their shortness, is valued, and is accentuated with uncomfortable, pointed shoes. The body paintings and other decorations worn by the Nuba people appear colorful to members of other cultures, but not attractive in the same way as they are to other Nuba.

Although the focus of this chapter is on how people alter their bodies to express cultural messages, it should be noted that femaleness or maleness itself can symbolize cultural values. In Botswana, South Africa, the Tswana people regard the female body as being "open" to whatever hostile forces

• Ask Yourself •

Do you ever feel "crowded" while standing and conversing with someone? If so, what do you usually do about it? How does the physical distance between you and someone you're speaking with affect you? How do you feel about conversational partners who occasionally touch your arm or shoulder?

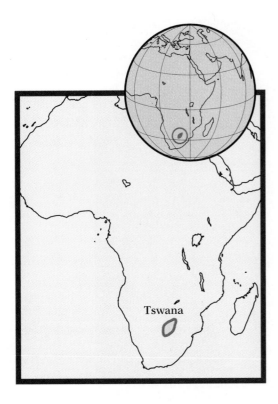

Tswana

plague Tswana life. In contrast, the bodies of males are "closed," making males more able to resist such forces (Comaroff 1985:67–68, 81). "Open" female bodies are classified as "hot," and "closed" male bodies are "cool." Since heat is unstable and liable at any moment to spill over into other individuals, women are seen as dangerous to men, whose coolness makes them more socially stable. These distinctions—which are among the oppositions with which structural anthropology concerns itself—fit neatly into a holistic picture of Tswana culture. To take Tswana subsistence activities as an example, horticulture (a risky, uncertain enterprise) is best suited to the "unstable" female sex; pastoralism (far more predictable and controllable) is best suited to the "steadier" male sex.

Thus, among the Tswana, not only do bodies themselves have symbolic meaning; body symbolism is also integrated with other aspects of Tswana culture. Likewise, in a provocative examination of the symbolism surrounding femaleness in North America, Emily Martin (1987) argues that American female bodies also serve as metaphors that affect how American women view themselves and their world. American women's bodies, Martin suggests,

are seen both as systems controlled by the brain and as factories for the production of babies. Depending in part on their socioeconomic status, American women both accept and resist the cultural meanings these metaphors impose on female body processes such as menstruation, birth, and menopause.

Thinness and Fatness

In contemporary North America, thinness is considered by most people to be more attractive than fatness. In fact, so important is thinness in the current North American ideal of attractiveness, especially for women, that many people are prepared to endure the discomfort of continuous caloric deprivation in order to stay slim. Some even develop an unrealistic view of themselves as too fat, become hooked on the habit of starving themselves, and suffer dangerous and occasionally fatal weight loss, a mental and physical condition known as **anorexia nervosa.** The hallmark of anorexia among Westerners is not so much the appearance of the body or the meagerness of the diet but the fact that starvation is not required to adapt successfully to a career or social position. In contrast to those considered anorexic, thin jockeys or high-fashion female models are not usually considered to be ill, because their professions require extreme thinness.

Anorexia is a functional disorder, meaning that it has no apparent cause, occurring as a disruption of bodily functioning in otherwise healthy individuals. More interestingly for our purposes, anorexia is also culture-bound: even though self-starvation occurs in all cultures and among people of both sexes and all ages, the ways in which it manifests itself among those who suffer from it, the ways in which it is interpreted by others in society, and the ways in which it is treated differ from society to society.

In the West, anorexia was first identified as a disease in 1873 by the English physician Sir William Gull. Outside of the medical community, however, its existence was not widely recognized until the middle of this century. Previously, individuals whose eating habits kept them in a state of

anorexia nervosa a mental and physical disorder characterized by an unrealistic view of oneself as too fat, self-induced starvation, and severe weight loss

Most North Americans view stoutness as unfashionable and unhealthy, but a century ago it was admired. By today's standards, President Grover Cleveland looks unfit for the presidency, but when photographed in 1888 he appeared the ideal man for the job: big, successful, confident.

semistarvation were usually not diagnosed as suffering from any disease. Since mid-century, however, anorexia in the West has received growing attention and has been strongly associated with young, "sexually conflicted" females from affluent, educated, backgrounds (Stevenson 1989). Indeed, most Western sufferers fall into this group. However, since in other cultures the condition afflicts males as well as females of any age, anorexia seems to be as much a product of cultural attitudes toward the body as it is a pathology of mind or body (Wolf 1991).

Various anthropological explanations for Western anorexia have been suggested. One is that the disease is a product of the Western notion that nature can and should be controlled (Stevenson 1989). Another is that it is a "symbolic struggle" on the part of Western females against male power and authority (B.S. Turner 1984:202). That power is in some way involved in anorexia in Western females

is also suggested in a recent study by Naomi Wolf (1991), who takes a feminist stance. Imposing impossible standards of thinness, she asserts, is society's way of "punishing" women for their new-found political power. Perhaps more convincing and certainly less political is the view expressed by Aimee Liu in an autobiographical account of her anorexia. Extreme dieting, she wrote, was her first "totally independent exhibit of power" (B.S. Turner 1984:194). In other cultures, the causes of self-starvation are believed to include sorcery, soul loss, the breach of some taboo, and loss of face (Stevenson 1989:299.) What is clear, then, is that Western culture has helped to "shape and exacerbate" the disease as it manifests itself in Westerners (Stevenson 1989: 298).

Stoutness has also been fashionable in many societies, including Western society. Portraits of past American presidents Grover Cleveland, Benjamin Harrison, William McKinley, Theodore Roosevelt, and William Howard Taft show that at the end of the nineteenth century and the beginning of the twentieth, big men were deemed best suited for big jobs. All of these men were what would be regarded today as unfit and unfashionably overweight, but at the time corpulence was considered proof of having dined often and well—and therefore of having the wealth necessary to do so. Americans felt they could place their trust and confidence in a beefy president. The ideal late Victorian woman, too, was as handsomely solid and well upholstered as her furniture (Lurie 1981:119).

Today, slimness is by no means admired everywhere. In Indonesia, where David Hicks carried out fieldwork, local people claim they can assess the wealth and social importance of a man by the size of his waistline. The fatter a man is, the more likely he is to be a leader. Ordinary villagers tend

• Ask Yourself •

What in your opinion are the physical attributes that make a male body attractive? A female body? Are the attributes you listed universally agreed upon within your culture? Can you think of any widely agreed-upon attribute of attractiveness that you do not find attractive, in either males or females?

to be skinny, headmen rather less so, local district leaders distinctly pudgy, civil servants of higher rank downright fat, and so on up the financial and social scale. But Indonesians know that corpulence is only an ideal body type. The body shape of many individual officeholders does not conform to this image.

Body Hair

Notions of physical attractiveness are highly culture-bound; what is acceptable or attractive or intensely erotic in the context of one culture may be unacceptable, unattractive, or even sexually repellent in another. And when it comes to notions about what is beautiful as opposed to what is ugly about the human body, there are probably few attributes that are more culture-bound than body hair.

The amount and distribution of hair on the body varies greatly in human beings, both between the sexes and among and within ethnic groups. But some societies are not content to leave the existence, let alone the amount, of body hair entirely to the mercy of nature. Each society has its (sometimes unrealistic) ideals, but these are often very different across cultures. Most young North American women scrupulously shave the hair from their underarms and legs, but some of their European counterparts allow underarm hair to grow and make no effort to conceal it. One American male wrote:

> Several years ago, I was in Berlin having dinner with a German [male] friend. A beautiful woman entered the restaurant, [and was] escorted to the next table. She wore furs and a sleek dress—she was a sensation. But when she removed her cloak, I could see her hairy underarms. I was instantly turned off. I told my friend, who said it turned him on (he was visibly titillated). Now that's culture shock! (Herdt and Stoller 1986:411)

To be beautiful, an Indian bride must have any hair on her forearms shaved before the wedding, but North American brides have no such ideal. Within societies, ideals can also vary between the sexes. Facial hair is not only acceptable on North American men, it is often viewed as attractive. Facial hair on women is unacceptable.

Teeth

In Western society, to be considered really attractive, a person must have a full set of teeth, and the teeth themselves must be straight and near-white. Altering the natural appearance of the teeth to achieve these standards, by straightening, capping, or bleaching, is common. Decorating one or more teeth by embedding a precious stone and capping or replacing natural teeth with gold ones are somewhat less common practices, but are by no means unheard of in Western culture. Westerners are not so different from most other societies in this regard; cross-culturally, changing the natural appearance of the teeth is common. Depending on the society, teeth may be shaped artificially, inlaid with substances such as jade or gold, or removed altogether (Milner and Larsen 1991:357).

Beauty is the most common reason for such alterations. While North Americans are whitening or straightening their teeth, the Krikati of Brazil are filing theirs to attractive points, and the Balinese are blunting theirs, since long teeth are considered dog-like and ugly (see photo, page 336). Another reason for altering the appearance of the teeth is health. While Americans are having their decayed teeth filled, people in the West Indian nation of Dominica, where modern dental services are not universally available, are having them extracted. In Dominica, having a few gaps between the teeth is not considered unattractive. A third reason for altering the teeth is social status. While some North Americans are having their front teeth capped with gold or inlaid with diamonds, young men in East Africa are having theirs removed in rites of passage marking their new, adult status (Milner and Larsen 1991:363).

Conclusion

All human beings start out in infancy with bodies that are quite similar physically, and that proceed to grow and change in fairly predictable ways. But we human beings are not content to let nature dictate our physical appearance. Universally, we alter our appearance with clothing, jewelry, hairdressings, cosmetics, or more permanent physical changes, and we adopt a wide range of physical stances and gestures as well. After these changes have been made, our outward appearances may be quite different from those nature originally provided. Adorning our bodies temporarily or altering them permanently thus transforms what were once completely natural objects into what we may certainly regard as cultural artifacts. Could any behavior be more cultural, more human, than this?

Summary

- The human body serves as a medium of expression in all cultures.

- Bodily adornments (clothes, jewelry, cosmetics, and hairdos), as well as more permanent forms of body alteration (labrets, scarification, and various forms of body mutilation), all reflect human beings' beliefs, attitudes, ideals, and preferences.

- Body language, which can be conscious, unconscious, or (like the body language with which males and females signal sexual interest) both, is an important form of human communication.

- Attitudes toward the body vary widely cross-culturally. Obesity, for example, is disfavored in some societies, but highly regarded in others.

- Ideals regarding the amount and distribution of hair on the body and the presence or absence and alteration of the teeth also vary.

- The cultural messages that can be communicated by manipulating the body's natural form include social status, group membership, the wish to be more attractive, or the wish to be either more conforming or nonconforming.

- Human bodies also convey messages about individuals' inner states, such as modesty, mourning, and pride.

Key Terms

anorexia nervosa
body language (kinesics)
cicatrization
clitoridectomy
cosmetics
infibulation
labret
mutilation
purdah
scarification

Suggested Readings

Barnes, Ruth, and Joanne B. Eicher (eds.). 1992. *Dress and Gender*. New York: Berg. The essays in this book, one of the series *Cross-Cultural Perspectives on Women*, show how clothing functions as an expression of social identity in Indonesia, Guatemala, India, Israel, Nigeria, and other cultures including the West.

Blacking, John (ed.). 1977. *The Anthropology of the Body*. Association of Social Anthropology, Monograph 15. London: Academic Press. Essays dealing with the body in a wide range of contexts. Subjects include kinesics, health, sexuality, and dance.

Lightfoot-Klein, Hanny. 1989. *Prisoners of Ritual*. New York: Haworth Press. An overview of female genital mutilation in Africa, written by a social psychologist.

Marwick, Arthur. 1988. *Beauty in History: Society, Politics, and Personal Appearance, c. 1500 to the Present*. London: Thames & Hudson. A scholarly history of Western standards of beauty from 1500 to the present.

Verswijver, Gustaaf (ed.). 1993. *Kaiapó, Amazonia: The Art of Body Decoration*. Seattle: University of Washington Press. Gorgeous photographs of body paintings, feather ornaments, bracelets, necklaces, ear decorations, headdresses, and adornments worn by the Kaiapó (or Kayapó) of central Brazil provide a vivid summary of how expressive culture can transform the human body into a work of art.

Wolf, Naomi. 1991. *The Beauty Myth*. New York: Morrow. A look at America's attitudes toward the female body from a feminist perspective. The book suggests that setting nearly impossible standards of thinness is society's way of "punishing" women for their newfound political power.

Introduction

Where Western rock music once blared from doorways, silence now prevails.

Where women once wore high-fashion, off-the-rack dresses designed in New York and

made in Hong Kong, lengths of dark-colored cloth now envelop them from head to toe. Where laborers once lined up to buy pints of vodka at the end of a long workday, sweetened tea now revives the weary. Where high noon once came and went with little interruption in the bustle of city life, hundreds of thousands now stop whatever they are doing, unroll their prayer rugs, and kneel, facing the direction of Mecca, when they hear the Muslim call to prayer. Teheran is not the same city it was only 20 years ago.

The change in Iran is countrywide, and occurred with dramatic swiftness. Disenchanted with the enthusiasm their hereditary ruler, Shah Reza Pahlavi, showed in embracing Western technology and culture, and demoralized by the abuses that accompanied his great wealth and power, the Iranian people, traditional Muslims at heart, decisively rejected the shah in 1978, throwing their allegiance behind an elderly Muslim cleric—a religious fundamentalist and cultural conservative. The Iranian upheaval was only one of a number of profound, sudden, state-level cultural changes that have taken place in the recent past. The collapse of communism in eastern Europe and of official apartheid in South Africa are others.

In small-scale societies, as in modern nations, change is a constant in human life. Forever thinking, reorganizing, experimenting, and innovating, human beings continually challenge established patterns of thought, and in so doing change their cultures for better or for worse.

This chapter approaches culture diachronically, focusing on why and how culture change occurs, what happens when it does, and how anthropologists can—or if they should—get involved. Should they restrict themselves merely to documenting culture change and attempting to explain it, or should they try to influence the course of change?

• Culture Change •

In Chapter 3, in which cultural evolution was defined as a gradual, continuous process of adaptive change, we mentioned the neoevolutionary idea that change need not imply forward progress or improvement, but only "process." Occasionally, features of a culture become simpler with time; the agricultural system in the American South, for instance, became less rather than more complex after the Civil War. Yet even though the passage of time does not always bring increased cultural complexity, throughout human history cultures have generally tended to move in this direction. The political developmental model presented in Chapter 12 is an example: it is based on the observation that, through history, sociopolitical organizations have tended to become increasingly complex—more populous, more highly stratified, more diverse, more technologically sophisticated—as they change from bands to tribes to chiefdoms to states.

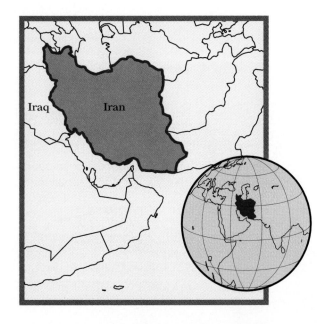

What are the processes that bring about culture change? One theory that has received much attention over the years was advanced by Leslie White (1971), whose explanation was a cultural materialist one. White distinguished three subsystems of culture: technological, sociological, and ideological. The technological subsystem, he wrote, consisted of all those elements of material culture that human beings use to exploit their environment. The sociological consisted of interactive behavior among individuals, and the ideological consisted of the nonmaterial elements of culture. The technological subsystem, according to White, was the most basic, since it strongly "conditioned" the other two. For White (390), "Technology is the hero of our piece," because, as he saw it, the development of culture depends upon technological advances. These advances include tapping new energy sources and improving the efficiency of tools. Through technological advances, cultures increase the amount of energy they are able to harness per capita per year. White formulated a "basic law of cultural evolution" as follows: "Other factors remaining constant, culture evolves as the amount of energy harnessed per capita per year is increased, or as the efficiency of the instrumental means of putting the energy to work is increased" (1971:368–369).

Anthropologists distinguish between two types of culture change: internal and external. **Internal change** comes from within a society; **external change** comes from without. White's law correctly identifies technology and energy as important to culture change, but it is flawed because it takes into account only the internal factors that bring about change, ignoring the impact of external forces.

Internal Change

For most of the history of humankind, cultures existed in some degree of isolation from one another; widespread cultural contact is a relatively recent development, certainly no older than the Neolithic Revolution. As recently as the nineteenth century, hundreds of isolated societies still existed in remote parts of South America, Africa, Asia, the Arctic, and the Pacific. Thus, during the infancy of anthropology as an academic discipline, anthropological fieldworkers were able to observe small-scale societies and their cultures in relative isolation from one another and from Western culture. This isolation did not mean that these societies had not changed, only that whatever changes had occurred were more likely to have come from within rather than from the outside.

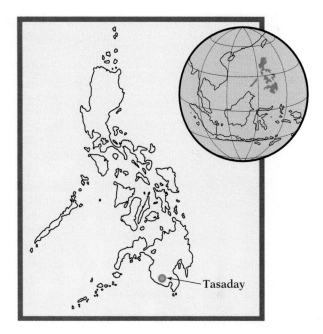

So far as is known, there no longer exists, anywhere on earth, a society that is changing only from within—one that has never been in contact with some other culture. All formerly existing "living laboratories," as isolated societies have been called, have been influenced to one degree or another by other cultures. Yet the romantic appeal of "undiscovered" cultures remains powerful—even among anthropologists. Thus the report, in 1971, that a tiny group of previously unknown, cave-dwelling gatherers and hunters, the Tasaday, had been discovered in the dense interior rainforest of the Philippine island of Mindanao (Headland 1992) excited much anthropological attention. Could the Tasaday be the last never-before-contacted, totally isolated human group on earth? To protect the Tasaday as a valuable cultural treasure, Philippine government officials soon staked out a vast area of forest in which the little group could live in isolation from outside influences.

Fifteen years later, after Philippine President Ferdinand Marcos had fallen from power, anthropologists visiting the Tasaday discovered much evidence

internal change change originating within a society

external change change originating outside a society

When they came to the world's attention in 1971, the cave-dwelling Tasaday of the Philippines were touted as an uncontacted, totally isolated human group, but later some said they were a hoax. In this photo taken in 1978, Tasaday display the results of a day's food-gathering efforts.

of culture change. Some Tasaday were wearing Western T-shirts; others were using steel-bladed knives and smoking cigars. "We're seeing a textbook case of social change, compressed in time," said one of the anthropologists (Mydans 1986). Others, however, were not so sure. In fact, some claimed that the Tasaday were not the world's last previously uncontacted group at all, but a hoax created by Marcos so that he and his supporters could mine, log, and farm the rich interior of Mindanao, free of outside interference (Iten 1986).

A recent review of the evidence concludes that although the Tasaday were not "rain forest phonies who were paid or coaxed to move into the forest and masquerade as Stone Age cavemen," neither were they previously uncontacted foragers (Headland 1992:215). Instead, they seem to be an indigenous group that had long been living in the interior of Mindanao in some degree of cultural isolation— exactly how much has never been determined. Although dwelling in a cave when discovered, the Tasaday possessed iron knives, glass beads, and tin

cans (216). And they *had* been manipulated by the Marcos regime; government emissaries, for instance, had asked them to wear clothing made from leaves instead of commercially manufactured cloth when visitors arrived.

In spite of the many unanswered questions surrounding the Tasaday, their rights and lands should undoubtedly be protected. This concern is at least as important as the still-debated details of their past and present life (Headland 1992:222–223).

• Ask Yourself •

If a heretofore totally isolated society should be discovered living in some remote part of our planet, what do you think the world's reaction would be? What should it be? Would the situation be different if a society of humans or humanlike creatures were discovered living on another planet?

India, where the average couple has four children, may overtake China as the world's most populous country by the middle of the twenty-first century (G. Moffett 1994:14). Such growth will inevitably result in culture change. In crowded Delhi, buyers and sellers at a market jostle for elbow room.

The Influence of the Natural Environment. One reason cultures change from within is in response to changing conditions in their natural surroundings. These may be relatively short-term climatic events, like the severe drought in the early 1990s that disrupted agriculture in southern Africa and forced many farmers to leave their homes and migrate to cities in search of food. Other environmental changes occur over much longer periods of time. The retreat of glaciers from northern Europe at the end of the Upper Palaeolithic period caused a gradual warming trend and the slow replacement of forests by grasslands. These environmental changes resulted in a decrease in the big game animals on which the region's cave-dwelling gatherers and hunters had long depended. Slowly but completely, their way of life changed in response.

Population Growth. Population growth can also stimulate culture change. Especially in beneficent natural environments, human groups often experi-ence a natural rate of population increase. Such increases may be prevented or mitigated by natural or cultural restrictions such as disease, warfare, emigration, or the development of cultural ideals favoring small family size or the survival of children of only one sex. But barring such restrictions, population growth may be relatively rapid, since—where conditions favor it—human populations may increase exponentially rather than linearly. And growth may be encouraged by aspects of culture such as the existence of competing descent groups, a cultural phenomenon that favors large families. Growing populations require more and more resources, and whatever its size, a population that has increased to the point at which it has outstripped the resources upon which its members depend must make some changes. Territorial expansion or agricultural intensification are typical cultural responses under such circumstances. Both of these inevitably precipitate additional changes.

Inventions.   Another cause of change from within a society is invention. The changes resulting from new ideas, born of the unique capacity of humans for insight and experimentation, may be material (like the idea of propelling a sharply tipped shaft of wood with the help of a taut bowstring rather than human muscle alone) or nonmaterial (like a newly invented folktale). In either case, inventions are the products of the creative abilities of members of a society, individually or collectively. They may come about in response to pressing needs, or they may be products of the human creative impulse and enough leisure time to exploit it, chance associations of ideas, or even the urge to find an aesthetically pleasing order. The discoverers of the structure of DNA, James D. Watson and Francis Crick, hoped that the physical shape of the molecule they were seeking would prove to be "pretty," and so it did: a double helix.

Necessity has been called the mother of invention, but this is not invariably true; more frequently, it seems, necessity is the mother of improvements on what already exists. Historians of technology have suggested that metallurgy (the science of extracting useful metals from their ores) may have come about not because Palaeolithic people realized they needed knives for domestic purposes or arrowheads for war, but because they wished to express themselves artistically by fashioning metal beads or armbands. Knives and arrowheads may have been a later development. Likewise, pottery may have been accidentally invented when it was discovered that figurines or counting beads, fashioned of soft clay, would harden if left near a fire. Early human beings may have been cultivating flowers for pleasure long before this hobby was translated into planting grain for food, and playing with pets may have given them the idea of domesticating animals for subsistence (Smith 1975).

But an invention does not necessarily produce internal change, for a novel idea must win acceptance before culture change occurs, and some societies accept innovation more readily than others. The personality of the innovator can be decisive; a charismatic innovator is more likely to win approval among his or her colleagues than some-

one who is disregarded or disliked. Based on this observation, it has been suggested that a single forceful individual can change the course of history, an idea known as the **great man theory** of history. There is less general agreement about the validity of this notion, however, than about the proposition that a climate of openness to new ideas greatly affects culture change.

Leslie White (1971), whose theory of culture change was mentioned earlier in this chapter, used the fourteenth-century B.C. Egyptian pharoah Ikhnaton (sometimes spelled Akenaton) to illustrate the relative effects on culture change of individual greatness and the cultural climate in which change occurs. It was Ikhnaton who first devised the idea of monotheism (Chapter 13). In the process of promoting this new idea, he swept away his people's old polytheistic religion, reorganized the government, and revitalized Egyptian art. The cultural impact of this one man can still be felt today. But White argued that great innovators like Ikhnaton are themselves products of the cultural forces and historical circumstances of their times; it is these forces, not individuals, that bring about culture change. The outstanding individual, according to White, is "best understood as an effect" rather than as a primary cause (190). As cultures become increasingly complex, the "community of scientific and technological workers" becomes more and more decisive (224–225) and it is less and less possible for a "great man" singlehandedly to instigate change (224–225).

In the nineteenth and early twentieth centuries, the impression that technologically simpler cultures were slow to change internally was reinforced by anthropologists' fieldwork among groups of gatherers and hunters. Sometimes, compared with what was happening in Western culture as the result of the Industrial Revolution, these groups appeared to be clinging to obsolete beliefs, customs, and especially material culture. Some ethnographers, unable to observe much evidence of technological development, assumed that other aspects of these cultures had not changed much either. Later fieldworkers showed that nonliterate communities do change internally, sometimes—as revitalization movements (Chapter 13) demonstrate—very rapidly. In general, however, the rate of change in nonliterate societies does tend to be slower than in our own fast-paced Western society.

Yet even in Western society, new ideas may be slow to catch on, or rejected outright, because of

---

great man theory the idea that a single forceful individual can cause major change in a society

ignorance, prejudice, personal dislike of an inventor, a strong commitment to tradition, or plain disinterest. The economist Thorstein Veblen noted that nineteenth-century Britain, reliant on steam power, was so slow to convert to electricity that its iron and steel industry was quickly outstripped by those of Germany and the United States (Barrett 1991:103–104). Similarly, when Charles Darwin (1809–1882) proposed natural selection as an explanation for the existence and physical form of human beings, the idea was greeted with great skepticism. Only later, after earlier theories had been disproven, was the idea accepted as valid. The Scopes "monkey trial" (Chapter 13) demonstrates how vigorously new ideas may be resisted in twentieth-century Western societies.

External Change

External culture change comes from outside a society, as the result of **cultural diffusion,** the spread of ideas and technology between cultures. Figure 16.1, which traces the spread of religious ideas throughout the old World, provides an example. The process is so common that it has inspired **diffusionism,** the idea that much culture change can be explained by contacts between representatives of different cultures. In the early decades of the twentieth century, diffusionism was championed in perhaps its most extreme form by *diffusionists* who argued, implausibly, that the roots of all civilizations lay in the culture of ancient Egypt. Anthropologists now acknowledge that, while diffusion is a powerful impetus to culture change, it is far from being the only agent.

Direct and Indirect Diffusion. Anthropologists distinguish two types of cultural diffusion: **direct** and **indirect**. When a Christian missionary succeeds in his or her evangelical work among a previously non-Christian group, this exemplifies the direct diffusion of Christianity from the missionary's culture to another. Not all new ideas or artifacts diffuse so directly, however. Some spread from one society to another through an intermediate culture. When Christianity diffuses from a culture into which it was first introduced from the outside to yet another culture, this exemplifies indirect diffusion.

Sometimes the spread of a new idea is affected by both direct and indirect diffusion. In 1586, Sir Walter Raleigh returned to England from the New World colony of Virginia with leaves of tobacco, which Native Americans had shown him how to grow, dry, and smoke in pipes. Smoking immediately became popular among the English, a case of direct diffusion. Some four years later, English medical students in Holland introduced smoking to the Dutch; Dutch sailors then exported it to other Northern European countries, thus spreading the custom by indirect diffusion. Sailors also took the custom to Spain, from where it spread eastward across the Mediterranean into the Near East. By 1605, less than two decades after Raleigh introduced tobacco to the English, the custom had reached far-off Japan. Smoking is now universal.

Diffusion and Adaptation. Rather than accepting a diffused idea in its entirety, people often use it selectively, adapting and changing it to suit their own special needs. Sequoia, a Native American of the Cherokee tribe who observed the many advantages Europeans enjoyed as a result of knowing how to read and write, adapted the English alphabet to suit the Cherokee language. Changing some characters and inventing new ones, Sequoia gave his people their own syllabary, making it possible for his language to be written and read.[1] Alternatively, people may use only certain elements of a diffused idea, blending these with elements from their own cultural tradition to produce a new idea, better suited to their particular cultural context. In Chapter 14, reggae music served as an example of syncretism, the blending of elements from two cultural traditions. Reggae combines elements of both Western and African music to produce an entirely new musical category. But

---

cultural diffusion the spread of ideas and technology between cultures

diffusionism the idea that culture change can be explained by intercultural contacts

direct diffusion the diffusion of an idea or custom from one culture to another without passing through an intermediary culture

indirect diffusion the diffusion of an idea or custom from one culture to another after passing through an intermediary culture

---

[1] A syllabary differs from an alphabet. Each is a system of representational characters, but in a syllabary each character represents an individual syllable; in an alphabet, a character may or may not represent a single syllable.

Cherokee

syncretism is not just a musical phenomenon; it can take place in any area of culture.

Beneficial Versus Destructive Diffusion.   When a new idea or artifact diffuses into a society, its members might be expected to accept it only if they think they will benefit from it (unless, of course, more powerful outsiders have imposed it upon them). But ideas that are beneficial in the context of one culture often work well in others, too. The Native American Mattapoisett people showed the Pilgrims of Plymouth Colony how to plant corn, an instance of beneficial diffusion that resulted in the harvest celebrated at the first Thanksgiving. In the late twentieth-century world of rapid and relatively easy global communication, beneficial diffusion is commonplace. Japanese improvements to cameras and cars mean that Americans can have better photographs and more

The work of Christian missionaries where Christianity was previously unknown is an example of direct diffusion, the spread of ideas or customs directly from one culture to another. In a scene from the movie At Play in the Fields of the Lord, *two missionaries confront their intended converts.*

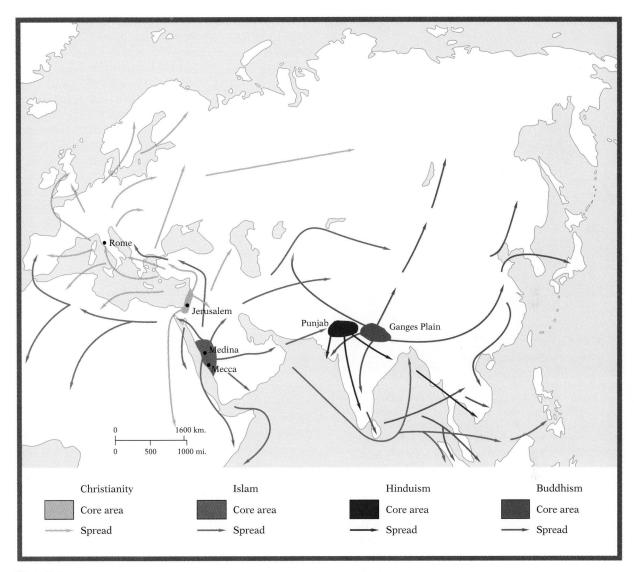

Figure 16.1

Four world religions—Christianity, Islam, Hinduism, and Buddhism—all originated in their own core areas and diffused very widely. This map shows their diffusion around Eurasia and into North Africa. Source: Jordan et al. 1994:223.

efficient transportation, Middle Eastern oil powers Western European generators, and AIDS test kits produced in the United States protect supplies of blood in Latin American hospitals.

The Inuit of Canada's Northwest Territories (see map on page 17), whose lives retain elements of their recent gathering-and-hunting past, readily incorporate new ideas they consider helpful into their lives. In the mid-1980s, their regional council, made up of representatives from 14 isolated Inuit communities, decided to use computers to store information on the game that hunters brought home to their remote hamlets (Wren 1986). If one hamlet found itself with plenty of caribou meat but few seal, it could easily locate a hamlet with an excess of seal, and trade one kind of meat for the

The blending of elements from two or more cultural traditions into a single new one is called syncretism. *In Zimbabwe, southern Africa, followers of a syncretic religion combining Christianity with traditional beliefs pray together in the rocky, uninhabited countryside outside the capital, Harare.*

other. Both the hardware and software had to be user-friendly, since many Inuit had little formal education and not all of them spoke English. The Apple Macintosh, which uses images rather than words to execute commands, was chosen for the job, and a software program made up of the lines and circles of the Inuit alphabet was written. Ultimately, even the remotest Inuit villages will be able to communicate easily with one another and the outside world.

In Chapter 11 (pages 282–283), we described how a consortium of women's groups in Kenya succeeded in placing new wells and pumps in rural communities suffering a lack of clean water, an example of the beneficial diffusion of water-related technology. But diffused technology can sometimes have unexpected or even destructive social, cultural, and economic results, as a similar project in rural India demonstrates (Wicker 1987). A solar-powered water pump, installed on a village

well, freed local women from the time-consuming task of drawing water by hand, but the women found they were spending much less time chatting with one another around the well. The easy availability of water attracted unwanted wanderers from outside the village; moreover, local boys whose job it had been to draw water from the well in buckets had nothing to do, and with time on their hands some turned to petty crime. Meanwhile, the gap between rich and poor widened; the rich, who owned land, used the pump for irrigation, but the poor had no land to irrigate. The new pump was definitely a mixed blessing. Eventually, women of the village intentionally broke it so they could once more gather around the well that had been the center of their social lives.

Resisting or Rejecting Diffusion. For all its power to alter cultures, for worse as well as for better, diffusion can be resisted, and many societies have energetically preserved their traditional ways rather than accept "progress" in the form of customs or technologies invented elsewhere. Alternatively, societies may be able to incorporate the best of both the traditional and modern worlds. Native Americans may live in modern brick houses, drive station wagons, watch television, cook in microwave ovens, and speak English in addition to their native Navajo or Choctaw. At the same time, their homes may be decorated with Native American crafts, they may visit traditional healers when sick, and their food (like that of their ancestors) may be home-grown.

Sometimes people sample ideas and artifacts that have diffused into their culture or even accept them for a time, but ultimately reject them. In Zaire in Central Africa, once the Belgian Congo, the Mbuti (see map on page 163) were persuaded by Belgian administrators to abandon their gathering-and-hunting life-style and plant crops. The Mbuti were competent farmers, but—as was the case with the Indian villagers described above—the new technology introduced unwanted changes in other aspects of their culture. Gathering and hunting had given meaning to their lives, but as farmers, the Mbuti "degenerated socially and physically at an alarming rate, losing all sense of individual or family responsibility and dying from sunstroke and stomach disorders" (Turnbull 1965:313). So they rejected horticulture and returned to gathering and hunting.

Cultural diffusion, the spread of ideas and technology between cultures, has sometimes been aided by sea travel. Near Moorea, Tahiti, sailors steer their tiny wooden craft much as their ancestors must have done.

• Ask Yourself •

A businessman bought a hand-held tape recorder with which to record notes and remember appointments, only to find he never used it. Jotting down appointments and notes with pencil and paper was easier and faster. Have you ever had a similar experience?

Barriers to Diffusion. In the past, the oceans that cover our planet sometimes provided a means of relatively easy communication between cultures, as linguistic similarities between North America and England demonstrate. However, mountain ranges, glaciers, swamps, forests, and deserts have since prehistoric times provided natural barriers to cultural exchange between different populations.

For example, the Indonesian island of Timor (see map on page 139), although small, is home to more than 12 different language groups; the island's mountainous landscape proved an effective barrier to intercultural communication.

Increasingly through history, natural and cultural barriers have fallen to cultural innovations. To get his troops across the Alps into Italy in the third century B.C., the Carthaginian general Hannibal used elephants, common enough in the context of his own North African culture but no doubt an astonishing sight to the Italians. Today, highways, ships, planes, television, and the internet represent only some of the ways in which intercultural contact can be made and maintained. Contact is so powerful a force for change that totalitarian political leaders, threatened by the possibility that ideas introduced from the outside might undermine their authority, may try to prohibit their followers' exposure to other cultures. Following World War II, in an attempt to keep Western values from diffusing to their own citizens, the leaders of the Soviet Union did their best to cut off channels of communication with the West, a policy that prompted Winston Churchill's famous remark that "an iron curtain has fallen down upon eastern Europe."

• The Status of Small-Scale • Societies

Although culture change takes place continually in all societies, today small-scale societies are apt to be as much its victims as its beneficiaries. Perhaps no global trend is more alarming to anthropologists than the increasing rate at which the world's remaining small-scale societies are being weakened or even exterminated by external change. When the members of such societies realize that their cultural individuality is threatened, some strongly resist efforts to bring their aims, values, and ways of life into line with other, usually national, ideologies. Instead, they may strive to protect their cultural traditions from **Westernization,** the diffusion of technologies, ideas, values, and customs from the West.

Westernization the process by which non-Western societies become more like Western ones by adopting Western technologies, ideas, values, and customs

Maintaining their cultural heritage worries not only non-Westerners; ethnic minorities living in the context of modern Western societies have the same concern. Wales (see map on page 304) is part of Great Britain, and many Welsh people speak both English and their native Welsh language. Some years ago, road signs in Wales were entirely in English. Today, most highway signs are in both English and Welsh, a change resulting from a strong movement among Welsh nationalists to preserve their country's ancient language. Some are even lobbying and demonstrating for their country's complete political separation from Great Britain.

The Welsh are an ethnic group (see Chapters 1 and 11), a self-perpetuating group distinguished by others (and whose members distinguish themselves) by their shared traditions, values, and language. Termed *ethnic minorities* when they are smaller than other groups within their larger society, ethnic groups are parts of nations and their members may participate fully in national events, yet also take pride in their unique cultural traditions. *Tribal groups* (such as the Kayapó) also have distinct cul-

Like the members of many other societies, the Welsh are struggling to preserve their language, culture, and identity. Some even advocate the political separation of Wales from Great Britain. Near Conwy in northern Wales, separatist graffiti incorporates the word Cymru, *the Welsh term for Wales.*

tural traditions, but unlike ethnic groups they are less integrated into the nations where they are found. The two kinds of groups confront similar problems in the face of culture change.

Ethnic and tribal groups may face an uphill battle when their interests and values are not shared by the governments of the countries within whose borders they live. It is not uncommon for a government to attempt to absorb these less powerful groups into the national culture, typically for political reasons. In trying to create the nation of Iran in the 1920s, Reza Shah (father of the shah overthrown by Khomeini) found himself at odds with the tribal Qashgai (see map on page 135), who refused to recognize his authority and whose nomadic pastoralist way of life was not "modern" enough for the new Iran Reza Shah planned. To convert the nomads into sedentary peasants and bring them into the mainstream of twentieth-century Iranian culture, he used tanks and airplanes to cut off their migration routes, and bullied them into building huts and settling down in villages. Ultimately, he failed. After Reza Shah abdicated the throne of Iran in 1941, most Qashgai burned their huts and resumed their transhumant existence.

National leaders may seek to assimilate tribal or ethnic minorities into the national culture for several different reasons. First, at the national level minorities may be thought "backward," and the leaders of countries struggling for economic development may find their presence an embarrassment. Second, the health and education of members of minority groups are often poor, and governments' attempts to bring modern health care and education—"progress"—to all their people may be weakened by the determination of minority groups to maintain their traditional ways. Third, the traditional subsistence practices employed by minority groups sometimes cause long-term environmental damage, especially when growing population numbers mean increased environmental exploitation. Fourth, national leaders realize that the more strongly people feel about their ethnic identity, the less loyalty they have toward their country. This makes it difficult, for example, to conscript soldiers to fight for the country's interests. National leaders may thus regard it as necessary to force members of ethnic or tribal groups to follow the national agenda.

Taken to extremes, the forceful attempt to assimilate an ethnic or tribal group can degenerate into

Anthropology and the Environment

Guardians of the Rainforest?

Small-scale societies play an essential part in the future of Planet Earth's environment—whether for its benefit or to its detriment. Once new values have diffused into such societies, the changes they effect make the reactions of local populations unpredictable. For example, the lure of western material culture has caused some of the Kayapó of Brazil (see map on page 383) to adopt contradictory attitudes toward the environment that has harbored them for generations, the mahogany-rich rainforests (see map on page 383).

Like other hardwoods, mahogany is fast becoming scarce. As a result, the rainforests where it grows have become the focus of a worldwide environmental battle aimed at stopping their wanton destruction (M. Moffett 1994:A6; anon. 1993:54). In 1988, the Kayapó, to the cheers of Western environmentalists, brought together over 600 tribes to oppose a World Bank-financed project to build a dam that would drastically alter the local environment by flooding almost 500 square miles of rainforest. The environmentalists chose to ignore the earlier Kayapó record of dealings with lumber interests, and hailed them as heros. The Kayapó emerged as "icons of the global green movement" (M. Moffett 1994:A6) and were jetted around the world as celebrities in feathered headdresses and body paints. The Brazilian government eventually ceded to these "guardians of the Rainforest" a vast tract of land about the size of West Virginia as a reserve for their exclusive use. Lumber companies were excluded.

Six years later, however, it developed that local Kayapó chiefs had been making illegal deals with loggers that brought them money and an array of western gadgets (such as the video camera shown on page 22 of Chapter 2), but also brought destruction to the rainforest. The environmental group "Friends of the Earth" discovered that chiefs in the village of Kikretun had permitted loggers to extract some 1500 truckloads of mahogany logs in exchange for an airplane, motor vehicles, and Western-style houses. In late 1994, chiefs in another village allowed a logger to cut down so much mahogany that 60 miles of new roads had to be built to truck the logs out. Environmental agents seized the booty; in response, the chiefs made four flights (paid for by the loggers) to lobby the government—successfully—to release the timber. These incidents evidently involved only a few Kayapó leaders; other members of the tribe firmly opposed the logging (Schwartzman 1995:A23).

The environmentalists were not above adding an ethnocentric "westerners know best" argument to their efforts to halt the logging. Pointing to the huge satellite dish a lumber company had installed in the center of A-Ukre village, they asserted that the Kayapó were selling off their natural resources too cheaply, and were using their money to buy what the environmentalists viewed as frivolous products instead of realizing that "what the village really needs is better medical care" (M. Moffett 1994:A6).

The Body Shop International PLC, a retail chain specializing in natural personal-care products, has had a contract with A-Ukre for several years to harvest and process Brazil nuts used in a popular hair conditioner—a use of natural resources of which the environmentalists approve. During a meeting with officials from the company, however, Kayapó leaders protested that they were excluded from the marketing end of the business, and received too little income for their efforts. "You get much more money selling timber," one chief confided (A6).

In 1975, the Indonesian army invaded East Timor, and thousands of Tetum and other citizens were massacred. Later, at a ceremony commemorating one of the dead, troops again opened fire, killing and wounding hundreds. Here, mourners gather up the victims' bloodstained clothes.

ethnocide, the deliberate attempt to destroy the culture of such a group. But absorption is not the only or even the cruelest threat to the continued existence of ethnic and tribal groups. Sometimes the members of one group try to destroy not only the culture of another but also the people themselves, often under circumstances in which traditional ethnic rivalries, which may have been simmering for years, are brought to the surface by contemporary struggles for political supremacy. This is called **genocide.** This century's most notorious case of ethnocide combined with genocide was the Nazi attempt, declared an official policy of the German state in 1942, to exterminate the Jewish people and their culture. Some estimates have put the number of Jews killed during this dark period of

human history as high as 7 million. More recent attempts to eradicate the members of ethnic or tribal groups and their culture, such as the "ethnic cleansing" of Bosnian Muslims by Serbs in the former Yugoslavia, and the mass slaughter in Rwanda of members of an ethnic minority by a rival group, remind us that attempts to exterminate people and their culture continue even today.

Although not as well publicized as these atrocities, attempts by the government of Indonesia since 1975 to eradicate the traditional cultures of East Timor—home of the Tetum, mentioned in previous chapters—have been no less horrifying. Until 1975, East Timor, occupying half of the island of Timor (see map on page 139), was a colony of Portugal, and adjacent West Timor was part of Indonesia. When the Portuguese gave up control of East Timor, its political leaders declared it an independent country. But East Timorese independence was to last for only about a month. On December 7, 1975, President Suharto of Indonesia ordered his armed forces to invade the new country.

---

ethnocide the deliberate attempt to destroy the culture of an ethnic group

genocide the deliberate attempt to exterminate the members of a culture

As a result of this order, an unknown number of Tetum and other citizens of East Timor were killed. Many were massacred by the Indonesian military; others died of starvation following the fighting. A conservative estimate put the death toll at over 100,000 out of a total population of no more than 500,000—20 percent of the population. East Timor was quickly incorporated into the Republic of Indonesia as a mere province. Since then, the Indonesians have forcibly imposed their own customs, beliefs, and values on the Timorese, some of whom continue a guerilla struggle inside their country, as well as a public information campaign outside it, in order to preserve their traditions and regain their former independence.

• Anthropology's Role in • Solving Global Problems

The earth's human population is growing at a tremendous rate, while the limited resources available to this growing population are being consumed ever more hungrily. Two imbalances affect this ultimately unsustainable course of events: the industrialized nations consume much more than their proportional share of resources, and the developing world produces a disproportionate share of the population increase (see Figure 16.2). Related problems affecting both our natural and cultural environments are environmental mismanagement; the disregard of basic human rights, particularly those of minority groups; the poor health and nutritional status of many of the world's people; large-scale warfare and other, smaller-scale regional and ethnic hostilities and the refugees they create; and glaring economic inequalities among individuals, groups, and nations (Bradford and Gwynne 1995). These and other global problems cause anthropologists and nonanthropologists alike to wonder about the future of *Homo sapiens sapiens,* and present anthropologists and others with continuing opportunities and challenges. Increasingly, anthropology's response has been to address such problems head-on, in either of two ways: through development anthropology or cultural advocacy.

Development Anthropology

Chapter 1 introduced the subfield of anthropology called *applied cultural anthropology,* the use of anthropological ideas (like holism and cultural relativism) and methods (especially participant observation and field interviewing) to achieve practical ends in areas such as government, business, medicine, and law. In that context, we briefly discussed **development anthropology,** anthropologists' contribution to multidisciplinary efforts to improve human well-being by helping local people solve practical problems in such fields as health care, education, and agriculture. Development anthropology in the form of economic development was again discussed in Chapter 7.

Development anthropology is part of a broad field called **international development,** a comprehensive term for a broad range of efforts—on the part of indigenous people, specialists of many kinds, and institutions—to improve human welfare, particularly in developing countries (Pottier 1993). The institutions involved include world bodies like the various agencies and programs of the United Nations, national governments, and public and private agencies. All of them employ experts of many kinds, including social scientists, physicians, teachers, and agronomists, to undertake international development projects (see Skar 1985).

A guiding premise of international development today is that both its broader scientific aims and its narrower practical goals are best achieved at the invitation of and with the full cooperation of the communities that are its intended beneficiaries. Another basic premise is that development projects should be **sustainable:** their intended beneficiaries should be able to continue to achieve the desired results after development assistance ends. These two premises may seem obvious enough, but they were often lacking in development projects in the past. Both were arrived at after trial and error.

---

development anthropology efforts by anthropologists to improve the well-being of people in the "developing" countries in areas such as health care, education, and agriculture

international development a comprehensive term for international efforts to improve the well-being of the world's people

sustainability the capacity of the beneficiaries of a development project to continue to achieve results after development assistance ends

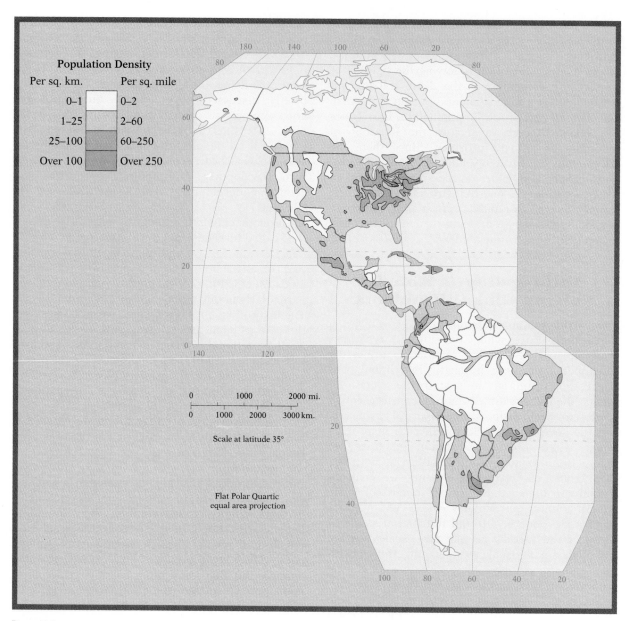

Figure 16.2

Population Density of the World in 1993. Source: Jordan et al. 1994:38–39.

In its formative period in the years following World War II, international development consisted largely of donations of money, facilities, or equipment from rich nations to poor ones. Sometimes the recipients put these resources to good use, but all too frequently such donations did not have the intended results. Equipment given to hospitals might work as advertised for awhile, but later require servicing or parts unavailable in a developing country. A newly introduced crop might not find a local market because local people preferred their customary food. As our example of the unwelcome effects of a solar-powered water pump in a rural Indian village showed, technological changes sometimes have adverse side effects.

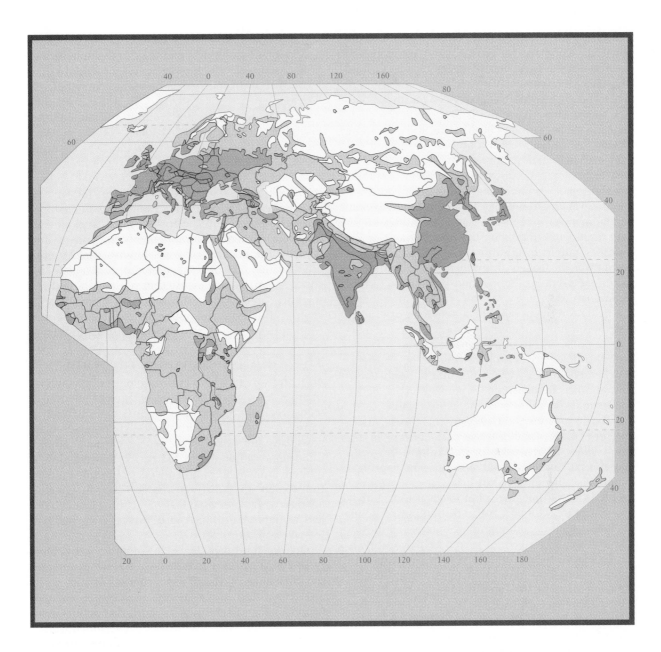

This early approach to development assistance—called the **top-down approach** because donations and assistance were imposed by outsiders without the full participation of the local people they were intended to benefit—proved ineffective and unsustainable. Today, people in developing countries often initiate and manage much of their own development, actively participating in identifying, designing, implementing, and evaluating development projects. International organizations such as the World Bank, government agencies like USAID, and private agencies like the Rockefeller Foundation continue to give money and provide technical assistance to developing countries, but they do not do it alone. They rely for their success on the active participation of people in the countries in which they work, from government officials to the residents of local communities.

top-down approach in international development, providing assistance to local people without their full participation

Perhaps the most daunting challenge to international development in general, and development anthropology in particular, is suggesting ways to satisfy what development workers term *basic human needs* and to provide basic services for those who lack them. These basic needs and services include food and shelter, primary health care, and education. Closely tied to the provision of these needs and services are such goals as increased economic production, technological improvements, a more equitable distribution of resources, and sound management of the natural environment. Thus, an international development project in a developing country might have as its goal improving the management of the country's public health system, resettling refugees fleeing war or drought, introducing to farmers new and more productive crops and better agricultural techniques, recording a body of oral literature that is fast being forgotten, building a new road or sewage system, retraining unemployed rural women in marketable skills, or informing teenagers about AIDS.

Anthropologists' best opportunity to be of service may lie in helping governments, international agencies, and private charitable organizations to better understand the cultures of the people whose needs they wish to address. Development efforts affect different cultures and different social groups in different ways; what works for one culture or group may not be suitable for all. A development project might raise the standard of living of one group of people (for example, men) but lower it for another (for example, women). An anthropologist knowledgeable about the ethnographic details of a particular culture, and aware of it as a holistic entity, is ideally placed to point out to governments and aid organizations how certain changes, while benefiting some, may at the same time make the lives of others even more difficult.

A long-delayed but welcome addition to the practice of development anthropology has been the growing recognition, over the last decade or two, of the importance of women in developing countries (Young 1993). For too long, development anthropologists and other development "experts" saw women primarily as mothers or, when their economic role outside the household was recognized at all, as providers of services: domestics, teachers, nurses. Today, recognizing the enormous variety of women's economic as well as cultural contributions to their societies, development workers are more aware of such issues as women's reproductive rights and the impact of traditional gender hierarchies. Without taking women's roles into account at every level of development thinking, planning, and implementation, sustainable development is impossible (147).

Despite anthropology's potential to contribute to development projects, the jury is still out on this subject. Some critics, both within and outside the discipline, doubt that Western outsiders are morally entitled to interfere in the lives of non-Western people, even if their intentions are admirable. Others point out that national leaders in developing countries have been known to ignore the wishes of local communities in pushing through "progressive" reforms, and development funds earmarked for improvements sometimes vanish into the pockets of government officials. Still other critics question whether anthropologists, as social scientists, are justified in relinquishing their scientific objectivity and committing themselves to change. But criticisms such as these come from what appears to be a minority of anthropologists.

The Anthropologist as Advocate

A second way in which anthropologists can involve themselves in world problems is through advocacy: using their influence and expertise to defend a cause. A number of anthropologists now serve as advocates for small-scale societies and ethnic minorities. Although the distinction between development anthropology and advocacy is a fine (and at times even an indistinguishable) one, in general advocacy is a somewhat less hands-on, although no less valuable, anthropological strategy for helping to solve world problems.

One of anthropology's best-known advocates is David Maybury-Lewis, whose fieldwork among the Shavante of Brazil (see pages 274–275, 291, 331) convinced him that this society needed and wanted help in retaining its cultural identity and defending its interests against government-sanctioned encroachments on their land by big business. In 1972, Maybury-Lewis founded a nonprofit organization called Cultural Survival, to encourage tribal peoples' participation in national market economies, to secure their land rights, and to fund projects

• Ask Yourself •

What do you consider the single major global problem we face today? What solutions can you think of to solve it?

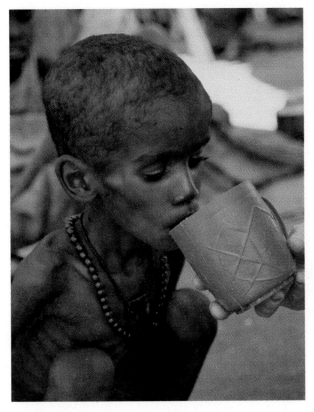

Among the most acute of contemporary world problems, mass starvation challenges anthropologists to help through development efforts or advocacy. In Somalia, western Africa, a starving child is offered a cup of milk.

designed and carried out by the people themselves. Cultural Survival also keeps Westerners informed about tribal groups and ethnic minorities by publishing information that results from its research.

Organizations like Cultural Survival are founded in the belief that some tribal and ethnic groups are being wronged and that their rights should be protected (Maybury-Lewis 1988:376). Adopting the stance of cultural relativism, anthropologists in their role as advocates examine, analyze, and attempt to understand the goals of minorities and the factors that might prevent these goals from being achieved, then work to develop effective strategies for dealing with injustices. But, as Maybury-Lewis emphasizes, it is the minority groups themselves, not the anthropologists, who should determine the direction and pace of cultural preservation efforts. Organizations such as Cultural Survival reject the paternalistic notion that tribal people need to be told what to preserve or how to respond to change.

Thus, the aim of organizations like Cultural Survival is not necessarily to encourage minorities to remain "true to their traditions," a romantic notion that may not serve minority groups well, but instead to assist people who request help to maintain those aspects of their culture they themselves regard as important (Maybury-Lewis 1988:380). A recent example from southern Brazil, where a tribal group was offered what for them was a huge amount of money to grant lumber companies the right to cut down trees on their land, illustrates the point (Maybury-Lewis 1988:386). The tribespeople thought the impact of the lumbering on their forest, which they considered an inexhaustible resource, would be trivial. Anthropologists acting as advocates tried to persuade them to decline the offer, but they decided to accept it nonetheless. At that point, the anthropologists ceased their opposition to the project. They felt they had made its ecological consequences clear, and were confident the local people had all the information that was available on which to base a decision. This respect for local choice contrasts with the ethnocentric attitude assumed by some environmentalists who believed they knew what was best for the Kayapó (see map on page 383; see also Anthropology and the Environment box, page 407), in their dealings with the loggers.

Addressing World Problems

In this section, we consider only three of the major global problems that anthropologists, through development work or cultural advocacy, can help solve: uncontrolled population growth, the planetary loss of species diversity, and poor health and nutrition.

Stemming Overpopulation. Between 1801 and 1974, the world's population grew from 1 billion to 4 billion people. By 1994—less than 20 years later—it was well over 5 billion, and it is projected to reach 7 billion by the year 2000. Although some of the more industrialized countries have made great strides in this century in slowing, halting, or even reversing their rate of population growth, many other countries have yet to do so, despite the family planning efforts of national and international organizations. Mexico, for example, grew from 28 million people to almost 86 million people in a little over a generation, between 1950 and 1991. The problem is that earlier population booms in some countries resulted in huge increases in the number of women now of reproductive age. These women are having fewer babies each year than their moth-

Particularly in some developing nations, rapid population growth rates are alarming, since they may result in future urban overcrowding, insufficient public assistance funds, and shortages of food, housing, health care, and employment opportunities. Despite the family planning efforts of national and international organizations, families as large as this one in Afghanistan are still common in many countries.

ers did, but since there are so many of them, the total number of children they will bear is much greater than the total born to their mothers.

Some of the implications of unchecked population growth are obvious. Overpopulation often means there is not enough food, health care, or employment available to satisfy people's needs. The result is that more people are likely to be undernourished, sick, and unemployed or underemployed. Other consequences are more subtle but also pose serious problems, especially for the poorer nations of the world. The changing age structure of a country's labor force may drain its public assistance and social security funds; the depletion of local resources may encourage rural-to-urban migration, placing heavy demands on urban housing and services.

Opportunities for anthropologists to help stem the tide of uncontrolled population growth are many. As employees of governments, international aid agencies, religious or other cultural organizations, or private charitable foundations, anthropologists are increasingly involved in population projects ranging from social marketing studies of family planning devices to helping formulate national population policies.

Preserving Biodiversity. In the Anthropologist at Work box in Chapter 6, we described the environmental adaptation of Maasai cattle pastoralists in Tanzania, which showed that environmental conservation and the subsistence needs of small-scale societies are not necessarily incompatible. But in some parts of the world, governments and international agencies find themselves faced with a difficult question: which is more important, people or nature? If nature is to be left undisturbed, how are people who depend on natural resources to obtain their subsistence?

Of the many natural resources on which people depend, few are more important than tropical rainforests. These tracts of unspoiled land, with their enormous diversity of species (**biodiversity**), have been described as the lungs of the planet, for they

biodiversity the diversity of species

convert the huge quantities of carbon dioxide produced by cars and factories into oxygen. Destroying rainforests removes the planet's best means of removing carbon dioxide from the atmosphere, and greatly contributes to global warming through the greenhouse effect. Rainforests are also home to plant and animal species found nowhere else, some of which are of proven or potential medicinal or other value.

Yet an estimated 50 million acres of rainforest are being destroyed every year—1½ acres per second (Survival International 1990). Prominent among the causes are large-scale tree cutting by the logging industry and slash-and-burn agriculture by indigenous people. As a response, and with the help of anthropologists, international environmental conservation and development organizations such as the World Wildlife Fund and USAID have developed plans and provided funds for protecting rainforests. Economic development may be prohibited in forested regions, and local populations may be either relocated or prohibited from exploiting newly protected animal and plant resources as they once did.

Improving Health and Nutrition. Anthropologists are also at work in the area of international health, studying practices that may lead to illness; the impact of disease and malnutrition on individuals, families, and cultures; how health care, both traditional and modern, is provided in developing countries; and how health care can be better organized and delivered to alleviate suffering and improve health (Hull 1991; Pillsbury 1991).

The close link between AIDS and various aspects of culture has made this socially transmitted disease a focus of much anthropological attention, and a number of anthropologists are working to identify cultural factors that may inhibit or promote the spread of AIDS. In Indonesia, for example, people who need medication prefer to take it by injection rather than orally. In view of the well-known impact of needle use on the spread of AIDS, Indonesian society may be at more risk of an AIDS epidemic than societies in which oral medication is preferred. Applied anthropologists are also helping to identify the best ways of educating people about AIDS in the context of particular cultures, and culturally acceptable behavioral measures that might help to prevent this scourge.

Even as economic growth raises local standards of living, at the same time it may bring about **diseases of affluence**—health problems such as cancer, hypertension, heart disease, and diabetes, which were once much more typical of industrialized than traditional societies. Poor nutrition, lack of exercise, stress, smoking, and alcohol and drug abuse are some the culprits. Injury and death from automobile accidents and urban violence are also increasingly afflicting members of non-Western societies.

The diffusion of values and material culture to Kayapó society (see Anthropology and the Environment box, page 407) that resulted in some Kayapó chiefs developing an unquenchable thirst for Western goods was sensational in the case of a chief known as Tutu Pombo, who had taken the lead among the Kayapó chiefs in making deals with land developers (M. Moffett 1994:A6). By 1990, he owned three ranches, several cars, and an airplane with his likeness painted on the fuselage. Two years later he died of hypertension, his doctor placing some of the blame on the chief's fondness for "white man's food"—chocolate and sugar.

In some Pacific island nations, the customary diet is changing from one based on high-fiber, low-fat foods like root crops, fresh fish, green leaves, and coconuts to one based on white flour or rice, canned meat and fish, and large quantities of sugar and salt. In Fiji, the proportion of total energy deriving from

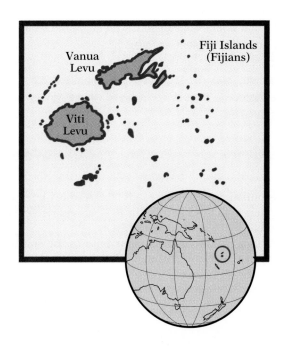

diseases of affluence diseases that result from a rise in living standards

The Anthropologist at Work

Patricia Wright

In Madagascar, a huge island lying off the southeast coast of Africa, lies Ranomafana National Park, one of the richest yet at the same time most endangered natural areas in the world. The park is so extensive and remote that parts of it have yet to be explored. At one time, Ranomafana was home to a thriving population of lemurs, rare primates that exist only in Madagascar. By 1985, however, environmentally destructive practices such as hunting by local people, slash-and-burn agriculture, and cattle herding in the forest, as well as deforestation resulting from fuel-wood collection and industrial logging, had seriously depleted Ranomafana's lemur population. If the lemurs and their habitat were to be protected, these practices would have to be halted.

An international conference was convened to help the Malagasy government decide how both the rainforest and its rare denizens could best be protected. Participants realized they needed to formulate policies that would simultaneously preserve the land and its animal and plant species, and also address the economic needs of the local people, the Tanala and Betsileo, who depended on the rainforest for their livelihood. A project to achieve these goals was established.

Anthropologist and primatologist Patricia Wright was appointed director of the new Ranomafana National Park Project. Wright quickly realized that any plan of action that failed to combine conservation with development, or to win the cooperation of the Tanala and Betsileo people in maintaining the park, would be doomed to failure. To learn what the villagers' needs would be if the use of their traditional lands were denied to them, she led a survey team on foot over rugged hillsides to

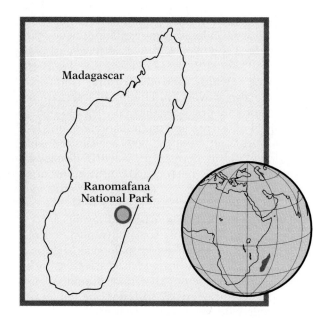

less nutritious imported foods has steadily increased: high enough at 43 percent in 1977, it had risen to 63 percent by 1981 (Hull 1991:25).

Some anthropologists contribute to the solution of health problems through **ethnobotany,** the study

ethnobotany the study of the ways cultures classify local plants

• Ask Yourself •

If you are majoring not in anthropology but in one of the natural sciences, humanities, or a social science other than anthropology, can you think of possible ways you might apply your knowledge to help alleviate global problems mentioned in this chapter, as some anthropologists hope to do?

Ranomafana National Park in Madagascar, one of the richest yet most endangered natural areas in the world, is home to an internationally funded development project combining environmental conservation with economic development. The park is home to several species of rare primates, found only in Madagascar, called lemurs.

Tanala and Betsileo villages. In each village, the team first met with the elders, then called a general meeting of village members at which their need for schools, health clinics, women's cooperatives, and agricultural assistance could be discussed. As the team listened, the scope of the project increased (Wright 1992:28).

Their survey completed, Wright and her team were able to recommend to the Malagasy government sustainable alternatives to villagers' traditional subsistence practices. These alternatives included beekeeping, raising fish in ponds, and cultivating wet rice. Subsequently, studies of the need for health care, primary education, and technical assistance with agricultural and forestry projects were carried out. Since Ranomafana is one of very few places in Madagascar where lemurs can be seen in their natural habitat, the team recommended **ecotourism**—tourism based on viewing wildlife—as a new way in which local villagers could make a living. Soon, some villagers had given up their traditional but ecologically harmful subsistence activities to work as tourist guides.

Wright's overall plan for Ranomafana includes biodiversity studies, conservation education, and ecotourism, but also focuses on the present and future needs of local people. She and her team are working toward providing health care for 28 remote villages, improving agriculture through better water management techniques, and training local people to monitor the health of the rainforest. Wright's multifaceted work illustrates how economic development and tropical conservation can be successfully linked.

of the way cultures classify and use local plants. Until recently, North American medical researchers paid little attention to the curative properties of plants used in non-Western societies. Now they are increasingly turning to these plants in their search for ways to cure, mitigate, or delay the onset of AIDS, cancer, heart disease, and other medical problems. Scientists, governments, environmental conservationists, pharmaceutical companies, and indigenous healers are coming together in an unusual coalition in which all parties might profit.

ecotourism tourism based on viewing wildlife

In San Antonio, western Belize, Mayan herb gatherer Antonio Kuk prepares a medicinal herb for a traditional therapist. North Americans searching for ways to cure cancer, heart disease, and AIDS have recently begun to study the curative properties of plants used by non-Western healers.

• Ask Yourself •

A tropical rainforest contains medicinal plants known to cure AIDS. The people who live in the forest regard these plants as so sacred they refuse to allow them to be gathered. Should their national government ignore these people's religious beliefs to harvest plants that could save the lives of millions? Or should government adopt a hands-off policy? Do you see any other options?

Conclusion

Anthropologists are often tempted to view their discipline as one of the bricks in an ivory tower. Some, those who still regard their work as a pure quest for scientific information, consider attempts to apply anthropology to practical ends as somehow unsuited to this lofty aim. One of the themes of this book has been that theoretical studies can be usefully pursued alongside more practical activities. Neither interest need suffer. This is not a new idea; mixing theory with practice has had a long and respectable history within cultural anthropology. Franz Boas, who thought a knowledge of other cultures could be an antidote to racism, was an anthropological activist as early as 1919.

Anthropology can be put to work for both theoretical and applied purposes in every culture and subculture. Its research methods, its analytical techniques, and the incalculable quantity of empirical data anthropologists have accumulated offer a unique perspective on small-scale and large-scale societies, both Western and non-Western, past and present; on females and males; on rural people and urbanites; on the newly enculturated and the elderly.

But whether we are able to take advantage of what anthropology offers depends on our capacity to suspend value judgments arising from ethnocentrism. Sometimes it is difficult to reject the notion that our modern, industrialized, twentieth-century way of life is somehow "better" than that of other cultures. Most Westerners think that, despite the costs associated with modern energy use, houses with central heating make "better" homes than houses built around open fires, because they are more comfortable breathing clean air in 72-degree surroundings than they would be inhaling smoky air in homes unevenly warmed by open fires. Most also regard passenger jets as "better" for transportation than donkeys, because jets move people from place to place much faster. Perhaps not everyone would agree, and no such value judgments can be applied to other aspects of culture. No one can say whether the languages we speak, the ideas and beliefs we hold, or the customs we have devised to order our social lives represent improvements over the languages, ideas, and customs of other cultures, past or present.

A conscious suspension of ethnocentrism is one of the best ways to put an education in cultural anthropology to use.

Summary

- Change, for better or for worse, is as inevitable and as constant in small-scale societies as in modern, industrialized ones.

- Because culture change does not necessarily imply improvement or even movement in the direction of greater complexity, it must be considered in terms of process rather than progress.

- However, in the evolution of cultures, there *has* been a general movement toward increasing complexity and (for Westerners, at least) improvement in at least one aspect of culture, the material.

- Change can come from within a culture (internal change) or from outside it (external change).

- In ancient times, when intercultural contacts were relatively few, culture change was more apt to be internal—a product of environmental shifts or inventions—than external.

- More recently, culture change has mainly resulted from contact between societies, and has occurred very rapidly.

- The mechanism through which external change comes about is diffusion: the spread of ideas, customs, artifacts, or language from one culture to another, directly or indirectly.

- Changes can be either beneficial or destructive. Beneficial changes are often modified, by the society that receives them, to suit its particular needs; destructive changes are sometimes resisted or rejected.

- Small-scale societies are more apt to be victims than beneficiaries of "progress," and anthropologists are concerned about the plight of these societies.

- The deliberate attempt to destroy the culture of an ethnic group is called *ethnocide*. Attempting to destroy the members of a society as well as their culture is called *genocide*. Both are occurring today.

- Some anthropologists serve as cultural advocates for minority groups, attempting to understand these groups' problems and helping them to develop effective strategies for achieving their goals.

- Development anthropologists are applied anthropologists involved in international development, a multidisciplinary effort intended to improve the well-being of people in "developing" countries.

- Two basic tenets of development anthropology are that it should be undertaken at the request and with the full participation of the intended beneficiaries, and that any improvements it helps to bring about should be locally sustainable once development assistance ends.

- Global problems with which today's development anthropologists often concern themselves include overpopulation, the loss of biodiversity, and poor health and nutrition.

- In helping to solve these and other problems, anthropologists are playing an important part in our changing world.

Key Terms

biodiversity
cultural diffusion
development anthropology
diffusionism
direct diffusion
diseases of affluence
ecotourism
ethnobotany
ethnocide
external change
genocide
great man theory
indirect diffusion
internal change
international development
sustainability
top-down approach
Westernization

Suggested Readings

Bodley, John H. 1985. *Anthropology and Contemporary Human Problems* (2nd ed.). Palo Alto, CA: Mayfield. An anthropological look at some of the most urgent problems we face today. The author discusses overconsumption, hunger, war, overpopulation, and the depletion of natural resources.

Bodley, John H. (ed.). 1988. *Tribal Peoples and Development Issues: A Global Overview*. Mountain View, CA: Mayfield. An outstanding collection of 39 articles yielding theoretical insights about cultural change and development and a wealth of empirical case studies from societies throughout the world.

Bodley, John H. 1990. *Victims of Progress* (3rd ed.). Mountain View, CA: Mayfield. This book gauges the impact of change on the indigenous cultures of the world. Among the many topics discussed are ethnocide, the effect of tourism on tribal people, progress and the quality of life, technological change, diseases of development, and ethnocentrism.

Cernea, Michael M. 1985. *Putting People First: Sociological Variables in Rural Development*. New York: Oxford University Press for the World Bank. A collection of articles on problems resulting from development projects in various countries. The editor is a noted social scientist affiliated with the World Bank.

Denslow, Julie Sloan, and Christine Padock (eds.). 1988. *People of the Tropical Rain Forest*. Berkeley: University of California Press. Twenty-three experts collaborated on this multidisciplinary study of how human beings use and misuse one of our most important natural resources. Case studies from Indonesia, Brazil, Africa, Thailand, Central America, and other regions are combined with more theoretical discussions on big business, logging, sustainability, resettlement, and Native Americans' rights in Amazonia. Anthropologists are well represented.

West, Patrick C., and Steven R. Bechin (eds.). 1991. *Resident Peoples and National Parks: Social Dilemmas and Strategies in International Conservation*. Tucson: University of Arizona Press. Over two dozen articles dealing with the human problems raised by creating environmentally protected areas in South Korea, the United States, Nepal, Costa Rica, Israel, and other countries.

Glossary

acculturation the process by which important changes take place within a culture as the result of contact with another culture

achieved authority authority that is earned

adaptation a complex of ideas, activities, and technologies that add up to a particular way of making a living

adjudication the process by which a dispute is settled after the disputants agree that a mediator's decision will be binding

affinal alliance ties between affines

affines relatives by marriage

affinity relationships created by marriage

age grade a period of life through which an individual passes as he or she grows older

age set a group of individuals of about the same age who move as a group through successive age grades

agnates (patrikin) consanguines who trace their descent from a common male ancestor

ambilineal descent the kind of descent in which one may choose to join either one's father's or mother's side of the family

ambilocal residence the residence pattern by which couples choose whether to live with the husband's relatives or the wife's

animism the belief that souls or spirits inhabit animals, plants, or inanimate objects

anorexia nervosa a mental and physical disorder characterized by an unrealistic view of oneself as too fat, self-induced starvation, and severe weight loss

anthropological linguistics (linguistic anthropology) the field of anthropology that focuses on languages

apartheid a former policy of the government of South Africa, under which nonwhite South Africans were physically, politically, and economically segregated from the white minority

applied anthropology the use of anthropological ideas and methods to achieve practical ends outside the academic community

archaeology the field of anthropology that focuses on the material remains of people of the past

armchair anthropologist an anthropologist who collects data from documents written by others rather than carrying out fieldwork

artifact any material thing created by people

ascribed authority authority that is inherited rather than earned

authority the socially granted right to exercise power

avunculocal residence the residence pattern by which male ego resides with his mother's brother

balanced reciprocity the immediate (or fairly prompt) return of goods equal in value to what has been given

band a group of gatherers and hunters; alternatively, a particular kind of political organization (see Chapter 12)

barter economic transactions in which goods and services are swapped without the use of money

berdache in some midwestern and western Native American societies, a transvestite and perhaps also transsexual male who was prompted by visions to dress and behave like a woman

bifurcate merging terminology a terminology in which F and FB are known by the same term, whereas MB is known by a different term; and where M and MZ are known by the same term whereas FZ is known by a different term

big man in Melanesia, a politician whose power depends on the influence he exerts over his followers rather than on a political office

bilateral exchange a form of cross cousin marriage in which the men of two nuclear families or descent groups, related to one another as cross cousins, exchange women in marriage; sometimes called direct exchange

bilineal descent (double descent) a combination of patriliny and matriliny

bilingualism being able to speak more than one language with equal, or roughly equal, competence

biodiversity the diversity of species

biological (physical) anthropology the field of anthropology that focuses on the biological aspects of being human

biomedicine the Western system of medical belief and practice

Black Vernacular English (BVE) a dialect of English spoken by black youths in the inner cities of the United States

body language (kinesics) nonverbal communication through body movements or facial expressions

bride-capture (bride-theft) the forcible and frequently symbolic carrying off of a bride

bride-service an arrangement in which a son-in-law is obliged to work for his father-in-law as a way of compensating the father-in-law for the loss of his daughter's services

bridewealth (bride-price) property transferred from a groom's family to his bride's at marriage

bullroarer an elongated piece of bone or other material, which when whirled about on a cord produces a tone

business anthropology the work undertaken by anthropologists who study workers and workplaces, and act as consultants to management

capital resources not consumed in the process of production

capitalist mode of production a system of production in which capital is controlled by capitalists, and workers, denied access to ownership of capital, must sell their labor to the capitalists in order to make a living

421

cargo cult a popular movement for social change in Melanesia, whose followers believe that certain rituals will bring ships loaded with valuable cargo

carrying capacity the maximum number of people who can live indefinitely within a given area at a given level of technology

case study a detailed ethnographic study focusing on a single individual or episode

caste a hereditary social group associated with a particular occupation; bound by distinctive rights, duties, and prohibitions; and occupying a permanent place in a hierarchy of similar groups

casual informant an informant from whom an ethnographer obtains information from time to time

charisma personal magnetism capable of inspiring agreement, loyalty, and enthusiasm

chiefdom a relatively complex political organization controlling a large, sedentary population

cicatrization a form of scarification in which the skin is repeatedly punctured in an intricate pattern

clan (patriclan, matriclan) a descent group whose members believe they are descended from (or in some special way related to) the same founding ancestor or ancestress

class a group defined by the amount of control it exerts over factors of production

clitoridectomy the partial or complete removal of the clitoris and sometimes the labia minora as well

closed peasant society a type of peasant society characterized by production for household use, old-fashioned technology, isolation from mainstream city life, and resistance to change

code switching switching from one language or dialect into another language or dialect

cognate a word or language historically derived from the same source as another word or language

cognation (cognatic descent) a form of descent reckoned through both males and females

cognitive anthropology a specialty whose practitioners attempt to explain cultures by examining the different categories people create in order to organize their universe

committee an advisory group, most common in states, that meets in private and usually achieves agreement by voting

common-interest group a group defined by the common needs and concerns of its members

comparative linguistics an alternate term for historical linguistics

conditional curse a verbal formula, containing a conditional phrase, designed to establish innocence or guilt

conjugate to change a verb to reflect different tenses, persons, and moods

consanguines (consanguinal kin) individuals related by ties of consanguinity

consanguinity a relationship based on the tie between parents and children that also includes more distant relatives

conservative art art that sustains the existing social order

consumption all the ways in which the goods, services, and nonmaterial things produced within a society are used

contagious magic magic based on the idea that even after they have been separated, things once in contact can influence each other

control group a group similar in size and composition to a study group, used for purposes of comparison or as a cross-check on the data provided by the study group

cooperation explanation an explanation for the incest taboo that emphasizes the social advantages that come from obliging members of the same family to marry outside of it

core vocabulary the most basic words of any language

cosmetics preparations designed to improve the appearance of the body, or part of it, by directly but temporarily applying them to the skin

council an advisory group, typical of simpler political organizations, that is usually informally appointed, meets in public, and resolves conflicts by consensus

court a group of people with the authority to hear the cases of disputants and their witnesses, to determine innocence or guilt, and to decide on punishment

creole a pidgin language that has become the mother-tongue of a community

cross cousin children of siblings of the opposite sex

cross cousin marriage a marriage between two cross cousins

Crow terminology a bifurcate merging terminology sometimes accompanying matrilineal descent in which, among other identifications, FZ = FZD

cultural anthropology the study of culture

cultural audit in business anthropology, a study of discrepancies between the ideal and actual conduct of business within a company

cultural diffusion the spread of ideas and technology between cultures

cultural ecology a cultural materialist perspective emphasizing the natural environment as a factor influencing culture

cultural evolution the notion that cultures evolve, usually gradually, steadily, and in the direction of greater efficiency and complexity

cultural materialism the idea that concrete, measurable things, such as the natural environment or technology, are more responsible for specific aspects of culture than other factors

cultural pluralism the meeting of many cultural traditions within a society, particularly a large-scale, modern society

cultural process what happens to cultures through time, whether change or stability, increasing or decreasing complexity

cultural relativism a central idea in modern cultural anthropology—that a culture must be evaluated in terms of its own values, not according to the values of another culture

culture everything that people collectively do, think, make, and say

culture hero a mythological being, animal, or inanimate object thought to be associated with the origins of a clan

culture and personality an area of special interest within anthropology, whose adherents see a significant link between culture and human psychology

culture of poverty the ideas and behavior of poor people in some capitalist societies

culture shock the sense of confusion and disorientation fieldworkers may experience upon entering the field

cuneiform ancient writing consisting of an arrangement of tiny wedge-shaped dents impressed into wet clay

cyclical age set a system in which an age set is continually recycled

decline to change a noun to reflect case, number, or gender

dependency ratio the number of people in a nation's work force compared with the number who are too young or too old to work

descent a relationship defined by a connection to an ancestor through a series of parent-child links

descent group a group made up of individuals who trace their descent to a common ancestor

descriptive linguistics the branch of linguistics that seeks to describe the features of languages

destructive potlatch a variety of potlatch in which Kwakiutl hosts destroyed their most valued possessions

development anthropology efforts by anthropologists to improve the well-being of people in the "developing" countries in areas such as health care, education, and agriculture

diachronic approach the study of societies and cultures as they develop through time

dialect a variety of a language resulting from the speaker's region, occupation, or class

diffused sanction a spontaneous expression of either approval or disapproval

diffusionism the idea that culture change can be explained by intercultural contacts

direct diffusion the diffusion of an idea or custom from one culture to another without passing through an intermediary culture

diseases of affluence diseases that result from a rise in living standards

distribution the way in which goods and services are allotted in a society

divination a ritual designed to foretell the future or interpret the past, with the help of supernatural agents

diviner a person who performs a divination ritual

domestic (private, household) domain the social sphere that centers on the home and is associated with such activities as child-rearing and food preparation for household consumption

double standard the notion that within a single society the rules governing sexual behavior should be different for males and females

dowry goods given by a bride's family to the family of her groom

ecofact a natural object used or modified by human hands

economic development strategies for improving national economies based on the assumption that they will lead to improvements in human welfare

economic system the interrelated production, distribution, and consumption of goods and services in a society

economy in the most general sense, all the ways in which the members of the society satisfy their wants and needs

ecotourism tourism based on viewing wildlife

ego the individual from whose perspective a kinship diagram is drawn

ego-centered network a network centering on a particular individual and including all the links between this person and others in his or her community

emic perspective the anthropological use of the concepts meaningful to the members of a society to understand their culture.

enculturation the process by which an individual absorbs the details of his or her particular culture, starting from birth

endogamy the custom in which one's spouse must be chosen from within one's own group

ends the goals achieved by expending resources

Eskimo terminology a terminology found in many cognatic societies, in which members of the nuclear family are distinguished from all other relatives

ethnic association a common-interest group based on ethnicity

ethnic group a group whose members share basic cultural traditions and values and a common language, and who identify themselves (and are identified by others) as distinct from other such groups

ethnicity the identification of individuals with particular ethnic groups

ethnobotany the study of the ways cultures classify local plants

ethnocentrism the belief that one's own society or culture is superior to all others

ethnocide the deliberate attempt to destroy the culture of an ethnic group

ethnographer a cultural anthropologist in the process of collecting data on contemporary people

ethnography a written work about a particular culture; also, the collection of data on contemporary people

ethnology an alternative term for cultural anthropology

ethnomedicine non-Western systems of medical belief and practice

ethnomusicology the study of music in its cultural context, either in a single society or cross-culturally

etic perspective the anthropological use of the concepts meaningful to the anthropologist to understand a culture

exogamy the social rule that one must marry someone from outside one's own group, however that group is defined

expressive culture the purposeful arrangement of forms, colors, sounds, language, and/or body movements in ways that have meaning and/or are aesthetically appealing to those who do the arranging, and usually to others as well

extended family a larger family group than the nuclear, whose membership is more variable

external change change originating outside a society

fable a category of folktale that teaches some important moral lesson

faction an informal, adversarial political group existing within a larger unit, such as a political party or village

family two or more individuals who consider themselves related, who are economically interdependent, and who share the responsibility for rearing any children in their group

feminist anthropology a topic within cultural anthropology that focuses on women

feud a prolonged but usually intermittent hostile relationship between two groups

fieldwork the process of collecting original information about people, ancient or modern

focus group a small group of informants brought together to shed light on a particular topic

folk art the art produced by traditional societies

folktale a fictional story about the adventures of animals or of animals and human beings

fraternal polyandry the custom whereby two or more of a polyandrous woman's husbands are brothers

functionalism the idea that aspects of culture function to fulfill the biological, psychological, or other needs of individuals

gamelan an Indonesian orchestra containing as many as 75 different instruments

gathering and hunting the nonproducing method of subsistence

gender learned maleness or femaleness, as reflected in sexual orientation and sex roles

gender hierarchy a ranking of cultural notions of maleness and femaleness, as opposed to a ranking of individual males and females

gender identity an individual's self-identification as male or female

genealogy a record of a person's relationships by blood or marriage

general-purpose money objects of value that can be used to purchase anything available for purchase

generalized reciprocity gift-giving with the expectation that sooner or later this act will be reciprocated

genetic explanation an explanation for the incest taboo that emphasizes the genetic advantages of marrying outside the family

genocide the deliberate attempt to exterminate the members of a culture

ghost marriage the custom in which the ghost of a man who has died "marries" and is considered able to father a child

glottochronology a method for establishing the approximate time at which two languages branched off from a common ancestor

good magic magic performed to achieve ends that society considers beneficial

government a formal organization through which the political process is carried out

grammar the rules governing word order, prefixes and suffixes, and other aspects of a language

graphic art two-dimensional forms of art such as painting or drawing

great man theory the idea that a single forceful individual can cause major change in a society

Great Tradition the wider, literate culture in which peasants exist

group marriage a form of marriage involving two or more men and two or more women as marriage partners at the same time

gullah a creole language spoken by black residents of coastal South Carolina

Hawaiian terminology a terminology found in many cognatic societies, in which all relatives of the same sex in the same generation are included under the same term

herding camp the pastoralist residence, consisting of the temporary homes of families that herd and travel together

hermaphrodite an individual who has both male and female physical characteristics

hijada (hijra) in northwestern India, a man who cross-dresses, begs for charity, and entertains like a woman at ceremonies

historical linguistics the branch of linguistics that studies histories of languages, both living and dead, and the relationships between languages and dialects

historical particularism the idea that every culture, because it is the product of specific historical circumstances, is unique

hominids contemporary human beings' prehuman ancestors

horticulture a method of subsistence based on growing crops with simple tools and technologies

hydraulic society a society in which crops are irrigated by a complex system of water management

illiterate lacking the ability to read and write while living in a literate society

image of the limited good the view that the world is a place in which there are not enough good things to go around

imitative magic a ritual that imitates the result desired

incest taboo the prohibition of sex between relatives

incorporation final stage of a rite of passage, in which an individual is integrated into a new status in society

indirect diffusion the diffusion of an idea or custom from one culture to another after passing through an intermediary culture

infibulation the process of stitching together the two sides of the vaginal opening

informant an individual who provides an ethnographic researcher with information

instinct explanation an explanation for the incest taboo suggesting that members of the same family instinctively find one another sexually unappealing

internal change change originating within a society

international development a comprehensive term for international efforts to improve the well-being of the world's people

interpretive anthropology the idea that an ethnographer's job is to describe and interpret what members of the culture being studied find meaningful

interview a conversation between an ethnographer and one or more informants

invented tradition symbols, ideas, or customs that members of a society claim as traditional parts of their culture but that in reality are of more recent origin

Iroquois terminology a bifurcate terminology associated with unilineal descent in which the matrilateral cross cousin and patrilateral cross cousin are known by the same term, which may sometimes be the same term as spouse

key informant an informant upon whom, because of specialized knowledge or influence, an ethnographer relies heavily

kibbutz an agricultural collective in Israel whose main features include communal living, collective ownership of all property, and the communal raising of children

kin-oriented mode of production a system of production in which labor is organized according to descent and marriage

kindred a group of relatives who all have at least ego in common

kinship (relationship) terminology the complete set of terms by which relatives are known

labret a plug inserted through the flesh of the lower lip

law an institutionalized body of rules, created over time and ratified by a society or its leaders

legend a narrative that describes events set in a specific place in the real world, at a time less remote than the mythological past

leveling mechanism any of various cultural devices or rules according to which individuals are obligated to redistribute their material wealth, so that no one can accumulate more than anyone else

levirate the custom in which a widow marries her dead husband's brother

life history an informant's story of his or her life and the influences upon it

liminality second stage of a rite of passage, in which an individual has no established status

lineage (patrilineage, matrilineage) a descent group made up of consanguines who can trace their precise genealogical links, through known ancestors, to a founding ancestor

lineal age set a system in which an age set ceases to exist when all of its members have died

magic a ritual intended to bring about some desired practical result without the intervention of spirits

market exchange the kind of exchange in which transactions are impersonal rather than based on descent, marriage, social position, or political relationships

marriage a socially sanctioned contract spelling out the domestic and civic rights and duties of the people who enter into it

matriarchy a society dominated by females politically and economically

matrigroup a matrilineal descent group, whether matriclan or matrilineage

matrikin (uterine kin) consanguines who trace their descent from a common female ancestor

matrilateral cousin cousin on the mother's side

matrilateral cross cousin marriage a man's marriage to his mother's brother's daughter or a woman's marriage to her father's sister's son

matrilateral parallel cousin marriage a man's marriage to his mother's sister's daughter or a woman's marriage to her mother's sister's son

matriliny (matrilineal descent) a system of descent in which females provide the links by which property descends to the next generation

matrilocal residence residence for a husband near or with his wife's parents

means all the material and nonmaterial resources people use to fulfill their wants and needs

mediator a person who is neutral to a dispute and charged with negotiating its settlement

medical anthropology a topic within cultural anthropology that focuses on the attitudes, beliefs, and practices surrounding illness and healing in different cultures

mental universals fixed patterns of thought common to human beings all over the world

military association a group of males who have fought or may fight together

millenarian movement a response made by a deprived community, characterized by anticipating a time when its hopes will be fulfilled

minority an ethnic group typically numerically smaller than the dominant group in its society

modal personality in any culture, the personality type that is statistically the most common

money objects accepted by a society's members as tokens of specific amounts of worth

monogamy the marriage of one husband and one wife

monotheism the belief that there is only one god

morpheme (morphology) the smallest combination of sounds that has meaning in a language

multilineal evolution the notion that different cultures evolve along multiple, if similar, lines, depending on their natural and cultural environments

mutilation any irreversible alteration of a healthy human body

myth a story describing the origins of the world, some natural phenomenon, or some aspect of culture, which contains at least one physically or humanly impossible event or situation

negative reciprocity an economic interaction between hostile parties in which each partner tries to get the better of the other

neoevolution any of several twentieth-century variations on cultural evolution

Neolithic revolution the shift in human subsistence from collecting to producing subsistence needs

neolocal residence residence for a married couple in a location separate from the residences of their families

neopaganism a modern revival of a pre-Christian religion

network analysis gathering and organizing data by focusing on individuals or small groups and their interrelationships, in order to establish patterns of association and assess their effects

nomads pastoralists who travel constantly throughout the year, within a large area, to provide their animals with grazing land

nonliterate lacking a tradition of reading and writing

nonmechanized agriculture agriculture using wooden or metal plows, pulled by animals

norm an informal rule for behavior

nuclear (elementary, simple) family a social unit consisting of a father, a mother, and unmarried children

octave a set of eight primary tones

office a position in which a certain kind and amount of authority is inherent, and that exists independently of its occupant at any given time

Omaha terminology a bifurcate merging terminology sometimes accompanying patrilineal descent in which, among other identifications, MB = MBS = MBSS

open peasant society a type of peasant society characterized by substantial participation in a national or international economy

opposition thinking in terms of opposing categories

oral art art in the form of spoken words

organized sanction a formalized and institutionalized expression of approval or disapproval

Oriental Despotism a kind of political system, highly developed in ancient China, in which some individuals achieved power by controlling water and labor

origin myth a story describing the origins of some feature of the physical environment, of a society, or of a culture; often describes the appearance of a clan's culture hero and how the clan was founded

ostracism a diffuse sanction in which the offender is shunned

paralanguage the use of voice effects to convey meaning

parallel cousin children of siblings of the same sex

parallel cousin marriage a marriage between two parallel cousins

participant observation ethnology's major research tool, involving sharing in people's lives as well as observing them

pastoralists those who practice a method of subsistence based on herd animals

patriarchy a society politically and economically dominated by males

patrigroup a patrilineal descent group, whether patriclan or patrilineage

patrilateral cousin cousin on the father's side

patrilateral cross cousin marriage a man's marriage to his father's sister's daughter or a woman's marriage to her mother's brother's son

patrilateral parallel cousin marriage a man's marriage to his father's brother's daughter or a woman's marriage to her father's brother's son

patriliny (patrilineal descent) a system of descent in which males provide the links by which property descends to the next generation

patrilocal residence residence for a husband near or with his father after marriage

peasants typically agricultural people who share the same general cultural tradition as members of the larger and more technologically complex societies in which they live

percussion toneless sounds made by striking something

peripheral market a market of relatively little economic importance, in which only objects, as opposed to land or labor, are bought and sold

personal survey a survey undertaken personally by a researcher

phoneme (phonology) the smallest meaningful unit of sound in a language

pictograph a simple pictorial representation of an object

pidgin a language in which the syntax and vocabulary of two other languages are simplified and combined

pitch the highness or lowness of a musical sound, largely determined by the frequency of its sound vibration

plastic art sculpture and other three-dimensional forms of art

political organization (political system) a mechanism, formal or informal, for establishing and maintaining social control

politics the process of regulating the behavior of members of a group

polyandry marriage between a wife and more than one husband

polyethnic made up of different ethnic groups

polygamy a form of marriage in which a person has more than one spouse at the same time.

polygyny marriage between a husband and more than one wife

polytheism the belief in the existence of many gods

postmodernism an anthropological specialty, developed in the 1980s, that encourages anthropology to focus on the analysis of ethnographies, examining how they are written from a reflexive point of view

potlatch among Native Americans of the Northwest coast, a form of institutionalized consumption consisting of a huge party given by a chief for a rival chief and for all the villagers under the sway of both chiefs

power the capacity to control the behavior of others, using means such as education, persuasion, coercion, punishment, or reward

prefix a morpheme that is added at the front of a word to alter its meaning

prestige social reputation based on a subjective evaluation of social statuses relative to one another

price the worth, expressed in the form of some agreed-on medium of exchange, of goods and services

priest a religious specialist whose authority comes from the office he or she occupies

prime a formal unit of American Sign Language, corresponding to the sounds of spoken language

production transforming natural resources into things people want and need

prophet a charismatic leader who emerges after some intense spiritual experience

protolanguage a hypothetical language thought to be the ancestor of a known language

psychoanalytic explanation an explanation for the incest taboo that suggests its origin in an attempt to control the unconscious desire of children to have sex with the parent of the opposite sex

psychological anthropology an anthropological specialty focusing on the relationship between culture and the psychological makeup of individuals and groups

public domain the social sphere that centers on the wider social world outside of the home and is associated with political and economic activity above the household level

purdah the physical seclusion of women, a custom common in the Middle East

race a term commonly used to identify groups of people supposedly sharing certain specific physical attributes, or, alternatively, physical plus cultural similarities. The word is not useful for distinguishing either biological or cultural categories of people

rank a position in a hierarchical system of social classification

realistic ethnography an ethnography that claims to represent a "real" portrait of a culture or society

reciprocity mutual exchange of gifts or services

redistribution a way of distributing goods in which the goods are gathered into the possession of a particular individual or group and then parceled out among the members of a society

respondent a person who provides information for a survey

respondent survey a survey consisting of a prearranged series of questions, in questionnaire form, asked of respondents

revitalization movement a popular movement for radical change, led by a charismatic figure and usually prompted by social, economic, or political upheaval

revolutionary art art that generates new ideas and values

rite of passage a ritual performed at a period of transition in the life cycle

ritual stereotyped, repetitive behavior, either religious or nonreligious, that uses symbols to communicate meaning

ritual of propitiation a ritual intended to appease a spirit

role a combination of the attitudes associated with a given status and the behavior that expresses them

sacrifice an offering made to a spirit; the term also denotes the ritual itself

sampling using a small part of something to represent a larger whole

sanction a positive or negative reaction by society to approved behavior (positive sanction) or disapproved behavior (negative sanction)

Sapir-Whorf hypothesis (Whorfian hypothesis) the idea that the way in which the members of a society order their world is conditioned by their language

scale a fixed set of tones on which music is based

scarification designs made by the intentional wounding and subsequent healing and scarring of the skin

separation first stage of a rite of passage, in which an individual is separated from an established status

serial monogamy consecutive monogamous marriages to a number of different spouses

set-centered network a network based on groups of individuals linked to one another

sex the biological category into which a person is born, male or female, as determined by chromosomal and anatomical characteristics

shaman a religious figure, believed to be chosen by spirits, who functions as an intermediary between the world of spirits and human beings

sibling language one of two or more languages that branched off from a common ancestral language

sign language a language in which hand and body gestures, instead of sounds, are used to express meaning

silent barter a kind of barter in which the trading partners never meet each other face to face

social anthropology especially in England, the brand of anthropology focusing on societies rather than on culture

social classification a systematic way of distinguishing among individuals or groups according to their different socially defined attributes

social explanation an explanation for the incest taboo that suggests it arose to prevent family disintegration

social stratification (social ranking) a system of social classification in which various statuses are viewed as unequal to one another

social structure the web of relationships binding members of a society

society a group of people whose members live in the same place and whose lives and livelihoods are interdependent

sociocultural anthropology a term for cultural anthropology that emphasizes society

sociolinguistics a branch of linguistics that focuses on the relationship between language and society

sorcery bad magic, performed to achieve ends society regards as evil

sororal polygyny the custom in which two or more of a polygynous man's wives are sisters

sororate the custom in which a widower marries his dead wife's sister

special-purpose money objects of value that can be used to purchase only specific goods and services

state a large, complex, autonomous political unit, consisting of many communities and large numbers of people under a centralized government that can conscript labor, make and enforce laws, collect taxes, and create and maintain institutions to support itself

status the place an individual occupies in the social structure

STD sexually transmitted disease

structural anthropology a specialty within cultural anthropology whose followers attempt to discover orderly patterns common to languages, myths, kinship systems, and other aspects of culture

structural-functionalism an anthropological perspective in which aspects of culture are viewed in terms of the part they play in maintaining the social structure

subculture a small group, within a larger one, whose members distinguish themselves (or who are distinguished by others) as different from others on any cultural basis

subsistence all the ways in which people get the things they need to subsist

Sudanese (descriptive) terminology a terminology often associated with unilineal descent, with separate terms for F, FB, MB, MZ, FZ, siblings, and cousins

suffix a morpheme that is added to the end of a word to alter its meaning

survey the counting and classifying of items, events, or opinions

sustainability the capacity of the beneficiaries of a development project to continue to achieve results after development assistance ends

swidden, slash-and-burn, or shifting cultivation a form of horticulture in which a plot of land is cultivated for some years and then abandoned in favor of a new one

symbol something that stands for something else

symbolic anthropology the anthropological study of symbols

synchronic approach the study of how aspects of societies and cultures fit together at any given point in time

syncretism the blending of two or more cultural traditions into a single new one

syntax the rules governing the way morphemes can be arranged in order to make sense

tone a sound of distinct duration, quality, and pitch

top-down approach in international development, providing assistance to local people without their full participation

totem a plant, animal, or object from which members of a clan are believed to have descended, or which plays some central role in its history

transhumance a pastoral way of life in which people move with their herds according to the seasons

transsexual an individual who adopts the social role of the sex opposite to his or her anatomical one

transvestite (cross-dresser) a man who dresses like a woman or a woman who dresses like a man

trial by ordeal a physical test of an accused person for the purpose of revealing the truth

tribe a political organization often occurring among horticulturalists or herders whose members identify themselves as distinct from members of other groups based on their common heritage, and often common ancestry

tributary mode of production a system of production in which producers must pay tribute to people who control things needed for production in order to gain access to them

unilineal descent a line of descent that runs through either males or females but not both

unilineal evolution the notion that all cultures follow the same trajectory, from savagery to civilization

universal grammar a hypothetical grammatical ability inherent in all human beings from birth

urban anthropology a topic within ethnology that focuses on the adaptations of urban dwellers

varna one of four traditional divisions of Hindu Indian society

vernacular the standard language or dialect of a population

voluntary association a self-help group

Westernization the process by which non-Western societies become more like Western ones by adopting Western technologies, ideas, values, and customs

wicca a pre-Christian European religion

witchcraft the belief that certain individuals, called witches, can injure others by psychic means

writing the graphic or visual representation of a language

References

Abdalla, Raqiya Haji Dualeh
1982. *Sisters in Affliction: Circumcision and Infibulation of Women in Africa*. London: Zed Press.

Abu-Lughod, Lila
1986. *Veiled Sentiments*. Berkeley: University of California Press.
1987. Bedouin Blues. *Natural History* 98(7):24–32.

Ackroyd, Anne V.
1984. Ethics in Relation to Informants, the Profession, and Governments. In Roy F. Ellen (ed.), *Ethnographic Research: A Guide to General Conduct*, pp. 133–154. ASA Research Methods in Social Anthropology No. 1. London: Academic Press.

Adam, Peter
1992. *Art of the Third Reich*. New York: Abrams.

Adra, Najwa
1985. Achievement and Play: Opposition in Yemeni Tribal Dancing. In *The Consulting Symposium on the Collecting and Documenting of the Traditional Music and Dance of the Arabian Gulf*, pp. 69–75. Doha, Qatar: Arab Gulf States Folklore Centre.
1992. Personal communication.

Agar, Michael H.
1980. *The Professional Stranger: An Informal Introduction to Ethnography*. New York: Academic Press.

American Anthropological Association
1971. *Principles of Professional Responsibility*. Washington, DC: American Anthropological Association.

Anderson, Richard L.
1992. *Art in Small-scale Societies* (2nd ed.). Englewood Cliffs, NJ: Prentice Hall.

Anonymous
1993. The Savage Can Also Be Ignoble. *The Economist*, June 12, p. 54.

Anonymous
1994, September 3. Experiment in Tribal Justice: 2 Youths Are Banished. *New York Times*, p. A6.

Anthropology Today
1988. News 4(3):29.

Applebaum, Richard P., and William J. Chambliss
1995. *Sociology*. New York: HarperCollins College Publishers.

Ardener, Shirley
1984. Gender Orientations in Fieldwork. In Roy F. Ellen (ed.), *Ethnographic Research: A Guide to General Conduct*, pp. 118–129. ASA Research Methods in Social Anthropology No. 1. London: Academic Press.

Ardrey, Robert
1961. *African Genesis*. New York: Atheneum.

Arens, W.
1981 (1976). Professional Football: An American Symbol and Ritual. In W. Arens and Susan P. Montague (eds.), *The American Dimension:*

Cultural Myths and Social Realities, pp. 3–14. Sherman Oaks, CA: Alfred Publishing.

Århem, Kaj
1985. *Pastoral Man in the Garden of Eden: The Maasai of Ngorongoro Conservation Area, Tanzania*. Uppsala, Sweden: University of Uppsala.

Armstrong, W. E.
1967. Rossel Island Money: A Unique Monetary System. In George Dalton (ed.), *Tribal and Peasant Economies: Readings in Economic Anthropology*, pp. 246–253. Garden City, NY: American Museum of Natural History Press.

Austin, Charles
1983, October 15. New Bible Text Makes God Male and Female. *New York Times*, pp. 1, 8.

Axtell, Roger E. (ed.)
1985. *Dos and Taboos Around the World*. New York: Wiley.

Bachtiar, Harsja
1967. Negri Taram: A Minangkabau Village Community. In Koentjaraningrat (ed.), *Villages in Indonesia*. Ithaca, NY: Cornell University Press.

Bailey, F. G.
1965. Decisions by Consensus in Councils and Committees. In Michael Banton (ed.), *Political Systems and the Distribution of Power*. ASA Monographs 2. London: Tavistock.

Barnes, J. A.
1981. Ethical and Political Compromise in Social Research. Manuscript quoted and cited in Ackroyd (1984:154).

Barnes, Ruth, and Joanne B. Eicher (eds.)
1992. *Dress and Gender: Making and Meaning*. New York: Berg.

Barrett, Richard A.
1991. *Culture and Conduct* (2nd ed.). Belmont, CA: Wadsworth.

Barringer, Felicity
1992, July 17. Rates of Marriage Continue Decline. *New York Times*, p. A20.

Barth, Frederik (ed.)
1981. Ethnic Groups and Boundaries. *Process and Form in Social Life*, Vol. I, pp. 198–227. London: Routledge & Kegan Paul.

Bateson, Gregory (ed.)
1972. Style, Grace and Information in Primitive Art. *Steps to an Ecology of Mind: Collected Essays in Anthropology, Psychiatry, Evolution, and Epistemology*, pp. 128–152. San Francisco: Chandler.

Beals, Alan R.
1980. *Gopalpur: A South Indian Village*. New York: Holt, Rinehart & Winston.

Beck, L.
1980. Herd Owners and Hired Shepherds: The Qashgai of Iran. *Ethnology* 19(3):327–351.

429

Bender, Barbara
1975. *Farming in Prehistory: From Hunter-Gatherer to Food Producer*. London: John Baker.

Benedict, Ruth
1989 (1934). *Patterns of Culture*. Boston: Houghton Mifflin.

Benthall, Jonathan
1988. The Bonham's Head Affair. *Anthropology Today* 4(4):1–2.

Berman, Paul (ed.)
1992. *Debating P. C.: The Controversy over Political Correctness on College Campuses*. New York: Laurel/ Dell.

Bernard, H. Russell
1994. *Research Methods in Anthropology: Qualitative and Quantitative Approaches* (2nd ed.). Thousand Oaks, CA: Sage Publications.

Bickerton, Derek
1983. Creole Languages. *Scientific American* 249(1):116–122.

Boas, Franz
1897. *The Social Organization and the Secret Societies of the Kwakiutl Indians*. Report of the U.S. National Museum, 1895. Washington, DC: U.S. National Museum.
1911. *The Mind of Primitive Man*. New York: Macmillan.
1948. *Race, Language, and Culture*. New York: Macmillan.
1966. *Kwakiutl Ethnography* (Helen Codère, ed.). Chicago: University of Chicago Press.
1973 (1919). Scientists as Spies. In Thomas Weaver (ed.), *To See Ourselves: Anthropology and Modern Social Issues*, pp. 51–52. Glenview, IL: Scott, Foresman.

Bock, Philip K.
1988 (1980). *Rethinking Psychological Anthropology: Continuity and Change in the Study of Human Action*. New York: Freeman.

Boe, S. Kathryn
1987. Language as an Expression of Caring in Women. *Anthropological Linguistics* 29(3):271– 285.

Bott, Elizabeth
1971. *Family and Social Networks* (2nd ed.). London: Tavistock.

Boyer, Paul, and Stephen Nissenbaum
1974. *Salem Possessed: The Social Origins of Witchcraft*. Cambridge, MA: Harvard University Press.

Bradford, Bonnie, and Margaret A. Gwynne (eds.)
1995. *Down to Earth: Community Perspectives on Health, Development, and the Environment*. West Hartford, CT: Kumarian Press.

Brandes, Stanley
1985. Women of Southern Spain: Aspirations, Fantasies, Realities. In David D. Gilmore and Gretchen Gwynne (eds.), Sex and Gender in Southern Europe: Problems and Prospects. *Anthropology* 3(1–2):111– 128.

Brooke, James
1991, 19 November. Brazil Creates Reserve for Imperiled Amazon Tribe. *New York Times*, p. A3.

Brown, B.
1991. *State of the World, 1991*. Washington, DC: WorldWatch Institute.

Brown, Donald E.
1991. *Human Universals*. Philadelphia: Temple University Press.

Bullard, Robert D.
1993. *Confronting Environmental Racism*. Boston: South End Press.

Burkhalter, S. Brian
1986, June. The Anthropologist in Marketing. In Hendrick Serrie (ed.), *Anthropology and International Business*, pp. 113–124. Studies in Third World Societies, Publication No. 28. Williamsburg, VA: Department of Anthropology, College of William and Mary.

Burton, Michael, Lilyan Brudner, and Douglas White
1977. A Model of the Sexual Division of Labor. *American Ethnologist* 4(2):227–251.

Butler, Nilak, and Winona LaDuke
1995. Economic Development and Destruction of Indigenous Lands. In Bonnie Bradford and Margaret A. Gwynne (eds.), *Down to Earth: Community Perspectives on Health, Development, and the Environment*, pp. 113–122. West Hartford, CT: Kumarian Press.

Callender, Charles, and Lee M. Kochems
1983. The North American Berdache. *Current Anthropology* 24(4):443–470.

Cameron, Deborah, et al.
1989. Lakoff in Context: The Social and Linguistic Functions of Tag Questions. In Jennifer Coates and Deborah Cameron (eds.), *Women in Their Speech Communities: New Perspectives on Language and Sex*, pp. 74–93. White Plains, NY: Longman.

Campbell, J. K.
1964. *Honour, Family, and Patronage: A Study of Institutions and Moral Values in a Greek Mountain Community*. Oxford: Clarendon Press.

Capps, Lisa L.
1994. Change and Continuity in the Medical Culture of the Hmong in Kansas City. *Medical Anthropology Quarterly* 8(2):161–177.

Carneiro, Robert L.
1970. A Theory of the Origin of the State. *Science* 69:733–738.
1978. Political Expansion as an Expression of the Principle of Competitive Exclusion. In Ronald Cohen and Elman R. Service (eds.), *Origins of the State: The Anthropology of Political Evolution*, pp. 205–223. Philadelphia: Institute for the Study of Human Issues.

Carrier, J. M.
1980. Homosexual Behavior in Cross-Cultural Perspective. In Judd Marmor (ed.), *Homosexual Behavior*, pp. 100–122. New York: Basic Books.

Carroll, J. B. (ed.)
1956. *Language, Thought and Reality: Selected Writings of Benjamin Lee Whorf*. Cambridge, MA: M.I.T. Press.

Chagnon, Napoleon
1983. *Yanomamo: The Fierce People* (3rd ed.). New York: Holt, Rinehart & Winston.
1992. *Yanomamo* (4th ed.). Orlando, FL: Harcourt Brace Jovanovich.

Chodorow, Nancy
1974. Family Structure and Female Personality. In Michelle Rosaldo and Louise Lamphere (eds.), *Women, Culture, and Society*, pp. 43–66. Stanford, CA: Stanford University Press.

Chomsky, Noam
1972. *Language and Mind* (2nd ed.). New York: Harcourt Brace Jovanovich.

Clammer, John
1984. Approaches to Ethnographic Research. In Roy F. Ellen (ed.), *Ethnographic Research: A Guide to General Conduct*, pp. 63–85. ASA Research Methods in Social Anthropology No. 1. London: Academic Press.

Clatts, Michael
1991. Order and Change in a Southeast Asian Community: An Ethnographic Perspective on Development Initiatives. Ph.D. dissertation, Department of Anthropology, State University of New York at Stony Brook.

Clendinnen, Inga
1987. *Ambivalent Conquests: Maya and Spaniard in Yucatan, 1517–1570.* Cambridge: Cambridge University Press.
1991. *Aztecs: An Interpretation.* Cambridge: Cambridge University Press.

Clifford, James, and George E. Marcus (eds.)
1986. *Writing Culture: The Poetics and Politics of Ethnography.* Berkeley: University of California Press.

CNP (Consejo Nacional de Poblacion)
1984. *Guia Demografica y Socioeconomica.* Lima, Peru: CNP.

Cohen, A. P.
1984. Types of Informant. In Roy F. Ellen (ed.), *Ethnographic Research: A Guide to General Conduct*, pp. 224–225. ASA Research Methods in Social Anthropology No. 1. London: Academic Press.

Cohen, Ronald, and Elman R. Service (eds.)
1978. *Origins of the State: The Anthropology of Political Evolution.* Phildelphia: Institute for the Study of Human issues.

Coles, Catherine, and Beverly Mack (eds.)
1991. *Hausa Women in the Twentieth Century.* Madison: University of Wisconsin Press.

Collinge, N. E. (ed.)
1990. *An Encyclopaedia of Language.* London: Routledge.

Comaroff, Jean
1985. *Body of Power, Spirit of Resistance: The Culture and History of a South African People.* Chicago: University of Chicago Press.

Coon, Carleton S.
1962. *The Origin of Races.* New York: Knopf.

Coote, Jeremy, and Anthony Shelton (eds.)
1992. *Anthropology, Art and Aesthetics.* Oxford: Clarendon Press.

Corwin, Miles
1984, December 7. It's Only a Cardboard Box—But It's Home to Them. *Los Angeles Times*, Part 1, pp. 3, 24.

Crewe, Emma
1995. Energy, Appropriate Technology, and Health in the Household: Women and the Indoor Environment in Sri Lanka. In Bonnie Bradford and Margaret A. Gwynne (eds.), *Down to Earth: Community Perspectives on Health, Development and the Environment*, pp. 92–99. West Hartford, CT: Kumarian Press.

Crystal, David
1975. Paralinguistics. In Jonathan Benthall and Ted Polhemus (eds.), *The Body as a Medium of Expression*, pp. 162–174. New York: Dutton.

Cushing, Frank Hamilton
1896. *Outlines of Zuni Creation Myths.* Bureau of American Ethnology Annual Report, No. 16. Washington, DC: Smithsonian Institution.
1990. *Cushing at Zuni: The Correspondence and Journals of Frank Hamilton Cushing, 1879–1884*, Jesse Green, ed. Albuquerque: University of New Mexico Press.

Dahlberg, Frances (ed.)
1981. *Woman the Gatherer.* New Haven, CT: Yale University Press.

Dalton, George
1968. Economic Theory and Primitive Society. In Edward E. LeClair and Harold K. Schneider (eds.), *Economic Anthropology: Readings in Theory and Analysis*, pp. 143–167. New York: Holt, Rinehart & Winston.

Davis, D. L., and R. G. Whitten
1987. The Cross-Cultural Study of Human Sexuality. *Annual Review of Anthropology* 16:69–98.

Delmonaco, Joe
1986. *"Communicative Tension" in Rural Greece: Toward a General Theory of the Evil Eye.* Unpublished manuscript.

D'Emilio, John, and Estelle B. Freedman
1988. *Intimate Matters: A History of Sexuality in America.* New York: Harper & Row.

Demos, John Putnam
1983. *Entertaining Satan: Witchcraft and the Culture of Early New England.* New York: Oxford University Press.

Dentan, Robert Knox
1979. *The Semai: A Nonviolent People of Malaya.* New York: Holt, Rinehart & Winston.

di Leonardo, Micaela
1991. *Gender at the Crossroads of Knowledge: Feminist Anthropology in the Postmodern Era.* Berkeley: University of California Press.

Dinnerstein, Dorothy
1990 (1976). *The Mermaid and the Minotaur: Sexual Arrangements and Human Malaise.* New York: Harper Perennial.

Donnelly, Nancy D.
1994. *Changing Lives of Refugee Hmong Women.* Seattle: University of Washington Press.

Doughty, Paul L.
1987. Vicos: Success, Rejection, and Rediscovery of a Classic Program. In Elizabeth M. Eddy and William L. Partridge (eds.), *Applied Anthropology in America* (2nd ed.), pp. 433–459. New York: Columbia University Press.

Dover, K. J.
1989. *Greek Homosexuality.* Cambridge, MA: Harvard University Press.

Dubin, Lois Sherr
1987. *The History of Beads.* New York: Abrams.

DuBois, Cora
1961 (1944). *The People of Alor: A Social-Psychological Study of an East Indian Island.* New York: Harper Torchbooks.

Dundes, Alan
1968. The Number Three in American Culture. In Alan Dundes (ed.), *Every Man His Way: Readings in Cultural Anthropology,* pp. 401–424. Englewood Cliffs, NJ: Prentice-Hall.
1981. *The Evil Eye: A Casebook.* New York: Garland.
1989. *Folklore Matters.* Knoxville: University of Tennessee Press.

Dunkel, Tom
1992, January 13. A New Breed of People Gazers. *Insight,* pp. 10–13.

Durkheim, Émile
1965 (1915). *The Elementary Forms of the Religious Life.* New York: Free Press.

Earle, Timothy
1989. The Evolution of Chiefdoms. *Current Anthropology* 30(1):84–88.

Egan, Timothy
1994, August 31. Indian Boys' Exile Turns Out to Be Hoax. *New York Times,* p. A 12.

Ellen, Roy F.
1982. *Environment, Subsistence, and System: The Ecology of Small-scale Social Formations.* Cambridge: Cambridge University Press.
1984. *Ethnographic Research: A Guide to General Conduct.* ASA Research Methods in Social Anthropology No. 1. London: Academic Press.

Ellis, Pat (ed.)
1986. *Women of the Caribbean.* London: Zed Books.

Ember, Melvin
1978. Size of Color Lexicon: Interaction of Cultural and Biological Factors. *American Anthropologist* 80:364–367.

Escobar, Arturo
1991. Anthropology and the Development Encounter: The Making and Marketing of Development Anthropology. *American Ethnologist* 18:658–682.

Estioko-Griffin, Agnes, and P. Bion Griffin
1993. Woman the Hunter: The Agta. In Caroline B. Brettell and Carolyn F. Sargent (eds.), *Gender in Cross-Cultural Perspective,* pp. 206–215. Englewood Cliffs, NJ: Prentice-Hall.

Evans-Pritchard, E. E.
1940. *The Nuer.* Oxford: Clarendon Press.
1951. *Social Anthropology.* London: Cohen & West.
1962. *Essays in Social Anthropology.* London: Faber & Faber.
1965. *Theories of Primitive Religion.* Oxford: Clarendon Press.
1971. *The Azande: History and Political Institutions.* Oxford: Clarendon Press.
1974 (1956). *Nuer Religion.* Oxford: Clarendon Press.
1985 (1937). *Witchcraft, Oracles and Magic Among the Azande* (abridged, with an introduction by Eva Gillies). Oxford: Clarendon Press.

Fallers, Lloyd
1977. Equality and Inequality in Human Societies. In Sol Tax and L. Freeman (eds.), *Horizons of Anthropology* (2nd ed.), pp. 257–268. Chicago: Aldine.

Faris, James C.
1972. *Nuba Personal Art.* Toronto: University of Toronto Press.

Feeley-Harnick, Gillian
1985. Issues in Divine Kingship. In *Annual Review of Anthropology* 14:273–313.

Ferguson, R. Brian, and Leslie Farragher
1988. *The Anthropology of War: A Bibliography.* New York: Harry Frank Guggenheim Foundation.

Fernandez, James
1971. Principles of Opposition and Vitality in Fang Aesthetics. In Carol F. Jopling (ed.), *Art and Aesthetics in Primitive Societies,* pp. 356–373. New York: Dutton.

Fernea, Elizabeth W., and Robert A. Fernea
1987. Behind the Veil. In James P. Spradley and David W. McCurdy (eds.), *Conformity and Conflict: Readings in Cultural Anthropology* (6th ed.), pp. 104–112. Boston: Little, Brown.

Firth, Raymond
1950. The Peasantry of South East Asia. *International Affairs* 26(4):503–514.
1960 (1957) *Man and Culture: An Evaluation of the Work of Bronislaw Malinowski.* London: Routledge & Kegan Paul.
1963 (1936). *We the Tikopia* (abridged by the author). Boston: Beacon Press.

Fisher, Helen
1992. *Anatomy of Love: The Natural History of Monogamy, Adultery, and Divorce.* New York: Norton.

Flandrin, Jean-Louis
1991. *Sex in the Western World.* Cooper Station, NY: Harper Colophon.

Flannery, Kent V.
1973. The Origins of Agriculture. *Annual Review of Anthropology* 2:271–310.

Ford, Clellan S., and Frank A. Beach
1951. *Patterns of Sexual Behavior.* New York: Harper and Brothers, and Paul B. Hoeber, Inc., Medical Books.

Forde, Daryll
1961. The Governmental Roles of Associations among the Yako. *Africa* 31(4):309–323.

Forth, Gregory L.
1981. *Rindi: An Ethnographic Study of a Traditional Domain in Eastern Sumba.* Verhandelingen van het Koninklijk Instituut voor Taal-, Land- En Volkenkunde 93. The Hague: Martinus Nijhoff.

Fortune, R. F.
1989 (1932). *Sorcerers of Dobu.* Prospect Heights, IL: Waveland Press.

Foster, George M.
1965. Peasant Society and the Image of the Limited Good. *American Anthropologist* 67:293–315.
1972. A Second Look at the Limited Good. *Journal of American Folklore* 83:304–317.

Fox, Robin
1983 (1967). *Kinship and Marriage: An Anthropological Perspective.* New York: Cambridge University Press.

Frankenberg, Ronald
1957. *Village on the Border.* London: Cohen & West.

Fraser, Douglas
1972. The Symbols of Ashanti Kingship. In Douglas Fraser and Herbert M. Cole (eds.), *African Art and Leadership*, pp. 137–152. Madison: University of Wisconsin Press.

Frayser, Suzanne G.
1985. *Varieties of Sexual Experience: An Anthropological Perspective on Human Sexuality.* New Haven, CT: HRAF Press.

Frazer, James George
1890. *The Golden Bough.* London: Macmillan.

Freedman, Maurice
1967. *Rites and Duties, or Chinese Marriage.* London: G. Bell & Sons.
1970. Ritual Aspects of Chinese Kinship and Marriage. In Maurice Freedman (ed.), *Family and Kinship in Chinese Society*, pp. 163–187. Stanford, CA: Stanford University Press.

Freud, Sigmund
1918. *Totem and Taboo.* New York: A. A. Brill.

Friedl, Ernestine
1984. *Women and Men: An Anthropologist's View.* Prospect Heights, IL: Waveland Press.
1985 (1978). Society and Sex Roles. In David E. K. Hunter and Phillip Whitten (eds.), *Anthropology: Contemporary Perspectives* (4th ed.), pp. 228–232. Boston: Little, Brown.

Fromkin, Victoria, and Robert Rodman
1988. *An Introduction to Language* (4th ed.). Fort Worth, TX: Holt, Rinehart & Winston.

Gailey, Christine Ward
1987. *Kinship to Kingship: Gender Hierarchy and State Formation in the Tongan Islands.* Austin: University of Texas Press.

Galbraith, John Kenneth
1983. *The Anatomy of Power.* Boston: Houghton Mifflin.

Gardner, John, and John Maier
1985. *Gilgamesh* (trans. from the Sin-leqi-unnini version). New York: Vintage Books.

Geertz, Clifford
1966. Religion as a Cultural System. In Michael Banton (ed.), *Anthropological Approaches to the Study of Religion.* A.S.A. Monographs 3. London: Tavistock.
1973. *The Interpretation of Cultures.* New York: Basic Books.

George, Alexander (ed.)
1989. *Reflections on Chomsky.* Oxford: Basil Blackwell.

Gilligan, Carol
1982. *In a Different Voice: Psychological Theory and Women's Development.* Cambridge, MA: Harvard University Press.

Gilmore, David D.
1980. *The People of the Plain: Class and Community in Lower Andalusia.* New York: Columbia University Press.

Gilmore, David D., and Gretchen Gwynne (eds.)
1985. *Sex and Gender in Southern Europe: Problems and Prospects.* Anthropology Special Issues #3. Stony Brook: Department of Anthropology, State University of New York.

Givens, David B., and Susan N. Skomal
1992. The Four Fields: Myth or Reality? *Anthropology Newsletter* 33(7):1, 17.

Gluckman, Max
1969. Concepts in the Comparative Study of Tribal Law. In Laura Nader (ed.), *Law in Culture and Society*, pp. 349–373. Chicago: Aldine.

Gmelch, George
1985 (1971). Baseball Magic. In Arthur C. Lehman and James E. Myers (eds.), *Magic, Witchcraft, and Religion: An Anthropological Study of the Supernatural* (2nd ed.), pp. 231–235. Mountain View, CA: Mayfield.

Gmelch, George, and Walter P. Zenner (eds.)
1980. *Urban Life: Readings in Urban Anthropology.* New York: St. Martin's Press.

Goldman, Irving
1980. Boas on the Kwakiutl: The Ethnographic Tradition. In Stanley Diamond (ed.), *Theory and Practice: Essays Presented to Gene Weltfish.* The Hague: Mouton.

Goldstein, Melvyn C.
1987. When Brothers Share a Wife. *Natural History* 96(3):39–48.

Gombrich, E. H.
1979a, September 27. Letter. *The New York Review of Books.*
1979b. *The Sense of Order.* Ithaca, NY: Cornell University Press.

Gonzalez, Nancie L.
1972. Patron–Client Relationships at the International Level. In Arnold Strickon and Sidney M. Greenfield (eds.), *Structure and Process in Latin America*, pp. 179– 210. Albuquerque: University of New Mexico Press.
1974. The City of Gentlemen: Santiago de los Caballeros. In George M. Foster and Robert V. Kemper (eds.), *Anthropologists in Cities*, pp. 19–40. Boston: Little, Brown.
1984. The Anthropologist as Female Head of Household. *Feminist Studies* 10(1):97–114.

Goody, Jack (ed.)
1981. *Literacy in Traditional Society.* New York: Cambridge University Press.

Goody, Jack, and S. J. Tambiah
1973. *Bridewealth and Dowry.* Cambridge: Cambridge University Press.

Gough, Kathleen
1962. Nayar: Central Kerala. In David M. Schneider and Kathleen Gough (eds.), *Matrilineal Kinship*, pp. 298–384. Berkeley: University of California Press.

Graburn, Nelson H. H., and B. Stephen Strong
1973. *Circumpolar Peoples: An Anthropological Perspective.* Pacific Palisades, CA: Goodyear Publishing.

Gregory, James R.
1975. Image of Limited Good, or Expectation of Reciprocity? *Current Anthropology* 16:73–92.

Grobsmith, Elizabeth S.
1992. Applying Anthropology to American Indian Correctional Concerns. *Practicing Anthropology* 14(3):5–8.

Gross, Jane
1992, March 1. Does She Speak for Today's Women? *New York Times Magazine*, pp. 16–19, 38, 54.

Gulliver, P. H.
1969. Dispute Settlement Without Courts: The Ndendeuli of Southern Tanzania. In Laura Nader (ed.), *Law in Culture and Society*, pp. 24–68. Chicago: Aldine.

Haas, Jack
1984. A Study of High Steel Ironworkers' Reactions to Fear and Danger. In Herbert Applebaum (ed.), *Work in Market and Industrial Societies*, pp. 103–119. Albany: State University of New York Press.

Hall, Edward T., and Mildred Reed Hall
1987 (1971). The Sounds of Silence. In James P. Spradley and David W. McCurdy (eds.), *Conformity and Conflict: Readings in Cultural Anthropology* (6th ed.), pp. 80–92. Boston: Little, Brown.

Hallpike, C. R.
1973. Functionalist Interpretations of Primitive Warfare. *Man* 8:451–470.

Hamilton, David L., et al.
1991. Stereotypes and Language Use. In Gun R. Semin and Klaus Fiedler (eds.), *Language, Interaction and Social Cognition*, pp. 102–128. London: Sage.

Hardin, Kris L.
1988. Aesthetics and the Cultural Whole: A Study of Kono Dance Occasions. *Empirical Studies of the Arts* 6(1):35–57.

Harris, Marvin
1980. *Cultural Materialism: The Struggle for a Science of Culture*. New York: Random House/Vintage Books.
1993. *Culture, People, Nature* (6th ed.). New York: Harper-Collins.

Hayden, Brian
1993. *Archaeology: The Science of Once and Future Things*. New York: Freeman.

Headland, Thomas N. (ed.)
1992. *The Tasaday Controversy: Assessing the Evidence*. AAA Scholarly Series Special Publication No. 28. Washington, DC: American Anthropological Association.

Headland, Thomas N., Kenneth L. Pike, and Marvin Harris (eds.)
1990. *Emics and Etics: The Insider/Outsider Debate*. Newbury Park, CA: Sage Publications.

Heider, Karl
1979. *Grand Valley Dani: Peaceful Warriors*. New York: Holt, Rinehart & Winston.

Hekimian, Kim
1995. The Post-Soviet Legacy of Industrial Pollution in Armenia. In Bonnie Bradford and Margaret A. Gwynne (eds.), *Down to Earth: Community Perspectives on Health, Development and the Environment*, pp. 49–59. West Hartford, CT: Kumarian Press.

Heller, Monica (ed.)
1988. *Codeswitching: Anthropological and Sociolinguistic Perspectives*. New York: Mouton de Gruyter.

Henretta, James, W. Elliot Brownlee, David Brody, and Susan Ware
1987. *America's History*. Chicago: Dorsey Press.

Henry, Jules
1964. *Jungle People: A Kaingáng Tribe of the Highlands of Brazil*. New York: Random House.

Herdt, Gilbert, and Robert J. Stoller
1986. *Intimate Communications: Erotics and the Study of Culture*. New York: Columbia University Press.

Herrnstein, Richard J., and Charles Murray
1994. *The Bell Curve: Intelligence and Class Structure in American Life*. New York: Free Press.

Herzfeld, Michael
1985. Gender Pragmatics: Agency, Speech and Bride-Theft in a Cretan Mountain Village. *Anthropology* IX(1–2):25–44.

Hewes, Gordon W.
1973. Primate Communication and the Gestural Origin of Language. *Current Anthropology* 14(1–2): 5–24.

Hicks, David
1984. Getting into the Field and Establishing Routines. In Roy F. Ellen (ed.), *Ethnographic Research: A Guide to General Conduct*, pp. 192–197. ASA Research Methods in Social Anthropology No. 1. London: Academic Press.
1988 (1976). *Tetum Ghosts and Kin*. Prospect Heights, IL: Waveland Press.
1990. *Kinship and Religion in Eastern Indonesia*. Gothenburg: Acta Universitatis Gothenburgensis.
1991. The Timor Civil War. Manuscript.
1995. *Children of the Temple: Religion, Art, and Ecology on Bali*. The World and I 10(5):246–257.

Hill, Robert T.
1896. Descriptive Topographic Terms of Spanish America. *National Geographic* 7: 292–297.

Hobsbawm, Eric, and Terence Ranger (eds.)
1992. *The Invention of Tradition*. Cambridge: Cambridge University Press.

Hoebel, E. Adamson
1964. *The Law of Primitive Man*. Cambridge, MA: Harvard University Press.
1978. *The Cheyennes: Indians of the Great Plains*. New York: Holt, Rinehart & Winston.

Hoffman, Jan
1992, February 23. When Men Hit Women. *New York Times Magazine*, pp. 22–27, 65–66, 72.

Holm, John
1989. *Pidgins and Creoles* (2 vols.). New York: Cambridge University Press.

Holy, Ladislav
1984. Theory, Methodology and the Research Process. In Roy F. Ellen (ed.), *Ethnographic Research: A Guide to General Conduct*, pp. 13–34. ASA Research Methods in Social Anthropology No. 1. London: Academic Press.

Horowitz, I. L. (ed.)
1967. *The Rise and Fall of Project Camelot: Studies in the Relationship between Social Science and Practical Politics*. Cambridge, MA: M.I.T. Press.

Hudson, R. A.
1980. *Sociolinguistics*. Cambridge: Cambridge University Press.

Hull, Valerie
1991. Health and Development: Seeking the Best of Both Worlds. *Cultural Survival Quarterly* 15(2):24–27.

Huntington, Richard
1988. *Gender and Social Structure in Madagascar.* Bloomington and Indianapolis: Indiana University Press.

Hutchinson, Ellen
1977. Order and Chaos in the Cosmology of the Baffin Island Eskimo. *Anthropology* I(2):120–138.

Itard, Jean-Marc-Gaspard
1962 (1932). *The Wild Boy of Aveyron.* New York: Appleton-Century-Crofts.

Iten, Oswald
1986, June. The Tasaday: A Stone Age Swindle. *Swiss Review of World Affairs,* pp. 14–19.

Jacobs, Norman
1966. *The Sociology of Development: Iran as an Asian Case Study.* New York: Praeger.

Jankowiak, William R., and Edward F. Fisher
1992. A Cross-Cultural Perspective on Romantic Love. *Ethnology* 31:149–155.

Johnston, Barbara Rose, and Margaret A Byrne
1994. Defining the Crisis, Shaping the Response: An Overview of Environmental Issues in China. In Barbara Rose Johnston (ed.), *Who Pays the Price? The Sociocultural Context of Environmental Crisis,* pp. 69–85. Society for Applied Anthropology, Committee on Human Rights and the Environment. Washington, DC: Island Press.

Jonaitis, Aldona
1988. *From the Land of the Totem Poles.* New York: American Museum of Natural History; Seattle: University of Washingtom Press.

Jordan, Terry G., Mona Domosh, and Lester Rowntree
1994. *The Human Mosaic: A Thematic Introduction to Cultural Geography* (6th ed.). New York: HarperCollins.

Kaijuka, E. M., E. Z. A. Kaiji, A. R. Cross, and E. Loaiza
1989. Uganda: Demographic and Health Survey 1988/89. Entebbe, Uganda, and Columbia, MD: Demographic and Health Surveys, Institute for Resource Development/Macro Systems, Inc.

Kaiser, Susan B.
1990. *The Social Psychology of Clothing* (2nd ed.). New York: Macmillan.

Kak, Lily P., and Marjorie B. Signer
1993. *The Introduction of Community Based Family Planning Services in Rural Mali: The Katibougou Family Health Project. Working Paper No. 2.* Washington, DC: Centre for Development and Population Activities.
1995. Improving Access to Family Planning Services in Rural Mali. In Bonnie Bradford and Margaret A. Gwynne (eds.), *Down to Earth: Community Perspectives on Health, Development, and the Environment,* pp. 77–84. West Hartford, CT: Kumarian Press.

Kardiner, Abram
1945. *The Psychological Frontiers of Society.* New York: Columbia University Press.

Kehoe, Alice Beck
1989. *The Ghost Dance: Ethnohistory and Revitalization.* New York: Holt, Rinehart & Winston.

Kelly, Raymond
1976. Witchcraft and Sexual Relations. In P. Brown and G. Buchbinder (eds.), *Man and Woman in the New Guinea Highlands,* pp. 36–53. Special Publications No. 8. Washington, DC: American Anthropological Association.

Kennedy, John
1966. Peasant Society and the Image of the Limited Good: A Critique. *American Anthropologist* 68:1212–1225.

King, Victor T.
1985. *The Maloh of West Kalimantan: An Ethnographic Study of Social Inequality and Social Change among an Indonesian People.* Verhandelingen van het Koninklijk Instituut voor Taal-, Land-en Volkenkunde 108. Dordrecht-Holland: Cinnaminson-U.S.A. Floris Publications.

Klaw, Spencer
1993. *Without Sin: The Life and Death of the Oneida Community.* New York: Allen Lane/The Penguin Press.

Konner, Melvin
1982. *The Tangled Wing: Biological Constraints on the Human Spirit.* New York: Harper Colophon.

Krauss, Werner
1994. Raden Saleh: One Javanese—Two Personalities: An Exemplary Case of the Disastrous Effects of Dutch Language Policy in 19th Century Java. In Wolfgang Marschall (ed.), *Texts from the Islands: Oral and Written Traditions of Indonesia and the Malay World,* pp. 381–397. Berne, Switzerland: University of Berne.

Krueger, Richard A.
1988. *Focus Groups: A Practical Guide for Applied Research.* Newbury Park, CA: Sage.

Kulik, Don
1992. *Language Shift and Cultural Reproduction: Socialization, Self, and Syncretism in a Papua New Guinean Village.* New York: Cambridge University Press.

Kuper, Adam
1985. *Anthropology and Anthropologists: The Modern British School* (rev. ed.). Boston: Routledge & Kegan Paul.

Labov, William
1984 (1972). *Language in the Inner City: Studies in the Black English Vernacular.* Philadelphia: University of Pennsylvania Press.
1988. The Judicial Testing of Linguistic Theory. In Deborah Tannen (ed.), *Linguistics in Context: Connecting Observation and Understanding: Advances in Discourse Processes,* p. 24. Norwood, NJ: Ablex.

Ladurie, Emmanuel LeRoy
1979. *Montaillou: The Promised Land of Error* (Barbara Bray, trans.). New York: Vintage Books.

Lakoff, Robin
1975. *Language and Woman's Place.* New York: Harper & Row.

Landsberg, Marge E.
1988. *The Genesis of Language: A Different Judgement of Evidence.* New York: Mouton de Gruyter.

Lansing, J. Stephen
1983. *The Three Worlds of Bali.* New York: Praeger.

Lavi, Zvi
1990. *Kibbutz Members Study Kibbutz Children*. New York: Greenwood Press.

Leach, Edmund
1963. *Rethinking Anthropology*. London: Athlone Press.

Lederman, Rena
1990. Big Men, Large and Small? Towards a Comparative Perspective. *Ethnology* 19(1):3–15.

Lee, Dorothy D.
1959. *Freedom and Culture*. Englewood Cliffs, NJ: Prentice-Hall.
1985 (1950). How Languages Code Reality. In David E. K. Hunter and Phillip Whitten (eds.), *Anthropology: Contemporary Perspectives* (4th ed.), pp. 108–115. Boston: Little, Brown.

Lee, Felicia R.
1994. Lingering Conflict in the Schools: Black Dialect vs. Standard Speech. *New York Times*, January 5: 1, D22.

Lee, Richard
1969 (1966). !Kung Bushman Subsistence: An Input-Output Analysis. In A. P. Vayda (ed.), *Environment and Cultural Behavior*. New York: Natural History Press.
1984. *The Dobe !Kung*. New York: Holt, Rinehart & Winston.

Lehman, Arthur C., and James E. Myers (eds.)
1989. *Magic, Witchcraft, and Religion: An Anthropological Study of the Supernatural* (2nd ed.). Mountain View, CA: Mayfield.

Lepowsky, Maria
1993. *Fruit of the Motherland: Gender in an Egalitarian Society*. New York: Columbia University Press.

Lerner, Gerda
1986. *The Creation of Patriarchy*. New York: Oxford University Press.

Lévi-Strauss, Claude
1969 (French ed., 1949). *The Elementary Structures of Kinship*. Boston: Beacon Press.
1983 (1967). *Structural Anthropology*. Chicago: University of Chicago Press.

Lewis, I. M.
1986. *Religion in Context: Cults and Charisma*. Cambridge: Cambridge University Press.
1989. *Ecstatic Religion: An Anthropological Study of Spirit Possession and Shamanism* (2nd ed.). London: Routledge.

Lewis, Oscar
1961. *The Children of Sanchez: Autobiography of a Mexican Family*. New York: Random House.
1966a. The Culture of Poverty. *Scientific American* 215:19–25.
1966b. *La Vida: A Puerto Rican Family in the Culture of Poverty—San Juan and New York*. New York: Random House.

Lieberman, Philip
1984. *The Biology and Evolution of Language*. Cambridge, MA: Harvard University Press.

Liebow, Elliot
1967. *Tally's Corner*. Boston: Little, Brown.

Lightfoot-Klein, Hanny
1989. *Prisoners of Ritual: An Odyssey into Female Genital Circumcision in Africa*. New York and London: Haworth Press.

Lindholm, Cherry, and Charles Lindholm
1985 (1980). Life Behind the Veil. In David E. K. Hunter and Phillip Whitten (eds.), *Anthropology: Contemporary Perspectives* (4th ed.), pp. 233–236. Boston: Little, Brown.

Lindsey, Robert
1988, February 1. Circumcision under Criticism as Unnecessary to Newborn. *New York Times*, pp. A1, 20.

Little, Kenneth
1982. The Role of Voluntary Associations in West African Urbanization. In Johnetta B. Cole (ed.), *Anthropology for the Eighties: Introductory Readings*, pp. 174–194. New York: Free Press.

Locke, John
1979 (1690). *An Essay Concerning Human Understanding* (Peter H. Nidditch, ed.). Oxford: Clarendon Press.

Locke, John L.
1993. *The Child's Path to Spoken Language*. Cambridge, MA: Harvard University Press.

Lowie, Robert H.
1970 (1948). *Primitive Religion*. New York: Liveright.

Lurie, Alison
1981. *The Language of Clothes*. New York: Random House.

MacClancy, Jeremy
1990. Primitive Thinking about Sophisticated Art. *Anthropology Today* 6(4):1–2.

Macfarlane, Alan
1990. *Witchcraft in Tudor and Stuart England: A Regional and Comparative Study*. Prospect Heights, IL: Waveland Press.

Maher, Vanessa
1992. *The Anthropology of Breastfeeding*. New York: St. Martin's Press.

Malcolm, Andrew H.
1979, October 23. In Hands of Stone Carvers, Eskimo Tradition Clings to Life. *New York Times*, p. A13.
1981, February 1. A Dogrib Bible, "Enitl'e-cho," Takes Shape in Canada. *New York Times*, p. 14.

Malinowski, Bronislaw
1927. *Sex and Repression in Savage Society*. London: Routledge & Kegan Paul.
1954 (1948). *Magic, Science, and Religion*. New York: Doubleday.
1962 (1929). *The Sexual Life of Savages in Northwestern Melanesia*. New York: Harcourt, Brace and World.
1965 (1935). *Coral Gardens and Their Magic. Vol. I: Soil-Tilling and Agricultural Rites in the Trobriand Islands*. Bloomington: Indiana University Press.
1978 (1926). *Crime and Custom in Savage Society*. London: Routledge & Kegan Paul.
1984 (1922). *Argonauts of the Western Pacific*. Prospect Heights, IL: Waveland Press.

Mangin, William
1979. Thoughts on Twenty-four Years of Work in Peru: The Vicos Project and Me. In George M. Foster, Thayer Scudder, Elizabeth Colson, and Robert V. Kemper (eds.), *Long-Term Field Research in Social Anthropology*, pp. 65–84. New York: Academic Press.

Marcus, George E., and Dick Cushman
1982. Ethnographies as Texts. *Annual Review of Anthropology* 11:25–69.

Margolis, Maxine
1984. *Mothers and Such: American Views of Women and How They Changed*. Berkeley: University of California Press.

Marshack, Alexander
1972. *The Roots of Civilization: The Cognitive Beginnings of Man's First Art, Symbol and Notation*. New York: McGraw-Hill.

Martin, Emily
1987. *The Woman in the Body: A Cultural Analysis of Reproduction*. Boston: Beacon Press.

Martin, M. Kay, and Barbara Voorhies
1975. *Female of the Species*. New York: Columbia University Press.

Masson, Jeffrey Moussaieff (ed. and trans.)
1986. *A Dark Science: Women, Sexuality and Psychiatry in the Nineteenth Century*. New York: Farrar, Straus & Giroux.

Masters, William H., Virginia E. Johnson, and Robert C. Kolodny
1985. *Human Sexuality* (2nd ed.). Boston: Little, Brown.

Mattoon, Mary Ann
1981. *Jungian Psychology in Perspective*. New York: Free Press.

Mauss, Marcel
1979 (1950). *Seasonal Variations of the Eskimo: A Study in Social Morphology* (in collaboration with Henri Beuchat; James J. Fox, trans.). London: Routledge & Kegan Paul.
1990 (1920). *The Gift: Forms and Functions of Exchange in Archaic Societies* (W. D. Halls, trans.). London: Routledge.

Maybury-Lewis, David
1974 (1967). *Akwẽ-Shavante Society*. Oxford: Clarendon Press.
1988. A Special Sort of Pleading: Anthropology at the Service of Ethnic Groups. In John H. Bodley (ed.), *Tribal Peoples and Development Issues: A Global Overview*, pp. 375–390. Mountain View, CA: Mayfield.

McConochie, Roger P.
1994. Personal communication.

McKee, Lauris
1992. Men's Rights/Women's Wrongs: Domestic Violence in Ecuador. In Dorothy Ayers Counts et al. (eds.), *Sanctions and Sanctuary: Cultural Perspectives on the Beating of Wives*, pp. 139–156. Boulder, CO: Westview Press.

McKee, Victoria
1990, March 5. With My Body I Thee Threaten. *London Times*, p. 17.

Messina, Maria
1988. Henna Party. *Natural History* 97(9):40–46.

Michael, Robert T., John H. Gagnon, Edward O. Laumann, and Gina Kolata
1994. *Sex in America: A Definitive Survey*. Boston: Little, Brown.

Midelfort, H. C. Erik
1972. *Witch Hunting in Southwestern Germany, 1562–1684: The Social and Intellectual Foundations*. Stanford, CA: Stanford University Press.

Miller, G. Tyler, Jr.
1994. *Living in the Environment: Principles, Connections, and Solutions* (8th ed.). Belmont, CA: Wadsworth.

Milner, George R., and Clark Spencer Larsen
1991. Teeth as Artifacts of Human Behavior: Intentional Mutilation and Accidental Modification. In Marc A. Kelley and Clark Spencer Larsen (eds.), *Advances in Dental Anthropology*, pp. 357–378. New York: Wiley-Liss.

Mitchell, J. Clyde
1984. Social Network Data. In Roy F. Ellen (ed.), *Ethnographic Research: A Guide to General Conduct*, pp. 267–272. ASA Research Methods in Social Anthropology No. 1. London: Academic Press.

Mitter, Sara S.
1991. *Dharma's Daughters*. New Brunswick, NJ: Rutgers University Press.

Moffett, George D.
1994. *Critical Masses: The Global Population Challenge*. New York: Viking.

Moffett, Matt
1994, December 29. Kayapo Indians Lose Their "Green Image": Former Heroes of Amazon Succumb to Lure of Profits. *The Wall Street Journal*, p. A6.

Money, John, and A. A. Ehrhardt
1977. *Man and Woman, Boy and Girl: The Differentiation and Dimorphism of Gender Identity from Conception to Maturity*. Baltimore: Johns Hopkins University Press.

Morphy, Howard
1991. *Ancestral Connections: Art and an Aboriginal System of Knowledge*. Chicago: University of Chicago Press.

Mother Earth News
1984. Barter Mania 89:108.

Moynihan, Patrick
1965. *The Negro Family: The Case for National Action*. Washington, DC: U.S. Government Printing Office.

Ms.
1982, September. The Barter Brokers: From Backyard to Boardroom, pp. 70–72.

Mukhopadhyay, Carol C., and Patricia J. Higgins
1988. Anthropological Studies of Women's Status Revisited: 1977–1988. *Annual Reviews of Anthropology* 17:461–495.

Mukolwe, Jennifer, Therese McGinn, and Cynthia Carlson
1995. Linking Population and Environmental Conservation in Southwest Uganda. In Bonnie Bradford and Margaret A. Gwynne (eds.), *Down to Earth: Community Perspectives on Health, Development, and the Environment*. West Hartford, CT: Kumarian Press.

Murdock, George P.
1957. World Ethnographic Sample. *American Anthropologist* 59:664–687.

Murdock, George P., and Caterina Provost
1973. Factors in the Division of Labor by Sex: A Cross-Cultural Analysis. *Ethnology* 12:203–225.

Murphy, William P.
1978. Oral Literature. *Annual Review of Anthropology* 7:113–136.

Mwangola, Margaret
1995. Bringing Clean Water to Kenyan Households. In Bonnie Bradford and Margaret A. Gwynne (eds.), *Down to Earth: Community Perspectives on Health, Development, and the Environment*, pp. 85–91. West Hartford, CT: Kumarian Press.

Mydans, Seth
1986, May 13. The Tasaday Revisited: A Hoax or Social Change at Work? *New York Times*, p. C3.
1987, December 27. From Forest to Manila, Stranger in a Strange Land. *New York Times*, p. A16.

Myers-Scotton, Carol
1993. *Social Motivations for Codeswitching: Evidence from Africa*. New York: Oxford University Press.

Nanda, Serena
1990. *Neither Man Nor Woman: The Hijras of India*. Belmont, CA: Wadsworth.

Nash, Nathaniel C.
1992, March 30. Bolivia Is Helping Its Battered Wives to Stand Up. *New York Times*.

Nation's Business
1985. Barter Boom. 73:18–25.

Needham, Rodney
1970. "Introduction." In Arthur Maurice Hocart, *Kings and Councillors: An Essay in the Comparative Anatomy of Human Society*. Chicago: University of Chicago Press.
1974. *Remarks and Inventions: Skeptical Essays About Kinship*. London: Tavistock.
1975 (1963). Introduction to Durkheim, Émile, and Mauss, Marcel. In Rodney Needham (trans. and ed.), *Primitive Classification* (5th impression). Chicago: University of Chicago Press.
1978. *Primordial Characters*. Charlottesville: University Press of Virginia.
1979. *Symbolic Classification*. Santa Monica, CA: Goodyear Publishing Company.
1985. *Exemplars*. Berkeley: University of California Press.

Newsday
1979, August 2. Brother and Sister Guilty of Marrying Incestuously, p. 13.

New York Times
1986, March 11. Secrets of Bearing a Burden.
1986, March 27. Zimbabwe Still Divided on Rights for Women, p. A17.
1987a, August 18. Town in Montana Endures as an Outpost of Polygamy, p. A18.
1987b, November 22. From Subway Graffiti to the Canvas: Bronx Program Transforms Vandals, p. 68.

Obeyesekere, Gananath
1981. *Medusa's Hair: An Essay on Personal Symbols and Religious Experience*. Chicago: University of Chicago Press.

Offir, Carole W.
1982. *Human Sexuality*. New York: Harcourt Brace Jovanovich.

Ong, Walter
1982. *Orality and Literacy: The Technologizing of the Word*. London: Methuen.

Orion, Loretta Lee
1995. *Never Again the Burning Times: Paganism Revived*. Prospect Heights, IL: Waveland Press.

Parker, Sue Taylor, and Kathleen Rita Gibson
1979. A Developmental Model for the Evolution of Language and Intelligence in Early Hominids. *Behavioral and Brain Sciences* 2(3):83–85.

Pasztory, Esther
1989. Identity and Difference: The Uses and Meanings of Ethnic Styles. In Susan J. Barnes and Walter S. Melion (eds.), *Cultural Differentiation and Cultural Identity in the Visual Arts*, pp. 15–37. Hanover, NH: University Press of New England.

Paul, Robert A.
1989. Psychoanalytic Anthropology. *Annual Review of Anthropology*, 18:177–202. Palo Alto, CA: Annual Reviews.

Pfeiffer, John E.
1982. *The Creative Explosion: An Inquiry into the Origins of Art and Religion*. New York: Harper & Row.

Piddock, Stuart
1965. The Potlatch System of the Southern Kwakiutl: A New Perspective. *Southwestern Journal of Anthropology* 21:244–264.

Piker, Steven
1966. The Image of the Limited Good: Comments on an Exercise in Description and Interpretation. *American Anthropologist* 68:1202–1211.

Pillsbury, Barbara L. K.
1991. International Health: Overview and Opportunities. In Carole E. Hill (ed.), *Training Manual in Applied Medical Anthropology*, pp. 54–87. Washington, DC: American Anthropological Association.

Plattner, Stuart (ed.)
1989. *Economic Anthropology*. Stanford, CA: Stanford University Press.

Podolefsky, Aaron
1984. Contemporary Warfare in the New Guinea Highlands. *Ethnology* 23(2):73–87.

Pohorecky, Zenon
1992. Personal communication, University of Saskatchewan, Saskatoon.

Polanyi, Karl
1971. The Economy as Instituted Process. In George Dalton (ed.), *Primitive, Archaic, and Modern Economies: Essays of Karl Polanyi*, pp. 139–174. Boston: Beacon Press.

Polanyi, Karl, Conrad M. Arensberg, and Harry W. Pearson
1957. *Trade and Market in the Early Empires*. Glencoe, IL: Free Press.

Polomé, Edgar C.
1990. Language and Behaviour: Anthropological Linguistics. In N. E. Collinge (ed.), *An Encyclopaedia of Language*, pp. 458–484. London: Routledge.

Pospisil, Leopold
1974. *Anthropology of Law: A Comparative Theory*. New Haven, CT: HRAF Press.

Pottier, Johan (ed.)
1993. *Practising Development: Social Science Perspectives*. London: Routledge.

Price, Sally
1990. *Primitive Art in Civilized Places*. Chicago: University of Chicago Press.

Propp, Vladimir
1988 (1958). *Morphology of the Folktale* (Laurence Scott, trans.; 2nd ed., Louis A. Wagner, ed.). Austin: University of Texas Press.

Pryor, Frederic L.
1986. The Adoption of Agriculture: Some Theoretical and Empirical Evidence. *American Anthropologist* 88(4):879–897.

Public Health Reports
1991. Forum on Youth Violence in Minority Communities: Setting the Agenda for Prevention: A Summary. *Public Health Reports* 106(3):225–277.

Quinn, Naomi
1977. Anthropological Studies on Women's Status. *Annual Review of Anthropology,* 6:181–225. Palo Alto, CA: Annual Reviews.

Radcliffe-Brown, A. R.
1965 (1952). *Structure and Function in Primitive Society: Essays and Addresses.* New York: Free Press.

Redfield, Robert
1956. *Peasant Society and Culture.* Chicago: University of Chicago Press.

Renfrew, Colin
1987. *Archaeology and Language: The Puzzle of Indo-European Origins.* Cambridge: Cambridge University Press.
1989. Origins of Indo-European Languages. *Scientific American* 261:106–114.

Reyes, Elma
1986. Women in Calypso. In Pat Ellis (ed.), *Women in the Caribbean,* pp. 119–121. London: Zed Books.

Rice, Otis K.
1978. *The Hatfields and the McCoys.* Lexington: University Press of Kentucky.

Rice, Patricia C., and Ann L. Paterson
1985. Cave Art and Bones: Exploring the Relationships. *American Anthropologist* 87(1):94–100.

Robarchek, Clayton A.
1989. Primitive Warfare and the Ratomorphic Image of Mankind. *American Anthropologist* 91(4): 903–920.

Rosaldo, Michelle, and Louise Lamphere (eds.)
1974. *Women, Culture, and Society.* Stanford, CA: Stanford University Press.

Roscoe, Paul B.
1994. Amity and Aggression: A Symbolic Theory of Incest. *Man* 29 (1):49–76.

Rosman, Abraham, and Paula G. Rubel
1986 (1971). *Feasting with Mine Enemy: Rank and Exchange Among Northwest Coastal Societies.* Prospect Heights: IL: Waveland Press.

Ruhlen, Merritt
1987. Voices from the Past. *Natural History* 96(3) : 6–10.

Sahlins, Marshall
1968 (1965). On the Sociology of Primitive Exchange. In Michael Banton (ed.), *The Relevance of Models for Social Anthropology* (2nd impression), pp. 139–236. London: Tavistock.
1974. *Stone Age Economics.* London: Tavistock.

Saibull, Ole Solomon
1981. *Herd and Spear: The Maasai of East Africa.* London: Collins and Harvill Press.

Saitoti, Ole Tepilit
1988 (1986). *The Worlds of a Maasai Warrior.* Berkeley: University of California Press.

Sangren, P. Steven
1992 (1988). Rhetoric and the Authority of Ethnography. In Sydel Silverman (ed.), *Inquiry and Debate in the Human Sciences,* pp. 277–306. Chicago and London: University of Chicago Press.

Saussure, Ferdinand de
1983 (1916). *Course in General Linguistics.* London: Duckworth.

Schmandt-Besserat, Denise
1992. *Before Writing.* Austin: University of Texas Press.

Schwartz, Theodore, Geoffrey M. White, and Catherine A. Lutz (eds.)
1992. *New Directions in Psychological Anthropology.* New York: Cambridge University Press.

Schwartzman, Stephen
1995, February 14. "Most Kayapos Protect Their Patch of Amazon." Letter to the Editor, *The Wall Street Journal,* p. A23.

Senior, Olive
1991. *Working Miracles: Women's Lives in the English-speaking Caribbean.* Bloomington: Indiana University Press.

Serrie, Hendrick (ed.)
1986. *Anthropology and International Business.* Studies in Third World Societies No. 28. Williamsburg, VA: Department of Anthropology, College of William and Mary.

Service, Elman R.
1971. *Primitive Social Organization: An Evolutionary Perspective* (2nd ed.). New York: Random House.

Shaara, Lila, and Andrew Strathern
1992. A Preliminary Analysis of the Relationship Between Altered States of Consciousness, Healing and Social Structure. *American Anthropologist* 94(1):145–160.

Shanklin, Eugenia
1994. *Anthropology and Race.* Belmont, CA: Wadsworth.

Shepher, Joseph
1983. *Incest: A Biosocial View.* New York: Academic Press.

Shoumatoff, Alex
1985. *The Mountain of Names: A History of the Human Family.* New York: Simon & Schuster.

Silverblatt, Irene
1988. Women in States. In *Annual Review of Anthropology,* 17:427–460. Palo Alto, CA: Annual Reviews.

Skar, Harald O.
1985. *Anthropological Contributions to Planned Change and Development.* Gothenburg Studies in Social Anthropology, No. 8. Atlantic Highlands, NJ: Humanities Press.

Smith, Cyril Stanley
1975, August 24. Aesthetic Curiosity—The Root of Invention. *New York Times.*

Sowell, Thomas
1994. *Race and Culture: A World View.* New York: Basic Books.

Spradley, James P.
1970. *You Owe Yourself a Drunk: An Ethnography of Urban Nomads.* Boston: Little, Brown.
1980. *Participant Observation.* Orlando, FL: Harcourt Brace Jovanovich.

Stein, Steve
1985. Health and Poverty within the Sociopolitical Context of Peru, 1985. Unpublished manuscript, Department of History, University of South Florida, Coral Gables.

Stevenson, T. T. B.
1989. *Anorexia Nervosa as a Culture Bound Syndrome.* Ph.D. dissertation, Department of Anthropology, SUNY/Stony Brook, NY.

Steward, Julian
1955. *Theory of Culture Change.* Urbana: University of Illinois Press.

Stewart, David W., and Prem N. Shamdasani
1990. *Focus Groups: Theory and Practice. Applied Social Research Methods Series,* Vol. 20. Newbury Park, CA: Sage.

Stewart, Hilary
1993. *Looking at Totem Poles.* Seattle: University of Washington Press.

Stewart, Jon
1980. Every Man a Saint: Archives Beneath the Rocky Mountains. *Saturday Review* 7:8–9.

Sumarsam
1995. *Gamelan: Cultural Interactions and Musical Development in Central Java.* Chicago: University of Chicago Press.

Survival International
1990, October. *Survival for Tribal Peoples* (newsletter). Washington, DC: Survival International USA.

Sweet, Ellen
1980, December. A Tune-up for a Haircut, and Other Bartering Miracles. *Ms.,* p. 86.

Swindells, Neil
1987, January 17. Uncovered–The Roman Bikini! *Daily Mail* (London), p. 23.

Todd, Alexandra Dundas, and Sue Fisher (eds.)
1988. *Gender and Discourse: The Power of Talk.* Norwood, NJ: Ablex.

Tully, Mark
1991. *No Full Stops in India.* London:Viking.

Turnbull, Colin
1965. The Mbuti Pygmies of the Congo. In J. C. Gibbs, Jr. (ed.), *Peoples of Africa,* pp. 281–317. New York: Holt, Rinehart & Winston.

Turner, Bryan S.
1984. *The Body and Society: Explorations in Social Theory.* Oxford: Basil Blackwell.

Turner, Terence S.
1987 (1969). Cosmetics: The Language of Bodily Adornment. In James P. Spradley and David W. McCurdy (eds.), *Conflict and Conformity: Readings in Cultural Anthropology* (6th ed.), pp. 93–103. Boston: Little, Brown.

Turner, Victor
1967. *The Forest of Symbols: Aspects of Ndembu Ritual.* Ithaca, NY: Cornell University Press.

Tyler, Stephen A.
1973. *India: An Anthropological Perspective.* Pacific Palisades, CA: Goodyear Publishing.

Tylor, Edward Burnett
1873. *Primitive Culture* (2 vols.). London: John Murray.
1889. On a Method of Investigating the Development of Institutions. *Journal of the Royal Anthropological Institute* 18:245–272.

U.S. News & World Report
1976, April 19. Unsolved Mystery: Who'll Get the Riches Howard Hughes Left Behind? *U.S. News & World Report* 80:21–23.

Valentine, Charles
1968. *Culture and Poverty: Critique and Counter-Proposals.* Chicago: University of Chicago Press.

Vander, J.
1989. From the Musical Experience of Five Shoshone Women. In R. Keeling (ed.), *Women in North American Indian Music: Six Essays.* Bloomington, IN: Society for Ethnomusicology.

van de Walle, Francine, and Mariam Maiga
1991. Family Planning in Bamako, Mali. *International Family Planning Perspectives* 17(3):84–90, 99.

van Gennep, Arnold
1961. *The Rites of Passage.* Chicago: University of Chicago Press.

van Willigen, John
1986. *Applied Anthropology: An Introduction.* South Hadley, MA: Bergin & Garvey.

Vargas, Marjorie Fink
1986. *Louder Than Words: An Introduction to Nonverbal Communication.* Ames: Iowa State Press.

Varisco, Daniel Martin
1989. Beyond Rhino Horn: Wildlife Conservation for North Yemen. *Oryx* 23(4):215–219.
1992. Personal communication.

Vaughan, J. Daniel
1984. Tsimshian Potlatch and Society: Examining a Structural Analysis. In Jay Miller and Carol M. Eastman (eds.), *The Tsimshian and Their Neighbors of the North Pacific Coast,* pp. 58–68. Seattle: University of Washington Press.

Vayda, Andrew P.
1961. Expansion and Warfare among Swidden Agriculturalists. *American Anthropologist* 63:346–358.

Vayda, Andrew P., and Bonnie J. McCay
1975. New Directions in Ecology and Ecological Anthropology. *Annual Review of Anthropology* 4: 293–306. Palo Alto, CA: Annual Reviews.

Wallace, Anthony F. C.
1985. Nativism and Revivalism. In Arthur C. Lehman and James E. Myers (eds.), *Magic, Witchcraft, and Religion: An Anthropological Study of the Supernatural* (2nd ed.), pp. 340–345. Mountain View, CA: Mayfield.

Wallman, Sandra, and Yvonne Dhooge
1984. Approaches to Ethnographic Research. In Roy F. Ellen (ed.), *Ethnographic Research: A Guide to General Conduct*, pp. 257–267. ASA Research Methods in Social Anthropology No. 1. London: Academic Press.

Wang, Zhusheng
1991. Road of Change: A Jingpo Village on China's Border. Ph.D. dissertation, Department of Anthropology, State University of New York at Stony Brook.

Ward, Colleen A. (ed.)
1989. *Altered States of Consciousness and Mental Health: A Cross-Cultural Perspective*. Newbury Park, CA: Sage.

WASH (Water and Sanitation for Health)
1992, May. Peri-Urban News 1(1).

Weaver, Thomas (ed.)
1973. *To See Ourselves: Anthropology and Modern Social Issues*. Glenview, IL: Scott, Foresman.

Weber, Anne
1986, December. Anthropologists Look at the Office. *Business Monthly*, pp. 40–42.

Weber, Max
1947. *The Theory of Social and Economic Organization*. New York: Free Press.
1963 (1922). *The Sociology of Religion*. Boston: Beacon Press.
1971. Class, Status and Party. In K. Thompson and J. Tunstall (eds.), *Sociological Perspectives*, pp. 250–264. Harmondsworth, England: Penguin Books.

Weinberg, Arthur (ed.)
1957. *Attorney for the Damned*. New York: Simon & Schuster.

Weiner, Annette B.
1976. *Women of Value, Men of Renown*. Austin: University of Texas Press.
1988. *The Trobrianders of Papua New Guinea*. New York: Holt, Rinehart & Winston.

Weisman, Steven R.
1987, October 27. Many Faces of the Mahabharata. *New York Times*, p. C17.

Westermarck, Edward
1922 (1891). *History of Human Marriage*. New York: Allerton.

White, Douglas R., Michael L. Burton, Lilyan A. Bradner, and Joel D. Gunn
1975. *Implicational Structures in the Sexual Division of Labor*. Social Science Working Paper No. 83. Irvine: School of Social Science, University of California.

White, Leslie A.
1971 (1949). *The Science of Culture: A Study of Man and Civilization*. New York: Farrar, Straus & Giroux.

Wicker, Tom
1987, September 14. The Pump on the Well. *New York Times*.

Wilkerson, Isabel
1987, December 20. New Studies Zeroing in on Poorest of the Poor. *New York Times*, p. 26.

Williams, Walter L.
1986. *The Spirit and the Flesh: Sexual Diversity in American Indian Culture*. Boston: Beacon Press.

Winkelman, M. J.
1986. Trance States: A Theoretical Model and Cross-Cultural Analysis. *Ethos* 14:174–203.

Wiser, William H., and Charlotte Viall Wiser
1971. *Behind Mud Walls: 1930–1960* and *The Village in 1970*. Berkeley: University of California Press.

Wittfogel, Karl
1957. *Oriental Despotism: A Comparative Study of Total Power*. New Haven, CT: Yale University Press.

Wolf, Eric R.
1955. Types of Latin American Peasantry: A Preliminary Discussion. *American Anthropologist* 57:452–471.
1957. Closed Corporate Peasant Communities in Mesoamerica and Central Java. *Southwestern Journal of Anthropology* 57:451–471.
1966. *Peasants*. Englewood Cliffs, NJ: Prentice-Hall.
1982. *Europe and the People without History*. Berkeley: University of California Press.

Wolf, Margery
1992. *A Thrice-Told Tale: Feminism, Postmodernism, and Ethnographic Responsibility*. Stanford, CA: Stanford University Press.

Wolf, Naomi
1991. *The Beauty Myth*. New York: Morrow.

World Bank
1993. *World Development Report 1993*. New York: Oxford University Press.

Wren, Christopher S.
1986, March 27. Computer Age Comes to Eskimos in Canada. *New York Times*, p. A15.

Wright, Patricia
1992. Primate Ecology, Rainforest Conservation and Economic Development: Building a National Park in Madagascar. *Evolutionary Anthropology* I(1):25–33.

Wurm, Stephen A.
1991. Language Death and Disappearance: Causes and Circumstances. In Robert H. Robins and Eugenia M. Uhlenbeck (eds.), *Endangered Languages*. New York: Berg (distrib. by St. Martin's Press, New York).

Young, Gayle
1986, June 12. Anthropologists Wade into the Dark Mystery of the Corporate Jungle. *Chicago Tribune*, Sect. 5, p. 4.

Young, Kate
1993. *Planning Development with Women: Making a World of Difference*. New York: St. Martin's Press.

Young, Michael W. (ed.)
1979. *The Ethnography of Malinowski: The Trobriand Islands 1915–18*. London: Routledge & Kegan Paul.

Zenani, Nongenile Masithathu
1992. *The World and the Word: Tales and Observations from the Xhosa Oral Tradition* (Harold Scheub, ed.). Madison: University of Wisconsin Press.

Zubrow, Ezra B. W.
1975. *Prehistoric Carrying Capacity: A Model*. Menlo Park, CA: Cummings.

Credits

Photos

Note: Images in the upper left-hand corners and bottom right-hand corners of the chapter-opening spreads are from The Detroit Industry murals, detail of the races. Fresco painted by Diego Rivera, 1932–1933. © Photograph, The Detroit Institute of the Arts, Gift of Edsel B. Ford. Dirk Baker, photographer.

Chapter 1 Page iii: J. T. Gwynne; **xx:** J. T. Gwynne; **2:** Delores Newton; **5:** Elizabeth Stone; **7L:** Elliott Erwitt/Magnum; **7R:** TOMPIX/Peter Arnold; **8:** Maxine Hicks; **9:** Superstock; **10:** Irven DeVore/Anthro-Photo File; **11:** Roger P. McConochie; **13:** Bettmann Archive; **15:** Smithsonian Institution; **16:** Neg. No. 351: Courtesy Department Library Services, American Museum of Natural History; **20:** Yale University Library. **Chapter 2 Page 22:** Stephen Ferry/JB Pictures; **25:** © from "Wolf Child and Human Child" by A. Gesell, Methuen & Co., Ltd., London; **26:** Twentieth Century Fox; **27:** Martin Rogers/Woodfin Camp & Assoicates; **28:** Maxine Hicks; **29:** Irven DeVore/Anthro-Photo File; **30:** Maxine Hicks; **31:** Anthro-Photo File; **32:** J. T. Gwynne; **34:** Steve Swope/Allsport USA; **35:** Anthro-Photo File; **37:** Topham/The Image Works; **39:** Focus On Sports; **40:** from "The People of Alor" by Cora DuBois, © 1944 the University of Minnesota Press; **41:** Superstock. **Chapter 3 Page 44:** J. T. Gwynne; **49TL:** Dan Budnik/Woodfin Camp & Associates; **49TR:** Robert Frerck/Odyssey; **49BR:** Mavournea Hay/Daemmrich; **51:** Maxine Hicks; **52:** from "Witchcraft, Oracles and Magic Among the Azande" by Evans-Pritchard, © Oxford, Clarendon Press, 1968; **54:** Clive Brunskill/Allsport USA; **57:** Alinari/Art Resource; **58:** Bill Anderson/Monkmeyer Press Photo Service; **60:** Prof Gananath Obeyesekere, Princeton University; **63:** J. T. Gwynne; **64:** Irven DeVore/Anthro-Photo File. **Chapter 4 Page 68:** Napoleon Chagnon; **71:** Maxine Hicks; **74:** Irven DeVore/Anthro-Photo File; **77:** Catherine Koehler; **78:** Irven DeVore/Anthro-Photo File; **79:** Robert Frerck/Odyssey; **80:** Irven DeVore/Anthro-Photo File; **82:** Bruno Barbey/Magnum; **83:** Leroy Catherine/Sipa Press; **87:** Scott, Foresman. **Chapter 5 Page 90:** The Gorilla Foundation; **93:** Andrew Malcolm/NYT Pictures; **94:** Navy photo by PH2 Dante M. DeAngelis; **96:** David Rose/Sygma; **99L:** Alexander Marshack; **99R:** Alexander Marshak; **100:** Erich Lessing/Art Resource; **101:** Irven DeVore/Anthro-Photo File; **111:** Irven DeVore/Anthro-Photo File; **112:** Harold Scheub; **113:** Superstock; **117:** Jeff Guerrant; **118:** M. A. Gwynne. **Chapter 6 Page 124:** Robert W. Hernandez; **126:** Larry Downing/Woodfin Camp & Associates; **129:** Jason Laure; **130:** National Museum of American Art, Smithsonian Institution, gift of Mrs. Joseph Harrison, Jr./Art Resource; **134:** David Harvey/Woodfin Camp & Associates; **136:** J. T. Gwynne; **137:** J. T. Gwynne; **138:** Superstock; **139:** Maxine Hicks; **140:** J. T. Gwynne; **141:** Irven DeVore/Anthro-Photo File; **142:** J. T. Gwynne; **143:** J. T. Gwynne; **145:** Alexis Diclos/Gamma-Liaison. **Chapter 7 Page 150:** J. T. Gwynne; **154:** Gerd Ludwig/Woodfin Camp & Assoiciates; **157:** Eastcott/The Image Works; **158:** David Hicks; **160:** J. T. Gwynne; **161:** Doug Ogden/Alaska Stock Images; **165:** J. T. Gwynne; **167:** Irven DeVore/Anthro-Photo File; **171:** Division of Rare and Manuscript Collections, Carl A. Kroch Library; Cornell University, Ithaca, NY; **172:** Superstock; **175T:** Irven DeVore/Anthro-Photo File; **175B:** Anthro-Photo File. **Chapter 8 Page 178:** Jay Dickman; **181:** AP/Wide World; **182:** Andy Sacks/Tony Stone Images; **183:** Worcester Art Museum, Worcester, MA, The Charles E. Goodspeed Collection, March 1910; **187:** Jason Laure; **188:** Alexandra Boulat/Sipa Press; **189:** Raghu Rai/Magnum; **191:** J. T. Gwynne; **193:** J. T. Gwynne; **195:** Heidi Larson; **197:** Smithsonian Institution. **Chapter 9 Page 200:** Eva Momatiuk/John Eastcott/Woodfin Camp & Associates; **203:** Maxine Hicks; **204:** Irven DeVore/Anthro-Photo File; **205:** LDS Church Vis. Res. Lib.; **209B:** 1994 Capital Cities/ABC; **212:** David Alan Harvey/Woodfin Camp & Assoiciates; **215:** Neg. No. 332987; photo © R. A. Gould; courtesy Department Library Sciences, American Museum of Natural History; **219:** Robert Caputo/Stock Boston; **220:** Superstock; **222:** David R. Frazier Photolibrary; **224:** Tony Freeman/Photo Edit. **Chapter 10 Page 234:** J. T. Gwynne; **236:** Ira Wyman/Sygma; **238TL:** Lindsay Hebberd/Woodfin Camp & Associates; **238TR:** Alan Dolgins/Leo de Wys; **238BL:** David Simson/Stock Boston; **238BR:** Paul Fusco/Magnum; **241:** Maxine Hicks; **242:** Reprinted from Peter Rigby, *Cattle & Kinship among the Gogo: A Semi-pastoral Society of Central Tanzania*. Copyright © 1969 by Cornell University. Used by permission of the publisher, Cornell University Press; **243:** Gerard Rancinan/Sygma; **250:** R. Maiman/Sygma; **252:** Superstock; **254:** Alex Webb/Magnum; **255:** Henry H. Bagish/Anthro-Photo File. **Chapter 11 Page 262:** D. Aubert/Sygma; **266:** Cameramann International; **269:** Edward Gargan/NYT Pictures; **271:** The Illustrated London News Picture Library; **272:** A. Tannenbaum/Sygma; **273:** Lori Grinker/Contact Press Images; **274:** Anthro-Photo File; **277:** J. T. Gwynne; **278:** Irven DeVore/Anthro-Photo File; **280:** M. Granitsas/The Image Works; **281:** Ricky Rogers/NYT Pictures; **282:** Superstock. **Chapter 12 Page 286:** Brad Rickerby/Sipa Press; **290L:** Bill Nation/Sygma; **290R:** Richard Saunders/Leo de Wys; **292:** Irven DeVore/Anthro-Photo File; **294:** Eastcott/Momatiuk/Woodfin Camp & Associates; **295:** Jack Fields/Photo Researchers; **296:** Maxine Hicks; **305:** Irven Devore/Anthro-Photo File; **306:** Yves Forestier/Sygma; **309:** Jason Laure; **310:** Scott, Foresman; **311:** T. F. Hunt/Bettmann Archive; **312:** Irven DeVore/Anthro-Photo File. **Chapter 13 Page 316:** J. T. Gwynne; **319:** Brown Brothers; **322:** David Hicks; **325:** J. T. Gwynne; **326:** *Washington Post*/Frank Johnston/Woodfin Camp & Associates; **327:** Kal Muller/Woodfin Camp & Associates; **329:** Tom Haley/Sipa Press; **330:** Montana Historical Society; **332:** Superstock; **333:** David Hicks; **335:** Library of Congress; **336:** Robert Frerck/Odyssey; **339:** Anthro-Photo File; **340:** Rare Book Department; Free Library of Philadelphia. **Chapter 14 Page 344:** J. T. Gwynne; **349:** Jean Clottes/AP/Wide World; **350:** Irven DeVore/Anthro-Photo File; **351:** Mary Strong; **354:** Historical Pictures Service, Chicago; **356:** Robert Frerck/Woodfin Camp & Associates; **358:** Najwa Adra; **359:** Printed by permission of The Norman Rockwell Family Trust, Copyright © 1946, The Norman Rockwell Family Trust, *A Country School* by Norman Rockwell, 1946; **360:** Andrew Malcolm/NYT Pictures; **361:** J. Gwynne; **362:** Photofest; **367T:** Penny Tweedie/Woodfin Camp & Associates; **367B:** © Peter Brooks and the *Times*, London, June 6, 1988; Times Newspapers Limited. **Chapter 15 Page 370:** Chris Johns/Tony Stone Images; **374:** Henry Bagish/Anthro-Photo File; **375:** Hubertus Kanus/Photo

Researchers; **377:** Will McIntyre/Photo Researchers; **378:** Christopher Arnesen/Tony Stone Images; **379:** Irven DeVore/Anthro-Photo File; **380:** Charles D. Miller, III; **381:** T. Campion/Sygma; **382:** J. Gwynne; **383:** Bamberger/Anthro-Photo File; **385:** Oliver Blaise/Gamma-Liaison; **386:** Film Study Center, Harvard University; **389:** Tom Campbell; **391:** Library of Congress. **Chapter 16 Page 394:** Sally Wiener Grotta/The Stock Market; **398:** Toby Bankett Pyle/Photo Researchers; **399:** J. T. Gwynne; **402:** The Kobal Collection; **404:** M. A. Gwynne; **405:** Rick Rusing/Tony Stone Worldwide; **406:** J. T. Gwynne; **407:** Superstock; **408:** Emmy Nuraheni/Reuters/Bettmann; **413:** Bruce Brander/Photo Researchers; **414:** Klaus Reisinger/Black Star; **416:** Irven DeVore/Anthro-Photo File; **417:** Nuridsany et Perennou/Photo Researchers; **418:** M. J. Balick.

Figures

Figures 5.2, 11.2, 12.1, 13.1, 16.1 From Jordan et al., *The Human Mosaic*, 6th ed. Copyright © 1994 by HarperCollins Publishers. Reprinted by permission of HarperCollins College Publishers.

Figure 12.2 From *Archaeology: The Science of Once and Future Things* by Brian Hayden. Copyright © 1993 by W. H. Freeman and company. Used with permission. **Figure 5.4** From Colin Renfrew, "The Origin of Indo-European Languages," *Scientific American*, October 1989, p. 112. Copyright © 1989 by Scientific American, Inc. All rights reserved. **Figure 16.2** Adapted from *Goode's World Atlas*, 18th ed. Copyright © 1993 by Rand McNally. Reprinted with permission.

Index